Regionalism and Rivalry

A National Bureau
of Economic Research
Conference Report

Regionalism and Rivalry

Japan and the United States
in Pacific Asia

Edited by Jeffrey A. Frankel
and Miles Kahler

The University of Chicago Press

Chicago and London

JEFFREY A. FRANKEL is professor of economics at the University of California, Berkeley, and a research associate of the National Bureau of Economic Research, where he is also associate director for the program for International Finance and Macroeconomics. MILES KAHLER is professor of international relations and adjunct professor of political science at the University of California, San Diego.

The University of Chicago Press, Chicago 60637
The University of Chicago Press, Ltd., London
© 1993 by the National Bureau of Economic Research
All rights reserved. Published 1993
Printed in the United States of America
02 01 00 99 98 97 96 95 94 93 1 2 3 4 5
ISBN: 0-226-25999-4 (cloth)

Library of Congress Cataloging-in-Publication Data

Regionalism and rivalry: Japan and the United States in Pacific Asia
    / edited by Jeffrey A. Frankel and Miles Kahler.
        p.   cm.—(A National Bureau of Economic Research conference
    report)
    Includes bibliographical references and index.
        1. East Asia—Foreign economic relations—Japan—Congresses.
    2. Japan—Foreign economic relations—East Asia—Congresses. 3. Asia,
    Southeastern—Foreign economic relations—Japan—Congresses.
    4. Japan—Foreign economic relations—Asia, Southeastern—Congresses.
    5. Investments, Japanese—East Asia—Congresses. 6. United States—Foreign economic relations—East Asia—Congresses. 7. East Asia—Foreign
    economic relations—United States—Congresses. 8. United States—Foreign economic relations—Asia, Southeastern—Congresses. 9. Asia,
    Southeastern—Foreign economic reltions—United States—Congresses.
    10. East Asia—Economic integration—Congresses.   I. Frankel, Jeffrey A.   II. Kahler, Miles, 1949-.   III. Series: Conference report (National Bureau of Economic Research).
    HF1600.5.R43   1993
    337.52073—dc20   93–21519
                                                                CIP

309439

Contents

Preface

A redefinition of United States interests, and a debate over the shape of a desirable world order, are under way following the end of the Cold War. Interests as well as desirable order will acquire different meanings in different parts of the world. In some parts of the world, where the transitions to a market economy and stable democracy are far from assured, the goal is surely to facilitate those transitions. In East Asia, on the other hand, economic success is already an accomplished fact, beyond anything that could have been hoped forty years ago. In this region, some Americans have begun to fear success rather than to welcome it. Many see a regional bloc centered on Japan, concentrating its economic activity inward, and rivaling the power of American and European blocs.

In early 1992, the National Bureau of Economic Research held two conferences sponsored by the Pew Charitable Trusts, one on economic reform in Eastern Europe and the former Soviet Union, the other on the activities of Japan and the United States in Pacific Asia. This volume contains the papers and comments presented at the second conference, which was held in Del Mar, California, April 2–5. A preconference meeting held in Cambridge, Massachusetts, November 9, 1991, helped narrow the range of variation of author wavelengths.

Half the participants were economists (many of them NBER research associates), and half political scientists. Many skills and combinations of skills were represented: specialized knowledge of individual East Asian countries, familiarity with the Pacific Rim as a whole, and expertise with the tools of international relations, international political economy, comparative politics, technology policy, international economics, economic theory, econometrics, and history. It is safe to say that no single participant possessed all, or even most, of these skills.

To narrow the focus manageably, many issues at the nexus of economics, politics, and security in East Asia and the Pacific were not directly addressed by the conference. The spotlight fell principally on the activities of Japan in the region, more than on those of the United States or of China and others. But any expectations that conference participants would offer evidence of a plan on the part of Japan Inc. to convert economic power into political power in Pacific Asia were disappointed. Instead, the economic nature of Japanese goals was taken for granted, and the debate centered more on whether observed economic trends differ from what could be explained by natural factors in international competition.

The editors wish to thank the participants for obeying the dictates of a rigorous timetable, designed to preserve the timeliness of the volume. They wish as well to thank the Pew Charitable Trusts for support, Martin Feldstein and Stanley Fischer for their encouragement, and the staffs of the NBER conference and publications departments, particularly Kirsten Foss Davis and Lauren Lariviere, for performing with the usual flawless efficiency.

Jeffrey A. Frankel and Miles Kahler

Introduction

Jeffrey A. Frankel and Miles Kahler

A common historical reading of the 1930s and World War II has long colored evaluations of regional monetary and trading blocs. Economists have typically appraised the global welfare implications of blocs negatively in comparison to a global, multilateral economic order. Political scientists have associated a regionalized international order with heightened economic and even military conflict, although some have accepted the possibility of a benign regionalism. Policymakers, influenced by these views, have hedged regional experiments with rules meant to reduce their discriminatory impact on nonmembers, most notably Article 24 of the General Agreement on Tariffs and Trade (GATT), governing preferential trading arrangements.

Until recently, with the important exception of the European Economic Community (formed in 1957), experiments in regionalism were more common among the developing countries, and even there, more likely to fail than not.[1] Even the European Community seemed limited to a customs union (with a liberalized external tariff) and several joint policies, of which only agriculture had serious implications for the global trading system. The European Monetary System (founded in 1979) initially seemed to augur little more than its expressed aim of forming a zone of monetary stability in Europe, a goal viewed with skepticism by many outsiders despite the eventual success of the EMS.

With the adoption of the Single European Act in 1985 and the subsequent

Jeffrey A. Frankel is professor of economics at the University of California, Berkeley, and a research associate of the National Bureau of Economic Research, where he is also associate director for the program in International Finance and Macroeconomics. Miles Kahler is professor of international relations and adjunct professor of political science at the University of California, San Diego.

1. A recent study by the International Monetary Fund notes that "significant difficulties have generally been encountered in implementing trade and other integration measures on schedule" in the case of regional schemes involving developing countries (de la Torre and Kelly, 1992, 32).

movement toward economic, monetary, and political union in Europe in the 1990s, the terms of debate shifted drastically. The United States and Canada have signed a free trade agreement and have entered into negotiations with Mexico to extend that agreement to a North American Free Trade Agreement (NAFTA). Only Pacific Asia has not actively engaged in a regional project, and many have asked whether the economic prerequisites for a regional bloc, centered on Japan and similar to those in North America and Europe, are not already in place in East and Southeast Asia.

If evidence for such a bloc-in-formation could be marshaled, the implications for the future of the global trading and monetary systems could be profound. Encompassing the most dynamic trading economies in the international economy and the world's largest creditor nation, East and Southeast Asia have represented a major influence in favor of strengthening the multilateral trade and monetary systems.[2] Their retreat into a regional project would knock away a major support for the global rules governing trade and monetary relations. In addition, the emergence of an East Asian bloc, however defined, could supply another item for the agenda of bilateral conflict between the United States and Japan.

The economists and political scientists contributing to this volume, then, are concerned with the ways in which the United States and Japan contribute to and are potentially affected by regionalism in East Asia. This is not, however, another work about United States–Japan bilateral economic relations or a consideration of the emerging tripolar global order. One could view each of these papers as dealing with Japan's use of its newfound economic power in one part of the post–Cold War world—East and Southeast Asia.

In part I the case for an emerging East Asian trading and financial bloc is scrutinized and tested. Part II deals with other elements in a possible Japan-centered bloc—particularly foreign direct investment—and the ways in which they might be expected to heighten the competitiveness of Japanese firms and increase Japanese influence in the region. The incentives and obstacles to Japanese leadership in Pacific Asia are described in part III.

A Bloc for the 1990s? Japan's Trade, Finance, and Direct Investment in Pacific Asia

Any Japan-centered economic bloc taking shape in Pacific Asia is not based on explicit, region-specific political arrangements. Such regional institutions have historically been weak or absent, whether the region is defined to include East and Southeast Asia only, extended to incorporate Australia, New Zealand, and the South Pacific, or equated with the Pacific Rim (including North and

2. In 1991, a year in which the volume of world trade grew at a sluggish 3 percent (its slowest rate since 1983), "the six leading non-OECD traders [in Asia] reported growth rates of 10 to 20 per cent for exports and 8 to 30 per cent for imports" (GATT Press Communiqué, 12 March 1992).

South America). The reasons for such weakness and the absence of "hard," politically determined regionalism include a preference on the part of the United States for bilateral relationships with its major allies in Asia and the radical asymmetry (at least during the early years of the Cold War) between the economic and military capabilities of the United States on the one hand, and Japan and the other noncommunist Asian states on the other. Large quantities of ink have been spilled on proposals for regional integration, but only the Association of Southeast Asian Nations (ASEAN) has emerged as a persistent (and largely political) regional entity.

As Stephen Haggard argues in his comment on Peter Petri's paper, however, such a "hard," politically driven route to regionalism is not the only route possible. Peter Petri elaborates a path to regional political institutions through a functional response to growing economic interdependence among Pacific Asian economies: politics follows economics, serving to manage the interdependence that is independently or "naturally" created by the actions of private agents. Petri, Jeffrey Frankel and Gary Saxonhouse scrutinize the evidence for growing "soft" regionalism of this variety, particularly regionalization centered on Japan. The *level* of trade interdependence within the region has been high during the postwar period, higher than one might expect from features such as geographical proximity. Both Petri and Frankel agree, however, that the *trend* in regional trade interdependence does not demonstrate a clear intensification of any intraregional bias during the post-1945 period. Indeed, Petri situates the post-1945 low point in regional trade interdependence in the mid-1980s. All three authors fail to find any pattern of Japan as a metropole in the regional pattern of trade; Frankel in particular suggests that the overseas Chinese (concentrated in entrepôts such as Hong Kong and Singapore) are more likely to provide an explanation for the high levels of intraregional trade.

Given Japan's growing global financial role, one might expect to find a stronger "Tokyo effect" through the financial markets. Any international effects on national financial markets in the region, however, are muted by the late, and still partial, liberalization of financial flows. Although Japan's influence over interest rates has grown, it rivals that of the United States in only a few regional markets. The yen's use as a peg for exchange rates in the region, in central bank reserves, and in invoicing trade and finance has also grown somewhat, but its role is far from dominant even after the expansion of Japan's financial presence in the 1980s.

To regard even these trends in the region as purely economic would be mistaken. As Petri points out, one explanation for the historical level of regional trade interdependence in the region is investment in the infrastructure of particular trade links, investment decisions that may be influenced by political or strategic calculations as well as economic ones. Larger international political changes also affect these patterns. The dismantling of the Japanese colonial empire ended one variant of "hard" regionalism that had forceably induced a high degree of regional trade interdependence. The decolonization of Southeast Asia after 1945 and the Cold War encouraged an extraregional trade strategy based on the U.S. market, as colonial entrepôts such as Singapore saw their role decline temporarily, and Japan was cut off from its traditional markets in China.

If current trends in trade and finance fail to demonstrate a clear intensification of flows within the Pacific Asia region, and institutionalization at the political level has lagged behind other regions, it may be that our image of a bloc depends too heavily on past models of "hard" regionalism based on politically determined discriminatory arrangements. It is in the area of foreign direct investment in the region by Japan and the use of foreign aid that some have identified the emergence of a "1990s model" bloc, different in external appearance from the European Community or NAFTA but closely integrated and centered on the Japanese economy.

The economic basis for such arguments lies in the changing composition of foreign direct investment in the region since the mid-1980s. All of the significant activities of foreign investors are not adequately captured by the most readily available data—those of flows of foreign direct investment. Both investment financed within the country (or in offshore financial markets) and other overseas activities on the part of firms may have important economic effects (such as cooperative arrangements with foreign firms and cooperation in production; see Doner, chap. 5 in this volume). Despite these shortcomings, it is worth noting a shift in the pattern of Japanese overseas investment flows associated with rapid appreciation of the yen that took place in the late 1980s. The absolute value of Japanese foreign direct investment increased dramatically, and even though the share directed to the Asian developing countries declined somewhat, the absolute amount of investment going to the Asian newly industrializing countries (NICs) and the rapidly industrializing ASEAN countries increased sharply. Equally important, Japan's significance to these countries as an investor (compared to the United States and the European Community) grew, and, among developing areas, the importance of developing Asia as a field for Japanese investment became clearer (Doner, chap. 5 in this volume; Petri, chap. 1 in this volume; Omori and Takata 1992, 146–47).

The search for cost advantages in East and Southeast Asia following *endaka* (strong yen) is clear in the pattern as well as the direction of Japanese foreign direct investment during these years. Unlike earlier emphasis on import substituting investments in the region (encouraged by local policies), this wave of Japanese investment, concentrated in manufacturing, served to develop a dynamic division of labor in the region. It reinforced the popular "flying geese" model of regional development in which Japanese manufacturers gradually reduce the production of labor-intensive manufactures and transfer those parts of the manufacturing process abroad. In this regard, Japanese manufacturers in East and Southeast Asia were simply following the established model of the global factory already apparent in Western Europe and the United States. As a result, Japanese investment in the region was more export-oriented than it had been previously, including a high share of intrafirm trade and an increase in exports to the Japanese market (Doner, chap. 5 in this volume; Petri, chap. 1 in this volume).[3]

Evaluating the effects of this influx on host country economic performance is controversial and difficult. Petri notes that the trade balance effects of the new investments have to date not been as positive as might have been predicted, despite their greater export orientation, because they continue to require a high level of imported components from abroad. Richard Doner notes that even the overall effect of the foreign investment surge on the level of Thailand's exports is disputed, with one study estimating that it accounts for only 10 percent of export growth in manufactures (Petri 1992, 24–25). Whatever its effects on levels of economic growth and export expansion, however, Japanese investment in manufacturing in Pacific Asia after 1985 has intensified regional economic integration in new ways.

More important than Japanese direct investment for the two most populous Asian countries—China and Indonesia—are Japanese flows of aid. Even for rapidly industrializing Thailand, which has recently been a magnet for Japanese investment, aid flows from 1989–91 totaled 35 percent of investment. The bilateral aid dominance of Japan in Asia is far more pronounced than is Japan's presence in foreign investment: the United States and Europe are hardly players in bilateral aid flows in East and Southeast Asia (Islam, chap. 8 in this volume). The integrating function of aid, however, may rest in its characteristics rather than its volume. Observers of Japanese aid policy agree that it is concentrated more in economic infrastructure than is the aid of most of the industrialized countries (Islam, chap. 8 in this volume). Considerable attention has been directed to explicit attempts on the part of the Japanese government to link the aid program to infrastructural improvements that would benefit Japanese investors, most notably in the New Aid Plan announced by MITI in 1987. Critical observers saw an effort to replicate Japanese industrial policy on a grand scale. Others, including some of the authors in this volume (Islam, Katzenstein and Rouse, and Doner), see a new label for an old pattern of aid, a grandiose program designed to expand the bureaucratic influence of MITI in the foreign aid process that is contested by its bureaucratic foes, one that is unlikely to be implemented according to the designs of ministries in Tokyo.

The investment-aid nexus has produced a weak set of institutions on the bilateral and national levels and none at the regional level, although the proposal of Malaysian prime minister Mahathir for an East Asian Economic Group or Caucus might be seen as a functional response to the new Japanese production network in Southeast Asia. If a new investment-based regionalization can be identified, it may be grounded more on diverse institutions that encourage collaboration between governments and business, institutions that

3. For a model of the effects of foreign direct investment on an ASEAN economy, see Petri (1992).

are quasi-public at best. Such institutions are being established between Japan and both public and private actors in Pacific Asia. Doner notes several institutional innovations that can be traced to the new pattern of investment and aid, such as imitation of Japanese patterns of industrial policy and public-private collaboration and the development of subcontracting networks similar to those in Japanese manufacturing. Japan has sponsored nothing as ambitious as the Singapore-backed growth triangle that aims to link infrastructural improvement and Singaporean capital with Malaysian and Indonesian land and labor.[4]

Does the new pattern of investment and aid in Pacific Asia augur a new-model "bloc" centered on Japan? Clearly, economic regionalism of this kind, weakly institutionalized, would be based on a particular form of economic integration, encouraged but not directed by government policy, producing in turn weak bilateral and international institutions. Hints of this sort of a "bloc" can be teased out of some of the contributions in this volume, but this type of grouping, even if it were to emerge, would bear little resemblance to the tightly organized and politically circumscribed blocs of the 1930s or even to the contemporary European Community. It would be a "bloc" for the era of fiber optics and informatics rather than for the age of coal, steel, and agriculture. Should it take shape, it would be aid- and investment-driven, not trade-driven (although presumably investment would influence regional trade patterns). It would be sectoral rather than territorial in scope: integration of the electronics or automobile industries throughout the region rather than all of the economic activities in Pacific Asia. Japanese government involvement would be oblique, supporting informal institutions that would offer information and infrastructure to Japanese investors, reducing the risks for private investment (Doner, chap. 5 in this volume). Finally, the channels of Japanese influence would include the influence that key investors in important industrial sectors are likely to have on host governments, host government calculations of anticipated Japanese reactions to their policy initiatives, and above all, differential access to information.[5]

The authors offer no conclusive evidence that such a 1990s-model bloc is taking shape in Pacific Asia. Indeed, to use the term *bloc* precisely, a demonstration of discrimination against European or American investors and exporters must be demonstrated. One could imagine that some of the "neural networks"[6] taking shape in the region might have such discriminatory implications, particularly the subcontracting webs described by Doner. Nevertheless,

---

4. On the current status of this plan, see Lee (1991).

5. As Albert O. Hirschman (1980, 16–17) noted in his classic study of international influence and economic transactions, "For the political or power implications of trade to exist and to make themselves felt, it is not essential that the state should exercise positive action, i.e., organize and direct trade centrally; the negative right of veto on trade with which *every* sovereign state is invested is quite sufficient."

6. This phrase was coined at the Del Mar conference by Gregory Noble.

many of the activities of the Japanese government in the region, particularly in the provision of infrastructure, are public goods from which other investors and exporters cannot be excluded (Katzenstein and Rouse, chap. 6 in this volume; Islam, chap. 8 in this volume). Without discrimination, the assertions of a bloc-in-formation lose much of their meaning.

The authors in this volume offer several powerful reasons to doubt that even a regional grouping of this "softer" variety will emerge. The public goods character of many of the instruments at Japanese disposal has already been mentioned. The leveling off and decline of Japanese foreign direct investment after 1990 suggests that at least part of the post-1985 surge in investment was a portfolio adjustment. The level of Japanese manufacturing investment in Southeast Asia appears likely to remain stable, however, within the constraints of infrastructural bottlenecks (Petri, chap. 1 in this volume; Omori and Takata 1992, 142, 146). The apparently unstoppable outflow of Japanese capital after 1985 may have been misread as a permanent feature in the life of the region.

More important, Japan is not the only actor whose investment is weaving together a regional pattern of production and trade. The East Asian NICs have recently rivaled and even surpassed Japan as investors in some of the countries of Southeast Asia. By 1991, for example, the cumulative investment position of the four Asian NICs in Indonesia had begun to approach that of Japan; it was the substantial investment of the NICs in the late 1980s and 1990s that spurred the export of manufactures from Indonesia (Kuntjoro-Jakti 1992). Taiwan was among the top three foreign investors in Malaysia; it also occupied a very strong position in Thailand. The immediate stimulus to overseas investment in these cases was the same real exchange rate appreciation and cost considerations that had spurred Japanese investment. Although the evidence is anecdotal at this point, investment from the NICs does not seem related primarily to Japanese investment networks or global production strategies: these are in large measure new investment entrants in the regional economy. Their rapid emergence does not suggest a sphere of unchallenged Japanese investment predominance.

The prominence of NIC investment in recent years suggests further diversification of the sources of foreign investment. The national governments of the region have demonstrated that they have both the instruments and the will to push diversification despite the perceived benefits of Japanese investment and aid. Peter Katzenstein and Martin Rouse document the efforts of Thailand to award infrastructure contracts to non-Japanese firms. Understandably, the ASEAN governments have no desire to award Japanese investors or the Japanese government the bargaining leverage of a monopolist.

A final barrier to a regional arrangement that might be both more formal and more discriminatory is the continuing dependence of both Japan and the Pacific Asian economies on the American market. The threat of American displeasure and even sanctions in the face of movement toward an institutionalization of the Japanese aid-investment network in the region is likely to prove an imposing obstacle, as it did for the modest proposal of Dr. Mahathir.[7]

Regionalism and International Conflict

Although concern over conflict between Japan and the United States has centered on bilateral trade conflict and its possible spillovers into political and security collaboration, any move toward Japan-centered regionalism also threatens conflict with the United States. Fifty years ago, worsening conflict between the two countries was owed to Japan's expansionist policies in East and Southeast Asia. No one is predicting a reappearance of conflict of that intensity, but an array of models suggests that movement toward regional blocs could intensify international conflict between the United States and Japan.

One familiar argument holds that declining power differentials between a dominant power and its rivals produce heightened conflict. Some political scientists have elaborated this view in the vocabulary of hegemonic cycles; others have proposed a more general power-transition theory of conflict. Such models suggest that a Japan-centered region in Asia would add to the anxieties of a United States already concerned over Japan's rapid economic rise: "Other things being equal, the greater (and more rapid) the relative economic decline of the United States vis-à-vis Japan (*and* Germany), the more difficult will be the problem of global security adjustment, as well as global economic adjustment" (Destler 1991). As Destler argues, the probability of Japan's becoming the single dominant power is small, but its regional dominance must be assigned a higher likelihood. For Pacific Asia to be seen as a power resource for an ascendant Japan, however, the organization of the region would need to acquire the character of a "hard" regionalism, politically determined, with much greater institutional development and economic concentration than currently exists.

Quite apart from the addition of economic dependents to a rival's power resources, it was long a matter of received faith in American policymaking that a regionalized world economy would not only lower world economic welfare but also produce heightened political and military conflict. That influential reading of the history of the 1930s shaped American attitudes toward postwar institutions—biasing the United States toward multilateralism and globalism—but it is not clear that a world organized in regional blocs would necessarily succumb to such conflict (unless the blocs were led by predatory powers such as Nazi Germany or prewar Japan). In any case, none of the contributors to this volume suggest that we are moving independently to a Pacific Asia organized on these lines. Only if the United States and the European Community adopted hard regionalist organizations or if United States–Japan bilateral

---

7. The continued importance of the American market as a barrier to further regional economic integration is emphasized by Yung Chul Park and Won-Am Park (1991).

conflict worsened do some argue that an East Asian regional bloc might emerge.[8]

Even a weak form of regionalism—the aid and investment network described above—could spur United States–Japan conflict. Any perceived discrimination against American firms would be read as the export of Japanese business practices (such as the *keiretsu*) that have attracted American attention and hostility in Japan itself. Such conflict could, as noted earlier, feed back into the political dynamics of Japan and other Pacific Asian countries to create the impetus for the regionalization that the United States sought to avoid. Much of this conflict would derive as much from American *perceptions* of the emerging Pacific Asian system as from the reality of discrimination or closure.

A final source of conflict, ironically, is the mirror image of concerns over an ascendant Japan: the belief that Japan does not contribute enough to the provision of international public goods, that it has been a free rider internationally and shows no signs of becoming a leader. If in the first instance, Japan is viewed as threatening because it might overtake the United States, in this case it is condemned for failing to assume some of the burdens of leadership in Pacific Asia.

Does the Public Goods Paradigm Fit the Issues of United States–Japan Cooperation in Pacific Asia?

How can we give substance to the ideas of leadership and responsibility? It is to be hoped that Japan is beginning to exercise more leadership and that the United States will not feel threatened by an expanded role for Japan. Both adjustments require a kind of maturity often lacking. The theory of international public goods at first seems the most powerful analytical tool for thinking about the issues that surround the respective roles of the United States and Japan in the region. The provision of a public good inevitably involves politics and institutions; by definition, the international private market cannot provide public goods unaided. The theory states that the optimal cooperative solution is for two countries to share the burden of helping to promote common goals in the region. In the broadest sense, these common goals include promoting peace, democracy, and stable, market-oriented economic development.

Table 1 illustrates the game for the case in which the public good is spending on defense. It could as easily be spending on foreign aid. The noncooperative (or Nash) solution is a choice by both countries to save resources by choosing low levels of defense spending. The cooperative solution appears in the last cell, where both countries choose high defense spending. Americans have accused the Japanese of free riding; this would imply a movement to the upper-right cell, where Japan leaves the United States to carry the spending burden

---

8. Notably, Ito, chap. 9 in this volume.

Table 1   **When Spending on Defense Is a Public Good**

	United States cuts spending	United States increases spending
Japan cuts spending	Underprovision of public good	Japan a free rider
Japan increases spending	United States a free rider	Cooperative solution

alone. What better analytical tool to apply to this problem than the Nash bargaining game—in its simplest form, the prisoner's dilemma—a tool that is shared by economists and political scientists?

Many policy issues examined by the papers in this volume can be cast in terms of the bargaining game. In addition to defense spending and aid (standard instances of "burdensharing"), there are issues of monetary and financial policy, protectionism, regional trading blocs, and foreign direct investment. But in virtually every case, this paradigm is crippled by a simple problem: a lack of general agreement as to whether the spending or other policy measure under consideration is properly considered a public good or a public bad.

Beginning with the case of defense spending, Americans naturally assume that their own defense spending is a public good, but not everyone agrees. Shafiqul Islam raises the possibility that it may be a public bad. More importantly, as several conference participants pointed out, Americans, Japanese, and Asians cannot agree—even among themselves, let alone with each other—whether Japanese defense spending is a public good or a public bad. Identification of Japanese military spending as a public bad was clear during the American occupation, when the United States imposed the peace constitution. But Americans today accuse Japan of free riding on United States defense spending. The United States evidently has changed its mind in response to changed circumstances. One wonders, however, how Americans would react to a full-fledged Japanese military buildup. There is no doubt that most Asian countries would be alarmed, as Islam, Wing Thye Woo, and others point out.

In game theory terms, we may be playing the game illustrated in table 2, where defense spending is a public bad. Here the noncooperative solution is for both players to increase spending—the arms race that is all too familiar from history. The cooperative solution is for both sides to reduce arms expenditures. Here "cheating" on a cooperative agreement means spending more than the other party, not less.

American complaints that Japan is not living up to its international commitments because it is spending too little should be viewed in a special light, if the level of spending is the outcome of a bargain urged on Japan by past American governments in the belief that it would be in everyone's interest, as Islam points out. Similarly, any future American (or Asian) complaints that Japan is spending too much on defense will have to be viewed in a special light to the extent that the increased spending is the outcome of bargains urged on Japan by American governments. The conclusion is that it is difficult to apply the game

Table 2   **When Spending on Defense Is a Public Bad**

	United States cuts spending	United States increases spending
Japan cuts spending	Cooperative solution	United States perceived as aggressive
Japan increases spending	Japan perceived as aggressive	Arms race: overprovision of public bad

theory paradigm if we are not sure among ourselves whether Japanese defense spending is good or bad.

One might think that Japanese official development assistance (ODA), such as assistance to Southeast Asian countries in developing infrastructure, would be a clear public good, especially if it is conducted via a multilateral lending institution such as the Asian Development Bank. But some observers question whether such aid is benign. It is suggested explicitly that Japan uses such aid in its own economic interest, and it is suggested implicitly that this trend may not be in the interests of the recipients or other participants in the regional economy, such as the United States.

Other public goods issues arise in the financial area. The policy of the U.S. Treasury, beginning with the 1984 Yen-Dollar Agreement, has been that Japan should promote international use of the yen (for example, in the invoicing of trade, denomination of loans, and use by central banks) and that yen internationalization is a public good. Jeffry Frieden adds banking regulation and monitoring of international lending to the list of supposed public goods in the world financial system. Yet, he points out, it is far from clear that internationalization of the yen is in fact in anyone's interest. Except, perhaps, the interest of Japan: the Yen-Dollar Agreement was perhaps the first major example of Takatoshi Ito's second type of United States–Japan bilateral negotiations. The United States makes demands on Japan that are not obviously in America's interest, but rather, if anything, in Japan's interest, and Japanese leaders use the *gaiatsu* (foreign pressure) to bring about useful reforms. The 1990 Structural Impediments Initiative is the best example of this type of negotiation (Frankel 1990).

Contributing to the maintenance of open international markets is a clear public good. One would expect the issue of cooperation in the trade area to come up most clearly in connection with GATT, specifically the Uruguay Round of trade negotiations, because this is the major international institution for cooperation on trade issues. Japan has been a supporter of the Uruguay Round. But a true test of the strength of its commitment to the liberal trading regime, particularly on the question of rice imports, has been repeatedly postponed by the failure of the Europeans and Americans to come to an agreement on agriculture. Partly because of this delay and partly because many view GATT as passé, attention has shifted to other aspects of trade.

The formation of a Pacific Asian trading bloc, which is the focus of the first four contributions to this volume, can be viewed in light of the public goods paradigm. Formation of a trading bloc, by such steps as preferential trading arrangements among the countries of a region, can hurt the rest of the world by diverting trade away from nonmembers. The classic proposition of Jacob Viner is that world efficiency is improved if trade creation within the bloc is greater than trade diversion. Krugman (1991b) reviews reasons why nonmembers may be made worse off. First, the presumption is that there will be a shift in demand and therefore in the terms of trade away from nonmembers, even with no increase in the level of trade barriers, such as tariffs, applied against them. Second, if each political unit sets its level of trade barriers in an economically maximizing way, the formation of a trading bloc will lead to a higher level of barriers against the rest of the world. The grouping has an enhanced incentive to protect, as it seeks to exploit a degree of joint monopoly power that is greater than that possessed by the individual countries. This is a clear prisoner's dilemma situation, as other regions of the world have an incentive to retaliate by forming their own trading blocs, raising barriers, and exploiting their own monopoly power. In this model (Krugman 1991a), the formation of trading blocs is a public bad (and an equilibrium of three blocs turns out to be particularly bad!).[9]

"New wave" international trade theory, which emphasizes imperfect competition, increasing returns to scale, and endogenous technology, has reinvigorated questions of strategic trade policy with findings that unilateral U.S. government activism can under certain conditions pay off (such as subsidizing aircraft manufacture, where oligopolistic rents are important, or semiconductors, where learning-by-doing is important). But in each case, the logic generally leads to the conclusion that the Nash noncooperative equilibrium in which the United States, the European Community, and Japan *all* subsidize aircraft or semiconductors is an equilibrium in which everyone is worse off, contrary to widespread impressions. New wave trade theory is a strong argument in favor of worldwide cooperation to refrain from such activity, in favor of negotiation and enforcement of international agreements such as GATT.

These implications of the theory extend to trading blocs. Everyone will be better off under an international agreement that forbids regional organizations from seeking to exploit their monopoly power. GATT adopted the most-favored nation principle and allowed for deviations from it to form free trade areas only under certain restrictions. GATT's Article 24 forbids, for example, an increase in tariffs by regional trading arrangements. Those rules have been bent in Europe, the Western Hemisphere, and other parts of the world. Japan does not in fact have any sort of preferential trading arrangements in Asia, so that the issue of GATT compatibility does not arise. As noted above, the au-

---

9. But Krugman (1991b) can just as easily come up with a model (one in which transportation costs between continents are extremely high, in contrast to his earlier model where they are assumed to be zero) in which a world of trading blocs is good. If this type of model is the right one, then a regional power, such as Japan in Asia, the United States in the Western Hemisphere, or Germany or France in Europe, who is large enough to take the initiative to organize a trading bloc is doing a public service. Once again, we have trouble telling a public good from a public bad.

thors in this volume endorse the view that trade in East and Southeast Asia, in contrast to North America and the European Community, does not demonstrate a trend toward intraregional concentration. To the contrary, Japan and other East Asian economies remain highly dependent economically on trade with North America.

Kenneth Froot and David Yoffie add foreign direct investment to a model of the Krugman type, where the formation of a trading bloc is a public bad because of the incentive to raise protectionist barriers. Their conclusion is that, when a bloc lets in such investment, it creates a constituency for trade liberalization and reduces its incentive to protect. Here a country's willingness to let in direct investment is a public good. This logic naturally leads to concerns about Japan, as far more direct investment is seen originating in Japan than entering there.[10] On the other hand, fears of domination by foreign investors often have more of a home in populist politics than they have a basis in reality. Some point out, in contrast to the Froot-Yoffie argument, that a country that is host to foreign direct investment has a ready hostage that increases its bargaining power, whether in economic or military competition.[11] This argument suggests that it is Japan, not its Asian neighbors or the United States, that should fear a vulnerability arising from transplanted Japanese firms on foreign soil. Concerns about sensitive technologies can amplify the case for the United States to encourage Japan to locate operations in the United States.

It is striking that in so many of the most significant issues—military spending, ODA, internationalization of the currency, regional integration, foreign direct investment—Americans (and Asians) have trouble agreeing whether they want Japan to do more or to do less. In some areas of policy, public goods can more easily be distinguished from public bads. This should be the case in areas of environmental protection, weapons proliferation, and human rights, which were not examined in this project. Even in these areas, however, different countries have different views about the relative importance of protecting marine mammals versus addressing global warming, of reducing the arsenals of the superpowers versus slowing proliferation to developing countries, or of protecting free speech versus accepting refugees.

Japanese are themselves divided over many of these issues. In some cases the outlines of the political divisions within Japan are strikingly similar to divisions within the United States and other countries. The debate between those in favor of a renewal of Japanese military capability and those opposed is a Right-versus-Left debate that is familiar from recent history in the West. Frieden points out that the debate between internationalists and nationalists in Japan (or what Funabashi [1988] calls internationalists and domesticists) is analogous to debates in the United States, particularly in the 1920s when it

10. As pointed out by Dennis Encarnation (1992), among others at the conference.
11. Graham and Krugman (1991). This argument was also made by Robert Lipsey at the conference.

was the isolationists who carried the day. Frieden argues that the internationalists may be gaining the upper hand in Japan, just as they eventually did in the United States during the 1940s. Even the alignment of economic interest groups is often similar in Japan and the West: nationalist farmers oppose economic liberalization, by appealing to the much larger urban population with nostalgic recollections of the country's cultural traditions, while internationalist financiers support economic liberalization, by appealing to the country's international obligations.

In other respects the outlines of political divisions in Japan are different from those in the United States. Ito points out the importance in Japan of a division between bureaucrats and politicians, as compared to a division in the United States between a market-oriented White House and a trade-hawk Congress. Institutional specifics are important in each case. In Japan the method whereby districts choose members of the Diet encourages candidates to cater in direct economic ways to special interest groups, as Frances Rosenbluth emphasizes in her comment. But at least the Japanese social system, through the process of *nemawashi* (consensus building), allows the country to speak in the international arena with a relatively unified position. In the United States, divided government has precluded the country from speaking to its trading partners with a single voice. Such divisions in each country lead to what Putnam (1988) calls two-level games: any internationally agreed position must be ratified by the domestic groups who are enfranchised on a given issue.

Japan and the United States as Leaders in Pacific Asia

The ambiguities in a public goods analysis of collaboration between the United States and Japan in Pacific Asia lend support to predictions that development of joint leadership in the region will prove difficult or impossible. Neorealist analysis, in which narrowing power differentials produce heightened conflict, could suggest an even more pessimistic view—that overt United States–Japan conflict is inevitable. Two features of the present international situation might be singled out in this view in support of this bleaker image of the future. The dissolution of the Soviet threat will place pressure on the United States–Japan security relationship—alliances do not long survive the threats that called them into being. Equally important, as Japan increases its economic weight and technological capabilities, a logic of relative gains will—in the absence of a common enemy—swamp the joint interests that the two countries still have in the region and undermine collaboration. A United States fearful of its new economic challenger will increasingly view Japanese success and initiative as a threat, even though American pressure may have originally encouraged Japanese assertiveness.

Despite this forbidding possibility, broad agreement between the two powers in their aims for Pacific Asia is likely to prevent any leap from present-day levels of cooperation to open conflict or mutual perceptions of threat. Both countries still share a strong interest in maximizing the extent to which people in this region are living in stable, democratic, market-oriented societies that do not impose negative externalities or spillovers (such as pollution or weapons proliferation) on other countries. Conflict has already occurred and remains very likely, however, in designing a structure of joint leadership in the region that will maximize these goals. In part, the difficulty lies, as described above, in defining the precise policies to be undertaken by both the United States and Japan and the relative sharing of the burdens, both military and economic, of a leadership role. More important, a stable structure of joint leadership will require wrenching political adjustments on both sides in order to construct a political base for that structure, a base as stable as the existing supports for an alliance relationship that is now under strain.

Americans worry that Japan is not ready politically to take on the leadership role that would be commensurate with its economic importance. Some Japanese share this concern and would prefer the United States to remain the leader. Frieden's account of America's disengaged international stance in the 1920s and 1930s poses the possibility that Japan will shift toward greater leadership and that the transit may take some time. The Japanese political system, in particular, is already demonstrating the difficulties of adjusting to a new role. The old "Yoshida line" held that Japan's international business would be business. Many Americans and Japanese alike (e.g., Ito, chap. 9 in this volume) worry that Japan continues to lack the ideals or principles required for international leadership. To the degree that it has a national ideology, it is based on the hoarding of technology (as David Friedman and Richard Samuels argue in this volume) or on a simple sense of national uniqueness.

New internationalists such as Yoichi Funabashi and Shinichi Kitaoka now argue that Japan should break from the Yoshida line and pursue a more active international policy based on such fundamental principles as promoting democracy, economic development, and environmental protection. This school is an encouraging alternative to the traditional extreme choices of Right and Left: on the one hand, Shintaro Ishihara and others who argue for a strong independent international presence but arouse suspicions of resurgent Japanese militarism; on the other, unreconstructed socialists who have long opposed any Japanese military capabilities and distrust American hegemony and whose economic ideology has never come to terms with the facts of East Asian dynamism. When Kiichi Miyazawa became prime minister, it was thought that he might break from the Yoshida line. But he encountered deep and persistent resistance in his efforts to push new initiatives—such as involvement by Japan in peacekeeping operations—through the scandal-weakened Japanese political system.

The United States must undertake an adjustment equal in difficulty to that of Japan. Americans must adjust to the fact that sharing leadership with Japan does not mean simply sending Tokyo the bill, whether it is for military operations in the Middle East or financing for troubled debtor countries. As C. Fred

Bergsten has said of transfers to the United States in connection with the 1991 Gulf War, "We now know the definition of collective leadership: the United States leads and the United States collects."[12] Saudi Arabia and Kuwait paid the most, followed by Japan, Germany, and the United Arab Emirates in that order. The total, with $37 billion of international commitments actually received by mid-1991, was enough to wipe out the United States trade deficit in goods and services in the first half of the year and produce a small surplus on the overall current account.

The United States must grant Japan a share of power in decision making that is commensurate with its financial contribution. "No taxation without representation" is not simply an ideal of American democracy; it is also a positive statement that a people who are denied a say in how their money is spent will eventually refuse to continue paying. In concrete terms the United States may need to support granting Japan expanded voting power in the Asian Development Bank, top management positions in the International Monetary Fund or the World Bank, and a permanent seat on the United Nations Security Council. Greater attention will be required to the alternative model of economic development that Japan has begun to offer in the International Monetary Fund and the World Bank.

Several of the authors in this volume make clear that it is the American political system that may prove the most recalcitrant to the demands for a new structure of joint leadership in the region. Perhaps the worst outcome would be an American withdrawal from Pacific Asia after assessing few economic gains (given Japanese ubiquity in the region) and many, largely military, costs. Such a policy shift could induce both a "hardening" of regional structures under Japanese leadership and eventually a remilitarization of Japan. This negative dynamic works primarily through American perceptions as played out in the American political process. But if the domestic adjustments in Japan and the United States are successful—a daunting prerequisite—then there are reasons to believe that conflicts over leadership and burdensharing in the provision of public goods may persist at only at a relatively low (and familiar) level.

Many of the international public goods to be provided are not regional but global, and Western Europe, particularly Germany, is as likely to be the target of American displeasure as Japan. (This was the pattern after the Gulf War.) The end of the Cold War means an erosion of common agreement on external security threats and divergence over defining public goods and bads, as described earlier. But the more relaxed security environment also means that the most contentious public good—military security—can be provided at lower levels. It is also worth noting that a suboptimal provision of international public goods, however defined, need not mean chaos or catastrophe in every instance. For example, should the Cambodian peacekeeping operation break down be-

12. "Burdensharing in the Gulf and Beyond," testimony before the House Committee on Ways and Means, 13 March 1991.

cause Japan and the United States are unable to agree with the other interested parties on an acceptable sharing of military and economic costs, the Cambodian people will face continued military conflict and much collective suffering, but the rest of the Pacific Asian region could continue its economic progress with little effect.

Finally, it is worth considering the perspective of the other countries in the region on the balance between cooperation and rivalry in U.S. relations with Japan. Intensified conflict at the levels of the 1930s would clearly be damaging to the development prospects of societies in the region. On the other hand, a certain degree of competition between the United States and Japan may be beneficial. Duopoly power awarded the United States and Japan by a structure of close collaboration in, for example, the provision of development assistance or the management of trade, may not be the preferred outcome for smaller countries economically dependent on American and Japanese capital and markets. For lesser powers in the region, a preferred future order for Pacific Asia may be one of restrained competition between the two economic giants, not two-power condominium, one-country dominance, or unbridled rivalry.

References

Destler, I. M. 1991. The United States and Japan: What Is New? Paper presented at the annual meeting of the International Studies Association, March.

Encarnation, Dennis J. 1992. *Rivals beyond Trade: America versus Japan in Global Competition.* Ithaca: Cornell University Press.

Frankel, Jeffrey A. 1990. The Structural Impediments Initiative: Japan Again Agrees to Make Its Economy More Efficient. *International Economy* 4(5): 70–72.

Funabashi, Yoichi. 1988. *Managing the Dollar: From the Plaza to the Louvre.* Washington, DC: Institute for International Economics.

Graham, Edward, and Paul Krugman. 1991. *Foreign Direct Investment in the United States.* Second edition. Washington, DC: Institute for International Economics.

Hirschman, Albert O. 1980. *National Power and the Structure of Foreign Trade.* Expanded edition. Berkeley: University of California Press.

Krugman, Paul. 1991a. Is Bilateralism Bad? In Elhanan Helpman and Assaf Razin, eds., *International Trade and Trade Policy.* Cambridge: MIT Press.

———. 1991b. The Move toward Free Trade Zones. In *Policy Implications of Trade and Currency Zones,* a symposium sponsored by the Federal Reserve Bank of Kansas City, Jackson Hole, Wyo., August, 7–42.

Kuntjoro-Jakti, Dorodjatun. 1992. Changing Pattern of Foreign Direct Investment in Indonesia. In *Changing Patterns of Foreign Direct Investment in the Asia Pacific Region: Background Papers for the Final Report,* 2:120–34. Osaka: Japan Committee for Pacific Economic Outlook.

Lee Tsao Yuan, ed. 1991. *Growth Triangle: The Johor-Singapore-Riau Experience.* Singapore: Institute of Policy Studies/Institute of Southeast Asian Studies.

Omori, Takashi, and Kiyoshi Takata. 1992. Changing Pattern of Direct Foreign Investment. In *Changing Patterns of Foreign Direct Investment in the Asia Pacific Region:*

Background Papers for the Final Report, 2:135–63. Osaka: Japan Committee for Pacific Economic Outlook.

Park, Yung Chul, and Won-Am Park. 1991. Changing Japanese Trade Patterns and the East Asian NICs. In Paul Krugman, ed., *Trade with Japan: Has the Door Opened Wider?* 85–120. Chicago: University of Chicago Press.

Petri, Peter. 1992. Platforms in the Pacific: The Trade Effects of Direct Investment in Thailand. *Journal of Asian Economics* 3(2): 173–96.

Putnam, Robert. 1988. Diplomacy and Domestic Politics: The Logic of Two-Level Games. *International Organization* 42(3): 427–60.

de la Torre, Augusto, and Margaret R. Kelly. 1992. *Regional Trade Arrangements.* Washington, DC: International Monetary Fund.

I   Is Pacific Asia Becoming a Regional Bloc?

1   The East Asian Trading Bloc: An Analytical History

Peter A. Petri

1.1   Introduction

The phenomenal expansion of East Asia's[1] intraregional trade—from $116 billion to $265 billion between 1985 and 1990—has raised the prospect of an East Asian economic bloc that could more than match the scale of either the European or North American trading area. This bloc would inevitably be dominated by Japan, and thus trade frictions between Japan and the United States could be generalized into a massive confrontation among giant economies. Against the background of declining U.S. competitiveness and suspicions about the "fairness" of global markets, some observers see sinister motives behind growing East Asian interdependence. Some scholars even go so far as to argue that Japan's recent investment, aid, and trade patterns "cloak political and conquistadorial designs similar to those in the past" (Montgomery 1988, xiii).

These issues are examined here in a historical and analytical context. I will show that East Asia has been and continues to be a trading bloc in the sense that its trade is more regionally oriented than would be expected on the basis of random trade patterns. As Frankel shows in chapter 2 of this volume, this is true even while controlling for geographical proximity. Moreover, East Asian interdependence has intensified in the last five or so years. But I will also show that recent increases in interdependence are small in a historical context, and that the East Asian economy has steadily *dis*integrated during the previous three decades. East Asia is *less* interdependent today than it was for most of

Peter A. Petri is Carl Shapiro Professor of International Finance and director of the Lemberg Program in International Economics and Finance at Brandeis University.

1. The regions referred to in this paper will be North America (Canada and the United States), East Asia (China, Hong Kong, Indonesia, Japan, Korea, Malaysia, Philippines, Taiwan, Thailand, and Singapore), and Pacific Rim (North America, East Asia, Australia, and New Zealand).

the twentieth century, save for short periods of time in the aftermath of World War II and during the mid-1980s. The key long-term story has been the shift of East Asian linkages from regional partners to a more diversified group of countries, including the United States.[2]

Nevertheless, there is reason to see 1985 as a turning point in these trends. East Asian interdependence has not greatly intensified so far, but the break with previous trends is clear. In addition, still larger changes have taken place in investment linkages, and these foreshadow future trade changes. These developments, combined with anecdotal evidence on how individual agents and governments are stepping up investments in regional linkages, suggest that from now on the East Asian trading bloc may be strengthening rather than continuing to dissolve.

The analytical base of this paper is a simple model of bloc formation. The model begins with the idea that a trading bloc's intrabloc bias—its preference for inside rather than outside partners—rests on low intrabloc transaction costs compared to outside-bloc transaction costs. Intrabloc transaction costs can be reduced by investments in intrabloc linkages—for example, in transport links, economic policies that facilitate integration, or information about regional business opportunities. These investments, in turn, depend on economic and/or political developments that draw the bloc's countries closer together. The process of bloc formation is dynamic, because a growing volume of intrabloc trade itself provides incentives for investing in linkages. Thus "historical accidents" that bring economies together may well be amplified and perpetuated by the linkage investments that they induce.

Three major historical developments are important for understanding East Asian interdependence. The first is the development of Asian treaty ports in the nineteenth century, which established a network of trade driven by major ports such as Singapore, Hong Kong, Manila, and Shanghai. A second is Japan's imperial expansion, which created a very high level of economic integration among the economies of northern East Asia. Finally, the spectacular growth of the region's economies is emerging as a new force for integration today: as East Asian countries are becoming increasingly important to each other, they are beginning to invest heavily in linkages that are very likely to increase their intraregional bias.

It is also possible to identify forces that have worked against regional integration in the postwar period. These include the central role of the United States in the postwar Pacific economy, the rapid economic development of the region, which enabled its economies to enter many new global markets, and the general integration of the world economy due to trade liberalization and improvements in transport and communications. This paper attempts to trace

2. The importance of the United States in the Pacific trade network is examined in some detail in Petri (1992). That study concludes that these transpacific connections make it unlikely that any exclusionist East Asian bloc could develop in the near future.

how the changing balance of these pro- and antiregional forces has led to the complex pattern of rises and declines that have characterized East Asian economic integration.

1.2   Measures of Interdependence

There is no single, widely accepted measure of interdependence. As we shall see, the reason for this is that the appropriateness of a particular measure depends on the uses to which it is put. Briefly, three different types of measures are frequently used. Let x_{ij} represent exports from country i to country j, and the subscript $*$ (in place of i or j) represent the summation across all i or j. Thus x_{i*} represents the total exports of country i, x_{*j} the total imports of country j, and x_{**} total world trade. In this notation, the three commonly used concepts of interdependence are (1) *absolute* measures of trading intensity, which deflate a particular bilateral (or intraregional) trade flow with overall world trade:

$$A = x_{ij}/x_{**};$$

(2) *relative* measures of trading intensity, which deflate absolute intensity with *either* the worldwide export share of the exporting country, or the worldwide import share of the importing country:

$$B = A/(x_{i*}/x_{**}) = x_{ij}/x_{i*} \quad \text{or} \quad B' = x_{ij}/x_{*j};$$

and (3) *double-relative* measures of trading intensity, which deflate absolute intensity with *both* the worldwide export share of the exporting country and the worldwide import share of the importing country:

$$C = A/\{(x_{i*}/x_{**})\,(x_{*j}/x_{**})\} = x_{ij}x_{**}/x_{i*}x_{*j}.$$

In effect, measure A compares the scale of a particular bilateral (or intraregional) trading relationship to worldwide averages, measure B compares it to the trade shares of one or the other of the two partners participating in the relationship, and measure C compares it to the product of the trade shares of both partners. These indexes of trading intensity can evolve quite differently over time. For example, exports from X to Y could grow rapidly compared to world trade (rising A measure), but could still fail to keep pace with X's rapidly increasing share of world exports or Y's rapidly increasing share of world imports (declining C measure). The double-relative measures calculated as the C measure in this study are commonly described as "gravity coefficients" in the literature.[3]

Each of these measures of trading intensity is appropriate for answering a particular type of question. For example, if one is interested in the relative stakes or influence of different groups of countries in global trade negotiations,

---

3. Some of the early studies based on gravity coefficients include Linnemann (1966) and Leontief and Strout (1963).

it may make sense to compare their trade volumes to world levels by using an absolute intensity index. Alternatively, if one wants to know to what extent a country will respond to the interests of a particular partner (or group of partners), then the intensity of the bilateral (intrabloc) trading relationship is best judged using a relative measure (in effect, the share of the partner[s] in the country's trade). Finally, if one wants to assess the extent of trade biases toward particular partners (or groups of partners) relative to the neutral of assignment of trade across all partners, then double-relative indexes, or gravity coefficients, provide an appropriate answer.

The evolution of East Asian interdependence is summarized, using each of three measures defined above, in table 1.1 and figures 1.1–1.3. The data used represent the longest consistent time series available on international trade flows, and were assembled from the International Monetary Fund's *Direction of Trade* and its many precursor publications. The measures shown are all calculated for *two-way* trade, that is, with x_{ij} defined as the sum of both exports and imports between i and j (not just as exports from i to j as in the previous discussion).

In absolute terms (table 1.1 and fig. 1.1), East Asian intratrade is only slightly larger than North American intratrade, and considerably smaller than Western European intratrade. Indeed, East Asia's share of world trade is still smaller than it was during the height of the Japanese empire before World War

Table 1.1 **Measures of Regional Interdependence (exports plus imports)**

	1938	1955	1969	1979	1985	1990
Absolute measure: intratrade as share of world trade						
North America	0.030	0.067	0.069	0.042	0.064	0.053
Western Europe	0.182	0.196	0.287	0.293	0.271	0.338
East Asia	0.100	0.022	0.029	0.042	0.064	0.079
Pacific Rim	0.180	0.135	0.169	0.156	0.248	0.246
Relative measure: intratrade as share of regional trade						
North America	0.227	0.334	0.379	0.287	0.330	0.313
Western Europe	0.461	0.491	0.647	0.664	0.654	0.712
East Asia	0.671	0.313	0.293	0.332	0.363	0.407
Pacific Rim	0.583	0.450	0.566	0.545	0.643	0.649
Double-relative measure: gravity coefficients						
North America	1.73	1.65	2.09	1.95	1.71	1.84
Western Europe	1.16	1.23	1.46	1.51	1.58	1.50
East Asia	4.48	4.45	2.97	2.64	2.05	2.09
Pacific Rim	1.89	1.49	1.90	1.91	1.67	1.71

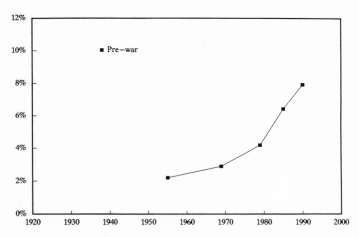

Fig. 1.1   East Asian interdependence: absolute

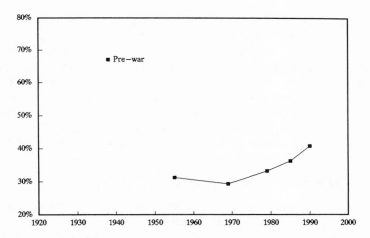

Fig. 1.2   East Asian interdependence: relative

II. Nevertheless, over the postwar period East Asian intratrade has grown very fast, nearly quadrupling its share of world trade.

In relative terms, East Asian intratrade shows a U-shaped pattern (fig. 1.2). By this measure, East Asian interdependence fell sharply as the Japanese empire was dismantled, and continued to decline well into the postwar period. During this period, despite the rapidly growing absolute volume of East Asian intratrade, the relative importance of regional trade fell, since the region's third-country trade developed even more rapidly. Eventually, the region's rapid growth caught up with the diversification of its trade patterns, and intratrade began to increase.

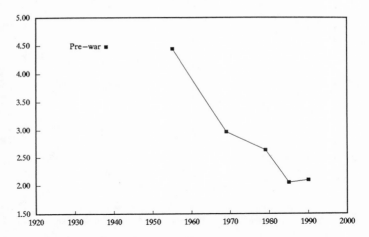

Fig. 1.3   East Asian interdependence: double-relative

Still a third story emerges from the double-relative measure (table 1.1 and fig. 1.3). This index shows a steady and sharp decline in the regional bias of East Asian trade in all but the last five years of data. It also shows that the level of interdependence was initially very high, and that it remained high even in the initial years after World War II. By this measure East Asia was more highly integrated than either North America or Western Europe both before and after the war, and remains so today. Moreover, even the Pacific Rim as a whole, with East Asia and North America combined, is more interdependent than Western Europe, although its trading bias has diminished somewhat in the 1980s.

1.3   Determinants of Interdependence

Bilateral trade patterns and their determinants usually receive little attention in the economic analysis of international trade flows. Economists usually chide noneconomists for concerning themselves with bilateral or regional trade flows when, at least according to some popular theoretical models, bilateral trade flows are analytically uninteresting and even indeterminate.[4] Yet the pattern of bilateral flows is far from random and exhibits remarkable stability over time. It would be difficult to understand this stability without reference to large differences in transaction costs across alternative bilateral linkages.

The most obvious candidate for explaining the differential intensity of bilateral linkages is transport cost. Studies of bilateral trade patterns typically show that bilateral trade is negatively related to the distance separating the partners.[5]

4. For example, the bilateral pattern of trade is indeterminate in a Heckscher-Ohlin model with more products than factors, assuming zero transport costs.
5. For example, Linnemann (1966) and Frankel (chap. 2 in this volume) provide clear evidence of distance effects.

Yet the strong empirical effect of distance is hard to reconcile with the facts of transport technology. Transport costs amount to only a few percentage points of the value of international trade, with much of the cost accounted for in arranging for shipment and the loading and unloading of products (Leontief 1973). Thus, while transport costs can vary greatly across products and modes of transport, they do not vary much with distance itself.[6] Nor is there evidence that bilateral flows were much affected by the large fluctuations in transport costs that took place, for example, during the oil price shocks of the 1970s.

So the empirical importance of distance is most likely due, not to distance itself, but to factors correlated with distance. Important among these may be human and physical assets that facilitate trade, on both sides of a trading relationship. Investments in such assets are more likely to be made among physically and culturally proximate trade partners.[7] These assets may include knowledge about the partner's language, culture, markets, and business practices. They may also include a network of personal or business relationships and business reputations abroad.

The importance of these factors is underscored by the pervasive role of institutions that economize on transactions costs in international trade. International trade is often intrafirm trade (Lawrence 1991); it is likely to be mediated by international banks (e.g., through letters of credit and other instruments that enable the firm to shift the risks and information requirements involved in international deals to banks); and in many countries it is dominated by large, specialized international trading companies.

The level of international transactions costs depends in part on past investments in physical infrastructure, information, and education. Often, the investments required to reduce transactions costs involve substantial scale economies, and so transactions costs across a bilateral link will be lower in proportion to the activity across the link. For example, it is generally cheaper (per unit of output) to establish and operate a transport or telecommunications link across a high-density linkage. This is even more true for investments in information, which generate an essentially public asset, whose services can be costlessly shared by all. Interestingly, the provision of trading information was an important early objective of Japanese policies in East Asia, and is among the first objectives of the Asia Pacific Economic Cooperation (APEC), the region's new forum for economic cooperation.

6. Linnemann (1966) concludes a survey of transport cost data by saying that "one cannot help feeling that these magnitudes [of transport costs] (for instance in comparison to prevailing profit margins) are in a sense too small to justify the emphasis on transportation costs as the major natural obstacle to international trade."

7. In an early empirical study of trade patterns Beckerman (1956) concluded that, "while transport costs paid (directly or indirectly) by an Italian entrepreneur on a raw material supplied by Turkey may be no greater (as the material may come by sea) than the same material supplied by Switzerland, he is more likely to have contacts with Swiss suppliers, since Switzerland will be 'nearer' to him in a psychic evaluation (fewer language difficulties and so on) as well as in the economic sense that air travel will absorb less of his time."

In still other cases, intrabloc transactions costs will be reduced through political mechanisms. For example, a free trade agreement will be easier to negotiate among partners who already have intense linkages. Similarly, the arguments for stabilizing an exchange rate will be much more compelling for countries with substantial bilateral trade than for those that are not highly interdependent. Such mechanisms presume, to be sure, that the trade linkage is valued highly by all of the bloc's countries; asymmetric trade, by contrast, may not lead to reinforcing agreements even if the (one-way) flow is very intense.[8]

The key point is that developments that increase bilateral contacts may trigger strong, positive feedback effects through their impact on trade-facilitating investments. A shock to a bilateral link may be significantly amplified as the initial increase in contacts leads to new investments in the bilateral linkage, which in turn reduce bilateral transaction costs. In some respects, these mechanisms are similar to those that generate irreversible changes ("hysteresis") in trade flows in reaction to exchange rate changes.[9]

The endogeneity of trade-facilitating investments, and thus transactions costs, suggests a simple model of bloc formation. Suppose that a relatively loosely connected group of economies becomes more interdependent due to an economic or noneconomic shock. The increased intensity of contacts will make it attractive to invest further in the bilateral relationship. Bilateral transactions costs will fall, leading to further increases in the intensity of the bilateral relationship. The cycle may repeat itself over time. This story is consistent with Europe's integration process in the 1950s and 1960s. After the war, European peace and economic recovery increased the importance of European partners to each other and provided incentives for reducing intra-European trade barriers. The Common Market undertook a massive effort to eliminate trade barriers and later to reduce the volatility of European Community exchange rates. These steps substantially raised the regional bias of European trade and, arguably, resulted in further efforts to reduce intra-European barriers.

If international transactions costs are endogenous, then history matters. The extent to which countries are "shocked" into close trading relationships, and the extent to which their periods of rapid growth are parallel, affects their investments in their bilateral trade and shapes their subsequent trading relationships.

This paper will examine how various historical events have shaped East Asian interdependence. A key piece of the argument is that various "accidents" of history—that is, close international contacts that cannot be traced to market

8. Petri (1992) argues that strong asymmetries in East Asian trade, including especially the fact that many East Asian countries run large trade deficits with Japan and large trade surpluses with the United States, explain why purely East Asian trading agreements are unlikely.

9. Baldwin (1990), for example, presents a model in which firms establish a "beachhead" (say, an export distribution system) in a foreign market after the appreciation of that country's currency and then continue to sell in the market even after the currency depreciates. The argument here subsumes such investments, but especially focuses on investments that affect transactions costs in the bilateral trading relationship.

forces alone—have changed the international pattern of transactions costs and have permanently affected East Asia's bilateral trading patterns. Three such accidents appear particularly important. First, the imperialist policies of the Western countries established an initial network of East Asian trade. Later, Japanese imperialism provided an impetus for the integration of East Asia's northern economies. As it was often observed at the time, "trade followed the flag." Finally, the rapid growth of various East Asian countries is now making them loom increasingly large to each other and is providing a new impetus for regional integration.

1.4   East Asian Interdependence before 1931

East Asia has a long history of trade, dating back to Arab and Chinese trade among East Asian countries and with Europe. The volume of East Asian trade in general, and of East Asian intratrade as well, appears to have gained momentum with the stepped-up involvement of European powers in the nineteenth century. Subsequently, the expansion of Japan's economic sphere of influence became the main force driving interdependence.

1.4.1   The Treaty Port System

Toward the middle of the nineteenth century, prompted by British leadership, a wave of liberalization spread through Europe. Britain sought similar objectives in East Asia: it abolished the monopoly of the East India Company and moved aggressively to obtain free access to Chinese markets. The Treaty of Nanking, which Britain concluded with China at the end of the Opium War of 1840–42, opened five ports where British subjects could carry on trade "without molestation or restraint" and ceded Hong Kong "in perpetuity" to Her Majesty. Export and import duties were fixed at an average of 5 percent, and consular courts were established to keep British subjects safe from local laws.

As in Europe, Britain also included most favored nation clauses in this and other treaties. Thus it paved the way for "cooperative" imperialism, with France and the United States, and eventually Russia, Prussia, Portugal, Denmark, the Netherlands, Spain, Belgium, and Italy all signing treaties guaranteeing access to Chinese and other ports (Beasley 1987).

A surge of trade ensued, both regionally within East Asia, and with Europe. The profitability of this trade led to a lively competition for new ports. The United States focused on Japan, and following Matthew C. Perry's landings eventually concluded a treaty in 1858. Russia, the Netherlands, Britain, and France followed with similar treaties of their own. Japan's early trade thus came to be oriented toward the West: silk, tea, and coal were exported to France, Italy, and the United States, while textiles, weapons, and machinery were imported from Britain and the United States.

Thus, by the turn of the twentieth century, when relatively comprehensive regional trade data become available, the level of East Asian regional interdependence was already high. As table 1.2 shows, by 1913 about 42 percent of the region's trade was intraregional, compared to 46 percent in 1938 and 47 percent today. Most of this trade was mediated by the great ports developed by the European powers—Hong Kong, Manila, Shanghai, and Singapore. In addition to maintaining bilateral ties between the colonies and their home countries—between Malaysia and Singapore and England, Indonesia and the Netherlands, and the Philippines and the United States—the ports also played a key role in coordinating the trade of a vast region stretching from India to Japan. Roughly 70 percent of Thailand's trade, for example, was mediated by Singapore, which sent some of Thailand's rice on to China and Japan, in exchange for Indian and British textiles.

1.4.2 Japanese Expansion

A second impetus for the intensification of regional ties came from Japan's industrialization and expanding economic influence. By the end of the nineteenth century Japan had established a role parallel to or surpassing those of other powers in Korea and China. It continued to gain economic and military power in the early twentieth century, and began to displace the exports of European powers in their own colonies.

Japan's role in the treaty port system quickly changed from host to protagonist. By 1876 Japan had itself opened three Korean ports and began competing aggressively with China to reexport Western textiles to Korea. In 1895 Japan won a major military victory over China, gaining a large indemnity, further influence in Korea, commercial privileges in China, and two important territories: the Liaotung Peninsula (including Dalien, Manchuria's most important port) and Taiwan. Japan was eventually forced to back down on the Liaotung claims, but its victory had clearly established it as a rising imperial power.

Table 1.2   **East Asian Trade as Share of Total Trade for Different Countries (exports plus imports)**

	1913	1925	1938	1955	1990
China	0.53	0.46	0.70	0.43	0.59
Indonesia	0.32	0.38	0.26	0.32	0.60
Taiwan			0.99	0.50	0.42
Japan	0.41	0.47	0.70	0.22	0.29
Korea			1.00	0.35	0.40
Malaysia	0.44	0.39	0.35	0.30	0.37
Philippines	0.18	0.15	0.11	0.17	0.43
Thailand	0.62	0.71	0.65	0.52	0.51
Simple average	0.42	0.43	0.59	0.35	0.45
Excluding Korea, Taiwan	0.42	0.43	0.46	0.33	0.47
Excluding Korea, Taiwan, Japan	0.42	0.42	0.41	0.35	0.50

Sources: League of Nations, Long-Term Economic Statistics of Japan.

Scholars tend to agree that the conquest of Korea reflected primarily military, rather than economic, objectives—as the Japanese army's Prussian advisor put it, Korea was "a dagger thrust at the heart of Japan" (Myers and Peattie 1984, 15). But the economic potential of a broader sphere of influence was not lost on the Meiji leadership. Foreign Minister Komura Jutaro explicitly recognized the importance of economic objectives and their relationship to military power.

> Competition through commercial and industrial activity and through overseas enterprises is a phenomenon of grave importance in recent international relations. . . . [Western countries] have been zealous in expanding their rights in mining, or in railroads, or in internal waterways, and in various other directions on the Asian continents, especially in China. . . . However, when we look at the measures [taken by] our own empire, which has the most important ties of interest in the area, separated by only a thin stretch of water, there is not much to be seen yet. Both those in government and those outside it regard this as highly regrettable. (Duus 1984, 133)

In any case, Japan's military triumphs in Korea were quickly followed by investments in communications infrastructure related to bilateral trade, and eventually modifications in the Taiwanese and Korean economies that helped to make them more complementary to the Japanese economy. Meiji-style agricultural reforms, such as comprehensive land surveys, were introduced, establishing clear criteria for the ownership and taxation of land and facilitating the sale of land.[10] A combination of these administrative measures and new agricultural technologies imported from Japan resulted in a dramatic surge of agricultural production.[11] By the late 1920s Korea and Taiwan supplied 80 percent of Japan's rice imports,[12] two-thirds of its sugar, and substantial shares of other minerals and lumber (Peattie 1984, 32).

But it was China that was regarded as the great prize. In 1905 Japan defeated Russia in Manchuria and acquired control over the Liaotung Peninsula (known as the Kwantung Leased Territory), all of Korea, the southern half of Sakhalin Island (Karafuto), and the Chinese Eastern Railway. There followed a substantial wave of investments in communications, coordinated by the Southern Manchuria Railway Company (SMR), a quasi-public company that remained a key player also in later phases of Japanese expansion. A key objective of the company was to shape the transport infrastructure of Manchuria—that is, to ensure

10. According to some historians, the land surveys made it easier for Japanese investors to acquire land from Korean and Taiwanese owners.

11. Colonial farmers did not benefit, however; despite substantial growth in output, per capita rice consumption was essentially flat in both Korea and Taiwan in the 1920s and declined substantially in the 1930s (Ho 1984, 379).

12. In light of the considerable current emphasis on full self-sufficiency in rice, it is interesting to note that Japan depended extensively on rice imports during much of the prewar period, generally importing 20 percent of its requirements.

that the network fed into Dalien, the Japanese-controlled port (Beasley 1987, 90–92).

The Japanese government also moved aggressively to improve information on the Chinese economy. The Ministry of Finance proposed a wide-ranging study of Chinese demand, exhibitions in treaty ports, visits by Japanese entrepreneurs, and new ways of disseminating information, including a China Association in Japan that would encourage businessmen to take interest in China. The minister of agriculture and commerce (the precursor of the modern-day MITI) provided a particularly eloquent argument for investments in information.

> There was a time when Japan hoped to find her chief field of commercial enterprise in the west; but today the mind of Japan is all toward China as the commercial hope of our future, not to say anything of our geographical and racial advantages with that country. It is our ambition to be to the East what Great Britain is to the West. We have left no means untried in making a thorough investigation of the present conditions of China. . . . We think we know a good deal about commercial conditions in China because we know a little more than the merchants of the West; but we really know nothing as we ought to know; and I would advise all those who hope to share in trade with China, to make careful and constant investigation into the conditions prevailing there; for I am sure there is much yet to be learned, if our trade with China is to achieve its best. Instead of our business men staying at home and waiting for orders, let them go or send representatives into central China, and they will find a more remunerative field of demand and consumption than they ever dreamed of, reclining in their offices at home. (Whelpley 1913, 247–48).

But as Japan became good at imperialism, the Western powers began to change the rules of the game. The powers started to relax their control over their colonies by revising the treaties on foreign ports; soon after World War I, for example, China was granted substantial tariff autonomy. At the same time, powers moved to control Japan's growing regional influence. The Washington Conference in 1921 sharply limited the size of the Japanese navy, and a period of economic and political frictions ensued.

Despite the strained political circumstances, the sphere of influence established at the turn of the century resulted in a sharp increase in Japan's regional economic role. By the late 1920s Japan had essentially caught up with Western interests in China, and by 1931 the stock of Japanese investments in China equalled those of Great Britain and exceeded those of all other countries combined (Beasley 1987, 133). Japanese investments reached deep into Manchuria; for example, by the end of World War I, the Hanyehping Coal and Iron Company supplied 60 percent of Yawata Steel's iron ore requirements (Beasley 1987, 137). This period of the so-called Shidehara diplomacy was characterized by frequent Japanese-Western clashes, repeated concessions on both military and trade rights, yet considerable economic gains.

1.5   Interdependence between 1931 and 1945

The era of political compromise ended in 1931. This turn of events was hastened by Chinese resistance to Japan's economic advance and by world depression. Subsequently, Japan's economic strategy dramatically changed. The colonial-style exchange of manufactures for raw materials gave way to a concerted effort to develop independent bases of industrial strength in several parts of Japan's economic empire. The new strategy led to substantial industrial investments outside Japan proper, and eventually gave rise to increasingly sophisticated economic linkages among Japan, Korea, Taiwan, and eventually China.

1.5.1   Military Expansion

Three factors helped to replace the economic approaches of the 1920s with a strategy based on military power. The first was China's emerging nationalism. By the late 1920s Japan's influence in China came under increased threat from the Kuomintang. In 1927, for example, the northern Chinese warlord Chang Tso-lin, under Kuomintang influence, withdrew permission for the construction of five new Japanese railway lines into northern Manchuria. A year later, Chiang Kai-shek defeated his Beijing rivals and set his sights on the north Chinese provinces dominated by Japan. Japan's Kwantung Army responded with a complex series of intrigues that eventually led to the invasion of Manchuria in 1931 (Barnhart 1987).

A second factor involved trade frictions that increasingly limited Japan's conventional access to international markets. As the world economy began to decline starting in 1929, Japan's trade relations sharply deteriorated, since many trade partners blamed Japan for the particularly large gains that it had achieved during the previous decade. For example, by 1932 Japan had displaced the Netherlands as Indonesia's largest trade partner, and had made similar inroads in Malaysia. During the 1930s Japan became embroiled in one trade dispute after another; conflicts with India, the Dutch East Indies, and Canada each resulted in a trade war or reciprocal boycott. As one contemporary writer put it, it was

> the bad fortune of the Island Empire that it has come of age industrially at a time when economic theory and, still more, economic practice have drifted far away from the ideals of Bright and Cobden. . . . [Its] export trade has been considerably retarded by a multitude of economic barbed-wire entanglements in the shape of quota restrictions, high tariffs, and other measures designed to check the sweep of "Made in Japan" products. . . . More than sixty countries have imposed special restrictions on Japanese textiles; less than thirty have left the door open on equal terms. (Chamberlin 1937, 219)

The final factor that pushed Japan toward a military strategy was a severe agricultural recession. Policies designed to generate rice surpluses in Taiwan and Korea coincided with worldwide commodity deflation. As rice prices fell, conditions in Japanese agriculture worsened, and the government rapidly shifted its colonial investments toward industry.

In any case, the 1931 invasion of Manchuria, like previous Japanese colonial moves, was followed by a large wave of public and private investments. But there was little room in this picture for non-Japanese companies; by the early 1930s Anglo-Dutch Petroleum, Standard Oil, Siemens, and Skoda had all liquidated major interests (Jones 1949). Manchuria, Korea, and to a lesser extent Taiwan became thoroughly transformed. In the meantime, the complementarity of the Manchurian, Korean, and Japanese economies came to be based on manufacturing; Nissan, for example, a manufacturer of armaments, airplanes, automobiles, and machinery, moved its headquarters to Changchun, and its president eventually went on to direct the Manchuria Industrial Development Company (MIDC; Jones 1949). Manchuria was to become a self-sufficient industrial base, supplying basic materials, including coal, iron and steel, electricity and synthetic oil, rolling stock, and ships to itself and Japan in exchange for machinery (Beasley 1987, 216).

Toward the end of the 1930s Japan's expansion into China became increasingly ominous and continued to accelerate. In 1937 a minor clash between Chinese and Japanese troops provided a pretext for capturing Nanking and much of the Yangtze valley. Soon afterward, Prime Minister Konoe announced a "new order" that called for close cooperation ("coprosperity") among China, Japan, and Manchuria.

A broad southern advance also began to emerge as part of Japan's increasingly expansionist strategy. In 1939 the Showa Research Institute developed an extensive plan for an East Asian Economic Bloc (Lebra 1975, 100–103), which would be self-sufficient by relying on tin, rubber, bauxite, tungsten, nickel, and chromium from Thailand, the Philippines, the Dutch East Indies, and Malaya (Beasley 1987, 225).

As World War II approached, the scope of Japan's sphere of influence was expanded to include Indochina in the so-called Greater East Asia Coprosperity Sphere (GEACS). In the event, not much economic integration took place during the GEACS period, aside from the diversion of some raw materials to Japan, because the sea-lanes were not safe enough to permit large-scale transport. Instead, the region suffered a deep economic decline as its trade with the West collapsed.

1.5.2   Legacies and Parallels

Japan's role in the prewar economy substantially increased East Asian interdependence, particularly among China, Korea, Taiwan, and Japan in the 1930s. Japan's activities in these countries focused on developing transport infrastructure and information, and in the end on developing complementarities with the Japanese economy. The result, naturally enough, was a surge in Japan's regional trade, as shown in figure 1.4. GEACS expanded Japan's influence into

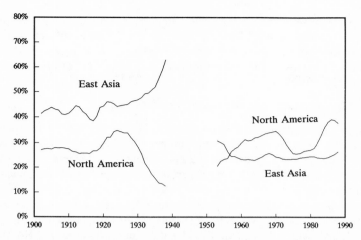

Fig. 1.4   Partner composition of Japanese exports (five-year moving averages)

Southeast Asia, but the economic connections between this region and Japan were brief and overshadowed by the imperatives of war. The Japanese occupation, however, did drive European colonial governments from Southeast Asia and laid the foundations for independence after the war. Thus the economic links that emerged after the war were more Asian than before.

Japan's intense style of imperialism has left long-lived legacies. Unlike the European imperialist powers, Japan was close to its colonies and, in Korea and Manchuria, had excellent communications with them through rail transport. Also, because it was concerned not only with the economic exploitation of the colonies but also with their role as buffers against Russian and Western forces, Japan developed dense political and military organizations to control its empire. Finally, given rice exports as a key early objective, Japan could not restrict its economic activities to an "enclave," but was forced to penetrate local economic structures (Ho 1984, 385).

By the early 1930s Japan's style of complementarity differed dramatically from that of other colonial powers; as Cumings (1984, 482) has observed, Japanese imperialism "involved the location of industry and an infrastructure of communications and transportation *in* the colonies, bringing industry to the labor and raw materials, rather than vice-versa." Although the linkage between the Japanese occupation and the subsequent spectacular development of Manchuria, Korea, and Taiwan is extremely controversial, there is no doubt that powerful industrial centers developed in each of these areas and that these centers evolved along the same technological lines as Japan's own industries.

The notion of a large regional bloc that would also include Southeast Asia does not appear to have been a part of Japan's strategy until 1939. Prime Minister Konoe's 1938 announcement made no mention of southern areas, and the inclusion of Southeast Asia did not arise until the fall of France. By that time, GEACS was clearly designed to obtain raw materials needed for war. As Peattie has argued, GEACS is best seen as a response to a "sudden turn in international events . . . rather than the consequence of long-considered or widely-held interest in the co-prosperity of Asian peoples" (1991, 42).

1.6   Interdependence from World War II to 1985

As table 1.1 and figure 1.4 show, World War II thoroughly disrupted the trade patterns established in the prewar years. Trade flows shifted toward the United States, now the leading military power in the Pacific and the only country with its economy largely intact. Linkages between Japan and Taiwan and Korea were sharply curtailed. China's trade also collapsed as the country sank into civil war. Insurrections erupted also in Indonesia, Indochina, and Malaysia. As a result, trade flows declined sharply throughout the Pacific, especially among China, Japan, Korea, and Taiwan, the "core" countries of GEACS.

Postwar U.S. policy recognized that this sharp dislocation in trade patterns would undermine the prospects for economic recovery in all of the countries that once formed the Japanese empire. The influential Institute of Pacific Relations, for example, concluded at its 1947 conference on the reconstruction of East Asia that, for the sake of Japan and the rest of the region, "Japan must be actively helped to regain something of her old position as the mainspring of the Far Eastern economy as a whole" (Institute of Pacific Relations, 1949). The U.S. occupation authorities in turn began to use the leverage provided by their influence over aid and Japanese reparations to China, Korea, and Taiwan, as well as in Southeast Asia, to revive these countries' trade with Japan.

The data show the magnitude of this challenge. Japan's two-way trade with East Asia fell from 73 percent of her trade around 1940 to only about 31 percent in 1951. At the same time, the partner composition of this East Asian trade shifted from the "core" economies of GEACS to Southeast Asia. The decline in the importance of East Asian countries in general, and of the core partners in particular, can be traced almost entirely to the general decline of their economies, rather than to a decline in their special gravitational linkages with Japan. The analysis of gravity coefficients suggests that regional biases within East Asian trade remained at essentially the same high level in 1955 as they were in 1938. While East Asian linkages remained strong, they were now driven, not by Japanese policy, but by economic structures inherited form the prewar period and by U.S. policies designed to restart this group of highly interdependent economies.

The subsequent story of East Asian economic growth is well known and has been recently reviewed by Kuznets (1988), Noland (1990), Wade (1990), and others. What is of interest here is that the spectacular growth of the region's economies was accompanied by a substantial decline in their regional trade bias. As shown in table 1.3, the gravity coefficients of East Asian trade—coefficients that summarize each country's bias toward East Asian trade partners—

Table 1.3   **Intensity of the East Asian Trade Linkages of Different Countries and Regions (gravity coefficient measure)**

	1938	1955	1969	1979	1985	1990
Japan	4.66	3.13	2.07	2.02	1.46	1.50
North America	0.92	1.16	1.48	1.53	1.48	1.44
Australia, New Zealand	0.53	1.35	2.70	2.85	2.24	2.11
Taiwan	6.63	7.15	4.83	2.82	1.72	2.14
Korea	6.68	4.92	4.83	2.91	1.96	2.04
Hong Kong	3.96	7.55	3.72	3.22	3.09	2.96
Malaysia, Singapore	2.31	4.22	3.34	3.11	2.05	1.88
Thailand	4.34	7.36	5.38	3.64	2.69	2.61
Philippines	0.70	2.45	4.58	3.17	2.54	2.22
Indonesia	1.76	4.60	5.52	4.89	3.34	3.10
China	4.70	6.13	2.91	2.76	3.23	3.04
Western Europe	0.26	0.49	0.33	0.34	0.31	0.36
Middle East	0.46	1.05	1.39	1.84	1.36	1.33
Rest of world	0.30	0.67	0.81	0.62	0.70	0.76
Total imports	1.00	1.00	1.00	1.00	1.00	1.00
East Asia	4.48	4.45	2.97	2.64	2.05	2.09
Pacific Rim	2.61	1.95	2.05	2.08	1.77	1.80
Average	2.72	3.51	2.93	2.44	1.94	1.91

which survived World War II at relatively high levels, fell steadily in the following years. The pattern of decline is similar for most East Asian countries, and the few anomalies that do occur (an unusually rapid decline in the case of China, and an unusual increase in the case of the Philippines) can be understood in terms of major political changes in the countries involved.

Equally remarkable is a parallel decline in the *dispersion* of gravity coefficients (that is, in variations in the intensity of linkages across different trade partners) in the region. As shown in table 1.4, the standard deviations of the gravity coefficients of most East Asian countries fell steadily during the postwar period. In effect, each country's bilateral trade pattern came to look more and more like the world's trade pattern—the importance of any particular partner to a given country came to resemble the importance of that partner in world trade as a whole. (If each partner's share of a country's trade were equal to that partner's share in world trade, then all gravity coefficients would be one.) Country-specific biases became less and less important in explaining the distribution of East Asian trade, both between East Asia and other regions and across different East Asian partners.

Three types of factors help to explain the diversification and homogenization of the region's trade. The first was the general integration of the global economy during most of the postwar period, which was spurred by several successful rounds of trade negotiations, steady progress toward convertibility, and considerable improvements in international communications and transport. All of these factors worked to pull East Asia's trade (as well as the trade

Table 1.4   **Dispersion of Gravity Coefficients, by Country and over Time (standard deviations of gravity coefficients)**

	1938	1955	1969	1979	1985	1990
Japan	5.55	4.25	2.50	1.75	1.26	1.22
North America	1.41	0.85	0.62	0.50	0.55	0.47
Australia, New Zealand	0.65	0.66	0.94	1.19	0.97	1.23
Taiwan	4.08	4.51	2.60	1.53	1.07	1.13
Korea	4.18	5.45	2.01	1.19	0.91	0.97
Hong Kong	6.81	10.22	2.79	2.61	3.36	4.02
Malaysia, Singapore	9.25	4.21	3.78	2.74	1.95	1.24
Thailand	9.59	4.92	3.14	2.18	1.80	1.26
Philippines	1.52	1.42	1.96	1.19	1.23	0.86
Indonesia	3.11	3.53	3.45	2.58	1.49	1.30
China	6.15	9.51	2.77	2.57	3.47	4.09
Western Europe	0.56	0.43	0.33	0.32	0.36	0.33
Middle East	1.12	0.68	0.74	0.63	0.41	0.49
Rest of world	0.41	0.38	0.58	0.48	0.37	0.37
Total imports	0.00	0.00	0.00	0.00	0.00	0.00
East Asia	2.28	2.52	1.68	1.15	0.88	0.80
Pacific Rim	0.97	0.76	0.77	0.64	0.49	0.46
Average	3.39	3.19	1.80	1.37	1.21	1.19

of all other countries) away from its regional partners toward more global sources and destinations.

A second important factor was the rapid development of the region's economies. The expansion of each economy's overall trade provided the scale needed to justify investments in trading linkages with an increasingly large number of countries. More frequent shipping and air schedules could now be maintained; additional investments could be made in communications; and a greater stock of information could be developed to link firms and their foreign counterparts. All these trends undoubtedly contributed to the broadening of East Asian marketing efforts. These trends presumably operated in all countries, but it is likely that their effect was especially pronounced in the context of East Asia's "miracle" economies.

A third factor driving East Asia's diversification was the similarity of East Asian development patterns. Each country rapidly shifted its output from raw materials to manufactures, and within manufactures from labor-intensive to more capital- and technology-intensive sectors. These patterns have been described as the "flying geese pattern" of development by the Japanese economists (Akamatsu 1960) and are consistent with Heckscher-Ohlin explanations of how trade patterns are likely to change with the accumulation of human and physical capital.[13]

13. A case can be made that East Asian development trajectories are *more* similar than would be justified by Heckscher-Ohlin considerations because they "follow" a common East Asian de-

The similarity in development patterns is important for two reasons. First, it explains how each country acquired an increasingly sophisticated basket of exports and thus positioned itself to compete in a wider world market. Second, it explains why East Asian countries developed competitive rather than complementary economies, and thus why they had to look to outside markets, rather than regional markets, for new trading opportunities.

An important exception of this story involves linkages based on the importation of intermediate inputs and capital goods. The commonality of East Asian development trajectories has meant that each country would typically look to neighboring countries for appropriate technology. These supply-side linkages in turn gave rise to substantial imports of machinery and components. As a result, several East Asian economies acquired asymmetrical linkages. On the one hand, they relied heavily on the region's more advanced economies—Japan, Korea, Taiwan, Singapore—for imports of machinery and components, and on the other, they looked outside the region to sell their exports.

1.7   Interdependence Today

The intensity of East Asian interdependence appears to have reached a trough in 1985–86. The turning point came at the end of a period when the real value of the U.S. dollar was unusually high; in the preceding years, several East Asian countries had sharply shifted their trade toward the United States. In addition, the high value of the dollar permitted Japanese companies to maintain their exports despite sharply higher wages and declining competitiveness against other East Asian economies.

The large exchange rate adjustments of 1985 and 1986 affected interdependence in a complex way. Initially, the appreciation of the yen was not matched by other East Asian currencies; thus other countries became more competitive against Japan in both U.S. and Japanese markets. For a while, East Asian imports surged in both markets, and Korea, Taiwan, and other countries began to run substantial trade surpluses. These export surges also led to accelerating imports from Japan and Singapore. As a result, East Asian interdependence intensified; intraregional trade expanded very rapidly, and the long-run decline of the region's gravity coefficients ceased.

Many observers assumed at that time that the trade flow adjustments described above represented the beginning of a new historical trend toward the

---

velopment model, as pioneered by Japan. This case is most easily made for Korea, which systematically researched and adopted Japanese policies during its high-growth period. Petri (1988) has shown that the composition of Korean industry resembles the composition of Japanese industry more closely than would be expected on the basis of resource similarities alone. These similarities are in part due to the similarity of external opportunities; for example, the dynamics of foreign protection systematically "capped" import surges from Japan and thus created systematic incentives for Korean producers to move into the same industries in which Japan excelled.

greater integration of the East Asian economy. This may still be the case, but
the events of 1985–88 were in large part driven by the staggered adjustment of
exchange rates in different East Asian countries. By the late 1980s the second
phase of the exchange rate adjustments took hold, as most of the region's currencies appreciated to close the gap that had opened between them and the yen
in the mid-1980s. These corrections slowed the surge of Japanese imports from
East Asia and stopped the increase in the region's gravity coefficients. To be
sure, the absolute volume of East Asian trade continued to expand at a rapid
pace due to the high growth of the region's economies.

The more significant impact of the appreciation of the yen was a sharp increase in regional investment flows (see table 1.5). Malaysia, Thailand, and
Indonesia had two-thirds as much investment in 1988–89 alone as in all previous years until then. The cause of this wave is widely accepted; the exchange
rate changes of the late 1980s reduced the competitiveness of Japanese firms
and led firms to shift some production activities closer to markets and to countries with lower labor costs. While most of these investments went into the
United States and other developed countries, a substantial amount also occurred in East Asia.

Table 1.5 **Foreign Direct Investment in East Asia (millions of U.S. dollars)**

Host/Source	Total	Japan	U.S.	Korea	Taiwan	Hong Kong	Singapore
Thailand							
Up to 1987	11,536	2,773	1,910	9	675	445	351
1988–89	7,868	4,431	570	66	530	278	408
Malaysia							
Up to 1987	4,200	1,741	202	0	34	262	594
1988–89	3,690	967	179	49	1,314	138	231
Indonesia							
Up to 1987	17,284	5,928	1,244	222	144	1,876	299
1988–89	11,159	1,304	783	728	1,126	867	489
Philippines							
Up to 1987	2,830	377	1,620				
1988–89	275	71	98				
Korea							
1984–88	3,648	1,857	876				
Taiwan							
1984–88	4,170	1,343	1,251				
Singapore							
1984–88	6,529	2,200	2,814				
Sum (Thailand, Malaysia, Indonesia only)							
Up to 1987	33,020	10,442	3,356	231	853	2,583	1,244
1988–89	22,717	6,702	1,532	843	2,970	1,283	1,128
Shares of sum							
1987	1.000	0.316	0.102	0.007	0.026	0.078	0.038
1988–89	1.000	0.295	0.067	0.037	0.131	0.056	0.050

Sources: Tho (1993); Holloway (1991).

By the late 1980s, as the newly industrializing countries (NICs) also adjusted their exchange rates and began to face competitive strains similar to Japan's, they too joined Japan as major investors in East Asia. Thus an entirely new channel of interdependence began to operate: cross-investments among a large number of East Asian countries. This is a natural result of the region's prosperity; it recalls patterns of integration that have evolved in Europe.

The investment wave of the late 1980s differed from earlier investments in developing country production facilities not just in magnitude and origin, but also in structure. Japan's investments in East Asia in the 1970s, for example, were primarily focused on local markets, often encouraged by policies that sought to increase local participation in industry, for example, through the importation of automobile kits instead of assembled automobiles. The recent wave of investments, by contrast, is the product of new, global strategies by regional firms. Nearly all firms have adopted such strategies, and some have gone to some length to plan a comprehensive distribution of their activities across different regional markets. Toyota, for example, has selected locations that will permit it to build a regional automobile, with components produced in different countries, depending on the advantages of the location in terms of supplier infrastructure and local resources (fig. 1.5).

Since the recent investment wave has been driven by production strategy rather than by market considerations, it has included a larger share of export-oriented industries. More so than in the past, the firms established in foreign

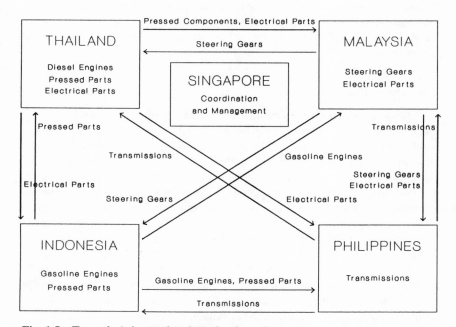

Fig. 1.5   Toyota's Asian regional production scheme

locations have also been intended to serve home (e.g., Japanese) markets. At the same time, since these investments were closely tied to Japanese technologies and suppliers that have remained at home, they have typically required a higher ratio of imported inputs than earlier investments. Because of these characteristics, the recent wave of intra–East Asian investment flows has helped to intensify regional linkages by facilitating exports into Japan and other regional markets and by spreading technologies that require regional inputs and capital goods.

The market forces that have helped to intensify regional linkages through trade and investment have been also supported by government aid policies. Japan's aid program has been always oriented toward Asia, but its growing scale has made it an important factor in recent economic linkages. Japanese aid flows to East Asia have been substantial compared to private investment flows. These flows have helped to finance the infrastructure that supports private investment.

The volume of intraregional investment has slackened somewhat recently but is likely to remain relatively high compared to historical levels. Some of the reasons for the current slowdown are permanent: the investment wave of late 1980s represented, in part, a onetime adjustment in corporate sourcing policies, triggered by the appreciation of the yen and the NICs' currencies. But other reasons are temporary. As a result of the rapid inflow of capital, infrastructure bottlenecks developed in several of the receiving economies, including especially Thailand, and labor and real estate costs rose sharply due to the overheated economy. At the same time, the accumulation of Japanese firms has contributed to the development of an economic infrastructure—consisting of suppliers and service companies—that will make it easier for other firms to invest in the future.

1.8 Policy Reactions

Postwar trends in East Asian interdependence have been driven by market rather than political forces. These forces initially worked to diversify the region's trade, as the growing scale of the region's economies permitted more diversified links, and as the region's competitive development strategies forced each country to look for markets outside the East Asian region. But even as the *intensity* of the region's trade declined, its volume dramatically increased. Over the past two decades, East Asia's share in world trade doubled, and even in the face of declining regional intensity, this meant that East Asia's internal trade increased from 30 to 41 percent of its total trade.

The importance of a particular partner in a country's transactions is likely to be closely related to the country's investments in linkages with that partner. It is thus not surprising that a wide array of regional initiatives have recently emerged to address the new issues generated by East Asian interdependence. From an analytical perspective, these initiatives can be seen as attempts to reduce transactions costs in regional trade, manage intraregional trade frictions, and marshal regional economic forces against external economic challenges.

The institutions that are emerging from these initiatives are still very much in flux. But to the extent that they manage to accomplish the objectives cited, they will further encourage intraregional transactions. In the pattern of European and North American interdependence, private sector trends and policies designed to accommodate these trends may lead to reinforcing political mechanisms that encourage interdependence.

The development of regional institutions is complicated both by the great diversity of the region's countries and by the preference of many of the region's countries for informal, negotiated (as opposed to formal, legalistic) approaches to policy. Regional trade policies range widely from the virtual absence of trade barriers in Hong Kong and Singapore, to the relatively liberal regimes of Malaysia and Thailand, the intermediate and more opaque regimes of Korea, Indonesia, and the Philippines, and the still extensive protection in China. The picture is further complicated by the fact that some highly outward countries—for example, Korea and Thailand—still use protection to promote infant industries and exports. And even countries that have little formal protection, such as Japan, have policy and business structures that are difficult to penetrate.

Regional cooperation is also tempered by the "style" of East Asian policymaking. At the risk of excessive generalization, many East Asian countries pursue informal and relatively opaque approaches to policy. Relationships among businesses and between business and government are often characterized by long-term collaboration, reciprocal favors, and continuous negotiations, rather than market-mediated transactions and explicit contracts. Most East Asian governments, even in countries with modest trade barriers, actively participate in the management of the economy and administer complex arrays of incentives and barriers (Arndt 1987). Bureaucrats and influential industrialists have high stakes in maintaining this system of intervention and thus prefer to respond to new policy challenges with administrative instruments such as VERs, VEIs, and regulatory interventions.

In this context cooperation on a modest, practical level has proved more possible than the development of large-scale agreements and institutions. Small, local free trade areas (especially the Shenzhen Free Trade Zone and the Singapore growth triangle) are especially well suited to this policy setting and appear to be developing very fast. In what follows, each of the region's cooperative structures is reviewed in the context of its history and likely evolution, moving from the least to the most comprehensive.

Mini–Trading Areas (MTAs). Though not unique to East Asia, international trading schemes involving small geographical areas of two or more countries have multiplied. These areas feature special provisions to exempt international trade from national tariffs until the products leave the MTA, as well as transportation and other infrastructure to support international trade and investment. The oldest and perhaps most successful such area is the Shenzhen Free Trade Zone, which forms a bridge between Guangdong Province and Hong Kong. A new initiative along these lines is the "growth triangle" formed by Singapore, Johore province of Malaysia, and Batam Island of Indonesia. Similar zones have been proposed to link (1) China, the Koreas, eastern Siberia, and western Japan (North-East Asia Economic Cooperation); (2) Japan, China up to Liaoning, and Korea (Yellow Sea Cooperation); (3) Hong Kong, Taiwan, and China south of Shanghai (Southern China Economic Cooperation); (4) Hong Kong, Guangdong, Guangxi, northern Thailand, Laos, and Vietnam (Tongking-Mekong Economic Cooperation); (5) Thailand, Cambodia, and southern Vietnam (Southern Indochina Economic Cooperation); (6) Myanmar, Thailand, and Indochina (Souvannaphoum); and (7) Thailand, northern Sumatra, and northern Malaysia (ITM Nexus).[14]

Not all of these MTAs will get off the ground, but the proliferation of the idea is interesting. MTAs fit the region's pragmatic approach to policy, and especially its reluctance to adopt more complex agreements than warranted by immediate economic needs. Such pragmatism is likely to be especially helpful in cooperations with the formerly socialist economies, which may not have the institutions to offer credible large-scale agreements for some time to come. So MTAs offer a potentially important model for linking China, Russia, Indochina, and North Korea with East Asia's market economies.

Association of Southeast Asian Nations (ASEAN). This association, comprising Brunei, Indonesia, Malaysia, the Philippines, Thailand, and Singapore, was initially focused on political and security issues. Due to competing industrial objectives, the organization made little progress toward integrating the region's economies until recently. A Preferential Trade Area Agreement was signed in 1977, but the proportion of trade covered by this agreement has remained small. As the association's economies came to pursue more liberal economic strategies, however, the possibilities for regional cooperation improved.

In February 1992 ASEAN adopted an ambitious program to establish a free trade area in fifteen years. Some tariffs have already been lowered with this objective in mind. But ASEAN's internal trade is modest, and the great similarity of ASEAN's economies (Brunei and Singapore aside) raises the possibility of substantial trade diversion within an ASEAN free trade area, particularly if external tariffs remain high. Against this, the opportunity to serve a larger regional market may improve prospects for attracting large-scale foreign investment. Overall, ASEAN's political divisions and the doubtful economic merits of the free trade area will tend to limit the influence of ASEAN in the region's institutional framework.

14. Some items on this list are drawn from Noordin Sopiee (1991).

East Asian Economic Caucus (EAEC). In late 1990, with the Uruguay Round negotiations heading for stalemate, President Mahathir of Malaysia called for the formation of an East Asian Economic Group (EAEG), consisting of Japan, the East Asian NICs, China, and the remaining ASEAN countries. Perhaps the plan emerged in President Mahathir's mind as a natural extension of his "Look East" program, which aimed to shift Malaysia's economic perspectives closer to the development models of Japan and Korea. Although the objectives of the EAEG were not spelled out, it appeared to create an alliance of East Asian states to counter emerging blocs in Europe and the Western Hemisphere. The plan was strongly opposed by Australia, New Zealand, and the United States, because it was viewed as undermining the Asia Pacific Economic Cooperation (APEC), the emerging OECD-like institution that includes countries from both sides of the Pacific (see below). Japan also publicly opposed the plan, but some Japanese government officials and senior business executives were more positive in private statements.

The opposition of the United States and the lack of a clear agenda for the EAEG(roup) eventually led President Mahathir to recast the idea as an EAEC(aucus). The concept now calls for periodic consultations among East Asian states—a mission no clearer than that of the EAEG. Three interpretations are possible. First, the EAEC may be a face-saving device for abandoning the EAEG idea. Second, the EAEC may be represent a threat against exclusionist U.S. and European policies. Third, the EAEC could be a step toward accelerating the integration of East Asian economies by promoting the coordination of their policies. Given the conflicting styles of East Asian and Anglo-Saxon policymaking, the EAEC may be better suited for this purpose than a broader group such as the APEC, which also includes Anglo-Saxon countries.

Asia Pacific Economic Cooperation (APEC). The idea of forming a Pacific region–wide organization has been pursued for several decades through informal, quasi-private organizations such as the Pacific Basin Economic Conference (PBEC), Pacific Economic Cooperation Council (PECC), and Pacific Association for Trade and Development (PAFTAD). Since 1989, however, the foreign ministers of twelve Pacific Rim countries—Australia, Brunei, Canada, Indonesia, Japan, Korea, Malaysia, New Zealand, the Philippines, Singapore, Thailand, and the United States—agreed to meet annually to review issues of mutual interest. APEC's initial work program consisted of a series of tasks, managed by member countries, on cooperation in areas such as the collection of trade and investment data, and the analysis of policies in sectors such as energy, tourism, transportation, and fisheries. At its 1991 meeting APEC also established a modest secretariat.

APEC's mission is still evolving. The organization has been most comfortable with tasks involving technical cooperation and information exchange. Its stiffest challenge has been the "China problem"—resolved by admitting

China, Taiwan, and Hong Kong to APEC membership. Beyond this, APEC meetings have dealt with noncontroversial issues such as support for international trade liberalization through the Uruguay Round. It remains to be seen whether APEC can assume functions beyond the technical, for example, whether it can facilitate movement toward regional liberalization, the harmonization of regulations, or the resolution of trade frictions. APEC's membership is very diverse, and few members seem willing to trust this new institution with significant responsibilities.

1.9   Conclusions

This paper has explored the hypothesis that blocs are, in part, the product of historical accidents. Reinforcing mechanisms of integration can be set into motion by military force or other developments that make countries important to each other. In East Asia important initial investments in regional linkages were triggered by imperial conquest—first by the Western powers under the treaty port system, and then by Japan during its imperialist period. By the advent of World War II these investments had transformed East Asia into perhaps the most interdependent region in the world.

After World War II the intensity of East Asian interdependence resumed its prewar level. Subsequently, however, the region diversified its trade patterns, due to the important role of the United States in postwar Pacific relations and to the growing sophistication of the region's industries. The trend toward diversification has been reversed in the last five or so years. Since 1985, spurred in part by investment and aid, trade flows within East Asia have grown sharply and have become more regionally biased.

An interesting question is how the recent flurry of regional policy initiatives will affect these trends. It is likely that the institutions created by these initiatives will not be strong enough to liberalize regional trade. Even if growing intraregional linkages create a demand for cooperation, the diversity of the region's policy approaches makes broad, formal agreements difficult and unlikely. So far, collaboration has focused on narrow, highly pragmatic objectives—trade cooperation in the context of MTAs and ASEAN, and technical cooperation in the context of APEC.

For the time being, then, much of the region's business will be conducted through bilateral rather than multilateral institutions. Japan is raising its profile in regional diplomacy as well as in economic cooperation and consultation. Intense series of Asian visits are scheduled for the emperor and the prime minister. Japanese ministries are also developing country-specific development plans and are encouraging their implementation with aid, expert advice, infrastructure lending, and support for private investment.

The East Asian trading bloc has a long and complex history. Investments in this bloc, some made more than a century ago, have proved surprisingly durable. Today's developments, likewise, may shape the pattern of East Asian trade far into the future. If there are externalities associated with investments in bilateral trade, as the evidence here suggests, then the factors and policies that affect bilateral trade deserve more attention than they usually receive.

References

Akamatsu, K. 1960. A Theory of Unbalanced Growth in the World Economy. *Weltwirtschaftliches Archiv* 86 (2).

Arndt, H. W. 1987. Industrial Policy in East Asia. *Industry and Development* (22): 1–65.

Baldwin, Richard. 1990. Some Empirical Evidence on Hysteresis in Aggregate U.S. Import Prices. In Peter A. Petri and Stefan Gerlach, eds., *The Economics of the Dollar Cycle*, 235–73. Cambridge: MIT Press.

Barnhart, Michael A. 1987. *Japan Prepares for Total War: The Search for Economic Security, 1919–1941.* Ithaca: Cornell University Press.

Beasley, W. G. 1987. *Japanese Imperialism: 1894–1945.* Oxford: Clarendon Press.

Beckerman, W. 1956. Distance and the Pattern of Intra-European Trade. *Review of Economics and Statistics* 28: 38.

Chamberlin, William Henry. 1937. *Japan over Asia.* Boston: Little Brown and Company.

Cumings, Bruce. 1984. The Legacy of Japanese Colonialism in Korea. In Ramon H. Myers and Mark R. Peattie, eds., *The Japanese Colonial Empire, 1895–1945,* 478–96. Princeton: Princeton University Press.

Duus, Peter. 1984. Economic Dimensions of Meiji Imperialism: The Case of Korea, 1895–1910. In Ramon H. Myers and Mark R. Peattie, eds., *The Japanese Colonial Empire, 1895–1945.* Princeton: Princeton University Press.

Ho, Samuel P. 1984. Colonialism and Development: Korea, Taiwan, and Kwantung. In Ramon H. Myers and Mark R. Peattie, eds. *The Japanese Colonial Empire, 1895–1945,* 347–98. Princeton: Princeton University Press.

Holloway, N. 1991. *Japan in Asia.* Hong Kong: Review Publishing Co.

Institute of Pacific Relations. 1949. *Problems of Economic Reconstruction in the Far East.* New York: Institute of Pacific Relations.

Jones, F. C. 1949. *Manchuria since 1931.* New York: Oxford University Press.

Kuznets, Paul. 1988. An East Asian Model of Economic Development: Japan, Taiwan, and South Korea. *Economic Development and Cultural Change* 36 (3): S11–43.

Lawrence, Robert Z. 1991. How Open Is Japan? In Paul Krugman, ed., *Trade with Japan: Has the Door Opened Wider?* 9–50. Chicago: University of Chicago Press.

Lebra, Joyce C. 1975. *Japan's Greater East Asia Co-prosperity Sphere in World War II: Selected Readings and Documents.* Kuala Lumpur: Oxford University Press.

Leontief, Wassily. 1973. Explanatory Power of the Comparative Cost Theory of International Trade and Its Limits. In H. C. Bos, ed., *Economic Structure and Development: Lectures in Honor of Jan Tinbergen.* Amsterdam: North-Holland.

Leontief, Wassily, and Alan Strout. 1963. Multiregional Input-Output Analysis. In T. Barna, ed., *Structural Interdependence and Economic Development,* 119–50. London: Macmillan.

Linnemann, Hans. 1966. *An Econometric Study of International Trade Flows.* Amsterdam: North-Holland.

Montgomery, Michael. 1988. *Imperialist Japan: The Yen to Dominate.* New York: St. Martin's Press.

Myers, Ramon H., and Mark R. Peattie, eds., 1984. *The Japanese Colonial Empire, 1895–1945*. Princeton: Princeton University Press.

Noland, Marcus. 1990. *Pacific Basin Developing Countries: Prospects for the Future*. Washington DC: Institute for International Economics.

Peattie, Mark R. 1984. The Nan'yo: Japan in the South Pacific: 1885–1945. In Ramon H. Myers and Mark R. Peattie, eds., *The Japanese Colonial Empire, 1895–1945*. Princeton: Princeton University Press.

————. 1991. Nanshin: The "Southward Advance" 1931–1941, as a Prelude to the Japanese Occupation of Southeast Asia. Paper presented at the Conference on the Japanese Wartime Empire in Asia, 1937–1945, Hoover Institution, Stanford University, August 23–24.

Petri, Peter A. 1988. Korea's Export Niche: Origins and Prospects. *World Development* 16 (1): 47–63.

————. 1992. One Bloc, Two Blocs, or None? Political-Economic Factors in Pacific Trade Policy. In Kaoru Okuzumi, Kent E. Calder, and Gerrit W. Gong, eds., *The U.S.-Japan Economic Relationship in East and Southeast Asia: A Policy Framework for Asia-Pacific Economic Cooperation*, 39–70. Washington, DC: Center for Strategic and International Studies.

Sopiee, Noordin. 1991. Introductory Remarks. Paper presented at the Fifth Trade Policy Forum, Pacific Economic Cooperation Conference, August 18–21, Kuala Lumpur.

Tho, Tran Van. 1993. Technology Transfer in the Asian Pacific Region: Some Recent Trends. In T. Ito and A. O. Krueger, eds. *Trade and Protectionism*, 243–68. Chicago: University of Chicago Press.

Wade, Robert. 1990. *Governing the Market: Economic Theory and the Role of Government in East Asian Industrialization*. Princeton: Princeton University Press.

Whelpley, James D. 1913. *The Trade of the World*. New York: Century Company.

Yamazawa, Ippei, and Yuzo Yamamura. 1979. Trade and Balance of Payments. In Kazushi Ohkawa and Miyohei Shinohara, eds., *Patterns of Japanese Economic Development: A Quantitative Appraisal*, 134–58. New Haven: Yale University Press.

Comment   Stephan Haggard

Peter Petri's paper provides an excellent introduction to the question of regionalism in the Pacific. It combines an interesting theoretical idea, centered on transactions costs, the collation of new data on the extent of regional interdependence, and a stylized history that is attentive to political as well as economic variables. I want to begin by placing Petri's paper, and others in the volume, in the context of the larger debate about the regionalization of the world economy, before turning to several specific comments.

Recent debates have employed *regionalism* and *regionalization* to mean two quite different things. Regionalization may be used to refer to an *economic* process in which trade and investment within a given region—however defined—grow more rapidly than the region's trade and investment with the rest of the world; this is the definition typically adopted by economists, including Petri. Regionalization has also been used to refer to the formation of political

Stephan Haggard is professor at the Graduate School of International Relations and Pacific Studies, University of California, San Diego.

groupings, or "blocs," that aim to reduce intraregional barriers to trade and investment.

Any discussion of regionalism must begin by keeping these two meanings of the terms separate, since the relationship between the two phenomena is far from clear. In this regard, it is useful to make a further distinction between economic and political explanations for the two types of regionalism, yielding the typology of different analytic approaches outlined in table 1C.1.

The economic explanation for increased regional integration (cell I) rests on "natural" economic forces of proximity, income convergence, and intrafirm trade; in this view, regionalism may owe very little to policy-induced discrimination. Proximity implies lower transport costs, higher information flows, and increased investment aimed at reducing transactions costs, the factor emphasized by Petri.

According to this view, the tendency toward greater intra-Asian trade should reflect only marginal preferences. There is no necessary tendency for these patterns to continue or deepen; the opposite may be the case. At some point, the advantages of extraregional diversification outweigh the economies associated with regionalization, thus providing a mechanism checking the tendency toward continuing regional concentration.

The "economic" perspective explains the emergence of regional political cooperation in functional terms (cell II). Regional agreements and institutions provide governance structures for managing increased economic integration; cooperation follows, rather than leads, trade and investment flows. Petri states this position succinctly when he argues that "a wide array of regional initiatives have recently emerged to address the new issues generated by East Asian interdependence. From an analytical perspective, these initiatives can be seen as attempts to reduce transactions costs in regional trade, manage intraregional trade frictions, and marshal regional economic forces against external economic challenges."

The economic perspective suggests several structural and policy conditions

Table 1C.1   Alternative Approaches to Regionalism

| | Causes of Regionalism | |
	Economic	Political
	I	III
Regionalism defined as economic integration	Proximity, income convergence, intrafirm trade, policy convergence	Preferences favor intraregional over extraregional trade and investment
	II	IV
Regionalism defined as political cooperation	Governance structures established to manage increased economic interdependence	Hegemonic power exploited, response to rival blocs. Dependence on domestic coalitions in member countries

that are likely to be necessary for successful regional political groupings to form. First, some threshold of economic integration is necessary for there to be an interest in the formation of a regional political arrangement in the first place. Second, the expected gains from discrimination must apply universally, and not only to some members of the group. Cooperation can founder when gains are unequally distributed.

Finally, the initial trade, investment, and macroeconomic policy stances of the countries should be broadly similar. Wide divergence in policies will make it more difficult to reach regional consensus because of the asymmetric nature of the concessions required of the more closed members. Divergent macroeconomic policies will imply unstable exchange rates, inhibiting both trade and investment, and differences in tax or regulatory regimes will create conflicts between countries with high and low levels of taxation and between countries with more or less strict regulatory norms.

From a normative perspective, this economic view of integration emphasizes the welfare gains to be achieved through trade creation and political cooperation, and assumes that the adverse effects to the rest of the world are limited. Under two conditions, regional organizations can provide "building blocks" for deeper integration: the arrangements must be liberalizing; and they must be nonexclusive in their membership. Arguably, this is what happened in the North Atlantic "region" in the immediate postwar period, flowering gradually into what we now know as multilateralism.

The political view of regionalization tends to see the growth of intrabloc trade primarily as a consequence of policy decisions, either already taken or potential (cell III). The emphasis is on an "unnatural" regionalism constructed on the basis of intraregional preferences that discriminate against extraregional trade and investment. The main puzzle, therefore, is to explain these policy choices. In doing so, the political economy view draws attention to both the internal and domestic factors that the functional economic view ignores (cell IV).

Countries may be motivated to construct regional "fortresses" for a number of international political as well as economic reasons. First, and most obviously, the formation of blocs provides a means of countering competitive pressures from outside the region by providing more assured markets within it. Second, blocs might initially be formed to gain bargaining leverage vis-à-vis other regional blocs. Interbloc negotiations could eventually produce liberalizing outcomes, but it is also possible that bargaining dynamics could degenerate into competitive protectionism rather than a liberal equilibrium.

Finally, intraregional arrangements between larger and smaller countries may reflect hegemonic power relations. Regional hegemons can exploit bilateral asymmetries in interdependence to exercise monopoly and/or monopsony power over smaller and poorer trading partners and to extract policy changes that favor the regional hegemon. Under such a scenario, regionalism will not be multilateralism in miniature, but will rest on a network of bilateral deals.

Such power can ultimately be turned to political objectives, as is seen in extreme form in Japan's Greater East Asia Co-prosperity Sphere or Nazi trade policy in central Europe during the 1930s.

The economic view emphasizes the aggregate welfare gains from integration and thus implicitly assumes the easy reallocation of resources necessitated by increased trade. The political perspective, by contrast, places greater emphasis on the distributional effects of economic integration *within* countries. Integration will have adjustment costs, and thus the viability of regional agreements will hinge in part on domestic political coalitions and conflicts within potential members. This is the main theme of the Frieden and Froot and Yoffie contributions to this volume, though they stress different cleavages: Frieden's is rooted in a real exchange rate analysis, Froot and Yoffie's distinguishes between sectors with declining versus rising returns to scale.

Before situating Petri's arguments, it is important to tackle a prior question: whether there is in fact any evidence of increased economic regionalization in East Asia. There is no reason to repeat the findings that are neatly summarized in table 1.1, except to note that Petri pays particular attention to trends in the East Asian figures, when on both the absolute and relative measures, there is also evidence of a deepening of the Pacific Rim region as a whole; I will return to this point below.

Petri's explanation for East Asian regionalism has two steps. First, a shock increases interdependence; second, this shock increases returns to investments that further reduce transactions costs, creating a virtuous circle of further transactions. It is not theoretically clear why this virtuous cycle would continue. Why don't the advantages of diversification come to outweigh continued investment in regional linkages? Put differently, why does Petri believe there are increasing, rather than decreasing, marginal returns to such transactions costs–reducing investments?

My second broad comment concerns a kind of asymmetry in the historical argument of the paper. The first two phases of integration are attributed to imperialism, but the third is not. This suggests an alternative argument that is familiar to political scientists, namely, that patterns of economic integration are determined by hegemonic actors.

What Petri's account shows, however, is that hegemons operate in quite different ways. British imperialism was aimed primarily at overcoming Chinese resistance to free trade. But the British conception was essentially nondiscriminatory, in that other imperial powers were allowed to benefit from the opening of the treaty ports. From the perspective of the other imperial contenders in the region, including the United States, Britain's victory in the Opium War constituted a pure public good.

Petri's assertion about the effects of these arrangements on regional interdependence are somewhat misleading, however, because they include entrepôt trade via Hong Kong, Shanghai, and Singapore, most of which was directed to Europe and India. If this entrepôt trade is removed, the degree of intraregional interdependence fostered by British penetration would be much less. Rather, as a theory of hegemony would predict, the region's trade was ultimately directed toward the European metropolitan powers or their colonies, particularly India.

The Japanese empire, of course, was organized on a fundamentally different basis, and suggests that the term "reducing transactions costs" can be somewhat euphemistic. Though Japan reduced transactions costs for Japanese exporters and investors, the government was clearly intent on raising them for everyone else through the imposition of formal and informal preferences. In developing the transactions costs approach, therefore, it is crucial to consider the extent to which the transactions cost–reducing investment is a private, club, or public good.

The U.S. strategy resembles to a greater extent the British one, though initially without the same emphasis on forcing liberalization on strategic allies. The result of this strategy was a steady increase in Pacific Rim interdependence on all three of Petri's measures between 1955 and 1979, and conversely, a decline in the intraregional share. The reason for this pattern was that first Japan, then the East Asian newly industrializing countries (NICs), and then the ASEAN countries adopted export-led growth strategies that were targeted on the United States. Moreover, the United States encouraged them to do so, both through its exchange rate policy and through bilateral influence on economic policy in Japan, Korea, and Taiwan.

Thus, while Petri emphasizes transactions costs in his model of regionalism, there is an implicit political explanation of regionalism lurking in the paper, in which the preferences of the hegemonic actor play a crucial role in the pattern of trade and investment. Petri's conclusion that "postwar trends in East Asian interdependence have been driven by market rather than political forces" ignores the role of the grand strategy of the United States in reconstructing the region as a component of its political-military effort to contain China and the Soviet Union.

This political argument also explains why the emergence of an exclusive East Asian bloc, or even the further deepening of intra-Asian trade and investment, is unlikely. First, Japan, the NICs, and ASEAN all remain heavily dependent on the U.S. market and thus ambivalent about political initiatives that would exclude the United States. Second, it is highly unlikely that Japan will be able economically to play the role of absorber of regional exports that the United States has played. And finally, even if Japan could play this role economically, the countries of the region may have valid political reasons to diversify their trade and investment relationships in order to guarantee that Japan would not be in a position to exercise undue influence.

2 Is Japan Creating a Yen Bloc in East Asia and the Pacific?

Jeffrey A. Frankel

2.1 Introduction

A debate got under way in 1991 over the advantages and disadvantages of a global trend toward three economic blocs—the Western Hemisphere, centered on the United States; Europe, centered on the European Community (EC); and East Asia, centered on Japan. Krugman (1991a), Bhagwati (1990, 1992), and Bergsten (1991) argue that the trend is, on balance, bad. Krugman (1991b) and Lawrence (1991b) argue that it is, on balance, good.[1] Most appear to agree, however, that a trend toward three blocs is indeed under way.

There is no standard definition of an "economic bloc." A useful definition might be a group of countries that are concentrating their trade and financial relationships with one another, in preference to the rest of the world. One might wish to add to the definition the criterion that this concentration is the outcome of government policy, or at least of factors that are noneconomic in origin, such as a common language or culture. In two out of the three parts of the world, there have clearly been recent deliberate political steps toward economic integration. In Europe, the previously lethargic European Economic Com-

Jeffrey A. Frankel is professor of economics at the University of California, Berkeley, and a research associate of the National Bureau of Economic Research, where he is also associate director for the program in International Finance and Macroeconomics.

The author would like to thank Menzie Chinn, Benjamin Chui, Julia Lowell, and Shang-jin Wei for extremely efficient research assistance, and Warwick McKibbin for data. He would also like to thank Miles Kahler, Robert Lawrence, and other participants at the Del Mar conference, Tamim Bayoumi, and participants at a seminar of Stanford University's Asia/Pacific Research Center, for useful comments. Finally, he would like to thank the Japan–United States Friendship Commission (an agency of the U.S. government) for research support.

1. Those who fear the blocs do so because they think they will tend to be protectionist. Froot and Yoffie (1991; chap. 4 in this volume) pursue this logic, and point out some implications of foreign direct investment. Krugman (1991b) argues in favor of the three blocs on the grounds that they are "natural," in a sense explained below. Lawrence's (1991b) argument in favor of blocs is that they can politically cement proliberalization sentiment in individual countries.

munity has burst forth with the programs of the Single Market, European Monetary Union, and more. In the Western Hemisphere, we have the Caribbean Basin Initiative and (more seriously) the Canadian-U.S. Free Trade Agreement, followed by the North America Free Trade Agreement and Enterprise for the Americas Initiative.[2]

In East Asia, by contrast, overt preferential trading arrangements or other political moves to promote regional economic integration are lacking, as has been noted by others (e.g., Petri 1992). The Association of Southeast Asian Nations (ASEAN), to be sure, is taking steps in the direction of turning what used to be a regional security group into a free trade area of sorts. But when Americans worry, as they are wont to do, about a trading bloc forming in Asia, it is generally not ASEAN that concerns them. Rather it is the possibility of an East Asia– or Pacific-wide bloc dominated by Japan.

Japan is unusual among major countries in *not* having preferential trading arrangements with smaller neighboring countries. But the hypothesis that has been put forward is that Japan is forming an economic bloc in the same way that it runs its economy: by means of policies that are implicit, indirect, and invisible. Specifically, the hypothesis is that Japan operates, by means of such instruments as flows of aid, foreign direct investment, and other forms of finance, to influence its neighbors' trade toward itself.[3] This is a hypothesis that should not be accepted uncritically, but needs to be examined empirically.

After examining some of the relevant statistics, this paper argues that the evidence of an evolving East Asian trade bloc centered on Japan is not as clear as many believe. Trade between Japan and other Asian countries increased substantially in the late 1980s. But *intraregional trade bias did not increase,* as it did, for example, within the EC. The phrase *yen bloc* could be interpreted as referring to the financial and monetary aspects implicit in the words, rather than to trade flows. The second half of this paper does find a bit of evidence of Japanese influence in the Pacific via financial and monetary channels, rather than via trade flows. But it does not find evidence that the country has taken deliberate steps to establish a yen bloc.

2.2   Is a Trade Bloc Forming in Pacific Asia?

We must begin by acknowledging the obvious: the greatly increased economic weight of East Asian countries in the world. The rapid outward-oriented growth of Japan, followed by the four East Asian newly industrialized countries (NICs) and more recently by some of the other ASEAN countries, is one of the most remarkable and widely remarked trends in the world economy over the last three decades. But when one asks whether a yen bloc is forming in

2. Reviews of recent developments in regional trading arrangements are offered by Fieleke (1992) and de la Torre and Kelly (1992).

3. For one of many examples, see Dornbusch (1989).

Table 2.1   **Summary Measures of Intraregional Trade Biases**

		East Asia	Western Hemisphere	European Community
Intraregional trade/	1980	.23	.27	.42
total trade[a]	1985	.26	.31	.42
	1990	.29	.29	.47
Intraregional bias,	1980	.91	.79	.72
holding constant	1985	.84	.78	.79
for size of trade[b]	1990	.93	.85	.80
Bias, holding	1980	.70	.53	.23
constant for	1985	.40	.34	.44
GNP, population,	1990	.60	.97	.46
distance, etc.[c]				

[a]Computed from IMF *Direction of Trade* data.

[b]Computed as the ratio of (intraregional trade/total trade) to shares of world trade, as described in text.

[c]Gravity regressions, reported in tables 2.2–2.4. They include significant coefficients on the APEC bloc, among other variables.

East Asia, one is presumably asking something more than whether the economies are getting larger, or even whether economic flows among them are increasing. One must ask whether the share of intraregional trade is higher, or increasing more rapidly, than would be predicted based on such factors as the GNP or growth rates of the countries involved.

2.2.1   Adjusting Intraregional Trade for Growth

Table 2.1 reports three alternative ways of computing intraregional trade bias. The first part of the table is based on a simple breakdown of trade (exports plus imports) undertaken by countries in East Asia into trade with other members of the same regional grouping, versus trade with other parts of the world.[4] For comparison, the analogous statistics are reported for Western Europe (the EC Twelve) and for North America (the United States, Canada, and Mexico).

The share of intraregional trade in East Asia increased from 23 percent in 1980 to 29 percent in 1990. Pronouncements that a clubbish trading bloc is forming in the region are usually based on figures such as these. But the numbers are deceptive.

All three regions show increasing intragroup trade in the 1980s. The region that has both the highest and the fastest-increasing degree of intraregional trade is not Asia but the EC, reaching 47 percent in 1990.

Quite aside from the comparison with Europe, it is easy to be misled by intraregional trade shares such as those reported in the first three rows of table

4. Similar statistics are presented in more detail in table 1 in Frankel (1991a).

2.1. If one allows for the phenomenon that most of the East Asian countries in the 1980s experienced rapid growth in *total* output and trade, then it is possible that there has in fact been no movement toward intraregional bias in the evolving pattern of trade. The increase in the intraregional share of trade that is observed in table 2.1 could be entirely due to the increase in economic size of the countries. To take the simplest case, imagine that there were no intraregional bias in 1980, that each East Asian country conducted trade with other East Asian countries in the same proportion as the latter's weight in world trade (25 percent). Total trade undertaken by Asian countries increased rapidly over this ten-year period, while total trade worldwide increased less rapidly. Even if there continued to be no regional bias in 1990, the observed intraregional share of trade would have increased by one-third (to 31 percent) due solely to the greater weight of Asian countries in the world economy.

Consider now the more realistic case where, due to transportation costs if nothing else, countries within each of the three groupings undertake trade that is somewhat biased toward trading partners within their own group (East Asia, North America, and the EC). Although East Asian trade with other parts of the world increased rapidly, trade with other Asian countries increased even more rapidly. Does this mean that the degree of clubbishness or within-region bias intensified over this period? No, it does not. *Even if there was no increase at all in the bias toward intra-Asian trade,* the more rapid growth of total trade and output experienced by Asian countries would show up as a rate of growth of intra-Asian trade that was faster than the rate of growth of Asian trade with the rest of the world.

Think of each East Asian country in 1980 as conducting trade with other East Asian firms in the same proportion as their weight in world trade (25 percent) *multiplied* by a regional bias term to explain the actual share reported in table 2.1 (23 percent). Then the regional bias term would have to be 0.91 (.23/.25). An unchanged regional bias term multiplied by the East Asians' 1990 weight in world trade would predict that the 1990 intraregional share of trade would be 28 percent (.91 ×.31 = .28). This calculation turns out to explain almost all of the increase in the actual intraregional share (to .29). Thus even with this very simple method of adjustment, the East Asian bias toward within-region trade did not rise much in the 1980s. The implicit intraregional bias rose only from 0.91 to 0.93 (.29/.31), as shown in the middle rows of table 2.1.[5]

2.2.2   A Test on Bilateral Trade Flows

The analysis should be elaborated by use of a systematic framework for measuring what patterns of bilateral trade are normal around the world: the so-

---

5. Petri (1991) calls this measure the "double-relative," while Drysdale and Garnaut (1992) and Anderson and Norheim (1992) use similar calculations of "intensity-of-trade indexes." All find that, once one holds constant for growth in this simple way, the existing intraregional bias in Asia did not increase in the 1980s.

called gravity model.[6] A dummy variable can then be added to represent when both countries in a given pair belong to the same regional grouping, and one can check whether the level and time trend in the East Asia–Pacific grouping exceeds that in other groupings. We do not currently have measures of historical, political, cultural, and linguistic ties. Thus it will be possible to interpret the dummy variables as reflecting these factors, rather than necessarily as reflecting discriminatory trade policies. Perhaps we should not regret the merging of these different factors in one term, because as noted there are in any case no overt preferential trading arrangements on which theories of a Japanese trading bloc could rely.[7]

The dependent variable is trade (exports plus imports), in log form, between pairs of countries in a given year. I have sixty-three countries in my data set, so that there are 1,953 data points ($63 \times 62/2$) for a given year. There are some missing values (245 of them in 1985, for example), normally due to levels of trade too small to be recorded.[8] The possibility that the exclusion of these data points might bias the results, or that the results might be subject to heteroscedasticity because country size varies so much, is considered in Frankel and Wei (1992a). The results appear to be robust with respect to these problems.

One would expect the two most important factors in explaining bilateral trade flows to be the geographical distance between the two countries and their economic size. These factors are the essence of the gravity model, by analogy with the law of gravitational attraction between masses. A large part of the apparent bias toward intraregional trade is certainly due to simple geographical proximity. Indeed, Krugman (1991b) suggests that most of it may be due to proximity, so that the three trading blocs are welfare-improving "natural" groupings (as distinct from "unnatural" trading arrangements between distant trading partners such as the United States and Israel). Although the importance of distance and transportation costs is clear, there is not a lot of theoretical guidance on precisely how they should enter. I experiment a bit with functional forms. I also add a dummy *ADJACENT* variable to indicate when two countries share a common border.

The basic equation to be estimated is

$$\log(T_{ij}) = \alpha + \beta_1\log(GNP_iGNP_j) + \beta_2\log(GNP/pop_iGNP/pop_j) \\ + \beta_3\log(DISTANCE) + \beta_4(ADJACENT) \\ + \gamma_1(EC_{ij}) + \gamma_2(WH_{ij}) + \gamma_3(EA_{ij}) + u_{ij}.$$

The last four explanatory factors are dummy variables. The goal, again, is to see how much of the high level of trade within the East Asian region can be

---

6. See Deardorff (1984, 503–4) for a survey of the (short) subject of gravity equations. Wang and Winters (1991) and Hamilton and Winters (1992) have recently applied the gravity model to the question of potential Eastern European trade patterns.

7. Krugman (1991b) made a crude first pass at applying the gravity model to the question of whether Europe and North America are separate trading blocs, but did not get as far as including other countries or including a variable for distance.

8. The list of countries and regional groupings appears in the appendix.

explained by simple economic factors common to bilateral trade throughout the world, and how much is left over to be attributed to a special regional effect.[9]

The practice of entering GNPs in product form is empirically well-established in bilateral trade regressions. It can be easily justified by the modern theory of trade under imperfect competition.[10] In addition there is reason to believe that GNP per capita has a positive effect, for a given size: as countries become more developed, they tend to specialize more and to trade more. It is also possible that the infrastructure necessary to conduct trade—ports, airports, and so forth—becomes better developed with the level of GNP per capita.

The results are reported in tables 2.2–2.4. I found all three variables to be highly significant statistically (>99 percent level). The coefficient on the log of distance was about −0.56, when the adjacency variable (which is also highly significant statistically) is included at the same time. This means that when the distance between two nonadjacent countries is higher by 1 percent, the trade between them falls by about 0.56 percent.[11]

I tested for possible nonlinearity in the log-distance term, as it could conceivably be the cause of any apparent bias toward intraregional trade that is left after controlling linearly for distance. Quadratic and cubic terms turned out to be not at all significant. An alternative specification that fits at least as well as the log is to include the level of distance and its square. The significant positive coefficient on the latter confirms the property of the log that "trade resistance" increases less than linearly with distance. The results for the other coefficients are little affected by the choice of functional form for proximity. I report here only results using the log of distance.

The estimated coefficient on GNP per capita is about 0.29 as of 1980, indicating that richer countries do indeed trade more, though this term declines during the 1980s, reaching 0.08 in 1990. The estimated coefficient for the log of the product of the two countries' GNPs is about 0.75, indicating that, though trade increases with size, it increases less than proportionately (holding GNP per capita constant). This presumably reflects the widely known pattern that small economies tend to be more open to international trade than larger, more diversified economies.

If there were nothing to the notion of trading blocs, then these basic vari-

---

9. Bilateral distances were computed between the main cities reported in the appendix.

10. The specification implies that trade between two equal-sized countries (say, of size .5) will be greater than trade between a large and a small country (say, of size .9 and .1). This property of models with imperfect competition is not a property of the classical Heckscher-Ohlin theory of comparative advantage (Helpman 1987; Helpman and Krugman 1985, sec. 1.5). Foundations for the gravity model are also offered by Anderson (1979) and other papers surveyed by Deardorff (1984, 503–6).

11. The coefficient on the log of distance is about 0.8 when the adjacency variable is not included.

Table 2.2 Gravity Model of Bilateral Trade, 1980

C	GNPs	Per Capita GNPs	Distance	Adjacent	EC	Western Hemisphere	ASEAN	EAEC	Asian Pacific	APEC	Pacific Rim	$R^2/\bar{R}^2$	SEE[a]
-11.36**	.763**	.268**	-.597**	.649**	0.092	0.449**	2.308**					.68/.68	1.26
(.56)	(.018)	(.021)	(.041)	(.185)	(.186)	(.157)	(.408)						
-12.05**	.759**	.283**	-.538**	.775**	0.193	0.498**		2.363**				.70/.70	1.23
(.55)	(.017)	(.020)	(.041)	(.180)	(.181)	(.153)		(.212)					
-12.05**	.759**	.283**	-.538**	.772**	0.193	0.499**	0.081	2.341**				.70/.70	1.23
(.55)	(.017)	(.020)	(.041)	(.181)	(.181)	(.153)	(.462)	(.247)					
-11.97**	.753**	.287**	-.543**	.764**	0.214	.527**			2.066*			.71/.71	1.21
(.54)	(.017)	(.020)	(.040)	(.178)	(.179)	(.151)			(.158)				
-12.13**	.753**	.290**	-.532**	.770**	0.227	0.535**		0.730*	1.650**			.71/.71	1.21
(.55)	(.017)	(.020)	(.040)	(.179)	(.179)	(.151)		(.332)	(.232)				
-11.09**	.733**	.281**	-.586**	.694**	0.207	0.503**				1.863**		.71/.71	1.21
(.53)	(.017)	(.020)	(.039)	(.177)	(.178)	(.150)				0.133			
-11.58**	.739**	.287**	-.557**	.724**	0.234	0.526**	0.062	0.704*	0.355	1.319**		.71/.71	1.20
(.55)	(.017)	(.020)	(.040)	(.177)	(.178)	(.150)	(.451)	(.330)	(.335)	(.248)			
-10.83**	.762**	.259**	-.638**	.701**	0.033	0.268					0.018	.68/.68	1.27
(.56)	(.018)	(.021)	(.021)	(.187)	(.184)	(.188)					(.014)		
-11.55**	.739**	.288**	-.563**	.716**	0.227	0.474**	0.062	0.699*	0.350	1.321**	0.0076	.71/.71	1.20
(.55)	(.017)	(.020)	(.041)	(.178)	(.174)	(.178)	(.452)	(.330)	(.335)	(.248)	(.0129)		

Notes: * and ** are significance at the 95 and 99 percent levels, respectively. Standard errors appear in parentheses. LHS variable (bilateral exports and imports) and first three RHS variables are in log form. All others are dummy variables.

[a]Standard error of estimate.

Table 2.3   Gravity Model of Bilateral Trade, 1985

C	GNPs	Per Capita GNPs	Distance	Adjacent	EC	Western Hemisphere	ASEAN	EAEC	Asian Pacific	APEC	Pacific Rim	R²/R̄²	SEEª
-10.54** (.53)	.791** (.017)	.242** (.020)	-.729** (.040)	.708** (.184)	.306†† (.179)	.276†† (.162)	1.735** (.392)					.72/.72	1.21
-10.92** (.52)	.784** (.017)	.248** (.020)	-.683** (.040)	.804** (.181)	.397* (.176)	.312* (.159)		1.841** (.205)				.73/.73	1.19
-10.92** (.52)	.784** (.017)	.248** (.020)	-.683** (.040)	.806** (.182)	.397* (.176)	.311* (.159)	-.046 (.448)	1.854** (.239)				.73/.73	1.19
-10.85** (.51)	.778** (.017)	.251** (.019)	-.685** (.039)	.796** (.178)	.424* (.174)	.341* (.157)			1.697** (.153)			.73/.73	1.18
-10.91** (.51)	.778** (.017)	.252** (.019)	-.679** (.039)	.802** (.179)	.431* (.174)	.343* (.157)	-.045 (.442)	.414 (.322)	1.474** (.225)			.73/.73	1.18
-10.07** (.51)	.761** (.017)	.243** (.019)	-.720** (.038)	.739** (.178)	.418** (.156)	.323†† (.173)				1.522** (.130)		.74/.74	1.17
-10.42** (.52)	.765** (.017)	.247** (.019)	-.698** (.039)	.766** (.179)	.439†† (.173)	.339* (.156)	-.071 (.440)	.398 (.321)	.469 (.327)	1.029** (.244)		.74/.74	1.17
-10.09** (.53)	.791** (.017)	.239** (.020)	-.778** (.041)	.731** (.185)	.239 (.179)	-.024 (.183)				.041** (.013)		.72/.72	1.20
-10.28** (.53)	.766** (.017)	.250** (.019)	-.723** (.040)	.738** (.179)	.415* (.173)	.142 (.177)	-.073 (.439)	.378 (.320)	.450 (.327)	1.034** (.244)	.030* (.013)	.74/.74	1.17

Notes: ††, *, and ** denote significance at the 90, 95, and 99 percent levels, respectively. Standard errors appear in parentheses. LHS variable (bilateral exports and imports) and first three RHS variables are in log form. All others are dummy variables.
ªStandard error of estimate.

Table 2.4   Gravity Model of Bilateral Trade, 1990

C	GNPs	Per Capita GNPs	Distance	Adjacent	EC	Western Hemisphere	ASEAN	EAEC	Asian Pacific	APEC	Pacific Rim	$R^2/\bar{R}^2$	SEE[a]
2.77**	.787**	.078**	-.589**	.732**	.341*	.934**	1.879**					.75/.75	1.11
(.36)	(.016)	(.017)	(.038)	(.166)	(.166)	(.148)	(.378)						
2.54**	.779**	.082**	-.559**	.794**	.412*	.957**		1.997**				.76/.76	1.09
(.35)	(.016)	(.017)	(.038)	(.162)	(.163)	(.145)		(.215)					
2.54**	.779**	.082**	-.559**	.797**	.412*	.955**	-0.109	2.032**				.76/.76	1.09
(.35)	(.016)	(.017)	(.038)	(.163)	(.163)	(.145)	(.450)	(.261)					
2.57**	.773**	.86**	-.561**	.790**	.437**	.983**			1.746**			.77/.77	1.08
(.35)	(.016)	(.016)	(.037)	(.160)	(.160)	(.143)			(.152)				
2.52**	.773**	.087**	-.555**	.794**	.446**	.986**	-0.107	0.612††	1.456**			.77/.77	1.08
(.35)	(.016)	(.016)	(.037)	(.160)	(.160)	(.143)	(.443)	(.331)	(.213)				
3.02**	.756**	.083**	-.597**	.730**	.444**	.948**				1.597**		.77/.77	1.07
(.34)	(.016)	(.016)	(.036)	(.158)	(.159)	(.141)				(.128)			
2.83**	.760**	.085**	-.579**	.750**	.460**	.967**	-0.144	0.604††	0.289	1.194**		.77/.77	1.07
(.35)	(.016)	(.016)	(.037)	(.159)	(.159)	(.142)	(.440)	(.328)	(.309)	(.231)			
3.04**	.788**	.073**	-.619**	.780**	.296††	.789**					0.015	.75/.74	1.12
(.37)	(.017)	(.017)	(.040)	(.167)	(.167)	(.170)					(.013)		
2.87**	.760**	.086**	-.584**	.743**	.454**	.925**	-0.143	0.600††	0.284	1.196**	6.39×10^{-3}	.77/.77	1.07
(.38)	(.016)	(.016)	(.038)	(.160)	(.159)	(.163)	(.440)	(.328)	(.309)	(.231)	(.012)		

Notes: ††, *, and ** denote significance at the 90, 95, and 99 percent levels, respectively. Standard errors appear in parentheses. LHS variable (bilateral exports and imports) and first three RHS variables are in log form. All others are dummy variables.

[a]Standard error of estimate.

ables would soak up most of the explanatory power. There would be little left to attribute to a dummy variable representing whether two trading partners are both located in the same region. In this case the level and trend in intraregional trade would be due solely to the proximity of the countries and to their rapid rate of overall economic growth. But I found that dummy variables for intraregional trade *are* statistically significant, both in East Asia and elsewhere in the world. If two countries are both located in the Western Hemisphere, for example, they will trade with each other by an estimated 70 percent more than they would otherwise, even after taking into account distance and the other gravity variables $(\exp(.53) = 1.70)$. Intraregional trade goes beyond what can be explained by proximity.

The empirical equation is as yet too far removed from theoretical foundations to allow conclusions to be drawn regarding economic welfare. But it is possible that the amount of intraregional bias explained by proximity, as compared to explicit or implicit regional trading arrangements, is small enough in my results that those arrangements are welfare-reducing. This could be the case if trade diversion outweighs trade creation. Inspired by Krugman's (1991a, 1991b) "natural trading bloc" terminology, we might then refer to the observed intraregional trade bias as evidence of "super-natural" trading blocs. The issue merits future research.

When the boundaries of the Asian bloc are drawn along the lines of those suggested by Malaysian prime minister Mahathir in his proposed East Asian Economic Caucus (EAEC), which excludes Australia and New Zealand (in the second row of tables 2.2–2.4), the coefficient on the Asian bloc appears to be the strongest and most significant of any in the world. Even when the boundaries are drawn in this way, however, there is no evidence of an *increase* in the intraregional bias of Asian trade during the 1980s: the estimated coefficient actually decreases somewhat from 1980 to 1990. Thus the gravity results corroborate the back-of-the-envelope calculation reported in the preceding section. The precise pattern is a decrease in the first half of the decade, followed by a very slight increase in the second half, matching the results of Petri (1991).[12] None of these changes over time is statistically significant.

It is perhaps surprising that the estimated *level* of the intraregional trade bias was higher in East Asia as of 1980 than in the other two regions. One possible explanation is that there has historically been a sort of trading culture in Asia. To the extent that such a culture exists and can be identified with a particular nation or ethnic group, I find the overseas Chinese to be a more plausible factor than the Japanese. But there are other possible regional effects that may be showing up spuriously as an East Asian bloc, to be considered below.

Of the three trading blocs, the EC and the Western Hemisphere are the two that show rapid intensification in the course of the 1980s. Both show an ap-

---

12. Petri infers, from the data on intraregional trade shares, a decrease in East Asian interdependence up to the middle of the 1980s, followed by a reversal in the second half of the decade.

proximate doubling of their estimated intraregional bias coefficients. As of 1980, trade within the EC is not strong enough—after holding constant for the close geographical proximity and high incomes per capita of European countries—for the bias coefficient of 0.2 to appear statistically significant. The EC coefficient increased rapidly in level and significance in the first half of the 1980s, reaching about 0.4 by 1985, and continued to increase a bit in the second half. The effect of two countries being located in Europe per se, when tested, does not show up as being nearly as strong in magnitude or significance as the effect of membership in the EC per se.

The Western Hemisphere coefficient experienced all its increase in the second half of the decade, exceeding 0.9 by 1990. The rapid increase in the Western Hemisphere intraregional bias in the second half of the 1980s is in itself an important new finding. The recovery of Latin American imports from the United States after the compression that followed the 1982 debt crisis must be part of this phenomenon. The Canada-U.S. Free Trade Agreement signed in 1988 may also be part of the explanation.

I consider a sequence of nested candidates for trading blocs in the Pacific. The significance of a given bloc effect turns out to depend on what other blocs are tested at the same time. One logical way to draw the boundaries is to include all the countries with eastern coasts on the Pacific, adding Australia and New Zealand to the EAEC group. I call this grouping Asian Pacific in the tables. Its coefficient and significance level are both higher than the EAEC dummy. When I broaden the bloc search and test for an effect of the Asia Pacific Economic Cooperation (APEC) group, which includes the United States and Canada with the others, it is highly significant. The significance of the Asian Pacific dummy completely disappears. The EAEC dummy remains significant in 1980 and 1990, though at a lower level than the initial results that did not consider any wider Pacific groupings.

APEC appears to be the correct place to draw the boundary. When I test for the broadest definition of a Pacific bloc, including Latin America, it is not at all significant, and the other coefficients do not change. (It is called Pacific Rim in the tables.) It remains true that the intraregional biases in the EC and Western Hemisphere blocs each roughly doubled from 1980 to 1990, while intraregional biases in the Asia and Pacific areas did not increase at all. The only surprising new finding is the APEC effect: the United States and Canada appear to be full partners in the Pacific bloc, even while belonging to the significant but distinct Western Hemisphere bloc. The APEC coefficient is the strongest of any. Its estimate holds relatively steady at 1.3 (1980), 1.0 (1985), and 1.2 (1990). The implication is that a pair of APEC countries trade three times as much as two otherwise similar countries (exp (1.2) = 3.3).[13]

---

13. Others have emphasized the high volume of transpacific trade. But it has been difficult to evaluate such statistics when no account is taken of these countries' collective size. A higher percentage of economic activity will consist of intraregional trade in a larger region than in a smaller region, even when there is no intraregional bias, merely because smaller regions tend by

One possible explanation for the apparent intraregional trade biases within East Asia and within the APEC grouping is that transportation between Asian Pacific countries is mostly by water, while transportation among European or Western Hemisphere countries is more often overland, and that ocean shipping is less expensive than shipping by rail or road. This issue bears further investigation. (Wang [1992] enters land distance and water distance separately in a gravity model. She finds a small, though statistically significant, difference in coefficients.) The issue of water versus land transport should not affect results regarding *changes* in intraregional trade bias in the 1980s, however, given that the nature of shipping costs does not appear to have changed over as short a time span as five or ten years.

Several further questions naturally arise. ASEAN negotiated a preferential trading arrangement within its membership in 1977 although serious progress in removal of barriers did not get under way until 1987 (Jackson 1991). In early 1992 the members proclaimed plans for an ASEAN free trade area, albeit with exemptions for many sectors. Does this grouping constitute a small bloc nested within the others? I include in my model a dummy variable for common membership in ASEAN. It turns out to have a significant coefficient only if none of the broader Asian blocs are included. The conclusion seems to be that ASEAN is not in fact functioning as a trading bloc.[14]

We know that Singapore and Hong Kong are especially open countries and engage in a large amount of entrepôt trade. A dummy variable for these two countries' trade with other Asian Pacific countries is highly significant when it is included, as shown in the first row of table 2.5. Its presence reduces a bit the coefficient on the East Asian grouping, but does not otherwise change the results.

We also know that most East Asian countries are very open to trade of all sorts. So I added a dummy variable to indicate when *at least* one of the pair of countries is located in East Asia, to supplement the dummy variable that indicates when both are. Its coefficient is significant. It is also positive, which appears to rule out any "trade-diversion" effects arising from the existence of the East Asian bloc: these countries trade an estimated 22 percent more with all parts of the world, other things equal, than do average countries (exp[.20] = 1.22). The addition of the openness dummy reduces a bit more the level and significance of the East Asian bloc dummy. Indeed, when the APEC bloc dummy and East Asian openness dummy are both added at the same time, the East Asian bloc term becomes only marginally significant in 1980 and insignificant in 1985 and 1990. There may be no East Asian bloc effect at all!

their nature to trade across their boundaries more than larger ones. In the limit, when the unit is the world, 100 percent of trade is intra-"regional."

14. In tests similar to mine, Wang (1992), Wang and Winters (1991), and Hamilton and Winters (1992) found the ASEAN dummy to reflect one of the most significant trading areas in the world. That they did not include a broader dummy variable for intra-Asian trade may explain the difference in results.

Table 2.5 Gravity Estimates with Allowance for Asian Openness

GNP	Per Capita GNP	Distance	Adjacent	WH	EA	APEC	EC	JapEA	HKSEA	HKS1	EA1	Adj. R²/SEE	# of Observations
							1980						
.78**	.24**	−.64**	.62**	.58**	.51††	1.29**	.18	−.11		1.33**		.73/1.16	1708
(.02)	(.02)	(.04)	(.18)	(.15)	(.34)	(.17)	(.18)	(.16)		(.12)			
.73**	.31**	−.66**	.63**	.65**	.31	1.22**	.18	−.12	1.06**		.52**	.72/1.18	1708
(.02)	(.02)	(.04)	(.18)	(.15)	(.34)	(.17)	(.18)	(.49)	(.41)		(.07)		
.78**	.26**	−.67**	.59**	.64**	.53†	1.19**	.15	−.16	.01	1.16**	.25**	.73/1.16	1708
(.02)	(.02)	(.04)	(.18)	(.15)	(.34)	(.17)	(.17)	(.48)	(.42)	(.14)	(.08)		
							1985						
.78**	.22**	−.74**	.69**	.37*	.36	1.18**	.45**	.09		.76**		.74/1.16	1647
(.02)	(.02)	(.04)	(.18)	(.15)	(.26)	(.17)	(.17)	(.16)		(.12)			
.76**	.26**	−.77**	.69**	.42**	.16	1.10**	.44**	−.08	.80*		.34**	.74/1.16	1647
(.02)	(.02)	(.04)	(.18)	(.15)	(.34)	(.17)	(.18)	(.48)	(.40)		(.07)		
.78**	.23**	−.77**	.67**	.41**	.26	1.09**	.44*	−.10	.28	.59**	.20*	.74/1.16	1647
(.02)	(.02)	(.04)	(.18)	(.15)	(.34)	(.17)	(.18)	(.48)	(.42)	(.14)	(.08)		
							1990						
.80**	.04**	−.63**	.69**	.97**	.40†	1.18**	.49**	−.15		1.23**		.79/1.03	1573
(.02)	(.02)	(.04)	(.18)	(.13)	(.23)	(.15)	(.16)	(.14)		(.11)			
.75**	.10**	−.66**	.69**	1.06**	.14	1.11**	.49**	−.27	1.09**		.50**	.78/1.05	1573
(.02)	(.02)	(.04)	(.18)	(.14)	(.30)	(.15)	(.16)	(.43)	(.37)		(.07)		
.79**	.06**	−.67**	.65**	1.03**	.34	1.08**	.49**	−.31	.15	1.06**	.25**	.79/1.02	1573
(.02)	(.02)	(.04)	(.18)	(.14)	(.30)	(.15)	(.15)	(.42)	(.38)	(.12)	(.07)		

Notes: †, ††, *, and ** denote significance at the 85, 90, 95, and 99 percent levels respectively. Standard errors appear in parentheses. All regressions have an intercept, which is not reported here. All variables except the dummies are in logs. JapEA=trade between Japan and other East Asian countries, HKSEA=trade between Hong Kong or Singapore and other East Asian countries, HKS1=trade between Hong Kong or Singapore and any other countries, EA1=trade involving at least one East Asian country.

I tried a few more extensions as well. I disaggregated trade into manufactured goods, agricultural products, fuels, and other raw materials. The results changed little. Raw materials show the greatest Asian bloc effect if judged by the estimated coefficient. Manufactures shows the greatest effect if judged by t-statistics. Desirable extensions for the future, besides further disaggregation, include adding factor-endowment terms.

What about bilateral trade between Asian Pacific countries and Japan in particular? Like intraregional trade overall, trade with Japan increased rapidly in the second half of the 1980s. Most of this increase merely reversed a decline in the first half of the 1980s, however (Petri 1991). More important, the recent trend in bilateral trade between Japan and its neighbors can be readily explained as the natural outcome of the growth in Japanese trade overall and the growth in trade levels attained by other Asian countries overall. Lawrence (1991a) has calculated that, out of the 28 percentage-point increase in the market share of Asian Pacific developing countries in Japanese imports from 1985 to 1988, 11 percentage points is attributable to the commodity mix of these countries' exports. There is no residual to be attributed to Japan's development of special trading relations with other countries in its region.[15]

I confirmed this finding (though without as yet decomposing trade by commodity) by adding to my gravity model a separate dummy variable for bilateral Asian trade with Japan in particular. It was not even remotely statistically significant in any year, and indeed the point estimate was a small negative number, as is shown in table 2.5. Thus there was no evidence that Japan has established or come to dominate a trading bloc in Asia.

To summarize the most relevant effects, if two countries both lie within the boundaries of APEC, they trade with each other a little over three times as much as they otherwise would. The nested EAEC bloc is less strong (especially if one allows also for the openness of East Asian countries) and has declined a bit in magnitude and significance during the course of the 1980s. The Western Hemisphere and EC blocs, by contrast, intensified rapidly during the decade. Indeed, by 1990 the Western Hemisphere bloc was stronger than the EAEC bloc, if one takes into account the existence of the APEC effect. There was never a special Japan effect within Asian Pacific.

In short, beyond the evident facts that countries near each other trade with each other, and that Japan and other Asian countries are growing rapidly, there is no evidence that Japan is concentrating its trade with other Asian countries in any special way, nor that they are collectively moving toward a trading bloc in the way that Western Europe and the Western Hemisphere appear to be. I now turn from trade to finance.

---

15. The empirical literature on whether Japan is an outlier in its trading patterns, particularly with respect to imports of manufactures, includes Saxonhouse (1989), Noland (1991), and Lawrence (1991c), among others.

2.3 Japan's Financial Influence in the Region

In the case of financial flows, proximity is less important than it is for trade flows. For some countries the buying and selling of foreign exchange and highly rated bonds is characterized by the absence of significant government capital controls, transactions costs, or information costs. In such cases, there would be no particular reason to expect greater capital flows among close countries than among distant ones. Rather, each country would be viewed as depositing into the world capital pool, or borrowing from it, whatever quantity of funds it wished at the going world interest rate. Thus even if we could obtain reliable data on bilateral capital flows (which we cannot), and whatever pattern they happened to show, such statistics would not be particularly interesting.

2.3.1   Tokyo's Influence on Regional Financial Markets

Many Asian countries still have substantial capital controls, and financial markets that are in other respects less than fully developed. Even financial markets in Singapore and Hong Kong, the most open in Asia, retain some minor frictions. Where the links with world capital markets are obstructed by even small barriers, it is an interesting question to ask whether those links are stronger with some major financial centers than with others. This question is explored econometrically below.

Information costs exist for equities, and for bonds with some risk of default. These costs may be smaller for those investors who are physically, linguistically, and culturally close to the nation where the borrower resides. Proximity clearly matters as well in the case of direct investment, in part because much of direct investment is linked to trade, in part because linguistic and cultural proximity matter for direct investment. We begin our consideration of capital links by looking at direct investment.

2.3.2   Foreign Direct Investment

Table 2.6 shows the standard Ministry of Finance figures for Japanese direct investment. The steady stream of direct investment by Japanese firms in East Asia and the Pacific (including Australia) has received much attention. But the table shows that, whether measured in terms of annual flows or cumulated stocks, Japan's direct investment in the region is approximately equal to its investment in Europe, and is much less than its investment in North America (see also Komiya and Wakasugi 1991).

It has been argued that, once one scales the table 2.6 figures for GNP among the host countries, an Asian bias to Japanese direct investment might indeed appear (Holloway 1991, 69). But if one scales the foreign direct investment figures by the host region's role in world trade, one finds that Japan's investment in Asia and Oceania is almost exactly in proportion to their size. There is no regional bias. Its direct investment in the United States and Canada, on the

Table 2.6 Japan's Foreign Direct Investment, by Area and Country (amounts in millions of dollars)

	FY 1990			FY 1991			Cumulative Total FY 1951–91		
	Cases	Amount	% of Total	Cases	Amount	% of Total	Cases	Amount	% of Total
United States	2,269	26,128	45.9	1,607	18,026	43.3	24,551	148,554	42.2
Canada	157	1,064	1.9	107	797	1.9	1,388	6,454	1.8
Subtotal (North America)	2,426	27,192	47.8	1,714	18,823	45.3	25,939	155,008	44.0
Latin America	339	3,628	6.4	290	3,337	8.0	7,487	43,821	12.4
Middle East	1	27	0.0	10	90	0.2	350	3,522	1.0
Europe	956	14,294	25.1	803	9,371	22.5	8,228	68,636	19.5
Africa	70	551	1.0	76	748	1.8	1,534	6,574	1.9
Australia and the South Pacific	572	4,166	7.3	394	3,278	7.9	4,351	21,376	6.1
Indonesia	155	1,105	1.9	148	1,193	2.9	2,021	12,733	3.6
Hong Kong	244	1,785	3.1	178	925	2.2	3,921	10,775	3.1
Singapore	139	840	1.5	103	613	1.5	2,662	7,168	2.0
Republic of Korea	54	284	0.5	48	260	0.6	1,895	4,398	1.2
China	165	349	0.6	246	579	1.4	1,105	3,402	1.0
Thailand	377	1,154	2.0	258	807	1.9	2,723	5,229	1.5
Malaysia	169	725	1.3	136	880	2.1	1,645	4,111	1.2
Taiwan	102	446	0.8	87	405	1.0	2,487	3,135	0.9
Philippines	58	258	0.5	42	203	0.5	892	1,783	0.5
India	7	30	0.1	9	14	0.0	176	210	0.1
Sri Lanka	9	4	0.0	7	4	0.0	126	102	0.0
Brunei	—	—		1	0	0.0	32	109	0.0
Pakistan	3	9	0.0	2	14	0.0	60	124	0.0
Others	26	69	0.1	12	39	0.1	166	175	0.0
Subtotal (Asia)	1,499	7,054	12.4	1,277	5,936	14.3	19,911	53,455	15.2
Total	6,589	67,540	100.0	5,863	56,911	100.0	63,236	310,808	100.0

Source: Financial Statistics of Japan (Tokyo: Ministry of Finance, 1992), 95.

other hand, is more than twice what one would expect from their share of world trade. Japan's investment in Europe is about half the continent's share of trade.

Furthermore, Ramstetter (1991a, 8–9; 1991b, 95–96) has forcefully pointed out that the standard Ministry of Finance figures on Japanese foreign direct investment actually represent statistics on investment either approved by or reported to the government, and greatly overstate the extent of true Japanese investment in developing countries. The more accurate balance-of-payments data from the Bank of Japan show a smaller percentage of investment going to Asia.

2.3.3   Tokyo versus New York Effects on Asian Interest Rates

Statistics also exist on Japanese portfolio investment. But, in the case of portfolio capital, looking at quantity data is not as informative as looking at price data—that is, at interest rates. For one thing, the quality of the data on interest rates is much higher than the quality of the data on capital flows. For another, the interest rate test is more appropriate conceptually. If the *potential* for arbitrage keeps the interest rate in a given Asian country closely in line with, say, Tokyo interest rates, then this constitutes good evidence of close links between the two national capital markets, even if the amount of actual arbitrage or other capital flow that takes place within a given period happens to be small.

Many East Asian countries have moved to liberalize and internationalize their financial markets over the last ten to fifteen years.[16] A number of studies have documented Japan's removal of capital controls over the period 1979–84 by looking at the power of arbitrage to equalize interest rates between Tokyo and New York or London.[17] Australia and New Zealand, while lagging behind Japan, also show signs of liberalization during the course of the 1980s.[18] Hong Kong and Singapore register impressively open financial markets, showing smaller interest differentials even than some open European countries like Germany. (Hong Kong has long had open capital markets. Singapore undertook a major liberalization in 1978, though it has tried to segment its domestic money market from its offshore "Asia dollar market."[19]) Malaysia has officially liberalized, following Singapore (Abidin 1986; Glick and Hutchison 1990, 45), though its covered differential has remained considerably higher.

16. Frankel (1991c) presents the 1980s evidence for Japan, Australia, New Zealand, Singapore, Hong Kong, and Malaysia. Faruqee (1991) examines interest differentials for Korea, Malaysia, Singapore, and Thailand (vis-à-vis yen interest rates in London) but does not take into account exchange rate expectations.

17. These include Otani and Tiwari (1981), Ito (1986), and Frankel (1984). The interest rates in the calculations are covered on the forward exchange or Eurocurrency markets so as to avoid exchange risk. (Tests that look at real or uncovered interest differentials, rather than covered interest differentials, include Ito [1988] and Fukao and Okubo [1984].)

18. The frequently large negative covered differential that had been observed for Australia up to mid-1983 (see, e.g., Argy 1987) largely vanished thereafter.

19. See Moreno (1988). Edwards and Khan (1985) include another test of covered interest parity for Singapore.

We can apply a simple test to the hypothesis that a particular Asian country is dominated financially by Japan, versus the alternative hypothesis that ties to capital markets in the other industrialized countries are equally strong. I ran the following OLS regression to see how the interest rate in a typical Asian country depends on interest rates in Tokyo and New York:

$$i_t^a = \alpha + \beta_1 i_t^T + \beta_2 i_t^{NY} + \varepsilon_t.$$

Under the null hypothesis that the country's financial markets are insufficiently developed or liberalized to be directly tied to any foreign financial markets, the coefficients on foreign interest rates should be zero. Under the alternative hypothesis that the country's financial markets are closely tied to those in Tokyo, the coefficient on Tokyo interest rates should be closer to one than to zero, and similarly for New York.[20]

Table 2.7 presents estimates for three-month interest rates in Hong Kong and Singapore, on quarterly data. For the Hong Kong interest rate, the influence of the New York market appears very strong. This is not surprising: not only does the colony have open financial markets, but its currency has since October 1983 been pegged to the U.S. dollar (see, e.g., Balassa and Williamson 1990, 32), so that there is nothing to inhibit perfect arbitrage between its interest rates and U.S. interest rates. Tokyo, London, and Frankfurt had no significant influence in Hong Kong on average over the sample period (from 1976 to 1989). For the Singapore interest rate, the influence of New York is again very significant, but now there is also a significant, though smaller, weight on Tokyo. The evidence suggests that both countries have had open financial markets ever since the mid-1970s, with New York having the dominant influence, but with Tokyo also having a one-quarter effect in the case of Singapore.

To see whether the influence of the foreign financial centers changed over the course of the sample period, we can allow for time trends in the coefficients, also reported in table 2.7. For Hong Kong, it is clear that London used to have a strong influence, and equally clear that the British influence has been diminishing over time. For Singapore, there is no sign of change in New York's role, but there is weak evidence of a gradually increasing role for Tokyo.

The next step is to expand the sample of countries. Some Asian countries, such as Korea and Taiwan, did not seriously begin to open their financial markets to external influence by *any* foreign center until the late 1980s. To obtain more observations, one can switch to monthly data. Preliminary results for the period 1988–91 found a dominant role for Tokyo interest rates in Singapore and Taiwan, a dominant role for New York interest rates in Hong Kong and Australia, and apparently strong roles for both in Korea (Frankel 1991a, table

20. It should be noted that if capital markets in Tokyo and New York are closely tied to *each other*, as they indeed are, then multicollinearity might make it difficult to obtain statistically significant estimates. But this does not mean that there is anything wrong with the test. A finding that the coefficient on the Tokyo interest rate is statistically greater than zero, or than the coefficient on the New York interest rate, remains valid.

Table 2.7   **Japanese, U.S., U.K., and German Interest Rate Effects in Hong Kong and Singapore**

	Hong Kong		Singapore	
	Without Trend	With Trend	Without trend	With Trend
Constant term	−2.41††	−1.70	−1.16††	−0.65
	(1.08)	(1.13)	(0.67)	(0.67)
Tokyo effect	−0.23	−0.11	0.23**	−0.36††
	(0.17)	(0.69)	(0.07)	(0.22)
Time trend in Tokyo effect		−0.00		0.02††
		(0.01)		(0.01)
New York effect	1.32**	0.61	0.75**	0.65††
	(0.15)	(0.52)	(.09)	(0.33)
Time trend in New York effect		0.01		0.00
		(0.01)		(0.01)
London effect	0.10	1.38**	−0.07	−0.09
	(0.11)	(0.47)	(0.06)	(0.16)
Time trend in London effect		−0.03**		−0.00
		(0.01)		(0.00)
Frankfurt effect	0.14	−1.74††	0.19	1.02††
	(0.20)	(1.13)	(0.12)	(0.54)
Time trend in Frankfurt effect		0.04††		−0.02††
		(0.02)		(0.01)
R^2	.83	.85	.87	.88
Durbin-Watson	1.50	1.61	1.53	1.92
Sample period	1976.4 to 1989.3		1974.1 to 1988.1	

†† and ** denote significance at the 90 and 99 percent levels, respectively. Standard errors appear in parentheses.

4; or NBER Working Paper no. 4050, table 7). Tests that also allowed a role for Frankfurt and London interest rates found apparently significant effects for the latter in Australia and New Zealand. But most of these results were tainted by high levels of serial correlation.

In table 2.8 I use conservative standard errors, to allow for the problem created by serial correlation. I expand the set of countries still further, to a set of ten (with three alternative measures of the Korean interest rate). The time trends in the coefficients tell us that New York seems to be gaining influence at the expense of Tokyo in the English-speaking countries of the Pacific Rim (Australia, Canada, and New Zealand), while the reverse is occurring in a number of East Asian countries. The observed shift in influence from New York interest rates to Tokyo interest rates is highly significant in the case of Indonesia, and somewhat less so in the case of Korea. It is positive but not significant (when the conservative standard errors are used) for Hong Kong, Singapore, and Malaysia.

These tests leave some important questions unanswered. Are the barriers

Table 2.8   Trends in the Influence of Dollar versus Yen Yen Interest Rates (September 1982–March 1992)

	Constant	Eurodollar	Eurodollar Trend	Euroyen	Euroyen Trend	R^2	$\overline{\text{DW}}$	Q
Australia	8.473*	−1.992**	0.429**	3.470**	−0.539**	.52	0.409	141.47**
	(1.143)	(0.277)	(0.041)	(0.411)	(0.054)			
	[3.428]	[0.479]	[0.071]	[0.712]	[0.094]			
Canada	0.535	0.487*	0.086**	0.670*	−0.057	.79	0.477	158.12**
	(0.458)	(0.111)	(0.016)	(0.165)	(0.022)			
	[1.375]	[0.192]	[0.028]	[0.285]	[0.038]			
Hong Kong	−4.115	1.691**	−0.068	−0.353	0.104	.71	1.047	41.35**
	(0.857)	(0.208)	(0.031)	(0.308)	(0.041)			
	[2.570]	[0.360]	[0.053]	[0.533]	[0.071]			
Indonesia	14.010**	1.852**	−0.267**	−2.337*	0.410**	.33	0.700	N.A.
	(1.483)	(0.356)	(0.053)	(0.529)	(0.070)			
	[4.449]	[0.616]	[0.091]	[0.916]	[0.121]			
Korea 1	9.094**	−0.037	−0.031*	−0.103	0.002	.82	0.488	124.18**
	(0.194)	(0.039)	(0.009)	(0.065)	(0.011)			
	[0.581]	[0.067]	[0.015]	[0.113]	[0.019]			
Korea 2	16.294**	−0.754	0.097	−0.929	0.086	.64	0.671	57.01**
	(1.087)	(0.527)	(0.077)	(0.704)	(0.091)			
	[3.262]	[0.913]	[0.133]	[1.219]	[0.158]			

Korea 3	10.079**	0.320	−0.061	−0.019	0.124*	.69	0.204	194.35**
	(0.690)	(0.143)	(0.026)	(0.231)	(0.031)			
	[2.070]	[0.248]	[0.045]	[0.400]	[0.053]			
Malaysia	5.520	−0.057	−0.072	0.700	0.016	.41	0.463	N.A.
	(1.262)	(0.286)	(0.049)	(0.453)	(0.059)			
	[3.785]	[0.496]	[0.086]	[0.784]	[0.102]			
New Zealand	18.573**	−2.584**	0.379**	3.405**	−0.599**	.37	0.327	204.22**
	(2.063)	(0.500)	(0.074)	(0.742)	(0.098)			
	[6.291]	[0.866]	[0.129]	[1.285]	[0.169]			
Singapore	−2.768*	0.960**	−0.052*	0.174	0.056	.86	0.842	103.64**
	(0.413)	(0.093)	(0.014)	(0.142)	(0.019)			
	[1.239]	[0.161]	[0.025]	[0.246]	[0.032]			
Taiwan	−4.144	0.635	0.017	0.811	0.049	.45	0.422	109.01**
	(1.217)	(0.292)	(0.043)	(0.437)	(0.057)			
	[3.651]	[0.505]	[0.075]	[0.757]	[0.099]			
Thailand	−3.846	0.780	−0.069	1.363*	0.097	.78	0.461	N.A.
	(1.114)	(0.232)	(0.039)	(0.363)	(0.049)			
	[3.341]	[0.402]	[0.068]	[0.628]	[0.085]			

Notes: figures in parentheses are asymptotic standard errors. Figures in brackets are standard errors assuming $N/3$ independent observations. The Q-statistic indicates the Ljung-Box Q-statistic. * and ** denote significance at the 5 and 1 percent level, respectively, using the adjusted standard errors.

that remain between a given country and the major world financial centers due to currency factors or country factors? Most of the Asian countries experience frequent changes in their exchange rates against the yen and the dollar. Financial markets in a country like Singapore could be very open, yet observed interest rates could differ from those in Tokyo or New York because of premiums meant to compensate investors for the possibility of changes in the exchange rate. The question of whether the yen is playing an increasing role in the exchange rate policies of East Asian countries is important to address, but it should be kept distinct from the question of whether financial links to Tokyo (irrespective of currency) are strengthening.

We can take out currency factors by using the forward exchange market. The necessary data are available for six of the countries. I simply express the foreign interest rates so as to be "covered" or hedged against exchange risk. Doing so changes the 1988–91 results for Australia and Singapore toward a Tokyo effect that is smaller than the New York effect. Most coefficients remain significant, despite the obvious multicollinearity between covered U.S. and Japanese interest rates.[21]

Returning to the longer 1982–92 time period to look for trends in the coefficients of the covered interest rates, we find that the observed upward trends for Tokyo influence in Singapore and Malaysia are not statistically significant (when conservative standard errors are used). Singapore, like Hong Kong, rather appears to obey a covered interest parity relationship vis-à-vis dollar interest rates.[22]

For six of these countries, there exists another way of correcting for possible exchange rate changes: direct data on forecasts of market participants collected in a monthly survey by the *Currency Forecasters' Digest* of White Plains, New York.[23] One advantage of using the survey responses to measure expected exchange rate changes is that the data allow us to test explicitly whether there exists an exchange risk premium that creates an international differential in interest rates even in the absence of barriers to international capital flows. Such a differential would be compensation to risk-averse investors for holding assets that they view as risky.[24] An advantage of the *Currency Forecasters' Digest*

21. Table 4 in Frankel (1991a), or table 7 in NBER Working Paper no. 4050. (The Durbin-Watson statistics improve substantially when the forward rates are included, confirming that the equation that uses covered interest rates is a more appropriate specification.)

22. These results are from tables 12a and 12b in Chinn and Frankel (1992).

23. The *Currency Forecasters' Digest* data is proprietary and was obtained by subscription by the Institute for International Economics.

24. The forward rate data allow us to eliminate factors associated with the currency in which countries' assets are denominated, but they do not allow us to distinguish between two currency factors: the exchange risk premium and expectations of depreciation. For the case of Australia, for example, the support for covered interest parity suggests that barriers to the movement of capital between Sydney and New York are low, and so differences in interest rates are due to currency factors. But when the Australian interest rate is observed to exceed the U.S. interest rate, is this because the Australian dollar is confidently expected to depreciate, or is it because investors have no idea what the exchange rate will do and demand to be compensated for this risk? The survey data may be able to distinguish between these two hypotheses, whereas the forward rate data cannot.

data in particular is that they are available even for countries like Taiwan and Korea, where financial markets are less developed. A potential disadvantage is the possibility that survey data measure the expectations of market participants imperfectly.

For Singapore, the survey data corroborate the finding from the forward rate data that, once expected depreciation is eliminated as a factor, the New York effect dominates the Tokyo effect. For Korea, the survey data also show that the Tokyo effect becomes smaller than the New York effect. For Australia and Taiwan, both effects largely disappear.[25]

2.3.4   The Role of the Yen in Asian Exchange Rate Policies

The finding that eliminating exchange rate expectations from the calculation leaves Tokyo with relatively little effect on local interest rates in most of these countries does not necessarily mean that the Japanese influence is not strong. It is possible, rather, that much of the influence in the Pacific comes precisely through the role of the yen. If Pacific countries assign high weight to the yen in setting their exchange rate policies, then their interest rates will be heavily influenced by Japanese interest rates.

No Asian or Pacific countries have ever pegged their currencies to the yen in the postwar period. But neither are there any Pacific countries that the International Monetary Fund (IMF) classifies as still pegging to the U.S. dollar. (As already mentioned, Hong Kong pegs to the dollar, although the colony is not an official member of the IMF.) Malaysia, Thailand, and a number of Pacific island countries officially peg to a basket of major currencies and are thought to give weight to both the dollar and yen, but the weights are not officially announced.

It is interesting to estimate econometrically the weights given to the dollar, yen, and other major currencies in exchange rate policies of Asian Pacific countries, especially those who follow a basket peg but do not officially announce the weights. This involves regressing changes in the value of the currency in question against changes in the value of the yen, dollar, and so forth. (I work in changes rather than in levels, among other reasons, because exchange rates have been widely observed to behave as unit-root processes.)

There is a methodological question of what numeraire should be used to measure the value of the currencies. A simple solution is to use the special drawing right (SDR) as numeraire. This approach suffers from the drawback that the SDR is itself a basket of five major currencies, including the dollar and yen. An alternative approach is to use purchasing power over local goods (the inverse of the local price level) as the numeraire. Whatever the numeraire, under the null hypothesis that a particular currency is pegged to the dollar or yen, or to a weighted basket, the regression results should show this clearly, featuring even a high R^2. I focus here on the purchasing-power measure.

---

25. Table 4 in Frankel (1991a), or table 7 in NBER Working Paper no. 4050. Time trends are estimated in tables 13a and 13b in Chinn and Frankel (1992).

Table 2.9   **Weights Assigned to Foreign Currencies in Determining Changes in Value of Malaysian Ringgit**

	Constant	Yen	Dollar	Mark	Pound	Franc	R^2	Durbin-Watson
74.1–91.10	−.0028	.01	.16	.07	.01	−.01	.28	1.59
	−7.97**	0.55	6.74**	2.35**	0.33	−0.22		
74.1–76.12	−.0044	.05	.15	.09	−.06	−.01	.24	1.59
	−2.74**	0.37	1.29	0.90	−0.69	−0.17		
77.1–79.12	−.0017	.05	.29	.15	.04	−.07	.45	1.73
	−1.82††	1.27	3.38*	2.19*	0.76	−0.78		
80.1–82.12	−.0041	.00	.11	.15	.03	−.06	.35	1.52
	−4.14**	0.08	2.17*	2.13*	0.83	−0.88		
83.1–85.12	−.0014	.07	.17	−.07	.00	.12	.32	1.90
	−1.55	1.24	2.65**	−0.59	0.00	0.98		
86.1–88.12	−.0021	−.04	.12	.06	−.06	−.02	.44	1.49
	−3.78**	−1.45	2.86**	0.70	2.55**	−0.24		
88.1–90.12	−.0025	−.01	.17	−.10	.04	.09	.30	1.55
	−5.52**	−0.50	2.75**	−0.76	1.56	0.71		

Notes: ††, *, and ** denote significance at the 90, 95, and 99 percent levels, respectively. *t*-statistics are reported below coefficients. The value of currencies, both domestic and foreign, refers to purchasing power over Malaysian goods, as measured by the CPI.

Regressions of changes in the real value of the Hong Kong dollar against changes in the value of the five major currencies show highly significant coefficients on the U.S. dollar during the periods 1974–80 and 1984–90 (not reported here). The weight on the dollar is statistically indistinguishable from 1 during most of the latter seven-year period, and the R^2 reaches 0.96 during the last four years. Occasional subperiods show apparently significant weights on other currencies (the yen during 1979–81, the franc during 1983–85, and the mark during 1986–88). Overall, however, the numbers bear out Hong Kong's peg to the dollar.

Regressions of changes in the real value of the Malaysian ringgit against the five major currencies, reported in table 2.9, give a large significant weight to the dollar. Some subperiods show a significant weight on the mark, and during 1986–88 even the pound is significant. But the yen is not significant during any three-year subperiod. The constant term is negative (and statistically significant), indicating a trend depreciation, and the R^2 is fairly low, indicating that the basket peg was loose, even if one allows for a crawling peg.[26]

The Singapore dollar shows significant weights (of about .2 each) on the U.S. dollar and mark during the period 1974–77, as reported in table 2.10. The regression for 1977–79 shows a rough basket peg ($R^2 = .83$) with significant

26. This turns out to be true of almost all currencies worldwide that purport to be on a basket peg (excluding a peg to the SDR).

Table 2.10   **Weights Assigned to Foreign Currencies in Determining Changes in Value of Singapore Dollar**

	Constant	Yen	Dollar	Mark	Pound	Franc	R^2	Durbin-Watson
74.1–91.13	−.0015	.06	.24	.13	−.01	−.04	.45	1.55
	−3.96**	3.93**	9.68**	4.19*	−0.58	−1.26		
74.1–76.12	−.0025	.02	.24	.26	−.07	−.00	.46	1.40
	−1.74††	0.20	2.32*	2.84**	−0.97	−0.05		
77.1–79.12	−.0010	.09	.47	.25	.09	−.09	.83	1.90
	−1.32	3.53**	8.07**	4.820**	2.32*	−1.44		
80.1–82.12	−.0013	.11	.22	.22	.07	−.12	.74	1.42
	−1.50	3.72**	4.73**	3.82**	2.05*	−2.04*		
83.1–85.12	−.0012	.20	.19	−.08	−.02	.07	.41	1.55
	−1.70††	3.87**	3.09**	−0.78	−0.53	0.77		
86.1–88.12	−.0004	.01	.14	.02	.02	.01	.46	2.59
	−0.83	0.36	3.93**	0.33*	1.14	0.12		
88.1–90.12	−.0010	.02	.15	−.05	.04	.06	.32	2.31
	−1.65††	0.87	3.29**	−0.42	1.29	0.46		

Notes: ††, *, and ** denote significance at the 90, 95%, and 99 percent level, respectively. *t*-statistics are reported below coefficients. The value of currencies, both domestic and foreign, refers to purchasing power over Singapore goods, as measured by the CPI.

weights of .09 on the yen, .47 on the dollar, .25 on the mark, and .09 on the pound. The weight on the dollar diminishes thereafter, and the weight on the yen increases. By 1983–85, the yen weight (at a significant .20) has temporarily passed the dollar weight (at a significant .19). From 1986 to 1990 only the dollar is significant.

The results for the real value of the Thai baht, reported in table 2.11, show a very close peg to the dollar from 1974 to 1980, whereupon the dollar weight falls somewhat. Beginning in 1986, a pattern emerges of significant weights on the yen and pound, in addition to the dollar. During the period 1988–90, the baht exhibits a close to perfect peg ($R^2 = .99$) to a basket with estimated weights of .82 on the dollar, .13 on the yen, .06 on the mark, and .02 on the pound.

Korea also claimed to have a sort of basket peg in the 1980s, but with large adjustments. Regressions of the change in the real value of the won show a statistically significant weight on the value of the dollar during the period April 1980–March 1986, with an estimated coefficient of .4 to .5. (The Canadian dollar, which was reputed to be included in the Korean basket, also shows up with a significant coefficient of .2 during part of the period.) There is a significant constant term (the "alpha") during this period: the value of the won declined during the early 1980s, whether measured by inflation or depreciation, relative to foreign currencies. The dollar, like the other major currencies, is insignificant during the period April 1985–March 1987. Its influence reemerges from April 1986 to March 1988. But during the final two-year subperiod, April 1988–March 1990, the yen (with a highly significant coefficient

Table 2.11 **Weights Assigned to Foreign Currencies in Determining Changes in Value of Thai Baht**

	Constant	Yen	Dollar	Mark	Pound	Franc	R^2	Durbin-Watson
74.1–91.3	−.0039	.01	.30	−.01	−.02	.03	.38	1.43
	8.05**	0.61	9.37**	−0.03	−0.63	0.85		
74.1–76.12	−.0000	−.00	1.00	.00	−.00	−.00	1.00	2.05
	−0.90	−0.00	240.71**	.42	−.36	−.10		
77.1–79.12	−.0010	.03	.89	.02	−.00	−.05	.96	1.70
	−2.35*	2.69**	22.16**	1.10	−0.01	−1.72††		
80.1–82.12	−.0061	.01	.47	.11	.00	−.10	.58	1.47
	−3.71**	0.15	5.82**	0.96	0.04	−0.80		
83.1–85.12	−.0020	.01	.03	−.01	−.07	.09	.32	1.51
	−2.45*	0.29	0.91	−0.06	−2.04*	0.89		
86.1–88.12	−.0006	.06	.63	−.03	.05	.08	.80	2.04
	−1.72††	3.52**	10.02**	−0.69	3.29**	1.76††		
88.1–90.12	.0001	.13	.82	.06	.02	−.01	.99	1.77
	0.61	19.35**	45.42**	1.99*	2.72**	−0.22		

Notes: ††, *, and ** denote significance at the 90, 95, and 99 percent levels, respectively. *t*-statistics are reported below coefficients. The value of currencies, both domestic and foreign, refers to purchasing power over Thai goods, as measured by the CPI.

estimated at .18) suddenly eclipses the dollar (with an insignificant coefficient of .11).[27]

To summarize, there is some evidence of increased yen influence in the case of the Singapore dollar in the early 1980s and the Thai baht in the late 1980s. The only place where the yen appears to have become as important as the dollar is Korea in the last two years of the decade.[28]

2.3.5   The Role of the Yen in Reserves and Invoicing

There is other evidence that the yen is playing an increasing role in the region. As table 2.12 shows, Asian central banks in the course of the 1980s increased their holdings of yen from 13.9 percent of their foreign exchange reserve portfolios to 17.1 percent.[29] Foreign exchange market trading in the regional financial centers of Singapore and Hong Kong, though still overwhelmingly conducted in dollars, now shows a much higher proportion of trading in yen than is the case in Europe (Tavlas and Ozeki 1992, 35).

The yen is also being used more widely to invoice lending and trade in Asia.

27. The results for the won are reported in Frankel (1992) (with value measured in terms of purchasing power. Value is measured also in terms of the SDR in a related paper to be published by the Hoover Institution, but the regressions are against the dollar and yen alone).

28. Further results on a set of nine East Asian currencies are reported in Frankel and Wei (1992b). The Indonesian rupiah turns out to be the clearest case of significant yen influence, which is of interest in that Indonesia is also the case where Japanese interest rates are seen to have the most strongly increasing influence (table 2.8 here).

29. The deutsch mark and Swiss franc are the two currencies that suffered the largest loss in share in the region.

Table 2.12   **Share of the Yen in Debt-Denomination and Official Reserve Holdings (percentage)**

	Yen Share in External Debt						Yen Share in Official Holdings	
	Indonesia	Korea	Malaysia	Philippines	Thailand	Total	Asia[a]	World
1980	20.0	16.6	19.0	22.0	25.5	19.5	13.9	4.4
1981	19.3	14.1	16.9	20.6	23.2	17.8	15.5	4.2
1982	21.0	12.3	13.3	19.2	24.0	17.2	17.6	4.7
1983	23.3	12.5	14.2	20.0	27.3	18.5	15.5	5.0
1984	25.0	12.8	21.2	20.0	29.2	20.3	16.3	5.8
1985	31.7	16.7	26.4	24.9	36.1	25.8	26.9	8.0
1986	33.9	22.0	30.4	25.5	39.9	29.3	22.9	7.9
1987	39.4	27.2	35.7	35.2	43.1	36.0	30.0	7.5
1988	39.3	29.5	37.1	40.5	43.5	37.9	26.7	7.7
1989	35.2	26.6	36.6	32.6	40.9	35.7	17.5	7.9
1990							17.1	9.1

Source: Tavlas and Ozeki (1992, 39).

[a]Selected Asian countries (not including Japan).

The countries that incurred large international debts in the 1970s and early 1980s subsequently shifted the composition away from dollar-denominated debt and toward yen-denominated debt. Table 2.12 shows that the yen share among five major Asian debtors nearly doubled between 1980 and 1988, entirely at the expense of the dollar. Table 2.13 shows that the share of trade denominated in yen is greater in Asia than in other regions, and that there was an especially rapid increase from 1983 to 1990 in the share of Asian imports denominated in yen.[30] Overall, however, it must be concluded that the role of the yen in East Asia is still not proportionate to Japan's importance in trade.

2.4   Conclusions

1. The *level* of trade in East Asia, like trade within the EC and within the Western Hemisphere, is biased toward intraregional trade, to a greater extent than can be explained naturally by distance. When one allows for the greater openness of the East Asian countries, however, the significance of the bloc effect largely disappears.

2. There is no evidence of a special Japan effect within Asia.

3. Although growth in Japan, the four NICs, and other East Asian countries is rapidly increasing their weight in world output and trade, the statistics do not bear out a *trend* toward intraregional bias of trade and direct investment flows.

4. The intraregional trade bias did increase in Europe in the 1980s, in the

30. Tavlas and Ozeki (1991, 1992) give further statistics and discussion.

Table 2.13   Share of the Yen in Denomination of Foreign Trade (percentage)

	Denomination of Exports		Denomination of Imports	
	Southeast Asia	All Regions	Southeast Asia	All Regions
1983	48.0	40.4	2.0	3.0
1986	37.5	35.5	9.2	9.7
1987	36.3	34.7	13.9	11.6
1988	41.2	34.3	17.5	13.3
1989	43.5	34.7	19.5	14.1
1990	48.9	37.5	19.4	14.4

Source: Japanese Ministry of Finance, Annual Report, as reported in Tavlas and Ozeki (1992, 33).

Western Hemisphere in the late 1980s, and in the grouping that includes the United States and Canada with the Asian Pacific countries, that is, APEC.

5. The APEC trade grouping appears to be the world's strongest, whether judged by rate of change of intragroup bias or (as of 1990) by level of bias. Far from being shut out of a strong Asian bloc centered on Japan, the United States and Canada are in the enviable position of belonging to *both* of the world's two strongest groupings.

6. There is a bit of evidence of Japanese influence in East Asia's *financial markets,* as opposed to trade. Tokyo appears to have increasing influence over interest rates in Singapore, Korea, and Indonesia. Overall, however, its influence is still smaller than that of New York.

7. Some of Japan's financial influence takes place through a growing role for the yen, at the expense of the dollar. There has been a gradual increase in the yen's relative importance in invoicing of trade and finance in the region, and in some countries' exchange rate policies.

This still leaves a question raised at the beginning of this essay. Is Japan undertaking deliberate policy measures to increase its monetary and financial role? Gradually increasing use of the yen internationally is primarily the outcome of private decisions by importers, exporters, borrowers, and lenders. It is difficult to see signs of deliberate policy actions taken by the Japanese government to increase its financial and monetary influence in Asia. To the contrary, until recently the Japanese government has resisted whatever tendency there may be for the yen to become an international currency in competition with the dollar.

It has been the U.S. government, in the Yen-Dollar Agreement of 1984 and in subsequent negotiations, that has been pushing Japan to internationalize the yen, to promote its worldwide use in trade, finance, and central bank policies (Frankel 1984). It has also been the U.S. government that has been pushing Korea and other East Asian NICs to open up their financial markets, thereby allowing Japanese capital and Japanese financial institutions to enter these countries. It has again been the U.S. government that has been pushing Korea and Taiwan to move away from policies to stabilize the value of their currencies against the dollar.[31] The increasing role of the yen in the Asian Pacific may or may not be a good idea. But it is an idea that originated in Washington, not in Tokyo.

Appendix
Countries Used in the Gravity Equation

The list shows regional groupings and main city. The distance between countries was computed as the great-circle distance between the relevant pair of cities. (APEC consists of East Asia, Australia, New Zealand, Canada, and the United States.)

Americas (WH, 13)

Argentina	Buenos Aires	Mexico	Mexico City
Bolivia	La Paz	Paraguay	Asunción
Brazil	Saõ Paulo	Peru	Lima
Canada	Ottawa	United States	Chicago
Chile	Santiago	Uruguay	Montevideo
Colombia	Bogotá	Venezuela	Caracas
Ecuador	Quito		

European Community (EC, 11)

Belgium	Brussels	Netherlands	Amsterdam
Denmark	Copenhagen	Portugal	Lisbon
France	Paris	Spain	Madrid
Greece	Athens	United Kingdom	London
Ireland	Dublin	West Germany	Bonn
Italy	Rome		

European Free Trade Area (EFTA, 6)

Austria	Vienna	Norway	Oslo
Finland	Helsinki	Sweden	Stockholm
Iceland	Reykjavik	Switzerland	Geneva

31. Balassa and Williamson (1990), Noland (1990), and Frankel (1989). Financial negotiations between the U.S. Treasury and the governments of Korea and Taiwan were a response to congressional passage of the 1988 Omnibus Trade bill.

Eastern Europe (3)

| Hungary | Budapest | Yugoslavia | Belgrade |
| Poland | Warsaw | | |

East Asia (EAEC, 10)

China	Shanghai	Philippines	Manila
Hong Kong	Hong Kong	South Korea	Singapore
Indonesia	Jakarta	Singapore	Seoul
Japan	Tokyo	Taiwan	Taipei
Malaysia	Kuala Lumpur	Thailand	Bangkok

Other Pacific (2)

| Australia | Sydney | New Zealand | Wellington |

Africa and West Asia (18)

Algeria	Algiers	Libya	Tripoli
Egypt	Cairo	Morocco	Casablanca
Ethiopia	Addis Ababa	Nigeria	Lagos
Ghana	Accra	Pakistan	Karachi
India	New Delhi	Saudi Arabia	Riyadh
Iran	Tehran	South Africa	Pretoria
Israel	Jerusalem	Sudan	Khartoum
Kenya	Nairobi	Tunisia	Tunis
Kuwait	Kuwait	Turkey	Ankara

References

Abidin, A. Z. 1986. Financial Reform and the Role of Foreign Banks in Malaysia. In *Financial Policy and Reform in Pacific Basin Countries,* ed. Hanson Cheng, 305–9. Lexington, MA: Lexington Books.

Anderson, James. 1979. A Theoretical Foundation for the Gravity Equation. *American Economic Review* 69 (1): 106–16.

Anderson, Kym, and Hege Norheim. 1992. History, Geography, and Regional Economic Integration. GATT Secretariat Conference, Geneva, October. Forthcoming in *Regionalism and the Global Trading System,* ed. Kym Anderson and R. Blackhurst. London: Harvester Wheatsheaf, 1993.

Argy, Victor. 1987. International Financial Liberalisation—The Australian and Japanese Experiences Compared. *Bank of Japan Monetary and Economic Studies* 5 (1): 105–68.

Balassa, Bela, and John Williamson. 1990. *Adjusting to Success: Balance of Payments Policy in the East Asian NICs.* Policy Analyses in International Economics 17. Washington, DC: Institute for International Economics, April.

Bergsten, C. Fred. 1991. Comment on Krugman. In *Policy Implications of Trade and*

Currency Zones, 43–57, a symposium sponsored by the Federal Reserve Bank of Kansas City, Jackson Hole, WY, August.

Bhagwati, Jagdish. 1990. Regional Accords Be-GATT Trouble for Free Trade. *Wall Street Journal,* December 5.

———. 1992. Regionalism vs. Multilateralism: An Overview. Paper presented at the Conference on New Dimensions in Regional Integration, World Bank, Washington, DC, April 2–3.

Chinn, Menzie, and Jeffrey Frankel. 1992. Financial Links around the Pacific Rim: 1982–1992. Forthcoming in *Exchange Rate Policies in Pacific Basin Countries,* ed. Reuven Glick and Michael Hutchison. Cambridge: Cambridge University Press.

Deardorff, Alan. 1984. Testing Trade Theories and Predicting Trade Flows. In *Handbook of International Economics,* ed. R. Jones and P. Kenen, 1:467–517. Amsterdam: Elsevier Science Publishers.

Dornbusch, Rudiger. 1989. The Dollar in the 1990s: Competitiveness and the Challenges of New Economic Blocs. In *Monetary Policy Issues in the 1990s* (Kansas City: Federal Reserve Bank of Kansas City).

Drysdale, Peter, and Ross Garnaut. 1992. The Pacific: An Application of a General Theory of Economic Integration. Paper presented at the Twentieth Pacific Trade and Development Conference, Washington, DC, September 10–12.

Edwards, Sebastian, and Mohsin Khan. 1985. Interest Rate Determination in Developing Countries: A Conceptual Framework. *IMF Staff Papers* 32 (September): 377–403.

Faruqee, Hamid. 1991. Dynamic Capital Mobility in Pacific Basin Developing Countries: Estimation and Policy Implications. IMF Working Paper 91/115, November.

Fieleke, Norman. 1992. One Trading World, or Many: The Issue of Regional Trading Blocs. *New England Economic Review* (May/June): 3–20.

Frankel, Jeffrey. 1984. *The Yen/Dollar Agreement: Liberalizing Japanese Capital Markets.* Policy Analyses in International Economics no. 9. Washington, DC: Institute for International Economics.

———. 1989. And Now Won/Dollar Negotiations? Lessons from the Yen/Dollar Agreement of 1984. In *Korea's Macroeconomic and Financial Policies,* 105–27. Seoul: Korean Development Institute, December.

———. 1991a. "Is a Yen Bloc Forming in Pacific Asia?" In *Finance and the International Economy,* ed. Richard O'Brien, 4–20. Oxford: Oxford University Press.

———. 1991b. The Japanese Cost of Finance: A Survey. *Financial Management* (Spring): 95–127.

———. 1991c. Quantifying International Capital Mobility in the 1980's. In *National Saving and Economic Performance,* ed. B. Douglas Bernheim and John B. Shoven, 227–60. Chicago, University of Chicago Press.

———. 1992. The Recent Liberalization of Korea's Foreign Exchange Markets, and Tests of U.S. versus Japanese Influence. *Seoul Journal of Economics* 5 (1): 1–29.

Frankel, Jeffrey, and Shang-jin Wei. 1992a. Trade Blocs and Currency Blocs. NBER Working Paper no. 4335. Cambridge, Mass.: National Bureau of Economic Research.

———. 1992b. Yen Bloc or Dollar Bloc? Exchange Rate Policies of the East Asian Economies. In *Macroeconomic Linkage,* ed. Takatoshi Ito and Anne Krueger. Chicago: University of Chicago Press, forthcoming.

Froot, Kenneth, and David Yoffie. 1991. Strategic Trade Policies in a Tripolar World. Working Paper no. 91-030, Harvard Business School. Revised.

Fukao, Mitsuhiro, and Takashi Okubo. 1984. International Linkage of Interest Rates: The Case of Japan and the United States. *International Economic Review* 25 (February): 193–207.

Glick, Reuven, and Michael Hutchison. 1990. Financial Liberalization in the Pacific Basin: Implications for Real Interest Rate Linkages. *Journal of the Japanese and International Economies* 4:36–48.

Hamilton, Carl, and L. Alan Winters. 1992. Opening Up International Trade in Eastern Europe. *Economic Policy* (April): 77–116.

Helpman, Elhanan. 1987. Imperfect Competition and International Trade: Evidence from Fourteen Industrial Countries. *Journal of the Japanese and International Economies* 1:62–81.

Helpman, Elhanan, and Paul Krugman. 1985. *Market Structure and Foreign Trade.* Cambridge, MA: MIT Press.

Holloway, Nigel. 1991. Half Full, Half Empty. *Far Eastern Economic Review* (December): 64.

Ito, Takatoshi. 1986. Capital Controls and Covered Interest Parity. *Economic Studies Quarterly* 37:223–41.

———. 1988. Use of (Time-Domain) Vector Autoregressions to Test Uncovered Interest Parity. *Review of Economics and Statistics* 70:296–305.

Jackson, Tom. 1991. A Game Model of ASEAN Trade Liberalization. *Open Economies Review* 2 (3): 237–54.

Komiya, Ryutaro, and Ryuhei Wakasugi. 1991. Japan's Foreign Direct Investment. *Annals of the American Academy of Political and Social Science* (January).

Krugman, Paul. 1991a. Is Bilateralism Bad? In *International Trade and Trade Policy,* ed. Elhanan Helpman and Assaf Razin. Cambridge: MIT Press.

———. 1991b. The Move toward Free Trade Zones. In *Policy Implications of Trade and Currency Zones,* 7–42, a symposium sponsored by the Federal Reserve Bank of Kansas City, Jackson Hole, WY, August.

Lawrence, Robert. 1991a. An Analysis of Japanese Trade with Developing Countries. Brookings Discussion Papers no. 87. April.

———. 1991b. Emerging Regional Arrangements: Building Blocks or Stumbling Blocks? In *Finance and the International Economy,* ed. Richard O'Brien, 24–36. Oxford: Oxford University Press.

———. 1991c. "How Open Is Japan? In *Trade with Japan: Has the Door Opened Wider?* ed. Paul Krugman, 9–50. Chicago: University of Chicago Press.

Moreno, Ramon. 1988. Exchange Rates and Monetary Policy in Singapore and Taiwan. In *Monetary Policy in Pacific Basin Countries,* ed. Hanson Cheng, 173–200. Boston: Kluwer Press.

Noland, Marcus. 1990. *Pacific Basin Developing Countries: Prospects for the Future.* Washington, DC: Institute for International Economics.

———. 1991. Public Policy, Private Preferences, and the Japanese Trade Pattern. Washington, DC: Institute for International Economics, November.

Otani, Ichiro, and Siddarth Tiwari. 1981. Capital Controls and Interest Rate Parity: The Japanese Experience, 1978–1981. *IMF Staff Papers* 28 (December): 793–815.

Petri, Peter. 1991. Market Structure, Comparative Advantage, and Japanese Trade under the Strong Yen. In *Trade with Japan: Has the Door Opened Wider?* ed. Paul Krugman, 51–84. Chicago: University of Chicago Press.

———. 1992. One Bloc, Two Blocs, or None? Political-Economic Factors in Pacific Trade Policy. In *The U.S.-Japan Economic Relationship in East and Southeast Asia: A Policy Framework for Asia-Pacific Economic Cooperation,* ed. Kaoru Okuzumi, Kent Calder, and Gerrit Gong, 39–70. Washington, DC: Center for Strategic and International Studies.

Ramstetter, Eric. 1991a. An Overview of Multinational Firms in Asia-Pacific Economies: An Introduction to the Commonplace Ignorance. Faculty of Economics, Kansai University, Osaka.

————— 1991b. Regional Patterns of Japanese Multinational Activities in Japan and Asia's Developing Countries. Economic and Political Studies Series no. 74. Osaka: Kansai University.

Saxonhouse, Gary. 1989. Differentiated Products, Economies of Scale, and Access to the Japanese Market. In *Trade Policies for International Competitiveness,* ed. Robert Feenstra, 145–74. Chicago: University of Chicago Press.

Schott, Jeffrey. 1991. Trading Blocs and the World Trading System. *World Economy* 14, (1): 1–17.

Tavlas, George, and Yuzuru Ozeki. 1991. The Japanese Yen as an International Currency. IMF Working Paper no. 91/2. Washington, DC: International Monetary Fund, January.

————. 1992. *The Internationalization of Currencies: An Appraisal of the Japanese Yen.* IMF Occasional Paper no. 90. Washington, DC: International Monetary Fund, January.

de la Torre, Augusto, and Margaret R. Kelly. 1992. *Regional Trading Arrangements.* IMF Occasional Paper no. 93. Washington, DC: International Monetary Fund, March.

Wang, Zhen Kun. 1992. China's Potential Trade: An Analysis Based on the Gravity Model. Department of Economics, University of Birmingham, United Kingdom.

Wang, Zhen Kun, and L. Alan Winters. 1991. The Trading Potential of Eastern Europe, Centre for Economic Policy Research Discussion Paper no. 610. London, November.

Comment   Robert Z. Lawrence

In choosing me to comment on this paper, Jeffrey Frankel showed an unusual amount of trust, since I find it hard to view the paper with impartiality. An earlier version of the paper won first prize last year in a competition organized by the American Express Company. It so happens, a paper that I wrote obtained the second prize.

Notwithstanding my unusual perspective on this work, my overall appraisal of the paper is favorable. I certainly agree with its central conclusion that in the trade area, thus far, growth rather than inherent discrimination is primarily responsible for the increased regionalization of Asia. While the work on financial integration is illuminating, it is much less convincing because of the difficulties associated with providing a structural interpretation of the relationships between the variables.

I would like to focus my first comment on the basic methodology of the paper. Frankel defines a regional bloc as "a group of countries that are concentrating their trade and financial relationships with each other, *in preference to the rest of the world*" (emphasis added). He then tests (1) whether trade blocs are forming in Asia by examining if intraregional trade has increased more

Robert Z. Lawrence is Albert L. Williams Professor of International Trade and Investment at the John F. Kennedy School of Government, Harvard University.

rapidly than a gravity model would predict, and (2) Japan's financial influence by using regression analysis.

Let me deal first with trade. In thinking about the implications of regional arrangements, it is important to be precise as to what we mean by the phrase "in preference." The term *preference* could imply some form of deliberate discrimination against outsiders—imposed by policy or prejudice. However, preferences could also reflect developments driven purely by efficiency considerations. The evidence from the gravity model tests cannot, of course, distinguish between these causes. While Frankel found that intra-Asian trade flows were not growing more rapidly than might be expected, even had he found that they were, this need not have implied that this development was harmful to the rest of the world.

The conventional answer to the question of whether regional arrangements enhance global welfare relates to the relative magnitudes of trade diversion and trade creation. These magnitudes, it should be stressed, do not correspond to the relative ex post growth of intra- and extraregional flows. Trade diversion harms welfare only when the inefficiency cost of buying from a higher-cost regional partner is greater than the deadweight gain to consumers of buying goods that are not subject to tariffs; that is, global (if not extraregional welfare) can be enhanced even when trade is shifted toward a regional partner. For the rest of the world, even if trade is thus diverted, there could be offsetting effects if regional integration has dynamic effects that stimulate growth.

Let me argue, moreover, that to evaluate regional arrangements properly, we need to move beyond the traditional approach that looks only at the role of the removal of border barriers. Regional arrangements such as EC92 involve deeper integration with an extensive program involving increased institutional harmonization to complete the internal market. We should really be evaluating the precise nature rather than simply the quantity of Asian economic integration. A growth in intraregional competition that reflects the weakening of domestic market power and the ability of domestic firms to collude and prevent entry might show up in data in a rapid increase in regional trade, but it could also increase the relative access of outsiders.

I think it is also important to distinguish between the aggregate trade flows that Frankel examines and behavior in particular sectors. While I agree that overall trade flows are driven by Asian growth, I think that in a few sectors, particularly machinery and electronics, there is more evidence that *keiretsu* activities are particularly strong. In these industries there appears to be an extensive and growing network associated with the activities of Japanese firms. These practices have made it relatively difficult for foreigners to enter the Japanese market, and there is a concern that the spread of such arrangements throughout Asia could have similar effects. So while I applaud Frankel's efforts as an important first step, I think we need to move beyond simply examining trade flows, toward examining institutional and industrial practices.

I had more problems with the evidence on financial behavior. In particular, the regressions can be thought of as statistical summaries of the historic relationships between some highly endogenous variables, but it is hard to provide a structural interpretation for the results. The increased correlation between variables does not necessarily imply increased integration. It could simply reflect similar responses to common external shocks. Indeed, a major reason for similar responses within Asian countries could of course be similar pressures from the United States. In other words, closer links with the United States could lead to increased correlation in Asian behavior but reduced correlation with the United States, if U.S. policies brought pressures to shift Asian exchange rates.

I am particularly concerned about several of the regressions in which the coefficients sum to far more than unity. We might expect, for example, that a 1 percent increase in expected global inflation would raise nominal interest rates throughout the world by 1 percent, yet these regressions, if taken literally, suggest that such a shock would lead to changes far in excess of (or below) this effect.

3 Pricing Strategies and Trading Blocs in East Asia

Gary R. Saxonhouse

3.1 Introduction

From the mid–eighteenth century until the First World War, the scale of political units around the world grew ever larger. At least part of the motivation for large political size during these years was economic. The past few years have seen an increasingly rapid unraveling of this process. Looking at the European Community (EC), the North American Free Trade Agreement (NAFTA), and even the Asia Pacific Economic Cooperation (APEC), it's hard not to think of strong, regional customs unions as the wave of everyone's future. Yet the experience of the Soviet Union, Yugoslavia, and Czechoslovakia really does suggest otherwise. The GATT-governed multilateral trading system has made possible the extraordinary economic success of microstates like Hong Kong and Singapore. And it is this success that has surely emboldened Estonians, Slovaks, and Tadjiks to assume that separation from large political units need not mean economic disaster. The great continental superpowers that came into existence before 1914 and that ran roughshod over cultural diversity may well have been made anachronistic not so much by increasing ethnic identification as by the open, multilateral global trading system of the late twentieth century. The multilateral trading system has been capable of providing a substitute for much of the special economic advantages of large political size. The door is now potentially open for a plethora of economically viable microstates organized, following East Asia, on the basis of cultural affinity.

The aspirations of regional economic arrangements do collide with the multilateral system. Slovaks may seek political independence, confident that the GATT will guarantee markets for their products even as it protects their access to vital imports. When Slovaks, however, attempt to negotiate the terms

Gary R. Saxonhouse is professor of economics at the University of Michigan.

of their access to the European Community, they may be in for a nasty surprise. Of course, it is the new vitality of regional arrangements such as the European Community and NAFTA, and not the obsolescence of dinosaurs like the Soviet Union and Yugoslavia, that provides the context for this paper.

In the first section of this paper, the consequences of trading bloc formation for countries left outside such blocs will be reviewed. In particular, the case where the formation of such a bloc will leave outsiders worse off will be highlighted. This can happen even without the trading bloc violating Article 24 of the GATT. Still worse, such blocs can make insiders better off than in the case of global free trade. In this circumstance, insiders may have no incentive to let in additional members, except where the formation of a rival bloc is threatened. The formation of a regional trading bloc may not be a way station on the road to global free trade.

The case outlined in the first section of this paper reflects the concerns of the East Asian economies. Trading blocs are being formed elsewhere in the world. Even without violating existing GATT provisions, such blocs can lower East Asian welfare. These trading blocs may have no incentive to expand their membership to include East Asian economies except insofar as they fear provoking the formation of an East Asian trading bloc.

The second section of this paper reviews the prospects for a regional trade regime in East Asia. Intra–East Asian trade is currently not large by historical standards. Nor does the rapid growth in intra–East Asian trade reflect much more than the very rapid overall economic growth in this region relative to the rest of the world. Estimation of a bilateral model of intraindustry trade using a factor-endowment-based version of the gravity model suggests no East Asian bias in the trading patterns of the leading economies there. There is no evidence as yet that a rival trading bloc is being formed in East Asia in response to developments in Europe and North America.

In the final section of this paper, the exchange rate–induced pricing strategies of East Asian firms across East Asian markets are examined. The results suggest that country-specific pricing strategies seem characteristic of East Asian markets. Commodity arbitrage may be more difficult in East Asia than elsewhere. Despite considerable progress in trade liberalization by many of the East Asian economies over the past two decades, there is some indication that regionwide liberalization could still be of considerable benefit.

3.2   The International Economic System and New Trading Blocs

Since 1945 international trade theory has developed to the extent that it is now well understood that the formation of a regional trading bloc may be detrimental to the international economic system (Machlup 1977). It is possible that the benefits for members of a trading bloc through trade creation may be less than the costs imposed on nonmembers through trade diversion (Viner 1950). Indeed, shifts in the terms of trade in favor of members at the expense of nonmembers are responsible for many of the benefits that follow the organization of a trading bloc. This can happen even if a trading bloc leaves its protective barriers against nonmembers unchanged. Of course, matters can get worse. A newly formed bloc may succumb to temptation and attempt to exploit its newfound market power by raising its barriers against nonmembers and still further improving its terms of trade. Even without assuming such GATT-inconsistent behavior, provided not all countries belong to trading blocs, trading blocs may be able, not just to improve member welfare, but to push it beyond what might be expected with global free trade.

By way of illustration consider a world with N countries of equal size (see Krugman 1991). Each country is specialized in the production of a single good that is an imperfect substitute for the products of all other countries. These countries are not only equal in size; they also have identical preferences and produce their goods with the same technology. Each country imposes identical tariffs on the imports of all other countries, except trading bloc member countries impose no tariffs on the products of fellow members. While Krugman puts each of his symmetric countries in one of a number of equal-sized trading blocs and assumes that each country produces the same number of units of its single good, here it will be assumed that the global economy is divided up between members and nonmembers of a single bloc and that each country's production of its single good is variable.

Analysis of such a simple system cannot explain why a particular group of countries join together in any particular trading bloc. It can illuminate, however, what happens to member welfare, nonmember welfare, and global welfare when a single trading bloc is first organized and then grows in size. Analysis of a global economy made up of countries of equal size with virtually identical characteristics may seem remote from the substance of trade policy, but as will be seen, it does appear to capture the concerns of many of the East Asian economies.

Let

(1) $$X_{ki} = x_{ki}P_k,$$

where $X_{ki} \equiv$ value of exports from country k to country i; $x_{ki} \equiv$ volume of exports from country k to country i; and $P_k \equiv$ price of country k's production.

The demand for country k's product by country i is given by

(2) $$X_{ki} = \frac{Y_i}{N} - \frac{\beta}{N^2}\left[P_k(1 + t_{ki}) - \frac{1}{N}\sum_g P_g(1 + t_{gi})\right],$$

where $N \equiv$ number of countries; $Y_i \equiv$ country i's income; and $t_{ki} \equiv$ tariff imposed by country i on country k's product.

Equation (2) states that country i's income will be spent equally on each country's products except to the extent that the prices of a country's product diverge from the average price level of all commodities. As noted above, the same demand relationship governs the behavior of each of the N countries. In consequence, β has no subscript. Where countries belong to the same trading bloc, $t_{ki} = 0$; where countries do not, $t_{ki} = t$. Except between bloc and nonbloc members, the N countries do not discriminate among their trading partners.

The demand for country k's product by country i is met by country k's supply. The supply of country k's production is given by

$$(3) \qquad \pi_{ko} = \frac{\bar{\alpha}}{N} - \alpha \sum \frac{P_g(1 + t_{gk})}{N^2 P_k},$$

where $\pi_{ko} \equiv$ production of country k. Equation (3) is a standard supply function. Country k's production of its single product is a positive function of its price and a negative function of its costs. Since country k produces a single good, all intermediate inputs must be imported from abroad.

If the impact of the formation and growth of trading blocs on individual country welfare and global welfare is to be assessed, it is helpful to discuss the determinants of gross global product π_{oo}, and y_k, country k's real income. From equation (3) and summing over k, the expression for gross global product is

$$(4) \qquad \pi_{oo} = \bar{\alpha} - \frac{\alpha}{N^2} \sum_k \sum_g \frac{P_g(1 + t_{gk})}{P_k}.$$

Multiplying country k's production from equation (3) by real prices, real income for country k is given by

$$(5) \qquad y_k = \frac{\pi_{ko} P_k}{\sum_g P_g} = \frac{\bar{\alpha} P_k}{\sum_g P_g} - \alpha \frac{\sum P_g(1 + t_{gk})}{N \sum_g P_g}.$$

Equations (4) and (5) are expressions for gross global product and real income for country k in terms of prices. The analysis here requires that gross global product and real income for country k be evaluated as a function of bloc size and levels of protection. To do this, the system defined by equations (1), (2), and (3) must be solved for the determinants of these prices, and the resulting expression substituted back into equations (4) and (5).

Assuming that markets clear, the system defined by equations (1), (2), and (3) will be in equilibrium when nominal gross global product

$$(6) \qquad \pi_{oo} = \left[\bar{\alpha} + \beta(1 + t_k)\right] P_k - \frac{1}{N} \sum_g P_g \left[\alpha(1 + t_{gk}) + \beta(1 + t_g)\right],$$

where

$$(7) \qquad t_k = \frac{1}{N} \sum_i (1 + t_{ki})$$

and

$$(8) \qquad \pi_{oo} = \sum_i Y_i.$$

Because countries in this system have the same size with identical preferences and technology, beyond their complete product differentiation they differ only to the extent that they are in or out of the trading bloc. In consequence, the only prices in this system will be the price of goods produced by trading bloc members and the price of goods produced by nonmembers. From equations (6), (7), and (8) the ratio of these prices can be obtained by

$$
(9) \qquad \frac{P_o}{P_b} = \sigma = \frac{\bar{\alpha} + \beta\left(1 + \dfrac{m}{N}t\right) + \alpha\dfrac{n}{N}t}{\bar{\alpha} + \beta\left(1 + \dfrac{N-1}{N}t\right) + \alpha\dfrac{t}{N}} = 1 - \varphi,
$$

where $P_b \equiv$ price of good produced by trading bloc; $P_o \equiv$ price of good produced outside of trading bloc; $n \equiv$ number of trading bloc members; and $m \equiv$ number of outsiders; and where

$$
(10) \qquad \varphi = \frac{n-1}{N}\frac{\beta - \alpha}{\bar{\alpha} + \beta}t.
$$

This price information can be substituted into gross global product equation (4) such that

$$
(11) \qquad \pi_{oo} = \bar{\alpha} - \frac{\alpha}{N^2}\left[n^2 + mn(1 + t)(1 - \varphi + \frac{1}{1 - \varphi})\right.
$$
$$
\left. + m(m - 1)(1 + t) + m\right].
$$

The price information from equation (9) can also be substituted into equation (5) to yield expressions for the national income of both bloc members and nonmembers:

$$
(12) \qquad y_b = \left[\bar{\alpha} - \frac{\alpha}{N}(N + mt - m\varphi) - m\varphi t\right]/(N - m\varphi),
$$

and

$$
(13) \quad y_o = \left\{\bar{\alpha}(1 - \varphi) - \frac{\alpha}{N}(1 + t)(1 - \varphi)\left[\frac{n}{(1 - \varphi)} + (m - 1)(1 - \varphi)\right.\right.
$$
$$
\left.\left. + \left(\frac{1 - \varphi}{1 + t}\right)\right]\right\}/(N - m\varphi).
$$

With equations (11), (12), and (13) it's possible to examine what happens to gross global product and its distribution between bloc members and nonmembers as the bloc grows in size. In figure 3.1 the gross global product equation (11) is evaluated for different bloc sizes and for different levels of protection. Gross global product π_{oo} is measured along the y-axis, while bloc size varies from one to thirty and tariff levels move from 0 to 150 percent. Clearly, in this simple world the creation and growth of a trading bloc is not detrimental to global welfare. As can be seen from figure 3.1, at any given level of t as n increases from 1 to 30, π_{oo} increases in value. That is to say, at any given level

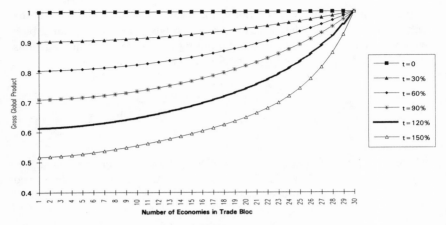

Fig. 3.1   Gross global product and trading bloc size
Note: t = tariff rate.

of protection the larger the bloc, the greater the gross global product. In this world, with every expansion of the size of the trading bloc, trade creation dominates trade diversion.[1] Of course, a bloc that includes all countries is global free trade, the equivalent of $t = 0$, which is the best situation of all.

At the same time that for any given level of protection an increase in the size of a trading bloc will increase gross global product, for any given size of trading bloc an increase in protection will diminish it. As can be seen from figure 3.1, for any given n, an increase in t will diminish π_{oo}. In this world a trading bloc that complies with Article 24 of the GATT cannot damage global welfare. A trading bloc that as it increases in size, however, takes full advantage of its increased market power to increase its barriers can do considerable damage. From figure 3.1 the trade-offs between the benefits to gross global product of a bigger trading bloc and the risks to it from increased protection are apparent.

The gain in gross global product that comes from a larger trading bloc when protection against outsiders is held constant will not be shared equally between members and nonmembers. As seen from equations (10)–(13), the distribution

1. Because all the countries in this model are alike except for the complete differentiation of their products, and because output is not fixed, the expansion of the size of a trading bloc does not lead to a decline in global welfare. In Viner (1950), trade diversion can outpace trade creation because links between natural trading partners can be severed by the creation of a customs union. Here there are no natural trading partners because all countries are alike or otherwise they are symmetrically different. As figure 3.1 indicates, gross global product accelerates in proportion to the number of tariff walls eliminated. The results here differ not only from Viner but also from Krugman (1991). In Krugman, even with countries that are virtually identical except for complete product differentiation, the relationship between bloc size and global welfare is not monotonic. Krugman's results depend critically on having each country's output fixed and having all countries being members of some equal-sized bloc. In this paper, by contrast, country output is variable, and there is only one bloc. If a country does not belong to this bloc, all its exports must bear a tariff *t*.

of gains between members and nonmembers will depend critically on the relative values of α and β. For example, when α, the supply parameter, is just equal to β, the demand parameter, the entire gain in global product will go to bloc members and the real income of nonmembers will stay constant unless they join the bloc.

With full employment of resources, however, it is likely that β will be considerably larger than α. This is the situation that's analyzed in figures 3.2 and 3.3, the counterparts to figure 3.1. In figures 3.2 and 3.3 the nonmember national income equation (13) and the bloc member national income equation (12) are evaluated for different trading bloc sizes and for different levels of protection. National income is in each case measured along the y-axis, while bloc size once again varies from 1 to 30 and tariff levels move from 0 to 150 percent.

As seen from figure 3.2, in the case where the demand parameter substantially exceeds the supply parameter, countries remaining outside the trading bloc don't just lose out relatively. National income actually declines for any given level of protection as the trading bloc increases in size. As is apparent from equations (9) and (10), this result reflects the continuous decline of non–bloc member producer prices relative to member producer prices. As the trading bloc increases in size, more and more of what nonmembers want to buy becomes increasingly more expensive in terms of what they produce. Under such conditions, the nonmember incentives to join the trading bloc are overwhelming. This incentive becomes ever stronger even though the bloc, by leaving the level of *t* constant, does not violate Article 24. From figure 3.1 it is also clear that if bloc members and nonmembers can mutually agree to lower *t*, nonmembers can be easily compensated for the loss in national income they suffer as the trading bloc grows.

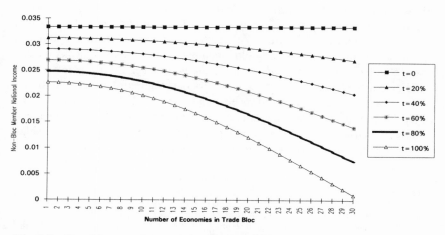

Fig. 3.2   Non–bloc member national income and trading bloc size
Note: t = tariff rate.

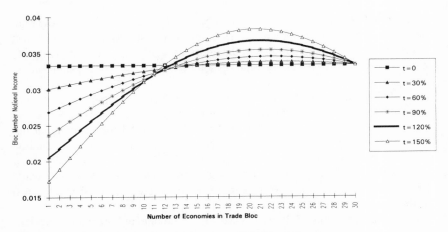

Fig. 3.3   Bloc member national income and trading bloc size
Note: t = tariff rate.

While the national income of each nonmember declines monotonically, as seen from figure 3.3, trading bloc member national income increases as the trading bloc grows in size from its very first members. A larger trading bloc means members can buy more products without trade restrictions, and it means, as noted earlier, increasingly favorable terms of trade with nonmembers. As long as admitting new members to the trading bloc increases the national income of each bloc member, the bloc has no incentive to be exclusive. As is apparent in figure 3.3, after the trading bloc has approximately twenty out of a possible thirty members (Europe and North America?), the incentive to admit additional members (East Asia?) and move on to free trading evaporates. At this point, the benefits to trading bloc members from being able to buy additional products without trade restrictions becomes less than the losses suffered from having fewer countries outside the trading bloc trading with members on unfavorable terms. With further expansion of the trading bloc, the national income of each trading bloc member declines monotonically as each new member joins, up to *and including the point* when no one is left outside and global free trade is achieved. Members of a trading bloc can achieve real income above what they would receive under free trade if they agree to keep their bloc exclusive. They certainly have no incentive to admit new members on a symmetric basis.[2] This important result will hold only so long as outsiders don't organize themselves into a competitive trading bloc.[3]

2. See Kemp and Wan (1976, 95–97). Since global free trade maximizes global welfare, there will always be some system of side payments that will allow nonmembers to bribe members into allowing them entry to the trading bloc. The terms of such side payments leaving symmetric economies in vastly different circumstances may make this an unappealing alternative.
3. The structure of the game that might result in this event is analyzed empirically in Stoeckel, Pearce, and Banks (1990), among other places.

Once again, nothing in the preceding analysis assumes that the trading bloc will attempt to exploit the growing market power that comes with increasing size and raise its barriers against nonmembers. Trading bloc members can achieve real income levels better than global free trade, and nonmembers can face continuous declines in real income as the trading bloc expands its membership, even while the trading bloc behaves consistently with GATT Article 24 and makes no attempt to exploit its increasing market power.

3.3 The East Asian Trade Regime

The case just outlined captures many of the concerns of the economies on the Pacific Rim of Asia. Very comprehensive regional trading arrangements have been organized or have been greatly strengthened in North America and in Europe. The possibility that, even without raising new barriers at all, the growing role of such blocs in the global economy could lower East Asian welfare is very real. The proliferation of voluntary export restraints, orderly marketing agreements, local content rules, new dumping regulations, and other aggressive unilateral measures against some of these economies suggests it may even be naïve to assume that such trading blocs are the necessary way stations to a newly invigorated global trading system. The optimum size of such blocs, from the existing members' point of view, makes it naïve to assume that as a matter of course they will be nonexclusive. It may not make sense to continuously expand the size of such trading blocs. In particular, it's not hard to imagine some or all East Asian economies being excluded from European or Western Hemispheric regional trading arrangements.

Exclusive arrangements will be preferred to global free trade by members of regional trading blocs only so long as there remain a nontrivial number of nonmembers who retain protective barriers against each other as well as against the trading bloc itself. If nonmembers organize their own rival trading bloc, free trade may once again become a superior outcome for all concerned. It is with this perspective that the prospect of new trading arrangements in East Asia should be examined. While no formal trading bloc has as yet arisen in East Asia, do emerging trading patterns there suggest that this is happening implicitly? In particular, do intraregional trading patterns suggest a Japan-centered rival to the European Community and NAFTA is being created? Is the scenario suggested by the trade theory in section 3.2 coming to pass?

At present, intraregional trade is approximately 40 percent of all East Asian trade. This is modest by comparison with Western Europe, where intraregional trade is over 70 percent of total trade, but it's considerably larger than the role played by intraregional trade in North America. Not only is intraregional trade more important in East Asia than in North America, its relative importance has been growing rapidly. Twenty years ago intraregional trade was no more than 30 percent of East Asian trade. By marked contrast, intraregional trade in North America has actually been declining over the past twenty years. Interestingly, if North America, East Asia, Australia, and New Zealand are combined into a single region, the share of intraregional trade in the total trade of the Pacific grouping approaches Western European levels. And over the past two decades, as over the past decade, intra-Pacific trade has been growing more rapidly than intra–Western European trade.

These intraregional trade trends provide some perspective on East Asia's position in a possibly regionalizing global economy. Regional trade is becoming more important for East Asia. This need not reflect increasing isolation at all. Trade with East Asia is not only increasingly important for the East Asian economies themselves. It's also increasingly important for North America and for Europe. The increasing bias toward East Asia itself in East Asian trade might reflect a nascent trading bloc, or since East Asian trade is also increasingly more important for North America and for Europe, it may reflect no more than the increasing economic weight of East Asia in the global economy.

Since there is no reason to expect one country's trade to be proportionally distributed to all other countries, the issue of whether there is regional bias in East Asia trade really needs to be addressed systematically by estimating a model of bilateral trade. The model that will be used to make such estimates can explain both cross-country and cross-commodity net and gross trade by making allowances for economies of scale and monopolistic competition, as well as for the more familiar differences in natural resources, capital, skills, and other national endowments.[4]

3.3.1   Factor-Endowment-Based Gravity Equations

Assume that all manufactured goods are differentiated by country of origin. Given the same homothetic preferences usually assumed in empirical work making use of Heckscher-Ohlin-style trade models, each economy will consume identical proportions of each good (Leamer 1984). This means that country k's export of good j to country i will be given by

$$(14) \qquad x_{ki}^j = S_i\, \pi_{ko}^j$$

where $x_{ki}^j \equiv$ export of variety k of good j to country i, $\pi_{ko}^j \equiv$ production of good j in country k, $\pi_{ko} \equiv \Sigma_j\, \pi_{ko}^j \equiv$ GNP of country k, $\pi_{oo} \equiv \Sigma_i\, \pi_{io} \equiv$ global GNP_i, and $S_i \equiv \pi_{oo}/\pi \equiv$ share of country i in global GNP.[5]

$$(15) \qquad S_i = \frac{\pi_{io}}{\pi_{oo}} = \frac{\displaystyle\sum_s W_{si} L_{si}}{\displaystyle\sum_k \pi_{ko}}$$

---

4. The model presented here is an extension to bilateral trade of earlier work presented in Saxonhouse (1989). See also Saxonhouse (1992).

5. The properties of π, the GNP function, are described in more detail in Saxonhouse and Stern (1989).

where $L_{si} \equiv$ endowment of factor of production s in economy i, and $W_{si} \equiv$ rental for factor of production s in economy i.

Following the approach taken in Heckscher-Ohlin comparative advantage analyses, if factor price equalization is assumed, then by Hotelling's lemma, if π_{ko} is differentiated,[6]

$$(16) \qquad \pi_{ko}^{j} = \sum_{s=1}^{K} R_{js} L_{sk},$$

where R_{js} is a function of parameters of π_{ko} and output prices, which are assumed to be constant.

Substituting equations (15) and (16) into equation (14), we get

$$(17) \qquad x_{ki}^{j} = \sum_{s=1}^{K} \sum_{r=1}^{K} B_{jsr} L_{sk} L_{ri}, \qquad i = 1, \ldots, N,$$

where B_{jsr} are functions of π_{ko}^{j} and π_{io} and where output prices will be constant under the assumptions already made. Equation (17) is a factor-endowment-based version of the gravity equation, which has been used for years as a framework for estimating bilateral trade relationships (Anderson 1979). Plausibly, it explains bilateral trade flows by the interaction between exporter and importer factor endowments. Alternatively, if equation (14) is divided by π_{io} before equations (15) and (16) are substituted into it, we get export shares as a simple linear function of exporter factor endowments:

$$(18) \qquad \frac{x_{ki}^{j}}{\pi_{io}} = \sum_{s=1}^{K} B_{jsr}^{*} L_{sk}, \qquad i = 1, \ldots, N.$$

The structure embodied in equations (17) and (18) results from relaxing many of the strictest assumptions of the Heckscher-Ohlin model in order to incorporate hitherto neglected phenomena in a bilateral trade model. Still further relaxation is possible. Suppose that the assumption of strict factor price equalization across countries is dropped. Suppose, rather, that international trade equalizes factor prices only when factor units are normalized for differences in quality. For example, observed international differences in the compensation of ostensibly unskilled labor may be accounted for by differences in labor quality.[7] Instead of equations (17) and (18) we get

$$(17') \qquad x_{ki}^{j} = \sum_{s=1}^{K} \sum_{r=1}^{K} B_{jsr} a_{sk} a_{ri} L_{sk} L_{ri}, \qquad i = 1, \ldots, N,$$

and

---

6. The GNP function, π, has been defined to allow for differentiated products and economies of scale. This can be done by including optimal firm scale in π, following the approach taken by Helpman and Krugman (1985). Provided optimal firm scale is small relative to market size, change in industry output can be achieved by changes in the number of firms in the industry. Firms are assumed to be identical. This means that at the industry level there will be constant returns to scale.

7. This was first pointed out by Leontief (1956) as a possible explanation for the empirical failure of the simple Heckscher-Ohlin model.

$$(18')\qquad\qquad \frac{x^j_{ki}}{\pi_{io}} = \sum_{s=1}^{K} B^*_{jsr}a_{sk}L_{sk},$$

where $a_{sk} \equiv$ quality of factors in country k.

3.3.2 Estimation Procedures

Equations $(17')$ and $(18')$ can be estimated for N commodity groups and K countries using cross-country data. For example, the terms a_{sk} are not directly observable but can be estimated from equation $(18')$. Formally, the estimation of equation $(18')$ with the a_{sk} differing across countries and unknown is a multivariate, multiplicative errors-in-variables problem. Instrumental variable methods will allow consistent estimation of the B^*_{jsr}. For any given cross-country sectoral equation, the a_{sk} will not be identified. In particular, for the specification adopted in equation $(18')$, at any given time there are N cross-sections that contain the identical independent variables. This circumstance can be exploited to permit consistent estimation of the a_{sk}.[8] Since the same error will recur in equation after equation owing to the unobservable quality terms, it is possible to use this recurring error to obtain consistent estimates of the quality terms. These estimates of the a_{sk} can then be used to adjust the factor-endowment data in equations $(17')$ and $(18')$ to obtain more efficient estimates of B_{jsr} and B^*_{jsr}.[9]

3.3.3 Estimation of the Trade Model

Equations $(17')$ and $(18')$ are estimated with data taken from the forty-two countries listed in table 3.1.[10] Equations $(17')$ and $(18')$ are estimated for each of the twenty-nine manufacturing sectors listed in table 3.2 for 1985. The six factor endowments used in this estimation include directly productive capital, labor, educational attainment, petroleum reserves, arable land, and transport resources.[11] The Heckscher-Ohlin equations $(17')$ and $(18')$ are assumed to hold up to an additive stochastic term.

---

8. The approach taken here is analogous to the two-step "jackknife" procedure first proposed in Guilkey and Schmidt (1973). As an example of the approach taken here, let $a_{sk} = 1 + a'_{sk}$, assuming $E(a'_{sk}) = 0$. Using instrumental variable techniques in the presence of multiplicative errors allows consistent estimates of the B^*_{jsr}. Using these estimates, for each economy an $N(J-1)X1$ vector $[v_j]$ of the net trade residuals can be formed. Consistent estimates of the quality terms can be obtained from

$$(B^*_{jsr}L_{sk})'(B^*_{jsr}L_{sk})^{-1}(B^*_{jsr}L_{sk})'(v_j)$$

9. Following Durbin (1954), and in common with two-stage least squares, the approach taken here uses synthetic instrumental variables. Factor endowments are ordered according to size, and rank is used as an instrument.

10. Since the factor-endowment variables in equation (18) explain national development, there is no need to limit the sample used here to just the most advanced economies. In general, less-advanced economies impose more protection than the most-advanced economies. This development-related protection is explained by changes in the levels of the factor endowments. Typically, the higher the level of factor endowments, the less the protection.

11. Following the suggestion of Dixit and Norman (1980), transport costs are incorporated in the Heckscher-Ohlin framework by treating them as another factor of production. Transport costs

Table 3.1   **Country Sample for Empirical Work**

Argentina	Indonesia	Philippines
Australia	Ireland	Portugal
Austria	Italy	Singapore
Belgium	Jamaica	Spain
Brazil	Japan	Sri Lanka
Chile	Korea	Sweden
Denmark	Malaysia	Switzerland
Finland	Malta	Taiwan
France	Mexico	Thailand
Germany	Netherlands	Turkey
Greece	New Zealand	United Arab Republic
Honduras	Nigeria	United Kingdom
Hong Kong	Norway	United States
India	Peru	Yugoslavia

Table 3.2   **Trade Sectors in Sample**

ISIC#	Sector
311	Food manufacturing
312	Other food manufacturing
313	Beverage industries
314	Tobacco manufactures
321	Manufactures of textiles
322	Manufactures of wearing apparel except footwear
323	Manufactures of leather products except footwear and apparel
324	Manufactures of footwear except rubber or plastic
331	Manufactures of wood and cork products except furniture
332	Manufactures of furniture and fixtures except primarily metal
341	Manufactures of paper and paper products
342	Printing, publishing, and allied industries
351	Manufactures of industrial chemicals
352	Manufactures of other chemical products
353	Petroleum refineries
354	Miscellaneous products of petroleum and coal
355	Rubber products
356	Plastic products not classified elsewhere
361	Pottery, china, and earthenware
362	Glass and glass products
369	Other nonmetallic mineral products
371	Iron and steel basic industries
372	Nonferrous metal basic industries
381	Fabricated metal products except machinery and equipment
382	Manufactures of machinery except electrical
383	Electrical machinery, apparatus, appliances, and supplies
384	Transport equipment
385	Professional and scientific measuring and control equipment
390	Other manufacturing industries

Table 3.3   The Estimation of $x_{ki}^j = \sum_{s=1}^{K} \sum_{r=1}^{K} B_{jsr} a_{sk} a_{ri} L_{sk} L_{ri}$

ISIC#	R^2	$F(35,957)$	ISIC#	R^2	$F(35,957)$
311	.334	13.7**	354	.544	32.6**
312	.019	0.498	355	.283	10.8**
313	.336	13.8**	356	.013	0.383
314	.323	13.0**	361	.220	7.7**
321	.195	6.6**	362	.302	11.8**
322	.515	28.5**	369	.283	10.8**
323	.538	31.8**	371	.491	26.3**
324	.515	29.0**	372	.544	32.6**
331	.197	5.87**	381	.389	17.4**
332	.266	9.89**	382	.331	13.5**
341	.592	39.6**	383	.174	5.75**
342	.454	22.7**	384	.063	1.83**
351	.505	27.8**	385	.254	9.29**
352	.011	0.331	390	.017	0.472
353	.605	41.8**			

** $\equiv$ significant at the .05 level, $F(35,957) = 1.43$.

Unlike the Heckscher-Ohlin net trade equations, the dependent variable in these bilateral equations will never be negative, but they will occasionally be zero. As most of the twenty-nine equations to be estimated will contain some zero observations, equations $(17')$ and $(18')$ can be specified as a Tobit model.[12]

Some of the results of estimating equation $(17')$ using the a_{sk} obtained from estimating equation (18) and excluding the East Asian economies from the sample are presented in tables 3.3 and 3.4. As can be seen in table 3.3, twenty-six out of the twenty-nine bilateral trade equations are statistically significant. These results mean it is possible to get a good explanation of the structure of bilateral trade when full advantage of the many available degrees of freedom is taken by including a large number of cross-country factor-endowment interaction terms. Table 3.4 identifies the statistically significant role played by the interaction between exporter and importer factor endowments in explaining bilateral trade flows. The signs of these coefficients will reflect the degree of complementarity or substitutability between the various factors of production and their relative importance in the various sectoral production processes.

are treated as proportional to the weighted average of country distance from potential trading partners. Countries are weighted in this calculation by their GNPs or GDPs. This particular approach allows the incorporation of transport costs within the bilateral Heckscher-Ohlin framework without abandoning the possibility of factor price equalization up to some multiplicative constant.

12. The Tobit estimation methods used here for equations $(17')$ and $(18')$ are described in Greene (1981, 1983) and Chung and Goldberger (1984).

Table 3.4   **Number and Sign of Significant (.05) Coefficients on Factor-Endowment Interaction Terms** (B_{jsr})

	$CAPITAL_{Exp.}$		$LABOR_{Exp.}$		$EDUC_{Exp.}$		$OIL_{Exp.}$		$TRANS_{Exp.}$		$LAND ARA_{Exp.}$	
	+	−	+	−	+	−	+	−	+	−	+	−
$CAPITAL_{Imp.}$	5	17	8	6	10	5	14	6	9	4	14	7
$LABOR_{Imp.}$	14	4	5	16	10	8	10	4	6	7	13	8
$EDUC_{Imp.}$	15	6	12	11	7	12	11	5	8	3	9	6
$OIL_{Imp.}$	7	7	7	3	9	7	4	14	5	6	7	11
$TRANS_{Imp.}$	5	3	6	8	10	14	6	8	10	8	5	6
$LAND ARA_{Imp.}$	11	5	17	3	12	3	5	12	7	8	8	12

Note: The rows in this table index the factor endowments of importers. The columns index the factor endowments of exports. The cells in this table indicate how many significant coefficients of each sign are found for the associated interaction terms in the twenty-nine estimated equations.

3.3.4   Is There Regional Bias in East Asian Trade?

The results presented in tables 3.3 and 3.4 have been obtained by estimating equation (18′) without using East Asian observations. Using these estimated structures and introducing observations on East Asian factor endowments, tolerance intervals have been constructed for East Asian regional trade and for the major flows in East Asia's extraregional trade. The constructed tolerance intervals indicate with a probability of .99 that .99 of the normal distribution of a trade flow will be found within the interval. Observed trade flows are then compared with these tolerance intervals. Observations that fall outside these tolerance intervals are considered evidence of regional bias (Christ 1966).

The findings for East Asian intraregional exports compared with East Asian exports to much of North America and the European Community are striking. East Asian intraregional exports appear to be well-explained by the factor-endowment-based gravity equations. As seen in table 3.5, out of a total of 2,088 trade flows only 325 are outside the tolerance interval. This relatively small number of extreme observations suggests there may be little regional bias in East Asian trade. Neither policy initiatives by the Association of Southeast Asian Nations (ASEAN) nor very large intraregional East Asian investment has resulted in intraregional distortions in East Asian trade patterns. What is true for the region as a whole is also true at the individual country level. Japan, South Korea, Taiwan, Hong Kong, Malaysia, the Philippines, Singapore, Thailand, and Indonesia have no more than a small number of extreme observations on their intraregional bilateral trade flows.

By comparison with intraregional trade, East Asia's extraregional trade is marked by many observations that fall outside the constructed tolerance intervals. Whereas there are an average of thirty-nine extreme observations per in-

Table 3.5   Extreme Observations on East Asian Intraregional Exports

	Japan		Korea		Taiwan		Hong Kong		Malaysia		Philippines		Singapore		Thailand		Indonesia	
	+	−	+	−	+	−	+	−	+	−	+	−	+	−	+	−	+	−
Japan	0	0	1	2	1	1	1	0	0	3	2	5	3	1	3	0	0	1
Korea	2	3	0	0	2	1	0	0	4	1	3	3	0	2	2	2	3	1
Taiwan	1	2	0	4	0	0	4	0	3	4	2	2	2	3	1	1	4	2
Hong Kong	3	0	3	3	5	3	0	0	4	2	1	0	3	1	2	3	1	3
Malaysia	2	1	0	2	2	1	1	2	0	0	3	3	3	2	1	4	3	1
Philippines	2	2	4	1	2	0	3	5	3	1	0	0	3	0	4	5	0	2
Singapore	0	5	1	0	1	4	2	4	4	3	3	2	0	0	2	3	5	1
Thailand	3	1	2	6	3	1	3	5	2	1	2	4	5	4	0	0	4	0
Indonesia	3	2	2	0	4	0	3	4	0	7	3	0	6	2	5	3	0	0

Note: Rows in this table index imports. Columns index exports. Each cell indicates the number of extreme observations, + indicates overexporting and − underexporting. Maximum number of extreme observations for any bilateral pair is twenty-nine. Critical value for tolerance interval $T(.99, .99, 957) = 2.51$.

traregional market, as seen from table 3.6 for East Asian extraregional export markets there are more than twice as many extreme observations per market. The factor-endowment-based gravity equations estimated without East Asian data do a much better job of explaining the trade among East Asian economies and overall East Asian trade, than of explaining the pattern of East Asian trade with non–East Asian trading partners.

The extraregional biases in East Asian trade are striking. Particularly interesting are the patterns of East Asian exports to the European Community by comparison with East Asian exports to North America. In some 332 instances East Asian exports to the European Community appear lower than what might have been expected, given the economic characteristics of the various East Asian economies. In each of these cases actual East Asian exports to the European Community are below the lower limit of the tolerance interval. In only a comparatively few (forty-eight) cases are actual East Asian exports to European Community markets above the upper limit of the tolerance interval. Despite very rapid growth in East Asian exports to the European Community over the past two decades, still greater exports might have been expected.

As with East Asian exports to the European Community, there are also a comparatively large number of extreme observations on East Asian exports to North America. By marked contrast with the extreme observations on East Asian exports to the European Community, the extreme observations on exports to North America are disproportionately above the upper limit of the tolerance interval. While 85 percent of the 380 extreme observations of exports to the European Community are below the lower limit of the tolerance interval, only 19 percent of the 195 extreme observations of exports to North America are below the lower limit of the tolerance interval. If East Asian exports are less to the European Community than might be expected on the basis of global relationships, they appear to be more to North America than might be expected. While there is no intraregional trade bias if East Asia is defined as a region, if the region is expanded to include the Pacific Basin, then intraregional bias does become apparent.

Does Japan play a special role in East Asia? Japan's level of productivity and its industrial skills and experience remain well ahead of even the most rapidly growing economies elsewhere in East Asia. It's hardly surprising that Japan is exporting sophisticated capital goods to its East Asian trading partners, at the same time that it's importing processed raw materials, components, and manufactures from them. There is at present little evidence of a regional bias in Japan's relations with the rest of East Asia that goes beyond the existing pattern of East Asian resource endowments. Out of 464 instances of bilateral trade flows between Japan and the other East Asian economies, only 56 extreme observations have been uncovered. These divide neatly into 16 cases of Japan overexporting, 16 cases of Japan underexporting, 11 cases of Japan overimporting, 13 cases of Japan underimporting.

What is particularly interesting about the regional pattern of Japanese trade

Table 3.6   Extreme Observations on East Asian Extraregional Exports

	Japan		Korea		Taiwan		Hong Kong		Malaysia		Philippines		Singapore		Thailand		Indonesia	
	+	−	+	−	+	−	+	−	+	−	+	−	+	−	+	−	+	−
United States	9	3	11	4	14	6	8	1	12	3	6	0	12	3	7	2	4	1
Canada	11	2	9	4	11	3	12	0	7	1	4	0	9	0	6	0	5	4
Germany	0	8	2	12	3	7	4	14	4	10	2	4	2	11	4	6	2	3
Netherlands	1	6	0	4	0	3	2	6	2	7	1	3	1	8	0	2	0	4
United Kingdom	0	3	2	5	0	4	3	7	1	4	0	5	2	5	0	3	0	6
France	0	7	0	8	2	10	1	11	0	8	2	7	0	13	2	8	3	8
Italy	1	13	0	10	1	9	0	13	0	14	0	5	0	11	0	10	0	6

Note: Rows in this table index imports. Columns index exports. Each cell indicates the number of extreme observations; + indicates overexporting and − underexporting. Maximum number of extreme observations for any bilateral pair is twenty-nine. Critical value for tolerance interval $T(.99, .99, .957) = 2.51$.

is not how it differs from the rest of the countries in East Asia but rather how it is similar. In common with the rest of the economies, in East Asia, Japan exports less to the European Community and more to the United States than might be expected. While the European Community appears to exhibit some negative bias against imports from East Asia and overall North America appears to exhibit considerable bias in favor, Japanese import behavior, at least insofar as the model estimated here is concerned, appears virtually neutral with respect to the rest of East Asia.

3.4 Pricing Strategies in East Asia

If there is no special intraregional bias in East Asian trade patterns and if the growth in East Asian intraregional trade merely reflects the growing global economic importance of East Asia, are regional initiatives superfluous except as a tactical exercise to prevent discrimination and exclusion elsewhere? Not necessarily. The absence of regional bias does not necessarily mean the absence of regional trade barriers. The estimated parameters of equation (18') may embody all manner of protective barriers. The absence of intraregional bias simply means there is no special discrimination in favor of or against East Asian trading partners (Saxonhouse 1983). This is quite a different matter from concluding, for example, that commodity arbitrage across East Asia is near perfect. How integrated are East Asian markets? One helpful way to examine this issue might be to look at East Asian firms' pricing behavior across different East Asian markets. If East Asian economies are not closely integrated with one another, East Asian firms may have greater latitude to employ widely different pricing strategies in different markets.

3.4.1 Lags in External Adjustment

The slow pace of adjustment to exchange rate realignment in the mid- and late 1980s resembled the reaction of trade flows to exchange rate realignments of the early and late 1970s. In both cases special emphasis has been placed on contractual obligations and habit persistence in explaining both the slow response of prices to exchange rate changes and the slow response of trade flows to the relative price changes that do take place (Magee 1973; Wilson and Takacs 1980). In something of a departure from earlier analyses of the impact of exchange rate change on trade flows, in recent years considerable emphasis has been placed on the role of market structure in shaping this process. This new approach suggests that, in any given sector, whether exchange rate changes lead to large relative price changes or negligible price changes will depend on industrial structure considerations such as the degree of market concentration, the extent of product homogeneity and substitutability, and the relative market shares of domestic and foreign firms (Krugman 1986; Dornbusch 1987). Even absent long-term contracts and habitual behavior, strategic behavior will indicate widely varying price responses across industries to exchange rate changes. Less than full pass-through will be an equilibrium response for many industries.

3.4.2   Pricing Strategies and the Pacific Adjustment Process

In pursuing questions about the Pacific adjustment process, work that stresses the role of market structure in understanding global pricing will be helpful. Whereas most of this literature emphasizes the distinction between pricing decisions in the home market on the one hand and all overseas markets collectively on the other, the empirical research presented here will make some effort to allow for differences in pricing strategies employed across overseas markets.[13] Bear in mind that different pricing strategies across markets are only possible where barriers to arbitrage exist.

The International Price Discrimination Model[14]

Assume that commodity arbitrage across markets is ineffective such that

(19) $$P_k^j \neq r_i P_i^j,$$

where $P_k^j \equiv$ price of good j in home market k in home currency; $P_i^j \equiv$ price of good j in foreign market i in foreign currency; and $r_i \equiv$ exchange rate between home currency and foreign market i currency.

In general, the differences in prices across markets will be determined by the differences in demand conditions across markets and their relationship to the producer's common marginal cost. As is well known, the gap between price in each of the markets (expressed in domestic currency) and the marginal cost will be given by

(20) $$G_k^j = \frac{D_k^j}{D_k^j - 1}, \qquad \text{and} \qquad G_i^j = \frac{D_i^j}{D_i^j - 1},$$

where $D_k^j \equiv$ price elasticity of demand for good j in the home market k, and $D_i^j \equiv$ price elasticity of demand for good j in the foreign market i.

Full pass-through. If the demand functions in domestic and overseas markets have constant price elasticities, relative prices for good j across markets will be invariant. This means exchange rate changes will have no impact on relative prices. With constant price elasticity of demand curves, exchange rate changes will always be fully passed through to foreign markets.

Less than full pass-through. Less than full pass-through of exchange rate changes will occur when demand curves are less convex than the constant elasticity of demand curve. In such cases the elasticity of demand will vary directly

---

13. Recent papers that disaggregate among overseas markets include Froot and Klemperer (1989) and Knetter (1992, forthcoming).

14. See Krugman 1986; Dornbusch 1987; Marston 1990; Feenstra 1989.

with price changes. In particular, a fall in price will lower price elasticity and a rise in price will raise it. From equation (20) it is seen that in this instance a fall (rise) in price will raise (lower) the gap between price and marginal cost.

Under these demand conditions when the yen appreciates, the price of the good in foreign markets rises and the gap between foreign prices and marginal cost must narrow. If marginal costs are constant, the gap between price and marginal cost will remain the same in the domestic market. This is an obvious case of less than complete pass-through.

In this case pass-through will vary across markets inversely with the convexity of the demand functions in price. Alternatively, the more elasticity of demands varies directly with price, the less pass-through will be observed.

Greater than full pass-through. By contrast with the case just described, when demand functions are more convex than the constant elasticity of price case, exchange rate changes will lead to greater than full pass-through (Marston 1990; Knetter 1992). In this case a price increase will make demand less elastic. For example, a yen appreciation by raising the foreign price of a good will increase the gap abroad between price and marginal cost. Once again with constant marginal costs, the gap between price and costs at home will remain the same. With yen appreciation, prices in terms of yen for goods abroad will rise relative to the yen price of the same goods at home. In this simple case yen appreciation may lead to a rush to concede markets abroad in the interest of profits.

Cost factors. Just as differences in the shape of demand functions are critical for explaining differences in the reactions of foreign markets to exchange rate changes, in this price discrimination framework they are also critical for explaining the influence of other factors on the differences between prices at home and abroad for the same good. For example, in the constant elasticity of demand case, since price is invariant to any kind of change, no change in wages or any other cost factor can change price, so relative prices at home and abroad will not change. More generally, if the demand functions have variable elasticities but have the same curvature, a change in cost will change prices, but always by the same rate in all markets.

In light of the above discussion and considering that income in domestic and foreign markets can be expected to affect relative prices at home and abroad, the following function can be adopted as an explanation of the gap between the domestic price of good j and its price in foreign markets i:

$$(21) \quad \log\delta_j = \log\frac{P_k^j}{r_i P_i^j} = \rho_{1k}\log q_{ki} + \rho_{2k}\log\frac{w_k}{p_k} + \rho_{3k}\log\frac{m_k}{p_k} + \rho_{4k}\log y_k + \rho_{5k}\log y_i,$$

where $q_{ki} \equiv$ real exchange rate between economy k and economy i, $w_k/p_k \equiv$ real wages in economy k, $m_k/p_k \equiv$ real raw material prices in economy k, $y_k \equiv$ real income in economy k, and $y_i \equiv$ real income in economy i.

Note equation (21) assumes firms set prices instantaneously in response to changes in the right-hand-side variables. If prices are preset, however, variations in δ_j may simply reflect unanticipated events such as change in the exchange rate, rather than destination specific price strategies.

To allow for this possibility and following Marston (1990) and Meese and Rogoff (1988), it is assumed that both r_i and q_{ki} follow random walks. This means equation (21), with time subscripted by t, becomes

$$(22) \qquad \log\delta_{jt} = \log(r_{it} - E_{t-1}\log r_{it}) + \rho_{1k}E_{t-1}\log q_{kit} + \rho_{2k}E_{t-1}\log\frac{w_{kt}}{p_{kt}}$$
$$+ \rho_{3k}E_{t-1}\log\frac{m_{kt}}{p_{kt}} + \rho_{4k}E_{t-1}\log y_{kt} + \rho_{5k}E_{t-1}\log y_{it},$$

where $E_{t-1} \equiv$ expectation on variable in period t from information available at $t - 1$.

Equation (22) indicates that, if no strategic pricing behavior is being employed and the $\rho_k = 0$, then the impact of exchange rate surprises on δ_{jt} will be short-lived. In the absence of further changes after a single period, δ_{jt} will return to its original level. Equation (22) is estimated to throw light on the role of the price mechanism in the Pacific adjustment process. The coefficient on the change in nominal exchange rate in equation (22) indicates whether there is a lag in price setting. Recall the coefficient on the real exchange rate measures the proportion of the real exchange rate change passed through into prices.

Data

Ideally, equation (22) should be estimated for exports based in each of the East Asian economies. Currently, comprehensive data are only available for exporters based in Japan. Table 3.7 lists the forty-seven product lines for which equation (22) has been estimated. Each of these forty-seven product-line equations have been separately estimated for each of the six markets, including South Korea, Taiwan, Hong Kong, Singapore, Malaysia, and Thailand.

Within the much larger number of capital goods exports, these products have been chosen on the basis of data availability for all countries in the sample. Monthly data are used for each of the countries from June 1984 to December 1989. For each of the product lines, the Bank of Japan's wholesale price index for that product is used as the Japanese domestic price. In place of detailed country-specific compatible export price data, unit value indexes have been constructed for each product line and each country from the Japan Tariff Association trade data. Admittedly, making use of bilateral unit value indexes for relatively narrow specific product lines in place of authentic price data may introduce a great deal of error into this estimation procedure. Nonetheless, because it is a relative price equation and not an import demand or export supply equation that is being estimated, the problems posed by using such data

Table 3.7   **Japanese Capital Goods Exports to East Asia (sample)**

Excavators	Milling cutters	Conveyors
Graders	Electric welding machinery	Forklift trucks
Construction tractors	Rectifiers	Ball bearings
Shovel trucks	Magnetic switches	Roller bearings
Lathes	Diamond tools	Speed changers
NC lathes	Pneumatic tools	Roller chains
Drilling machines	Electric machinery tools	Copying machines
Boring machinery	Spinning machines	Refrigerating machines
NC milling machinery	Knitting machines	Woodworking machinery
Grinding machinery	Pumps for liquid	Printing machinery
NC electric discharge machinery	Air and gas compressors	Centrifugal machinery
Machining centers	Blowers	Electric generators
Press machines	Elevators	Elecric motors
Forging machines	Escalators	Transformers
Rollers for metal industry	Overhead traveling cranes	Switchboards
Drills	Winches	

Note: NC = numerically controlled.

are not insurmountable. After all, this variable appears only on the left-hand side of all the equations being estimated here.[15]

The one truly non-Japanese source of data in this estimation is the monthly production indexes used as the active variable in equation (22). These indexes have been gathered from the monthly or yearly statistical bulletins of each of the six countries in this sample as well as from Japan. The remaining variables, including the Japanese manufacturing wage, Japanese raw material prices, and the bilateral exchange rates, are all readily available. Finally, in each instance, nominal variables are converted to real variables by deflating with the Japanese wholesale price index.

Estimation

Two hundred and eighty-two relative price equations have been estimated with the data just outlined. Each equation is estimated with seventy-seven observations after logarithms of each variable have been first differenced and distributed lags applied. The general results of this estimation are presented in tables 3.8 and 3.9.

As indicated, interest should focus on the coefficients of the change in the nominal exchange rate and the coefficients on the level of the real exchange rate. No less than 201 cases out of a possible total of 282 coefficients on the level of the real exchange rate are statistically significant from zero.

At the level of the individual foreign market level, these results confirm findings from many studies for aggregated overseas markets. Strategic pricing

---

15. Froot and Klemperer (1989) and Knetter (forthcoming) follow a similar path in constructing destination-specific export price data.

Table 3.8   **Foreign Price–Domestic Price Gap Equation: Statistically Significant Variables by Country (47 equations estimated for each country)**

	Korea	Taiwan	Hong Kong	Singapore	Malaysia	Thailand
Statistically significant price selling lag	12	10	12	8	20	15
Statistically significant strategic price setting due to real exchange rate change $H_0:\rho_1 = 0$	45	39	32	25	32	33
Satistically significant strategic price setting due to changes in other variables $H_0:\rho_2 = 0$; $\rho_3 = 0$; $\rho_4 = 0$; $\rho_5 = 0$	17	18	10	7	12	8
$R^2 = .000-.333$	6	7	4	6	8	9
$R^2 = .334-.666$	16	14	14	11	12	13
$R^2 = .666-.991$	25	26	29	30	27	25

Note: The numbers in each cell refer to the number of equations in which a statistically significant variable corresponding to the row heading appeared. Forty-seven is the maximum number of equations in which a variable can appear as statistically significant.

is a pervasive phenomenon. Of particular interest here, Japanese exporters exhibit this behavior in the majority of their Pacific markets. Such behavior is most pronounced in the Korean market and is practiced by Japanese machinery exporters for the vast majority of the capital goods they sell in East Asia. Among types of machinery exports, machinery components, for whatever reason, seem less subject to strategic pricing than the complete machine.

Not all 201 statistically significant coefficients on the real exchange rate are positive. In no less than twenty cases here this coefficient is negative, illustrating the case where rate changes are more than passed through into foreign prices. The distribution of such cases by country is given in table 3.10. These cases typically reflect the very small size of some of the overseas markets being investigated here and the resulting instability of some of the unit value indexes being used as dependent variables.

While strategic pricing is a pervasive phenomenon among Japanese machinery exporters to elsewhere in East Asia, tables 3.8 and 3.9 indicate that this is almost exclusively a response to exchange rate changes. In only 72 out of a possible 1,126 cases is there any indication that the gap between foreign prices and domestic prices adjusts in a statistically significant way as a response to changes in domestic costs or to shifts in income in either foreign or domestic markets.[16] Given the extreme volatility of the real exchange rate compared with these other variables, this result should not be surprising.

More surprising are the relatively few instances where there are significant

16. Marston (1990) and Knetter (forthcoming) have similar findings.

Table 3.9 **Foreign Price–Domestic Price Gap Equation: Statistically Significant Variables by Capital Good**

Market	Statistically Significant Price Setting Lag	Statistically Significant Strategic Price Setting due to Real Exchange Change $H_0: \rho_1 = 0$	Statistically Significant Strategic Price Setting due to Changes in Other Variables
Excavators	2	3	—
Graders	1	2	2
Construction tractors	3	5	1
Shovel trucks	1	3	3
Lathes	4	3	4
NC lathes	3	5	2
Drilling machines	3	3	—
Boring machinery	—	6	1
NC milling machinery	1	6	—
Grinding machinery	1	5	—
NC electric discharge machinery	1	4	2
Machining centers	—	6	—
Press machines	1	1	1
Forging machines	—	4	1
Rollers for metal industry	4	5	4
Drills	2	5	2
Milling cutters	1	6	—
Electric welding machine	1	3	—
Rectifiers	3	5	3
Magnetic switches	3	5	1
Diamond tools	2	3	2
Pneumatic tools	4	4	2
Electric machinery tools	1	6	1
Spinning machines	—	6	—
Knitting machines	1	6	—
Pumps for liquid	3	6	5
Air and gas compressors	4	5	3
Blowers	3	3	4
Elevators	2	6	2
Escalators	5	5	2
Overhead traveling cranes	—	6	—
Winches	3	4	3
Conveyors	2	4	4
Forklift trucks	—	6	3
Ball bearings	5	5	—
Roller bearings	2	4	3
Speed changers	2	2	1
Roller chains	2	1	2
Copying machines	—	4	2
Refrigerating machines	—	5	2
Woodworking machinery	—	6	—

(*continued*)

Table 3.9   (continued)

Market	Statistically Significant Price Setting Lag	Statistically Significant Strategic Price Setting due to Real Exchange Change $H_0: \rho_1 = 0$	Statistically Significant Strategic Price Setting due to Changes in Other Variables
Printing machinery	—	6	2
Centrifugal machinery	—	4	—
Electric generators	—	6	1
Electric motors	1	4	—
Transformers	4	4	1
Switchboards	—	6	—

Notes: Coefficients here are statistically significant at the .05 level.

Table 3.10   **Cases of More than Full Pass-Through by Country**

Korea	2	Singapore	5
Taiwan	—	Malaysia	3
Hong Kong	4	Thailand	6

lags in the resulting prices after exchange rate changes unaccompanied by strategic price behavior. Overall, there are seventy-seven cases where the coefficient on the change in the nominal exchange rate variable is statistically significant. In only twenty-eight of these cases, however, are $\rho_k = 0$ and the lags in resetting export prices solely responsible for the change in the gap between export prices and home market prices.

What is particularly interesting here is not just that Japanese firms practice strategic price setting in all their East Asian markets for almost all the capital goods in this sample. This simply tells us that the Japanese market is not fully integrated with the rest of East Asia. What is of special importance here is the degree to which strategic price setting by Japanese firms varies across East Asian markets. As seen in table 3.11, in no less than thirty-seven out of forty-seven product lines, the hypothesis cannot be accepted that the coefficient on the real exchange rate is the same across East Asian markets. Significant barriers to commodity arbitrage in East Asia appear to exist. Considering the interest in regional trade and investment initiatives in East Asia, further investigation is clearly needed as to why pricing behavior by exporters of the same machinery should vary so much across geographical markets. Do Japanese firms really have the capacity to effectively segregate proximate markets in the absence of host government connivance of some sort?

The results on the weakness of commodity arbitrage rest on a very simple model of international price discrimination. The limitation of this model

Table 3.11   **Do Japanese Firms Use Different Price Strategies across East Asian Markets?**

	$F(6,432)$		$F(6,432)$
Excavators	3.5	Knitting machines	11.4*
Graders	4.3	Pumps for liquids	0.6
Construction tractors	12.5*	Air and gas compressors	45.6*
Shovel trucks	6.8*	Blowers	3.1
Lathes	22.5*	Elevators	11.4*
NC lathes	15.9*	Escalators	8.2*
Drilling machines	41.0*	Overhead traveling cranes	7.0*
Boring machinery	23.6*	Winches	19.7*
NC milling machinery	7.4*	Conveyors	53.5*
Grinding machinery	8.2*	Forklift trucks	7.6*
NC electric discharge machinery	8.5*	Ball bearings	17.6*
Machining centers	6.8*	Roller bearings	23.2*
Press machines	4.3	Speed changers	2.3
Forging machines	6.8*	Roller chains	3.6
Rollers for metal industry	7.1*	Copying machines	8.3*
Drills	11.6*	Refrigerating machines	6.5*
Milling cutters	9.8*	Woodworking machinery	7.9*
Electric welding machinery	1.4	Printing machinery	9.4*
Rectifiers	26.1*	Centrifugal machinery	11.5*
Magnetic switches	12.8*	Electric generators	17.0*
Diamond tools	2.7	Electric motors	34.5*
Pneumatic tools	29.3*	Transformers	21.5*
Electric machinery tools	6.7*	Switchboards	8.3*
Spinning machines	4.8		

Notes: Following Leamer (1978),* $\equiv F(6,432) > 5.88$ is chosen as the criterion for statistical significance. $H_0 : \rho_{1\text{Korea}} = \rho_{1\text{Taiwan}} = \rho_{1\text{Hong Kong}} = \rho_{1\text{Singapore}} = \rho_{1\text{Malaysia}} = \rho_{1 \text{Thailand}}$

should not be forgotten (see Knetter 1992). Even apart from issues of specification, further evidence for other product lines and for firms based in other East Asian home markets needs to be examined. Despite the extraordinary growth in intraregional trade in East Asia, the price evidence presented here suggests the continuing importance of official and nonofficial barriers to intraregional trade in East Asia. Are these barriers, however, significantly different from barriers to intraregional trade in North America or Western Europe? The results of estimating equation (22) for Japanese firm behavior in the U.S. and Canadian markets for forty-three capital goods are presented in table 3.12. Surprisingly, in less than half the cases in either the U.S. or the Canadian market is the real exchange rate coefficient statistically significant. Despite all the complaints about lack of Japanese pass-through of exchange rate changes in the North American market, strategic pricing is far less pervasive there than in East Asia. Moreover, as indicated in table 3.12, while there may be as many as twenty product lines in the sample examined here where the U.S. and Canadian markets do not appear well integrated with the rest of the global economy, in

Table 3.12   Japanese Strategic Price Setting in North America

	Canada $\rho_{1Canada} = 0$	United States $\rho_{1U.S.} = 0$	$F(2,152)$ $\rho_{1Canada} = \rho_{1U.S.}$
Excavators	—	—	0.6
Graders	—	—	1.2
Construction tractors	*	*	7.3*
Shovel trucks	—	—	3.5
Lathes	—	—	0.1
NC lathes	—	*	2.7
Drilling machines	—	—	2.4
Boring machinery	*	—	3.9
NC milling machinery	*	*	11.3*
Grinding machinery	*	—	5.7*
NC electric discharge machinery	—	*	3.9
Machining centers	*	*	17.4*
Press machines	—	—	3.0
Forging machines	*	—	4.7
Rollers for metal industry	—	*	4.3
Drills	*	*	6.3*
Milling cutters	*	*	11.4*
Electric welding machinery	—	—	2.3
Rectifiers	—	*	5.8*
Magnetic switches	*	—	4.0
Diamond tools	—	—	1.8
Pneumatic tools	—	*	3.6
Electric machinery tools	*	*	3.8
Pumps for liquids	*	*	8.8
Air and gas compressors	—	—	2.1
Blowers	—	—	0.9
Escalators	—	*	2.5
Winches	—	—	3.2
Conveyors	—	*	4.3
Forklift trucks	*	*	11.8*
Ball bearings	*	—	3.7
Roller bearings	—	—	2.9
Speed changers	—	—	0.8
Roller chains	—	—	0.3
Copying machines	*	—	4.3
Refrigerating machines	*	*	3.9
Woodworking machinery	*	*	3.6
Printing machinery	*	*	8.4*
Centrifugal machinery	—	—	2.2
Electric generators	*	—	9.3*
Electric motors	—	—	3.7
Transformers	—	—	1.4
Switchboards	*	—	3.2

* $\equiv$ Statistically significant; $F(2,152) > 4.797$, following significance levels correction suggested in Leamer (1978).

only half as many cases do Japanese firms act as if commodity arbitrage is not an easy matter across the U.S.-Canadian border. By comparison with their behavior in East Asia, Japanese firms appear to treat the U.S.-Canadian markets as very well integrated. This is true even for the period before the Canada-U.S. Free Trade Agreement was ratified.

Despite the absence of intraregional bias in East Asian trade, evidence on the ability of Japanese firms to behave as if East Asian markets are substantially segregated from one another and their inability to behave the same way in North America does suggest that important barriers to East Asian trade remain. Quite apart from the tactical benefits in global negotiations that an East Asian grouping might bring, new East Asian–wide liberalization could still have substantial trade-creating effects within the region.

3.5   Finale

Regional initiatives in Europe and North America have triggered considerable interest and concern in the Pacific Basin. New trade initiatives by ASEAN, the Mahathir proposal for an East Asian economic group, the rapidly evolving APEC now with its own secretariat reflect, at least in part, a reaction to developments elsewhere. This is quite apart from the somewhat more familiar, smaller subregional trading zones, proposals for which are once again proliferating wherever there is proximity in East Asia. These proposals are not being made in the face of long-dormant East Asian economic interaction. Quite the contrary. In absolute terms, East Asian regional trade and East Asian cross-investment have grown very rapidly.

In the perspective of these developments, this paper concludes

1. It is certainly possible that trading blocs being formed elsewhere in the world might lower East Asian welfare. This can happen even in the absence of any explicit or implicit effort by these blocs to exploit their market power at the expense of East Asia. These trading blocs may have no incentive to expand their membership to include East Asian economies except insofar as they fear provoking the formation of an East Asian trading bloc. In the presence of a substantial group of disorganized, nonretaliating outsiders, a trading bloc, even without violating GATT Article 24, can achieve outcomes for its members that might be superior to global free trade.

2. The rapid growth in intraregional East Asia reflects not much more than the very rapid overall growth in this region relative to the rest of the world. Estimation of a bilateral model of intraindustry trade using a factor-endowment-based version of the gravity model suggests no East Asian bias in the trading pattern of the leading economies there. When the Pacific region is defined to include North America, however, substantial regional bias will likely be present. This reflects the positive bias found in East Asian exports to North America. By contrast, there is a negative bias in East Asian exports to Western Europe.

3. Despite the absence of intraregional bias in East Asian exports, evidence on the ability of Japanese firms to behave as if East Asian markets were substantially segregated from one another and their inability to behave the same way in North America does suggest that important barriers to East Asian trade remain. Despite much recent progress, further regionwide liberalization could be of particular benefit.

References

Anderson, James E. 1979. A Theoretical Foundation for the Gravity Equation. *American Economic Review* 69:106–16.

Christ, Carl F. 1966. *Econometric Models and Methods*. New York: John Wiley.

Chung, Ching-fan, and Arthur S. Goldberger. 1984. Proportional Projections on Limited Dependent Variable Models. *Econometrica* 52:531–34.

Dixit, Avinash, and Victor Norman. 1980. *Theory of International Trade*. Cambridge: Cambridge University Press.

Dornbusch, Rudiger. 1987. Exchange Rates and Prices. *American Economic Review* 77:93–106.

Durbin, James. 1954. Errors in Variables. *Review of the International Statistical Institute* 22:23–32.

Feenstra, Robert. 1989. Symmetric Pass-through of Tariffs and Exchange Rates under Imperfect Competition: An Empirical Test. *Journal of International Economics* 27:25–45.

Froot, Kenneth A., and Paul D. Klemperer. 1989. Exchange Rate Pass-through When Market Share Matters. *American Economic Review* 79:637–54.

Greene, William H. 1981. On the Asymptotic Bias of the Ordinary Least Squares Estimation of the Tobit Model. *Econometrica* 49:505–13.

———. 1983. Estimation of Limited Dependent Variables by Ordinary Least Squares and Method of Moments. *Journal of Econometrics* 21:195–212.

Guilkey, D. K., and P. Schmidt. 1973. Estimation of Seemingly Unrelated Regressions with Autoregressive Errors. *Journal of the American Statistical Association* 68:642–47.

Helpman, Elhanan, and Paul R. Krugman. 1985. *Market Structure and Foreign Trade*. Cambridge: MIT Press.

Kemp, Murray C., and Henry Y. Wan. 1976. An Elementary Proposition Concerning the Formation of Customs Unions. *Journal of International Economics* 6:95–97.

Knetter, Michael. 1992. Exchange Rates and Corporate Pricing Strategies. NBER Working Paper no. 4151. Cambridge: National Bureau of Economic Research.

———. Forthcoming. International Comparisons of Pricing to Market Behavior. *American Economic Review*.

Krugman, Paul, 1986. Pricing to Market When the Exchange Rate Changes. NBER Working Paper no. 1926. Cambridge: National Bureau of Economic Research.

———. Is Bilateralism Bad? In *International Trade and Trade Policy,* ed. Elhanan Helpman and Assaf Razin. Cambridge: MIT Press.

Leamer, Edward E. 1978. *Specification Searches*. New York: John Wiley.

———. 1984. *Sources of Comparative Advantage*. Cambridge: MIT Press.

Leontief, W. W. 1956. Factor Proportions and the Structure of American Trade: Further Theoretical and Empirical Analysis. *Review of Economics and Statistics* 38:386–407.

Machlup, Fritz. 1977. *A History of Thought on Economic Integration*. New York: Columbia University Press.

Magee, Stephen P. 1973. Currency Contracts, Pass-through, and Devaluation. *Brookings Papers in Economic Activity* 1:303–23.

Marston, Richard C. 1990. Pricing to Market in Japanese Manufacturing. *Journal of International Economics* 29:217–36.

Meese, Richard, and Kenneth Rogoff. 1988. "Was It Real? The Exchange Rate–Interest Rate Differential over the Modern Floating Period. *Journal of Finance* 43:933–48.

Saxonhouse, Gary R. 1983. The Micro- and Macroeconomics of Foreign Sales to Japan. In *Trade Policy in the 1980's,* ed. W. Cline, 259–304. Cambridge: MIT Press.

———. 1989. Differentiated Products, Economies of Scale, and Access to the Japanese Market. In *Trade Policies for International Competitiveness,* ed. Robert Feenstra, 145–74. Chicago: University of Chicago Press.

———. 1992. Europe's Economic Relations with Japan. In *Singular Europe,* ed. William James Adams, 347–69. Ann Arbor: University of Michigan Press.

Saxonhouse, Gary R., and Robert M. Stern. 1989. An Analytical Survey of Formal and Informal Barriers to International Trade and Investment in the United States, Japan, and Canada. In *Trade and Investment Relations among the United States, Canada, and Japan,* ed. Robert M. Stern, 293–353. Chicago: University of Chicago Press.

Stoeckel, Andrew, David Pearce, and Gary Banks. 1990. *Western Trading Blocs*. Canberra: Center for International Economics.

Viner, J. 1950. *The Customs Union Issue*. Washington, DC: Carnegie Endowment for International Peace.

Wilson, John F., and Wendy E. Takacs. 1980. Expectations and the Adjustment of Trade Flows under Floating Exchange Rates: Leads, Lags, and J-Curve. International Finance Discussion Paper no. 160. Washington, DC: Board of Governors of the Federal Reserve System.

Comment   Robert Gilpin

The theme of my comments is that institutions are important in understanding how market forces affect international affairs. As political scientists at this conference have been emphasizing, economists too frequently omit institutions just as political scientists too frequently underestimate the role and efficacy of markets in human affairs. In my comments, however, I am interested only in pointing out the limitations of economic analysis of developments in East Asia.

The world of the economist is composed primarily of individual firms and consumers responding to changes in prices and quantities. Such neoclassical methods of analysis are very powerful tools indeed, and needless to say, many political scientists envy the economists their models and equations. But it is important to recognize that market signals take place in an institutional setting. As economists since Ronald Coase have taught us, institutions can do many good and useful things, that is, decrease transactions costs, reduce uncertainties, and enhance efficiency. But as several political scientists have emphasized

Robert Gilpin is the Dwight D. Eisenhower Professor of International Affairs, Princeton University, and a faculty associate of the Center of International Studies.

over the past few days, institutions also create *differential* opportunities and constraints on economic activities. Institutions do not create opportunities and constraints equally for all firms and consumers. By their very nature, institutions exclude some participants and have powerful distributive effects both domestically and internationally. In fact, as we all know but too frequently forget, institutions are created for purposes of rent seeking and redistribution perhaps as frequently as they are created to increase efficiency.

As economists have taught those of us who might be called "political economists," or as one of my Princeton economist colleagues prefers, "economical politicians," what transforms the world are major price changes, supply shocks, and the like. From this perspective the most significant transforming event in the recent history of the Pacific economy has been the dramatic appreciation of the yen (*endaka*) following the Plaza Accord of September 1985. Before this development, Japan had been interested in Southeast Asia, especially Malaysia and Thailand, primarily as sources of raw materials. There was relatively little Japanese foreign direct investment (FDI) in the region and almost none in the manufacturing and services sectors.

The effect of *endaka* was suddenly to make many Japanese products noncompetitive in world markets. In response to this development, Japanese multinational corporations, with the support of the Japanese government, began to invest heavily and to establish subsidiaries in Southeast Asia. In particular, they established overseas manufacturing subsidiaries in those low-tech industries in which Japan was losing comparative advantage because of yen appreciation. At the same time, these Japanese firms moved up the technological ladder at home to high-tech industries and exports. While these developments were a rational response to market forces, it is important to understand that they are an outgrowth of Japanese industrial organization and the relations of the Japanese corporation to the Japanese state.

Through the combination of Japanese FDI, intrafirm trade, and the infrastructure investments financed by Japanese official development assistance (ODA), the Southeast Asian economies are being linked closely to the Japanese home economy. In a number of industrial sectors such as automobiles and consumer electronics, a regional division of labor and complementary economic ties under Japanese leadership are being created. Whereas Japan is the primary producer of high-tech, high value–added products and components, the subsidiaries of Japanese firms in Southeast Asia are either assembly operations or producers of labor-intensive goods that employ lower-cost local labor. Products produced by Japanese subsidiaries in Southeast Asia are for local consumption, for export back to Japan itself, or for third markets, especially the United States. Peter Petri in his paper gives us a wonderful picture of one example of this evolving regional division of labor in what he calls Toyota Motor's regional interdependence structure. In effect, a regional institutional structure uniting Japan and the Southeast Asia economies is taking shape that will have significantly distributive effects on third countries.

It is quite obvious that developments in East Asia have great economic and potential political significance. However, this development is not adequately captured by Gary Saxonhouse's paper. His analysis does not really address the changing economic and institutional relationships. I do not and in fact cannot challenge his economic analysis of intraregional and extraregional trade flows. His careful analysis of the data is certainly reasonable and convincing on its own terms. But one wants to know whose trade and what trade are benefiting from the increasing economic and institutional ties in the region that are being created by Japanese investment and ODA flows. For example, as has been suggested above, we know that Japanese firms control the production and trade in almost all high-tech industries such as automobiles and consumer electronics. This fact is a datum point that is as important as Saxonhouse's gross trade figures. Institutional ties really capture the economic and political significance of what is happening in the region.

It is undoubtedly true, as many participants in this conference have emphasized, that Japanese FDI, trade, and ODA are of great benefit to the region. Furthermore, I personally do not fear, at least for the moment, the reestablishment of a Japanese-led coprosperity sphere in the region. However, the overall results of the integration of vital sectors of these regional economies with the Japanese home economy does raise issues of long-term significance. These developments appear to be the following:

1. The increasing importance of the Japanese model of political economy in the economic development strategies of the economies in the region. This model has at least three elements that distinguish it from the American model of political economy: the primacy of producer over consumer interests, an industrial organization based on industrial groupings, and the crucial role of state interventionism in guiding economic development.

2. The internationalization of Japanese industrial policy, that is, the effort of Japanese firms backed by the Japanese state to create in the region a group of complementary economies and a regional division of labor.

3. The creation of a Japanese-led system of international production, especially in high-tech sectors, closely integrated with the Japanese home economy. As some commentators have suggested, it is unnecessary for Japan to create a formal regional bloc because Japanese corporations in the region are creating a de facto regional bloc.

Whether the long-term result of these developments will be an East Asian trading region within a larger multilateral global economy, an exclusive East Asian trading bloc, or a revival of the 1930s coprosperity sphere has yet to be determined. A great deal will obviously depend on what happens in North America and especially in Western Europe. Will these regional economies remain open or will they become closed systems? Japan and the other East Asian economies are highly dependent on world markets and are hardly likely to initiate moves that would encourage an intensification of regional trading arrangements. Meanwhile, several questions need to be posed. The first is whether nations with fundamentally different economic institutions will want to play by basically different rules. For example, the United States and Japan have very different concepts of antitrust and collusive behavior. Are Japanese firms establishing such an overwhelming presence in the region that non-Japanese firms will be effectively excluded? A lot of evidence suggests that this development is already occurring. Will the United States continue to provide a security umbrella over a region in which its economic interests are declining? Again, there is much evidence to suggest that such a pullback has already begun. These questions are but a few that suggest that political analysis, however intuitive it may sometimes be, is a necessary complement to the more rigorous methods of the economist.

I said earlier that economists are very sensitive to price changes and are alert to their effects. By the same token, political scientists tend to be very sensitive to changes in power relations and their effects. When one observes major shifts in the global or regional distribution of economic and hence political power, there will inevitably be profound security and diplomatic effects. For this reason, it is important to ask what these political and security consequences could be rather than to imply that nothing of political significance is occurring. In East and Southeast Asia, we must be alert to the significant shift in the distribution of economic power that is taking place and that in time will profoundly affect the security relations in the regions.

Comment   Lawrence B. Krause

The excellent papers by Peter Petri, Jeffrey Frankel, and Gary Saxonhouse make a similar point in different ways, namely, that trade and other economic relations in the Pacific Basin do not reflect a line down the Pacific that separates the western Pacific from North America. Instead economic forces seem to be integrating the two sides of the Pacific into a single region.

Nevertheless, because of there being three very large industrial countries with currencies to match (German D-mark, Japanese yen, and U.S. dollar), it is commonplace for reference to be made to triad power, or even more pointedly to a three-bloc world. This literary shorthand would not be of much concern except that, if three blocs were to become a reality, it could mean a disaster for the world economy. There is little doubt that Europe is a distinct region, and that Germany is its most powerful member. However, the question remains as to whether Japan and the United States are in economically distinct regions,

Lawrence B. Krause is Pacific Economic Cooperation Professor and director of the Korea-Pacific Program at the Graduate School of International Relations and Pacific Studies, University of California, San Diego.

or whether they are part of the same economic entity. The three papers give support to the latter conception.

What would be so bad about a three-bloc world? Analysis of a three-bloc configuration with Germany, the United States, and Japan being the regional hegemonies suggest that they would be internally contentious and externally aggressive. Game theory suggests that such a trading system would be very unstable in that there would be frequent changes in alliances, regions would follow aggressive tit-for-tat strategies, and short-term considerations would overwhelm long-term interests. The most serious problems would arise if Japan and the United States were to be in different and rival regions, for these two countries represent the most extreme examples of economic integration among nonneighboring countries anywhere in the world. It is unlikely that the global system as it exists today could be sustained in such an atmosphere.

What gives the three-bloc concept some saliency is the formalization of the already existing close economic integration of North America into NAFTA, and the ill-considered trade elements in President Bush's Enterprise of the Americas Initiative (EAI), which could extend NAFTA to the whole of the Western Hemisphere. While analysis can clearly show that even an expanded NAFTA cannot replace global economic linkages for the United States, fear has been created that the United States may be turning inward within the confines of a protected subregion. This has led to suggestions for an East Asian economic group or caucus.

How can the breakup of the world economy into three rival trading regions be prevented? Would it not be better to have just a multilateral system without any regions at all? In the abstract, it might have been better if the European Community had not been a political necessity, but it was, and no one should believe that breaking up the EC today would be beneficial for any country. It should also be noted that NAFTA is desirable on its own terms and should not disadvantage nonmember countries. Canada, Mexico, and the United States are special cases of neighbors well along in the process of integration. In reality, capital markets and labor markets are already integrated. Only the goods and service markets were separated, which NAFTA is designed to correct.

Could NAFTA turn inward and cause the problems that others fear? It is probably less likely that the North American countries would collectively turn inward than they would individually. NAFTA is simply too small to serve the needs of the United States. The United States requires access to global markets and particularly the growing markets of the Pacific Basin. The United States could not confine its economic activity to North America without severe economic hardship.

If a rival East Asian bloc were to be created in the absence of any real need, it would raise concerns elsewhere as to what its real intentions were. Hence the onus of undermining the world economy would fall on East Asia, not on the EC or NAFTA (although NAFTA should not be enlarged).

With the end of the Uruguay Round of GATT negotiations, attention will turn to regional initiatives. The time will be ripe for solidifying an institutional structure that reflects the economic reality analyzed in the three papers. This can be done by building an APEC, which includes the United States, Japan, and the other outwardly oriented countries of the Pacific. With a strong APEC, the world trade regime would be headed toward a benign two-region world rather than a three-bloc configuration.

4   Trading Blocs and the Incentives to Protect: Implications for Japan and East Asia

Kenneth A. Froot and David B. Yoffie

4.1   Introduction

The Single European Act of 1985, the Canada-U.S. Free Trade Agreement, and the current talks among the United States, Canada, and Mexico may signal the beginning of a sea change in international trade policies. Government decisions to form larger trading blocs have been construed by many as a precursor to the return of trade warfare that dominated international trade in the 1930s. Just as the absence of international leadership in the interwar period produced trade rivalry among nations and intense competition for markets, so too have there been fears that the tripolar world of the 1990s will be too unstable to promote freer trade. In this context, the momentum created by Europe's 1992 program and North America's free trade zone could have severe consequences for Japan and East Asia.

There is a political as well as an economic logic for believing that the 1990s will produce fortresses in Europe and North America. On the political front, the declining competitiveness of the United States and many European nations has produced increasing pressure to protect industry and employment. In the absence of a hegemon, the countervailing forces for free trade may be difficult to find. These political arguments become reinforced by the economics of bloc formation. Medium and small countries have never made a pretense of becoming self-sufficient: it makes little sense for Luxembourg or Canada to produce its own brands of airplanes and cars. Once small countries become part of a larger economic bloc, however, domestic production becomes more feasible in

Kenneth A. Froot is visiting professor at Harvard Business School and a research associate of the National Bureau of Economic Research. David B. Yoffie is professor at Harvard Business School.

The authors thank the Division of Research of Harvard Business School for generous research support.

many industries. Therefore, it is often argued that, as trading blocs grow larger, the potential benefits of protectionism rise.

This paper explores the underlying incentives for protectionism in a world with economic blocs, and the consequences for trade, investment, and competition with Japan and East Asia. We argue that the incentives for protection vary by the type of industry: in traditional sectors not characterized by increasing returns, protectionism may not be appealing in large trading blocs. We suggest that, over time, trade barriers may even fall. Our logic is that factors of production, especially capital, are increasingly mobile. In industries without strong increasing returns, efficient production is possible in a variety of locations. As a consequence, any effort by one region to raise taxes will lead firms to establish operations abroad. As long as barriers to exit for capital are low, firms will seek to exploit lower-cost locations that take advantage of other large markets. Exit by domestic firms (as well as the possibility of inward investment by foreign firms) weakens the political case and the political coalition for protection in the long run. Much of the outward investment should benefit low wage but high productivity countries in East Asia, such as Korea, Taiwan, Singapore, Malaysia, and so forth.

High-technology industries, with increasing returns, offer a different picture. We argue that the emergence of regional trading blocs is more likely to produce an increase in trade restrictions in sectors characterized by large fixed costs in R&D, manufacturing scale economies, and/or steep learning curves. For these industries, there is not only a coherent case for import protection (to help promote exports as well as preserve the domestic market), but that case becomes even stronger as trading blocs emerge and grow.

Finally, we draw some implications from the model. One of the strongest findings is that there is a disjuncture between trade policies and investment policies, in both academic models and the real world. The mobility of capital undermines many of our precious assumptions about how trade policy and trade politics are supposed to work. Moreover, if our arguments are robust, they suggest some significant dangers for the future. Cross-investments between North America and Europe will undermine many of the forces for isolationism and protectionism in the long run only if cross-investment is symmetrical, that is, firms from all major regions invest in each others' territory. To date, however, cross-investment has been asymmetrical: European and Japanese firms have invested heavily in America; American and Japanese firms have invested heavily in Europe; but no significant American and European investment has gone to Japan.

If Japan remains reserved for the Japanese, incentives for strategic trade policy will continue in Japan, creating further trade tensions. Moreover, asymmetric access to Japan's markets could alter the structure of competition in the rest of Asia. Using the logic of our model, there are incentives for Japan to create a de facto trade bloc, at least for increasing returns sectors, that extends beyond the borders of Japan to the rest of East Asia. If European and North American firms lack (or even believe that they lack) trade and investment access to a larger East Asian trading bloc, the asymmetry between North American and Japanese firms in increasing returns industries could grow. The rational response for American and European firms might then be to prevent the creation of an even larger East Asian trading bloc by actively countering Japanese expansion in East Asia.

The paper is in four sections. Following this introduction, we construct a simple model of trade in industries that do not exhibit global economies of scale. In section 4.2, we show how static and dynamic forces for and against protectionism can interact. We conclude that the long-run outlook is optimistic for free trade in these sectors, even in a world with one or two trading blocs. Next, we extend the model to "battlefield" sectors like semiconductors, where increasing returns are critical. Here we argue that the temptation to use strategic trade policies will grow along with trading bloc size. Because the critical factors of production are not as mobile in the short run as industries with increasing returns, direct investment will not have the same effects, at least in the medium term. Only over the long run will direct investment produce similar results. We use brief illustrations of trade in semiconductors to illuminate the increasing returns part of the model.

In drawing implications from the model, we present a brief case study of competition in telecommunications equipment in East Asia. The combination of fear and frustration—fear of the long-term competitive strength of Japanese companies, and frustration over lack of access to the Japanese telecommunications market—have led firms such as AT&T to fight aggressively Japanese firms in East Asia to prevent a de facto trading bloc from emerging. Although the evidence is still anecdotal, it could suggest that East Asia—not Japan—may become the next battleground outside of North America and Europe for East-West competition in high-technology products.

4.2   A Model of Protection among Trading Blocs

Here we study how the formation of trading blocs affects strategic trade incentives for goods not subject to increasing returns in production. For these purposes, we adapt a simple model used first by Gros (1987) and developed in more detail by Krugman (1991b).

Imagine that the world is composed of N countries or distinct economic regions. Each of the N regions has its own variety of indigenous good, which is produced locally (and potentially abroad) and which may be sold to other regions. These regions are divided among B trading blocs. We assume that each bloc represents a "common" market within which goods and factors move freely. For simplicity we assume that all B blocs are symmetric, that is, that they each comprise N/B regions.

The consumers of all regions are exactly alike, in that they share the same preferences for goods produced locally as well as those produced in other regions. Again, for simplicity, we assume that their utility is of the form

$$(1) \qquad U = \left(\sum_{i=1}^{N} (C_i^{\theta}) \right)^{1/\theta},$$

where C_i is an individual's consumption of region i's good. The symmetry of the model implies that the elasticity of substitution between any two goods is given by $\sigma = 1/(1 - \theta)$, with $0 \le \theta < 1$. The higher is σ the greater is the substitutability of goods in consumption.

We also assume that, while goods move freely within the confines of each trading bloc, the domestic (intrabloc) market may be protected by levying import tariffs or export taxes. As long as goods are not perfect substitutes in consumption (which would be the case were $\theta = 1$), blocs will favor some type of protection at their common border. In our model, this protection takes the form of an optimal export tax. From the optimal tariff literature, we know that the optimal (ad valorem) export tax is given by

$$(2) \qquad \tau^* = \frac{1}{\varepsilon - 1}$$

where ε is the elasticity of the rest of the world's demand for a bloc's exports. We assume that each bloc sets its own external taxes or tariffs in isolation, treating other blocs' tax rates as fixed; that is, we assume that tariffs are set in a Nash bargaining process.

There is a great deal of literature on the desirability of trading blocs—typically called "customs unions" in the parlance of international trade. Much of this literature is concerned with the question of whether such blocs could ever be in participating countries' interests. By eliminating trade restrictions with one set of countries but maintaining restrictions with others, some of the newly created intrabloc trade is welfare-improving because it involves the expansion of efficient producers, but some of the new trade is welfare-reducing because it expands the production of firms that are inefficient by international standards. However, the positive effects of "trade creation" must dominate the negative effects of "trade diversion" as long as the trading bloc as a whole sets its external barriers optimally.[1] Thus, trading blocs naturally emerge in the above model, since bloc formation is in the individual interest of participating countries (although countries would be better off if all external barriers were completely removed).

There are two empirical difficulties with the theoretical proposition that protection improves a customs union's welfare. The first (and easiest to dismiss) is that protection rarely takes the form of an export tax, the type of trade barrier

1. See Kemp and Wan (1972) for a rigorous derivation.

described by equation (2). However, it should be noted that export taxes are used here for convenience only. In our model—as in many general equilibrium models with balanced trade—export taxes are equivalent to import tariffs. (Tariffs and export taxes discourage both imports and exports because both raise domestic prices of goods and factors relative to those on the world market.) This means that all of our results below hold when tariffs are used instead of export taxes.

A second, more telling objection to this model concerns the motivation for imposing protection in the first place. Here the assumption is that protection can improve a country's terms of trade: tariffs lower the world price of its imports, and export taxes raise the world price of its exports. Yet in the real world, these kinds of optimal-tariff arguments are often not the motivation behind the erection of trade barriers. Occasionally, countries impose trade barriers to capture gains from increasing returns to scale—the subject of the model in section 4.2.1 (see also Milner and Yoffie 1989). In most cases, however, governments use protection as a means of transferring resources to factors that are inefficient by international standards (Aggarwal, Keohane, and Yoffie 1987). Often these transfers are not the result of some kind of market failure in which there is a wedge between social and private returns that domestic protection altogether removes.

Despite these caveats, we believe that the Gros-Krugman model has relevance to the political economy of protection when economic blocs form. One of the great fears of "fortress Europe," for example, is that some export-oriented producers, like Italian footwear firms, makers of Belgian chocolate, and British banks, would prefer to have a larger Europe to themselves. Whether or not protection for such sectors can be justified on the basis of increasing returns is unclear. But it is clear that much of the 1992 debate is about making the benefits of the customs union available exclusively to local factors (and not to foreign factors). And this is just another way of phrasing the optimal tariff argument.

The absence of globally increasing returns is important in the model of this section because the model implies that protection *hurts* competitiveness, that is, that protection leads to a diminution, not an expansion, of interblock trade. The way that the domestic bloc benefits from imposing common external trade barriers is to limit its sales on international markets. This need no longer be true if the trade barriers are put in place to protect firms with globally increasing returns to scale. If, for example, the marginal costs of an import-competing firm fall fast enough as output increases, then tariffs may actually enhance international competitiveness: by protecting domestic production and assuring a domestic market base, the domestic producer may end up with lower costs in terms of world prices, so that its exports become more competitive.[2] The

2. For a series of models exhibiting these features, see Krugman (1991a).

implicit guarantee of domestic market share may lower total costs even though import protection tends to raise factor prices. We investigate the implications of increasing returns in section 4.2.1.

Thus far, we have not addressed the issue of whether government taxation of trade creates an incentive to locate production elsewhere. Consider, for example, the case of an import tariff. By raising domestic production of import-competing goods, tariffs tend to siphon factors of production out of export sectors and to drive up their costs. The corresponding erosion in international competitiveness may be offset through relocating production of exports abroad. The argument for producing abroad is even more direct in the case of an explicit export tax. Either way, protection may lead firms to reconsider their production-location decisions.

However, firm location decisions are usually moot in standard models of trade policy. Domestic "firms" produce local goods only locally. Firms do not consider relocation, and as a result, governments do not need to take relocation decisions into account in determining desired trade barriers. These assumptions are probably not very accurate—few Fortune 500 firms produce exclusively in the United States, and many have more than half of their labor force employed outside that country. Economists usually do not worry so much about the accuracy of the domestic-production assumption, but here we might expect firm location decisions to interact with the level of protection, especially when the world becomes dominated by a few trading blocs.

When blocs levy taxes on their own exports, exporting firms may find that they have a greater incentive to locate certain activities abroad. To be more precise, note that, on units to be sold abroad, each unit that is also produced abroad does not have to pay the export tax. Firms therefore receive $(1 + \tau)$ times as much on foreign sales produced abroad as they do on exported sales, where τ is the ad valorem export tax. As a consequence, domestic firms have an incentive to shift toward foreign-based production as long as the marginal cost of production abroad is less than $(1 + \tau)$ times as great as the marginal cost of domestic production. This leads to an equilibrium condition:

$$(3) \qquad \frac{MC_a(q_a)}{MC_h(q_h)} = 1 + \tau,$$

where MC_a and MC_h are marginal cost of production abroad and at home, and q_a and q_h are the quantities produced abroad and at home, respectively. We assume that q_a is less than the quantity consumed by foreign residents, that is, that some domestic production for export always takes place. As long as we have such an interior solution, equation (3) holds, and it yields a condition on the share of firm production that is done overseas.

Equation (3) holds only for "interior" levels of production. That is, it may be that marginal costs of production at home are much lower than those abroad, in which case all production will take place domestically, and equation (3) will not be satisfied. It could also be that there are fixed costs to starting up a foreign productive facility, so that even if marginal costs make overseas production attractive, firms may not produce abroad. Nevertheless, in what follows we presume that equation (3) holds, that we are not at a "corner" equilibrium.

Equation (3) should be thought of as applying to each productive location abroad. To simplify matters, suppose that firms treat production within each foreign bloc as an alternative to exports to that bloc. (This rules out locating in one foreign bloc as a means of exporting to others, which in any case would be economically inefficient in the equilibrium of the model. Because such foreign-produced exports would be subject to the foreign bloc's export tax, there would be no incentive for firms to locate export production overseas in the first place.)

In order for equation (3) to be operationally useful, we need to make some assumptions about how the ratio of marginal costs on the left-hand side behaves. In order to satisfy equation (3), the left-hand side must be locally increasing in q_a or decreasing in q_h; we cannot have an equilibrium in location of production if by exporting one unit fewer and producing it abroad, a company could lower its total costs of production and increase its incentive to produce even more units abroad. Perhaps the simplest assumption is that marginal costs of home production are a constant (represented by $\alpha > 0$), and that foreign marginal costs increase above the home level as output rises (represented by $\alpha + \beta q_a$, with $\beta > 0$). Equation (3) then has the form

$$(4) \qquad \frac{MC_a(q_a)}{MC_h(q_h)} = \frac{\alpha + \beta q_a}{\alpha} = 1 + \tau,$$

which implies that production in each of the $(B - 1)$ foreign blocs is $q_a = \tau/b$, where $b = \beta/\alpha$. It follows that total *production abroad* is given by $Q_a = (B - 1)q_a = (B - 1)\tau/b$.

This expression for production abroad is useful in several ways. First, it assumes that the marginal cost of production at home is always less than that abroad. This means that firms locate abroad only to avoid domestic taxation (relaxing this assumption is likely to strengthen the results below), and otherwise have a preference for domestic production. Second, by letting the parameter b vary with the number of blocs, we have an easy way of incorporating scale effects into the model, even while retaining local decreasing returns. For example, when the world trading system is fragmented into many blocs of small size, blocs may be too small to merit firms establishing separate operations in each. In such a case, we might expect relatively little (and perhaps no) production in each small foreign bloc (i.e., b is large). Alternatively, when there are few blocs, each of large size, marginal costs for large foreign operations might be expected to be close to those for home production (i.e., b is small).

To incorporate this latter notion simply, we let $b = B - 1$, so that overseas production of each region's product is simply $Q_a = \tau$. (If the incentives to produce abroad are stronger as bloc size grows, then we could let $b = (B - 1)^2$,

so that overseas production is increasing in the size of blocs, $Q_a = \tau/(B - 1)$.)
Since there are N/B regions in each bloc, the total amount of a given bloc's
product that is produced locally in the rest of the world is

$$(5) \qquad L^{row} = \frac{NQ_a}{B} = \frac{\tau N}{B}.$$

Next we need to determine the optimal tax for each bloc. Following Krugman
(1991b), we normalize each region's volume of output to equal 1. This implies
that a representative bloc's output is $Y = N/B$ and that output in the rest of the
world is $Y^{row} = N(1 - B^{-1})$. If trade is balanced, then rest-of-world demand
must equal rest-of-world output. Rest-of-world demand is spent on goods produced domestically, D^{row}, goods exported from our bloc, M^{row}, and overseas
production of our goods, L^{row}. Therefore,

$$(6) \qquad Y^{row} = D^{row} + p(M^{row} + L^{row}),$$

where p is the relative price (in rest-of-world prices) of goods from our bloc.

In this setting, unlike in standard models, the "optimal" export tax is, in a
sense, a question of political economy. Usually it is assumed that both production and ownership of the domestic firm are entirely domestic. This leads to
the presumption that an improvement in the terms of trade will be reaped only
by domestic residents, workers, and capital providers. Even if this presumption
is not realistic, it is consistent with the structure of the traditional model.

Once the foreign firm employs foreign factors of production, however, it is
no longer immediately clear that domestic factors will receive all of the benefits of protection. There is likely to be some leakage to foreign factors. That is,
these foreign factors may be able to extract some of the benefits of the domestic
good's higher price on world markets. Clearly, domestic residents cannot benefit from a tax or tariff to the extent that its proceeds are transferred to foreigners. And if the government is concerned only with domestic residents' welfare,
then leakage to foreigners will affect its choice of an optimal tax or tariff. In
the present model, the portion of production that is located abroad avoids the
export tax. Therefore the firm, not the domestic government, must distribute
some of the tax revenues, both in the form of higher marginal costs and in the
form of profits.

To keep things simple, we consider two types of revenue distribution by the
firm. The first is the traditional case in which all tax-generated revenues (i.e.,
the additional firm revenues earned by moving production abroad) are returned
to *domestic* factors. This assumption is probably not very reasonable in a world
in which firms have international work forces and equity holders. But it is
useful because it parallels the assumption in the standard model that all revenue gains accrue to domestic residents. This case might also be thought of as
a kind of "short-run" optimal tax. When first moving abroad, domestic firms
may be able to keep most of the excess revenues for domestic residents. But
over time, as the firm becomes more international in character, foreign factors

of production may become more able to extract excess revenues from their employers.[3] Thus, our short-run optimal tariff treats the leakage to foreigners as unimportant.

The other case—which we will call the "long-run" optimal tariff—is where the government considers only those revenues that are actually collected at the border as benefiting domestic residents. This would occur if the lost tax revenues accrue entirely to foreigners, which as mentioned above is more likely to occur over time. The distinction we are drawing here between short- and long-run is obviously extreme; neither is very realistic. But our goal is to strike a balance between positive and normative theories of commercial policy. Thus, while governments' actual commercial-policy objectives may remain unclear, the optimal tariff may nevertheless be changing over time, as the benefits of protection are increasingly lost to foreign factors of production.

Once we accept this distinction between short- and long-run taxes, it is straightforward to derive their optimal levels. Since in the short run we assume that governments ignore the distinction between L^{row} and M^{row}, we can simply take logs and then derivatives of the terms in equation (6):

$$(7) \qquad (1 - f)\hat{D}^{row} + f(\hat{p} + \hat{F}^{row}) = \hat{Y} = 0,$$

where $F^{row} = L^{row} + M^{row}$ is total sales to foreigners, circumflexes over the variables denote log derivatives, $\hat{D}^{row} = d\ln(D^{row}) = dD^{row}/D^{row}$, and $f = (L^{row} + M^{row})/Y^{row}$ is the share of our bloc's goods in rest-of-world consumption. Equation (7) tells us that the elasticity of foreign demand for our bloc's goods is

$$(8) \qquad \frac{\hat{F}^{row}}{\hat{p}^{row}} = -\left(f + (1 - f)\sigma\right).$$

Using equations (8) and (2), the optimal short-run tax is given by

$$(9) \qquad \tau^{sr} = \frac{1}{(1 - f)(\sigma - 1)}.$$

Equation (9) says that the optimal tariff is a function of the substitutability of domestic and foreign goods, and of the share of domestic goods in rest-of-world expenditure. The more substitutable are the goods (the higher is σ), the less there is room to extract rents, and the lower is the optimal tariff. Also, the tariff becomes smaller as share of domestic goods in foreigners' consumption falls. Note, however, that even if the domestic bloc is "small" (i.e., if $f = 0$), the optimal tariff is positive: there is still some monopoly power created by the imperfect substitutability among goods.

In the longer run, the government's perceived elasticity of substitution between domestic and foreign goods is not given by equation (9). The govern-

3. Porter (1990) suggests that workers ultimately are able to extract compensation gains from successful companies. That is, even if a firm can succeed in raising the price at which its product sells, over time it may not be able to raise its markup over costs.

ment recognizes that a tax increase stimulates additional overseas production, eroding the export-tax base. Thus equation (6) becomes

(10) $$(1 - f)\hat{D}^{row} + f(\hat{p} + l\hat{L}^{row} + (1 - l)\hat{M}^{row}) = \hat{Y} = 0,$$

where $l = L^{row}/(L^{row} + M^{row})$ is the share of overseas production in rest-of-world consumption of our bloc's goods.

Next we need to know how overseas production is affected by a change in relative prices. First, note that, since $p = 1 + \tau$, it follows that percentage changes in prices and tariffs are related by

(11) $$\hat{\tau} = \frac{(1 + \tau)\hat{p}}{\tau}.$$

Second, from equations (5) and (11) the percentage change in overseas production for a given percentage change in relative prices is given by

(12) $$\hat{L}^{row} = \hat{\tau} = \hat{p}\left(\frac{1 + \tau}{\tau}\right).$$

Combining equations (10) and (12), we have that the long-run elasticity of substitution is

(13) $$\frac{\hat{M}^{row}}{\hat{p}^{row}} = -\left(\frac{f + (1 - f)\sigma + l(1 + \tau)/\tau}{1 - l}\right) = \varepsilon^{lr}.$$

A little algebra yields that the optimal long-run tax is given by

(14) $$\tau^{lr} = \frac{1 - l}{(1 - f)(\sigma - 1) + 2l}.$$

Equation (14) is similar to (9), except that (14) is a decreasing function of l. This says that, as the foreign-produced share of the domestic good rises, the optimal long-run tariff falls. If l reaches one, so that all of the domestic good is produced abroad, the optimal tariff falls to zero.

In order to understand how these taxes move in equilibrium, we must first determine the consumption and production shares, f and l. Following Krugman (1991b) we note that, at world prices, a representative bloc's expenditure must equal its output,

(15) $$D + M + L = Y,$$

and the representative bloc's output is in turn

(16) $$Y = \frac{N}{B}.$$

Each of the other $(B - 1)$ blocs sells a total volume of $(M + L)/(B - 1)$ (expressed in world prices) to the representative bloc; the ratio of these expenditures to the representative bloc's expenditures on its own good is

$(M + L)/D(B - 1)$. The constant elasticity of substitution (CES) utility function then implies that this ratio is equal to the relative price of foreign to domestic goods, adjusted for the elasticity of substitution, $(M + L)/D(B - 1) = p^{-\sigma}$. Substituting, this yields

$$(17) \qquad \frac{M + L}{D} = (1 + \tau)^{-\sigma}(B - 1).$$

Using equation (17) and the definition of f, we have that the share of rest-of-world expenditure that falls on domestic goods is

$$(18) \qquad f = \frac{1}{(1 + \tau)^{\sigma} + B - 1}.$$

To determine the foreign-produced share of domestic goods consumed by foreigners, note that l can be written

$$(19) \qquad l = \frac{L^{row}/Y^{row}}{(M^{row} + L^{row})/Y^{row}} = \frac{\tau}{f(B - 1)},$$

where we have used equations (5) and (16) to get the last expression on the right-hand side.

Equations (18) and (19) together with an expression for the optimal tariff (either equation [9] or [14]) allow us to understand how optimal taxes are affected by changes in the number of trading blocs. Let us begin with the short-run tax, τ^{sr}. Here equations (9) and (18) are all that matter (the fraction of output produced abroad, l, has no effect on either equation). Figure 4.1 shows the equilibrium. On the horizontal axis is the level of the tax, τ^{sr}, and on the vertical axis is f, the fraction of the domestic bloc's goods in rest-of-world expenditure. The curve marked TT shows the trade-off between f and τ given by equation (9). The curve is an increasing function of f: as the expenditure

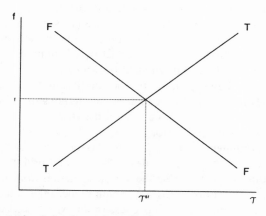

Fig. 4.1   The optimal short-run export tax

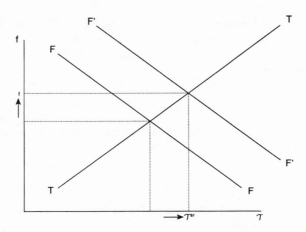

Fig. 4.2   The effect of an increase in bloc size on the optimal short-run export tax

share of domestic goods increases, the domestic bloc's monopoly power also increases. The other curve, marked *FF,* is given by equation (18). It shows that, all else equal, an increase in the tax encourages foreigners to substitute consumption away from domestic products, leading to a decline in f.

Figure 4.2 shows what happens to the optimal tariff as the number of blocs falls. The *T T* curve does not shift, since the optimal tax is a function only of a bloc's importance in foreigners' consumption, f, and not of the number of blocs, B. However, the *FF* curve in equation (18) shifts outward as the number of blocs falls: with fewer blocs, each bloc has a greater share in others' consumption at the preexisting tax rate. In equilibrium, the optimal short-run tax increases to reflect this higher degree of monopoly power. This simple model therefore suggests that protectionism rises as trading blocs become larger.

To see what is driving this result, ask why it is that, for any given number of trading blocs, governments are unwilling to raise taxes to even higher levels. The model's answer is that foreigners shift their consumption away from the domestic bloc's goods, reducing exports. That is, substitution in foreign consumption disciplines a bloc's ability to tax its own industries.

Now let us turn to the long-run tariff. The equilibrium here is described by equations (14), (18), and (19). These three equations are graphed in figure 4.3. The top panel shows the trade-off between f, the share of domestic goods in rest-of-world expenditure, and the long-run tax, τ. These two curves are similar to those shown in figures 4.1 and 4.2. In the bottom panel of figure 4.3, the relationship between l, the share of sales to the rest-of-world that is produced abroad, and τ is depicted. Note that the *T T* curve here is *downward* sloping: an increase in the share of overseas production reduces the domestic government's tax base, and limits the effectiveness of an export tax. At the margin this makes export taxes less worthwhile. On the other hand, the l schedule is upward sloping: an increase in the domestic tax induces domestic producers to locate more of their production abroad. The optimal long-run tax is determined both by the short-run substitutability of consumption by foreigners and by the long-run substitutability of where production is located.

What happens to the optimal long-run tax as the size of the representative trading bloc increases? To clarify the effect that production-location decisions have on optimal taxes, consider the case in which goods are not very close substitutes, $\sigma = 1$. (This implies that preferences are Cobb-Douglas, so that given B, a fixed share of income is spent on each region's good.) Figure 4.4 demonstrates what happens. With $\sigma = 1$, equation (14) becomes

$$(14') \qquad\qquad\qquad \tau^{lr} = \frac{1 - l}{2l},$$

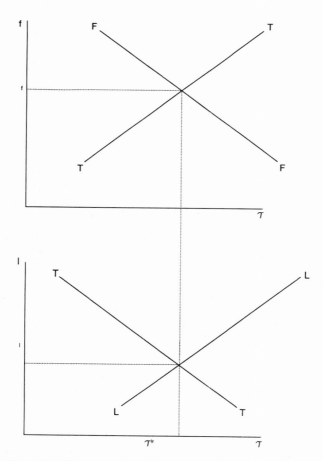

Fig. 4.3   The optimal long-run export tax

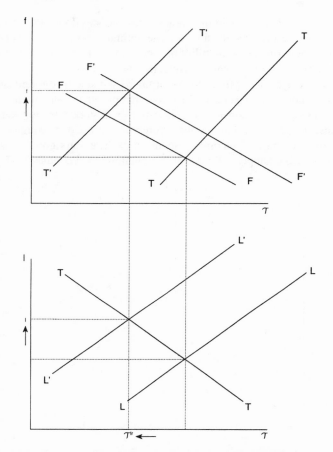

Fig. 4.4   The effect of an increase in bloc size on the optimal long-run export tax

which is a function only of l. By setting $\sigma = 1$, the sole cost of raising export taxes is that production moves abroad. Thus, when the number of trading blocs falls, the TT curve in the bottom panel of figure 4.4 does not shift.

When $\sigma = 1$, equation (18) becomes

$$(18') \qquad\qquad\qquad f = \frac{1}{\tau + B},$$

which implies that equation (19) can be written

$$(19') \qquad\qquad\qquad l = \frac{\tau(\tau + B)}{B - 1}.$$

Equation (19') says that a decrease in the number of blocs makes firms more willing to establish production abroad, which in turn makes the domestic government less willing to levy export taxes. This effect is captured by a shift outward in the *LL* curve in the bottom panel of figure 4.4. Thus, as the figure shows, the optimal long-run tax *falls* as the representative bloc increases in size.

Why is it that bigger bloc size implies a lower optimal long-run tax but a higher optimal short-run tax? Recall that the short-run tax increases because, when domestic goods are a larger share of foreign consumption, it becomes possible for the domestic government to extract more monopoly rents from foreign consumers. In the case of the long-run tax, we can for the moment suppress this effect: setting $\sigma = 1$ neutralizes the effect of bloc size on the monopoly power that a bloc's government has. Once we have suppressed the effects of substitution in consumption, the sole long-run effect is that created by substitution in production location. In the long run, firms have a greater incentive to locate abroad when foreign blocs are big, since bigger bloc size permits overseas production on a more efficient scale. The greater is the elasticity of substitution in production location, the lower is the tax that the government is willing to levy.

Of course, if we allow goods to be better substitutes for one another (by setting $\sigma > 1$), then the long-run tax will be determined by both forces: substitutability in consumption as well as substitutability in production. If bigger blocs lead to greater monopoly power in consumption, but to smaller monopoly power in firm-location choice, then the ultimate effect of bigger blocs on protection is ambiguous. However, the long-run tax will consistently be lower than the short-run tax.

This model therefore suggests that there are conflicting forces at work when trading blocs form or increase their size. On the one hand, there is a temptation to protect domestic producers from charging "too low" a price for their exports. This tends to keep external taxes high. On the other hand, the possibility of foreign direct investment helps to minimize how much the government gives in to protectionist temptations. Government interference in the best interest of the country (or of the export industry) is not necessarily in the best interest of each firm. Firms have a private incentive to avoid direct and indirect costs of protection. When firms can respond to this incentive, effective taxation remains low as trading bloc governments compete with one another to attract domestic production.

As always, it is best to think of the results from this model as suggestive. The forces that determine the optimal levels of protection discussed above do not provide a satisfactory description of the motivation behind many commercial policies. In practice, governments that impose protection (as well as industries that lobby for it) often do so in the name of *promoting* international competitiveness, not *discouraging* competitiveness, as standard optimal tariff arguments would have it. Regardless of the motivation, the general equilibrium effects of protection are clear: it raises the relative costs of domestic factors and therefore makes local production less competitive internationally. This creates the incentive to produce local goods with less expensive foreign factors. Countries that want to keep the cost of domestic factors down and domestic production for exports will have to avoid protectionist policies.

The economics of industries with increasing returns suggests a different rationale for protection, one that may represent a closer parallel to the real world. Through protection, firms may realize lower costs of production and therefore become more internationally competitive. We therefore turn to the effects of tripolarity on protection of increasing returns sectors.

4.3   Increasing Returns and Trading Blocs

Politicians and businessmen have long argued that a protected domestic market enhances international competitiveness. Traditionally, they based their arguments on the "infant industry" notion, which says that domestic market imperfections lower private (but not social) returns in new industries, and that these imperfections are best dealt with through trade restrictions. Among economists, however, the infant industry argument receives little support. While many economists accept the existence of market imperfections (incomplete capital markets, lack of complete appropriability of R&D, externalities in production, etc.), nearly all reject the idea that trade restrictions can be a first-best means of correction.

More recently, strategic trade theory has offered a better rationale for using protection as a means of helping domestic industries. With imperfect competition among firms, protectionist policies can alter foreign competitors' beliefs about the domestic firm's strategic behavior. Sometimes (though not always) it is possible to use government policies—trade restrictions in particular—to tip the equilibrium outcome not only in favor of domestic firms, but also in favor of the domestic economy as a whole. Trade policies may be a device for conveying credibly the future aggressiveness of domestic firms, which in turn may make foreign firms less aggressive.

For the whole economy to benefit, trade restrictions must create sufficient improvements in the efficiency of the productive sector to offset what would otherwise be an increase in the price paid by domestic consumers (as well as any tendency to "crowd out" other types of domestic production). Thus, it is necessary that some kind of economies of scale, either static or dynamic, be present. We show below that larger domestic markets help leverage the effects of increasing returns. That is, a larger domestic market can enhance the domestic government's ability to capitalize on the benefits from import protection. These forces suggest that protectionism should be even greater in these sectors when blocs are large compared to when the national markets are small.

Imagine that there are N firms that share the world market for a product, say RAM chips. The demand for the product is given by

(20)
$$p = a - \sum_{i=1}^{N} q_i = a - Q,$$

where p is the price of chips and q_i is the output of the ith firm. Suppose that each firm chooses its output in order to maximize profits, setting marginal revenues equal to marginal costs. This implies the standard equilibrium condition for profit maximization:

(21)
$$p\left(1 - \frac{s_i}{\varepsilon}\right) = MC_i,$$

where $s_i = q_i/Q$, the ith firm's share of the total market for chips; $\varepsilon = \dfrac{pdQ}{Qdp}$, the elasticity of demand for chips; and MC_i is the ith firm's marginal costs of production. From this setup it is straightforward to show that the ith firm's output is given by

(22)
$$q_i = (N + 1)^{-1}\left(a - nMC_i + \sum_{j \neq i} MC_j\right).$$

What happens if the domestic market is protected so that only the domestic firm can sell there? If there are no increasing returns (so that marginal costs remain the same once the protection is put in place), then the domestic firm's foreign market share remains the same in the short run. All that changes is its share of the domestic market. Under these circumstances, protection is likely to be bad for the domestic bloc as a whole: the domestic market for chips becomes less competitive, which hurts domestic consumers more than it helps domestic producers.

If there are increasing returns to scale, however, the domestic economy can benefit from protection. Increasing returns may take several forms, including dynamic effects such as learning by doing and the proliferation of new techniques. For our purposes, however, static increasing returns (in the form of decreasing marginal costs) have the same overall impact as these more complex dynamic effects.

Suppose, then, that marginal costs decline as output increases. This implies that, as the domestic market for chips becomes more efficient, domestic firms expand their foreign market share. In this situation protection is much more likely to make the domestic bloc better off. To see the effects on output, take equation (22) as a description of the domestic firm's foreign sales. When the domestic market is protected, the domestic firm's output rises and so its marginal costs fall (i.e., MC_i declines). This has a direct, positive effect on the domestic firm's foreign sales, raising its foreign market share.

There are also several strategic effects of the protectionist policy, which may be even more powerful than the direct effects. First, other firms reduce the absolute amount of their output in foreign markets, in deference to the lower costs achieved by the home firm. To see this in equation (22), note that q_i falls as MC_j, $j \neq i$, declines. But a foreign output reduction further spills over into *higher foreign* marginal costs, reducing foreign output even further. Finally, as equation (22) shows, higher foreign marginal costs directly raise the domestic firm's output. This then begins the cycle again, further raising domestic marginal costs and output, and lowering further foreign marginal costs and output. Once we arrive at a new equilibrium—at which point equation (22) is satisfied for all N firms—protection of the domestic market will have been translated into a competitive advantage for the domestic firm in its foreign markets as well. The greater the increasing returns, the greater is the spillover effect onto export competitiveness.

Clearly, these strategic effects are important beyond the large size of a domestic bloc. In larger blocs, domestic protectionist policies have a greater impact on the strategic outcomes abroad. Indeed, the domestic welfare consequences of protection depend importantly on how much marginal costs fall. All else equal, a larger domestic market makes it more likely that marginal costs fall substantially, and that the domestic firm gains a large strategic advantage in overseas markets. The greater the decrease in marginal costs, the greater the chance that the domestic bloc as a whole will benefit from the protection. The implication is that larger blocs have greater incentives to initiate strategic protectionism designed to take advantage of increasing returns.

Is the possibility of foreign direct investment likely to reverse this tendency toward greater protectionism, as it did in section 4.2? The answer partly lies in whether firms are willing to transfer abroad that part of the operations that is subject to increasing returns. Activities such as R&D, product development and design, and the actual production of new generation products may have the greatest increasing returns associated with them. Yet these activities may be the least likely candidates to be moved abroad—at least in the short to medium run. Production activities that are not associated with important increasing returns are probably better candidates for overseas production, to which the model of the previous section applies.

The modern semiconductor industry provides a good illustration of how this model might work in reality. Semiconductors is a relatively new industry, begun in 1959 with the invention of the integrated circuit (IC). Initially the industry had relatively low entry costs and only moderate scale economies (Intel Corporation built a state-of-the-art fabrication facility in 1972 for $3.2 million). Even R&D scale was modest: it was common for a few engineers with a good idea to design a new product. Most firms in the United States, Japan, and Europe built their manufacturing fabrication facilities in their home bases, but since transportation costs were insignificant, assembly and test operations were often moved to low-cost-labor locations.

In the mid-1970s, several changes occurred in the economics and technology of the industry. Perhaps most important was that production of chips moved from large scale integration (LSI) to very large scale integration (VLSI). A result of this change was that microelectronics became much more capital-intensive. Estimates for building a world-class production facility varied, but most analysts concurred that the cost had risen some ten- to twenty-fold from 1975 to 1985. By 1990, every step in the production process became more capital intensive, expensive, and intricate. A high-volume plant cost approximately $400 million and would take almost two years to build and qualify the products for sale. Learning effects were also significant, with costs declining about 30–40 percent for every doubling of production. One estimate suggested that a firm had to achieve 6 percent of the world market (up from 3 percent a decade earlier) from each new plant in order to justify the capital costs. R&D expenses also rose during this period, averaging as much as 15 percent of sales in some years. As product life cycles in the industry shortened on some high-volume products (like DRAMs) from five to three years, the advantage was won by firms that introduced early and had the capacity to fill demand (Yoffie 1988).

These features of the semiconductor industry make it an ideal-typical candidate for strategic trade policy, especially in the context of growing economic blocs. The largest part of demand for semiconductors is in the United States and Japan (approximately 39 percent and 51 percent, respectively, in 1989), with Europe consuming approximately 10 percent. No individual country in Europe had adequate demand to justify new plant capacity. Once Europe becomes a larger bloc, however, the incentives for more semiconductor production are obvious. A European government could hypothetically intervene in its semiconductor industry, reduce imports, and build local scale economies. Europe might then receive a disproportionate share of the benefits from the profits or spillovers generated by the semiconductor industry. And while capital mobility allows firms to move abroad easily in industries that broadly conform with the competitive paradigm, the capital-intensive and especially the R&D-intensive nature of semiconductors makes it much harder for firms to escape from a high-cost national base in the short to medium run, or for firms to invest directly in a foreign market to avoid import tariffs.

The incentive to protect semiconductors in Europe becomes even more compelling if one looks at the history of this industry. In the early 1970s, America dominated production and consumption—controlling over 60 percent of both. To build a competitive industry, the Japanese government explicitly and implicitly restricted foreign entry until the late 1970s. Even though many studies suggested that protectionism led to initially higher costs for Japanese producers, by the end of the period, Japanese firms successfully built scale economies, moved down the learning curve, and had become the lowest-cost producers in the world of certain leading-edge chips. The temptation for any individual country in Europe to replicate the Japanese experience should be low because even Germany and France have tiny markets for chips compared to Japan and the United States. But collectively, Europe's market for chips in the 1990s is only marginally smaller than Japan's market in the early 1970s.

Not only does larger market size increase incentives for protectionism in semiconductors, but the high fixed cost structure of manufacturing and the scale intensity of R&D make it difficult for firms to adapt to protectionism. Trade conflict between the United States and Japan in semiconductors has been intense since the mid-1980s. In other industries with comparable trade conflict, like TVs in the 1970s and autos in the 1980s, many Japanese firms invested heavily in the United States within a few years. But direct investment in semiconductors has been much slower; most firms in Japan (and the United States) have considered the cost penalties too great to move either the high value-added portion of manufacturing (i.e., wafer fabrication versus assembly and test) or large R&D facilities (many firms have small design centers in other countries where marginal changes are made in the home country designs). Even though protectionism was a reality in Japan throughout the 1970s and became a real threat in America and Europe in the mid-1980s, few plants actually moved overseas. Most companies that have announced their intentions to pursue direct investment will not be opening facilities in other countries until the mid-1990s (see table 4.1). Furthermore, most of the planned facilities are only manufacturing operations, without fully integrated R&D. Most firms continue to do the significant R&D at home and transfer designs to foreign plants.

While we do not yet know how trade, investment, and protectionism in semiconductors will evolve, experience to date is suggestive of several issues posed in our model. First, the Europeans have already showed signs of creating a fortress in semiconductors, even before the 1992 program was complete. Recent changes in antidumping laws (which had previously defined local content in chips as low value-added assembly and test, but now defines local content as "diffusion" or fabrication) have been widely interpreted within the industry as a sign that Europe wants to safeguard European chip demand for European companies. Second, the high cost of direct investment in an industry like semiconductors makes it harder for firms to adjust. The very slow pace of direct investment is evidence of this trend. But third, even if domestic firms do not like to move abroad their increasing returns activities, one should expect capital to move if it becomes a necessity for being competitive. It may take a much longer time, and not all of the increasing returns activities may relocate, but ultimately capital remains mobile. If firms penetrate each others' markets, and assuming that investment is not a perfect substitute for trade, the domestic incentives for protection could decline.

4.4   Implications

Thus far we have argued that strategic trade policies in a world with larger trading blocs will differ greatly across sectors. Incentives for protection will be greater and last longer in industries with increasing returns in production compared to industries that lack significant scale economies. For those goods that are not subject to increasing returns, the formation of large trading blocs may ultimately help lower tariffs, as firms quickly move production abroad.

Table 4.1   **Overseas Semiconductor Fabrication Facilities, Memory and Microprocessors**

Company	Date	Location	Product	Capacity (per month)
Mitsubishi	1989	Durham, North Carolina	1M DRAM, arrays, MCU	8,500
	1989	Taiwan	1M 4M DRAMS	
	1989	Alsdorf, W. Germany	4M DRAM, MCU, MPU, Arrays	22,000
Sony	1991	San Antonio, Texas	1M SRAM	12,800
	1996	San Antonio, Texas	SRAM	N.A.
	1992	Scotland	1M SRAM	22,000
NMB	1992	New Mexico	4M DRAM	20,000
NEC	1984	Roseville, California	256K DRAM, arrays	27,900
	1987	Livingston, Scotland	1M DRAM	12,000
	1991	Roseville, California	4M DRAM	16,000
	1994	Hillsboro, Oregon	16M DRAM	16,000
	1991	Livingston, Scotland	4M DRAM	10,000
Motorola	1970s	Aizu, Japan	Logic	365,210
		Aizu, Japan	MCU, SRAM, power ICs	304,341
		E. Kilbride, Scotland	MCU, MEM, logic	
		E. Kilbride, Scotland	1M DRAM, SRAM, MPU	N.A.
		E. Kilbride, Scotland	FET, AMPS, LED	N.A.
		Toulouse, France	Bipolar, power trans	12,000
		Seremban, Malaysia	Small signal	N.A.
	1991	Aizu, Japan	Consumer ICs	N.A.
	1992	Sendai, Japan	4M DRAM, MPU, custom	25,000
National	1975	Greenock, Scotland	NMOS, XMOS, bipolar	40,000
		Greenock, Scotland	Logic	N.A.
		Greenock, Scotland	Logic Custom	7,000
		Livingston, Scotland	1M DRAM, 4M DRAM	12,000
		Ha-Emek, Israel	32-Bit MPU	6,400
Intel	1987	Jerusalem, Israel	386 MPU	21,000
	1993	Kildare, Ireland	NA	N.A.
TI	1960s and 1970s	England	PWR, discrete	20,000
		W. Germany	Logic, LIN	15,000
		Hatogaya, Japan	MCU, logic	15,000
		Hatogaya, Japan	N.A.	28,000
		Hatogaya, Japan	N.A.	18,000
		Hiji, Japan	Arrays, logic, linear	50,000
		Hiji, Japan	Arrays, LISP, MPU	20,000
		Hiji, Japan	4M DRAM	7,000
		Mijo, Japan	64K DRAM	20,000

(*continued*)

Table 4.1   (continued)

Company	Date	Location	Product	Capacity (per month)
		Mijo, Japan	256K DRAM, 1M DRAM, 256K SRAM	23,750
		Mijo, Japan	256K DRAM	20,000
	1991	Ibaragi, Japan	16M, 64M DRAM	N.A.
	1990	Italy	4M DRAM	30,000
	1990	W. Germany	Logic	3,000
	1992	Italy	16M DRAM	20,000
	1991	Taiwan	1M DRAM	30,000
	1995	Taiwan	4M 16M DRAM	N.A.

Source: Compiled from *Dataquest Newsletters.*

For those goods that are subject to increasing returns, however, firms may actually become more efficient producers by locating production exclusively within the protected domestic market. Since the presence of increasing returns can lead the domestic economy as a whole to benefit from protection, the incentives to raise trade barriers increase in a world dominated by large trading blocs.

Yet over time, capital remains mobile, even in sectors with increasing returns. And to the extent that foreign direct investment occurs, and as long as it is an imperfect substitute for trade, it should diminish the force of increasing returns–based arguments for domestic protection. Foreign firms with local production (and local employment) will advocate liberalization. Moreover, one of the most important strategic advantages of protection to domestic firms disappears—the guarantee of a large domestic market base on which efficient production can be realized. If foreign producers invest in—and ultimately share—the domestic market, trade protection may not be a fully credible guarantee of market share. Without credibility, many of the strategic advantages to protection are lost. While strategic protection may provide some local employment, it may or may not provide the type of employment (e.g., semiconductor R&D) or spillovers that would be generated by domestically headquartered firms (see Tyson 1992; Porter 1990; Reich 1990).

To reap the strategic advantages associated with increasing returns, governments would need to insulate their economies from foreign direct investment and from foreign trade. Yet many countries (or blocs) actively protect certain sectors from imports but do not discourage foreign direct investment in those sectors. This suggests that either the motivation for protection is different than the assumptions underlying our model, or that trade and investment policies in many countries are not in harmony with one another.

One could draw an optimistic conclusion about the world economy from this disjunction between direct investment and trade. On the one hand, we have argued that growing economic blocs could produce more economic conflict in the short run, but as foreign investment grows in response to protectionism, countries will have incentives to liberalize trade. Even in increasing returns sectors, the mobility of capital will make it difficult for the European bloc or American bloc to preserve its domestic market for local firms. Over time, multinational companies will invest in each others' markets, undermining the effectiveness of strategic protectionism.

In reality, much of this process is already under way. In traditional sectors, such as autos, significant foreign investment has already taken place. A Honda produced in Ohio is difficult to distinguish from a Honda produced in Japan; one suspects the same will be true in Europe when Japanese firms bring their announced investments on stream. In the absence of restrictions on local investments, it becomes increasingly difficult for governments in Europe or North America to preserve the local market for local companies.[4] The level of cross-investment among industrial markets has reached historic proportions, partly in response to existing protectionism, and partly in anticipation of the short-run protectionism our model suggests.

If the cross-investment described above were symmetrical (i.e., each bloc invested roughly equally in each others' territory), one might predict that protectionism and strategic trade policy in a tripolar world might eventually disappear. Each bloc would have so much of each other's investment that it would be politically difficult to distinguish national origins of firms. While the outflow of investment has been fairly symmetrical across the three blocs (see figures 4.5 and 4.6), however, it has been highly asymmetrical on the inflow side. Japan appears to be the only major industrialized country whose domestic market remains effectively protected from foreign investment as well as trade in some increasing returns sectors. While there are no formal barriers to foreign direct investment into Japan (restrictions were removed in the 1970s), Japan permits far less foreign access to corporate control than it does even to its goods markets.[5] Figures 4.5 and 4.6 show the flows of foreign direct investment out of and into major countries, including Japan. Even in an era in which foreign direct investment around the world has mushroomed, inflows into Japan remain nil.

If increasing returns are important, Japan may be the only country that has pursued policies that are consistent with maximizing domestic welfare (either on purpose or by happenstance). In the presence of increasing returns, these policies also lower the rest of the world's welfare. Nevertheless, viewed in this way, Japanese policies are not hard to understand.

The possibility that Japan follows a coherent strategic trade policy has not

---

4. If there are going to be political consequences of direct investment, it is important that investment is not a perfect substitute for trade. In the extreme case, where trade and investments are substitutes, there is no reason to believe that the foreign firm will lobby for liberalization. Once established, the multinational might prefer to continue operating behind closed barriers. In reality, however, much of the investment among industrial countries has been to promote incremental sales without displacing all exports from the home country. Therefore, many foreign investors are likely to advocate freer trade.

5. See Froot (1991) for an analysis of Japanese foreign direct investment.

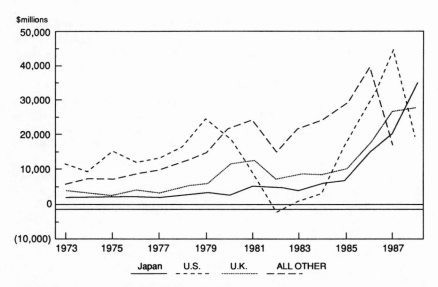

Fig. 4.5   Foreign direct investment outflows
Sources: International Monetary Fund, *Survey of Current Business,* Bank of England, Bank of Japan.

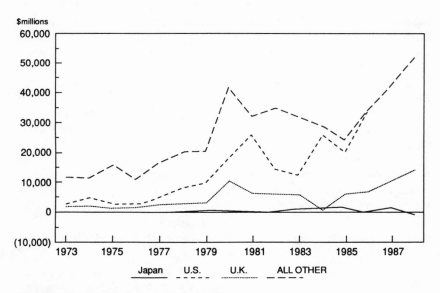

Fig. 4.6   Foreign direct investment inflows
Sources: International Monetary Fund, *Survey of Current Business,* Bank of England, Bank of Japan.

been lost on multinational corporations in increasing returns industries. In businesses like telecommunications equipment, firms based in Europe and America fear a repeat of Japan's performance in semiconductors. The strategy of companies like AT&T may be symptomatic of the coming battles for increasing return sectors in East Asia. Below we briefly describe the dynamics of trade and investment strategies in telecommunications equipment. While the information is still anecdotal, it suggests that concern over a Japanese trading bloc is real and that it is motivating changes in corporate behavior that could influence the structure of competition in the region.[6]

Central-office switches (COSs) form the heart of the public telecommunications network. For most equipment manufacturers, large digital switches are the flagship products of their entire equipment line. Physically, a digital COS consists of arrays of several hundred circuit boards, containing thousands of integrated circuits, wired together in metal cabinets of 400 to 1,000 cubic feet. Digital COSs range in size from 5,000 line units to more than 100,000 lines (connecting remote modules up to forty or fifty miles away). Switches were also highly differentiated products, which could be segmented by differences in size and degree of functionality. Ericsson switches, for instance, were originally designed for international markets and were traditionally more vanilla-like—that is, adaptable but simple, and deployable in relatively small increments. At the other extreme, AT&T switches, such as the 5ESS, were designed for a more advanced network, with larger concentrated volumes of usage, greater functionality (especially centrex), and extraordinary levels of reliability.

The R&D costs for COSs are large, and for the generic software, continuing. Only companies with considerable financial resources and technical personnel, or substantial government support, have entered this business. Fewer still survived the 1980s. In addition to initial development costs, which range from $800 million to more than $1 billion for each manufacturer's switch, there are annual expenses for software modifications of as much as $200 million per firm. To recover costs of this magnitude, most firms had to receive government subsidies (directly through transfers or indirectly through high domestic switch prices), or they had to win a significant share of their domestic markets as well as some share of the world market beyond their national borders. If a firm in a small country, such as GPT in the United Kingdom, could not sell overseas, its ratio of R&D to sales would inevitably become unsustainable without government subsidies, even with a monopoly at home.[7]

Manufacturing COSs also required very large scale plants. Although simple assembly can be done locally on a small scale, firms that manufacture their circuit boards and integrated circuits require large facilities. In the largest national market—the United States—the dominant supplier (AT&T) produces

---

6. This short case study is based on extensive interviews with AT&T and the other major telecommunications equipment companies worldwide. The full results are reported in Vietor and Yoffie (1993).

7. Ultimately, GPT had to sell out to Siemens (Cowley 1990).

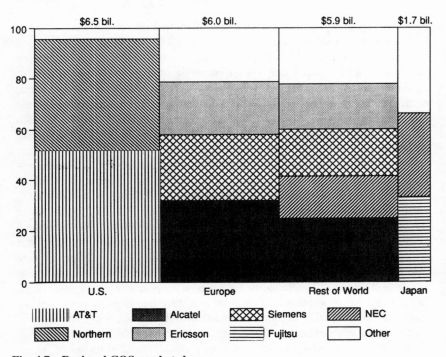

Fig. 4.7   Regional COS market shares
Note: Other in the United States consists of Siemens/Stromberg, Ericsson, and NEC;
Fujitsu is also trying to enter. *Other* in Europe consists primarily of ItalTel/AT&T,
Bosch, and TeDeWe. *Other* in Japan consists of Hitachi, Oki, and Northern Telecom.

all its 5ESS switches at a single plant and its 4ESS (interexchange) switches
at a single plant. Northern Telecom similarly produces its DMS switch at single plants in the United States. Since all other markets are smaller, one can
assume that efficient manufacturing scale for digital COSs is a single plant
with capacity of as much as 6.5 million lines. Under this assumption, the 1989
world market of 40 million lines could support at most six players, if equally
sized, at efficient manufacturing scale. In sum, this is a classic increasing returns business, where the advantages of strategic trade policy should be apparent to all parties.

The strategies of firms in this industry are depicted in figures 4.7 and 4.8.
National firms dominate their home markets. In addition, the American firms
are aggressively pursuing pieces of Europe, the European and Japanese firms
are aggressively pursuing the United States, but most of the non-Japanese players have given up or forgone opportunities to sell in Japan. Real or imagined
barriers, technical and political, have discouraged all of the major players (except Northern Telecom, which has less than 1 percent of the Japanese COS
market) from selling or investing in the Japanese market.

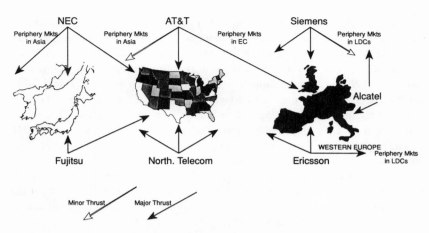

Fig. 4.8   Geographic thrusts in telecommunications

AT&T is particularly interesting in this regard. Starting in the mid-1980s, AT&T pursued a strategy of aggressive expansion into Europe and Japan. Its goal was to generate 25 percent of its revenues from non-US. sales. Recognizing its lack of international experience, AT&T launched a patchwork of "strategic alliances," one with Philips, the Dutch electronics giant, to help AT&T break into Europe's COS market; and a variety of distribution and joint venture manufacturing agreements were signed throughout Asia, including joint ventures in Korea and Taiwan for COSs, and two agreements in Japan—including a distribution arrangement with Toshiba for PBXs.

Japan and Asia were a major focus from the beginning. With NEC and Fujitsu each investing more than $500 million in manufacturing and software development for the U.S. market, AT&T management saw penetrating the Japanese market as a necessity. However, Japan's NTT, after considerable pressure from the United States, rejected the AT&T 5ESS switch. NTT decided to take on only one additional outside supplier, giving Northern Telecom a $650 million contract over five years. Toshiba also decided to develop and market its own PBX directly in competition with AT&T. At this point, AT&T's management concluded that it would be difficult, and perhaps impossible, to challenge Japanese suppliers at home. To counter the possible advantages gained by its Japanese competitors, AT&T concluded that every effort must be made to stop Japan from building a larger protected arena in East Asia. The joint ventures in Taiwan and Korea took on new importance, and AT&T decided to contest aggressively every new contract in Asia.

When Indonesia and Malaysia opened bidding for digital switches in 1990 and 1991, AT&T's responses were indicative of its strategy. Even though it would ship its initial products to Indonesia from its subsidiary in Holland rather than the United States, AT&T politicized the contract to the highest levels of the American government. It mobilized the U.S. government and especially the U.S. embassy in Jakarta in an effort to offset any influence of the Japanese government on behalf of the other major contender—NEC. A senior Indonesian official claims that "everyone is trying to push, pull, do this, do that" (*Wall Street Journal,* June 21, 1990). Ultimately Indonesia decided to double the size of the contract and give half to NEC and half to AT&T. A similar pattern was being repeated in Malaysia in late 1991: this time it was Fujitsu and AT&T going head to head (*Wall Street Journal,* October 11, 1991).

The logic of AT&T's strategy is consistent with the logic of our paper. With Japanese and European firms investing aggressively in AT&T's home market, the possibilities of strategic trade intervention in COSs becomes increasingly problematic for the United States. While AT&T has been able to counter the challenge of a European bloc, to a limited extent, by winning big contracts in Italy and Spain, it failed at penetrating Japan. AT&T's solution has been to attack the periphery of Japan to reduce the long-run Japanese advantage. The other major non-Japanese firms—Siemens, Northern Telecom, Alcatel, and Ericsson—have followed variations on this strategy.

This analysis suggests two conclusions. First, if firms in other increasing returns industries see Japan as a closed market, then East Asia may well become the next battleground for trade and investment. Second, we have to wonder about the stability of these arrangements when Japan seems to be in a position to follow coherent strategic policies, while the other blocs are politically confounded by cross-investment. Even with growing trade and investment by European and American firms in East Asia in increasing returns sectors, the ongoing asymmetry in direct investment between Japan and the rest of the world makes the outlook uncomfortable, at best.

References

Aggarwal, Vinod, Robert O. Keohane, and David B. Yoffie. 1987. The Dynamics of Negotiated Protectionism. *American Political Science Review* 81 (2): 345–66.

Cowley, Peter. 1990. Telecommunications. In *Europe, 1992,* ed. Gary Hufbauer. Washington DC: Brookings Institution.

Froot, Kenneth A. 1991. Japanese Foreign Direct Investment. In *U.S.-Japan Economic Forum,* ed. M. Feldstein. Chicago: University of Chicago Press.

Gros, Daniel. 1987. A Note on the Optimal Tariff, Retaliation, and the Welfare Loss from Tariff Wars in a Model with Intra-industry Trade. *Journal of International Economics* 23: 357–67.

Kemp, Murray, and Henry Wan. 1972. The Gains from Free Trade. *International Economic Review* 13: 509–22.

Krugman, Paul R. 1991a. Import Protection as Export Promotion: International Competition in the Presence of Oligopoly and Economies of Scale. In *Rethinking International Trade,* Cambridge: MIT Press.

————. 1991b. Is Bilateralism Bad? In *International Trade and Trade Policy*, ed. E. Helpman and A. Razin. Cambridge: MIT Press.

Milner, Helen, and David B. Yoffie. 1989. Between Free Trade and Protectionism: Strategic Trade Policy and a Theory of Corporate Trade Demands. *International Organization* 43 (2): 239–72.

Porter, Michael. 1990. *The Competitive Advantage of Nations.* New York: Free Press.

Reich, Robert. 1990. Who Is Us? *Harvard Business Review* 68 (1): 53–64.

Tyson, Laura. 1992. *Who's Bashing Whom?* Washington, D.C.: Institute for International Economics.

Vietor, Richard, and David B. Yoffie. 1993. Telecommunications: Deregulation and Globalization. In *Beyond Free Trade: Firms, Governments, and Global Competition*, ed. David B. Yoffie, 129–92. Boston: Harvard Business School Press.

Yoffie, David B. 1988. The Global Semiconductor Industry, 1987. Harvard Business School Note no. 9-388-052. Boston: Harvard Business School.

Comment   Marcus Noland

Kenneth Froot and David Yoffie have written an interesting and provocative paper. The paper first constructs a model of trading blocs based on optimal tariff arguments. It is shown that protection will tend to rise with the size of the bloc and that foreign direct investment will act as a counterweight to protection. This raises several questions.

First, Kemp and Wan (1976) have shown that, assuming constant returns to scale but permitting a very general set of impediments to trade, any welfare-maximizing customs union will iteratively expand until it encompasses the whole world in a free trade area in the limit. It is unclear why the Froot-Yoffie bloc wouldn't be subject to the same forces.

One reason that customs unions do not expand forever is that political systems are unable to make the necessary compensating transfers. By the same token, in the real world protection appears to be undertaken more often for narrow parochial reasons, not for optimal tariff reasons. This suggests that blocs could arise as an equilibrium solution in a model of international trade emphasizing transactions costs and the political economy of protection along the lines sketched out in Peter Petri's paper (chap. 1 in this volume). This could be a fruitful avenue for investigating bloc formation.

What this paper does is point to the role of foreign direct investment (FDI) as a counterweight to protection. In the Froot-Yoffie model this occurs because the benefits of optimal trade policies are diluted by the presence of foreign firms. This consideration must enter into policymakers' calculations. However, a number of recent cases (Brazilian infomatics, European autos) indicate that

Marcus Noland is a research fellow at the Institute for International Economics and visiting assistant professor of economics at Johns Hopkins University.

government officials behave in a more sophisticated (or at least in a more complicated) way than in the Froot-Yoffie model, restricting FDI as well as trade as part of an overall program.

Nonetheless, I suspect Froot and Yoffie have the impact of FDI on trade policy right, if for somewhat different reasons. Rather than reducing the incentives to protect because of dilution of benefits in the home country, FDI acts as a counterweight to protection by generating antiprotection lobbying by firms that fear retaliation against their own operations in the foreign target country. In other words, FDI creates hostages, and the existence of hostages discourages rash actions. In either view, Japan's distinctive position with regard to inward FDI is troubling.

While the Kemp-Wan argument holds under constant returns, the existence of increasing returns sectors gives rise to opportunities for rent shifting that are taken up in the second part of the paper. Here I think there is room for a significant extension. The paper assumes that countries can pursue optimal policies without any foreign reaction. I would argue that, as the size of the blocs increases (or, in the paper's terms, as the number of blocs decreases), the likelihood of retaliation increases. This, it seems to me, is central to the bloc story. The United States does not really care if Belgium inflicts its optimal policies on the United States; the United States would care (and certainly respond) if the whole European Community did. One can envision a first pass in which this is treated as a Nash bargaining game.

Permitting foreign response is important because once one allows for retaliation, my sense is that the case for activist policies is weakened, due to the possibility of mutually destructive trade wars. Under these circumstances, it would seem to me that the optimal policy response is twofold: announce a tit-for-tat strategy as a deterrent measure (which is what the United States' section 301 and super 301 can do), then try to negotiate some sort of accord to constrain policymakers' options (which is essentially what GATT does).

This leads me to the final section of the paper, which consists of a discussion of trade in telecommunications equipment. Because GATT does its job so well, the simple tools (tariffs, quotas, subsidies) to implement optimal trade policies are unavailable, policymakers are forced to use less traditional instruments, and there is a well-developed body of anecdotal evidence on this point for Japan. I would thus interpret the Structural Impediments Initiative talks as an attempt to constrain the use of policy tools not already covered under GATT.

However, a second issue arises with regard to Japan. What if the trade impediments do not take the form of governmental policy, but of private preferences. In this case, the natural response would be for foreign firms to form strategic alliances with Japanese firms. For example, the dominant tendency among innovative U.S. producers was not to go to the U.S. government seeking the creation of a bastion market in the United States, but was rather to form strategic alliances with foreign firms.

A question for the authors, then, is whether what is occurring in Japan is more akin to the traditional bloc formation analyzed in the first part of the paper, or the private alliance game described in the final section. If it is the former, then it would be useful to analyze the interests of each East Asian country in joining each potential bloc. Presumably the developing countries have their own interests, and these could conceivably involve siding with one bloc on certain issues and with the other on others. Neither part of the paper really speaks to this issue.

If the contest is more of a private game, however, this opens up an even larger set of issues. We would want to analyze the incentives of firms to join alliances, and what is the proper role of government policy in this situation. This in turn raises issues revolving around the definition of national interest (when, for example, the interests of putatively national firms and national residents diverge, or when the country is home to firms in competing alliances), and the structure of interest-group politics.

Reference

Kemp, Murray, and Henry Wan, Jr. 1976. An elementary proposition concerning the formation of customs unions. In Jagdish N. Bhagwati, ed., *International Trade*. Cambridge: MIT Press.

Comment   Jeffry A. Frieden

This very useful essay could be expanded to cover the political economy of foreign direct investment (FDI) more comprehensively if its approach to FDI itself were more complete. The principal gap in the presentation of the authors is the implicit notion that it is primarily shareholders of a mother firm who benefit from trade barriers that protect one of their foreign affiliates. This is incomplete and leads to a somewhat misleading view of the political economy of trade policy in the context of FDI.

It is widely recognized that FDI is mostly about the transfer of technological, management, and marketing skills and assets that are highly specific to an industry or a firm. In this context, while some of the benefits of increased business for the industry or firm accrue to shareholders, some of them are also realized by workers and managers (or suppliers and customers) whose skills and experience are especially important to the firm or industry.

In fact, industry-specific trade protection is beneficial to *all* factors of production specific to the industry, whether the factors are owned by locals or by foreigners. Workers with skills specific to an industry gain when that industry is protected and can be expected to support such protection. FDI does not

Jeffry A. Frieden is professor of political science at the University of California, Los Angeles.

change this fact; it only changes, if anything, the nationality of the shareholders who also gain from protection.

However, the protectionist rents accruing to an industry can accrue to different *firms* within the industry. In this sense, if a worker has skills specific to a particular *firm* rather than to an industry as a whole, and if protection draws in foreign firms that garner some or all of the rents from protection, the worker might not be better off.

Put differently, adding FDI to a picture of trade policy formation simply adds a new set of *firms* that can benefit from protection. We probably should expect some of the benefits from protection that go to new foreign firms to go to foreigners (shareholders or headquarters personnel of the mother firm), but this is not guaranteed: if the inward investment simply substitutes for lost export markets, the foreigners might in fact be worse off. In any case, even with FDI it is very likely that many of the benefits from protection will go to local people employed by the foreign firm. So those whose factors are specific to the industry as a whole have an incentive to lobby for protection; those whose factors are further specific to an existing domestic firm have an incentive to lobby for protection *and* against inward direct investment. This is simply a variant of the more general desire of members of a cartel to reduce the possibility of new entrants into the cartelized industry.

To take an example, protection of the U.S. auto industry should help those whose skills can be used in the auto industry generally. Inward direct investment in auto manufacture (the "transplant" phenomenon) harms those whose fortunes are tied not to the auto industry generally, but to the Big Three American firms. So auto parts producers and their employees who can sell to *all* assemblers will do well and support both protection and free FDI, while managers and workers with long-term implicit or explicit contracts with domestic auto firms will do less well and will support protection but oppose inward direct investment. I believe that this comes relatively close to describing the political economy of these issues.

The introduction of FDI does not *eliminate* protectionist rents, and probably does not reduce them substantially. It may not even have too appreciable an impact on the rents accruing to local residents (or at least this is purely an empirical question). But it does change the contours of the groups aided by various trade policies in important ways.

II Japanese Foreign Direct Investment in East Asia

5   Japanese Foreign Investment and the Creation of a Pacific Asian Region

Richard F. Doner

5.1 Introduction

This paper explores the sources, patterns, and consequences of Japanese foreign investment (FI) in the Pacific Asian region. My principal question is whether and how this investment promotes regional linkages among Japan and the two major groups of developing capitalist countries in East Asia: the newly industrialized countries (NICs), which include South Korea, Taiwan, Hong Kong, and Singapore; and four members of the Association of Southeast Asian Nations (ASEAN), which include Indonesia, the Philippines, Malaysia, and Thailand.[1] I define Japanese FI broadly to include not simply foreign direct investment (FDI) in the form of equity participation in overseas ventures, but also the intermediate forms of FI, such as technology agreements, licensing, and machinery sales that yield knowledge-based assets (Markusen 1992, 31; see also Lipsey 1992, 277).

East Asian regionalism has at least three dimensions: a dynamic division of labor brought about in large part by foreign trade and investment, a set of countries exhibiting increasingly common institutional characteristics, and a regional organization. This paper emphasizes regionalism in the first two senses. My principal argument is that East Asia is becoming a product-based region, one in which Japanese-style institutions show signs of extensive diffusion. Development of a regional division of labor and common production-related institutions has outpaced the growth of ASEAN or other regional organizations. This progress varies, however, across the region.

Richard F. Doner is associate professor of political science at Emory University.

He wishes to thank Alasdair Bowie, Miles Kahler, Greg Noble, Eric Ramstetter, Danny Unger, and participants in the NBER conference for useful comments.

1. ASEAN also includes Singapore and Brunei.

The argument proceeds in five major steps. Section 5.2 examines and largely confirms the argument that Japanese investment has promoted a "dynamic multitier catch-up process" in which the eight countries have become increasingly part of a regional division of labor (e.g., Lo, Song, and Furukawa 1989). I first examine the broad outlines of Japanese (as well as U.S. and NIC) FDI in the region, and then describe structural changes in the national economies and the evolving trade and production interdependencies. Considering the weak evidence for a regional trading bloc in this volume's other papers, the argument here suggests the emergence of a region that is outward-oriented in terms of trade and increasingly integrated in terms of production.

Section 5.3 addresses the supply side of Japanese investment flows to the Pacific Asian region. It explores the position of East Asia within Japan's global investment targets and argues that, despite a relative cut in Japanese funds to the region and a global move away from investments in manufacturing, Japanese FI will continue to promote upgrading in the region's economies and a shifting division of labor. This process has been encouraged by the political economy of structural changes in the Japanese economy itself, and by institutional mechanisms through which Japanese FI flows.

In section 5.4 I take this institutional focus one step further and explore the impact of Japanese investment on domestic institutions of recipient countries. Most observers acknowledge that Japan owes much of its industrial success to production innovations such as "lean production" systems (Womack et al. 1990; see also Yamashita 1991b). Such innovations involve a whole range of cooperative arrangements ranging from "trust-based" subcontracting to business associations, trading companies, and corporatist-like public-private-sector bodies. These can be considered part of the knowledge-based assets Japanese multinationals bring to the region. Section 5.4 explores whether and to what extent such Japanese practices have indeed spilled over into Asian host countries, thus linking the region institutionally.

Section 5.5 proceeds on the assumption that the countries of East Asia are far from passive recipients of FI. They have developed institutions, private as well as public, to resolve the collective action problems involved in screening and absorbing the managerial and technological components of FI. This section thus examines this host country side of the equation—the varying national and regional approaches to and capacities for FI management. This focus helps to explain the different national positions within the regional development hierarchy. It also illustrates the weakness of *regional* responses to FI and suggests that, where such responses emerge, they are consistent with the development of an investment-driven regional division of labor.

The preceeding issues are of course important for the United States in both security and economic terms. Section 5.6 reviews the implications of Japanese investment for U.S. interests.

5.2 Japanese FDI and the Regional Division of Labor[2]

5.2.1 Cumulative Flows

Japanese direct investment in East Asia trailed that of the United States until 1977, when cumulative totals of both countries were roughly $6 billion. This rough parity disappeared in subsequent years as a flood of Japanese investments exceeded even the threefold growth of U.S. funds.[3] On a cumulative basis, Japan is now the most important source of FDI in the region. Japan is the primary investor in Thailand, Indonesia, and South Korea, and the second most important source of FI in Malaysia, the Philippines, Hong Kong, Taiwan, and Singapore (tables 5.1–5.6).

It is true that the share of Japan's investment going to the Asian developing countries actually dropped during the latter 1980s. Up to 1980 the NICs and ASEAN-Four had accounted for 25 percent of Japanese FI. That portion dropped to roughly 12 percent of reported flows between 1986 and 1988, and the region's share of cumulative Japanese flows fell to roughly 17 percent (table 5.7). However, the absolute volume of Japanese capital going to developing Asia has increased significantly, in part as a function of the broader general growth of Japanese overseas investments.[4] Cumulative Japanese flows to the region (including the People's Republic of China) increased from $5.5 billion in 1976 to $19.5 billion in 1985 and $32.3 billion in 1988, an almost sixfold increase in a twelve-year period. The NICs and ASEAN-Four accounted for over 90 percent of these totals. Japanese flows contributed to a steady expansion in overall FI to the eight countries from $2 billion in 1976–80, to $4 billion in 1981–85, and then to $6 billion in 1986, $8 billion in 1987, $12 billion in 1988, and $15 billion in 1988. This expansion of funds to developing Asia stands in marked contrast to lower and in some cases stagnating FI in Africa, Latin America, and the Middle East (Ramstetter 1991a, table 1).

This expansion was also fueled by a significant new source of investment flows—and an important indicator of both changing comparative advantage and regional interdependence—investment funds from the NICs. Both Malaysia and the Philippines saw the relative share of their FDI from the NICs, espe-

2. Any attempt to evaluate the relative importance of diverse FI sources in East Asia must first recognize the severe comparability and validity problems involved. This paper does not pretend to resolve these two problems. As to the first, I hope simply to capture basic patterns of FDI, leaving more nuanced treatments to careful economists (e.g., Ramstetter 1992). I address the validity issue by exploring the technological and institutional benefits of FI captured by host countries. For an extended discussion of these problems see Ramstetter (1991a, 10).

3. Encarnation (1992, 176). Note that these data include investments in China and India. Given Japan's minimal investments in India, these inclusions do suggest patterns at variance with those limited to the NICs and ASEAN-Four. Further discussion of the evolution of Japanese FDI is found in section 5.3.

4. For example, after remaining relatively constant in 1977–80 and rising slightly in 1980–86, the number of Japanese affiliates worldwide roughly *doubled* from 1986 to 1988 (Ramstetter 1991b, 30).

Table 5.1   Cumulative FDI in Developing Asia by Country of Origin (percentage)

	Japan	Hong Kong	United States	Netherlands	Germany	India	Singapore
Indonesia ending Dec. 1986	34.2	12.3	7.9	4.5	3.3	2.9	2.0
Malaysia up to 1985	18.6	6.3	7.0	3.6	N.A.	N.A.	30.3
Philippines							
Up to 1983	16.5	5.9	51.5	4.2	N.A.	N.A.	N.A.
Up to 1986	15.7	6.2	54.0	4.1	N.A.	N.A.	N.A.
Thailand							
Up to 1983	23.1	N.A.	8.9	6.2	N.A.	5.4	N.A.
Up to 1986	20.5	N.A.	19.1	4.4	N.A.	4.2	N.A.
Taiwan 1981–86	20.0	N.A.	34.0	N.A.	N.A.	N.A.	N.A.
South Korea ending June 1987	51.6	4.3	28.6	1.5	1.6	N.A.	N.A.
Hong Kong ending Dec. 1986	20.5	N.A.	41.2	3.7	N.A.	N.A.	1.4
Singapore 1984	23.6	N.A.	30.0	12.8	2.2	N.A.	N.A.

Sources: Figures for Indonesia, Philippines, Thailand, South Korea, Hong Kong, and Singapore are from Japan External Trade Organization, "Foreign Direct Investment of Japan and the Rest of the World" (Tokyo), as cited in Healey (1992). Figures for Malaysia are from Steven 1990, table 6.9; for Taiwan from Lim and Fong 1988, table 10.

Table 5.2   **Cumulative FDI in Developing Asia by Country of Origin (percentage)**

	Indonesia	Australia	South Korea	U.K.	France	Taiwan	Malaysia
Indonesia ending Dec. 1986	N.A.	1.9	1.4	1.4	1.1	N.A.	N.A.
Malaysia up to 1985	N.A.	N.A.	0.08	17.3	N.A.	0.6	N.A.
Philippines							
Up to 1983	N.A.	2.0	N.A.	3.3	1.8	N.A.	N.A.
Up to 1986	N.A.	1.7	N.A.	3.4	1.5	N.A.	N.A.
Thailand							
Up to 1983	N.A.	1.3	N.A.	8.7	N.A.	6.2	N.A.
Up to 1986	N.A.	6.4	N.A.	5.3	N.A.	6.2	N.A.
Taiwan 1981–86	N.A.	N.A.	N.A.	N.A.	N.A.	N.A.	N.A.
South Korea ending June 1987	N.A.	N.A.	N.A.	2.7	1.2	N.A.	N.A.
Hong Kong ending Dec. 1986	N.A.	N.A.	N.A.	5.5	N.A.	N.A.	N.A.
Singapore 1984	N.A.	N.A.	N.A.	13.1	N.A.	N.A.	N.A.

Sources: Figures for Indonesia, Philippines, Thailand, South Korea, Hong Kong, and Singapore are from Japan External Trade organization, "Foreign Direct Investment of Japan and the Rest of the World" (Tokyo), as cited in Healey (1992). Figures for Malaysia from Steven 1990, table 6.9; for Taiwan from Lim and Fong 1988, table 10.

Table 5.3   **Cumulative FDI in Developing Asia by Country of Origin (percentage)**

	Philippines	Thailand	Switzerland	Canada	Panama
Indonesia ending Dec. 1986	N.A.	N.A.	N.A.	N.A.	N.A.
Malaysia up to 1985	N.A.	N.A.	N.A.	N.A.	N.A.
Philippines					
Up to 1983	N.A.	N.A.	2.7	2.0	N.A.
Up to 1986	N.A.	N.A.	2.5	1.6	N.A.
Thailand					
Up to 1983	N.A.	N.A.	N.A.	N.A.	5.4
Up to 1986	N.A.	N.A.	N.A.	N.A.	3.9
Taiwan 1981–86	N.A.	N.A.	N.A.	N.A.	N.A.
South Korea ending June 1987	N.A.	N.A.	N.A.	N.A.	N.A.
Hong Kong ending Dec. 1986	1.8	N.A.	1.7	N.A.	N.A.
Singapore 1984	N.A.	N.A.	2.7	N.A.	N.A.

Sources: Figures for Indonesia, Philippines, Thailand, South Korea, Hong Kong, and Singapore are from Japan External Trade Organization, "Foreign Direct Investment of Japan and the rest of the World" (Tokyo), as cited in Healey (1992). Figures from Malaysia from Steven 1990, table 6.9; for Taiwan from Lim and Fong 1988, table 10.

cially Taiwan, grow over threefold in the 1986–90 period.[5] Thailand and Indonesia experienced similar, albeit smaller, increases in the NICs' share of investment flows (table 5.8). In fact, 1988 NIC investment in the ASEAN-Four

---

5. At least some of the funds from Taiwan are reportedly recycled domestic capital from Malaysian Chinese restricted from investments in Malaysia. This further illustrates, however, the ways in which the region's economies may be gradually integrated despite legal impediments.

Table 5.4   **Cumulative FDI in Indonesia by Country of Origin (percentage)**

	Gross Investment Approvals, 1985–88	Realized Investment, 1967–88 (foreign equity)
Total (in millions of U.S. $)	7,563	6,687
Japan	16.4	30.0
Asian NICs	27.1	11.2
Hong Kong	6.0	8.8
Korea	4.0	1.4
Singapore	4.7	0.6
Taiwan	12.4	0.5
Other ASEAN	0.5	0.5
Malaysia	0.3	0.3
Philippines	0.1	0.1
Thailand	0.05	0.2
United States	14.0	4.3
Australia	1.3	1.5
Other	40.7	52.5

Source: Adapted from Pangestu 1992, table 3.4

Note: Gross investment approvals are new investments and expansion.

Table 5.5   **Cumulative FDI in Taiwan by Country of Origin, 1952–86, Share of Total (percentage)**

	1952–60	1961–70	1971–80	1981–86	1952–86
Total (in millions of U.S. dollars)	35.2	523.1	2,158.7	3,211.6	5,930.2
Overseas Chinese	29	29	37	8	21
Foreign nationals	71	71	63	92	79
United States	67	42	25	34	31
Japan	4	17	17	20	23
Europe	0	7	10	14	12
Others	0	5	11	15	12

Source: Reproduced from Lim and Fong (1988, table 10).

Note: Totals may not add up to 100 percent because of rounding.

exceeded that of Japan and was expanding more rapidly: these four countries contributed 31 percent of new ASEAN projects compared to Japan's 30 percent and increased their commitments by 334 percent compared to Japan's 125 percent (Holloway 1989, 71). Thus, as the ASEAN-Four have gained a comparative advantage in labor-intensive industries due to rising wages and currency appreciation in the NICs, investment from the latter has moved south (Kohama and Urata 1988, 333). In the case of the two largest NIC investors, Hong Kong and Taiwan, these flows have been facilitated by overseas Chinese networks.[6]

6. South Korea's low level of FDI relative to the other three NICs reflects at least two factors: its lack of a "Chinese connection" and the ability of the dominant *chaebol* to sustain higher costs

Table 5.6   **Cumulative FDI in Thailand by Country of Origin, 1974–89 (percentage)**

	1974	1981	1986	1989
Total (in millions of U.S. dollars)	$416	$1,282	$2,662	$5,871
Japan	28.0	27.4	29.5	37.2
United States	38.5	34.0	31.0	21.0
Other OECD	11.8	14.0	15.7	13.2
Europe	11.3	13.2	14.8	12.6
United Kingdom	5.5	5.7	5.3	3.3
West Germany	0.7	3.2	2.7	2.5
France	1.7	1.0	1.1	1.2
Netherlands	2.9	1.6	4.0	3.1
Switzerland	0.5	1.6	1.8	2.5
Australia	0.5	0.8	0.9	0.5
NICS	16.6	18.8	16.0	23.0
Hong Kong	11.1	10.5	10.3	11.1
Singapore	5.3	8.1	5.0	5.4
Taiwan	0.5	0.2	0.6	6.2
Other ASEAN-Four	1.7	1.2	0.9	0.5
Malaysia	1.2	1.0	0.8	0.4
Philippines	0.5	0.2	0.04	0.02
Other	3.6	4.8	7.2	4.1

Source: Adapted from Tambunlertchai and Ramstetter (1992, table 4.3).
Note: The figure for total FDI is year-end stock.

Finally, note that while U.S. investment flows did increase in the early 1980s, they largely stagnated in the last half of the decade (table 5.9). This pattern results in part from the fact that developing Asia is less important for U.S. multinationals than it is for Japanese multinationals. For example, U.S. affiliates in Asia accounted for 0.5–0.7 percent of U.S. employment and 7–8 percent of U.S. affiliate employment worldwide, whereas the ratios for Japan were 0.8 percent of employment and 50–54 percent of affiliate employment worldwide (Plummer and Ramstetter 1992, table 9.1).

5.2.2   Industry Concentration

The manufacturing emphasis of Japanese FI seems to have contributed to, as well as reflected, the region's dynamic division of labor. By 1988 Japanese manufacturing investments had become twice the size of comparable U.S. investments and constituted a larger share of total Japanese FDI in the region. This emphasis on manufacturing was not static, however; Japanese investment has become increasingly diversified across industries and countries, indeed

---

without moving overseas due to their high levels of R&D and financial strengths. Indeed, Lall argues that Korean FDI reflects "growing industrial strength rather than, as in Hong Kong or Singapore, domestic deindustrialization" (1991, 23).

Table 5.7   Japanese FDI Abroad: Net Flows and Reported Flows

Year	Net Flows[a] Total Amount	OECD Share	Total Non-OECD Share	Reported Flows[b] Total Amount	OECD share	Total Non-OECD Share	Developing Asia Share	Latin America Share	Africa and Middle East Share
1972	723	62.7	37.3	2,338	58.7	41.3	17.2	12.1	11.5
1973	1,904	60.8	39.2	3,494	40.4	59.6	28.6	23.5	6.2
1974	2,012	56.7	43.3	2,395	34.6	65.4	30.5	29.2	5.0
1975	1,763	48.7	51.3	3,280	38.8	61.2	33.6	11.3	11.8
1976	1,991	49.5	50.5	3,462	35.3	64.7	36.0	12.1	15.9
1977	1,645	49.2	50.8	2,806	39.4	60.6	30.8	16.3	13.0
1978	2,371	48.4	51.6	4,598	41.2	58.8	29.1	13.4	15.6
1979	2,898	48.5	51.5	4,995	48.5	51.5	19.5	24.2	6.0
1980	2,385	59.0	41.0	4,693	55.6	44.4	25.3	12.5	6.3
1981	4,894	66.1	33.9	8,932	41.7	58.3	37.4	13.2	7.5
1982	4,540	61.8	38.2	7,703	54.3	45.7	18.0	19.5	8.0
1983	3,612	61.3	38.7	8,145	47.5	52.5	22.7	23.1	6.6

1984	5,965	68.1	31.9	10,155	55.1	44.9	16.0	22.6	5.9
1985	6,452	69.9	30.1	12,217	64.7	35.3	11.7	21.4	1.8
1986	14,480	78.5	21.5	22,320	66.6	33.4	10.4	21.2	1.6
1987	19,519	76.4	23.6	33,364	69.5	30.5	14.6	14.4	1.0
1988	34,210	81.2	18.8	47,022	72.0	28.0	11.8	13.7	1.9
Average annual flows									
1965–71	207	56.3	43.7	521	54.1	45.9	22.9	13.4	8.0
1972–80	1,966	52.9	47.1	3,562	44.1	55.9	27.6	17.0	10.0
1981–85	5,093	66.1	33.9	9,430	53.6	46.4	20.4	20.1	5.6
1986–88	22,736	79.3	20.7	34,235	70.0	30.0	12.4	15.6	1.6
Cumulative flows									
1965–71	1,447	56.3	43.7	3,645	54.1	45.9	22.9	13.4	8.0
1965–80	19,139	53.2	46.8	35,706	45.1	54.9	27.1	16.7	9.8
1965–85	44,602	60.5	39.5	82,858	49.9	50.1	23.3	18.6	7.4
1965–88	112,811	71.9	28.1	185,564	61.1	38.9	17.3	16.9	4.2

Source: Bank of Japan and Japan Ministry of Finance, cited in Ramstetter (1991b, table 1).

Note: Amounts in millions of U.S. dollars; shares in percentage.

[a]Data refer to calendar years.

[b]Data refer to fiscal years ending March 31 of following calendar year.

Table 5.8   **Shares of FDI in ASEAN-Four, 1986–90 (percentage)**

	Total	Japan	NICs	Korea	Taiwan	Hong Kong	Singapore	U.K.	U.S.	China
Indonesia										
1986	100.0	39.8	27.6	1.5	2.2	11.6	12.3	N.A.	18.6	N.A.
1987	100.0	36.5	11.8	1.6	0.5	9.3	0.4	N.A.	5.0	N.A.
1988	100.0	5.6	36.0	4.5	20.6	5.4	5.4	N.A.	15.2	N.A.
1989	100.0	16.3	25.4	9.9	3.3	8.6	3.5	N.A.	7.4	N.A.
1990	100.0	13.3	34.7	6.4	8.5	15.8	4.0	N.A.	0.3	N.A.
Malaysia										
1986	100.0	6.9	15.1	0.3	0.6	3.4	10.9	2.9	3.2	N.A.
1987	100.0	34.7	28.9	0.2	11.7	4.3	12.6	3.8	7.9	N.A.
1988	100.0	25.1	32.6	0.9	17.0	6.1	8.6	4.0	11.0	N.A.
1989	100.0	31.1	41.8	2.2	25.0	4.1	10.6	8.8	3.7	N.A.
1990	100.0	12.0	54.9	0.7	48.4	3.0	2.6	4.2	1.4	N.A.
Philippines										
1986	100.0	28.2	9.6	0.0	0.4	9.0	N.A.	N.A.	28.2	2.6
1987	100.0	17.4	23.4	0.6	5.4	16.8	N.A.	N.A.	21.6	4.8
1988	100.0	20.3	30.0	0.4	23.3	5.7	N.A.	N.A.	32.3	5.5
1989	100.0	19.7	40.2	2.1	18.5	16.5	N.A.	N.A.	16.3	4.2
1990	100.0	37.1	31.3	1.7	23.4	5.6	N.A.	N.A.	6.0	2.3
Thailand										
1986	100.0	58.2	40.7	27.3	0.1	7.2	6.1	13.9	17.2	N.A.
1987	100.0	36.6	35.6	19.0	0.5	11.4	4.7	2.4	6.5	N.A.
1988	100.0	48.7	51.0	26.9	1.7	13.6	8.7	4.4	10.8	N.A.
1989	100.0	44.1	45.2	25.2	2.1	10.9	7.0	5.1	6.9	N.A.
1990	100.0	34.6	60.2	34.7	4.4	7.3	13.9	9.2	15.3	N.A.

Source: International Centre for the Study of East Asian Development Symposium, cited in Tan, Heng, and Low (1991, table 9)

Table 5.9   **U.S. Outward FI to East Asia, 1986–89 (millions of U.S. dollars)**

	Average 1976–80	Average 1981–85	1986	1987	1988	1989
Asian NICs	428	560	1,088	1,175	1,153	1,033
Hong Kong	211	289	720	321	707	370
Korea	8	20	68	190	237	222
Singapore	155	192	217	226	5	162
Taiwan	54	59	83	367	204	279
ASEAN-Four	161	772	54	−180	−143	996
Indonesia	−17	609	44	−310	−251	757
Malaysia	33	87	−55	−67	167	−32
Philippines	114	−33	66	9	90	155
Thailand	30	109	0	188	−149	116
China	N.A.	70	−116	102	96	54

Source: U.S. Department of Commerce, cited in Ramstetter (1991a, table 6).

Table 5.10   **Japanese FI Distribution across Sectors**

	Manufacturing	Mining	Trade	Other
Global				
1976	31.3	25.0	13.5	30.2
1985	29.2	14.1	15.2	78.7
1988	24.7	7.5	10.7	55.0
Asian NICs				
1976	60.8	0.24	8.3	30.6
1985	43.4	0.17	10.2	46.2
1988	36.9	0.09	10.1	52.9
ASEAN-Four				
1976	31.5	56.5	0.8	11.1
1985	35.8	54.3	2.4	7.5
1988	42.5	46.0	2.4	9.06

Source: Adapted from Ramstetter (1991b, table 3).

more so than U.S. investments (Encarnation 1992, 177–78). Together the industry and geographical distributions of Japanese FDI seem to mirror the region's evolving comparative advantage.

Manufacturing traditionally constituted a major portion of Japanese FDI in the NICs, 61 percent in 1976 (table 5.10). But this portion declined to 37 percent in 1988, while other industries (presumably non-trade-related services such as finance) became a more important focus of Japanese investment, expanding from 31 percent to 53 percent. Mining was never an important component of Japanese investment in the NICs. This shift away from manufacturing investments in the NICs does vary somewhat by country.[7] Hong Kong, South Korea, and Singapore all saw the percentage of Japanese FI in manufacturing reduced by at least 25 percent, and in none of these three does manufacturing investment account for more than 52 percent of cumulative Japanese FDI (table 5.11). In Taiwan, however, the concentration of manufacturing investment fell only 12 percent, with manufacturing investment accounting for 82 percent of all Japanese investment as of 1988.

Unlike in the NICs, the manufacturing component of Japanese FDI in the ASEAN-Four has tended to expand, from 32 percent to 43 percent (table 5.11). Again, however, there is cross-national variation (based on Ramstetter 1991b, table 3). Manufacturing investment in Indonesia has increased, from 25 percent to 30 percent, but remains the lowest of the ASEAN-Four because of the continued large volume of funds flowing to the Indonesian petroleum sector (mining accounts for some 63 percent of Japanese FI). Between 1976 and 1988, manufacturing has risen from 57 percent to 74 percent of Japanese flows in Malaysia and 26 percent to 45 percent in the Philippines. The portion of

7. This paragraph draws on data from Ramstetter (1991b, table 3).

Table 5.11   **Cumulative Reported Flows of Japanese FDI**

	Manufacturing, Percentage of All Industries		
	1976	1985	1988
Asian NICs	61.0	43.0	37.0
Hong Kong	6.2	8.4	7.97
Korea	70.0	56.0	49.0
Singapore	72.0	64.0	52.0
Taiwan	93.0	89.6	82.0
ASEAN-Four	31.5	35.8	43.0
Indonesia	25.2	27.7	30.0
Malaysia	57.6	70.3	73.6
Philippines	26.0	39.7	45.5
Thailand	75.0	70.0	73.0

Source: Adapted from Ramstetter (1991b, table 3).

manufacturing dropped slightly in Thailand but continues to account for the majority of Japanese FDI, shifting from 75 percent in 1976 to 73 percent in 1988.

Another indication of the role of Japanese investment in the region's changing structure of comparative advantage is the emphasis on what may be termed early, middle, and late industries. Applying Ramstetter's data (1991b, table 3) to the classification developed by Lo, Song, and Furukawa (1989), trends seem to be the following:[8] For the Asian NICs, cumulative Japanese FI shifted away from early industries toward middle and late industries between 1975 and 1988. Much of the reduction in early-industry concentration was due to a drop in emphasis on textiles. The increase in the middle industry reflects growth in investment in the chemical industries of Korea and Singapore. Growth in late-industry investments is due to increased concentration of Japanese FI in machinery, electrical machinery, and transport machinery in Hong Kong and South Korea and in transport machinery in Taiwan. Singapore, on the other hand, saw a reduced share of investment in basic metals, machinery, electrical machinery, and transport machinery. Thus for the NICs, Japanese FI seems to have shifted further along the product cycle by first moving out of manufacturing into the service industries and by increasingly concentrating on late industries within manufacturing.

The most dramatic shift for the ASEAN-Four is between early and late industries. In 1975 early industries accounted for almost 46 percent of cumula-

8. As presented in Lo, Song, and Furukawa (1989, 115), early industries include food, certain textiles, and leather. Middle industries include certain wood products, chemicals, petroleum, and nonmetallic products. Late industries include apparel, paper and printing, metal products, industrial and electrical machinery, and transport equipment.

tive Japanese manufacturing FI, but by 1988 this had dropped to 19.3 percent, while the proportion of late industries rose from almost 38 percent to 66 percent in the same period. These shifts reflected a reduction in Japanese emphasis on textiles (as in the NICs), and country-specific growth in different manufacturing industries. Indonesia saw Japanese investment in basic metals rise from 16.9 percent of total manufacturing investment to 47.7 percent but remained essentially stable across other categories. Malaysia saw the largest increase in electrical and transport machinery, with the former doubling its relative share and the latter growing from under 2 percent to over 13 percent of the total. The Philippines experienced a similar increase in transport-machinery investment, up from 4.2 percent in 1976 to 26.7 percent in 1988. Thailand saw increases in basic metals, machinery, and electrical machinery. Thus for ASEAN, Japanese investment evolved both away from mining toward manufacturing, and within manufacturing toward a concentration in the late industries.

Finally, shifts in the industry distribution of Japanese FDI are reflected in the production of Japanese affiliates in developing Asia.[9] In 1977 Asia accounted for 42.6 percent of Japanese manufacturing sales worldwide, with roughly 27 percent of these sales in textiles and apparel, 25 percent in electrical machinery, and only around 11 percent in transport machinery. By 1988 Asia's contribution to Japanese worldwide manufacturing sales had dropped to roughly one-third, but textiles accounted for only 8.4 percent of these sales, while the shares of electrical machinery and transport machinery had risen to 34.4 percent and 22.8 percent, respectively. In the Asian NICs, electrical machinery accounted for 40.4 percent of gross sales in 1988, followed by transport machinery with 18.2 percent and textiles and apparel with only 7.5 percent. In the ASEAN countries, transport machinery accounted for 25 percent of gross sales in 1988, followed closely by electrical machinery, accounting for 23.3 percent, with textile and apparel accounting for 12.1 percent.

As implied in the preceding paragraphs, the industry diversification of Japanese FDI has been accompanied by geographical diversity. In 1988 Singapore moved up to second place as a target of Japanese manufacturing investment. Yet it accounted for only one-sixth of such investment, compared to one-third for the United States. As a result Singapore "represents less of a regional manufacturing center for the Japanese than for the Americans."[10] Consistent with the shift of Japanese manufacturing investments south to the ASEAN-Four has been the expanding role of Thailand: in 1988 Thailand's manufacturing sector attracted more new Japanese investment than did the combined manufacturing sectors of the four NICs.

5.2.3   Trade Orientations of Japanese Overseas Investments

Broadly speaking, Japanese affiliates in East Asia have gradually become more export-oriented, with a trend toward greater exports back to Japan, an

9. This paragraph draws on data presented in Ramstetter (1991b, table 14).
10. Encarnation (1992, 178), from which the rest of this paragraph is drawn.

emphasis on labor-intensive exports, and a tendency toward greater linkages with local sources of inputs.

Compared to U.S. firms, Japanese investors have emphasized sales to host country markets rather than back to Japan or to third countries. In 1977 and 1988 some 60 percent of Japanese subsidiary sales in East Asia went to host country markets, whereas the role of host country markets for U.S. subsidiaries dropped from roughly 40 percent in 1977 to around 23 percent in 1988. Host country markets accounted for roughly 40 percent of sales of manufactured goods by U.S. subsidiaries in the region in both 1977 and 1988, compared to levels of some 65 percent and 60 percent for Japanese subsidiaries (Encarnation 1992, 155, 175). However, these relative figures do not reflect the significant absolute growth of exports by Japanese subsidiaries, especially since the Plaza Accord's yen appreciation in 1985. Since then, Japanese FDI in developing Asia has been increasingly oriented toward the exploitation of comparative advantage rather than simple maintenance of host country market. Exports by Japanese affiliates in Asia expanded over sixfold, compared to threefold growth for all Japanese affiliates.[11] The growth of manufactured exports for all affiliates was somewhat greater (over sevenfold) than that for Asian affiliates (over fivefold).

Exports of manufactured goods by Japanese affiliates have generally emphasized third-country markets over sales to the Japanese home market. But exports to Japan did expand slightly, from roughly 7 percent in 1977 to around 13 percent in 1988 (Encarnation 1992, 175, 181). More significant growth in exports to the home market has occurred in electrical machinery and other manufacturers, although even in electronics Japanese subsidiaries are less reliant on their home market than are U.S. affiliates. The growth of Japanese affiliate exports has been most pronounced in labor-intensive industries and in the NICs, not in the ASEAN countries (Ramstetter 1991b, 71). This consistency between exports and relative factor supplies and technology levels is also seen in U.S. affiliates but seems to be more pronounced for the Japanese (Lipsey 1992, 281–86). Although electronics occupies an important position in the exports of both Japanese and U.S. affiliates, the Japanese export emphasis is reportedly closer to that of local firms than is that of U.S. affiliates. The Japanese concentration in machinery exports is not as strong as that of the United States. And, as noted earlier, the Japanese tend to be more concentrated in other manufacturing, which includes textiles and apparel.

As to affiliate imports and the ratio of imports to local purchases, Japanese *trade* affiliates account for a declining but still sizable percentage of imports from Japan, down from 85 percent to 72 percent worldwide and 54 percent to 49 percent in Asia (Ramstetter 1991b, 80). There is a general trend toward lower import/purchase ratios in Asian affiliates, whereas these ratios stayed

11. Unless otherwise noted, information on exports and imports is drawn from Ramstetter (1991a, 1991b, especially table 20).

constant in affiliates worldwide. Import/purchase ratios vary somewhat by industry, being naturally higher for machinery than for food. The ratio also varies by region and country. Ratios for manufacturing affiliates in the NICs were "relatively low" but "relatively high" for affiliates in the ASEAN countries (here including Singapore). By 1988 NIC affiliates import ratios were low in electrical machinery and transport machinery relative to affiliates worldwide and in ASEAN, thus suggesting that NIC affiliates "have developed more extensive ties with local suppliers than elsewhere" (Ramstetter 1991b, 81). However, Japanese manufacturing affiliates in the NICs obtained a much larger portion of their imports from Japan than did affiliates in the ASEAN countries.[12] Finally, imports from Japan as a percentage of all Japanese manufacturing affiliate imports in Asia were high and growing, from 72 percent in 1980 to 78 percent in 1986 and 1988. In sum, although Japan remains a major source of inputs for Asian affiliates, the latter have gradually increased their links to host country economies, albeit with significant cross-national and cross-industry variation.

5.2.4   National Structural Change and Regional Division of Labor

There is no clear proof of a consistent relationship between Japanese investment in Asia on the one hand and the pattern of comparative advantage in developing Asia or Japan on the other (Ramstetter 1991b, 98). That said, it is presumably possible at least to identify general patterns of association between investment flows and indicators of change in the regional division of labor. I proceed first by examining structural changes in the region's national economies and indicators of shifting regional comparative advantage. I then examine some possible causal linkages between investment, trade, labor migration, and shifting comparative advantage.

The impressive changes occurring within the NICs and ASEAN-Four need little elaboration. Measured most crudely, the share of manufacturing in GDP has risen by at least 42 percent for six of the eight countries, the exceptions being Hong Kong and the Philippines, both of which were at fairly high levels by the mid-1960s (table 5.12).

These structural changes have translated into shifts in comparative advantage consistent with the flying geese analogy. That model involves each country capturing "increasingly sophisticated products from more advanced economies, which in turn are shifting their attention to still more advanced products" (Petri 1992a, 54). Several kinds of evidence seem to support the flying geese dynamic. One is Petri's calculation of the sophistication exhibited by the export bundle of different economies in developing Asia. Shifts in market shares between 1970 and 1986 suggest considerable dynamism consistent with dynamic comparative advantage (Petri 1992a, 56). Petri's general argument is reinforced

---

12. Since Ramstetter's data do not include country-specific figures, it's unclear whether excluding Singapore from ASEAN would make a difference (see 1991b, table 23).

Table 5.12   Share of Manufacturing in GDP, 1965–89

	1965	1989	Change (%)
United States	29	20	−31.03
United Kingdom	30	22	−26.67
France	29	25	−13.79
Germany	40	31	−22.50
Australia	28	17	−39.29
Japan	32	30	−6.25
NICs			
Korea	19	28	47.37
Hong Kong	24	24	00.00
Taiwan	20	36	79.97
Singapore	15	24	60.00
ASEAN-Four			
Malaysia	9	19	111.11
Indonesia	8	14	75.00
Thailand	14	20	42.86
Philippines	20	25	25.00

Source: World Bank, *World Development Report, 1987,* cited in Lo, Song, and Furukawa (1989, 86, table 1).

by evidence showing the NICs moving away from and the ASEAN countries moving toward unskilled labor-intensive products (table 5.13; see Alburo, Bautista, and Gochoco 1992).

The result has been an increasingly horizontal and intrafirm division of labor. Rather than the U.S.-European intraindustry trade driven by demand for differentiated products, FDI in Asia has promoted a more vertical type of horizontal trade involving the exchange of goods within similar industries at different stages of assembly or processing. This is reflected in (1) the expansion of NIC exports to Southeast Asia (Fransman 1986a, 170–71), (2) the expanded share of manufactures in Japan's imports from the NICs and especially ASEAN (tables 5.14 and 5.15), and (3) the increasing dependence of the NICs and ASEAN-Four on Japan for industrial goods.[13] The emergence of a horizontal division of labor has been especially sharp in the steel and textile industries. According to recent MITI figures, South Korea and Taiwan account for nearly half of Japan's steel imports, whereas Japan exports almost half of its higher-value steel and iron products to Taiwan and South Korea as well as to Singapore and the rest of ASEAN (do Rosario 1992, 38). In many cases, this regional division of labor occurs within firms as production departments move abroad and R&D and planning departments are strengthened at home (Nakakita 1988, 318). Indeed, Encarnation argues that intracompany trade is more characteristic of Japanese than of U.S. multinationals (1991, 9).

13. According to a recent MITI report, manufactured exports from the ASEAN-Four have been more successful in penetrating the Japanese market than those of the NICs (do Rosario 1992, 38).

Table 5.13   **Revealed Comparative Advantage Indexes**

	Year	Indonesia	Malaysia	Philippines	Thailand	Japan	Hong Kong	Korea	Singapore	Taiwan
Unskilled labor-intensive	1970	N.A.	0.15	0.08	0.21	2.61	7.10	5.43	0.94	N.A.
	1976	0.01	0.29	0.84	1.29	1.38	6.91	6.06	0.94	N.A.
	1980	0.07	0.44	1.29	1.63	1.17	6.48	5.63	0.93	6.14
	1985	0.45	0.56	0.67	1.89	0.89	5.74	4.18	0.72	5.58
Human capital-intensive	1970	0.02	0.12	N.A.	0.03	1.62	0.45	0.20	0.39	N.A.
	1976	0.001	0.10	0.02	0.05	2.25	0.70	0.76	0.61	N.A.
	1980	N.A.	0.12	0.05	0.13	2.42	1.23	1.19	0.51	0.81
	1985	N.A.	0.04	0.02	0.14	2.10	0.87	1.84	0.43	0.78
Technology-intensive	1970	N.A.	0.04	0.003	N.A.	2.46	1.59	0.62	0.63	N.A.
	1976	N.A.	0.64	0.041	0.17	2.10	2.06	1.39	1.75	N.A.
	1980	0.04	0.98	0.14	0.52	2.13	1.59	1.46	1.80	1.81
	1985	0.05	1.39	0.78	0.54	2.08	1.45	1.16	1.19	1.44
Physical capital-intensive	1970	0.05	0.93	0.06	0.53	1.37	0.13	1.16	0.26	N.A.
	1976	0.05	0.68	0.20	0.31	1.68	0.18	0.39	0.45	N.A.
	1980	0.12	0.58	0.25	0.65	1.80	0.23	0.74	0.56	0.43
	1985	0.24	0.40	0.42	0.23	1.50	0.44	0.53	0.59	0.48

Source: Chen (1989).

Table 5.14   Changes in Export and Import Structure of Japan

	1970	1975	1980	1985	1988
Export structure					
Textiles	12.5	6.7	4.9	3.6	2.6
Chemical	6.4	7.0	5.2	4.4	5.2
Metal	19.7	22.4	16.4	10.5	8.2
Machinery	46.3	53.8	62.8	71.8	74.3
Office machines	1.7	1.4	1.8	4.4	6.9
Semiconductors	0.4	0.8	1.8	2.7	4.7
Videotape recorders	—	—	1.5	3.8	2.3
Cars	6.9	11.1	17.9	19.6	18.4
Import structure					
Foodstuff	13.6	15.2	10.5	12.0	15.5
Raw material	35.4	20.1	16.9	13.9	15.0
Mineral fuels	20.7	44.3	49.8	43.1	20.5
Chemical	5.3	3.6	4.4	6.2	7.9
Machinery	12.2	7.4	7.0	9.6	14.2
Official machine	1.7	0.9	0.7	1.2	1.8
Other manufactures	12.8	7.4	11.4	15.2	26.9
Iron and steel	1.5	0.3	0.6	1.1	2.5
Textile	1.7	2.3	2.3	3.0	5.8
Manufactures subtotal	30.3	18.4	22.8	31.0	49.0

Source: Japan Tariff Association, cited in Yamazawa (1990, table 2).
Notes: Percentage of total export and import values. Manufactures subtotal is the sum of chemical, machinery, and other manufactures.

Table 5.15   Share of Manufactures in Japan's Imports

	1970	1975	1980	1985	1986
Asian NICs	38.1	52.2	57.3	57.3	61.7
Taiwan	34.4	44.7	55.2	57.0	54.8
Korea	42.3	61.2	73.0	64.0	68.9
Hong Kong	67.4	79.8	78.7	84.1	85.1
Singapore	6.2	21.6	20.7	27.6	40.2
ASEAN-Four	2.1	2.6	3.2	4.8	7.7
Malaysia	2.7	4.0	4.4	5.8	7.4
Thailand	6.5	10.6	14.7	21.7	22.3
Philippines	1.7	2.4	10.6	13.7	14.1
Indonesia	0.7	0.4	0.7	1.6	4.0
China	24.9	20.4	22.4	25.8	34.2
LDC total	7.1	7.5	8.3	13.6	21.5
World total	25.3	18.1	19.3	26.7	35.3

Source: Institute for Developing Economies Trade Data Search System, cited in Hirata and Nohara (1989).
Note: Manufactures include SITC less 68.

Finally, this Japanese-driven division of labor has entailed a wave of labor migration throughout the region. Some two million workers from East and Southeast Asia have left home to take work, not just as domestic helpers or unskilled labor, but as accountants and machine tool operators and cooks. As the Japanese work force has aged and moved into higher-technology areas, severe labor shortages have plagued the country's construction and basic industries. The Japanese work force reportedly now includes some 38,000 "trainees" from the region, over 150,000 ethnic Japanese foreigners, and an unknown number of illegal entrants. A similar pattern has occurred in Taiwan and South Korea. In Malaysia some 50 percent of construction and plantation workers are foreigners (mostly Indonesians), and manufacturers have begun to bring in foreign workers. Indonesia, itself an important source of labor flows to other countries, has been forced to employ Filipinos and other foreigners in white-collar and professional positions. Although these flows have the potential to generate numerous social tensions, they will also encourage further shifts up the product-cycle ladder. Labor shortages will encourage countries to improve productivity through technical innovation, while workers returning to Southeast Asia from Japan, Taiwan, and South Korea will constitute a source of new skills ("Asian Labor Shortages" 1992).

The preceding discussion presents only the general outlines of the ways in which Japanese FI influences the region's division of labor. In fact, the impact will vary by industry, as well as country. The following two cases provide some sense of this variation.

Textile and Apparel Industries

The evolution of the region's textile and apparel complex is probably the most advanced of all industries. Between 1968 and 1977 Japan's total textile and apparel trade with East Asia increased by over twofold, but its trade surplus with them declined by roughly one-half (Arpan, Barry, and Tho 1984). By 1972 textile and apparel exports of South Korea, Taiwan, and Hong Kong exceeded those of Japan for the first time, and widened considerably by 1977. By the end of this period, Japan maintained a comparative advantage in up-stream and midstream activities (e.g., yarns, fibers, and fabrics) but rapidly lost competitiveness in apparel. The NICs, on the other hand, expanded surpluses in apparel and began to catch up with Japan in synthetic fiber products, whereas the ASEAN countries gained competitiveness in apparel.

By 1987 Japan maintained an overall surplus in textiles but experienced increased competition from the NICs. NIC textile and apparel products increased their penetration of Japanese markets, prompting both intensified diversification by the stronger Japanese firms and demands for protection by others.[14]

---

14. Import penetration ratios for textile products between 1984 and 1987 went from 25.1 percent to 34.5 percent: for yarn from 11.6 percent to 13.7 percent, for cloth outergarments from 23.2 percent to 34.1 percent, and for knit outergarments from 26.7 percent to 46.7 percent (JICA 1989, A-III-1). On diversification see Johnstone (1988). On charges of dumping and demands for protection, see "When Japan Is Threatened by Imports" (1988).

The ASEAN countries, meanwhile, rapidly expanded apparel exports while some moved into midstream and upstream operations. Thailand, for example, was 100 percent self-sufficient in cloth made from synthetic fiber and 85 percent self-sufficient in synthetic yarn by the early 1970s (JICA 1989, II-1).

From the Japanese perspective, the textile and apparel complex is perhaps the quintessential example of the product cycle. This relatively rapid shift in comparative advantage was due to at least three factors, one of which involved the relatively low entry barriers for Asian firms in certain sectors of the industry. A second factor was Japan's effective restructuring of its own textile capacity and its low levels of protection, leading to a general reduction in textiles position within Japanese manufacturing (JICA 1989). And finally, these regional shifts reflected Japan's focus on East Asia as its primary focus of textile and apparel FI. Some 64 percent of the cases of Japanese FI in textiles between 1955 and 1985 were in the NICs and the ASEAN-Four (UNCTC 1987, 136). As host country firms have expanded their own capacity, however, the Japanese presence seems to have declined.[15] Simultaneously, textile investment from the NICs, especially Hong Kong and Taiwan, has expanded, in some cases bringing technology as well as capital (Tho 1988, 397). In some cases this has occurred via linkages with larger Japanese firms.[16]

Automobile Industry

The auto industry lies at the other end of the spectrum from textiles and apparel. As the share of textiles in Japanese manufacturing and exports declined, the role of autos and auto parts grew.[17] Auto exports (parts and components) by the NIC and ASEAN countries expanded as well, albeit much more slowly and from a smaller base. The East Asian countries, especially South Korea and Taiwan, accounted for between 5 percent and 9 percent of Japanese auto part imports in 1987. However, given the very low overall level of Japanese part imports, this is not a very large volume. Also, until recently the Japanese have not had much of an overseas manufacturing (as opposed to assembly) presence. Preferring to service overseas markets through exports, not offshore production, Toyota and Nissan had a combined average of only 1 per-

15. According to Plummer and Ramstetter (1992, 250), affiliate export shares declined in Taiwan and Thailand. Also, affiliate employment levels and shares of host country employment fell for South Korea, Taiwan, and Thailand.

16. The prime example of this pattern is Toray's tie-up with TAL in the 1970s. The latter, a Hong Kong-based textile converter, already had subsidiaries in Taiwan and Thailand. The two firms established several more subsidiaries in Thailand, Hong Kong, and Malaysia and by the mid-1970s had created a vertically integrated complex in the region (Arpan, Barry, and Tho, 1984, 139).

17. Transport equipment expanded as a percentage of total Japanese manufacturing from 5.3 percent in 1950 to 14 percent in 1987 (Tahara-Domoto and Kohama 1989, 3). Japanese exports of auto parts grew even more sharply, from a total of $3.8 billion to $15.5 billion from 1980 to 1987, compared with an increase of U.S. exports from $10.5 billion to $14.3 billion (auto parts = SITC 732.8 [bodies, chassis, and parts] and 7111.5 [internal combustion engines]; UNCTAD 1990, table 3).

cent of their production abroad in 1980, compared to 35 percent for the U.S. Big Three. And unlike U.S. firms, Japanese assemblers preferred not to export from their overseas plants or those of their East Asian partners (Doner 1991, 64). Quite clearly, regional shifts in comparative advantage in the auto industry have been much slower than in textiles (or in electrical equipment).

The regional production and trade of auto products is, however, far from stagnant. For one thing, Japanese assemblers and parts firms have helped to develop a modest automotive industrial base in the region through a fairly long history of operation in most of the countries. Toyota was involved in an early joint venture in South Korea, and Mitsubishi has established a close relationship with Hyundai. Until the proliferation of Japanese transplants in the West beginning around 1985, the ASEAN-Four accounted for 39 percent and 35 percent of the overseas production bases of Japanese assemblers and parts firms, respectively (Doner 1991, 72–73). The ASEAN facilities were largely devoted to assembly. However, host country localization policies and the growth of spare-parts markets both at home and overseas gradually gave rise to local automotive industries of varying strengths. This growth was of course most striking in the South Korean assembly industry. Elsewhere in the region the emphasis was on parts production. Exports of parts and components began to grow in the early to mid-1980s. Some of this growth was due to initiatives by local firms confronted with saturated domestic markets, especially in Thailand and Indonesia. But some was a function of initiatives by Japanese firms who dominate the region's markets and account for one-fourth of its auto exports.[18]

Several interrelated factors accelerated the investment and export activities of Japanese firms in the region. One was the assemblers' growing realization of the enormous growth potential of the Asian markets, especially when contrasted with relatively stagnant demand in Japan and in the developed countries more generally (e.g., LTCB 1987). Second, South Korea's emergence as an auto exporter has encouraged Japanese (as well as U.S.) auto makers to view the region as a potential source of vehicles and components for small car and developing country market niches.[19] The yen appreciation helped to crystallize these other factors. By increasing the import price of Japanese-made components used to produce vehicles in the NICs and ASEAN, this shift encouraged further use of locally made parts. It has also resulted in a further extension of competition in the Japanese market to the East Asian markets: individual Japanese assemblers have formed linkages with potential East Asian competitors to preempt any linkage between these firms and one of their competitors in Japan (LTCB 1987, 2). Finally, the most recent auto (as well as electronics)

---

18. According to Plummer and Ramstetter (1992, 272), Japanese affiliates accounted for $1.7 billion out of the total $5.9 billion in transportation equipment exported from Asia in 1986.

19. Hyundai has recently shown signs of establishing assembly operations in the Philippines and Thailand (MACPMA News [Kuala Lumpur], December 1991, 9).

investments in Southeast Asia reflect still another factor—the shortage of labor in Japan (author interviews).

These factors have prompted the Japanese to deepen and rationalize their auto manufacturing operations in the region. Deepening has involved increased investments and pressure on local firms to modernize production management. If overseas facilities are to be used for exports as well as domestic markets, quality must be raised by replicating Japanese practices. There thus seems to be a marked increase in efforts to implement quality circles, to organize suppliers' cooperative associations, to improve stamping lines, and so forth in overseas operations (discussed below).

Note that this process has occurred even in certain of the ASEAN-Four that are categorized above as the locus of simple assembly operations. In Thailand the FI inflow has resulted in labor scarcities and encouraged many firms to increase both capital equipment and required skill levels. The importance of both local and regional markets has also prompted several Japanese firms, including Kawasaki, to establish design and R&D centers in Thailand and elsewhere in the region.[20]

To rationalize their operations, the assemblers have begun to engage in limited cooperation among themselves (e.g., in engine manufacturing in Indonesia and Thailand). They have also begun to develop intrafirm production and trade arrangements within the region. Toyota, traditionally the most Japan-bound producer, has begun to ship engines from Indonesia to Malaysia, Taiwan, and Japan, and from Thailand to Portugal. The firm has also begun to use Southeast Asia as a source of press dies for its regional operations. Toyota's Thailand complex is slated to play a leading role in the firm's "planned Southeast Asian parts-production network" (*Japanese Motor Business,* July 1989 and various issues). Nissan has announced a regional complementarity program that would involve Taiwan selling Nissan auto bodies to Thailand and Thai-made Nissan engines going to Taiwan. Nissan's role would be to coordinate production and distribution among the Asian countries, to "administer the traffic" (*Asiaweek,*

20. The Kawasaki case highlights the importance of regional market niches and the potential for intraregional exports. Thai Kawasaki originally produced for the domestic market. After Kawasaki's plants in the Philippines and Indonesia ran into problems, the firm decided to focus its assembly activities in Thailand, where Kawasaki's facilities had initiated design changes to meet the specific requirements of Thai consumers. These were approved by the home office in Japan, proved quite popular in the Philippines and Indonesia, and have resulted in exports as well as a design center in Bangkok (author interviews). Note the following other cases: Isuzu has organized a special automotive engineering program with Thailand's King Mongkut Institute of Technology. Toyota plans to invest several hundred million baht to develop technology-transfer programs in Thailand; these will include establishing an automotive engineering department at one of Thailand's universities, setting up auto mechanics courses with local technical schools, opening a Toyota automotive vocational center to produce qualified mechanics, and granting scholarships to university students. Thailand's Federation of Thai Industries plans to join with Japan's Keidanren to establish an institute to train technicians and engineers. The Japan International Cooperation Agency provided financial and technical support for two materials testing centers in Thailand. Sony will establish a major research and manufacturing operation in Taiwan (*Bangkok Post,* various issues).

October 26, 1986). Mitsubishi has perhaps been the most active by initiating intraregional exchanges among its plants and promoting an ASEAN complementarity scheme. Honda has recently begun participating in this plan as well. Several of these projects involve overseas production and export of old models or older technologies (e.g., Mitsubishi is reportedly manufacturing an engine in Indonesia that has been phased out of production in Japan). But some also involve products used in Japan but cheaper to make in East Asia due to labor costs. Such products are not necessarily low-skilled goods. Nippondenso Tool and Die is exporting dies from Thailand to Japan due to a shortage of tool-and-die experts.

Many of these plans are still on the drawing board. Some will not come to fruition, and those that do will take some time to work out. The precise mix of "self-contained" investments versus "regional division of labor" also remains to be seen. It will, however, reflect efforts to reconcile (1) host country factors, such as localization policies and particular market characteristics; (2) pressure to increase efficiency through regional scale economies; and (3) tensions between regional and global strategies of particular firms. Japanese strategies will also have to take account of competition from South Korean firms, especially Hyundai, whose shrinking North American export markets have prompted new efforts to penetrate ASEAN as well as Japanese markets ("Update on South Korea" 1990; author interviews).

These two cases suggest that the impact of Japanese FI varies with factor endowments, entry barriers, and the degree of industry-specific restructuring within Japan itself. And they suggest that the emerging hierarchy will not be a neat alignment in which the ASEAN-Four are confined to simple assembly activities. The fact that much of this new Japanese investment builds on existing facilities and interests suggests greater potential for both local value added and continued tension between individual host country concerns and efficiency on a regional level.

More broadly, it appears that the impact of FI on the comparative advantage and exports of a particular host country is indirect, mediated by host country conditions, the shifting comparative advantage of neighbors, and the ways in which host countries screen and manage FI. Before addressing that management process in section 5.5, I turn to the supply side of Japanese investment in the Pacific Asian region.

5.3 Supply of Japanese Investment

To assess the impact of Japanese FI on East Asia from the supply side, I first examine the broad evolution of Japanese investment and the region's position as an investment target within that evolution. I then explore the domestic sources of Japan's ability to promote structural changes at home along with those it helps to engender abroad. I conclude with an analysis of the important institutional components of Japan's investment presence in the region.

5.3.1 Patterns of Japanese FI

Japanese FI in East Asia has passed through three general phases. Until the late 1960s, Japanese capital flows to the region were "quiescent and narrowly circumscribed" due to Japanese capital controls and pervasive anti-Japanese attitudes by host countries (Encarnation 1992, 167–68). Capital controls were probably the dominant factor here, since the low levels of investments in East Asia mirrored the modest global levels of Japanese investments, at least relative to those of the United States (tables 5.16 and 5.17). During this period, the largest share of Japanese investments in the region was devoted to natural resources.

Manufacturing investments jumped in the early 1970s as a result of several factors, including domestic capital liberalization, the 1971 yen appreciation, increased protectionist pressure from the United States, and host country performance requirements. Although the import and development of natural resources continued to play an important role, the expansion of Japanese textiles and electronics investments was especially striking (table 5.18). As host countries shifted from import substitution to a greater emphasis on exports, the portion of export-oriented investments in labor-intensive intermediate and final products expanded.

Japanese investments increased in overall volume during the 1980s, especially following the yen appreciation. Indeed, after remaining relatively constant in 1977–80 and rising slightly in 1980–86, the number of Japanese affiliates worldwide roughly doubled from 1986 to 1988 (Ramstetter 1991b, 30). This period also witnessed a more pronounced shift of emphasis from natural

Table 5.16   Japanese FDI

	1965	1970	1975	1980	1985	1988
Percentage of GNP	0.5	0.7	1.7	1.8	3.4	4.0
Amount (billions of U.S. dollars)	0.4	1.5	8.2	19.5	45.0	113.1

Source: Balance of payments figures cited in Yoon (1990, table 1).

Table 5.17   Components of Japanese FI (percentage)

Area	Contents	1951–71	1972–80	1981–84	1988
Developed	Resources	10.3	7.0	2.5	2.9
	Manufactures	9.2	11.4	15.0	16.4
	Other	31.3	26.9	32.6	42.2
Developing	Resources	14.3	14.4	9.9	5.5
	Manufactures	18.2	24.0	12.2	10.4
	Other	16.5	16.2	27.9	22.6
Amount (billions of U.S. dollars)		4.4	32.1	34.9	186.4

Source: Approved investments cited in Yoon (1990, table 2).

Table 5.18   **Distribution of Japanese FI in Manufacturing**

	Region	1975	1980	1985
Processing and assembling	North America	8.5	12.7	37.6
	Machinery	3.1	1.8	10.3
	Electrical machinery	4.7	9.8	17.1
	Transportation equipment	0.7	1.1	10.2
	Asia	9.3	7.7	11.9
	Other	14.0	14.1	13.9
Basic	North America	22.3	9.9	10.9
	Asia	24.3	30.7	5.2
	Other	12.2	19.8	11.6
Other	All regions	9.4	5.2	8.8

Source: Yoon (1990, 11).

Note: Basic industries include food, textiles, wood and wooden products, pulp and paper products, chemicals, iron and steel, and nonferrous metals.

resources and cheap labor in the developing countries to technology-based, market-oriented activities in the developed countries (table 5.17). The global percentage of Japanese FI going to the NICs and ASEAN-Four also declined, from roughly 26 percent of the 1953–83 cumulative total to 10 percent of the 1987 figure (table 5.19), as did the percentage going to developing countries overall. Nonmanufacturing investments, especially in U.S. finance and insurance sectors, expanded sharply after 1985.

This picture of a geographical shift away from East Asia and a sectoral shift away from manufacturing requires qualification. First, the statistics cited in table 5.19 do not cover direct investments by subsidiaries using money obtained abroad. Second and more important, the absolute volume of Japanese FDI to the NICs and ASEAN countries has expanded rapidly, averaging a $2 billion/year increase for all eight countries during the 1984–87 period in contrast to a roughly $485 million/year annual growth for the 1951–83 period (Nakakita 1988, table 3, 308, 310). This reflects not only complementarity in industry structures (wages, technological developments, and structural changes in Japan). It is also a function of "country bias" factors such as physical proximity and strategic interests (Pangestu 1987). Further, in the coming years Japan may shift the emphasis of its investment from North America and Europe to developing Asia. This may occur for several reasons: Asian investments yield relatively high profits; Japan's "trade friction–avoiding" investments are largely in place; Japanese firms are worried about economic uncertainty in the industrialized countries; and American and European trade blocs could push Japan to focus on its own backyard.[21]

21. According to a recent Export-Import Bank of Japan survey, 115 major Japanese firms said they would direct 26.1 percent of their foreign investment to the European Community between 1992 and March 1994. But ASEAN was slated to receive 25.1 percent and the NICs 12 percent (Rowley 1992a; see also Rowley 1992b; *Asian Wall Street Journal Weekly,* April 15, 1991, cited in Lim 1991, 93).

Table 5.19   Distribution of Japanese FI (percentage)

	1951–83	1984	1985	1986	1987
NICs	10.0	8.0	5.8	7.0	7.7
Korea	2.4	1.1	1.1	2.0	1.9
Taiwan	0.9	0.6	0.9	1.3	1.1
Hong Kong	3.9	4.1	1.1	2.3	3.2
Singapore	2.8	2.2	2.8	1.4	1.5
ASEAN-Four	16.3	6.8	4.8	2.5	3.0
Indonesia	12.5	3.7	3.3	1.1	1.6
Malaysia	1.5	1.4	0.6	0.7	0.5
Philippines	1.3	0.5	0.5	0.1	0.2
Thailand	1.0	1.2	0.4	0.6	0.7
China	0.1	1.1	0.8	1.0	3.7
Oceania	5.3	1.2	4.0	4.4	4.0
United States	27.0	33.1	44.2	45.5	44.1
Europe	11.6	19.1	15.8	15.5	19.7
World (in millions of U.S. dollars)	61,278	10,155	12,217	22,320	33,364

Source: Japan Ministry of Finance, cited in Nakakita (1988, table 3).

Third, these figures also exclude overseas activities that do not involve capital transfers but do offer host countries the opportunities to capture knowledge-based assets. One involves expertise provided to host country importers of production machinery by the machinery makers' sales engineers.[22] There are also, as noted earlier, several "intermediate" forms of overseas activity by firms who might otherwise engage in more direct FI. These include business tie-ups (cooperative links between Japanese and foreign firms involving the acquisition and provision of sales rights or brand names), technological tie-ups (the provision of new technologies between Japanese and foreign firms for joint efforts on R&D), and production cooperation (cooperative links involving commissioned and local production). The number of these intermediate forms has risen, with the greatest gain in technological tie-ups and production cooperation agreements in the NICs (Nakakita 1988, table 4). Indeed, there is evidence that in South Korea, at least, knowledge-based assets obtained from licensing, technical services contracts, turnkey plants, and machinery imports were more important than FDI (Westphal, Rhee, and Pursell 1984). The relative weight of intermediate forms versus FDI may also vary with industry and, as discussed below, with the level of development of local firms.[23]

22. This is the "major mechanism for technology acquisition" by Thailand's largest locally owned producer of consumer electronics (Shiowattana 1991, 182–83).
23. In South Korea, for example, technical licensing is the major source of foreign technology in the general machinery subsector. According to one study, this reflects the subsector's multitude of differentiated products, most of which involve several distinct processes, each of which can be licensed. Since no two products may be alike, no two processes or technologies may be alike (Amsden and Kim 1986, 100).

But it also appears that small and medium-sized Japanese firms (SMEs) prefer such intermediate forms and that most SME technical tie-ups have taken place in the Asian NICs, followed by ASEAN and the People's Republic of China (Phongpaichit 1988, 305–6). In addition, the contribution of SMEs to Japanese FI in Asia has increased since the mid-1980s. By the end of 1986, the yen appreciation raised the cost of Japanese goods overseas by some 40 percent. Supplier firms in Japan were asked to reduce the price of their components—by 30 percent in the case of firms supplying one auto assembler (Phongpaichit 1988, 304). This need for price reduction has translated into a powerful incentive to shift production overseas. Investments by Japanese SMEs may hold further benefits to the extent that these firms bring more standardized (and thus more accessible) technology, as well as marketing and managerial know-how needed by host countries. The growing number of investments by SMEs from NICs, especially Taiwan and South Korea, reportedly yield similar benefits (e.g., Ramstetter 1988).

The relative reduction of Japanese FDI to East Asia thus seems to have been offset by quantitative increases in investment flows as well as new forms of investment and particular knowledge-based assets brought by SMEs from the NICs as well as Japan. Two other factors reinforce this admittedly optimistic picture. One is the incremental nature of the investment process. A good portion of Japan's new investments in East Asia is reportedly going to restructure or expand existing investments ("Asia/Pacific" 1989, 50). This assertion is supported by the fact that the recent expansion of FI does not seem to have been a sudden shift caused solely by exchange rate shifts. For many Japanese SMEs, the yen appreciation simply accelerated a process, begun some seven or eight years before, during which they have collected information, made feasibility studies, and monitored economic and political trends in potential overseas investment sites (Phongpaichit 1988, 304–5). The process of globalization among larger firms was also well under way prior to the yen appreciation (Kohama and Urata 1988, 330).

Another factor offsetting the relative reduction in FDI going to East Asia is a tendency for Japanese investment, since the yen appreciation, to promote both a widening and a deepening of overseas manufacturing facilities. I have addressed this issue in the context of the Thai auto industry. Consider here some changes in the Thai electronics industry (Shiowattana 1991, 186–89). Since the exchange rate shift, several Japanese firms have encouraged their Thai partners to stop relying on Japanese suppliers and to begin obtaining components from South Korea and Taiwan. They also began to localize production tools such as press dies and plastic injection molds. Several have expanded their human resource development programs, and at least one has announced plans to establish an R&D center to put Japan-based research findings into product development. Similar developments have occurred in Malaysia (Sanger 1991).

Much of this additional investment, at least in the ASEAN cases, involves cooperation with established local firms. Local capitalists often have experience in working with foreign partners as well as the financial and managerial capacity to take advantage of new resources. The expansion of linkages between Japanese investors and major Thai firms such as Siam Cement, Saha Union, and Charoen Pokphand illustrates this point (Phongpaichit 1991, 42–43). But, at least in the Thai and Malaysian cases, the pattern extends to many medium-sized local firms that, through Japanese technology and local content regulations, had already become suppliers of parts and components to Japanese firms.

This pattern of building on existing investments and capacity suggests that the production expansion occurring in the ASEAN-Four as a result of new FDI may involve more than simple assembly and other low value-added operations. Thai firms producing under the country's largely import substitution regime have developed sufficient capacity in processes such as forging, mold making, die casting, and plastic injection to supply many parts needed by foreign appliance, electronics, and auto firms. Thai industries, according to one account, "are already well into the phase of developing central industries with satellite suppliers, of the type in Japan and Taiwan" (Handley 1991, 466). This process is certainly not uniform across or within countries. Cross-nationally it varies in large part as a function of policies and institutions (discussed below). But it may also vary within one industry and one country as a function of differences among Japanese investors. Some Japanese firms, for example, have responded to the yen appreciation with a "self-contained" approach (discussed above). Others have pursued the "division of labor" type of investment, in which each host country facility is part of a global production system and any technology introduced is highly fragmented (Shiowattana 1991, 186–88).

5.3.2   Domestic Sources of Japanese Structural Change

Japan's growing FI and its support for shifting comparative advantage in neighboring countries has required structural change at home—shifting resources out of declining and into advanced industries. Such change has been facilitated by particular political arrangements and high levels of investment leading to constant productivity improvements, especially in process innovation.

Japanese growth has relied on, among other things, a conservative coalition for which small business constitutes an "organized swing constituency," especially in periods of domestic crisis (Calder 1988, 348). This "structural bias toward the small" has entailed government policies promoting sectoral development in industries such as textiles, autos, and machine tools. Also, because the Japanese labor force has lacked strong political influence, it could be "eased out of old industries and retrained for new ones" (Cumings [1984] 1987, 65). Further moderating labor's response to structural change has been the Japanese distribution sector's capacity to function as a sponge for labor made redundant by automation.

There are questions as to the strength of these arrangements. The conservative coalition, especially the linkages among agriculture, small business, and big business, has begun to erode under the pressure of economic liberalization (Pempel 1989). To the extent that this occurs, we may see (1) increased conflicts among and within industries with regard to the adjustment capacity of smaller firms, and (2) a more rationalized distribution sector with reduced capacity to absorb redundant labor.

There are also concerns that the replacements of exports by FDI will lead to an industrial "hollowing-out" in Japan (Yoon 1990, 18–20). Growing FI, it is argued, has already reduced investment in, orders to, and employment in the traditionally most efficient industries such as autos. Although many of the unemployed have been absorbed into services and distribution, these are sectors with low productivity growth. Furthermore, shifts of production of lower-end products abroad will entail a loss of production experience, a phenomenon already apparent in the deterioration of Japan's tool-and-die-making capacity.[24] These shifts may also undermine the intraindustry linkages that have supported the development of higher-level products.

A thorough discussion of these concerns is beyond the scope of this paper. But if Japan's automotive, office machinery, computer, and machine tools industries relocate 30–50 percent of their production overseas within the next five to ten years, as suggested by MITI, the political arrangements surrounding this relocation will become increasingly important ("Japan's Drive into Asia" 1989, 50). In section 5.3.3, I explore some of the institutional channels through which relocation has occurred.

5.3.3   Institutional Sources of Japanese Investment in Pacific Asia

Japanese investment in the Asian region has been facilitated by a relatively proactive and institutional approach to regional development by the Japanese government and private sector. In concluding this section, I wish to explore the degree to which public and private sector actors in Japan attempt to manage shifts in the regional division of labor and the range of institutions through which they do so. I hope to avoid the pitfalls of the usual industrial policy debate between state- versus market-led explanations of Japanese economic success. My argument is not that the Japanese government has determined and directed public and private sector activities concerning shifts in the region's division of labor. Certainly the government has been important, especially since the mid-1980s. But its role has been one of promoting collective action toward goals already embraced by the private sector. In addition, private sector

24. This is reflected in Toyota's obtaining an increasing portion of its dies for Asian operations from Thai firms, as noted earlier. Nevertheless, Japan continues to produce dies. Chrysler recently looked for a die producer to provide the 210 pieces necessary for a model it intended to begin making in Thailand. The U.S. price was $35 million, the Thai price $14 million, and the Japanese price $10 million. Chrysler officials stated, however, the Japanese price was clearly a giveaway designed to maintain market share (author interviews).

institutions have themselves played important roles in promoting Japan's over-all investment position.

Ironically, given the region's importance to Tokyo, a coherent Japanese gov-ernment policy toward the developing countries of Asia has been fairly slow in coming. Early efforts included ASEAN technology support by the Associa-tion for Overseas Technical Scholarship (AOTS) followed trade tensions in the mid-1970s, Prime Minister Fukuda's 1977 pledge of major support to ASEAN projects, and Prime Minister Suzuki's effort to refocus Japanese aid on clearly designated priority areas.[25] But more focused attention on the region did not come until the mid-1980s. By that time, Japan was coming under significant pressure from ASEAN countries, then suffering from severe economic slumps, to correct trade balances and redirect FI from the United States and Western Europe to Asia (Unger 1990a, 1993); Awanohara 1986; Smith 1986). The United States was pushing Japan to stimulate domestic demand and expand foreign assistance. Increased protectionism in the United States, while not ne-gating the importance of the American market, did encourage the Japanese to look to Asia as a way of correcting an overreliance on Washington. This extended to an explicit recognition, at least by MITI, of the need to de-velop a horizontal division of labor between itself and its Asian neighbors. Such an arrangement, it was argued, would encourage the long-range indus-trial growth of its neighbors, thereby expanding markets for Japanese manufac-tured goods as well as reducing the destabilizing impact of Japan's economic self-sufficiency.

The yen appreciation, beginning in September 1985, added more immediate economic logic to these arguments. MITI calculated that, given exchange rate shifts, a given amount of industrial investment overseas would yield more jobs and thus create more long-term economic welfare than the same investment in Japan (Smith 1986, 56–57). The result of these concerns was a MITI draft called the "Project for Comprehensive Cooperation and Asian Industrializa-tion" (also known as the New Aid Plan). The plan drew on extensive discus-sions with private sector organizations such as Keidanren, as well as research by government organizations such as the Japan External Trade Organization (JETRO) and the Institute for Developing Economies. One of its goals was to facilitate Japanese domestic restructuring. The other was to provide assistance for export-oriented industries in developing Asia, including help in targeting particular sectors for development. These may be part of MITI's efforts to ex-tend its industrial planning and coordination activities into foreign economies

25. The creation of the Thai-Japan Technological Promotion Association (TPA) illustrates one type of Japanese response on which subsequent measures have been built. During the outbreak of anti-Japanese demonstrations in 1971 and 1972, MITI investigated ways to alleviate the tensions. Reportedly on the advice of the head of the AOTS, the ministry supported the creation of an institute devoted to technology transfer. The TPA was established in 1973 and operated with fi-nancial support from some one hundred Japanese firms. As a student in Japan during the early 1970s, the present director of the TPA had participated in anti-Japanese demonstrations in solidar-ity with his fellow students in Bangkok (author interview; TPA materials).

in response to the expansion of Japanese FI and the lack of coherent industrial policies in host countries (Wade 1992, 290).

This plan was reportedly never officially adopted, due in part to intrabureaucratic conflicts. The plan was more attractive to MITI than to other agencies because it would expand the former's funds and range of jurisdiction when factors such as private sector strength have weakened its traditional functions and leverage (Unger 1990a). But the plan's central thrust has been carried on by a variety of measures and state agencies. In Japan these include, among others, special Export-Import Bank of Japan loans for Japanese investors going abroad (Yoon 1990, 9; Doner 1991, 82), and industry-specific institutions to help in domestic restructuring.[26] Moreover, efforts at domestic restructuring in response to advances in the NICs have been initiated by business associations in industries such as textiles and machine tools (JICA 1989; Fransman 1986a, 171).

Outside of Japan, institutional support includes industry surveys, training, and development assistance by the Japan International Cooperation Agency (JICA), the Overseas Economic Cooperation Fund (OECF), the Japan Overseas Development Corporation, the AOTS, and JETRO. A recent addition is the Japan-ASEAN Investment Corporation, an organization funded by the OECF and designed to channel Japanese FI to worthy projects in ASEAN.[27] Although state or quasi-state agencies, these activities often involve and/or serve the Japanese private sector. For example, members of the private sector do much of the groundwork for projects to be funded by the Japan-ASEAN Investment Corporation. Similarly, in Malaysia a JETRO-sponsored evaluation of press-die and precision-molding capacity made use of Japanese industry experts, and in Thailand, JICA arranged for a visit by the founder of the Japanese mold-and-die association (Tsuruoka 1992; author interviews). The AOTS, which began as a pre–World War II center for overseas Asian students, works with MITI to manage the training of overseas buyers and technicians invited by Japanese industrialists to familiarize themselves with locally made machinery.[28] Further, many of these activities are industry-specific and result in a very impressive level of information. For example, JETRO and JICA officials are

26. The Export-Import Bank's Asia-related activities have shifted over time as a reflection of the region's changing comparative advantage. During 1957–67 and 1968–73, Asian textiles took a dominant portion of the bank's loans. But in 1974–80, the portion of loans going to textiles declined sharply. This reflected the NIC's movement out of light manufacturing into heavy industry, so that 90 percent of the bank's loans to East Asia went to heavy and chemical industries, compared to 7 percent for textiles and sundries (Ozawa 1986).

27. I am grateful to David Arase for bringing this organization to my attention. This organization probably had its genesis in an earlier (1981) body known as the ASEAN Finance Corporation, established by Japan's Committee for Economic Cooperation (Keizai Doyukai).

28. AOTS had enrolled over 27,000 students by 1984. Its trainees first undergo a five-week course in Japanese economy, society, culture, and language. They then spend four months in private companies, often the ones with which their own company has formed a joint venture. JICA also serves training functions but focuses on preparing employees for work in public enterprises and state agencies rather than in private corporations (Koike and Inoki 1990, 64–65).

probably better informed than most officials in Thailand's Ministry of Industry on the competitiveness of various sectors of Thai industry (Unger 1990a, 27; author interviews).

Finally, a number of private sector organizations have played direct roles in supporting this expansion of Japanese investment in Asia. Trading companies (*sogo shoshas*) were traditionally important sources of information and financing for Japanese firms making initial moves into overseas production. With the extensive experience gained by many Japanese firms, as well as the need for more direct control in pricing and marketing, the role of trading companies (and intercorporate networks in general) has declined (Yoon 1990, 12–13). Yet *sogo shoshas* remain important as sources of technical assistance and marketing channels for host country firms, and of information to smaller Japanese firms beginning overseas operations.[29] They are especially important in certain industries, such as textiles, and in certain countries, such as Taiwan, where they reportedly handle over 50 percent of trade with Japan (Baum and do Rosario 1991). And they continue to play a major role in opening up new geographical markets, such as Vietnam (Lehner 1992a).

The overseas branches of Japanese banks fulfill similar information functions. Also, business groups, or *keiretsu,* have at times facilitated the overseas expansion of firms within the group. This has certainly been the case in the auto industry, where Japanese parts and components suppliers have been asked by their primary assemblers to establish operations overseas, and where Mitsubishi Motors joined Malaysia's "national car" project in part through the activities of other Mitsubishi firms in Malaysia (Doner 1991). Also, large Japanese supermarkets and department stores help Asian producers to improve quality control, place orders, and bypass Japan's complex distribution system (Unger 1990b, 41).

Business associations have also been active. The Japan Chamber of Commerce and Industry provides information to Japanese SMEs at home through individual trade associations while gathering data in host countries (Phongpaichit 1988, 308). The Mitsubishi supplier cooperation association sponsored study trips to Southeast Asia when overseas production facilities were being considered (Smitka 1991, 44). Keidanren, reportedly backed by MITI, has established the Industrial Project Development Corporation, whose function is to identify targets for Japanese FI.[30] A think tank supported by the Japanese auto industry is currently undertaking a comprehensive study of present and future needs of the Southeast Asian auto industries (author interview).

The argument here is not that the Japanese government is orchestrating a private sector shift to Asia. The consensus of Japanese executives in the auto and electronic industries interviewed recently in Tokyo was that MITI has

29. Unger (1991c, 41) notes Marubeni's role in arranging for Japanese technical assistance to Thailand's Siam Cement as part of a joint venture operation.
30. I am grateful to David Arase for providing this information.

pressed Japanese firms to invest in the United States and Western Europe but not in East Asia.[31] This is to a large degree because such pressure has not been necessary. As interviewees noted, economic factors encouraged Japanese firms to build on overseas investments and facilities already in place.[32] The government has supplied collective goods necessary to reduce risks for such investments and encouraged private sector efforts to do likewise.

These efforts are clearly designed to promote trade and production linkages between Japan and its neighbors. Illustrative cases abound: public and private sector officials of the Thai textile industry note that JICA proposals for better machinery translate into calls for the import of Japanese equipment (JICA 1989; author interviews). The Japanese report on the Malaysian die industry recommends the adoption of certain grinding techniques that facilitate assembly into Japanese dies (Tsuruoka 1992, 45). U.S. firms attempting to interest Thais in American machinery found that the latter had already adopted Japanese specifications (author interviews).

5.4   Institutional Impact of Japan's "Organized Capitalism"

According to some observers, Japanese multinationals differ from their Western counterparts in their preferences for minority equity arrangements, their emphasis on developing countries and standardized industries, and the heavy trade orientation of their investments (e.g., Kojima and Ozawa 1986). Western analysts have cast serious doubt on this view, arguing that such differences are either exaggerated or tend to disappear as multinationals from both countries confront similar economic and political environments (Encarnation 1992; Ramstetter 1991b).

The one area in which differences do seem to exist involves the institutional forms of and supports for Japanese investments discussed in section 5.3.3. Indeed, as many have noted, these arrangements suggest the operation of a more organized form of capitalism in Japan than is common in the United States (e.g., Noble 1989). Here I wish to explore the possibility that Japanese FI, when combined with host country efforts to adopt best practices, can lead to a diffusion of Japanese-style institutions in the region. Rather than a process of mechanical replication, the hypothesis to be explored involves an uneven tendency toward institutional convergence. This section, which is meant to be suggestive, examines the potential for such convergence by focusing on specific institutional arrangements appearing in the region, identifying their

31. Interviews conducted in Tokyo, January–February 1992, by Patcharee Thanamai, Thammasat University, as part of a joint project with the author.
32. During the first half of 1986, "the rapidly improving competitive edge of the East Asian NICs in industries such as steel and electronics, and even in machine tools, has given rise to a stream of plans for shifting production out of Japan to the countries concerned" (Smith 1986, 57).

sources, and exploring possible causes for cross-national variation in their strength.

5.4.1   Looking East to "Japan Inc."

Unger has argued that "most of the capitalist countries of East Asia have already set about learning from Japan and drawing on Japan's successful experience in devising institutions suited to its developmental goals" (1993, 19). At its most general level, this has involved the promotion of public-private sector cooperation. South Korea is clearly the most striking and extensive case of this pattern (e.g., Ting 1985, 77). Also worth note, however, are efforts by Malaysia and Thailand. Malaysia's Prime Minister Mahathir has proclaimed the need for a "Malaysia Inc.," including admonitions to emulate Japan's work ethic. In Thailand, officials of the National Economic and Social Development Board joined with local industrialists to promote private sector peak organizations and joint public-private sector consultative committees during the governments of General Prem Tinsulanond (1980–88; Jomo 1985; author interviews). Both of the efforts have encountered serious political obstacles. In Malaysia, Malay antagonism toward Chinese-dominated business undermines real cooperation between the Malay-dominated state and local capitalists. In Thailand a more fragmented political arrangement under General Prem's successor seems to have stymied the corporatist-like developments of the consultative committees. But the efforts seem to have made a difference. Discussions between Malaysian businessmen and government officials at both industry and national levels are more extensive than before. And in Thailand, industry's peak association has continued to play a major role in aggregating and articulating the views of its members.

5.4.2   Interfirm Cooperation

The efforts to promote peak business association and public-private sector linkages described above came from Malaysian and Thai officials. At the sectoral level, however, at least in Thailand, there has also been pressure from the Japanese.[33] This has involved conditions attached to Japanese industrial support. JICA has been a major supporter of Thailand's Metalworking and Machinery Industries Development Institute (MIDI). MIDI's function is to provide both technical and organizational support for Thailand's SMEs. JICA has emphasized the critical role of business associations in Japan's industrial growth. It has arranged for a visit by the founder of Japan's mold-and-die association. And most critically, JICA has informed MIDI that its financial support is to be

---

33. This discussion draws on author interviews and on JICA (1989). Note also a case in which Japanese firms demonstrated the utility of cooperation through their own actions overseas: some one hundred Japanese companies in Malaysia reportedly agreed, informally, to restrain their competition for electrical engineers in the country's tight labor market (Tsuruoka 1991, 52).

distributed through such organizations, not through the government. In part under this pressure, MIDI sees itself as a sort of midwife whose function is to encourage the development of independent associations of metalworking firms.

The Japanese have also raised the importance of cooperation among firms through JICA's study of the country's largest industry—textiles and apparel—and, presumably, in other industry studies. In examining Japan's and Thailand's need for textile restructuring, the report stresses the importance of local industry associations and "linkage production units," that is, firms possessing "vertical links with different industries . . . to improve . . . information gathering, product development, and adaptation to wide variety in small lot production" (JICA 1989, A-III-26).

5.4.3   Trading Companies

A number of countries in the region have recognized the benefits of Japan's version of the general trading company (GTC) and have attempted to develop their own. Here I want to focus briefly on the two most extensive efforts, those of Taiwan and South Korea.[34] Both of these cases involved "conscious government attempts to adapt to their respective settings institutional arrangements borrowed from Japan" (Fields 1989, 1075). Yet their achievements were quite different. Korea's GTCs grew impressively, rapidly expanding the country's exports while assembling large, diverse business conglomerates. Taiwan's effort to graft the Japanese institution largely failed. By the mid-1980s, Japanese, not Taiwan, trading companies dominated the island's foreign trade.

Several factors account for these different outcomes. First, Taiwan GTCs encountered significant competition. Rivals included not only local manufacturers, government agencies, and trade associations, but also Japanese trading companies, which had free entry to the island and controlled some 50 percent of Taiwan's trade. In South Korea, on the other hand, Japanese trading companies were excluded until the 1960s. The two cases also differed with regard to support offered by large business groups. Korean GTCs benefited from financial support and a reliable source of export products from Korea's large business groups (*chaebol*). Taiwan's business groups, on the other hand, largely ignored the fledgling GTCs. These groups already had internal trading arms and were largely based in manufacturing, thus having little interest in expanding trading interests. Further, the Taiwan government did little to promote group-GTC ties, due to its own fears of business concentration. This stands in sharp contrast to South Korea's approach of development on the basis of large firms. Indeed, as Fields stresses, the government of Taiwan differed sharply from its Korean counterpart in offering "virtually no incentives" (1989, 1087).

---

34. On Malaysia, see Jomo (1985). Information on the Taiwan and Korean efforts is drawn from the work of Karl Fields (1989, 1990).

5.4.4   Subcontracting

Japan's success in manufacturing owes much to the strength of subcontracting relationships, whether between primary assemblers and component suppliers in autos (Smitka 1991) or between large fiber producers and downstream processors in textiles and apparel ("A Japanese Approach to Investment" 1991). I know of no study of subcontracting in the region as a whole. But evidence from Thailand, a country with probably average if not above-average levels of subcontracting, suggests that the phenomenon is a fairly recent one, emerging in the early 1970s as a response to local content regulation.[35]

There are also a number of factors impeding the growth of subcontracting in the region. As noted earlier, the positions of SMEs relative to dominant political coalitions helps to account for the weakness of subcontracting in South Korea and the Philippines (under Marcos). The predominance of large firms in Indonesia probably also discourages subcontracting. In Malaysia, ethnic differences also undermine subcontracting linkages. The Malaysian Ministry of International Trade and Industry has designed a subcontractor exchange scheme—a computerized data base designed to link small suppliers with larger primary firms. Yet the Chinese owners of many SMEs are reluctant to participate for fear that the data base will be used to force them to "restructure" their equity in favor of ethnic Malays. A second illustration: ethnic Chinese auto parts firms have refused to accept the Japanese-style supplier purchase agreement designed by Mitsubishi for firms supplying parts to the Malaysian national car. Their fear is that ethnic Malay employees of the national car firm will use price information from the suppliers to establish new parts firms.

There are also economic obstacles, even where the political factors are more propitious (Amsden and Kim 1986, 119). Subcontracting often involves a small group of large prime contractors amid a galaxy of small satellite subcontractors. Yet even in South Korea such large production units are just emerging in several industries. Based on the Japanese experience, subcontracting also seems to require excess demand, pushing prime firms gradually to increase their reliance on suppliers. Yet the problem for many firms in East Asia has been excess capacity. Subcontracting also seems to expand when prime contractors experience labor market rigidities and are not able to shift workers among assignments and extend the workday. Yet in most East Asian firms unions are weak, and there is little ostensible need to rely on subcontractors.

Finally, sociocultural factors may hinder the expansion of subcontracting in the region. As the Japanese experience has shown, trust is critical to subcontracting. Yet trust is not a strong point in several of the region's cultures. Many

---

35. Dahlman and Brimble (1990, 23). This study found "significant subcontracting activities" in textiles, wood products, metal products, machinery, electronic and electrical products, and transport equipment.

have, for example, stressed the tendency to defect from the group in Chinese business culture on Taiwan (Fields 1990). In Thailand, a country long known for its "loosely structured" social system, Seagate and Sharp abandoned efforts to establish links with domestic subcontractors due to a lack of trust when subcontractors released product designs to competitors (Dahlman and Brimble 1990, 24).

Despite these obstacles, there are indications that subcontracting linkages are becoming stronger in the region. Some pressure is coming from governments impressed with the Japanese model and convinced that subcontracting is necessary to strengthen local firms and the overall competitiveness of their country. The government of Taiwan, for example, has required Toyota to extend active support for the local auto parts and components industry as a condition of its operations (LTCB 1987, 8). The Thai Board of Investments, hardly a proponent of industrial policy, is encouraging local subcontracting through the Board of Investments Unit for Industrial Linkage Development (BUILD; *Business Asia,* May 27, 1991, 74).

Democratic and populist pressures may also encourage this development. In South Korea, popular opposition to economic concentration and the government's strategy of building up national champions prompted the Korean state to strengthen local subcontractors through measures such as tax incentives, the promotion of small-firm cartelization, requirements for frequent payments to vendors by large firms, and a ban on prime contractors' buying out suppliers (Moon 1988). I suspect that this kind of dynamic may emerge in Indonesia, where the Suharto government is constantly concerned with ethnic antagonism against Chinese-owned conglomerates.

There may also be situations in which the economic conditions discussed above encourage local firms to initiate or support subcontracting on their own. This may be the case for Siam Nawaloha, the foundry and casting firm within Thailand's giant Siam Cement group. A number of former employees of this firm have left to establish small machine shops close to the firm (author interviews).

But Japanese firms attempting to expand and improve quality are probably the major force promoting subcontracting. Let me conclude this discussion with a description of an institutional component of automotive subcontracting in Thailand—the cooperation club. This is the Thai analogue of the suppliers' cooperative association, a critical component in Japanese auto production. The associations are groups of auto parts and components suppliers organized by assemblers in Japan for purposes of technical, managerial, and, at times, financial support.[36] The Thai club described here was initiated by Isuzu. I do not know how it compares to those reportedly organized by Nissan, Toyota, and

---

36. The best discussion of these associations in Japan is Smitka (1991). The following draws on interviews.

Mitsubishi in Thailand. It does, however, conform to the outlines of suppliers' associations in Japan.

The Isuzu cooperation club is controlled by Isuzu's purchasing department. Its members are those suppliers with a fairly high level of original equipment sales to Isuzu. These are the suppliers on whom Isuzu depends heavily and who therefore share with Isuzu all information relevant to production (e.g., cost, price, technology, etc.). If a supplier is invited to join, membership is essentially compulsory if sales are to be maintained. The club's activities are a combination of the social and the professional. The former include various kinds of outings. The latter include the provision of information on issues such as projected model changes and quality problems, the organization of quality circles and QC competitions, and factory visits among the members. The diffusion of information is certainly a major objective of the club. But equally if not more important is the promotion of trust, a feature emphasized by Smitka for the Japanese associations. Trust is, moreover, seen by members as an important and inexpensive method for diffusing information.

Trust is promoted in part by the assembler's willingness to provide important technical and managerial support in exchange for each supplier's openness with regard to its own operations and its commitment to meet price and quality requirements. But the club also promotes trust among suppliers, even those producing the same item, as a way of diffusing best practices. Social outings, at first resented by parts makers as sophomoric, gradually became an opportunity to know and exchange views with other suppliers. QC contests, although intensely competitive, also encouraged trust because teams must openly discuss their problems and their proposed solutions.

Factory visits are also important instruments for diffusion of information and promotion of trust. These visits have reportedly become quite common and are appreciated by most concerned. This is significant, since the Thai auto parts association had previously failed at a similar attempt, due to mutual suspicions. Obviously some of the success of Isuzu's efforts is due to the Japanese firm's leverage as major client. But according to interviews, much credit is also due to the gradual way in which the visiting process evolved. The assembler encouraged firms to accept visitors from other plants, but recognized and attempted to deflate concerns about secrecy. Isuzu sent a list of prospective visitors to the plant to be visited. That plant had the option of striking a visitor, that is, direct competitor, off the list. Gradually, however, such exclusions ceased. This was in part due to assembler pressure. But to draw on game theory, it also reflected changes in the suppliers' payoff structure. Those interviewed talked of being ashamed to refuse to show their plants; they talked of pride in being able to impress visitors with innovations and new machinery; and they talked of the things they in turn would learn from visiting other plants. Finally, they mentioned an added benefit of these visits: the trust that developed helped to alleviate what they termed "domestic brain drain." That is, several firms stopped raiding other members of the club for skilled labor. This was no small achievement in Thailand's very tight labor market, especially for technicians.

Emphasis on these benefits should not negate the dangers raised by those interviewed—namely, the tendency for Isuzu to get its hands on every aspect of a Thai firm's operation. Several Thai businessmen repeatedly raised the specter of complete Japanese control. On the other hand, the subcontracting relationship had clearly provided local firms with managerial and technological assets that would not otherwise have been available.

There is clearly no teleological process of institutional development occurring in the region. The preceding discussion has indicated a number of factors, such as ethnicity, state fragmentation, loose labor markets, and industrial organization, that can impede institutional diffusion. But we have also suggested other factors, not the least of which is the learning effect of Japanese practices themselves, that can encourage such diffusion. Although inconclusive, the discussion does highlight the importance of research on this question, especially if such research draws on more explicitly theoretical analyses of institutional development in the industrialized countries (e.g., Hirst and Zeitlin 1991).

5.5 The Demand Side: Host Country Management of FI

The preceding sections have painted a relatively smooth and cooperative picture of Japan's contribution to industrial deepening and interdependence in developing Asia. This emphasis may reflect my focus on the post-1985 period, when Japanese firms exhibited willingness to expand overseas manufacture and procurement. Prior to the exchange rate shift, however, Japan was known for its relatively low level of overseas production (see, e.g., Encarnation 1992, 23). There were, of course exceptions, such as the textile case. But in many other industries the Japanese were often reluctant multinationals, reluctant to establish manufacturing facilities and reluctant to share the knowledge-based asset components of these investments.

Further, given the incremental nature of recent FI, it is plausible to expect that the countries benefiting the most from the recent expansion are those that had been relatively successful at inducing and learning from Japanese FI prior to the exchange rate shift. We thus turn to the "demand side" of the equation, the ability of host countries to attract and manage FI. Doing so can help to explain the relative position of different countries within the emerging regional production structures.

The following discussion, it should be noted, does not apply to host country management only of Japanese FI. But it is relevant to the discussion in that Japan is a major investor in each of these countries. Further, the Japanese have shown themselves quite flexible in adapting to the region's range of FI regimes. This flexibility is partly a function of the Japanese ability to operate successfully through minority equity, and partly a function of the institutions noted earlier.[37]

The discussion also makes certain basic assumptions, one of which is that host country policies can in fact influence the volume and composition of FI (e.g., Haggard 1990, 204–5). I also assume that each of the host countries considered here is exposed to similar potential "supplies" of FI. Different levels of development largely reflect national capacities to make use of that investment. Finally, I presume that while FI flows are not all that important quantitatively to any of the countries under consideration, with the exception of Singapore (table 5.20), each country considers FI an important factor in its growth. This is in part because the spillover of knowledge-based assets in FI is at least as important for host country economic growth as simple quantities of investment funds. But such spillover is neither automatic nor purely technical. It requires active institutional support from state and, as I argue below, private sector sources.

Host countries influence FI flows and benefits through three general types of policies: property rights, macroeconomic incentives and general development strategy, and sector- and firm-specific incentives (Haggard 1990, 192). I shall not address the role of property rights. With some exceptions (noted below), the developing countries of East Asia have generally shown much weaker nationalist tendencies toward expropriation or nationalization than seen in Latin America (e.g., Kobrin 1984). Variation in property rights thus seems to account for little if any cross-national ability to manage FI. Further, although Japanese firms are very aware of political shifts in host countries, their willingness to invest seems much less dependent than their U.S. counterparts on major changes in government and policy commonly subsumed under the term "macropolitical risks" (Doner 1991, 93–94).

The section thus begins with a discussion of the macroincentives of the region's various economies and then addresses sector-specific FI management designed to obtain knowledge-based assets. The section concludes with a brief discussion of East Asian regional efforts at FI management.

5.5.1   General FI Regimes

Host country FI regimes vary with regard to a combination of factors that, taken together, suggest a measure of openness to and selectivity about FI. Openness refers to rules on local equity ownership, profit repatriation, tax in-

---

37. The Japanese tendency to accept minority equity and the U.S. tendency to insist on majority ownership have been attributed to different investment foci: the Japanese on traditional industries for which Japan is no longer a low-cost location, the United States on more modern industries where American firms maintain monopolistic power. I believe that Japanese equity preferences have more to do with the institutional supports discussed above and with the Japanese tendency to maintain control through greater numbers of expatriate managers than used by most U.S. firms. See, for example, Stewart (1985, 12–14). Moreover, Dennis Encarnation has cast doubt on the prevailing assumption that Japanese multinationals tend to operate through minority equity. Like U.S. firms, the Japanese generally avoid minority shareholdings whenever possible.

Table 5.20   **Macroeconomic Significance of Direct Investment (percentage)**

Host Country	Year	Direct Investment	
		% of Producers' Fixed Capital Formation	% of GDP
NICs	1984	6.9	0.9
	1985	6.9	1.0
	1986	5.6	0.8
	1987	9.6	1.3
Korea	1984	4.2	0.5
	1985	4.8	0.6
	1986	2.6	0.4
	1987	6.3	0.9
Taiwan	1984	7.5	0.9
	1985	8.8	1.1
	1986	6.7	1.1
	1987	12.3	1.4
Singapore	1984	12.2	3.3
	1985	9.5	2.3
	1986	14.3	3.1
	1987	17.4	3.8
Philippines	1984	5.4	0.7
	1985	3.8	0.4
	1986	2.9	0.3
	1987	4.4	0.4
ASEAN-Four	1984	5.9	1.0
	1985	4.7	0.7
	1986	6.0	0.8
	1987	11.3	1.5
Malaysia	1984	1.9	0.3
	1985	2.8	0.4
	1986	7.1	0.7
	1987	9.7	1.0
Thailand	1984	7.0	1.0
	1985	3.4	0.4
	1986	5.2	0.6
	1987	12.0	1.5
Indonesia	1984	7.1	1.3
	1985	5.9	1.0
	1986	6.5	1.1
	1987	12.8	2.2
Total	1984	6.3	1.0
	1985	5.6	0.8
	1986	5.8	0.8
	1987	10.5	1.4

Source: Haseyama, Honobe, and O'uchi (1989, table 3).

Notes: Producers' fixed capital formation is defined as follows: South Korea and Singapore: non-residential buildings, transport equipment, and other equipment; Taiwan, Malaysia, and Thailand: gross fixed capital formation of private sector; Philippines: private construction and durable equipment; Indonesia: assumed as 70 percent of gross fixed capital formation.

Table 5.21   **Characteristics of FI Regimes**

Country	Openness	Selectivity
Korea	overall moderate: closed until early 1960s; moderate until late 1980s; increasingly open in 1989	high
Taiwan	high	moderate
Singapore	high	high
Hong Kong	high	low
Indonesia	overall moderate: low until 1965; moderate opening until 1974; opening after 1986	low
Malaysia	moderate; increasingly open after 1986	low/moderate
Philippines	moderate/high	low
Thailand	high	low

centives, foreign exchange controls, and so forth. Selectivity has to do with industry-specific restrictions on foreign operations, and performance requirements on local content, exports, training of local replacements, and technology transfer.

Does any particular combination of these factors seem best suited to derive potential benefits from FI? Table 5.21 provides a rough characterization of the East Asian cases with regard to openness and selectivity. If we assume (1) higher levels of development for the NICs than for the ASEAN-Four, and higher levels for Thailand and Malaysia than for Indonesia and the Philippines, and (2) some linkage between FI and development, then the East Asian cases suggest that no particular combination is optimal on its own. Instead, studies of national FI regimes suggest that the following factors are necessary for effective host country management of FI: a political consensus on the part of public and private sector interests as to the benefits of FI, open information channels between the state and business, clear linkage of investment policy to broader development policy, and the existence of a relatively insulated screening agency.[38] Effective policies designed both to attract and to channel foreign firms into priority areas were evident only in Singapore, South Korea, and, evidently to a lesser degree, Taiwan. Elsewhere, political conditions—ethnic tensions (Indonesia, Malaysia), ideological antipathy (Indonesia), extreme rent seeking (Philippines), and political fragmentation (Thailand)—undermined the kinds of institutions and development policies necessary for such management. To the degree that Taiwan does not seem to have been as selective as the

38. On South Korea see Haggard (1990); Fields (1990); Mardon (1990); *Business Asia* (February 4, 1991, 44). On Taiwan see Fields (1990); Lam (1991); Lim and Fong (1988); Noble (1987). On Singapore see Haggard (1990); Lim and Fong (1988); Phongpaichit (1991); *Business Asia* (January 22, 1990). On Hong Kong see Haggard (1990); Lam (1990). On Indonesia see Phongpaichit (1991); Doner (1991); Hill (1988). On Malaysia see Jomo (1985); Lim and Fong (1988). On the Philippines see Lindsey (1983); Doner (1991); *Business Asia* (various issues). On Thailand see Unger (1990a); Doner (1991); Phongpaichit (1991); Lim and Fong (1988); *Business Asia* (especially May 27, 1991).

other two NICs, we may identify still another factor that can help to account for its success—namely, its promotion of exports. Exports allow host countries low-cost access to a wide range of information provided by buyers of exports as well as machinery suppliers. This factor clearly operated in the other NICs as well (e.g., Westphal, Rhee, and Pursell 1984, 298).

This macroperspective does not capture the entire picture, however. Even if investment flows to areas considered strategic by host countries, there is no guarantee that investment will provide anything but funds and that the spillovers from knowledge-based assets will not be lost. As Fransman notes, factors of production "must not only be purchased on the market at the going rate. They must also be 'brought into the factory gates' so that inputs may be transformed into outputs" (1986a, 209).

Thus even in the NICs, effective public policy at the macrolevel cannot account for the largely beneficial impact of FI and related activities. Also, the macroperspective does not account for relatively impressive economic growth, including the expansion of domestic entrepreneurs, in the less efficient ASEAN-Four (McVey 1992). Although natural resource–based revenues were necessary to the emergence of many of these new capitalists, their growth in manufacturing was closely linked to the technical and managerial resources provided by foreign investors. Given the weaknesses of public policy in the ASEAN-Four, understanding more microlevel processes can help to explain the transmission of these resources.

5.5.2   Host Country Investment Management at the Sector and Industry Level

Host country firms can obtain knowledge-based assets from foreign firms through a variety of channels. These include joint ventures, "competitive imitation," subcontracting (supplier and vendor development), machinery purchases, and intermediate channels such as technology licensing. Regardless of the channel, increased local content requirements, common in most of the countries under consideration, increase the potential for technological spillovers. The pitfalls of localization requirements are well known, however. They often contravene the most basic rules of comparative advantage, resulting in inefficient (protected) local products and very high costs to local consumers. To some degree, the weaknesses of localization can be avoided by localizing simpler parts first and gradually moving to higher value-added items. The Philippines' decision to adopt the opposite strategy—to begin with major functional components beyond the reach of all local firms—was an important flaw in that country's auto localization plans (Doner 1991).

Assuming a realistic localization plan, however, what kinds of measures encourage and enable local firms to become more efficient within local content umbrellas? State policies, such as linking foreign exchange allocations to export performance, are obviously important. Here I want to emphasize other sets of measures—rationalization and technology import policy. In East Asia, these challenges are met by a wide range of institutions, private as well as public.

Rationalizing

Industries in developing countries are often characterized by a large number of producers in small markets. This market fragmentation can be beneficial: it can force local firms to expand production skills and develop "economies of scope," it can generate capacity to service new markets,[39] it can ensure competitive pressure, and it can help ensure that local suppliers are not the captive of one particular client. But multiproduct firms often encounter real problems in production management, and without some minimum demand, firms cannot hope to reach scale economies large enough to master relevant production processes and technology (Prendergast 1990). Thus rationalization—reduction in the number of firms, brands, and/or models—is an important challenge (Markusen 1992, 29).

As illustrated by the auto industry, the East Asian countries have addressed this problem with varying degrees of success and through different instruments (Doner 1992). South Korea has been the most successful, in part due to state mandates such as limits on the number of vehicle assemblers. But what is striking, given Korea's reputation as a strong-state country, is the degree to which the country's rationalization reflected private sector initiatives and bargaining between the state and private firms. Perhaps most important has been Hyundai's decision to focus on single models (first with the Ford Cortina and subsequently with the firm's own Pony). Malaysia has also achieved some success in reducing brands through a state-led joint venture with Mitsubishi, whose tariff preferences effectively excluded other makes from the most popular market niche. Elsewhere in the region, brand reduction efforts have not succeeded. But large business groups producing components and parts in Indonesia and Thailand have achieved some success in compelling foreign assemblers to accept standardized products. As the localization process continues and costs increase, we can assume that such commonization efforts will intensify.

Importing Technology

I have noted several channels for obtaining foreign technology. The private sector plays a much greater role in these processes than is usually acknowledged in the political science literature. At the same time, successful private efforts usually require political, as well as institutional, support from the state.

The choice of channel through which to obtain knowledge-based assets may, as noted earlier, vary with the industry. Public policy also influences this choice; Korea's efforts to limit Japanese penetration have resulted in greater

---

39. A Malaysian firm, having produced small volumes of a particular type of glass for several years, subsequently began to sell large quantities of this product to the North African replacement market (author interview).

use of licensing agreements than elsewhere in the region. But the most important influence on the source of foreign technology seems to be the strength of local firms. Joint ventures seem to predominate when host country firms are seeking to induce new technologies. Licensing and technical assistance become more common as local entrepreneurs begin to master technology and the technology becomes more standardized.[40] Note, however, that this pattern is not linear. For example, when Japanese assemblers decided to expand the value of parts obtained in Thailand, a long-standing licensing agreement between the major Thai radiator firm and its Japanese licenser changed to a joint venture. This certainly reflected the Japanese desire to control the transfer of new technology. But this was not a decision imposed on the Thai firm. The latter, although concerned about increased Japanese control, faced major investments in a new stamping line and in-house die production, and believed that a Japanese joint venture partner would provide more solid support than would a licenser (author interviews).

Host country firms have been especially influential with regard to the choice of and benefits derived from licensing and technical assistance contracts. Even in South Korea, where the Foreign Capital Deliberation Committee monitors and approves all technological transfer agreements, there is significant leeway for private sector initiative. Unlike other Korean auto firms, Hyundai has truly shopped around and diversified its technology sources. By 1979 Hyundai licensed over thirty different technologies. In some cases the firm looks to different sources for the same technology, obtaining fundamental concepts from a U.S. firm but then turning to the Japanese for help in practical applications. And although it maintains equity links with Mitsubishi, Hyundai reserves the right "to compete directly in Mitsubishi's own markets and to import technology and parts from Mitsubishi's competitors" (Amsden and Kim 1985).

Private sector decisions as to technology sources seem to have been equally important in the Korean heavy equipment industry as well as in the Taiwan machine tool industry (Amsden and Kim 1986; Fransman 1986a). Larger Thai and Indonesian firms in autos and textiles have also diversified their technology sources, in some cases playing Japanese firms off against each other. Some firms have also added a dimension that reflects the region's interdependence. They have established technology agreements with overseas Chinese firms, often from Hong Kong and Taiwan, who themselves have long operated as suppliers to or partners with Japanese firms. Such NIC sources allow ASEAN firms to obtain technology at significantly better terms than from the Japanese. In a variation of this pattern, Lam notes that Taiwan's small and medium-sized electronics manufacturers initially benefited from "extensive networks of

---

40. This was the case, for example, for South Korean firms attempting to obtain technology from the leading Japanese fiber producers, Toray and Teijin, during the 1960s (Tho 1988, 395–96). For similar patterns see Kim (1984, 85).

friends and relatives overseas, who helped them market their products and acquire new technology and knowhow" (1990, 33).

Foreign machinery suppliers are a further important source of technology for host country producers. One of several "specialized technological agents," machinery suppliers provide information on issues such as quality control, equipment maintenance, and process organization (Dahlman, Ross-Larson, and Westphal 1987, 772). To the extent that such suppliers are not linked to Japanese principals, they also offer technology that is cheaper, more accessible, and more adaptable by East Asian producers.[41] Thai textile firms, for example, obtained significant amounts of machinery from the People's Republic of China during the 1980s (author interviews, Bangkok, 1992). Quite often such machinery is obsolete secondhand equipment from Europe and Japan. Obsolescent Japanese machinery made possible the initial growth of Hong Kong and Taiwan textile exporters (Lam 1990, 33). Thai auto parts and components producers have developed extensive contacts with secondhand machinery suppliers in Japan. This has, for example, allowed one Thai firm to develop its own boring machines by using Thai-built and used imported components to build the machine around a new boring head purchased from Japan (author interview).

Finally, firms in developing Asia often obtain technology as subcontractors to Japanese producers. Such supply relationships, discussed earlier, potentially involve the provision of a wide range of knowledge-based assets, including blueprints, machinery and plant operation, quality control, training in Japan, and so forth. But such linkages should be seen less as an institution imposed by foreign firms and more as something reflecting host country conditions and influencing the decisions of foreign, especially Japanese, firms (e.g., Dahlman and Brimble 1990, 23). Indeed, what is striking in East Asia is the cross-national range of variation with regard to the development of subcontracting relations (e.g., Amsden and Kim 1986; Fujimori 1986). To a large degree, this variation is the result of differences in economic and political factors noted earlier, such as the structure of industrial organization and the role of small firms within the state's basic coalition.

Education and R&D constitute one final area in which politics interacts with private efforts to influence the technology absorption process. Where the state provides public goods–type incentives, we see not only public research institutes and quality education but also extensive private sector initiatives. This is clearly the case in South Korea, where, for example, all major synthetic fiber producers established their own research institutes by the end of the 1970s (Tho 1988, 397). In Thailand, on the other hand, where textiles and apparel

---

41. A Thai parts-firm director noted that his Japanese licenser constantly pushes for the most expensive machinery. He admits that such machinery will last for thirty years but searches for other machinery in large part because he does not benefit from the low interest rates on industrial loans common in Japan (author interview).

constitute the largest manufacturing industry and the principal source of manufactured exports, bureaucratic fragmentation, the lack of public-private sector
linkages, and the lack of a coherent R&D policy have blocked the establishment of a textile research institute proposed by the private sector several years
ago (see, e.g., Dahlman and Brimble 1990).

Private sector initiatives themselves, however, are important in several ways.
First, some firms make use of public sector incentives more than others. Hyundai Motor Company, in part by drawing on expertise from other firms in the
Hyundai group, established a Department of Planning in 1973 and an R&D
center in 1979 to obtain and adapt foreign technologies at the lowest price. The
other major firm, Daewoo, has not followed this path (Amsden and Kim 1985;
Back 1990). Second, there is evidence that R&D initiatives by large firms,
such as Siam Cement (Thailand) and Astra (Indonesia), have jumped ahead of
relatively passive government policies. And finally, as noted earlier, there is
evidence of Japanese support for an expansion of both public and private sector
research capacities in Southeast Asia.

5.5.3   Regional Management of FI

My emphasis has been on management of FI at the national level largely
because intraregional investments have largely been a function of market
forces and private sector preferences operating independently of any organizational efforts (Lim 1992). The one partial exception to this pattern illustrates
both the obstacles to regional investment management and the ways in which,
however slowly, Japanese and local capital have interacted to create some regional patterns. These programs, I argue, will encourage the development of a
regional division of labor.

The case discussed here involves efforts by ASEAN to establish an auto
complementarity program in order to overcome the inefficiencies of production
for fragmented, small markets. The initial impulse for this project came from
Ford's interest in building an "Asian car" during the early 1970s. Ford's effort
was defeated in part by Southeast Asian suspicions that such a vehicle would
simply facilitate the expansion of Ford's economic empire. Equally important,
however, were the objections of Japanese firms then in the process of establishing themselves in the ASEAN markets.[42]

The complementarity concept was revived in 1976 when a summit meeting
of the ASEAN heads of state revitalized both private and public sector activities in ASEAN. The meeting led to the establishment of regional industry
clubs, the most active of which was the ASEAN Automotive Federation
(AAF). Subsequent efforts led to the establishment of a program in which particular countries would specialize in the production of particular auto parts/
components. These products would enjoy tariff exemptions and local content

---

42. The emphasis on local suspicions is found in Young (1986). The emphasis on Japanese
influence is drawn from author interviews. This discussion draws on these two sources.

accreditation in the other ASEAN member states, thus encouraging their production for the regional market.

This effort also failed. The member states were not able to agree on levels of foreign involvement. They also differed with regard to potential trade imbalances resulting from the production of higher value-added goods in Singapore, say, compared to Malaysia. Indeed, in the late 1970s, the project prompted competing engine manufacturing projects in Thailand, Indonesia, and the Philippines. These were designed to ensure the position of each country in higher value-added products. Also hindering the project were overlapping production facilities in the countries. Thai firms were not willing to abandon or diversify out of their investments so that Philippine firms could dominate the manufacture of a particular product. Equally important, however, was Japanese opposition. By the late 1970s the Japanese dominated the Southeast Asian markets and auto production facilities. They participated in the regional discussions but refused to move forward, citing high transportation costs, intra-ASEAN disputes, and the impossibility of one assembler using components made under the umbrella of another.

By the mid-1980s, it had become clear that only a plan based on the strategic interests of each assembler, rather than each ASEAN country, would be feasible. The AAF thus developed a "brand-to-brand" (BTB) proposal. The initial Japanese response was largely indifferent, and the plan, along with the AAF, lay dormant for several years.

There has, however, been progress on two fronts. First, as described earlier, the deepening and expansion of Japanese auto production has prompted the assemblers to submit firm-specific plans for regional production within a modified BTB framework. This is an uneven process, with Mitsubishi taking the lead and Indonesia holding back, its government clinging to the objective of a completely integrated national auto industry. But it is a first step, and further progress will probably occur under the pressure of Japanese attempts to expand scale economies.

The second area of progress—the ASEAN Industrial Joint Venture program (AIJV)—has the potential to create networks somewhat more independent of Japanese production structures. With the failure of regionwide efforts, local entrepreneurs in 1980 began to design a lower-level model of cooperation in the form of a joint venture agreement between interests from at least two different ASEAN members with majority equity from local interests. The products of such ventures would enjoy tariff reductions and local content accreditation in the countries participating.

Although just getting started, the program's smaller scale has provided opportunities for local initiative and participation by non-Japanese firms. The first AIJV, for example, involves electrical motorcycle parts and is jointly held by Thai and Malaysian interests. Yamaha's Thai partner initiated the project with support from Thailand's major peak association, the Federation of Thai Industries. Yamaha itself reportedly still opposes the project. Other AIJVs involve the engineering firm of Siam Cement, Thailand's largest industrial group, as well as several European firms.[43]

Several features of these efforts merit note. Most importantly, regional programs in the auto industry will continue to follow rather than lead regional investment decisions by Japanese firms. However, prior regional and national efforts will accelerate and mold those investment decisions. On the regional level, it is likely that the BTB plan hastened Mitsubishi's efforts by establishing a rough set of institutional guidelines. On the national level, the Japanese are attempting to reconcile their regional plans with each country's existing strengths in parts production. It is also possible that the pressure to achieve greater economies of scale will lead to more cooperation among Japanese firms in the production of major components. The sharing of dieing and casting facilities for the manufacture of engines in Thailand is one such case (Doner 1991).

Finally, as ASEAN businessmen emphasize, the very process of attempting to design a complementarity scheme encouraged organizational development—the growth of assembler and auto parts associations in each country— and cross-national contacts among firms. The latter have reportedly led to the establishment of some of the AIJVs.

5.6   U.S. Interests: Implications

The Pacific Asian region described in this paper is characterized first and foremost by production linkages and shifting comparative advantage. The region also exhibits a less developed but potentially important feature, the gradual diffusion of Japanese-style institutions. But as other papers in this volume argue, the region is not a closed trading bloc. With most of the countries in the region strongly dependent on Western, especially U.S., markets, Japan and the other countries of the region are part of a triangular trading system. In broad terms Japan sells capital goods to the rest of East Asia, the rest of East Asia sells finished goods to the United States, and the United States sells raw materials to Japan. Japan is a critical contributor to each of these developments. Yet, as captured in Unger's phrase "Big Little Japan," Tokyo's political vision does not yet match its impressive economic strength (1993; see also Tamamoto 1990).

These features—strong production ties, growing institutional commonalities, outward trade orientation, and weak political vision by the strongest economic actor—challenge U.S. corporate interests in the region as well as Washington's broader concerns with economic stability and security.

5.6.1   U.S. Firms in East Asia

As developing Asia's dynamic growth becomes more evident, so does the declining position of U.S. firms in many (but certainly not all) industries in the

---

43. On an extensive auto-related AIJV undertaken by the truck firm DAF, see *Business Asia,* December 17, 1990, 433–34.

region. Preceding sections of this paper suggest several possible reasons for this state of affairs, including (1) host country adoption of Japanese industrial standards at odds with U.S. equipment; (2) the establishment of Japanese networks that are difficult to penetrate by outsiders; (3) the lack of institutional supports providing U.S. firms information about local economic and political conditions; (4) "country bias" factors such as general lack of information and interest about the region on the part of U.S. firms (one Malaysian supplier noted that some officials from U.S. auto firms viewed Southeast Asian markets as similar to Australia due to physical proximity); (5) short U.S. time horizons encouraged by the need for immediate returns on investment; (6) lack of fit between U.S. firms' mass production emphasis and the need for more flexible production in the region's smaller, fragmented markets; and (7) domestic protectionism discouraging U.S. FDI (as in many textile sectors).[44]

Although Japanese investment will most likely dominate capital from other sources in the region, there are several reasons to believe that this domination need not be so absolute. Anecdotal evidence suggests a strong desire on the part of many in the region to moderate the weight of Japanese capital with U.S. investment. As local firms expand their own bargaining leverage, they will presumably improve their capacity to draw on diverse sources of finance, technology, and managerial skills.

U.S. firms can also adopt several measures to improve their position in the region. At one level this involves making better use of corporate tie-ups. U.S. firms can pursue what one auto parts official termed a "shirttail strategy" involving joint ventures with Taiwanese firms to break into Japanese supplier networks in the region. In a related approach, U.S. firms can follow the example of Dana, an auto components firm with extensive experience in the region, by using sales to Japanese transplants in the United States to begin similar sales in East Asia (Lehner 1992b). Tie-ups with Japanese trading companies coordinating infrastructural investment offer still another channel (e.g., Lehner 1992a).

Linkages with politically and managerially strong host country firms are especially important. Dana itself quit Indonesia several years ago, in part due to a lack of a good local partner (Doner 1991, 146–48), whereas Guardian Industries, a major U.S. glass producer, succeeded in establishing a Thai production site in part through links to Siam Cement. Such tie-ups require better firm-level information, which in turn often hinges on extending the time period of expatriate managers. Perhaps more important, stronger linkages require shifts in U.S. managerial approaches. The simple fact is that many established local entrepreneurs, given the expansion of their operations and investments, are becoming more choosy about foreign partners. Local capitalists are some-

---

44. Recent articles decrying and analyzing the sources of U.S. weakness in Asia include Lim (1991); Lehner (1992b); Sanger (1991); and Darlin and White (1992).

times hesitant to engage in joint activities with U.S. firms because of the latters' narrow focus on price and delivery.

According to interviews, several U.S. electronic and auto firms operating in Southeast Asia have begun to address these concerns. They have essentially attempted to emulate Japanese-style supply networks by developing longer-term, trust-based relations with suppliers and clients. Whether such attempts succeed depends in large part on support from the home office. But they do signify East Asia's potential as a test site for U.S. firms attempting to improve production management, as well as a base for breaking into Japanese production networks and, potentially, the Japanese market. This is somewhat ironic, since Southeast Asia functioned in the 1960s and early 1970s as a test site for Japanese auto firms hoping to break into the U.S. market.

5.6.2   U.S. Economic and Security Interests

In a worst-case scenario, an economically more integrated and Japan-dominated East Asia might prompt a broader U.S. disengagement from the region. The demise of an ideological mission for the United States in the region, isolationist pressures in the United States, the outbreak of instability in other regions, and the weakness of U.S. corporate involvement in East Asia may all undermine domestic pressure for sustained U.S. involvement. These factors may be compounded by U.S. indignation at the structure of its triangular trade with the region and by tensions stemming from a more assertive Japanese voice with regard to broader economic questions. Japan may well be "bound by a wilful political innocence [and] a society devoid of ideas about what to give to the world, much less how to organize it" (Tamamoto 1990, 494). But that does not preclude a more forceful enunciation of Japanese views on issues, such as economic reform, that are relevant to its own economic interests (e.g., OECF 1991). Finally, tensions may increase if East Asian reactions to the formation of North American and European trading arrangements prompt regional trading arrangements perceived as exclusionary by the United States.

Washington's disengagement would not only reduce U.S. access to and influence over the world's most important source of economic growth. It would also find disfavor with Japan and the rest of the region for at least two reasons. A general U.S. withdrawal would weaken the region's ties with a critical export market. More important, it would deprive the region of a moderating influence on Pacific Asia's suspicions of Japan and thus weaken the broader political basis of the region's growth. Whether countries of the region are able and willing to influence U.S. policy remains to be seen. One hopeful sign is Japan's recognition of its own stake in maintaining the international trading and financing system (Rosecrance and Taw 1990). Where and to what extent Tokyo will extend such an attitude to regional affairs is yet unclear. But it may well be that East Asia's very ability to encourage a sustained U.S. presence depends on a greater leadership role for Tokyo.

References

Alburo, F. A., C. C. Bautista, and M. S. H. Gochoco. 1992. Pacific Direct Investment Flows into ASEAN. *ASEAN Economic Bulletin* 8 (3): 284–307.

Amsden, Alice H., and Linsu Kim. 1985. The Role of Transnational Corporations in the Production and Exports of the Korean Automobile Industry. Harvard Business School Working Paper.

———. 1986. A Technological Perpsective on the General Machinery Industry in the Republic of Korea. In Martin Fransman, ed., *Machinery and Economic Development*. London: Macmillan.

Arpan, Jeffrey S., Mary Barry, and Tran Van Tho. 1984. The Textile Complex in the Asia-Pacific Region. *Research in International Business and Finance* 4:B101–64.

Asian Labor Shortages Spur a Wage of Migration That Raises Economic and Social Questions. 1992. *Asian Wall Street Journal*, March 9.

Asia/Pacific: The New Kid on the Bloc. 1989. *Business Asia*, February 13, 7.

Awanohara, Susumu. 1986. The "Abe Doctrine." *Far Eastern Economic Review*, June 26, 22, 25.

Back, Johng Kook. 1990. Politics of Late Industrialization: The Origins and Processes of Automobile Industry Policies in Mexico and South Korea. Ph.D. diss., University of California, Los Angeles.

Baum, Julian, and Louise do Rosario. 1991. The Sumo Neighbour. *Far Eastern Economic Review*, February 21, 40–43.

Calder, Kent. 1988. *Crisis and Compensation: Public Policy and Political Stability in Japan*. Princeton: Princeton University Press.

Chen, Edward K. Y. 1989. The Changing Role of the Asian NICs in the Asian-Pacific Region towards the Year 2000. In Shinohara Miyohei and Lo Fu-chen, eds., *Global Adjustment and the Future of Asian-Pacific Economy*. Tokyo: Institute of Developing Economies.

Cumings, Bruce. [1984] 1987. The Origins and Development of the Northeast Asian Political Economy. Frederic Deyo, ed., *The Political Economy of the New Asian Industrialism*. Ithaca: Cornell University Press.

Dahlman, Carl J., and Peter Brimble. 1990. *Technology Strategy and Policy for Industrial Competitiveness: A Case Study of Thailand*. Washington, D.C.: World Bank Industry and Energy Department.

Dahlman, Carl J., Bruce Ross-Larson, and Larry Westphal. 1987. Managing Technological Development: Lessons from the Newly Industrializing Countries. *World Development* 15 (6): 759–75.

Darlin, Damon, and Joseph White. 1992. GM Venture in Korea Nears End, Betraying Firm's Fond Hopes. *Wall Street Journal*, January 16.

Defense Tactics. 1991. *Far Eastern Economic Review*, July 25, 52–53.

Doner, Richard F. 1991. *Driving a Bargain: Automobile Industrialization and Japanese Firms in Southeast Asia*. Berkeley: University of California Press.

———. 1992. Limits of State Strength: Toward an Institutionalist View of Economic Development. *World Politics* 44 (3): 398–431.

do Rosario, Louise. 1992. Engines of Growth: "Made in Asia"—on a Japanese Machine. *Far Eastern Economic Review*, May 21, 38.

Encarnation, Dennis J. 1992. *Rivals beyond Trade: America versus Japan in Global Competition*. Ithaca: Cornell University Press.

Fields, Karl J. 1989. Trading Companies in South Korea and Taiwan: Two Policy Approaches. *Asian Survey* 29 (11): 1073–89.

———. 1990. Developmental Capitalism and Industrial Organization: Business Groups and the State in Korea and Taiwan. Ph.D. diss., University of California, Berkeley.

Fransman, Martin. 1986a. International Competitiveness, International Diffusion of Technology, and the State: A Case Study from Taiwan and Japan. In Martin Fransman, ed., *Machinery and Economic Development*. London: Macmillan.

———, ed. 1986b. *Machinery and Economic Development*. London: Macmillan.

Fujimori, Hideo. 1986. Industrial Policy and Technology Transfer: A Case Study of the Automobile Industry in the Philippines. *Developing Economies* 24 (4): 349–67.

Haggard, Stephan. 1990. *Pathways from the Periphery: The Politics of Growth in the Newly Industrializing Countries*. Ithaca: Cornell University Press.

Handley, Paul. 1991. Make It Yourself. *Far Eastern Economic Review,* July 18, 46–47.

Haseyama Takahiko, Honobe Susumu, and O'uchi Minoru. 1989. New Issues of Economic Cooperation. In Shinohara Myohei and Lo Fu-chen, eds., *Global Adjustment and the Future of Asian-Pacific Economy*. Tokyo: Institute of Developing Economies.

Healey, Derek. 1992. *Japanese Capital Exports and Asian Economic Development*. Paris: OECD.

Hill, Hal. 1988. *Foreign Investment and Industrialization in Indonesia*. New York: Oxford University Press.

Hirata Akira, and Nohara Takashi. 1989. Changing Patterns in International Division of Labour in Asia and the Pacific. In Shinohara Miyohei and Lo Fu-chen, eds., *Global Adjustment and the Future of Asian Pacific Economy*. Tokyo: Institute of Developing Economies.

Hirst, Paul, and Jonathan Zeitlin. 1991. Flexible Specialization versus Post-Fordism: Theory, Evidence, and Policy Implications. *Economy and Society* 20 (1): 1–56.

Holloway, Nigel. 1989. The Numbers Game. *Far Eastern Economic Review,* November 16, 71–72.

A Japanese Approach to Investment. 1991. *Economist Intelligence Unit Textile Outlook International* (March): 33–41.

Japan International Cooperation Agency (JICA). 1989. A Study on Industrial Sector Development in the Kingdom of Thailand. Second year, final report draft, Bangkok.

Johnstone, Bob. 1988. Diversification Helps to Protect Profits. *Far Eastern Economic Review,* October 13, 54–56.

Jomo, K. S., ed. 1985. *The Sun Also Sets: Lessons in "Looking East."* (Kuala Lumpur: Institute for Social Analysis).

Japan's Drive into Asia: The Emerging Regional Bloc. 1989. *Business Asia* 21 (February 13): 49–53.

Kim Young Kee. 1984. American Technology and Korea's Technological Development. In Karl Moskowitz, ed., *From Patron to Partner: The Development of U.S.-Korean Business and Trade Relations*. Lexington, MA: D. C. Heath.

Kobrin, Stephen J. 1984. Economic Nationalism in the Developing Countries of the Asia-Pacific Region. In Richard Moxon, Thomas Roehl, and J. Frederick Truitt, eds., *International Business Strategies in the Asia-Pacific Region: Industry Studies.* Greenwich, CT: JAI Press.

Kohama Hirohisa and Urata Shujiro. 1988. The Impact of the Recent Yen Appreciation on the Japanese Economy. *Developing Economies* 26 (4): 323–40.

Koike Kazuo and Takenori Inoki, eds. 1990. *Skill Formation in Japan and Southeast Asia*. Tokyo: University of Tokyo Press.

Kojima Kiyoshi and Ozawa Terutomo. 1986. Japanese-Style Direct Foreign Investment. *Japanese Economic Studies* 14 (Spring): 52–82.

Lall, Sanjaya. 1991. Asia's Emerging Sources of Foreign Investment. *East Asian Executive Reports* (June): 7, 19–25.

Lam, Danny K. K. 1990. Independent Economic Sectors and Economic Growth in Hong Kong and Taiwan. *International Studies Notes* 15 (Winter): 28–34.

———. 1991. The Myth of State-Led Industrialization: The Origins of Electronics Manufacturing in Taiwan. Paper presented at the 1991 American Political Science Association meeting, Washington, D.C., September.

Lehner, Urban C. 1992a. Japanese Prepare for Vietnam Gold Rush. *Wall Street Journal,* February 21.

————. 1992b. Some U.S. Firms Profit in Booming Far East despite Mighty Japan. *Wall Street Journal,* January 1.

Lim, Linda. 1991. Explaining the Decline of U.S. Investment in Southeast Asia. *Journal of Southeast Asia Business* 7 (2): 90–93.

————. 1992. The Role of the Private Sector in ASEAN Regional Economic Cooperation. Paris: OECD Development Center.

Lim, Linda Y. C., and Pang Eng Fong. 1988. *Foreign Investment, Industrial Restructuring, and Changing Comparative Advantage: The Experiences of Malaysia, Thailand, Singapore, and Taiwan.* Paris: OECD.

Lindsey, Charles W. 1983. In Search of Dynamism: Foreign Investment in the Philippines under Martial Law. *Pacific Affairs* 56 (3): 477–94.

Lipsey, Robert E. 1992. Direct Foreign Investment and Structural Change in Developing Asia, Japan, and the United States. In Eric D. Ramstetter, ed., *Direct Foreign Investment in Asia's Developing Economies and Structural Change in the Asia-Pacific Region.* Boulder, CO: Westview Press.

Lo Fu-chen, Song Byung-Nak, and Furukawa Shunichi. 1989. Patterns of Development and Interdependence among the East and Southeast Asian Economies. In Shinohara Miyohei and Lo Fu-chen, eds., *Global Adjustment and the Future of Asian-Pacific Economy.* Tokyo: Institute of Developing Economies.

Long Term Credit Bank of Japan (LTCB). 1987. The Automobile Industries of Asia NICs and Globalization of Japanese Auto and Auto Parts Manufacturers. *LTCB Research Economic Review* 90 (May): 1–10.

McVey, Ruth. 1992. *Southeast Asian Capitalists.* Ithaca: Cornell University Southeast Asia Program.

Mardon, Russell. 1990. The State and the Effective Control of Foreign Capital: The Case of South Korea. *World Politics* 43 (October): 111–38.

Markusen, James R. 1992. The Theory of the Multinational Enterprise: A Common Analytical Framework. In Eric D. Ramstetter, ed., *Direct Foreign Investment in Asia's Developing Economies and Structural Change in the Asia-Pacific Region.* Boulder, CO: Westview Press.

Moon, Chung-in. 1988. The Demise of a Developmentalist State? Neoconservative Reforms and Political Consequences in South Korea. *Journal of Development Studies* (4): 67–84.

Nakakita Toru. 1988. The Globalization of Japanese Firms and Its Influence on Japan's Trade with Developing Countries. *Developing Economies* 26 (4): 306–22.

Noble, Gregory W. 1987. Contending Forces in Taiwan's Economic Policymaking. *Asian Survey* 27 (6): 683–703.

————. 1989. The Japanese Industrial Policy Debate. In Stephen Haggard and Chung-in Moon, eds., *Pacific Dynamics: The International Politics of Industrial Change.* Boulder, Colo.: Westview Press.

Overseas Economic Cooperation Fund. 1991. Issues Related to the World Bank's Approach to Structural Adjustment: A Proposal from a Major Partner. OECF Occasional Paper no. 1. Tokyo, October.

Ozawa, Terutomo. 1986. Japan's Largest Financier of Multinationalism: The Exim Bank. *Journal of World Trade Law* 20 (6): 599–614.

Pangestu, Mari. 1987. The Pattern of Direct Foreign Investment in ASEAN: The U.S. vs. Japan. *ASEAN Economic Bulletin* 3 (3): 301–28.

————. 1992. Foreign Firms and Structural Change in the Indonesian Manufacturing Sector. In Eric D. Ramstetter, ed., *Direct Foreign Investment in Asia's Developing Economies and Structural Change in the Asia-Pacific Region.* Boulder, CO: Westview Press.

Pempel, T. J. 1989. Japan's Creative Conservatism—Continuity under Challenge. In Francis G. Castles, ed., *The Comparative History of Public Policy*. Cambridge: Polity Press.

Petri, Peter A. 1992. One Bloc, Two Blocs, or None? Political-Economic Factors in Pacific Trade Policy. In Kaoru Okuzumi, Kent E. Calder, and Gerrit W. Gong, eds., *The U.S.-Japan Economic Relationship in East and Southeast Asia*. Washington, D.C.: Center for Strategic and International Studies.

Phongpaichit, Pasuk. 1988. Decision-Making on Overseas Direct Investment by Japanese Small and Medium Industries in ASEAN and the Asian NICs. *ASEAN Economic Bulletin* (March): 302–15.

————. 1991. Japan's Investment and Local Capital in ASEAN since 1985. In Shoichi Yamashita, ed., *Transfer of Japanese Technology and Management to the ASEAN Countries*. Tokyo: University of Tokyo Press.

Plummer, Michael G., and Eric D. Ramstetter. 1992. Multinational Affiliates and the Changing Division of Labor in the Asia-Pacific Region. In Eric D. Ramstetter, ed., *Direct Foreign Investment in Asia's Developing Economies and Structural Change in the Asia-Pacific Region*. Boulder, CO: Westview Press.

Prendergast, Renee. 1990. Causes of Multiproduct Production: The Case of the Engineering Industries in Developing Countries. *World Development* 18 (3): 361–70.

Ramstetter, Eric D. 1988. Taiwan's Direct Foreign Investment in Thailand: The Potential for Technology Transfer. *Development and South-South Cooperation* 4 (7): 113–27.

————. 1991a. An Overview of Multinational Firms in Asia-Pacific Developing Economies: An Introduction to the Commonplace Ignorance. Paper prepared for Asian Productivity Organization/Institute for Economic Development seminar on the Role of Foreign Direct Investment in Development, Seoul, September 16–20.

————. 1991b. *Regional Patterns of Japanese Multinational Activities in Japan and Asia's Developing Countries*. Osaka: Kansai University, Institute of Economic and Political Studies.

————, ed. 1992. *Direct Foreign Investment in Asia's Developing Economies and Structural Change in the Asia-Pacific Region*. Boulder, CO: Westview Press.

Rosecrance, Richard, and Jennifer Taw. 1990. Japan and the Theory of International Leadership. *World Politics* 42 (2): 184–209.

Rowley, Anthony. 1992a. The Asia Card. *Far Eastern Economic Review*, February 6, 50.

————. 1992b. Japan Looks Closer to Home. *Far Eastern Economic Review*, January 16, 40.

Sanger, David E. 1991. Power of the Yen Winning Asia: New "Co-prosperity" Is Displacing U.S. *New York Times*, December 5.

Shiowattana, Prayoon. 1991. Technology Transfer in Thailand's Electronics Industry. In Shoichi Yamashita, ed., *Transfer of Japanese Technology and Management to the ASEAN Countries*. Tokyo: University of Tokyo Press.

Smith, Charles. 1986. Tokyo's Neighbourly Urge. *Far Eastern Economic Review*, June 12, 56–58.

Smitka, Michael J. 1991. *Competitive Ties: Subcontracting in the Japanese Automotive Industry*. New York: Columbia University Press.

Steven, Rob. 1990. *Japan's New Imperialism*. London: Macmillan.

Stewart, Charles T. 1985. Comparing Japanese and U.S. Technology Transfer to Less-Developed Countries. *Journal of Northeast Asian Studies* (Spring): 3–19.

Tahara-Domoto Kenji and Hirohisa Kohama. 1989. Machinery Industry Development in Korea: Intra-industry Trade between Japan and Korea. Tokyo: International Development Center of Japan.

Tamamoto Masuru. 1990. Japan's Search for a World Role. *World Policy Journal* (Summer): 493–520.

Tambunlertchai, Somsak, and Eric D. Ramstetter. 1992. Foreign Firms in Promoted Industries and Structural Change in Thailand. In Eric D. Ramstetter, ed., *Direct Foreign Investment in Asia's Developing Economies and Structural Change in the Asia-Pacific Region*. Boulder, CO: Westview Press.

Tan Kong Yam, Toh Mun Heng, and Linda Low. 1991. ASEAN and the Asia Pacific. Paper presented at the Joint IPS-ISEAS ASEAN Roundtable, Singapore, June 27–28.

Tho Tran Van. 1988. Foreign Capital and Technology in the Process of Catching Up by the Developing Countries: The Experience of the Synthetic Fiber Industry in the Republic of Korea. *World Development* 26 (4): 386–402.

Ting Wenlee. 1985. *Business and Technological Dynamics in Newly Industrializing Asia*. Westport, CT: Quorum Books.

Tsuruoka, Doug. 1991. Gathering of the Clan. *Far Eastern Economic Review,* March 28, 52.

———. 1992. In the Same Mould. *Far Eastern Economic Review,* January 30, 44–45.

Unger, Daniel. 1990a. Japanese Manufacturing Investment and Export Processing Industrialization in Thailand. Harvard University Program on U.S.–Japan Relations, Occasional Paper, Cambridge, Mass.

———. 1990b. Japan's Export Processing Hinterland: Industrialization in Thailand. Paper presented at the Seminar on the Role of the State in Asian Pacific Nations and Mexico, El Colegio de Mexico, November.

———. 1993. Big Little Japan. In Robert O. Slater, Barry M. Schutz, and Stephen R. Dorr, eds., *Global Transformation and the Third World* (Boulder, CO: Lynne Rienner).

United Nations Conference on Trade and Development (UNCTAD). 1990. *Handbook of International Trade and Development Statistics*. New York: UNCTAD.

United Nations Centre on Transnational Corporations (UNCTC). 1987. *Transnational Corporations in the Man-Made Fibre, Textile, and Clothing Industries*. New York: United Nations.

Update on South Korea. 1990. *Economist Intelligence Unit International Motor Business* (April): 51–57.

Wade, Robert. 1992. East Asia's Economic Success: Conflicting Perspectives, Partial Insights, Shaky Evidence. *World Politics* 44 (2): 270–320.

Westphal, Larry E., Yung W. Rhee, and Garry Pursell. 1984. Sources of Technological Capability in South Korea. In Martin Fransman and Kenneth King, eds., *Technological Capability in the Third World*. London: Macmillan.

When Japan Is Threatened by Imports. 1988. *Economist,* June 25, 69–70.

Womack, James P., Daniel T. Jones, and Daniel Roos. 1990. *The Machine That Changed the World*. New York: Rawson.

Yamashita, Shoichi. 1991a. "Economic Development of the ASEAN Countries and the Role of Japanese Direct Investment. In Shoichi Yamashita, ed., *Transfer of Japanese Technology and Management to the ASEAN Countries*. Tokyo: University of Tokyo Press.

———, ed. 1991b. *Transfer of Japanese Technology and Management to the ASEAN Countries*. Tokyo: University of Tokyo Press.

Yamazawa, Ippei. 1990. Gearing the Japanese Economy to International Harmony. *Developing Economies* 28 (1): 3–12.

Yoon Young-kwan. 1990. The Political Economy of Transition: Japanese Foreign Direct Investments in the 1980s. *World Politics* 43 (1): 1–27.

Young, Evans. 1986. The Foreign Capital Issue in the ASEAN Chambers of Commerce and Industry. *Asian Survey* 26 (5): 688–705.

Comment   Robert E. Lipsey

As I read this paper, it occurred to me that economists tend to look for, and to find, the operations of impersonal forces—the invisible hand—and that political scientists tend to look for, and to find, the operations of conscious policy carried out by specific actors.

A basic theme of the paper is that an interdependent East Asian region is developing, and that the development is not simply a consequence of economic forces, such as trends in income and skill levels that change national comparative advantages. According to this view, the interdependent region is being constructed by conscious management of the response to economic developments by governments, by intergovernmental organizations, and by private companies and organizations representing private companies. Of course, even in the economists' world the invisible hand does not work without individuals and enterprises making choices and acting on them. One way of describing this paper is that Richard Doner is looking more at these actors and their behavior than at the underlying economic changes that are forcing them to act or at the outcomes of their actions taken in the aggregate.

It is not surprising to find that Japanese multinationals are organizing interdependent operations across national borders. That is what multinationals do. It would be interesting to know how these Japanese networks differ from those formed by American or European firms or by multinationals from developing countries, if they differ at all.

There is quite some discussion in various places in the paper about comparative advantage. Two kinds of comparative advantage are involved. One is the standard comparative advantage of countries, based on immobile factors of production. But the other determinant of direct investment is the comparative advantages of a country's firms, based on firm-specific advantages that are immobile between firms but mobile within firms across countries. The latter may stem from the former, but firms may retain some advantages, particularly those based on knowledge or technology, long after their countries have moved on to different comparative advantages, perhaps because factor endowments and factor prices have changed. And firms may develop advantages based on their own R&D, technology, or marketing skill quite apart from their countries' present or former comparative advantages.

There is a passing mention in the paper about the replacement of exports by foreign investment. The idea of such replacement by foreign *direct* investment, which, from the context, appears to be what is meant here, is highly questionable. The major empirical studies I am aware of do not find that such replacement is a general phenomenon and, more frequently than not, find that such investment raises exports. The reason is that the direct investment raises the

Robert E. Lipsey is professor of economics at Queens College and the Graduate Center, City University of New York, and a research associate of the National Bureau of Economic Research.

investor's market share in the host country and exports of components and of other finished products rise.

The explanation given in this paper of the greater willingness of Japanese firms than of American firms to accept minority equity in developing countries is an example of the rejection, or slighting, of an explanation in economic terms in favor of one based on institutional preferences. I am not sure such a difference between Japanese and American multinationals exists, but if it does, there are at least two economic explanations. One is the relative inexperience of Japanese firms in direct investment, which might make them more willing to accept partners. The other is the relatively low-tech industry composition of Japanese direct foreign investment in developing countries. The prevalence of 100 percent or majority ownership in U.S. foreign direct investment is clearly related to the technological level of the industry. To what extent could the difference between U.S. and Japanese firms be explained by industry composition? Or should the industry composition of investment itself be explained by different attitudes toward the employment of foreigners and the leakage of technological knowledge?

The paper argues that the spillover of knowledge to host country firms or nationals requires support from the state. There is certainly a large collection of regulations aimed at encouraging such spillovers, and I do believe that the spillovers are one of the main advantages of direct investment to the host country. But I do not know of strong evidence that the regulations have much effect, and there must be some level of regulation that would reduce spillovers by discouraging investment. Spillovers may depend more on the capacity of the host country to absorb technology than on regulations requiring technology transfer. Would a country gain more spillovers by raising the educational level of its citizens, by encouraging foreign study by its citizens, or by raising the technical level of local firms than by regulating foreign firms?

The reader's task is made a little harder by defining "foreign investment" in an extremely broad way, to include technology licensing and machinery sales, certainly not part of the economist's usual definition. Both of these can be arm's-length transactions involving no control over the use of the techniques or machinery, and neither one necessarily involves any transfer of capital.

There is a brief mention of political risk and of the apparent indifference of Japanese firms to it in making their investments. There have been suggestions recently that Japanese firms would shun direct investment and joint ventures in the states of the former Soviet Union because of fears of political instability. Perhaps their orientation toward investing in the United States and Southeast Asia, rather than in Latin America or Africa, reflects some concern about political stability.

6   Japan as a Regional Power in Asia

Peter J. Katzenstein and Martin Rouse

6.1   Introduction

The main protagonists of the Cold War, the United States and the Soviet Union, both "lost" the war to two trading and welfare states, Japan and Germany, whose leaders learned similar lessons from their disastrous involvement in power politics in the first half of the twentieth century. Recent events in world politics have created historic changes in international politics comparable in this century only to the years 1917–22 and 1947–53. This paper argues that Japan's future role in the international system will be affected deeply by a political regionalism in Asia that will supplement rather than replace the U.S.-Japan relationship. Will that regionalism be constructed largely around bilateral political bargains involving Japan and its Asian neighbors? Or will these bilateral bargains be embedded in a set of multilateral regional and global arrangements that also include the United States? Drawn from the experiences of two Asian nations, Thailand and Indonesia, where issues of regionalism have gained salience in the 1980s, evidence presented in this paper suggests that the answer to the first question is negative while the answer to the second is positive.

Any interpretation of Japan as a regional power requires an examination of how its political system organizes and exercises power at home and abroad. This is an issue on which Japan specialists are deeply divided. A decade of charged political debate and dispassionate scholarly discourse has created a tenuous consensus that discards the two polar views that dominated discussion in the 1970s. Power in Japan is organized neither by a monolithic coalition of

Peter J. Katzenstein is Walter S. Carpenter, Jr., Professor of International Studies at Cornell University. Martin Rouse is a Ph.D. candidate in government at Cornell University.

The authors would like to thank Benedict Anderson, Miles Kahler, Takashi Shiraishi, and Wing Woo for their detailed comments on an earlier draft of this paper.

business and government, "Japan Inc.," nor by a pluralistic system of market competition. Instead during the last decade the various interpretations that specialists have advanced stress the interaction between state and market, politicians and bureaucrats, social movements and political organizations in what Richard Samuels has aptly called a system of "reciprocal consent" (Samuels 1987). This consent balances the autonomy of the state against its embeddedness in civil society.

The behavioral consequences of this distinctive interaction between state and society in domestic politics have differed for Japan's industrial and political structures as well as for its public policies. Since 1945 Japan has succeeded in remaking its industrial structure twice, a feat not approached by any of the other advanced industrial states. At the same time Japan has been governed by the same political party without interruption since 1955, a record of political longevity that makes it unique among the world's major democracies. The flexibility of its industrial structure and the inflexibility of its political structure converge in a set of adaptable public policies. Energy and public spending are good examples. These two issues posed serious challenges to Japan and other states in the 1970s and 1980s. Through a number of deliberate policy choices in the 1970s Japan succeeded in establishing a foundation for future economic growth without increasing energy consumption. Likewise in the 1980s it succeeded in curtailing dramatically its debilitating public deficit.

The behavioral consequences of the distinctive interaction between state and society for Japan's foreign affairs are also noteworthy. Japan's approach to other states is marked by a great flexibility in how it calculates its interest and by a great inflexibility in how it conceives of Japan's identity in a world of multiple norms. For example, Japan's vulnerabilities in importing food and raw materials give rise neither to an urge for autarchy nor to a master plan for the world. Japanese policy elites believe firmly that Japan's inherent vulnerabilities can be mitigated through clever maneuvers in markets—they cannot be avoided. Thus what matters to the Japanese is the construction of vulnerabilities for other countries in areas of Japanese strength, such as manufacturing and technology. To date Japan's international conduct is not governed by any grand vision but by a sustained effort to reduce the enormous vulnerabilities it faces through altering the political leverage it has over other political economies, such as those in Asia.

The 1980s have witnessed a massive shift in relative power between the United States and Japan—exemplified by the surge in both Japanese economic and technomilitary capabilities. And in Asia there are signs of a growing regional orientation fueled by greater economic interdependence and a relative decline in the U.S. economic position vis-à-vis the Japanese and the newly industrializing countries (NICs). Japan has recently surpassed the United States as the country with the greatest amount of total foreign direct investment (FDI) in Asia. And according to the Japan Foreign Trade Council, Asia overtook the United States as Japan's largest export market in 1991 (*Far Eastern*

Table 6.1   Japan's Economic Relations with Asia (billions of dollars)

Aid/Trade FDI, September 1986–April 1989

Country	Aid	Trade	Investment
Thailand	1,307	26.5	1.81
Indonesia	1,433	48.26	1.72
Malaysia	777	29.49	.99
Philippines	1,364	13.30	.33
Singapore	—	36.93	2.35
South Korea	—	93.85	1.95
China	2,177	53.19	2.00
Taiwan	—	78.51	1.23

FDI in Asia, 1951–88

Country	Manufacturing	Resource Development	Commerce	Others	Total
ASEAN					
Thailand	1,456	38	416	82	1,992
Indonesia	2,955	6,441	400	8	9,804
Malaysia	1,350	179	294	11	1,834
Philippines	510	455	144	11	1,120
Singapore	1,990	5	1,744	73	3,182
NICs					
Hong Kong	492	33	5,515	127	6,167
South Korea	1,589	21	1,506	132	3,248
Taiwan	1,473	4	246	68	1,791
China	349	48	1,575	64	2,036
Rest of Asia	207	119	85	12	423
Total	12,371	7,343	11,925	588	32,227

Source: Far Eastern Economic Review, May 3, 1990 (MITI and Ministry of Finance).

Economic Review, July 25, 1991, 91). Much of this expansion in trade stems from the great increase in demand for Japanese capital goods in the wake of the rapid Japanese foreign investment expansion in Asia. Japan also provides more financial aid and loans to Asia than does the United States and is seeking an even greater role in the Asian Development Bank (Friedland 1988; Awano-hara 1991b).

With the continuing strength of the Japanese economy and the revaluation of the yen after the signing of the 1985 Plaza Accord, Japanese investment has flooded into the ASEAN nations (table 6.1).[1] The accelerated pace of Japan's economic involvement in the ASEAN nations built on an already significant Japanese presence developed since the end of World War II. During the period 1969–81, for example, 48 percent of ASEAN's FDI was from Japan, and from 1972 to 1981 45 percent of aid to the region came from Japan ("Uneasy Neigh-

1. The ASEAN countries include Brunei, Indonesia, the Philippines, Malaysia, Thailand, and Singapore.

bors" 1983, 94). The importance of Japan as a source of technology, loans, and investment has grown even more dramatically over the past six years. The total amount of FDI in ASEAN originating from Japan between 1985 and 1989 was two times the total amount invested from 1951 to 1985 (do Rosario 1990, 48).

As this influx of capital continues, governments in the region are considering carefully the long-term implications of their relationship with Japan. Specifically, they are exploring whether and how their relationship with Japan can be managed, restructured, or expanded. On the one hand, Japan's increasing economic involvement in the region has been encouraged by almost all governments in Southeast Asia. There is no better proof of this encouragement than the liberalization of economies in the region and the extension of lucrative privileges to attract foreign investors for export promotion policies, as Richard Doner's chapter in this volume illustrates. Furthermore, many ASEAN countries have actively sought to emulate Japan's model of development in both the private and public sectors. Many Thai and Malaysian businesses have established trading companies, for example, and as Prime Minister Mahathir's recent proposal for a trading bloc excluding the United States suggests, some ASEAN politicians and bureaucrats are interested in even greater ties to Japan.[2]

At the same time as ASEAN leaders observe a growing dependence on their northern neighbor, there is apprehension concerning their future relationship with Japan. The ASEAN nations have witnessed the winding-down of the Cold War in Europe and are uneasy about the potential unraveling of U.S.-Japanese security arrangements, a fear that has rekindled memories of the wartime Greater East Asia Co-prosperity Sphere.[3] Some countries view economic integration in Europe and America with growing trepidation, for it is difficult to envision a counterweight to Japanese power in Asia, were an Asian trading bloc to emerge in the near future. Most ASEAN nations depend heavily on the United States and Europe for export markets, and ASEAN alone neither generates significant internal trade nor provides adequate leverage against a Japan playing the role of "regional hegemon." The total GNP of the ASEAN nations is less than 10 percent of Japan's, and significant economic cooperation among the six countries is virtually nonexistent. To date ASEAN remains largely a political grouping with limited success in fostering industrial and

2. See Machado (1987). In the early 1980s Mahathir, irked that large neon signs of Japanese companies spoiled the view from his governmental palace, requested that the signs be turned off at night. After criminal activity increased sharply, however, he requested that the advertisements be relit. This is a small but revealing example of ASEAN dependence on Japan.

3. In Japan the right-wing nationalist Shintaro Ishihara openly talks of the recreation of the Dai Toa Kyoei-ken, the Greater East Asia Co-prosperity Sphere. In the 1991 July cover story of the Japanese journal *Sansarra* he writes: "Japan is now qualified to revive its global ideal, the Greater East Asia Co-Prosperity Sphere, which had no chance before the War." He argues that Japan "has no need to have a military presence in Southeast Asia." If other Asian countries resist Japan's leadership, "there are other ways to make them realize the consequences." For example, "We can cut off the flow of technology." See Doi and Willenson (1991, 6).

commercial cooperation. The January 1992 signing of an agreement to create an ASEAN free trade area over the next fifteen years represents one of the first significant steps toward greater economic cooperation. At present it remains much more of an ideal than a reality.[4]

This paper seeks to understand Japan's role as a regional power in Asia by analyzing Thailand's and Indonesia's policy toward Japan in section 6.2, examining Japan's role in the development of Thai and Indonesian infrastructure in section 6.3, and drawing some conclusions in section 6.4.

6.2   Thai and Indonesia Policy toward Japan

6.2.1   Case Selection

Within ASEAN, Thailand and Indonesia offer important test cases for the study of the emerging political and economic contours of Japanese-led regionalism. By observing the recent policies these countries have adopted to deal with Japan, it is possible to explore the present and future dimensions of Japan's role in Asia. A focus on Thailand and Indonesia is useful in several respects. Japan has historically been interested in both nations for markets and natural resources such as oil. It colonized or indirectly ruled both countries during World War II. Japan's continuing interest in both political economies, furthermore, is demonstrated by the fact that Indonesia presently receives a greater share of Japanese foreign aid than does any other nation in the world (approximately 11 percent of Japan's bilateral aid) and is a top destination for Japanese capital in Asia (Schwarz 1990). Thailand is the fourth largest recipient of Japanese aid and has received substantially increased amounts of Japanese manufacturing investment since 1985. Both countries are important strategically to Japan. Indonesia supplies Japan with 13 percent of its crude oil imports and 53 percent of its natural gas. The rest of Japan's oil imports pass through Indonesian waters. Because of its growing economy and its position in mainland politics, Thailand is viewed by the Japanese as the rising star among the ASEAN nations.[5] Both countries offer Japanese businesses large and growing

4. Proposals for a free trade zone among the ASEAN states have been justified to the public largely as a means of attracting greater foreign investment. The prime minister of Thailand, Anand Panyarachun, whose proposal was adopted January 28, 1992, has stated that "Japan, the U.S. and the E. C. would be more interested in investment following formation of a free trade area which would create a larger market" (*Nation,* August 3, 1991, B8). The new trade accord allows numerous loopholes that exempt hundreds of products from the proposed tariff reductions.

5. The recent progress toward a peace settlement in Cambodia and the liberal investment climates that have been created by the Laotian and Vietnamese versions of *perestroika* have led to a great expansion in the trade and investment opportunities in all three countries. The Thais hope that they will be well placed to take advantage of these new opportunities by serving as a partner to East Asian investors. Thailand's greatest fear is that Japan may move directly into Vietnam, especially if the United States–led embargo is lifted. There are growing indications that Japanese business is already dealing directly with Vietnam without using Thais as middlemen. Reportedly Japan is importing 80 percent of Vietnam's crude oil and has opened unofficial trade offices in Saigon and Hanoi. See Shenon (1992).

Table 6.2   Country Profiles, Thailand and Indonesia

	Thailand	Indonesia
Population (million)	56	178
Population growth rate (%)	2	2.1
Land area (square km)	514,000	1,919,443
GDP (US$ billions 1989)	66.2	95.59
Per capita GDP (US$)	1,180	504
GDP growth rate (% per annum)		
1971–80 (average)	9.9	7.9
1981	6.3	7.9
1982	4.1	2.2
1983	7.3	4.2
1984	7.1	6.7
1985	3.5	2.5
1986	4.5	5.9
1987	8.4	4.8
1988	12.0	5.7
1989	10.8	6.5
1990 (estimated)	9.9	6.4

Sources: Asian Business, February–March 1990; Asian Development Bank (1990).

markets—Indonesia with 178 million inhabitants, and Thailand with 56 million, with per capita incomes at US$504 and US$1,180, respectively (table 6.2). Japanese officials and businessmen have a clearly demonstrated interest in expanding their influence in these nations.

At the same time, these two countries are economically far behind Japan, and the amounts of aid and investment they are receiving from Japan are proportionally highly significant for the regimes of both countries. Thailand's GDP is 2 percent of Japan's, and Indonesia's is just under 3 percent. If, as some analysts suggest, the region is witnessing the emergence of a closed economic grouping (whether intentional or not), then it should be most evident among these dependent economies. In this regard Thailand and Indonesia can be viewed as important test cases for the hypothesis that Asia is an emerging, closed bloc. If there are few signs that these two smaller economies are trying to create, or are being drawn into, a closed bloc arrangement, however, this would cast doubt on the hypothesis of a trend toward a closed economic regionalism in Asia.

A focus on Thailand and Indonesia, specifically, is useful in that both countries differ significantly in their geopolitical position, their domestic political systems, and their historical relationship with Japan. Yet both are presently confronted with the same external stimulus: a semicooperative Japanese government-business endeavor to promote and expand Japan's economic and political presence within both countries, particularly in the area of infrastructure investment.

Examined in detail in section 6.3, infrastructure development policy is crucial for several reasons. First, it presents the clearest bottleneck so far to further Japanese investment in both countries. Hence it is an impediment to further regional integration. Second, the solution to these bottlenecks involves more explicitly political rather than market arrangements. The provision of infrastructure is closely tied to the political patronage systems in both Thailand and Indonesia. Japanese officials and businessmen are drawn into a political space held by the military, bureaucrats, politicians, and others. Many Thai and Indonesian officials have various political reasons for keeping infrastructure procurement the way it has been—disastrous in terms of efficiency, but savvy in terms of the calculus of power. In short, Japanese attempts to promote infrastructure improvement, as outlined, for example, in MITI's 1987 New Asian Industries Development Plan (New Aid Plan), represent the best example to date of expressly political attempts by outsiders to influence domestic politics for the purpose of promoting greater economic integration in Asia. A fundamental question then is the extent to which Japanese government and business officials are attempting to remold these two countries to suit their own purposes, and the extent to which Japanese initiatives are being modified by, or are seen as compatible or incompatible with, the interests of these two important regional actors.

6.2.2   Thai and Indonesian Policy toward Japan.

Thailand's and Indonesia's responses to Japan over the last six years reveal some important similarities. They support the thesis that Japan is exerting increasing political and economic influence in both countries. Despite differing historical legacies at the hands of the Japanese—the former Dutch East Indies were colonized during World War II, while Thai leaders formed a tenuous alliance with Japan—and important differences in domestic political and economic structures—Thailand's political economy is considerably more market-oriented than Indonesia's—both countries have moved steadily to clear obstacles and provide incentives for dramatic increases in the levels of Japanese investment for export manufacturing. Japanese foreign investment in both Thailand and Indonesia now exceeds U.S. totals, and the Japanese far outstrip foreign investments in manufacturing by other countries (Sanger 1991b). Japanese businesses in both countries, largely through joint ventures with local partners, have created a crucial presence in sectors such as textiles, automobiles, and electronics (Doner 1991). Why have both countries been so willing to open the doors to a flood of foreign, particularly Japanese, investment? A brief review of foreign investment in Indonesia and Thailand helps in answering this question.

In the early 1960s both Thailand and Indonesia pursued import substitution policies with the participation of multinational corporations. Supply-side limitations on private international credit helped to create import-substitution strategies in much of the Third World, Thailand and Indonesia included. The fact that access to international capital could be obtained only through multinational enterprises (MNEs) or development assistance required difficult choices as to the source of funds.

In Indonesia during the early 1960s Sukarno had largely repudiated both MNEs and foreign aid as sources of capital. Hyperinflationary economic policies, combined with a military buildup and conflict with Malaysia, however, helped precipitate the coup of 1965, which brought Suharto and the military to power. Suharto reversed many of Sukarno's policies in his New Order, including those concerning foreign investment and acceptance of development assistance (Anderson 1990). It was during the late 1960s that the Japanese established a growing presence both as investors behind high tariff walls and as foreign contributors to the Intergovernmental Group on Indonesia (IGGI), which provides Indonesia with an annual block of foreign aid.[6] In 1974 a growing perception that Japanese business was coming to dominate the Indonesian economy caused anti-Japanese riots in Jakarta.[7] Between 1974 and 1984 the economy grew at an annual rate of 7 percent, largely as a result of Indonesia's emergence during this period as a major exporter of oil and gas (Carey 1987). Much of the revenues obtained from the rise of oil prices in the 1970s funded government development projects such as the establishment of a shipbuilding and avionics industry as well as oil refineries and petrochemical plants.

When the price of oil collapsed in 1983, however, the Indonesian government faced a financial crisis, which it sought to stem by unraveling its import substitution strategies and by relying more heavily on foreign investors, particularly the Japanese. Until 1983 the government had relied on sales of oil for roughly 60 percent of its revenue and 70 percent of the country's foreign exchange. Faced with the loss of this revenue the government was forced to turn elsewhere for development capital. Suharto began borrowing heavily from foreign sources, mostly Japanese. Indonesia's foreign debt increased from US$27 billion in 1982 to US$51 billion in 1989 as a result of borrowing to meet the requirements of financing public development plans and restructuring the economy.[8] It was with the purpose of assisting the Indonesian government in its efforts at privatization that the Japanese government announced an aid package amounting to US$2.3 billion at the end of 1988. It included for the first time "special assistance," that is, quick disbursing loans and program aid (Edamura 1989).

As a result of its increasing debt burden and the continuing low price of oil on world markets, however, Indonesia has been forced to earn foreign ex-

---

6. The donor consortium, IGGI, provided the government with U.S.$4.75 billion in FY 1991. The Japanese, in this year as in the recent past, provided approximately half to two-thirds of this total. It is also important to note that the Japanese government has never attempted to change this multilateral aid consortium. And it has allowed the United States to retain significant influence over economic policy through the World Bank even when U.S. donations to IGGI have stagnated.

7. Another important target of the riots was a faction inside the Suharto regime, which could not be opposed directly.

8. The appreciation of the yen after 1985 and the devaluation of the rupiah also eroded Indonesia's foreign debt position.

change through other means. One of the few ways of obtaining scarce foreign currency has been Indonesia's increasing reliance on foreign investments for purposes of export promotion. Over the last ten years the Indonesian government has cleared away many tariff barriers. And it has actively promoted new foreign investment for export purposes while encouraging established MNEs to begin production for export (Hadiputranto 1988). For many segments of society the policy has met with considerable success. Nonoil exports have grown at 26 percent per year since 1983, and nonoil manufacturing has been growing at more than 12 percent per year ("Suharto and the Reins of Power" 1990, 38). But Indonesia's ability to get its economy back on track has come at the price of increased dependence on foreign investment, particularly Japanese. Indonesia's need for greater foreign investment to jump start its export industry coincided, especially after the 1985 revaluation of the yen, with the Japanese desire to provide capital. By the end of 1990 the Japanese had invested heavily in numerous sectors, with chemicals having received the most investment followed by banking, auto parts, machinery, and electrical goods (Tachiki 1990, 3). Without foreign investors interested in producing for export, it is fair to say that Indonesia today might not have achieved its recent high levels of growth.

A brief examination of Thailand's recent political-economic history, and foreign investment more generally, suggests a similar structure of incentives and constraints. Like Indonesia, Thailand adopted policies of import substitution in the early 1960s. When General Sarit obtained full authority over the government in his 1958 coup, he reversed previous policies of nationalizing various sectors of the economy. In a move to cut back on foreign imports he raised tariffs while welcoming the investment of multinationals. Many foreign companies and local businesses applauded these policies: the government guaranteed that it would neither nationalize companies at some future date nor compete with the MNEs through state-run firms (Baldwin 1988, 109).

More than 50 percent of the MNEs in Thailand were established between 1963 and 1972 (Hewison 1987, 56). Japanese automobile companies that had formerly exported cars to the Thai market, for example, linked up with local companies to build assembly plants behind new tariff walls. Similar investment took place in textiles. During this period most of the foreign investment capital—besides that of the MNEs—came to Thailand in the form of World Bank loans as well as grants and military aid from the U.S. government (Suehiro 1989, 82–83). As in Indonesia, the early 1970s were a period of public demonstrations against the growing Japanese presence in the economy. In November 1972 Thai students with the support of some politicians organized a boycott of Japanese goods to protest the continuing imbalance of trade between the two countries. Though the boycott itself was unsuccessful, the Japanese government introduced a new, lower–interest rate loan program, which it also extended to other nations in Asia (Sueo 1988, 221). Thailand's balance-of-payments problem, however, has persisted since the 1970s.

While retaining in some areas a policy of import substitution, in the 1970s Thailand's policymakers began to move the economy toward a more export-oriented development strategy.[9] This shift arose in part from the saturation of the domestic markets. More important, the change in policy was a response to the oil shocks of the 1970s. A net importer of oil, Thailand found itself— unlike Indonesia during this period—with growing trade imbalances and increasing public deficits. With the worldwide increases in private loans through the recycling of petrodollars, however, Thailand was able to borrow funds to cover these deficits. As Thailand's debt service ratio began to climb precipitously after the second oil shock of 1979, the Thai government was pressured by the World Bank and the International Monetary Fund (IMF) to initiate austerity measures (Hewison 1987, 75). Under austerity, massive public service programs were postponed and state-operated organizations, which in 1985 accounted for one-half of the government's foreign debt, were forced to restructure. Privatization of several of these organizations began,and public-private joint ventures were encouraged in several other cases.

Thailand cleared the way for export promotion almost a decade before Indonesia. But in an attempt to attract greater amounts of foreign investment, the government improved incentives for MNEs even further after 1986 (Rainat 1988, 32). As in the case of Indonesia, and for similar reasons, Japanese investment has become crucial to the success of Thailand's export promotion over the last six years. Thailand has been able to reduce its foreign debt substantially, and its rate of industrialization has accelerated. Profits from manufactured exports have overtaken those earned traditionally from the export of rice. Thailand's GDP growth rate over the last several years has been among the highest in the world. As in the case of Indonesia, Japanese investment and Thailand's policy toward it must be credited with much of the success of the economy during the late 1980s. Analysts claim that Japanese investment since 1986 accounts for at least 1.5 percent of the annual increase in Thailand's GNP (Tasker 1990, 49).

This brief overview of recent Thai and Indonesian economic development lends support to the hypothesis that Japan has indeed been acting as a regional economic hegemon, and that both countries have willingly supported this role. In reaction to the vagaries of the international marketplace, both Thailand and Indonesia have chosen to rely on the export interests and capabilities of mostly Japanese business to support their own as well as Japanese export promotion policies. While recent policies provide evidence that both governments have actively sought to encourage Japanese investment, there are indications that the nature of Thailand's and Indonesia's relationship with Japan may be undergoing important changes, calling into question Japan's role in further economic integration in Asia.

---

9. This change in strategy is reflected in the third economic plan for 1972–76. High tariff barriers still protect many agricultural products, textiles, and leather goods.

Direction-of-trade statistics for both countries, for example, indicate that for the past thirty years Thailand has become steadily *less* dependent on Japan for its imports and exports while Indonesia has become more dependent (table 6.3). Japan now accounts for a little more than one-tenth of Thailand's export and import markets, whereas Indonesia has become dependent on Japan for one-quarter of its imports and two-fifths of its exports. Thailand has been very successful in diversifying its imports and exports to other developing countries, thus alleviating to some extent its dependence on Japan. On the other hand, because of its oil assets Indonesia has consistently run trade surpluses with Japan. Trading relations have been largely devoid of friction because of Japan's willingness to accept this imbalance. In contrast, approximately 70–80 percent of Thailand's trade deficit over the last several years, compared with the 10 percent of Thailand's trade with Japan, has been with Japan ("Cracks Begin to Develop" 1990). Thus trading relations between Thailand and Japan have become increasingly strained, as the Thai government perceives Japanese reluctance to open domestic markets to Thai rice and manufacturing exports. In this trade dispute the Thais have actively supported U.S. efforts to open Japanese markets. Other analysts and government officials, however, accept this trade imbalance. They point to the fact that most of Thailand's Japanese imports are capital goods, which contribute to the overall industrialization of the country.

In the area of debt Thailand has been quite successful in reducing its external vulnerability, whereas Indonesia's dependence—particularly on the Japa-

Table 6.3   **Geographical Composition of Trade, Thailand and Indonesia**

Country	Exports		Imports	
	1963	1988	1963	1988
Thailand				
Developed Countries	43.5	62.4	83.5	55.5
Japan	18.1	15.9	32.9	11.7
Western Europe	17.7	22.7	30.8	22.9
United States	7.4	20.0	17.5	16.9
Developing Countries	55.6	36.3	15.6	41.6
East Asian NICs	19.4	15.5	6.1	19.3
Other ASEAN-Four	25.7	3.9	6.9	4.8
Indonesia				
Developed Countries	68.6	71.4	68.2	67.8
Japan	8.5	41.7	10.5	25.4
Western Europe	35.0	11.3	24.3	22.4
United States	15.8	16.2	33.1	12.9
Developing Countries	25.0	27.8	24.6	30.8
East Asian NICs	0.6	20.5	9.2	18.7
Other ASEAN-Four	15.7	2.2	7.7	3.2

Source: Adapted from Noland (1990).

nese—remains very large. Thailand has succeeded in lowering its foreign debt service ratio from 22.3 percent in 1986 to 16.2 percent in 1990 (Asian Development Bank 1990, 245). One-third of Indonesia's US$41 billion debt is held by Japanese creditors. This places Indonesia (and Tokyo bankers) in a vulnerable position (Schwarz 1990, 56). Indonesia's foreign debt service ratio has declined from 43.7 percent in 1988 to 35 percent in 1990, but even this rate is well above the 20 percent level the World Bank deems manageable.

Foreign investment is another area in which the two governments' relationship with Japan may be changing. The East Asian economic boom has led to increased interest on the part of the NICs in investing in Thailand and Indonesia. As a result of some of the same pressures driving the Japanese offshore, South Korea, Singapore, Taiwan, and Hong Kong have recently become major investors in both nations.[10] This investment lends support to the notion of a growing regionalism in Asia. In the long run, furthermore, it may free the hands of both the Thai and Indonesian governments. Fearful of becoming overly dependent on the Japanese, other Asian economies may provide alternative sources of investment and technology. The fear that the Japanese are obtaining too much leverage in Thailand has recently led the Thai Board of Investment (BOI) to a shift in policy away from a continued reliance on Japanese business and toward the active promotion of other pools of investment capital in Taiwan, South Korea, and Hong Kong (Handley 1991, 43). The Indonesian government at present is continuing to seek Japanese investment. But it has also begun to look for greater investment from other NICs and the United States (Mann 1990). Both countries are also actively encouraging technology transfers from the United States and the NICs, an area where leaders feel the Japanese have been remiss. Although the Thais may be attempting to gradually redirect investment sources away from Japan, such a shift may prove difficult. Because of Thailand's relatively liberal investment climate and relatively pluralistic political system, Japanese MNEs will be able to pursue their interests with comparatively greater freedom and less bureaucratic oversight than they have in Indonesia. The ability of Japanese investors to circumvent laws on foreign ownership of property in Thailand is but one example of this freedom (Sricharatchanya 1987).

It is difficult to characterize with certainty the future direction of Thailand and Indonesia's relationship with Japan. Although with the encouragement of governments the Japanese have established a crucial presence in certain sectors of both economies, there are signs that both countries are becoming aware of the perceived pitfalls of too heavy a reliance on their northern neighbor. At the same time Thailand and Indonesia are operating under various constraints. The

---

10. For a further discussion of NIC investment in Southeast Asia see "Give Me Your Huddled Hongkongers" (1989) and "ASEAN Prospects for Foreign Investment" (1990). At the end of 1989 Hong Kong and Taiwan had invested a total of US$3.7 billion in Indonesia compared to Japan's US$6.5 billion (Mann 1990). The investment ratios for Thailand are comparable.

need to export to service debts is very strong. And increasing technological dependence in a fiercely competitive global marketplace will also limit their room to maneuver.

6.3   Japanese Role in Thai and Indonesian Infrastructure Development

Arguably one of the most important policy issues likely to shape the two countries' relationship with Japan over the next several years is the area of infrastructure development. While the pace of Japanese investment in Southeast Asia has grown tremendously over the last five years, there are signs that it may be tapering off. In 1990 Indonesia continued to receive a positive increase in the amount of Japanese investment, but Thailand showed no increase over the previous year. Investment applications during the first four months of 1991 in Thailand were down 40 percent (*Bangkok Post,* July 25, 1991, 16). One important reason for this slowdown is the inability of Thai and Indonesian infrastructures to support a continuation in the volume of Japanese investment. Foreign investors report that the main impediment to further investment in both countries is infrastructural bottlenecks in communications, transport (roads, ports), and services ("Looking at Indonesia's Business Opportunities" 1990; Rim 1989). As recent accounts of the current situation in Eastern Europe indicate, it is very difficult to attract large foreign investment where infrastructural systems are inadequate. How the governments of Thailand and Indonesia deal with these problems will have a crucial impact on the future of Asian regionalism.

In the late 1980s the Japanese stepped up their attempts to alleviate infrastructural bottlenecks in Thailand and Indonesia, as well as in other Asian economies. This move supports the view that Japan has significant long-term interests in these countries and in Asian regionalism more generally. Japan pledged to distribute US$50 billion over a five-year period ending March 31, 1993. Thus far it has disbursed almost half this sum, mostly to Asian nations (Awanohara 1991a, 45). Much of this aid has supported major infrastructural projects aimed at alleviating serious deficiencies in communications, transport, and power-generating capacity in countries receiving Japanese technology transfers and investment ("Japan's Drive into Asia" 1989, 51).

More concretely, in January 1987 MITI unveiled in Bangkok a program known as the New Aid Plan, dealing specifically with the issue of infrastructural difficulties in Asia and their relation to the developmental needs of Japanese industry and the restructuring of the Japanese economy in general (Brown 1991). The program is an attempt to relocate selected Japanese businesses to Southeast Asia through loans and technical assistance to governments. These loans will be used for the improvement of infrastructure, including industrial estates, ports, and improved telecommunication services. The New Aid Plan reflects MITI's view that Japan must be prepared to meet the double challenge of the world's continuing drive toward globalization and Japan's need to move to higher value-added production ("Yen Bloc Survey" 1989; Sricharatchanya 1987). Various Japanese agencies, most importantly MITI, the Overseas Economic Cooperation Fund (OECF), and the Ministry of Foreign Affairs, are attempting (with apparently significant interministerial conflict) to coordinate different aspects of this plan, the details of which are negotiated bilaterally with each government.

The New Aid Plan envisages four stages. First, Japanese loans support the development of roads, ports, and other infrastructural supports. Second, the Japanese government sends technical experts to assist in coordinating industrial plans for each country. Third, Japanese loans are extended to various industries within participating countries. Finally, Japanese bureaucrats and businessmen take steps to facilitate access to Japanese markets and to ensure the distribution of products imported from offshore factories to Japan (Wysocki 1991). In short, the plan suggests that Japanese business and government elites view ASEAN (and the NICs) as one economy, requiring a comprehensive perspective on aid, trade, and investment. The provision of the necessary infrastructure, as one part of this plan, will serve the interests of Japanese companies and promote economic growth in Asia. The program is in some ways a continuation of previous Japanese policies toward Southeast Asia that focused on developing markets for Japanese goods and securing natural resources for Japanese industry. But the goals of the New Aid Plan depart significantly from past policies in emphasizing the extent to which the Japanese are seeking to take on a more prominent role in regional economic integration.[11]

Japanese bureaucrats have thus mapped out a comprehensive strategy for the future. But it is far less certain whether this plan will be heeded by Japanese business, and how it will be received in Bangkok and Jakarta. The Thai government agreed in 1988 to work with the New Aid Plan and established a joint steering committee with Japanese officials and businessmen to map out a future program of industrialization ("Yen Bloc Survey" 1989, 13). Several Japanese bureaucrats are presently working side by side with planners in Thai government ministries, and various agencies are attempting to coordinate these activities. The Indonesians have yet to formally sign on, but there is both pressure from the Japanese and interest from some sectors of the Indonesian government.

The implementation of the New Aid Plan will undoubtedly be affected by Japan's Overseas Development Assistance (ODA). It is often argued that Japanese aid cannot further larger Japanese objectives favoring business since aid typically is made on the "request principle." It dates back to the early postwar period, when the Japanese government paid reparations to Indonesia and other

---

11. U.S. aid agencies have responded to the New Aid Plan by altering their own policies. They now extend more mixed credits to four countries—Thailand, Indonesia, the Philippines, and Pakistan—in which they perceive markets for infrastructure development to be "spoiled" by the mixed credit advantages extended by Japanese aid agencies to Japanese firms. See Awanohara (1991a).

Asian nations for projects that were specifically requested by the governments (Kunihiro 1990). This policy continues today. Nevertheless, what governments in both Thailand and Indonesia request from Japanese aid officials often coincides fortuitously with the needs of Japanese multinationals on whom these same governments depend for tax revenues and technology transfers. An extremely small and powerful number of indigenous business conglomerates dominate the economies in both Thailand and Indonesia.[12] These conglomerates wield enormous power over government and are partners with numerous Japanese multinationals (Kunio 1988; Phongpaichit 1990; Suehiro 1989). They have a direct stake in getting governments to push through requests congenial to the interests they share with their Japanese business partners. Moreover, through personal networks Japanese partners are often able to steer through the intricacies of Japanese ODA procedures with considerable ease.

Thus it should come as no surprise, for example, that much of the recent Japanese ODA has gone to the alleviation of traffic congestion in Bangkok and Jakarta where Japanese auto assemblers dominate the market. Loans for the alleviation of rural poverty, on the other hand, are infrequent. The fact that the projects requested happen to benefit Japanese subsidiaries and their comparatively wealthy, car-driving customers is no coincidence. It is likely that Thailand and Indonesia would refuse to accept aid if the Japanese designated the use to which it should be put. Nevertheless, the explanation that aid is "requested" must be interpreted within the context of transnational coalitions of powerful business interests. Indeed, the Japan Federation of Economic Organizations (Keidanren) continually promotes a growing role for the private sector—both in Japan and abroad—in determining the developmental needs of ODA recipients. It implicitly acknowledges this pattern of "request" assistance and decries the lack of "efficiency" in some of the development projects carried out by the Japanese government.

> The Japanese government has extended its assistance in the building of industrial infrastructure, such as electric power, telecommunications, roads, railways, and port facilities. However, we believe that the scope of such assistance should be extended to areas that will support industrial modernization, such as information processing, in line with the development needs of the recipient countries. . . . Efforts to encourage private-sector investment and lending should emphasize the development of an improved investment environment in the recipient countries. This includes such areas as infrastructure development, privatization, improved legislative frameworks, protection of intellectual property rights and tax incentives. (Keizai Koho Center 1988)

---

12. The one major difference, however, is that in Thailand the economy is dominated by a Sino-Thai bourgeoisie with political power (through parties), whereas in Indonesia the private sector, which is smaller than the state sector, is dominated by Sino-Indonesians dependent on Suharto and his generals for power and protection.

But nowhere in this four-page brief is there mention of rural or urban poverty.

The extent to which the Thais and Indonesians are welcoming Japanese involvement in their infrastructure improvement via the "request principle" reveals the extent to which Japan will succeed in creating greater regional and economic integration. However, infrastructure development such as construction of ports, industrial estates, and telecommunication services involves sectors of the economy that, by their very nature, are close to the core of state sovereignty and political patronage. They typically resist the kind of intrusive interventions of local and foreign planners alike. The provision and care of infrastructure in both Thailand and Indonesia are handled by state-run agencies, which are typically intertwined with patronage networks and the military. This adds a highly political element to efforts for improving economic infrastructures. Elites and political coalitions in both countries are increasingly divided between the need to privatize and deregulate these agencies to improve their country's infrastructure on the one hand, and a desire to hold on to them for political reasons on the other. There is also uncertainty as to whether privatization is indeed the best means for upgrading infrastructure. And the issue of who wins and who loses under privatized infrastructural agreements continues to vex policymakers. The hard truth remains, however, that the high growth rates Thailand and Indonesia have enjoyed during the last decade, and on which military regimes have staked their claim to legitimacy, will increasingly hinge on their ability to improve infrastructure. How and whether infrastructure is upgraded will in turn influence the Japanese success in carrying out the New Aid Plan and its goal of inducing further Japanese investment in Southeast Asia.

Any analysis of the New Aid Plan must examine whether the intended results of the plan are achieved and the means by which such ends are sought. In many cases the provision of infrastructure for the benefit of Japanese multinationals is more important than the means by which it is provided. It is thus possible to view Japanese policies as successful even if Japanese contractors are not part of the actual building of roads and ports and the improvement of telecommunication services. A related issue is whether Japanese firms are allowed to participate in the design and building of infrastructure, a lucrative business considering the large sums budgeted recently for infrastructure investment in both Thailand and Indonesia. Japanese participation in the construction of roads, ports, and industrial estates is as notable as Japanese involvement in the upgrading of antiquated telecommunication services.

Evidence from Thailand suggests that the Japanese have met with some success both in creating the types of infrastructures that will benefit Japanese multinationals and their partners, and in obtaining large contracts for Japanese companies for building such infrastructure. Roughly 70 percent of Thailand's ODA comes from Japan. And since the early 1980s, following OECF funding guidelines, grant and aid loans have been used almost exclusively for heavy infrastructure planning and development (Handley 1990a). With the exception of several irrigation projects in the north, most of these projects are concentrated in and around Bangkok; the northeast, Thailand's poorest region, has received little Japanese ODA (Thaitawat 1991). The new Eastern Seaboard Project, a combination port, railroad, and industrial facility—designed to shift investment away from congested Bangkok—has been the most significant Japanese ODA project. It is financed by soft loans from the OECF and built by Japanese contractors with the assistance of the Japan International Cooperation Agency (JICA; Handley 1988, 69). The project makes use of plentiful supplies of natural gas, recently discovered in the Gulf of Thailand. It will provide cheap energy to those businesses relocating to new industrial parks. Energy-intensive Japanese businesses—particularly those that might produce potentially dangerous environmental waste that would be intolerable in Japan[13]—are being encouraged by both the Japanese and Thai governments to relocate to the new production site. One such project is a rare instance of successful economic cooperation among the ASEAN nations. It involves a potash plant, funded by the ASEAN governments and Japanese ODA, utilizing the facilities of the Eastern Seaboard Project. A second huge industrial project, the Southern Seaboard Development Programme, centers on a plan to create a pipeline system across the Kra Peninsula through which oil could be transported overland instead of being shipped through the Strait of Malacca. The oil would be refined in one of the two ports on either side of the pipeline before being sent to other Asian countries. Proposed by JICA, it is being designed by a consortium of engineering firms with a loan from the World Bank (Bangkok Bank 1991).

After a delay of several months following the February 1991 coup in Thailand, the four government agencies responsible for Japanese ODA, the Ministry of Foreign Affairs, the Ministry of Finance, MITI, and the Economic Planning Agency, approved an OECF funding package worth 84.7 billion yen (US$685 million) for infrastructural development in Thailand for 1992. The bulk of this aid is earmarked for infrastructural projects in and around the Bangkok area, such as viaducts on various trunk roads to alleviate the city's traffic problems ("Tokyo Grants Aid to Thailand" 1991). The Thai government allocated upward of US$7.3 billion for infrastructure in 1991 ("Cracks Begin to Develop" 1990). These numbers show that Japanese funds account for about one-tenth of Thailand's total infrastructure investment.

In recent years there have been major problems with many of the projects in Bangkok, due largely to a lack of coordination among the various roads and mass transit projects as well as interministerial conflicts. In an effort to privatize the provision of infrastructure, many of the contracts were awarded

---

13. With the unveiling of Japan's "Green Aid Program," to be headquartered in Bangkok, the Japanese have attempted to counter criticism that they are exporting the cost of pollution by setting up multinational operations of energy-intensive production in Southeast Asia. The ODA program will grant aid totaling 750 million yen to Thailand for 1992 to fight industrial pollutants. The five-year program will provide US$15 billion to Japanese ODA recipients. See "Tokyo Grants Aid to Thailand" (1991).

to private firms under the democratically elected Chatchai administration (1988–91). This circumvented the various public agencies charged with infrastructure development as well as the public sector labor unions, which opposed privatization. A political base of the military since the 1976 coup, these unions probably had the support of the military, which feared an erosion in its power because of these privatization schemes. Prime Minister Chatchai was ousted in 1991 by the military on charges that he had received kickbacks from the awarding of large infrastructure contracts to private industry. In the wake of the coup, and with the appointment of former diplomat Anand Panyarchun as prime minister by the military, many contracts for infrastructure development were renegotiated. However, public sector unions were abolished, clearing the way for an even brisker pace for privatization in the provision of infrastructure, in coordination with the government. Apparently even the military has realized the crucial importance of upgrading Thailand's infrastructure for continued economic development.

The lack of coordination arising from Chatchai's rapid privatization of infrastructure, without any government planning and regulation, suggests that the market may not be the best system for upgrading infrastructure. The recent return to greater state supervision over the planning of infrastructure is a hallmark of the new military government's first year in power. Prime Minister Anand has focused much of his energies on coordinating and renegotiating infrastructure contracts and attempting to root out the corruption blamed for the woeful state of Thailand's infrastructure. Japanese willingness to extend huge loans for infrastructure development so soon after the coup—when other countries, notably the United States, have frozen aid contingent on steps toward the restoration of democracy—gives tacit approval to the military government's approach to the alleviation of infrastructural bottlenecks.

Another important issue concerning infrastructural development is the question of who actually provides for its upgrading. There are presently more than seventy-two Japanese contracting companies in Thailand. With the continual opening of the door to foreign investment since the 1960s, Japanese contractors and engineering consultants have gained a reasonable share (2–4 percent) of the construction market, particularly for large projects such as the Eastern Seaboard Project. Japanese firms often form joint ventures with Thai partners, but they also operate on their own. Recently, however, due largely to a report published in 1988 by the Institute for Developing Economies concerning Japanese ODA and the construction industry, local developers and some politicians and bureaucrats have challenged the tying of Japanese aid for infrastructure to Japanese contractors (Chittiwatanapong, Karasudhi, and Itoga 1989). At an international conference on Japan's ODA held in Bangkok in March 1991, Yochi Aki, the OECF chief representative in Bangkok, refuted the notion of tied aid. He noted that the Japanese government-business relationship was no longer that close, and he cited statistics that showed that Japanese companies' worldwide share of projects funded by loans denominated in yen declined from a high of 67 percent in 1986 to 55 percent in 1987, and to 38 percent in 1989 (Thaitawat 1991). In addition, Aki pointed out that by law the Thai government is obligated to accept the lowest bid for government projects, a stipulation that consistently favors Japanese contractors with easier access to low–interest rate financing ("Cracks Begin to Develop" 1990).

Nevertheless, the perception of Japanese dominance in the construction industry, particularly in large and highly visible projects, has sparked attempts to diversify foreign project funding from the Japanese to more multilateral institutions such as the Asian Development Bank (Handley 1988). In a move that suggests an attempt to diversify away from Japanese contractors, the Southern Seaboard Development Programme is being engineered with Japanese, Thai, and American participation (Bangkok Bank 1991). And the awarding of the most recent contracts for infrastructural improvements in Bangkok to firms based in Canada (the Lavellin Skytrain) and Hong Kong (the Hopewell Expressway Expansion) is also a political attempt to diversify away from Japanese sources of capital and technology (*Bangkok Post,* August 8, 1991, 1).

In the case of Indonesia, Japanese aid for the provision of infrastructure is equally important. But participation by Japanese contractors has been less significant, due to Indonesia's generally more nationalistic policy toward foreign participation in the economy. Until recently Japanese aid to Suharto has been intended to buttress the power of his dictatorship, thereby securing Japanese access to oil and investment in Indonesia. From 1988 to 1990 Indonesia received US$13 billion in aid—more than half from Japan. In the category of special assistance—quick disbursing, nontied aid—Japan has provided approximately 70 percent of late (Schwarz 1990). Soft loans from Japan's OECF have financed an estimated 31 percent of Indonesia's power-generating capacity, 11 percent of regional roads, 14 percent of railroads, and 46 percent of Jakarta's water supply ("Indonesia Shows Evidence" 1989). The OECF loans extended to Indonesia since 1968 have reached a cumulative commitment of approximately 1,300 billion yen, or about one-fifth of the total OECF loans granted to developing countries. This makes Indonesia by far the largest recipient of Japanese ODA. The OECF program has covered more than four hundred projects, over one hundred in the transportation sector alone. They include many arterial roads and tollways, rehabilitation of railway track, and improvement of both seaports and airports. Power generation ranks second, with eighty-five projects and a share of 29.5 percent of total OECF project loans ("Indonesia Shows Evidence" 1989). These have included numerous hydroelectric dam projects, some of which have drawn criticism from nongovernmental organizations. Loans for this year will also fund a feasibility study on a proposed nuclear power project in northern Java, awarded to a subsidiary of Kansai Power, the second largest Japanese power company, which is also expected to receive the contracts to build up to twelve plants in the future ("RI Picks Japanese Firm" 1991). Telecommunications, with forty-three projects, ranks third in the number of OECF-funded projects.

The Indonesians have not ventured as far as the Thais in attempting to privatize infrastructure development. Nor have they signed on to the New Aid Plan. But de facto they are following the objectives of the plan, through the loans that Suharto's government requests. The Indonesian government has placed infrastructure improvements at the top of the state's agenda because it is concerned that Indonesia's recent export success could founder without it. Many state-led industrial projects were not funded in FY 1992, in order to support government infrastructural development (Stone 1991). Moreover, since 1988 the government has opened the industrial estate sector to private investors, including foreigners through joint ventures. Two Japanese groups, Marubeni and Sumitomo, as well as South Korea's Hyundai, are currently completing the construction of industrial estates outside of Jakarta. The estates are an attempt to circumvent the slow-paced upgrading of the infrastructure presently provided by the government. They have already leased space to numerous Japanese companies. In addition to these privately owned estates, the Indonesian government, in the hopes of attracting foreign investors to the archipelago, has poured millions of dollars into the Batam Island Industrial Estate over the last several years. It hopes that the land, labor, and infrastructure supplied by the Indonesians, with the aid of Singaporean management and capital, will promote growth and greater regional integration within ASEAN in the Singaporean growth triangle (Batam Industrial Development Authority 1991).

The Indonesian construction market, unlike Thailand's is largely dominated by state corporations. Over 80 percent of the construction companies in Indonesia are owned by the government. This dominance leaves very little room for either private or foreign contractors in gaining market shares in Indonesia. With the exception of the change in industrial estate laws, it is difficult to assess whether the Indonesian market will open up in the future. The Indonesian government seems willing to improve its infrastructure with Japanese aid. But it is considerably more hesitant to give foreign contractors a sizable share of the contracts. One large industrial project near Jakarta, built by Japanese contractors and financed with yen loans, continues to be a source of contention between the two governments.[14] Nationalist backlashes thus have limited Japanese participation in the Indonesian construction market to under 0.5 percent. Approximately twenty Japanese companies are currently working in the Indonesian construction sector (Informasi: Pusat Data Business Indonesia 1991).

Furthermore, foreign contractors are upset with a new law that removes their eligibility for automatic joint venture status. Instead, the government now grants joint venture status to international contractors on a project-by-project

14. The Asahan Project, a US$2.7 billion complex that includes dams, power transmission, and a giant aluminum smelter exporting ingots to Japan, is 59 percent owned by Japanese interests and 41 percent owned by the Indonesian government. When the yen rose sharply in 1985, the government was unable to pay interest due on loans borrowed to build the plant and pay the contractors. Even after further loans were extended by Tokyo, the Indonesian government in 1988 for a period of five months discontinued exports of the ingots to Japan. See Wysocki (1991).

basis. Rules for buying imported construction equipment have been eased but still favor locally made equipment. Imported equipment, according to law, must be sold to either the government or Indonesian contractors when the project is completed ("New Engine of Growth" 1988). According to numerous private sector contractors in Indonesia, the government's insistence on control over infrastructure projects through state-led companies is a major factor impeding the improvement of Indonesia's infrastructure. They maintain that the state is unaware of the needs of industry and often fails to see the links between a sound infrastructure and continued industrial success.[15] The liberalization of other sectors of the Indonesian economy may eventually create pressure to broaden private participation in the construction sector. But for now the political reasons for holding onto the construction industry, often described as one of the government's cash cows, remain intact.

In the area of telecommunications both Thailand and Indonesia have taken steps toward allowing foreign firms to invest. In Thailand private sector operation of telecommunications has expanded enormously since 1988, largely as a result of demand surging far beyond the capabilities of the state-run operators (Westlake 1991). Full privatization of the two state-run communications agencies, the Telephone Authority of Thailand (TOT) and the Communications Authority of Thailand (CAT)—the latter with strong links to the military—has been rejected. But due to a severe shortage of telephone lines and Bangkok's traffic congestion, both have begun to grant concessions to local and foreign business for paging and cellular services. In this area Motorola, Ericsson, and NEC have been major joint partners in the provision of these services. In addition, British Telecom recently won a US$1 billion contract with Charoen Pokphand, its Thai partner, to set up and operate two million new telephone lines for twenty years. In this initiative a British MNE beat out both NEC and Fujitsu for the first major contract. The awarding of this contract to the British was widely interpreted as an attempt of the new military government to diversity investment away from Japan. Thailand already relies heavily upon Japanese telecommunication equipment suppliers (Handley 1990b). The TOT, for example, which handles domestic services, is heavily dependent on Japanese foreign borrowings for development projects and must wait for each year's foreign loan commitments before granting contracts to suppliers. The Japanese are also trying to entice Thailand through OECF loans into joining its Sigma Project, which began in 1989. This is a plan for working with Asian countries to develop a regional, automated software industry to help counter a growing labor shortage in Japan ("Automating Software" 1988).

As in Thailand, Indonesia's state-run telecommunication agencies, Perumtel (which handles domestic calls) and Indosat (which services external communi-

---

15. The most recent example of this perceived misunderstanding is the tabling of many urgent projects in Indonesia so that government contractors could participate in the reconstruction of Kuwait to earn foreign currency.

cations), have run into major infrastructural bottlenecks. As a consequence, the Indonesian government has stepped up annual spending on telecommunications to US$600 million ("Competing in Indonesia's Telecommunications Market" 1988). Japanese OECF money finances a large portion of this investment. Many of the orders for purchases of telecommunication equipment have gone to Japanese firms as well as their European and American competitors. As in Thailand, Japanese foreign aid has been linked to Japanese telecommunication suppliers. In Indonesia typically 60–65 percent of telecommunication equipment is obtained through local contractors working in cooperation with foreign vendors; the rest is produced through a state monopoly working in conjunction with Siemens (Hukill and Jussawalla 1989). The newly introduced mobile telephone service uses Motorola's Advanced Mobile Telephone System (AMPS), but the mobile phones are supplied equally by Motorola, NEC, JRC, and Ericsson. In January 1991 a major telephone contract to supply digital switching equipment for 350,000 lines was initially awarded to NEC. After intervention by U.S. President Bush and acrimonious debate alleging favoritism by all parties involved, the contract was doubled, allowing for participation by both NEC and AT&T. Significant infighting among the members of Suharto's family over the selection of Indonesian partners to work with these two MNEs also occurred. In the end two companies in the hands of Suharto's sons were chosen after both NEC and AT&T had offered generous finance packages. As in the case of the construction industry, compared to Thailand the Indonesians are keeping a tighter grip on the telecommunication industry. The large share of public ownership and the regime's internal security concerns explain this difference. Nevertheless, the Indonesian government realizes the extent to which poor telecommunications can handicap economic growth. And it has taken significant steps toward improving Indonesia's telecommunications.

6.4   Japan's Future Role in Asia and the Regional World Economy

Japan is at the center of a new Asian regionalism that is complementing rather than replacing the multilateralism that has evolved since 1945. This regionalism differs from Japan's Greater East Asia Co-prosperity Sphere in the 1930s and 1940s. What separates the new from the old regionalism is the difference between autarchy and direct rule on the one hand and interdependence and influence on the other.

Greater Asian regional cooperation appears to be an idea whose time has come—both in terms of the larger public debate and in terms of initiatives such as the New Aid Plan and the ASEAN free trade area. Enhanced regional cooperation is often invoked as a necessary response to the process of European integration as well as the Canada-U.S. Free Trade Agreement, soon to be joined by Mexico. The Asia Pacific Economic Cooperation Conference (APEC) held its first meeting in Canberra in December of 1989. And in 1992 the ASEAN states began to work toward the creation of a common free trade zone by early next century. Like the Asian Development Bank, APEC and the ASEAN initiatives are providing forums for the discussion of economic policy and thus may turn out to be useful for strengthening regional economic cooperation.

Japan's interests in fostering greater Asian cooperation and the responses by Indonesia and Thailand can serve as test cases for how questions of regionalism and multilateralism are being negotiated. If Japanese government and business actions, either intentionally or unintentionally, were fostering a shift away from multilateralism toward the emergence of a closed form of regionalism in Asia, this should be particularly evident in those Asian countries where Japanese trade, aid, and investment power are strong. While Thailand and Indonesia have both opened their economies to extensive economic relationships with Japan, both governments have viewed their involvement with Japanese business largely in multilateral terms. They have welcomed the investment capital, technology, and loans provided by the Japanese as a means of restructuring their own economies and of becoming more important and more diversified participants in the global trading system. Although Indonesia's trade and debt dependence on Japan has risen while Thailand's has decreased over the last decade, Indonesia's movement away from a reliance solely on oil exports— due in part to the investment by Japanese MNEs—bodes well for its attempts to diversify its trade patterns in the future. Oil and gas reserves also provide Indonesia with valuable leverage and access to a wide variety of markets.

Despite the advantages accruing to an open relationship with Japan, the sharp growth in Japanese influence and power in these and other Asian countries has created some unease about the political consequences of intensifying Asian economic relations for an emerging regional political economy.[16] With the total GNP of ASEAN amounting to less than 10 percent of Japan's GNP, a world of self-contained regions in the northern half of the globe would leave the ASEAN members highly dependent on Japan. In the view of Thai and Indonesian leaders as well as other Asian countries, only the United States can act as an indispensable counterweight to Japan's growing power.

This is perhaps one reason why there has, as of yet, been no substantive move toward an Asia-wide free trade agreement similar to those negotiated in North America and Europe. When in the wake of the suspension of the Uruguay Round of GATT negotiations in December 1990 Malaysia's Prime Minister Mahathir proposed that Asian nations form a regional trading bloc that would exclude North America, his suggestion was promptly dismissed by the Japanese government and others within the region (Sanger 1991a). At the ASEAN ministerial meeting in July 1991, Mahathir's continuing attempts to promote his East Asian economic group sparked interest among the ASEAN

---

16. Rumor has it that the best way for ASEAN academics to get a free trip to Japan these days is to write an article critical of Japan.

partners only when the proposal was watered down by referring to it merely as a "consultative forum." Despite the growth of economic regionalism in Asia, few Asian nations—most notably the Japanese—want to upset their relationship with North America and Europe, on whom they depend so heavily for trade and investment. Asian nations still export well over a third of their products to the North American market. And Asian trade is significantly less interdependent than trade within the European Community. The chapters in this volume written by Frankel, Ito, Petri, and Saxonhouse all reinforce this conclusion. Furthermore, while expanding rapidly during the last few years, Japanese investment to other Asian nations still lags significantly behind Japanese investment in Europe and, especially, North America. To date, the desire to maintain open lines to the United States and Europe is not yet incompatible with a stepped-up economic and increasingly political role for the Japanese in Asia, particularly among the ASEAN nations.

With the American navy firmly committed to retaining a strong position in Asia and with the consolidation of U.S.-Japanese security arrangements in the 1980s, the United States is likely to remain an Asian power. Furthermore, since virtually all Asian countries, including Thailand and Indonesia, run a substantial trade deficit with Japan and a large surplus with the United States, the United States is essential for regional economic integration in Asia. An Asia that includes the United States has several virtues. It can diffuse the economic and political dependencies of the smaller Asian states away from Japan. And it can provide Japan with the national security that makes unnecessary a major arms buildup and the hostile political reaction it would engender among Japan's neighbors.

The case studies of Thai and Indonesian responses to Japanese interests suggest that Asia is not heading toward a Japanese-led autarchic order. Japanese efforts to improve infrastructure under the aegis of the New Aid Plan have encountered major political obstacles in both Thailand and Indonesia. Furthermore, where infrastructure has been built, it is serving to strengthen not only Japanese capital, but domestic, East Asian, and U.S. capital as well.

In addition to the numerous difficulties encountered with the New Aid Plan in Indonesia and Thailand, Japan's increasing power is limited in two further ways. First, the structure of Japanese politics makes the articulation of a clearcut view of Japan's role in global politics much less compelling than the creation of points of political leverage to counter Japan's numerous vulnerabilities. The criticisms levied against Japan in the wake of the Gulf War and anticipation of the substantial political changes that the end of the Cold War might bring about in Asia are providing a strong impetus for Japan's political leadership to remedy that shortcoming. International crises during the interwar years and the experience of World War II jolted the United States out of its isolationist stance. Crises of similar magnitude may do the same for Japan. But short of cataclysmic changes, Japan's leaders are likely to experience great difficulties in countering the political habit of redefining Japanese interests flexibly and of creating structures that reduce Japan's vulnerability by enhancing the vulnerabilities of others. The investment strategy of Japanese corporations, coupled with their technological dynamism, is very likely to drive political developments in the future, rather than the articulation and implementation of a political vision for Japan's future global role.

Second, political constraints, both domestic and international, militate against a dramatic rise in Japan's military power. Some shrill voices (magnified by American publishers with a good instinct for what it takes to sell books in Tokyo) talk of "the coming war with Japan" (Friedman and Lebard 1991). But hardly anyone in Asia or the United States takes such talk seriously at this time. Public sentiment among Japanese citizens and among the leaders of Japan's neighboring countries will continue to provide a check on the resurgence of the Japanese military.[17] The real change since the late 1970s, however, is rather a gradual Japanese military buildup that is creating technological options for a national strategy that did not exist ten or twenty years ago. But as long as Japan is not developing interballistic missiles, stealth technologies, and offensive, conventional military power in Asia on a large scale, we can be reasonably certain that Japan will operate within the political limits that it has imposed on its exercise of military power since 1945. This is hardly a surprise. Japanese policymakers define national security in comprehensive terms, to include economic, social, and political issues besides military considerations (Langdon 1976; Kurth 1990). They are thus much more attuned to finding an appropriate political role for Japan rather than to seeking to develop national military options in a world marked by decreasing international tensions. Playing a central, perhaps the central, role in an Asia that is defined broadly to encompass also the United States is a far more urgent and appealing task.

Japan's approach to international partners expresses a vision of national security rooted in political harmony, economic prosperity, and social stability rather than military preeminence. This vision is grounded in a notion of economic partnerships constituting an international society of states. According to this view, what holds the world together is not common norms that tie different nations together in common endeavors. Instead the world is governed by interests. International cooperation is made possible by the flexibility of redefining short-term interest into long-term interests. This ability to redefine interests presupposes a willingness to extend the notion of "self" to incorporate at least some relevant portions of the "other," so that the expectation of an ongoing interest-based relationship is met (Hamaguchi 1985). In the 1990s Japan is likely to extend and deepen its traditional approach to its international partners

17. The abortive attempt by the Japanese government to send a peace support group to the Persian Gulf and Japan's refusal to participate in joint military exercises with Thailand at the request of Thai Prime Minister Chatchai Chunhavan are just two of the more recent examples of the power of such sentiment (see Simon 1991, 672). See Haber (1990) for a trenchant discussion of how the power of both China and India will severely curtail any foreseeable Japanese military expansion in Asia.

in Asia. And it may choose to invest in global institutions and policies to help Japan play a larger role in Asia. Asian regionalism is likely to retain strong multilateral and global colors.

References

Anderson, Benedict. 1990. Old State, New Society: Indonesia's New Order in Comparative Historical Perspective. In *Language and Power,* 94–120. Ithaca: Cornell University Press.

ASEAN Prospects for Foreign Investment: North Asia Looks South. 1990. *Business Asia,* February 19, 62–64.

Asian Development Bank. 1990. *Asian Development Outlook.* Manila: Asian Development Bank.

Automating Software: Japan's Assistance Plan for Asia. 1988. *Business Asia,* October 17, 337.

Awanohara, Susumu. 1991a. Conditional Generosity. *Far Eastern Economic Review,* January 24, 45.

———. 1991b. The Shrinking Pie. *Far Eastern Economic Review,* January 24, 46.

Baldwin, Robert. 1988. U.S. and Foreign Competition in the Developing Countries of the Asian Pacific Rim. In *The United States in the World Economy,* ed. Martin Feldstein, 79–141. Chicago: University of Chicago Press.

Bangkok Bank. 1991. Southern Seaboard Development Programme. *Bangkok Bank Monthly Review,* April, 140.

Batam Industrial Development Authority. 1991. *Batam: Business Directory Investors and Tourist Guide.* Jakarta: Pt. Wahya Promospirit.

Brown, Donna. 1991. Whither Japan's MITI? *Management Review,* April, 54–55.

Carey, Peter. 1987. Indonesia: The Problem of the Post–Oil Boom Era. *Euro-Asian Business Review,* January, 4–9.

Chittiwatanapong, Prasert, Phisidhi Karasudhi, and Shigeru Itoga. 1989. *Japanese Official Development Assistance to Thailand: Impact on Thai Construction Industry.* Tokyo: Institute of Developing Economies.

Competing in Indonesia's Telecommunications Market: The U.S. Company Image. 1988. *East Asian Executive Reports,* February, 15.

Cracks Begin to Develop. 1990. *Business Asia,* July, 56.

Doi, Ayako, and Kim Willenson. 1991. Japan: Greater East Asia Co-Prosperity Sphere? *International Herald Tribune,* August 12, 6.

Doner, Richard. 1991. *Driving a Bargain: Automobile Industrialization and Japanese Firms in Southeast Asia.* Berkeley: University of California Press.

do Rosario, Louise. 1990. Drop in the Bucket. *Far Eastern Economic Review,* December 20, 48–49.

Edamura, Sumio. 1989. Indonesia Shows Signs of Wise Economic Policies. *Jakarta Post,* January 20, 3.

Friedland, Jonathan. 1988. Preparing for the Pacific Century? Asian Development Bank. *Institutional Investor,* April, 211–13.

Friedman, George, and Meredith Lebard. 1991. *The Coming War with Japan.* New York: St. Martin's Press.

Give Me Your Huddled Hongkongers Yearning to Be Free. 1989. *Economist,* August 26, 52.

Haber, Deborah. 1990. The Death of Hegemony: Why Pax Nipponica Is Impossible. *Asian Survey,* September, 892–905.

Hadiputranto, Sri Indrastuti. 1988. New Regulations Affecting Foreign Investment Companies. *East Asian Executive Reports,* June, 9, 19–21.

Hamaguchi, Esyun. 1985. A Contextual Model of the Japanese: Toward a Methodological Innovation in Japan Studies. *Journal of Japanese Studies* 11:289–321.

Handley, Paul. 1988. Thailand Remains Wary of Japan Inc.'s Generosity. *Far Eastern Economic Review,* March 10, 69–70.

———. 1990a. Japanese Builders Pile In. *Far Eastern Economic Review,* May 3, 50–51.

———. 1990b. Unequal Partners. *Far Eastern Economic Review,* May 3, 51–54.

———. 1991. Going by the Board. *Far Eastern Economic Review,* January 31, 43.

Hewison, Kevin. 1987. National Interests and Economic Downturn: Thailand. In *Southeast Asia in the 1980s: The Politics of Economic Crisis,* ed. Richard Robison, Kevin Hewison, and Richard Higgott, 52–79. Sydney: Allen and Unwin.

Hukill, Mark, and Meheroo Jussawalla. 1989. Telecommunications Policies and Markets in the ASEAN Countries. *Columbia Journal of World Business,* 24 (Spring): 43–57.

Indonesia Shows Evidence of Wise Economic Policies. 1989. *Jakarta Post,* January 30.

Informasi: Pusat Data Business Indonesia. 1991. Interview with Thomas Wibisono, researcher. July.

Japan's Drive into Asia: The Emerging Regional Block. 1989. *Business Asia,* February 13, 51.

Keizai Koto Center. 1988. Toward a New Development of Japan's Assistance Regime and the Role of the Private Business Sector. Brief 50, October, 1–4.

Kunihiro, Michihiko. 1990. RI, Japan Benefit from Economic Relations. *Jakarta Post,* October 13.

Kunio, Yoshihara. 1988. *The Rise of Ersatz Capitalism in Southeast Asia.* Singapore: Oxford University Press.

Kurth, James. 1990. East Asia plus Mitteleuropa. Paper presented to the conference, Beyond the Cold War in the Pacific, Institute on Global Conflict and Cooperation, University of California, San Diego, June 7–9.

Langdon, Frank. 1976. Japan's Concept of Asian Security. *Asian Forum* 8 (Autumn): 33–43.

Looking at Indonesia's Business Opportunities through Japanese Eyes. 1990. *Business Asia,* May 21, 175.

Machado, Kit. 1987. Malaysian Cultural Relations with Japan and South Korea in the 1980s. *Asian Survey,* June, 638–60.

Mann, Richard. 1990. *Business in Indonesia.* Toronto: Gateway Books.

The New Engine of Growth. 1988. *Asian Business,* December, 68.

Noland, Marcus. 1990. *Pacific Basin Developing Countries: Prospects for the Future.* Washington, DC: Institute for International Economics.

Phongpaichit, Pasuk. 1990. *The New Wave of Japanese Investment in ASEAN.* Singapore: Institute of Southeast Asian Studies.

Rainat, Joyce. 1988. Asia's New Land of Opportunity. *Asian Finance,* October, 32–34.

Rim: Pacific Business and Industries. 1989. Vol. 1.

RI Picks Japanese Firm to Study Nuclear Project. 1991. *Jakarta Post,* May 30.

Samuels, Richard J. 1987. *The Business of the Japanese State: Energy Markets in Comparative and Historical Perspective.* Ithaca: Cornell University Press.

Sanger, David. 1991a. Malaysia Trading Plan Seeks a Unified Voice. *New York Times,* February 12.

———. 1991b. Power of the Yen Winning Asia. *New York Times,* December 5.

Schwarz, Adam. 1990. The Price of Security. *Far Eastern Economic Review,* September 27, 56–61.

Shenon, Philip. 1992. Reaching for the Good Life. *New York Times Magazine,* January 5, 16–32.

Simon, Sheldon. 1991. U.S. Interests in Southeast Asia. *Asian Survey,* July, 668–78.

Sricharatchanya, Paisal. 1987. Strengthening Economic Links. *Far Eastern Economic Review,* January 29, 43–45.

Stone, Eric. 1991. Easing into the Fast Lane. *Asian Business,* June, 24–27.

Suehiro, Akira. 1989. *Capital Accumulation in Thailand, 1855–1985.* Tokyo: Yuuki Kikahu.

Sueo, Sudo. 1988. The Politics of Thai-Japanese Trade Relations: A Study of Negotiation Behavior. In *Thai-Japanese Relations in Historical Perspective,* ed. C. Khamchoo and E. B. Reynolds, 213–35. Bangkok: Institute of Asian Studies.

Suharto and the Reins of Power. 1990. *Economist,* November 17, 37–39.

Tachiki, Dennis. 1990. Going Transnational: Japanese Subsidiaries in the Asia Pacific Region. *Research for International Management,* November, 1–8.

Tasker, Rodney. 1990. Wedded to Success. *Far Eastern Economic Review,* May 3, 49.

Thaitawat, Nusara. 1991. Benefit from Tokyo's Aid in Question. *Bangkok Post,* March 15.

Tokyo Grants Aid to Thailand. 1991. *Nation,* August 8, 4.

Uneasy Neighbors: Japan and ASEAN. 1983. *Economist,* April 30, 94.

Westlake, Michael. 1991. The Big Switch. *Far Eastern Economic Review,* March 7, 45–46.

Wysocki, Bernard. 1991. In Asia, the Japanese Hope to Coordinate What Nations Produce. *Wall Street Journal,* August 20, 1–2.

The Yen Bloc Survey. 1989. *Economist,* July 15, 1–21.

Comment   Wing Thye Woo

This is an excellent paper. I agree with its conclusion that the bilateral relationship between Japan and its Asian neighbors will be embedded in a set of multilateral regional and global arrangements that will also include the United States. East and Southeast Asia is definitely not heading toward a Japanese-led autarchic regional order. Japan will not become the regional hegemon because (1) it does not want to do so presently; and (2) most of its Asian neighbors do not want to develop the kind of close bilateral relationship that would allow it to do so.

There are at least two important reasons not mentioned by Peter Katzenstein and Martin Rouse about why Japan does not want to be the regional hegemon. The first is that Japan approximates a country of peaceniks. Skeptics of this claim need only recall the domestic outcry when the prime minister wanted to send a Japanese noncombatant contingent to the Iraq conflict.

The second reason is that the benefits of being the regional hegemon are

Wing Thye Woo is associate professor of economics and head of the Pacific Rim Studies Program of the Institute of Governmental Affairs at the University of California at Davis.

exceeded by the costs of antagonizing the United States and Western Europe. The U.S. and Western European markets are far bigger than the Southeast Asian markets. This fact explains Japan's quick disassociation from the proposal by the Malaysian prime minister to form an exclusively East Asian trading community.

On the other side, there are two major reasons why Japan's neighbors do not want it to be the regional hegemon. The first is that they recognize the benefits of having multiple patrons. The strategy of playing one power against another during the Cold War is a proven winner.

The second reason, which was hinted at by Katzenstein and Rouse but was not developed, is that memories of World War II have created an atmosphere of suspicion toward Japan by its neighbors. These suspicions in the case of China verge on animosity. This is why Hirohito was never invited to China even though he had hinted many times to visiting Chinese officials that he would like to walk on the Great Wall. The Chinese reaction, according to the Beijing grapevine, was that this is exactly what the Great Wall is for—to keep out people like this.

To see how widespread the suspicions about Japan are, we should recall what happened in 1974 when Tanaka visited Southeast Asia. His visit was marred by big riots in Bangkok, Jakarta, and Manila. These riots occurred for domestic reasons, but Japan bashing provided an acceptable excuse to riot. These acts of patriotism were actually shows of defiance to the domestic dictators (Marcos in the Philippines, Soeharto in Indonesia, and Thanom Kittikachorn in Thailand).

The interesting question is why internal dissent was able to masquerade as patriotic acts. The answer is that the governing elite in 1974 in these three countries had in their youth been traumatized by the extreme brutality with which Japan rampaged through Southeast Asia during World War II. For example, General Yamashita earned the title of the Tiger of Malaya when he systematically shot all the people that had anything to do with the propagation of Chinese language or Chinese culture. (Yamashita was later transferred to the Philippines, where he ordered the Bataan Death March.)

Memories of acts like this explain why Lee Kuan Yew (with the implicit agreement of Malaysia and Indonesia) has offered military facilities in Singapore to the United States to replace its loss of the Subic Bay naval facility. This action came from Lee Kuan Yew's and Soeharto's recognition that Japan would immediately rearm if there were any threats to oil tankers traveling through Southeast Asian waters. Both leaders preferred U.S. warships rather than Japanese warships to do the patrolling.

Lee Kuan Yew and Soeharto are just fearful of Japan rearming if it were to become the regional hegemon. To paraphrase Lee Kuan Yew, the Japanese have an obsession with perfection—nothing but the best. The idea of a second-rate military force that is poorly armed just goes against the national grain. A rearmed Japan will be a nuclear Japan, and this, in Lee Kuan Yew's words, "is like giving chocolate liqueur to an alcoholic." Both Lee Kuan Yew and Soeharto want America to have continued strong economic interests in Southeast Asia in the hope of producing the following division of labor: America to continue the management of regional security, and Japan to develop high-definition television to perfection.

So far, I have developed the case that an important impediment to Japan's becoming the regional hegemon is painful historical memories about Japan. The question now is whether this impediment can be removed to speed up the progress of Asian-Japanese bilateral relationships. The answer to this question is the same as the answer Paul Samuelson gave when he was asked how progress is made in economics: progress is always made funeral by funeral.

The other Asians' suspicion of Japan will naturally fade out over time. To give an example, the Japanese embassy in Jakarta, in preparation for the emperor's visit, invited a group of prominent Indonesians for individual conversations. The question the Japanese embassy asked of their guests was whether the emperor should apologize for the World War II atrocities. The responses by the Indonesians coincided very nicely with their age group.

Those above fifty years old gave James Joycean answers: "Apologize, apologize or the eagles will pull out your eyes." Those under fifty years old felt that an apology was not necessary if the emperor would announce a big increase in development aid.

I maintain that the Japanese awareness of this historical memory variable plays a large part in formulating the basic Japanese vision of "national security rooted in political harmony, economic prosperity, and social stability" (section 6.4) rather than in political hegemony.

This excellent paper is unfortunately blemished in several places by poor use of economic theory and an overly suspicious tone. The most prominent examples of faulty theory follow.

In section 6.2.2, the authors attribute the import-substitution industrialization programs of the 1960s to the absence of "private international credit." I do not see the economic reason for this claim. Taiwan hardly borrowed in the 1960s, yet its industrialization program was export-oriented rather than import-substitution-oriented. "The fact that access to international capital could be obtained only through multinational enterprises (MNEs)" does not dictate that industrialization will be import-substituting. The MNEs will come to exploit whatever profit opportunities the government creates. They came in the 1960s when tariffs made it profitable to produce for the domestic markets, and they came in the 1980s when export-promoting policies (actually, industrial deregulation) made it profitable to use these countries as manufacturing bases. Since the authors are well aware of the latter too (see section 6.2.2), I am puzzled by their claim of a link between imperfect credit markets and import-substitution industrialization.

The authors write that in the aftermath of the second oil shock, "the Thai government was pressured by the World Bank and the International Monetary

Fund (IMF) to initiate austerity measures." Shouldn't it be "advised" rather than "pressured"? Why do the authors wish to imply that the IMF's action was detrimental to Thailand's welfare? The only choices the Thai government had were either take the IMF loans and implement the austerity programs, or forgo the IMF loans and still implement the austerity programs. The authors surely cannot be saying that the second choice would have been better than the first.

In section 6.3 the authors conclude from the "lack of coordination arising from Chatchai's rapid privatization of infrastructure, without any government planning and regulation, . . . that the market may not be the best system for upgrading infrastructure." But then, the authors had just noted that in the pre-Chatichai period there had "been major problems with many of the projects . . . , due largely to a lack of coordination among the various road and mass transit projects as well as interministerial conflicts." Since the authors make no claim that the Chatchai period was more chaotic, the only permissible conclusion from both observations is that neither market coordination nor bureaucratic coordination works.

I find the authors too quick to sound suspicious about Japanese investment and infrastructure aid in the following cases.

"But Indonesia's ability to get its economy back on track [since 1983] has come at the price of increased dependence on foreign investment, particularly Japanese" (section 6.2.2). I do not see the negative aspects suggested by the word *price,* because the final outcome was mutually advantageous, as the authors observe in the final sentence of the same paragraph. They also noted earlier that "Japan's increasing economic involvement in the region has been encouraged by almost all governments in Southeast Asia" (section 6.1).

I do not follow how documentation of growing Japanese investment in Thailand and Indonesia could have led to the conclusion that "Japan has indeed been acting as a regional economic hegemon" (section 6.2.2). Up to that point, the authors have presented no examples of how Japan has used its investments to influence public policies in these countries. Being a hegemon is more than simply being the biggest foreign investor. The hegemon conclusion should have been drawn only after the section on infrastructure investment, and even then would still be debatable.

The authors emphasize that the Japanese have not been truly altruistic because "loans for the alleviation of rural poverty . . . are infrequent" (section 6.3). Let us ask ourselves, Has the Japanese (and other foreign donors' and investors') way of getting the Indonesian economy back on track since 1983 been either bad or negligible for Indonesian welfare, particularly for rural poverty? The evidence is a resounding no. The Japanese and other foreigners in the pursuit of their self-interests have created a more export-oriented economy that, throughout the period of structural adjustment, has caused the poverty rate to fall, raised the real wages of rural and urban workers, and increased the caloric intake of the poorest 40 percent of the population.

Let me conclude with what I see to be the biggest flaw in this paper. It is quite remarkable that the possibility of Japan's becoming the hegemon of East Asia was analyzed without any reference to the other East Asian giant, China. Obviously, depending on economic growth in China, Japan may not want to assert itself as the regional hegemon. Moreover, Japan may not be able to assume that role even if it desires to. The recent establishment of diplomatic relations between China and South Korea (or equivalently, the jettisoning of North Korea by China and Taiwan by South Korea) reveals well the moves that are afoot by Japan's neighbors to prevent Japan from assuming such a position. There can be no autarchic regional order without the consent of China, least of all a Japanese-led one.

The authors' neglect of China led to two misstatements in the paper. The first is the claim that "it is difficult to envision a counterweight to Japanese power in Asia" (section 6.1). The second misstatement is the claim that the most important factor behind the decline in Japanese investment (and foreign investment, in general) in Thailand and Indonesia since 1990 is the inadequacy of their infrastructure. At least as important is that Japanese, Taiwanese, and Korean investments have been pouring into the lower-wage alternative, China, instead. President Bush's repeated vetoes of congressional efforts to remove China's most-favored-nation status has restored confidence in China as a suitable manufacturing base.

III Does Japan Have the Qualities of Leadership?

7   How to Succeed without Really Flying: The Japanese Aircraft Industry and Japan's Technology Ideology

David B. Friedman and Richard J. Samuels

7.1   Introduction

Since the end of World War II, the United States has spent billions of dollars more on military research and development (R&D) than Japan has.[1] Even today, despite an American recession and sustained increases in Japan's military expenditures, Japanese annual defense R&D spending—less than 100 billion yen—is dwarfed by U.S. spending of more than 5 trillion yen. In Japan, official defense R&D is just 5 percent of all government R&D, while in the United States, government expenditures account for more than 60 percent.[2] But despite the enormous postwar American efforts to foster defense technologies, a massive disparity in nominal spending, and the fact that Japan does not design or build military equipment for export, Japanese commercial manufacturers now exhibit dual-use production capabilities that match or exceed American capabilities in many areas.[3]

David B. Friedman is a research fellow of the MIT-Japan Program of the Massachusetts Institute of Technology. Richard J. Samuels is professor and head of the Department of Political Science and director of the MIT-Japan Program at the Massachusetts Institute of Technology.

The authors would like to thank the National Science Foundation (NSF #INA-9106045) and the Fulbright Commission for partial research support for this project. They are also grateful to Arthur Alexander, Gerald Sullivan, Mark Lovell, Gregory Noble, Naramoto Yukiya, Tak Seto, Suzuki Hideo, and Fujiki Hirō for their careful reading of an earlier draft. This analysis is elaborated in Richard J. Samuels, *"Rich Nation, Strong Army" and Japanese Technology* (Ithaca, NY: Cornell University Press, 1994). Any errors that remain are, of course, the sole responsibility of the authors.

1. Differences in yen/dollar rates, nominal versus adjusted expenditures, and accounting conventions make precise comparisons difficult, but American defense technology investments have, by any measure, been about two orders of magnitude beyond the Japanese effort. For Japan, see Bōeichō . . . Kikakubu (1991, 35). For the United States, see Alexander, (1989).

2. Bōeichō . . . Kikakubu (1991, 35).

3. Studies of the dependence of U.S. producers on Japanese and other foreign producers include Analytic Science Corporation (1990); Office of Technology Assessment (1989, 1990); Defense Science Board (1987); Defense Technical Information Center (1990); and Institute for Defense Analysis (1990).

This has been possible, we argue, in part because Japanese views about technology and national security sharply diverge from comparable American beliefs. It is this divergence between U.S. and Japanese defense technology strategies deriving from fundamentally different ideas about the economy and national security that concerns us here. Cold War U.S. technology strategy focused on making huge public outlays to specialized defense laboratories and contracting firms, justified by the military calculations of national security. While American defense planners recognized that technologies developed for the military might diffuse into the commercial economy, and many spin-offs—such as jet engines or new materials—did occur, no special effort was made to marry commercial and defense industrial capabilities. Indeed, American defense prime contractors developed design, manufacturing, and business practices, or responded to secrecy and classification requirements in ways that impeded effective exchanges of commercial and defense technology. While many U.S. subcontractors mixed military and commercial technologies more freely than the primes, they lacked the stability and resources necessary to expand into new civilian markets.[4] Over time, "spin-away" rather than "spin-off" may more accurately describe the relationship between U.S. military and civilian manufacturing.

In contrast, Japan's firms have made little distinction between military and civilian technology. They have focused instead on three principles: (1) obtaining and indigenizing foreign civilian and military design, development, and manufacturing capabilities; (2) diffusing these capabilities as widely as possible throughout the economy; and (3) nurturing and sustaining the primes and subcontractors to which commercial and military technologies could be diffused and from which indigenous development could be generated. Differences between military and civilian technologies were less important than differences between domestic capabilities and foreign dependence; making things that "go bang in the night" was not as crucial as nurturing the more fundamental ability to design and make "things," period. Whether these things—machinery, electronics, aircraft, vehicles, and so forth—were for military or commercial end use, the know-how enabling their production was diffused aggressively throughout the Japanese economy as a matter of national policy and private practice. Defense technology has been valued for its ability to elevate the fundamental capacities of the economy as well as a means for actually producing military hardware.

Crucial to implementing Japan's technology and security ideology are formal and informal linkages and bargains—which we call a system of *protocols*—that integrate Japan's industrial technology community. Technology protocols, such as informal industry cooperation practices, regional and national

---

4. One study of the 350 largest companies and corporate divisions participating in the U.S. defense industry shows that the top U.S. defense contractors rely on military production for well over 80 percent of their output (Alexander 1993, 45).

subcontractor associations, R&D consortia, semipublic industry research groups, or vertical and horizontal industrial "cooperation" associations, overlap and bind Japanese producers in ways that create and preserve opportunities for firms to build alliances within the economy. These alliances—metaphorically, sets of "open door" opportunities, or technology highways—stimulate competition while at the same time providing competitors with access to crucial manufacturing know-how. They enable Japanese firms to build and combine their skills with comparative ease to produce even the most complex products, including military equipment. Japanese defense production is simply one of many technology linkages that firms maintain within the domestic economy. Japan's defense prime contractors are far less specialized than their American counterparts, and subcontractors more readily combine defense and commercial production in a wider range of industrial undertakings. As a consequence, defense and commercial technologies interdiffuse—they spin-on and spin-off to each other with comparative ease in Japan.

In this paper, we illustrate the industrial consequences of Japan's technology and security ideology with the case of the aircraft industry. Aerospace provides an ideal case because, as in the United States, it has received the lion's share of military R&D expenditures, and aircraft production has been heavily geared towards defense; four-fifths of Japan's output and two-thirds of American aircraft production has been for the military.[5] Commercial aircraft development in Japan has been a major goal of industrialists and policymakers alike, and has been cherished within the United States as one of the industries in which America dominates global competition.

But the Japanese and American aircraft industrial strategies and structures have diverged. U.S. prime contractors and subcontractors heavily specialize in aircraft production. At the prime level, this specialization has proceeded to the point where there is a sharp, practically impenetrable barrier between civilian and military aircraft operations even within the same firm. American aircraft industry subcontractors more readily combine their commercial and defense capabilities, but generally do not diversify into nonaerospace fields. Japanese aircraft primes and subcontractors, however, are overwhelmingly dedicated to nonaerospace commercial production. The industry is, in effect, embedded in the civilian economy as a whole. Japan's aerospace capabilities result from the combination of skills possessed by companies whose primary business and technology strategies are oriented toward other industries. The disjuncture between commercial and military, aircraft and nonaircraft production characteristic of primes and subcontractors in America never emerged. Instead, even aerospace producers in Japan at the prime level, and especially the country's subcontractors, have been able to spin-on to military applications many of the fruits of their commercial investments, and spin-off defense skills for civilian purposes. In this fashion, Japan has built a thriving, if still small, aerospace

5. Aerospace Industries Association of America (1990, 22).

sector, and it has used aircraft industry technologies to enhance commercial and military capabilities throughout the economy. In short, judged by the criteria of Japan's technology and security ideology, the aircraft industry has succeeded without really flying.

Section 7.2 outlines the three basic tenets of that ideology: indigenization, diffusion, and nurturing. It shows that Japan has embraced and promulgated a vision of national security that elevates local control, national learning, and sustained development over the more conventional procurement criteria of cost, performance, and delivery schedules that dominate in America. Section 7.3 suggests that the Japanese aircraft industry arguably has flourished when measured in conventional terms of sales, output, profits, and growth, despite common perceptions to the contrary. Section 7.4 contends that, even if the caliber of Japan's aerospace capabilities is debatable in conventional terms, the industry is a success under the criteria that inform Japanese industrial thinking. Finally, in section 7.5 we conclude that, since differences in technology ideologies can lead to divergent standards for industrial achievement, different industrial development trajectories, and political and economic conflict, America, Japan, and the Asian region as a whole face significant conceptual and policy challenges in the near future.

7.2 The Origins and Contours of Japan's Technology and Security Ideology

From the moment Tokugawa Ieyasu united nation and state at the turn of the seventeenth century, the Japanese people have been exhorted to make sacrifices to enhance national security in a hostile world. At different times and in different measures, this mobilization has mixed xenophobia, religion, militarism, and nationalism. Japan's early industrialization was led by military industries to enhance national security by "catching up and surpassing the West"(*oitsuke, oikose*). Later, the Meiji era mobilization symbolized by the slogan, "Rich nation, strong army," proved calamitous. In the postwar era, sheltered by the U.S. security umbrella, Japanese citizens have been exhorted to sacrifice for more purely commercial purposes.

Technology has been central to national security in three consistent ways: (1) to achieve *independence and autonomy* through indigenization of technology (*kokusanka*); (2) to *diffuse* this learning throughout the economy (*hakyuu*); and (3) to *nurture and sustain* appropriate Japanese enterprises to which technical knowledge can be diffused and further refined (*ikusei*).

Indigenization, diffusion, and nurturing derive from a pervasive sense that Japan must compensate for its special vulnerabilities in a Hobbesian world. This feeling of insecurity and vulnerability (*fuan*) has been articulated repeatedly throughout Japanese history. In the eighteenth century, a Sendai nobleman, Hayashi Shihei, warned the shogunate (roughly at the same time Alexander Hamilton similarly admonished the fledgling U.S. government) to protect

Japanese manufactures or face foreign domination. A century later, bridling at having to purchase antiquated weapons from the west, Meiji leaders drove Japan to adopt "Western learning with Japanese spirit" (*wakon yōsai*) while they promoted a program of industrial nurturance (*shokusan kōgyō*).[6] Following Japan's defeat in the Pacific war, Navy Minister Yonai Mitsumasa proclaimed, "The loss of the war was a technological defeat."[7] Informed by this perspective, and afforded the luxury of U.S. security guarantees, over the next half century Japan set out to build its general technological capabilities to enhance its national security.

The same perceived vulnerabilities that justified Japanese militarism also influenced the country's commercial strategies. In postwar commercial Japan, direct foreign investments have been discouraged in favor of joint ventures that maximize technology transfers.[8] When domestic manufacturers have lacked capabilities in key areas, they have typically elected to buy licenses rather than to import products. Fundamental to Japan's technology and security ideology is the belief that "security" means comprehensively building the nation's productive and technological capabilities rather than simply amassing military hardware. Japan has sought to compensate for economic, technological, political, and social vulnerabilities that it believes demand special vigilance beyond merely responding to military threats and enhancing military preparedness. Japan's conception of "comprehensive security" (*sōgō anzen hoshō*) is merely the latest and most elaborate articulation of a technonational ideology that has driven its security concerns for more than a century.

Indigenization, diffusion, and nurturing have been, and continue to be, the core values that make up Japanese security thinking. Each reinforces the objectives of the other; together, they undergird Japan's remarkably successful industrial development. Technology indigenization is thought to be essential, so that, at least, Japan can derive higher value from leading-edge design, manufacturing, and production knowledge; at best, it can set the pace for world technology development. Once indigenized, domestic technical knowledge diffusion is essential, so that Japanese producers can collaborate to exploit fully the results of their efforts while competing vigorously to ensure that ultimate commercial (or military) applications are achieved. Finally, firms in Japan are nurtured and sustained by a system of alliances and protocols, so that the knowledge that has been diffused is not lost through calamitous economic dislocations (such as business cycle swings, short-term capital shortages, commercial product failures, market consolidations). Nurturing also assures that, in the future, technology can be diffused to enterprises that have steadily absorbed design and manufacturing knowledge, developing the economic wherewithal to produce first-rank products for civilian or military end-users.

---

6. Yamazaki (1961, 19).
7. Maema (1989, 169).
8. Mason (1992).

As used in this paper, *ideology* does not mean that Japanese or American technology and security strategies have been determined solely by each nation's national "culture." Rather, as each country has faced its own unique industrial and security challenges, certain basic principles have emerged to guide debates over how best it should respond. These ideas are now institutionalized through years of private and public practice, but they are not unchangeable or immutable. Indeed, we argue below that by understanding the divergence between U.S. and Japanese technology and security thinking, both nations may be able to modify their actions and beliefs to improve bilateral and regional prospects. In this fashion, we argue that ideology does shape a nation's choices about technology and security but it does not determine them; change, learning, and adaptation, however slow and halting, are not only possible but essential.

Let us explore the three interwoven strands of Japan's technology and security ideology in more detail.

7.2.1   Autonomy and Indigenization

Writing of the intellectual origins of modern Japanese bureaucratism, Tetsuo Najita has explained Japan's "unadorned, yet pervasive perception" that national development is a matter of "autonomy," and that "national integrity" can be achieved "only through economic power (*fukoku*)."[9] Japan's first national research institutes were established by MITI's forerunner, the Ministry of Agriculture and Commerce, to fortify Japan, achieve independence from foreign industrial products, and meet the Western imperialists on their own terms.[10] The Meiji leader Fukuzawa Yukichi wrote in his classic treatise, *The Outline of Civilization (Bunmeiron no gairyaku)*, that both civilization and wisdom were necessary to protect the nation. Wisdom, he argued, could be learned from abroad but was best nurtured and applied at home. From the start, influential Japanese taught that the advancement of independent knowledge and scientific competence were as necessary as military power to achieve security.

In response, throughout the Meiji period Japan strove to learn Western technologies—particularly military technologies—and to indigenize them as soon as possible. Foreign tutelage for national strength was enshrined in the Charter Oath of the emperor Meiji in 1868: "Intellect and learning would be sought throughout the world in order to establish the foundations of Empire."[11] Independent arms manufacture based on imported foreign design and manufacturing skills, the first modern industrial sector in the Meiji era, led Japan's forced march to industrialization.

This process of indigenization is called *kokusanka* in Japanese. From Meiji to the present, private and public procurement decisions have been guided by the "three unwritten principles of *kokusanka:* (1) domestic supply; (2) if do-

9. Najita (1980, 6). This *fukoku* is more familiar as the first half of the Meiji exhortation, *fukoku kyōhei* ("Rich nation, strong army") that defined Japan's course of military technonationalism.
10. Kamitani (1988).
11. Lockwood (1955, 9). See Samuels (1992) for a fuller account.

mestic supply is not possible, licenses should be secured using domestic manufacture and equipment; and (3) equipment should have broader application than specific to the project for which purchased."[12] In accordance with these principles, in both military and civilian cases, each subsequent generation of Japanese product has usually depended less than its predecessor on foreign technology. So crucial has *kokusanka* been in Japanese thinking that some of the most important debates over industrial development and industrial policy in Japan have centered on how to achieve local control of knowledge.[13]

The Defense Production Committee of Keidanren has justified *kokusanka,* which it has championed, in at least five ways: (1) Japan's unique policy of "defensive defense" requires different equipment than that manufactured in Europe and North America; (2) the "special spirit and body size" of Japanese military personnel, as well as Japan's special "land, water, and seas"; (3) licensing breeds dependence of the licenser on the licensee, making upgrading difficult; (4) licensers are less willing to transfer technology to Japan, now that Japan's technological level has improved; and (5) codevelopment with other nations can succeed only if Japan has something of its own to offer.[14] The significance of this and numerous other similar arguments is its almost total lack of any credible military rationale for autonomous weapons developments. Rather, *kokusanka* is justified to avoid foreign dependence generally and to specifically improve Japan's bargaining position when obtaining technologies from abroad. *Kokusanka* is more than self-serving propaganda at budget time; it has been implemented in Japan's procurement practice: using aggregate time-series budgetary data, for instance, Bobrow and Hill found that Japanese military budgets reflect military calculations only in part. In addition, autonomy and dependence concerns explain a significant portion of Japan's defense priorities.[15]

The struggle for technological autonomy has not slackened now that Japan has emerged as a technological superpower. To the contrary, parity with the United States (and the prospect of considerably more intimate bilateral transfers of defense technology) is frequently used by industry and by the bureaucracy to justify demands for increased funding for scientific and technological development and for *accelerated kokusanka.*[16] A group of industrialists convened by the Keidanren responded to demands from the United States for technology codevelopment by arguing for accelerated autonomous defense technology strategies to ensure against a U.S. technology blockade.[17]

Efforts to achieve autonomy are also central to the process of Japan's interna-

12. Adachi (1981, 14).

13. See Anchordoguy (1989) for computers; Mason (1988) for automobiles and electronics; Green (1991) for defense.

14. Keizai . . . Iinkai (1976, 31–33).

15. Bobrow and Hill (1991, 55).

16. Ueda (1991), for example.

17. Jikibō . . . (1990).

tional cooperation. Consider these opening lines of the most recent report on promoting international cooperative aircraft development of the Japanese Machinery Industry Alliance and the International Aircraft Development Fund (IADF):

> It goes without saying that in order to secure a stable rank in international society, it is essential to more fully utilize our nation's meager resources and, moreover, to develop high level industrial technologies, leading the world. In order to do this, we must stir up the will for a technological renovation . . . as well as to reinforce and nurture the capability to develop technology autonomously. . . . In order to overcome the fragility of our resource poverty it is necessary to shift our policies of promoting a technology-based nation, and establish our economic security; this is a major objective that we must aim at especially now.[18]

A survey of Japanese defense production capabilities by the Mitsubishi Research Institute in 1987 was even more blunt about the tactical use of international cooperation to foster autonomous technology development in Japan: "With the exception of some very advanced high technologies, the commercial base of Japanese electronics materials and vehicles technology is equal to or better than in the United States and Western Europe. We anticipate progress in commercial-led R&D for military application. However, in those areas of high technology where domestic technology is behind, it will be necessary to supplement [domestic efforts] with international cooperation."[19]

The drive to indigenize and autonomously control technology remains as vital as ever in Japanese strategic thinking.

7.2.2   Diffusion

But it is not just a concern to indigenize and develop autonomous technical capabilities that is noteworthy about Japan. After all, autonomy is widely accepted as a legitimate goal of every nation's security policy. But Japan is also uniquely committed to diffusing technologies as broadly as possible throughout the economy. In practice, technology is often treated as a quasi-public good that is developed and distributed through elaborate networks of producers and bureaucracies. Participants in the process believe that propriety technology can be distinguished from generic information and that each contributes significantly to Japanese national security. As a consequence, Japan has built an extensive network of "technology highways"—an infrastructure comprising at least as many lanes, but perhaps fewer roadblocks, as its U.S. counterpart. Indeed, because the Japanese system facilitates extensive inbound (but much less outbound) technology traffic from abroad, it is able to exploit the opportu-

---

18. Nihon Kikai . . . Kikin (1991, i). The term used in this text is *gijutsu rikkoku sokushin no seisaku.* Nakayama (1991), suggests this can also be translated "a policy of technonationalism," although most Japanese tend to restrict use of that term for U.S. policies of technoprotectionism.

19. Mitsubishi Research Institute, survey (1987, 34).

nities other countries have created to promote technology exchanges as well. As a result, Japanese technology highways more effectively acquire and diffuse global and domestic technologies than similar systems in other countries.

Further, roadblocks impeding the interdiffusion of military and civilian technologies are in evidence considerably less in Japan than in the United States. Unlike in the United States, Japan's technology highways can accommodate automobiles, trucks, or tanks with equal facility. We noted above that national power and industrial autonomy were interdependent in the view of Meiji leaders. So too were military and civilian technologies. The first machine tools were manufactured in a government arsenal in 1869, and modern communications technology was first used by the army to suppress the Satsuma Rebellion. As the academic/bureaucrat Kobayashi Ushisaburo explained in 1922, the diffusion of basic technologies initially absorbed for military purposes was later crucial in building Japan's commercial industries.

> While the manufactured articles made as war materials are seldom fit for general use, the tools and machines that manufacture them may for the most part be used for making other kinds of articles wanted by the people at large. . . . One industrial work is apt to cause another of a similar kind, and so on, and the result was the evolution of all sorts of new industries. But that is not all. Workmen who had been employed and trained in the military industry went to work elsewhere in private factories or started little works of their own. (166)

Kobayashi's analysis remains true today. The interdiffusion of military and civilian products, process technologies, and skills has been of incalculable benefit to Japanese national development. Indeed, it has become so ingrained that Japanese managers often disclaim any interest in tracking the diffusion of military technology because "we don't make any such distinction."[20]

The low barriers to the interdiffusion of civilian and military technologies profoundly shaped Japan's postwar development. The country's earliest export successes, such as cameras, watches, and small machinery, were developed under the supervision of former military engineers.[21] Senior executives of many of Japan's most successful firms—including Morita Akio and Ibuka Masaru, the founders of Sony—learned their first lessons about manufacturing and technology management in the laboratories and factories of the Imperial Naval Air Arsenal (Kugisho).

Once the United States began sourcing in Japan for goods and services during the Korean War, Japanese firms used U.S. military procurement as a technological locomotive for the entire economy. This "special procurement" (*tokuju*) resuscitated then-moribund Japanese industries by transferring American

---

20. Interview, General Manager Aircraft Division, Mitsubishi Heavy Industries, October 8, 1991. This is vigorously denied by some MITI and industry association officials (correspondence, February 3, 1993) but is acknowledged by other MITI officials (interview, August 22, 1991).

21. Maema (1989, 160).

engine and machinery technologies, and introducing production, quality control, and manufacturing process know-how.[22] According to surveys done in the 1960s for the Defense Production Committee of the Keidanren, military demand, and especially technologies first introduced for military production such as materials processing, wireless communications, and propulsion, actively contributed to Japan's commercial economy for at least two decades after the resumption of military production in 1952 (contrary to conventional wisdom).[23] Keidanren repeatedly demanded increased military production, claiming that "the diffusion of modern weapons production raises the technological level of general industry."[24] Engineers noted in surveys that participation in defense R&D "helps raise technological capabilities in other areas" such as systems integration and design.[25]

In part because of the limited size of aerospace and defense production, Japan's prime contractors make little distinction between military and civilian products, except at final assembly, unlike U.S. primes that isolate much defense from commercial production. Japanese components and subassemblies are produced by and tested on the same equipment, regardless of the project for which the equipment was initially obtained or the ministry from which subsidies may have been initially derived at both the prime and supply levels.[26] As long ago as 1966, more than 80 percent of the production equipment employed in the manufacture of military products was used for nondefense products as well.[27]

Knowledge diffusion in Japan occurs at several levels, both inside and among firms and between sectors. It is accomplished through parallel, undifferentiated efforts affecting both commercial and military technologies. In the case of military production, the major defense contractors are diversified manufacturing conglomerates that take special pains to establish mechanisms such as project teams, extensive corporation-wide study groups, and technology focus centers for functional area specialists, to share know-how and experience across divisional lines. Although Japanese prime contractors rarely transfer engineering personnel across applications, they actively seek to transfer knowledge accumulated in one area to others within the firm.[28]

The result is a cadre of multifunctional design and manufacturing specialists

---

22. Bōei Kiki . . . Iinkai (1968, 49).

23. Ibid.; Keizai . . . Iinkai, ed., 1970.

24. Nihon . . . Kōgyōkai (1987, 57). We acknowledge that many of Keidanren's claims are self-serving.

25. Keizai . . . Iinkai (1970, 180).

26. Kamata (1979) and our site visits to aerospace and defense plants of two of Japan's three largest prime defense contractors (December 1991).

27. Bōei Kiki . . . Iinkai (1968, 16). According to this survey, 80,000 to 92,000 machines were put to military and nonmilitary use. Even in the weapons sector, 83 percent of the production equipment was general use. In military vehicles it was 97 percent.

28. Usually this is organized through the technology headquarters (*gijutsu honbu*) of the firm (interviews with senior technology managers: Shin Meiwa, Mitsubishi Heavy Industries, Mitsubishi Electric, Toshiba, September–December 1991).

who understand their application area comprehensively and who are expected to systematically diffuse their accomplishments company-wide. Even though engineering and technical staff do not typically leave their specific application areas, they each participate in every phase within the program from design to production, and they participate in a range of intrafirm mechanisms that transfer their knowledge. It has thus been comparatively easy for statistical quality control appropriate for military production to diffuse throughout the machinery industry divisions of Japanese primes, for commercial automated manufacturing processes to rationalize fighter aircraft parts production beyond what even the American licensers can achieve, or for aerospace materials to improve automobile and bus body production.[29] In the United States, prime contractor defense production is something to protect, isolate, and classify within the firm. Defense designers only design; process engineers focus only on production. But in Japan, defense production is like any other resource for advanced basic and process technologies within a firm, from which technological wisdom is to be mined and integrated into the firm.

Technology also diffuses horizontally among competitors. Many of Japan's technological capacities were fostered by novel and borrowed organizational practices—institutions such as research consortia—that allow risk-averse competitors to achieve common technical goals before they compete with each other in the market. Japanese firms cooperate in consortia at every level of the development cycle, including basic research, systems development, and, especially in aircraft, manufacturing. While the form and function of these consortia vary, every government program since the 1970s designed to support technology development has provided incentives for additional collaborative research.[30]

The research consortia are just one of several other "external" information networks through which technology is exchanged, traded, or otherwise diffused among competitors in Japan. These networks, coupled with public policies and private practices that are "delocalizing" Japanese research include joint ventures, technology exchange agreements, cross-licensing, second

---

29. The diffusion of commercial automated machinery techniques in nonaerospace industries to aerospace uses has been achieved both by Japanese primes and by sectoral suppliers who draw on their expertise in other divisions to produce aircraft parts of higher quality and with greater efficiency than their foreign licensers can achieve. The diffusion of statistical quality control techniques has also flowed in the opposition direction, mediated by the technology headquarters of the primes and facilitated by technology study activities undertaken by representatives of suppliers, subcontractors, and the primes in joint consultation with each licensed production activity. Aerospace production has also been used to obtain new materials technology, such as braking devices, lightweight metals, and more pliable structural assemblies in train and bus construction in Japan. Information derived in a series of interviews performed by us in 1991 involving site visits to a major Japanese defense prime contractor in the aerospace sector and seven subcontractors of varying sizes and capabilities located in Kakamigahara, Gifu prefecture. Data collected from these interviews in Japan shall be referred to as "Kakamigahara field study, December 1991."

30. Levy and Samuels (1991).

sourcing, production sharing, and a wide range of informal technology trading and information sharing. Industry associations and regional and prefectural manufacturer associations (*kumiai*) also provide opportunities for specialty equipment or components vendors and subcontractors to exchange technological information.[31] As we will see, efforts to stimulate multiple technology-sharing relationships among competitors are particularly pronounced in the aircraft industry.

An additional technology highway connects suppliers and their customers. It extends to (and indeed defines) the vertical relationships among primes and subcontractors and facilitates both upstream and downstream learning. Japanese prime contracts have been the principal conduit through which knowledge gleaned from licensed production is diffused to supplier and vendors. Typically, with each new project, subcontractors will dispatch teams of engineers to the primes for several weeks or months of training to master design or manufacturing techniques imported from abroad. The primes will also provide technical guidance on equipment purchases such as autoclaves, new NC machinery, or specialty composite materials technology.[32]

There is also substantial bottom-up diffusion; indeed, one of the dominant trends in Japanese manufacturing is the increased role subcontractors play as specialists in applying technology to foster new products. As the subcontractors diversify into new fields, or undertake independent R&D, they often learn unique techniques or skills that they spin-on to their old lines of work. This knowledge is often transferred downstream in generic form, as the subcontractors become more involved in designing or manufacturing new products in collaboration with other firms.[33] As in the United States, prime defense contractors are directly responsible for only a fraction of their nominal production. A 1987 survey by the Mitsubishi Research Institute found that reliance by primes upon their subcontractors for defense production was already high and growing.[34] The volume of upstream and downstream technology diffusion differs among companies and industries; downstream transfer may be comparatively rare in Japanese defense manufacturing, given the heavy influence of licensed production. Nevertheless, it is yet another mechanism by which technologies flow between companies in Japan.

7.2.3 Nurturing

The third strand of Japan's technology security ideology, nurturing, is concerned with creating the conditions under which domestic firms can usefully

31. An example of a horizontal and a vertical organization designed to transfer technology to supply networks is the Kawasaki Gifu Kyōdō Kumiai, described in Kawasaki Gifu Kyōdō Kumiai (1990); Kakamigahara Shiyakusho (1987); Sanemoto (1989).

32. Kakamigahara field study, December 1991.

33. A discussion of bottom-up engineering in the automobile industry is provided in Womack, Jones, and Roos (1990, 104–37); Nishiguchi (1989, 183–94).

34. Mitsubishi Research Institute, survey (1987, 24).

apply and retain the technical knowledge they obtain. Market shifts or techno-logical revolutions can threaten long-term manufacturing capabilities if indus-trial players—firms, workers, designers—are not able to respond without threatening their very survival. It is therefore just as important to assure that networks and industrial participants survive as it is to obtain or develop tech-nology. As a director of Japan's Aircraft Technology Association explained, Japanese industrial policy is about "targeting technology, not an industry. We are nurturing capabilities, not a sector."[35]

Consistent with this philosophy, the Japanese have constructed an elaborate system of protocols—sometimes tacit and sometimes explicit—which induce domestic firms, even as they compete, to constantly bargain and negotiate with their managerial counterparts and with Japanese bureaucrats to share market jurisdiction and control. These protocols—sometimes as simple as legitimacy afforded to government advisory commissions or as complex as reciprocity accumulated over decades of interaction—force interests as varied as the largest industrial producers, small subcontractors, regional industrial associa-tions, local and national bureaucrats, and financial institutions to take account of each other's needs in shaping the economy. No single interest can ignore the others in making and implementing industrial strategies; no one bureaucracy, multinational firm, domestic industrial association, or union can significantly disadvantage the others through unilateral decision making.[36]

This system contrasts with American views that collaboration is the same as collusion and that economic competition is zero-sum. While U.S. economic bureaucrats have been historically preoccupied with the threat of excessive market concentration, their Japanese counterparts have feared that excessive competition may drive producers out of business that might otherwise contrib-ute to the economy. Bargaining and negotiation protocols help ensure that busi-ness cycles, differential access to capital, cutthroat regional development com-petition, or large-firm market power, which typically generate enormous industrial dislocation in other countries, are mediated so that even "sick" play-ers have a chance to recover, and none moves too far ahead of the other.

Consequently, small and large producers in Japan share the pain of eco-nomic downturns to a greater degree than in the United States; capital is allo-cated across the board to talented niche producers as well as brand-name cor-porations; and regions are not subject to huge currents of investment and disinvestment forcing painful social adjustments that endanger skills and man-ufacturing know-how.[37] Options to "exit" from the economy are made less at-

---

35. Interview, November 27, 1991.

36. Samuels calls this process of iterative bargaining among stable public and private actors "reciprocal consent." For an extended discussion of efforts to describe the Japanese economy's networks of power and authority, see Samuels (1987, 279–82).

37. Friedman (1988, 129–34) describes how postwar cyclical adjustments have increasingly been borne equally by larger and smaller firms, as the "dual structure" of the Japanese economy receded in the present period.

tractive than collaborative strategies that progressively build the skills of individual firms, regions, and the economy as a whole.[38] And when markets prove irresistible and exit is unavoidable—as in the case of Japan's coal mining districts in the 1960s—the state and consumers are expected to bear their "fair share" of the costs involved in restructuring regions or industries.[39]

Japanese nurturing strategies encompass the public, private, tacit, and explicit bargains that undergird the whole economy. Indeed, military production is so embedded in the commercial economy in Japan that it is difficult to distinguish between support strategies applicable only to military or defense manufacturing. Nevertheless, in several instances, Japanese nurturing has had especially clear effects on the nation's defense capabilities.

One is the creation of geographical regions where arms manufacturing knowledge is systematically strengthened and then retained over time. Unlike many American regions, such as the Rust Belt in general or Detroit in particular, Japanese industrial regions are "sticky"; once capital and technology flow into a region, they almost never flow out.[40] After design, manufacturing, and financial links are forged between producers and investors in specific industries, all of the participants exert considerable effort to keep them intact. In lean times, to diversify their options or learn new skills, regional producers often enter new industries, building relationships with new banks or firms. But these relationships supplement, rather than destroy, existing ties. New regional networks are built on top of the old.

Consequently, Japanese regions can sustain whole industries in suspended animation; like pictures burned into a television screen, certain regional capacities may dim with changing times, but they do not fade completely. Later, they can flare again into sharp definition should circumstances permit. As we shall see, this process has been characteristic of the aircraft industry. Immediately after the war, and then again in the late 1970s, Japanese producers kept alive the country's aerospace options during severe slumps by turning to other sectors while awaiting new military or commercial opportunities. In the immediate postwar period, aircraft industry intercorporate links were preserved for close to a decade and a half without significant production. Then, as defense orders blossomed in the early 1960s and commercial subcontracting expanded in the 1980s, the same firms and personnel successfully resuscitated Japanese aircraft production. Regional production skill development in Japan is cumulative rather than disjunctive, as is often the case in America.

As we will see, this strategy has been crucial in developing Japan's defense industries. Japanese military manufacturing has been limited by comparatively low, cyclical military expenditures. But as the country's defense was sustained by regional producers, aircraft, tank, or warship builders minimized the poten-

38. Basic concepts of exit, voice, and/or loyalty in response to change are first set forth in Hirschman (1970).
39. See Lesbriel (1991) and Samuels (1987, chap. 3) for reviews of this process.
40. See Friedman (1993) for an elaboration of sticky regions.

tial loss of accumulated know-how and skills during lean times, and could more readily meet the nation's procurement requirements as conditions changed for the better.[41] Not incidentally, they were also positioned to further enhance their capabilities through imports of foreign technologies or commercial R&D.

Horizontal and vertical relationships between firms also nurture long-term stability and skill retention by preventing debilitating intercorporate struggles for power. On the horizontal dimension (as we describe below in the case of aircraft), Japan's defense industry has been shaped by collaborative arrangements between the largest firms, which seem to ensure that each participates in at least a piece of every major project. Substantial market consolidations that would force many military production participants out of the industry—typical in other countries—rarely occur. Rather, historical players, and occasional new entrants, are able to share in learning and applying defense-related technology.

Similarly, primes and subcontractors have developed relationships that enhance skill retention by reducing the kinds of intercorporate exploitation that frequently threatens the existence of smaller producers in many other countries. In much of the prewar period and in the early postwar economy, Japanese primes—consistent with current and historical American practices—used their subcontractors as shock absorbers when the economy turned sour. Concerted political action on behalf of suppliers and subcontractors, the rise of producer associations that could bargain with the primes and with the government, the provision of massive financial and technological support to smaller firms, and the decline of mass, standardized production in Japan largely reversed this trend.[42]

Today, it is unusual for larger Japanese firms to force their supply networks to bear unequally the costs of economic adjustments. Indeed, when asked if they do, Japanese defense production managers often express genuine surprise that prime contractors in other countries could, or would want to, treat their suppliers in this fashion.[43] Conversely, representatives of U.S. primes and defense subcontractors are usually puzzled that the Japanese would *not* take ad-

41. An unpublished survey by the Mitsubishi Research Institute found in 1987 that "surge" capability in most sectors is considerable—ranging from 1.5 to 10 times current production during a rapid mobilization—including the rapid conversion of capital equipment in most sectors.

42. See Friedman (1988). See also Nishiguchi (1989) for discussion of the collaborative manufacturing strategies that have come to characterize Japanese manufacturing networks. In essence, Japanese firms both large and small rely on each other to market and produce the subsystems in which they specialize. As a result, it becomes extremely difficult for a large firm to cast off its smaller firm suppliers in bad times, since it is frequently closely relying on those firms for indispensable subsystems, technology, and manufacturing skills. See also the discussion by Asamuma (1989, 1–30). It states that Japanese firms increasingly specialize and rely on each other's skills in manufacturing hierarchies, which mitigates against buffer roles that would tend to disadvantage one part of the hierarchy to the advantage of another.

43. Kakamigahara field study, December 1991.

vantage of their suppliers to cushion themselves from market shocks.[44] The dense local, regional, national, political, and industrial networks that shape how firms are vertically organized in Japan do not facilitate the "cut and run" strategies typical in the United States. Rather, Japanese primes and subcontractors share market pain and grow together during economic upturns. The result is that the country's defense suppliers are better able to retain their military production skills, and can more easily experiment over the long term with spinons and spin-offs involving commercial and defense applications.

Japanese beliefs about the strategic contributions of technology to national security have therefore generated a national commitment to indigenizing technology, diffusing it throughout the economy, and nurturing firms that could benefit from indigenization and diffusion. Pursued separately and measured in conventional economic terms, each has effects that are costly and inefficient. Pursued jointly and understood in their ideological context, these principles have led to industrial strength and national security. Indeed, they have helped create a defense industry—if not an entire economy—organized differently than is typical in America. Industries are valued for the knowledge that they provide as well as for the products they can make. Relations between industrial players are guided less by price considerations than by the desire to continuously amass and apply knowledge over the long term.

In making this claim, however, we are not arguing that the defense sector in Japan has been the most important source of technology for the Japanese economy as a whole. Rather, as Japan's security and technology ideology has played out in practice, defense production has been subsumed within the commercial base, and defense technology is simply one of several technology options that Japanese firms engaged primarily in commercial production can and do draw upon. Further, we do not claim that this outcome resulted from state control, that industry has uniformly triumphed over politicians, that it has been uncontested politically, or that Japan's responses were preordained in accordance with the nation's basic security and technology ideology.

Finally, nothing about Japanese strategies reflects cultural peculiarities; non-Japanese thinkers such as Joseph Schumpeter and Friederich List have put forth ideas that coincide closely with the country's technology and security ideology. Schumpeter's claim that technology is the central component of economic competitiveness resonates throughout Japanese economic practice.[45] So does List's argument that a nation's independence and security depends on the independence and vitality of its manufacturers.[46] Japanese industrialists, secu-

44. Information regarding the manufacturing strategy, financial position, and intercorporate links in the U.S. aircraft industry is derived in part from a series of field interviews we conducted, first in Puget Sound, Washington, January 1992 with a major defense and commercial prime contractor and six affiliated subcontractors, and interviews with subcontractors in Los Angeles in January 1992. The Puget Sound study will be referred to hereinafter as "Puget Sound field study, January 1992"; the Los Angeles interviews will be referred to as "Los Angeles field study, January 1992."

45. Schumpeter (1950).

46. List (1927).

rity planners, and policymakers have been more informed by Schumpeter's belief in the centrality of technology and List's belief in the importance of domestic industrial and technological capabilities, than have their counterparts in America and other nations where different principles were widely adopted. Autonomy, diffusion, and nurturing, the core values of Japan's technology ideology, may not be uniquely Japanese, but Japan combined them to generate effective industrial practices, public policies, and criteria measuring the success of an entire industry. Japan is demonstrating that a nation may have less need for an explicit technology strategy if it embraces ideology that holds technology to be strategic. This is nowhere more apparent than in the case of the Japanese aircraft industry.

7.3   Aircraft Production and the Japanese Security Ideology

By the early 1990s, the Japanese aircraft industry was small but growing and carefully cultivated. Yet it is widely regarded as a failure. Certainly, the Japanese industry remains small by international standards. It is barely one-fifteenth the size of its $110 billion U.S. counterpart. Its exports are less than 0.1 percent of U.S. aircraft exports, and the production of the entire industry is just 10 percent of the production of Toyota Motors alone. It is less than 2 percent the size of the Japanese electronics or automobile industries. Few completed airplanes are built—just 188 in 1989 compared to 2,448 civil and 1,227 military aircraft in the same year for the United States.[47] No airline flies more than a handful of Japanese aircraft, and those that are flown are vintage-1960 YS-11 turboprops. The largest aeroengine manufacturer, Ishikawajima Harima Heavy Industries (IHI), has never designed and sold a commercial jet engine. How successful has Japanese industrial policy been? Has Japanese aircraft production been as disappointing as many suggest? Let us explore answers both conventional and unconventional.

Explanations for the "failure" of Japanese commercial aircraft production typically include some or all of the following.[48]

Late start.   Between 1945 and 1952, the U.S. occupation prohibited aircraft production. Japan missed the start of the jet engine technology age and has been behind ever since. Licensing established knowledge is a good way to keep up; it is not a good way to get ahead.

Military dependence.   For the past several decades, 70–80 percent of Japanese aircraft production has been for the Japan Defense Agency (JDA). Japanese

---

47. Aerospace Industries Association of America (1990, 30–31); Ono (1991, 15); data include transports, helicopters, and general aviation craft.

48. This litany is recited variously in Nihon Ritchi Sentaa (1982); Abegglen (1991); Nihon . . . Kōgyōkai (1979); Moxon, Roehl, and Truitt (1987); Long Term Credit Bank of Japan (1986); Frenkel (1984); Keizai Dōyūkai (1979); Mowrey, (1987); Rubin (1983).

government policy prohibits the export of military aircraft, and so the Japanese aircraft industry has had few opportunities to achieve economies of scale.

Small domestic market. Japanese travelers rely on trains rather than aircraft, and Japanese domestic airlines carry only 5 percent of the world's airline passengers.[49] This small home market makes it impossible for Japan to repeat the protected infant industry strategy that worked so well in steel and automobiles.

Lack of systems integration and design skills. Licensed production has deprived Japanese manufacturers of the opportunity to learn how to integrate complex aircraft systems. The point of successful design and systems integration is that the whole is more than the sum of its parts.

Inability to provide adequate aftermarket support. Japanese manufacturers lack an established marketing network in a global market where a large percentage of sales comes after delivery and payment for the original equipment.

Inappropriate industrial structure. Japanese heavy industrial firms are highly diversified, and not one of Japan's prime contractors specializes in either airframes or engines. Within the parents firms, the aircraft divisions have long been viewed as "poor cousins" that drain resources. Parent firms, with a considerable range of other options, reportedly have viewed aircraft as too risky.

Prohibitively high entry costs. This risk aversion is related to high entry costs. The cost per unit sold of aircraft is the inverse of that for integrated circuits. The significantly greater value added combines with the significantly smaller number of units sold to make aircraft a high risk. It is easier and more attractive to continue as coordinated, subsidized subcontractors than to set out as independent competitors.

Powerful foreign competitors. There are only three major integrated commercial airframe manufacturers in the world. The $29 billion Boeing Company enjoys more than half the world's civil transport market and has full order books into the twenty-first century. Airbus, now the number-two producer, needed billions in subsidies to enter the market. Today Japanese aircraft producers probably face even more substantial competition.

This is a formidable set of claims for one of Japan's more conspicuous commercial failures, but on consideration each claim becomes less compelling. In conventional terms the industry's performance is, at the very least, mixed.

Late starts can be advantageous. As the Japanese machinery industry demonstrated in the Meiji period and as the electronics industry has shown more

49. Frenkel (1984); Keizai Dōyūkai (1979, 70).

recently, a late start is not a permanent handicap and may even be an advantage. Later developers avoid the expensive mistakes made by market pioneers. Japanese firms have systematically learned from established world producers. The question is not whether latecomers will catch up but whether leaders will continue to innovate.

Military production can provide flexibility, experience, and stability. Military procurement actually provides substantial advantages. Though less profitable than commercial markets, military demand is more stable. Low barriers between military and civilian production enable producers to train and maintain a cadre of aerospace engineers and to nurture key technologies while preparing to compete in commercial markets. Moreover, gaps in Japan's technological capabilities can be and are reduced by defense programs. Finally, Japan's aerospace military dependence is not high by international standards, and commercial projects have followed military ones in Japan as elsewhere. Uchino Kenji, former vice president of the Commercial Airplane Company (the firm established to organize the subcontracting for Boeing's 767), has observed that "we cannot nurture an industry from collaborative development in commercial aircraft. The only way is to use military demand . . . to bring along civilian [demand]."[50] While the commercial market is more attractive to Japanese producers who look to wean themselves from dependence on the JDA, commercial production is neither a replacement for nor adversely affected by military demand.

Domestic market size is largely irrelevant. Like most markets for Japanese manufactures, the aircraft market is global. In the early 1980s, Japanese firms shifted strategy to cash in on significant opportunities as subcontractors and components manufacturers.[51] Even after the 1985 yen revaluation, which should have *reduced* Japanese exports and *increased* imports, exports increased 57.6 percent and imports decreased 27.1 percent.[52] Total nominal exports increased by nearly 40 percent between 1989 and 1991, and nominal exports do not include much electronics equipment and displays. The Society of Japanese Aerospace Companies (SJAC) projects exports will continue to grow at twice the rate of total production, amounting to more than 15 percent of total production by 1994.[53] In absolute terms, reported exports rose from $290 million in 1987 to $538 million in 1989; these figures, compiled by the Ministry of Finance, exclude exports of generic electronics, materials, or components. Ex-

50. Quoted in Takase (1979, 15).

51. See, for example, the "Long Term Vision" of the Society of Japanese Aerospace Companies, produced in 1990.

52. Kukita (1990, 43).

53. *Aerospace Japan,* November 1991, 29. This is partly accounted for by an expected decline in military production, until the FS-X comes on line.

ports reached nearly \$1 billion in 1991—growth of more than 200 percent in four years.[54]

Japan's domestic production steadily expanded from a very low base in both relative and absolute terms. In 1983, Japanese aircraft output was about one-thirtieth that of its U.S. competitors. In 1985, it was one-twentieth. In the early 1990s, it was one-fifteenth the size. In absolute terms, aircraft production rose nearly 250 percent between 1978 and 1988 alone and grew at nearly twice the rate (10 percent) of the Japanese economy (5.7 percent). Between 1981 and 1989, the Japanese aircraft industry grew slightly faster than the French, British, Canadian, or U.S. industries. Its growth lagged behind only Italy in the global industry. The industry is positioned for a near-term future in which 30 percent of the value added of aircraft will come from components, up from the current 20 percent.

Clearly, Japanese strategists have found a method—"international collaboration"—to overcome their small domestic market.[55] The calculation is quite deliberate—if Japanese airlines must import finished products, Japanese manufacturers should supply as high a share of the value added in those products as possible. One analyst observed sardonically that "the four Heavy Industries will never admit it publicly, but they are merely 'parts makers.' Everything in Japanese commercial aircraft is *parts*. Everyone knows this, but it is a matter of pride not to acknowledge it."[56] Still, derision aside, this has been a high growth strategy, as seen in table 7.1. Further, in 1990, the aircraft and engine divisions of Japan's heavy industrial parent firms enjoyed significantly higher operating profits than did the parent firms overall. Profits for aircraft systems/components divisions were 5.9 percent, versus 6.5 percent for the parent firms overall; those for engines/airframe divisions were 5.0 percent versus 3.3 percent.[57]

Although the industry's output declined slightly in 1993 due to the global recession and flagging Boeing orders, Japan's global aircraft industry entry strategy is overcoming its small domestic market limitations, generating sustained, if not spectacular, volume expansion, financial achievements, and growth in technical capabilities.

Japan already possesses, and readily can develop, systems integration and design skills. Japanese aircraft producers have already demonstrated the capability to design high-quality aircraft, and each of the major airframe makers has touted the "paperless" airplane—designed by computer—as the next challenge.

54. Using a different base line, SJAC reports that aircraft imports by Japanese airlines increased by nearly 116 percent between 1975 and 1984. By this calculation, Japan's trade deficit in aircraft-industry manufactured goods has continued to widen (private correspondence, February 3, 1993).

55. Adachi outlined this strategy in 1981; Kukita did so in 1990.

56. Interview, former official, SJAC, November 27, 1991.

57. Chōgin Sōgō Kenkyūjo (1991, 104). SJAC reports, however, that net profits for the aircraft and engine divisions remained lower than for the parent firms.

Table 7.1   **Japanese Aircraft Production, 1983 and 1988 (billion yen)**

	Military		Commercial			
			Domestic		Export	
	1983	1988	1983	1988	1983	1988
Aircraft (including helicopters)	109.9	188.6	0.5	—	8.4	9.2
Fuselage parts	28.9	68.7	2.3	32.8	4.3	37.0
Engines	52.0	56.0	2.0	—	—	1.1
Engine parts	21.3	36.2	5.3	11.8	1.1	5.5
Other parts						
Landing gear	0.96	1.6	—	—	—	—
Propellers/rotors	2.1	0.1	—	0.1	—	0.1
Auxiliary equipment	2.9	17.8	0.04	0.6	1.1	1.1
Actuators	1.3	11.5	0.01	0.1	0.2	1.3
Power systems	—	0.8	—	—	—	—
Instruments	10.6	22.2	2.0	0.1	0.1	0.9
Avionics	9.5	31.6	0.4	—	—	0.1
Training equipment	5.6	10.3	0.4	—	—	—
Other components (seats, galleys,						
lights, entertainment system)	5.1	0.4	0.1	—	0.3	1.4

Source: Nihon . . . Kōgyōkai (1992).

Note: These data are based on a survey of thirty-three large firms that excludes auto consumption, Toray and other materials makers, virtually all below-first-tier subcontractors, and repairs/maintenance. As a consequence, they probably underestimate the scope and breadth of the industry by a significant extent.

Through "mere" licensed production, Japanese producers obtain complex manufacturing knowledge and (in design changes) glimpse how major producers integrate new technology or parts into a completed aircraft.[58] Kukita Sanemori demonstrates in a series of case studies—including hydraulic systems, air pressure and climate control systems, automated flight management systems, surveillance radars, and fuel systems—how licensed production has combined with domestic projects and international collaboration to provide both the know-how and the market access that have enabled equipment suppliers to challenge foreign manufacturers. Over time, many Japanese firms have become key subsystems suppliers or even sole sources for products they once licensed.[59] According to data published by the Japanese National Institute of Science and Technology Policy, the number of patent applications in aerospace in the United States between 1971 and 1984 was virtually unchanged, while

58. Even machinists in extremely small shops will frequently redesign components that they make for the largest American primes. Moreover, even quite small subcontractors have CAD/CAM systems that can use digitized data to create on-screen cutting paths and blueprints, which subcontractors can then manipulate in collaboration with the prime to enhance part quality (Puget Sound field study, January 1992).

59. Kukita (1990, 66). Teijin Seiki, a division of the larger textile firm, is now sole source of flight control equipment for McDonnell Douglas's MD-11 and is designing the equipment for the MD-12. Its experience with the Defense Agency's T-2 CCV jet trainer qualified it to supply fly-by-wire flight controls for the Boeing 777.

during this same period the number more than doubled in Japan.[60] Finally, we note that Japanese manufacturers have considerable experience with other kinds of complex systems, including nuclear power plants, satellites, and the most elaborate rail transport network in the world.

Components production and subcontracting make after-service capabilities less important. The absence of a worldwide service network for Japanese aircraft products would be a critical problem if the Japanese actually wanted to build and sell their own commercial transports. But this goal is not an important part of Japan's short- to medium-term aerospace strategy. In the longer term, there is little question about Japan's ambition to design, build, market, and service its own aircraft. We are reminded that the absence of a service network, faced by Sony in the 1960s and Toyota and Nissan in the 1970s, has been ovecome by other Japanese producers.

Japan's aircraft industrial structure is a strength, not a weakness. Unlike U.S. aircraft manufacturers, Japanese producers build aircraft and construction equipment, nuclear power plants, and machine tools and jet engines. Eighty-five percent of the combined sales of Japan's major airframe and engine manufacturers is in nonaerospace businesses, compared to only 40 percent of the combined sales of U.S. manufacturers. Total sales of the entire Japanese aircraft industry are a small fraction of Boeing's or McDonnell Douglas's, but total sales of individual heavy industrial firms are larger than the total sales of any single foreign aircraft manufacturer save Boeing. As a consequence, Japanese firms enjoy enormous flexibility in deploying their considerable resources, in combining military and commercial capabilities, in marrying aircraft and nonaircraft production skills. By the late 1970s, the value-added rates of their aircraft businesses surpassed that in other sectors, and as a consequence manufacturers found it easier to compete for capital within their firms. Mitsubishi Heavy Industries' (MHI) aerospace sales, for example, grew 50 percent in the early 1980s, catapulting its aerospace division from last to first among seven. During the same period, IHI's engine business, once the weakest in a diversified portfolio of shipbuilding and machinery production, became the most profitable division in the firm. Highly innovative sectors, such as new materials and electronics, in which these firms excel, provide opportunities for rapid spin-on of nonaerospace technologies. As John Alic observes, "The family of design methods, production processes, and inspection techniques required for polymer matrix composites—ranging from filament winding to ultrasonic inspection—represents a shift as great as that faced in earlier years by the electronics industry in moving from vacuum tubes to transistors to integrated circuits."[61] Moreover, Japanese aerospace firms learned much earlier

60. Kagaku Gijutsuchō Shigen Chōsajo (1987, 86).
61. Alic (1989, 20).

than their foreign competitors how to share tasks and collaborate on major projects—one of the most important factors driving technological diffusion and reducing risks in the economy.

These structural advantages are acknowledged in a detailed report of Japan's IADF, which argues that the fact the industry does not focus on aircraft is a source of strength. The ability to apply advanced technologies in different businesses within the same firm "deepens the capabilities of the company and provides Japanese aircraft-related firms strength beyond what is visible." [62]

Entry costs are less significant for components manufacturing and subcontracting. Japanese producers do not currently have the physical infrastructure to produce commercial transports for the world market. But while the level of capital investment is still small by global standards, investments in aerospace-related capital equipment and the operating expenses of the top twenty-four Japanese aerospace producers have increased very rapidly: in 1975, total investment in aerospace-related capital equipment and operating expenses was 8.5 billion yen; in 1980, it was 52.3 billion yen; and in 1988 (even before tooling for the Boeing 777 began), it reached 85.6 billion yen. Government-endorsed strategies, such as risk-sharing subcontracting with overseas producers, and access to the enormous financial resources of *keiretsu* firms, further reduce entry barriers. Finally, in 1993, the JDA began construction of Japan's first high-altitude test facility, intended as a "means of research and development for the Japanese aviation industry [and to] enable Japan to establish an integrated development and production system, to include design, experimental production, testing, and volume production." [63] In Japan, aircraft are seen as integrated systems of the highest-technology, high-value-added components. The process of integrating these components adds value still.

Limited number of global competitors can facilitate market participation. Global market leaders are willing to cede portions of their aircraft production to Japanese manufacturers in the expectation of sales to Japanese airlines. Exploiting their leverage, Japanese firms have insisted on becoming integrated into the design phase. In every successive project with Boeing, for example, Japanese suppliers have achieved a larger work share and greater technological responsibilities. According to one analysis, 70 percent of Boeing's foreign procurement for the 767 came from Japanese firms, and Japanese designers are now integrated directly into the development and engineering phase of the 777. [64]

Despite contractual restrictions, Japanese producers seem able to apply knowledge gleaned from one foreign partnership to work with another—one

62. Nihon Kikai . . . Kikin (1991, 7).
63. *Mainichi Shimbun,* December 29, 1992.
64. Fuji (1990, 7). Boeing officials claim that this figure is far too high and that they "cannot recreate" it (correspondence, June 10, 1992).

well-known case is Boeing "Supplier of the Year Award" winner Fuji Heavy Industries (FHI), which provides McDonnell Douglas with composite fuselage subassemblies that it first learned to produce under contract with Boeing. Similarly, Kawasaki Heavy Industries (KHI) developed a fuselage panel mounting tool for Airbus from its commercial experiences with Boeing, enabling Airbus to perform tasks it was previously unable to achieve.[65] A variety of military and commercial producers and engine makers contract with the same Japanese firms (see appendix A).

At the very least Japan's aerospace producers have found a growing, profitable niche in the global industry and are far from a failure in conventional terms. Their strategy, to "develop the equipment used in the world's aircraft" rather than build complete aircraft, has already paid substantial dividends.[66] While the Japanese aircraft industry remains small, it has begun to succeed without really flying.

But there is more to the story than building aircraft and components. Measured against the criteria of Japan's technology and security ideology, the industry's success is far more unambiguous. Aerospace producers have achieved a remarkable degree of technological autonomy and have strengthened the domestic technology base. They have helped diffuse advanced technologies widely in the domestic economy. Finally, Japanese companies have nurtured relationships among producers so that acquired knowledge could be sustained and applied over the long term to aircraft production and to "unrelated" civilian industries.

7.4 Aircraft and Japan's Technology and Security Ideology

7.4.1 Indigenization: The Paradox of Autonomy through Dependence

Perhaps the most significant feature of the Japanese aircraft industry is the staggering number of technology-transfer relationships—including joint ventures, licenses, coproduction and codevelopment programs, maintenance, retrofit and overhaul contracts—it has sustained with leading-edge foreign military and commercial producers. There is no authoritative public accounting of these relationships, and those accounts that are available are widely divergent. According to unpublished data compiled by the Machinery and Information Industries Bureau of MITI, 556 separate inbound licensing agreements designed to acquire technologies applicable to aircraft production were completed between 1952 and 1987.[67] The SJAC, on the other hand, lists 672 *active* licensing relationships in 1992.[68] According to a study recently completed by the U.S. congressional Office of Technology Assessment (1991), in fiscal year

---

65. Interview, U.S. aerospace executive, Tokyo, November 8, 1991.
66. Nihon . . . Kōgyōkai (1987, 39).
67. Data provided by Aircraft and Ordinance Division, MITI.
68. Nihon . . . Kōgyōkai (1992).

1991 alone, Japanese royalties to the United States for aerospace licenses were reported to be to $816 million, roughly the same amount as Japan's official defense R&D budget. According to Department of Defense data, payments to the United States for military aircraft licenses (over the life of a program) can be as high as $2 billion for the SH-60J helicopter, $1.9 billion for the F-15, and $900 million for the P-3C antisubmarine aircraft; payments for missile systems amount to hundreds of millions of dollars each, and the licensed sale of Raytheon's Patriot missile is expected to result in a flowback of $2.4 billion to the United States. Excluding direct sales of U.S. military equipment under the terms of the Foreign Military Sales Program and current air defense and ground programs—excluding aircraft—will result in license fees of $3.9 billion over the course of these programs. Aircraft coproduction and licensing fees may add another $5.9 billion.[69]

Large firms may have dozens of such technology agreements with foreign firms, and it is not uncommon for even medium-tier suppliers to have ten to fifteen separate aerospace technology-transfer agreements with U.S. and European firms.[70] Consider the representative relationships shown in table 7.2.

Japanese aerospace producers use alliances with U.S. manufacturers to accumulate skills with broad competitive implications. Each of Japan's prime aircraft contractors has now worked with a range of U.S. licensers. As we shall see below, not only has this strategy enhanced the capabilities of each participant, but by maintaining stable alliances among the primes and their vendors, knowledge gleaned from international collaborations has been diffused throughout the economy. Even the Technical Research and Development Institute, the agency responsible for indigenization within the JDA, acknowledged the massive benefits of licensed production.

We began indigenous production based upon the introduction of licenses for U.S. and other military equipment. Although these new technologies were intended directly for military purposes, the special technologies to manufacture these exceptional products spilled over into the commercial world and before long they found their way into every area of the economy—superior large scale systems engineering, environmental testing, quality reliability control—such that it is impossible to ignore the huge contributions that licensed military production made to the rapid elevation of our nation's industrial technology base. . . . Even now, for a variety of reasons, in a variety of areas, licensed production continues to enable us to absorb many advanced foreign technologies."[71]

69. Unclassified data, current as of July 1989, made available by the Mutual Defense Assistance Office, U.S. Embassy, Tokyo.
70. According to published company data, Teijin Seiki, a Japanese aircraft supplier, had fifteen "major technological cooperation agreements," including a long-term joint venture housed with Sundstrand (STS Corp); another Japanese subcontractor, Kokukikaku Kōgyō (Aero-spec Products, Inc.), a company of 250 employees, sustains thirteen "technology tie-ups" with U.S. and German producers.
71. Bōeicho . . . Honbu (1977, 36).

Table 7.2   Selected Japanese Aircraft Industry Vendors and Their Foreign Technology Relations, 1991

Manufacturing Licensees	
Kayaba	
Allied Signal Industries	landing gear, hydraulics, brake lining
Aircraft Braking Systems	wheel brakes
Pneumo Abex	actuators, flight control systems
Murdoch Machine and Engineering	actuator parts
BF Goodrich	brake components
Aircraft Porous Media	helicopter modules
Loud Engineering	power steering
York Industries	helicopter parts
Arkin Industries	master cylinders, pumps, coolers
Ozone Industries	bumper parts
Carleton Technologies	cylinder bulbs
Dynapower and Stratopower	pumps
Vickers-Steerer	brake cylinders
Yokohama Rubber	
Aeroquip Products	hoses
Research and Chemical	sealing materials
Manville	heat-resistant materials
SSP	metal ducts and bellows
Vesper	metal/nonmetallic ducts and bellows
Engineered Fabrics	fuel tanks
Lucas Aerospace	spray mats
HR Textron	bulbs
Wyman-Gordon Composites	armor panels
Brunswick	radomes
Technit	radiation shielding
Ferro	prepreg composite materials
Alcoa-Tre	external tanks
Vickers/Tedeco	chip detectors

Trading Company Representation	
Yamada Yoko Corporation	
Emerson Electronics	antisubmarine electronics
Chandler-Evans	engine fuel controls
GE Aerospace	satellite equipment
	electronic countermeasures
General Instrument	equipment
Gould	towed sonar
GTE	laser radar
ITT	traveling tubes
Kelsey-Hayes	hydraulics, engine components
Loral	simulator, infrared countermeasures
	Sidewinder missile, laser target des-
Loral Aerospace	ignator
Lucas Western	pylon
Marquart	ramjet engine

Table 7.2   (continued)

Trading Company Representation	
Motorola	displays, radar equipment
Perkin-Elmer	optical equipment
Systron-Donner	security systems
Teledyne Brown Engineering	displays
Teledyne Ryan Electronics	doppler avionics
Tracor Aerospace	chaff/flare dispenser
Westinghouse Electric	target drones

Source: Nihon . . . Kōgyōkai (1992).

Technology-transfer arrangements include virtually all phases of commercial and military aircraft production, including airframes, electronic and mechanical equipment, and materials. Domestic firms specialize and operate as nodes within the Japanese economy for accessing and indigenizing foreign technologies applicable for aircraft production. As one senior procurement manager explained his company's military sourcing strategy, "First, we determine if a Japanese firm makes the required part or equipment. If not, then we try to find a domestic company that can either develop the capability quickly or obtain it from abroad. If not, we are forced to import. Then we worry about price and delivery." And while Japanese aircraft industrialists often argue that in commercial procurement there is less concern with indigenization, when asked they rarely recall an instance when a foreign company displaced orders let to Japanese firms despite countless instances where domestic companies displaced overseas producers.[72]

Consequently, Japanese aircraft industrial development, centered on military systems, has followed a nearly linear path in which successive projects usually—but not always—have a larger domestic share than the previous ones. When successive projects do create significant foreign dependencies as in the case of the F-15, internal program licensing is used to close these gaps; as noted above, Japanese firms eventually became key subcontractors to the F-15 program through licensing even though they lacked indigenous capabilities at the outset.[73] Further, subsequent projects are often designed to acquire or autonomously produce the technical skills or products that were not indigenized in earlier aircraft programs.[74]

72. Kakamigahara field study, December 1991. An SJAC official provides four examples involving hinges and serrated plate for the Boeing 767 subcontracted by KHI (correspondence, February 3, 1993).

73. Aboulafa (1991, 11–12).

74. The FS-X is such a program. See Samuels and Whipple (1989). Further, a respected aerospace reference service notes: "The size or nature of the threat Japan faces is not the primary consideration in the manufacture of the SX-3 [FS-X]. Rather, it is an effort to acquire the design and manufacturing know-how necessary to create a first-rate indigenous jet fighter. The SX-3 will not be canceled for budgetary reasons, or because 'peace has broken out'" (Aboulafa 1991).

In this way, Japan has been able to transform itself from a buyer to a developer of weapons systems, including jet fighters. Indeed, this process took place quite rapidly. In the early 1950s, Japanese defense aircraft were supplied by the United States, and then were purchased with borrowed funds. Within a decade and a half after the 1954 Mutual Defense Assistance Agreement, and after numerous technology transfer, retrofit, and overhaul agreements with (largely) U.S. firms, Japanese companies were able to provide most of the components and perform the final assembly for almost all of Japan's military aircraft.[75]

Licensed production, retrofit, overhaul, and coproduction arrangements are sometimes denigrated by foreign observers as transferring only the most limited technical or manufacturing knowledge. Japanese producers are said to learn simple "metal bending" or the "how" but not the "why" of aerospace production.[76] It is true that since 1952 Japanese firms have licensed or coproduced nineteen different U.S. airplanes and helicopters without developing a significant "fly-away" industry of its own. Licensed production does not teach everything the licensee needs to know to build a domestic industry, nor does it ensure the indigenous financial commitment required to establish a world-class aerospace industry. But, as the JDA openly acknowledges, Japan's aircraft technology indigenization effort has nevertheless enhanced its military and civilian industrial capabilities in several ways.[77]

First, Japanese producers obtain from their licensed production and retrofit/overhaul activities extensive basic production knowledge, including blueprints, machining techniques, quality control methods, and design methodologies. In some instances, U.S. licensers even provide the informal notes skilled machinists had made concerning manufacturing "tricks" they had learned in American factories.[78] Japanese firms use U.S. manufacturing standards and testing techniques to set goals for their own operations. Unless prohibited by contract, they typically develop their own manufacturing plans (including NC machine

75. This includes virtually all ships (99 percent) and ammunition (87 percent). The Japanese Ordnance Association claims that these figures would be even higher if Japan were not forced to purchase American weapons for political purposes. See Asahi Shimbun Shakaibu (1987, 116). Note also that the gun mounts, radar displays, data link receivers, VHF receivers, instrument displays, 20-mm guns, radar, and inertial navigation system of the F-15J are made in Japan. Adachi (1981) reports that in June 1955 virtually all the components of the T-33 and F-86 jets were "knock-down" kits supplied by the U.S. Air Force. But within two years, domestic content was 48 percent. Likewise, in the first phase of the F-104 project (Japan's follow-on to the F-86), less than 15 percent of the electronics were manufactured in Japan. In the second phase of the project, this figure rose to over 80 percent. By 1975, less than 5 percent of Japan's military equipment was supplied from abroad.

76. For a review of skeptical arguments relating to the effects of licensing, see the sources and materials cited in footnote 50 above; also interview, Boeing Asian managerial staff, July 1991.

77. For an official (and controversial) evaluation of how coproduction of U.S. military systems was used by Japanese contractors to enhance commercial technological development, see U.S. General Accounting Office (1982). The Defense Agency's own *Defense of Japan* (1976 and 1988) details the way Japanese firms have learned from licensing U.S. military technologies.

78. Hall and Johnson (1970).

routes) and quality control systems in an effort to meet or exceed American standards. They have been notably successful: the defect rate for Japanese parts can be ten to fifteen times less than that for imported products made by the licenser or the original vendor.[79]

Licensed production and retrofit/overhaul work also stimulates cost control and manufacturing process improvements. Japanese primes and their subcontractors are able to learn the best process practices of American aircraft companies and then set out to improve upon them. they have become so proficient that, unlike common practice with other countries, most foreign licensers now simply provide project specifications on the assumption that Japanese production skills match or exceed their own. Japanese supplier firms lead the world in automated, flexible aerospace parts production capabilities, which can increase actual machine tool cutting time from 60 to 90 percent. They also readily spin-on process technologies that they employ in other industries to improve on the standards they have learned from licenser companies. In some instances, aircraft producers measure their process technology success not by the standards of foreign aerospace firms but by the capabilities demonstrated by their nonaircraft production facilities.[80]

Nor do initially limited roles with foreign producers preclude more extensive design/systems integration opportunities. CAD-CAM equipment and specialized design divisions are a ubiquitous feature of even the smallest Japanese aircraft subcontractor doing build-to-print work for larger firms, suggesting a commitment to learning design skills together with manufacturing techniques.[81] From the inception of Japan's postwar aircraft technology tie-ups, domestic producers have participated in, or have themselves generated, program change orders that provide opportunities—if small in scope—to design subsystems or parts. Occasionally, Japanese firms have improved on U.S. designs with autonomous developments, solving structural or design problems with ingenious solutions. In 1991 alone, Japanese firms submitted 775 engineering change proposals (ECPs) to their U.S. coproduction partners. These ECPs provide general technical descriptions of engineering changes aimed at improving existing U.S. designs and production. Among these were 341 changes to the Patriot missile system. Five ECPs for the SH-60 helicopter have now been incorporated as part of Sikorsky's design, as have Japanese enhancements of the Lockheed P-3C antisubmarine aircraft.[82]

Further, as they have increasingly mastered sophisticated manufacturing processes, Japanese aircraft companies have insisted on sharing in the design of new commercial and military aircraft. In 1991, over 250 Japanese engineers were resident at Boeing facilities in the United States, and in 1993 designers

---

79. Kakamigahara field study, January 1992.
80. Ibid.
81. Ibid.
82. Personal correspondence, Mutual Defense Assistance Office, U.S. Embassy, Tokyo, February 7, 1992.

in Japan will soon be on line with Boeing's American computers to work on the 777. On the military side, Japan was induced by the United States to abandon a totally indigenous fighter project in favor of the FS-X codevelopment deal with General Dynamics.[83] At the very least, Japanese designers can obtain advice regarding their proposed designs by collaborating with experienced foreign engineers. But they are also now involved at the ground floor in world-class commercial design efforts like the 777, as well as advanced, if not cutting-edge, military development projects such as the FS-X and Patriot missile systems. In 1990, the governments of Japan and the United States agreed to pursue three military codevelopment projects, including ducted rocket engines.

Finally, years of pursuing aircraft licensed production, retrofitting, and overhaul work have indigenized ancillary industries, most notably machine tools and their electronic controllers. The NC machinery industry in the United States was initially created precisely to meet new machining needs for military aircraft. But licensed production enabled Japanese machine tool producers to adapt their products for the aerospace industry. In short order, they displaced American or European equipment in most Japanese factories, and then made significant inroads into U.S. facilities as well. Indeed, while American machinery still can be observed in U.S. and even some Japanese facilities, it is usually older in vintage than Japanese equipment. American aircraft prime and subcontractor managers often ruefully confess that their next purchase will be a Japanese product. A similar process can be observed in selected components and materials where specialist Japanese producers of items such as flight controllers or plastics have emerged as sole or dominant sources for many foreign manufacturers.[84]

Japanese indigenization contrasts with American strategies. U.S. firms, unlike their Japanese competitors, actively transfer technologies abroad. In part because U.S. programs are so mature by the time foreign production begins, U.S. firms make comparatively little effort, however, to obtain significant flowback of process, manufacturing, or design skills from the overseas firms to which they transfer technology. While it is typical for American managers involved in joint ventures or licensing programs to tour Japanese plants once or twice a year, few have developed a systematic program to monitor or acquire Japanese practices.[85]

83. Noble (1992).

84. Friedman (1988, 26–32); see also Noble (1984). The Puget Sound, Kakamigahara, and Los Angeles field studies, 1991–92, suggested current machinery purchases by both primes and subcontractors in America and Japan were of Japanese equipment. Some Japanese primes initially purchased American machines during the late 1960s and 1970s, but those that still have functioning American equipment are replacing them with new Japanese equipment.

85. According to one engineer involved in the FS-X General Dynamics/MHI collaboration in Nagoya, General Dynamics placed over seventy engineers on site in a special building at the MHI plant, none of whom spoke Japanese fluently. (Later, Japanese-speaking employees were added.) He reported Japanese designers frequently held detailed technical meetings either before the Americans come to work, or more frequently, after they leave at 5:00 P.M.

Japanese industrial leaders recognized early on the role of the aircraft industry in fostering technology indigenization in the economy. A Keidanren report concluded that "because [licensed military] aircraft technology has to respond to a demanding environment with high reliability, small scale, and light weight, it will clearly have a positive effect on commercial aircraft development and production, as well as on other general industries."[86] Indeed, by learning how to meet demanding industrial standards, producing new equipment and materials, and increasingly applying design skills to aerospace systems integration projects, the Japanese industry has fashioned an impressive (but as yet incompletely documented) record of commercial spin-offs of military technology that, taken together, constitute substantial indigenization of technology.[87]

7.4.2   Diffusion: From Highways to Jetways

The aircraft industry has also accomplished a remarkable degree of technology and manufacturing diffusion throughout the economy along four dimensions: (1) horizontally, between major domestic prime contractors; (2) vertically, among primes, subcontractors, and suppliers; (3) across military and commercial aircraft applications; and (4) between aircraft manufacturing and unrelated industries.

That aircraft manufacturing is valued in Japan for its capacity to promote diffusion has been evident in several influential industrial and policy analyses of the industry. MITI's famous 1970 "Vision," which identified aerospace, nuclear power, and information as Japan's three future "strategic" industries, treated aerospace as the archetypal "knowledge-intensive" sector that must be fostered for its capacity to stimulate widespread advances in economic capabilities. MITI depicted the industry's links to other industries in the form of a tree, whose roots (key materials, fabrication, control, and processing technologies) bear fruit in the form of innumerable products in virtually every other part of the economy, such as vehicles, machinery, energy, electronics, leisure, and housing.[88]

Even more revealing is the way that the Japanese aircraft industry itself characterizes why aerospace is important when bidding for financial support before an often skeptical political or bureaucratic audience. An official industry postwar history cites the four major contributions aerospace made to Japan in the

---

86. Kikai . . . Iinkai (1965, 283–84).

87. Comprehensive data regarding Japanese spin-offs from the defense industry to commercial uses are not available due to Japanese domestic and international political concerns. One of the few public sources, compiled in appendix B, describes a series of spin-offs from postwar military projects to the Japanese commercial sector as compiled by the Keidanren, which has incentives, of course, to portray the ancillary benefits of defense spending in as positive a light as possible. Given the magnitude of funding for these projects, some spin-off is to be expected. Whether or not this justifies the expenditure is an empirical question awaiting more definitive analysis.

88. See Nihon . . . Kōgyōkai (1987, 47–49); Keizai Dōyūkai (1979); and Kōkūki . . . Bukai (1985) for representative statements of this "roots to fruits" metaphor. Samuels and Whipple (1989) reproduce the tree.

following order: (1) the aircraft industry's knowledge intensity raised the level of the industrial base as a whole; (2) its high value added secured the Japanese economic base; (3) it contributed to Japanese national security by building defense systems; and (4) it contributed to the national transport system.[89] In this recitation, the industry's effect on national transportation is far down on the list. Contributions to industrial knowledge and economic capabilities generally are more highly touted.

In practice, the most striking evidence of a concern for diffusion is the systematic way that key prime contractors repeatedly cooperate in major aerospace programs in Japan. The Japanese aircraft industry is unlike any other industry in Japan in the extent to which rivals collaborate. Competition between primes is usually limited to upstream, precontract R&D. Downstream production and sales functions are accomplished in an exceptionally cooperative manner. Each of Japan's prime contractors has played a role in every major postwar aerospace project. While the firms compete to become prime contractors for JDA, they do so in the knowledge that their competition will not be winner take all. Failed bidders routinely become subcontractors and receive a fixed work share and participation in the design or licensing process.[90]

It is little different on the commercial side. The same airframe manufacturers who were partners in the domestic YS-11 (and every military project) are again cooperating as risk-sharing subcontractors in the Boeing 767 and 777 projects. KHI, MHI, and FHI share indirectly public funding through the IADF, created in 1986 to provide them guidance on prospective projects and loans. As a result of collaboration through this fund, these firms have created nominally independent "development corporations" to coordinate their collaboration in the 767, the 777, and other projects. They partner also with IHI in the Japan Aero-Engine Corporation—another IADF project to coordinate their collaboration with the V2500 engine project with Rolls-Royce and Pratt and Whitney (see table 7.3).

In short, the Japanese aircraft business is a cozy "friendship club" (*nakayoshi kurabu*) in which each of the participants has, over decades of cooperation, become intimately familiar with the capabilities of each of the others.[91] One defense contractor from the more competitive electronics sector said sardonically that "in aircraft, like in construction, it's all rigged [*dango*]."[92]

89. Nihon . . . Kōgyōkai (1987, 41).
90. In a typical case, a Japanese prime will subcontract over 65 percent of its total business; 20 percent goes to other primes; 45 percent is directed to domestic specialist parts suppliers; 17 percent is accounted for by work let to "backshops" or manufacturers with close links to the primes; and 18 percent is spent on imports (derived, with permission, from proprietary data received from one of Japan's prime aircraft contractors, January 1992). Sources indicated that they had knowledge of other primes' subcontracting ratios, and that they were generally similar. For a related account of the U.S. case, see Kurth (1990).
91. For example, the plant managers of Japan's two largest aerospace works, MHI-Nagoya and KHI-Gifu, worked together on collaborative projects in both the military and civilian sectors—both in Japan and in Seattle (interview, December 18, 1991).
92. Interview, senior manager, October 28, 1991.

Table 7.3   **Selected Postwar Japanese Aircraft Projects**

Japanese Prime	Project	Licenser
Mitsubishi Heavy Industries	F-86F	North American
	F-104J	Lockheed
	F-4EJ	MDD
	T-2	**Domestic**
	F-1	**Domestic**
	F-15	MDD
	FS-X	General Dynamics
Kawasaki Heavy Industries	T-33A	Lockheed
	P2V-7	Lockheed
	P-2J	**Domestic P2V-7**
	C-1	**Domestic**
	P-3C	Lockheed
Fuji Heavy Industries	T-34	Beechcraft
	T-1	**Domestic**
	T-3	**Domestic**
Nihon Kokuki	YS-11	Domestic
Shin Meiwa	PS-1	**Domestic**
	US-1	**Domestic**

Source: Ono (1991).

While some attribute this collaboration to the rising costs of aircraft projects (each being roughly four times that of the previous one) and to the fact that the number of projects has declined overall, in other economies the number of firms would have been reduced in response to the same pressures. But in Japan, partners are considerably more stable, even if they are simultaneously competitors. Sharing tasks, rather than ruthless industry consolidation, is the strategy most consistent with the diffusion goals of Japan's technology and security ideology.

Keidanren has been a leader in exhorting horizontal collaboration. In a 1965 report, it acknowledged that large-scale projects required the integration of enormously complex technologies from disparate fields. It urged that interfirm, interdisciplinary teams of engineers be created to undertake national projects: "While it is valuable that each firm in the aircraft industry undertakes its own research and development, it is even more important that each specialized firm come together in a comprehensive body in a spirit of fellowship, and that government-business cooperation be achieved."[93] Or, as a former deputy director of the MITI Aircraft and Ordinance Division put it, "When the Japanese aircraft industry was provided chances to develop aircraft, almost all related companies, determining each other's comparative advantage in advance, shared the tasks and integrated the work. . . . Through this process it was possible to take a step-by-step approach. In other words, the Japanese aircraft industry did

93. Kikai . . . Iinkai (1965, 282).

not simultaneously pursue more than one or two projects. . . . it put to use what was learned in previous projects, explored new areas, and strengthened its technological base."[94]

Private firm strategies closely track these sentiments. Companies argue for their inclusion in major projects, for example, on the grounds that technology diffusion will help them, and the economy as a whole, compete against the rest of the world. In 1986, when the Japanese government's Key Technology Center subsidized the country's advanced turboprop (ATP) engine project, corporate participants, many of whom duplicated each other's skills and capabilities, variously justified their roles on the basis of (1) how much the project would contribute to their ability to "confront Western makers" (MHI and Sumitomo Precision); (2) the capacity to expand Japanese global market share (Ishikawa-jima Harima Heavy Industries); or (3) "to be able to compete with Western firms" (FHI). Each of the leading participants also saw clear linkages between the ATP project and their commercial activities. KHI and Kobe Steel both expressed their expectation that the ATP project would afford access to advanced equipment and the "application of the results to other business activities."[95]

The ATP engine project is only one of at least a dozen separate consortia in aircraft propulsion, materials, or components that are undertaken with public support in Japan. In each case, virtually all of the major industry players are assured a substantial role. While Japanese firms compete vigorously, this vigor has its limits, and competition is rarely allowed to compromise prospects for access to resources that would stimulate technological advantage for domestic firms or the nation.

As in the United States, technology also diffuses through the vertical links that bind Japanese primes to their suppliers and subcontractors. Like many other industries in Japan, subcontracting is vital to aircraft manufacturing. Roughly 70 percent of Japanese aerospace work is subcontracted by the leading primes. Each maintains roughly 300–500 direct relationships with domestic materials, components, and parts vendors.[96] As the primes develop their networks of suppliers and affiliated firms, which in turn resubcontract, thousands of Japanese firms throughout the economy participate in the industry. As we shall see, unlike U.S. cases, these relationships are often exceptionally durable; like the *nakayoshi kurabu* the primes have created, subcontractors and suppliers, organized into horizontal cooperation associations (*kyōryoku-kai*) or vertical regional producer associations (*kumiai*), are each able to assure access to technology and skills from the primes in a fashion that does not favor or exclude selected firms, but diffuses knowledge as widely as possible.

94. Hasegawa (1987, 14).
95. Nihon Kiban Gijutsu Sentaa, internal planning document, 1987.
96. Derived, with permission, from proprietary data received from one of Japanese prime aircraft contractors, January 1992.

But unlike most sectors in Japan, aircraft industry subcontractors—and even many suppliers—have not yet assumed primary responsibility for product design and integration. The heavy emphasis on military and commercial licensing or subcontracting has generated what is usually a one-way flow of knowledge from the primes, or the specialist suppliers that have direct technology tie-ups of their own, to lower-tier producers.[97] In most cases, technology or manufacturing know-how is transmitted at the start of each commercial or military project when a team of engineers from the subcontractors will be dispatched to the primes for weeks or months of detailed training. The subcontractors are instructed in the techniques, quality goals, design specifications, and production roles that the primes have negotiated with their foreign partners. After both sides are satisfied that the subcontractors comprehend their tasks and can meet the production objectives of the project, the team will return to their firm and begin to apply what they have learned.

Over the course of the project, the subcontractors and primes monitor performance and solve production problems in a number of ways. A steady stream of supplier and subcontractor engineers and technical staff interact with their counterparts at the primes on close to a daily basis. Each subcontractor is also subjected to at least an annual, and sometimes a six-month, inspection during which a detailed report card, which actually grades the subcontractor in a variety of categories on an A–D basis, is generated. This report is then often used as an action plan by the subcontractor to upgrade its capabilities and performance.[98]

Many subcontractors also hire retired technical staff of the primes to obtain production knowledge or, in effect, to buy direct access to the prime's resources through the retiree's personal contacts. Through these and other regular contacts, primes and subcontractors exchange advice concerning manufacturing equipment purchases or other capital investments that will affect their collective capabilities to compete for and meet contract goals. NC machinery purchases for aircraft production are made in close consultation with the prime,

97. In fact, since the subcontractors have little opportunity in the industry to develop unique manufacturing niches as in most other sectors in Japan, and are required by JDA regulations to supply detailed financial data to the primes, they are extremely protective of *their* technology. Their primary economic leverage comes from developing some method for producing parts that the prime can make, and has a good idea of the cost for making, at a price that earns a profit. One strategy, using lower-wage workers, is increasingly difficult because of the labor shortage in Japan. No one will work in factories for a fraction of wages they could earn elsewhere. More common are efforts to devise new cutting methods or use novel equipment to beat the prime's cost standard. Very few subcontractors stated that they would freely supply such knowledge to the primes, although, when queried, they could not explain how they could assure that frequent visitors from the primes, or former prime employees, would not obtain such knowledge. There are, however, examples where subcontractors do teach larger firms (like electrochemical machining technology) how to use technologies that they imported into Japan (Kakamigahara field study, December 1991).

98. Ibid.

to complement or supplement the prime's internal machining capabilities, and to assure that the selected machinery meets required standards. Purchases of large-scale equipment such as autoclaves for metal bonding or composite manufacturing by subcontractors are similarly coordinated with substantial input from the primes.[99] In this fashion, supplier and subcontractors use their relationship with the primes to secure access to defense and commercial aircraft technologies.

The third axis of aircraft industry diffusion is between commercial and defense technologies. It is uniformly the case at the prime, subcontractor, and supplier level in Japan that commercial and military work are performed by the same shop personnel on the same equipment, usually in the same facility. At the prime level, large-scale projects are often managed by individuals who have, over time, become specialized in specific programs. But despite legal formal proscriptions, the interdiffusion of military with commercial aircraft production is apparent everywhere else. The same work groups, on the same machines, will produce batches of parts for jet fighters, missiles, and Airbus or Boeing with equal facility in the same day. Scattered around a typical factory are pallets of work intermingling titanium F-15 components, hardened missile cases, and aluminum 767, MD-11, or A-321 fuselage parts. Indigenous trainers such as the T-4 are equipped by teams that can and do shift with ease to civilian projects. Blueprints for military and commercial aircraft are stacked next to, if not on top of, one another in even the largest factory. And in assembly areas, military aircraft take shape next to subassemblies for commercial transports.[100]

Finally, there is substantial diffusion between aircraft technologies—commercial and military—and the general economy. A 1979 SJAC survey estimated, for instance, that the sales generated by products derived from aircraft industry technologies were *sixteen times greater* than other products the same technologies produced. In addition, the report concluded that there were substantial economy-wide process improvements fostered by the aircraft industry's production-technique diffusion: "Elevating the product quality in other industries through quality control systems designed for the aircraft industry was a consequence that began with the licensed production of aircraft and aircraft parts that rapidly spread, so that today quality control is just common sense in every sector, regardless of the scale of the firm."[101]

A decade later, SJAC completed Japan's most detailed study of technology diffusion between the aircraft industry and sixteen other sectors, identifying a range of mechanisms by which technologies are transferred.[102] In the case of submersible craft, marine engineers were dispatched to the aircraft divisions of their parent firms for training and for the collection of data on materials

99. Ibid.
100. Ibid. and MHI field study, December 1991.
101. Nihon . . . Kōgyōkai (1979, 6).
102. Nihon . . . Kōgyōkai (1985).

and manufacturing processes. They also received "technical leadership" from competing submersible manufacturers. In the case of the space industry, engineers and designers were transferred in-house across divisions to take advantage of their experience in aircraft materials and testing. The study also found that aircraft engine technology was transferred through technical exchanges between large and small manufacturers, through joint development projects involving users and makers, through technology exchange agreements between engine makers and systems controls manufacturers, and through the active use of "controlled leaks" of technological information.[103]

All told, the report suggests that product and process technologies in nine different aerospace areas, including general systems and control technologies, aerodynamics, flight control technologies, structural technologies, materials, electronics, and testing were applied in thirteen different product areas in the Japanese automobile industry, including shock absorbers, clutch linings, fuel tanks, air bags, manufacturing process controls and so forth. Aircraft know-how also contributed to the manufacture of submarines (materials, design, testing), industrial machinery (CAM, locknuts, materials), robots (encoders, alloys), materials (fabrication, design), petrochemicals (fasteners, high-function synthetic materials, sports equipment, tires), and electronics (displays, computers, switches). The study documented more than five hundred cases of technology diffusion, 60 percent of which originated in the aircraft sector.[104]

The capacity to spin-on or spin-off commercial and military aircraft technologies to other industries varies with the scale and organization of the firms involved. The process is least impressive at the prime level. Although Japanese primes are generally smaller divisions of larger, nonaerospace companies, they usually house their aircraft facilities in factories geographically separated from the rest of their commercial activities. Few workers, engineers, or managerial staff members are ever transferred interdivisionally. Yet most primes report that they foster interdivisional diffusion on a more systematic basis, by creating elaborate networks of research committees assigned to consolidate a firm's knowledge of technology in specific functional areas. At Shin Meiwa and at MHI, for example, the technology headquarters sponsors firmwide study teams that coordinate at both the plant and corporate level on functional topics such as electrical machinery, heat treatment, inspection, and so forth. Each study team meets quarterly to enable engineers responsible for disparate applications within diversified firms to share their know-how.[105]

Thus, despite the physical isolation of aircraft operations from other divisions at the prime level, there is considerable evidence of technology interdiffusion. In constructing an advanced phased-array radar (APAR) for the FS-X

103. Ibid., 208–9.
104. Ibid., 231.
105. MHI, Kakamigahara field study, December 1991; interview, general manager, Shin Meiwa Industries, October 18, 1991.

project, for example, Japanese engineers from Mitsubishi Electric's radar group briefly transferred to Mitsubishi Electric's (MELCO's) electronic devices group, where they received training in the gallium arsenide (GaAs) chip manufacturing technology they needed to make APAR high-frequency transponder modules. Leveraging MELCO's GaAs commercial memory technology, they were able to produce, with just a fraction of the government R&D support American firms received, an APAR prototype that many regard as fairly close to leading-edge U.S. capabilities. Aircraft and nonaerospace technology interdiffusion, with significant strategic implications, does occur even inside Japanese primes.[106]

Japanese subcontractors and suppliers achieve even more systematic interdiffusion of aerospace and nonaerospace technologies because their aircraft production is less segregated from other activities. Unlike the United States, Japanese lower-tier producers are primarily *not* aircraft manufacturers. Typically, 80–90 percent of their production is in nonaircraft industries; top-caliber aerospace manufacturing operations occupy just a corner of their facilities.[107] The resulting direct combination of aircraft and nonaircraft production in Japanese subcontracting plants facilitates an enormous cross-fertilization of technologies and skills. Consider four examples of this process.[108]

1. In one case, a firm of about 250 employees originally specialized in packaging for air defense ordnance and general machining. To enhance its capabilities, it imported electrochemical machining (ECM) technology from the United States and began using ECM techniques for Japanese aircraft production. To stimulate sales, the company launched a number of workshops for both primes and subcontractors, and began to supply technical support and machinery to implement ECM in Japanese aerospace factories. As demand for sophisticated routing and milling technology increased in the automobile industry, it adapted ECM technology for use in making auto parts. The firm now designs and builds an electrochemical device (ECD) for nonaerospace parts producers that is based almost entirely on the ECM technology it originally imported for aircraft industry use. One year after development, 15 percent of the firm's revenue was accounted for by ECD sales, which were expected to grow to 45 percent by 1993.

2. Cross-fertilization can also occur in a less direct fashion. A well-established aerospace machine-shop subcontractor of about one hundred employees discovered that chip removal for the sophisticated NC machine tools involved in aircraft production was quite difficult. It began experimenting with conveyor systems and telescopic covers for NC equipment, forming a joint venture with a German firm to import technology. At present, the company has designed and produced, under its own nameplate, world-renowned conveyors

106. Interview, general manager, MELCO Radar Group, October 8, 1991.
107. Kakamigahara field study, December 1991.
108. All examples are from ibid.

and covers and has made sales throughout Japan and the world. It also produces the speciality machines required to *make* the conveyors. While remaining an integral part of the Japanese aircraft industry's subcontracting network and participating in several prime contractors, the firm relies on aerospace work for just 15 percent of its revenues; machine tool accessories now account for about 85 percent of its business and nearly all of its profits.

3. A third example of the enormous cross-industrial interdiffusion Japanese aircraft subcontractors and suppliers can achieve is the case of a plastics and seat manufacturer. While a first-tier aerospace supplier, the company's aircraft machining and passenger-seat production earnings account for just 17 percent of its business. Nevertheless, the firm continuously applies technologies from one industry to another. By learning to make lightweight, durable military ejector seats, for example, the firm made significant improvements in commercial transport seat design. It sells its seats to aircraft equipment suppliers and primes worldwide. Both commercial and military aircraft seat technology made possible new designs of lighter Shinkansen, or bullet train, seats necessary to facilitate announced plans to speed up the trains. More fuel-efficient buses also resulted. The company has also leveraged its reinforced fiberglass and composites technology into aircraft and nonaerospace business. Aircraft manufacturing led the company to purchase a large autoclave, with technical assistance from a Japanese prime, to produce composite and fiberglass materials. Building in part on the knowledge it obtained, the company now constructs an impressive array of composite products, from aircraft fairings to ski-lift canopies, and from bus bodies to cars for Tokyo Disneyland attractions.

4. A final example illustrates nonaircraft commercial *spin-on* capabilities. One of Japan's most successful textile firms is also a highly sophisticated aircraft component supplier, specializing in fuel injectors and flight control equipment. Approximately 25 percent of the company's sales are in aerospace; the remainder are in textile equipment, robotics, and industrial machinery. The production of robotic transfer gear systems, the firm discovered, actually involved tolerances more acute than aircraft parts specifications. Further, many of its foreign competitors or licensers were unversed in state-of-the-art nonaircraft manufacturing techniques and therefore were unable to learn from process innovations made in other sectors. To improve efficiency and quality, the firm began to adapt its nonaircraft quality control and process techniques to its aerospace operations, dramatically increasing the quality and reducing the cost of its products. In turn, the firm achieved a commanding presence in certain segments of the world aircraft market in which it competes. In at least one case, the company is now a sole source of flight control equipment for a major overseas commercial aircraft program; in many others, it is one of two or three remaining sources worldwide.

Japanese horizontal, vertical, military/commercial, and aircraft/nonaircraft diffusion markedly contrasts with U.S. experiences. Competition among American primes does not ensure that losers in the process share in military and commercial projects; they rarely exchange information or know-how more extensive than requests for price quotes with their subcontractors (although they do collaborate, of necessity, in design with their specialist subsystems suppliers); and most studies suggest that interdiffusion between military and commercial or aircraft and nonaircraft functions is comparatively rare today. As one analyst notes, "Even among those firms [that have defense and military divisions] there is very little integration at the plant level between the defense operations and the civilian operations.[109]

American subcontractors and suppliers, however, can and do mix commercial and civilian aerospace technologies and machinery, but they have been generally unable to apply their skills in nonaircraft business.[110] Unlike the Japanese, who have found that there is often very little distinction between meeting customer needs in either the aircraft or other industries, comparable intersectoral diversification has eluded U.S. suppliers and subcontractors. Many, such as one first-tier U.S. supplier, admit that their firms lack the confidence that they can make a successful foray into industries "where standards are lower."[111] A survey of U.S. defense and aerospace subcontractor capabilities by an American defense consultant came to a similar conclusion.

> The foraging, casting (foundry) and fastener industries share several important characteristics. In each of these industries, firms which manufacture products for the defense industry do so almost exclusively for defense and aerospace customers. The products they sell are manufactured in very small quantities and are of high quality relative to products sold in . . . commercial markets. . . . As a consequence of the specialized production equipment, test equipment, and labor and management skills required to manufacture these products, these firms are generally unable to compete in commercial markets for high volume, low technology products. Although they are technically capable of making commercial products, they are usually unable to do so in an economic fashion. At the same time, firms which manufacture in large volume for commercial markets are usually unable to compete in de-

---

109. While it is often asserted that in the early postwar period military and commercial technology diffused quite rapidly at the prime level in the United States, most studies have concluded that this process has become less evident in the current period. There are numerous examples of efforts by defense firms to convert to commercial products that have failed, including Grumman's effort to build canoes and then city buses, and Rockwell's attempt to enter the aircraft overhaul business. Most studies of this issue conclude that there is very limited integration at the plant level or at the division level between commercial and defense activities of prime U.S. contractors. See, for example, Alic et al. (1992); Gansler (1989, 1984).

110. Unlike U.S. primes, for instance, studies show aerospace subcontractors in fact often perform military work jointly with commercial business. A survey of Puget Sound defense suppliers, for instance, showed that over 75 percent of the subcontractors in the region sold less than half of their output to the military or in military projects (Sommers, Carlson, and Birss 1992). Field studies of aircraft subcontractors and suppliers in both Los Angeles and Washington also demonstrated that nonprime U.S. manufacturers frequently combined defense and nondefense aerospace work with the same facility as did the Japanese (Los Angeles and Puget Sound field studies, January 1992). See also Kelley and Watkins (1992) for survey research that demonstrates significant dual-use activities among metalworking subcontractors.

111. Puget Sound field study, January 1992.

fense and aerospace markets because they lack the necessary skills and equipment. In those instances where it may be possible to manufacture a product, it generally cannot be done economically, again because of the inappropriateness of the equipment, the people and the organization to do the job.[112]

Most striking in this analysis is that virtually all of the matter-of-fact conclusions explaining why aircraft and nonaerospace production are incompatible apparently *do not* apply in Japan. Indeed, Japanese producers routinely achieve profound intersectoral diffusion.

7.4.3   Nurturing—Assuring that Technology Highway Travelers Stay in the Race

We now turn to the third strand of Japan's technology and security ideology, the importance of nurturing firms that can indigenize and diffuse technology. Through a variety of means, Japanese companies are afforded substantial resources to assure that, as they master industrial capabilities, they have sufficient stability to exploit what they have learned. We earlier referred to this system as an economy of protocols; while pursuing individual ends, players in Japanese industry are caught in a web of mutual obligations or "reciprocal consent" that moderates the chance that fratricidal competition, rapacious industry consolidations, or external cyclical market shocks will threaten their existence.[113]

We have already discussed some of the features of the protocol economy apparent in the aircraft industry. These include (1) the system of work sharing that virtually ensures that each Japanese aircraft prime contractor participates in every major aerospace project; (2) joint collaborative research consortia, such as the ATP project, which spreads public R&D funding across the widest possible range of industry players; and (3) networks of suppliers and subcontractors that leverage stable vertical and horizontal business into technological and market advantages.

The effects of Japan's protocol economy in nurturing opportunities in the aerospace industry can be further appreciated by focusing on a specific region, Kakamigahara in Gifu prefecture, which has been a center of Japanese aircraft production since before World War II. Kakamigahara illustrates how Japanese primes and their subcontractors accommodate each other's needs to generate a stable economic environment in which indigenization and diffusion can productively occur.

Kakamigahara is home to KHI's main airframe production and assembly facility, the Gifu Works, which employs about four thousand workers and adjoins a Japan Air Self Defense Force (JASDF) air base. The region was one of

112. Institute for Defense Analysis (1990, 3). (Contrast this finding to Kelley and Watkins 1992).

113. Ronald Dore calls this "relational contracting." See Dore (1987, 109–92).

the major fighter production centers in Japan during World War II. Major post-war military projects in which KHI has participated as a prime or subcontractor at the Gifu Works are shown in table 7.4.

In addition, KHI is a contractor for 737, 747, 757, A-321, and MD-11 production, is a principal participant in the FS-X and 777 development projects, and has performed extensive overhauls of close to six thousand commercial and military aircraft since 1955. The firm is the second largest Japanese aircraft prime contractor, accounting in 1990 for 29 percent of the aerospace production of the nation's top six firms and 11 percent of Japan's total defense contracts (150 billion yen). Its aircraft sales, exclusive of jet engines, more than tripled in 1981–90, rising from just under 60 billion yen to over 200 billion yen during the decade. Additional KHI factories in Akashi, west of Kobe, and Tobishima, south of Gifu, produce aircraft engines and assemble 767 fuselage components, respectively.[114]

Surrounding KHI is a network of suppliers and subcontractors with long-term roots in Kakamigahara. Most of its principal suppliers of components, subsystems, or materials are organized into a "cooperation committee" popularly known as *Kawajū*. In addition, KHI's thirty-six primary local subcontractors are organized into a regional production association called the *Kawasaki Gifu Kyōdō Kumiai*.[115] The *kumiai* represents a typical Japanese organizational innovation in which competing firms stabilize their relationships with key customers and each other, but do not constrict their industrial options.

Japanese aircraft manufacturing was suspended during the U.S. occupation, a devastating event for Kakamigahara's wartime aerospace subcontractors and KHI.[116] By 1948, however, newly reconstituted and renamed, KHI had developed a bus design, the KBC-1, around which the regional production network reformed.[117] Many of the former subcontractor managers, often working of necessity in the retail or restaurant business, began to reopen small machine shops to participate in the region's new bus-building activity.[118]

In 1951, the twenty-two largest subcontractors organized into the *Kawasaki-Gifu Seisakujo Kyōryoku Kōjo Kyōdō Kumiai* (literally, Kawasaki-Gifu Collaborative Association of Cooperating Factories) to address two problems.[119] The

114. KHI financial and promotional material for the Gifu Works, 1991.
115. Details on the regional organization of KHI suppliers and subcontractors are from several sources: Kawasaki Gifu Kyōdō Kumiai (1990); Kakamigahara Shiyakusho (1987); Sanemoto (1989).
116. During the war, aircraft production was accomplished in the forerunner to KHI, which bore a different name. For simplicity, we refer to KHI here for each of these entities.
117. Kakamigahara Shiyakusho (1987, 691–94).
118. Kakamigahara field study, December 1991.
119. *Kumiai* also perform numerous other services: (1) building apartment dwellings for member employees; (2) conducting technology seminars for members; (3) serving as a focal point for other industries to contact suppliers in the region; (4) conducting political lobbying and liaison with local, regional, and national bureaucracies; and (5) organizing social activities such as bowling clubs, travel, and so forth (Kawasaki Gifu Kyōdō Kumiai 1990, 10–24).

Table 7.4   **Kawasaki Heavy Industries, Gifu Works, Military Prime and**
                 Subcontracting Project Participation, 1959 to April 1, 1991

Type	Kind of Aircraft	Period of Manufacture	Remarks
Fixed-wing aircraft	T-33A jet trainer	1955–58	210 planes
	P2V-7 ASW patrol airplane	1958–65	48 planes
	F-104J jet fighter	1961–67	207 planes (coproduction)
	YS-11 medium transport plane	1962–72	182 planes (coproduction)
	P-2J ASW patrol airplane	1967–78	83 planes
	F-4EJ jet fighter	1969–81	138 planes (coproduction)
	C-1 medium transport airplane	1970–81	31 planes
	P-3C ASW patrol airplane	1978–	66 planes
	F-15J fighter	1978–	140 planes (coproduction)
	Boeing 767 passenger airplane	1978–	388 planes (coproduction)
	T-4 medium trainer	1985–	56 planes
	EP-3 utility airplane (EW)	1988–	1 plane
Helicopters	Kawasaki-Bell 47	1952–75	439 helicopters
	Kawasaki-Vertol 107 11A	1963–	160 helicopters
	Kawasaki-Hughes 369	1969–	300 helicopters
	Kawasaki BK 117	1982–	343 helicopters
	CH-47	1986–	28 helicopters
Missiles	Type 64 antitank	1964–	ATM
	Type 79 antilanding craft/antitank	1979–	H-ATM
	Type 87 antitank	1987–	M-ATM
Space equipment	geodetic satellite	1986–	
Repairs	fixed wing	1953–	3,990 planes
	helicopter	1954–	1,993 helicopters

Source: Kawasaki Heavy Industries, promotional data, Gifu Works (1991).

first, and most critical, was to ensure that KHI did not try to allocate work to select subcontractors due either to personal favoritism or in an effort to drive down contract prices. The *kumiai* operated as a collective interface with KHI, establishing basic expectations regarding contract procedures and work volume to which the entire region would adhere. In addition, the *kumiai* forged close alliances with regional, prefectural, and national authorities to create political resources with which to protect their interests. As their business relationship developed, KHI and the *kumiai* became enmeshed in a multilayered network of local and national contacts that precluded destabilizing, unilateral actions on both sides. Indeed, the extent of the *kumiai*'s ability to form visible links with influential political authorities can be appreciate in its forty-year commemorative publication of 1990. The handsome 152-page book offers messages of personal congratulations from the acting MITI minister, the Chubu region MITI bureau chief, the governor of Gifu prefecture, the head of the national small and medium enterprise association, the head of the Commerce Manufacturing Union Central Bank (a public small-firm lending institution), and the mayor of Kakamigahara.[120] From an early period, the *kumiai* members exploited their opportunities in the Japanese protocol economy to induce KHI to make long-term business commitments to their region.

The second goal was to facilitate joint applications for financing.[121] Despite their close contacts with KHI, itself affiliated with one of Japan's major *keiretsu* groups, none of the *kumiai* members received investment or other financial support from the firm or affiliated banks. They relied instead on family equity, retained earnings, and local bank financing to build and expand their businesses. To reassure regional banks during the postwar industrial slump, *kumiai* members applied for loans as a group, combining their collective manufacturing and management expertise into a single package.[122] They also benefited, like subcontractors in other industries, from the specialized regional financial institutions Japan created to fund sophisticated equipment purchases and capital expansion undertaken by smaller firms.[123] Consequently, Kakamigahara subcontractors organized to avoid price and wage exploitation by the region's dominant economic enterprise while collaborating to secure independent capital from dedicated small-firm lenders, as was true of other lower-tier producers throughout early postwar Japan.[124]

The result was a set of vertical and horizontal links that fostered the skills and stability of Kakamigahara's aerospace subcontractors in several ways. First, as we described above, KHI and its subcontractors maintained substantial personnel, management, and training contacts that helped indigenize and diffuse technology, especially licensed production techniques, in the course of military and commercial projects. The commitment to mutually foster business opportunities also led KHI to share the burden of aircraft production cutbacks more or less equally with its subcontractors. Unlike U.S. practice, no one in Kakamigahara could recall an instance where KHI used its suppliers as a buffer for economic shocks, retracting work to maintain its internal operations at the expense of its subcontractors. Nor could they remember a case where KHI refused to place orders with a *kumiai* member because of past production problems; rather, the preferred solution was for KHI to maintain business volume while insisting on improved performance.[125]

The subcontractors also used their stable relationship with KHI as a springboard into new industries and business networks. They initially diversified their production among various KHI divisions, especially aircraft and bus bod-

120. Ibid., 2–9.
121. Kakamigahara Shiyakusho (1990, 701).
122. Kakamigahara field study, December 1991; Kakamigahara Shiyakusho (1982, 701).
123. Friedman (1988, 192–95). Aircraft subcontractors in Kakamigahara also rely almost exclusively on regional banks rather than the *toshi ginkō,* or other *keiretsu* affiliates of the primes (Kakamigahara field study, December 1991).
124. For details of Japan's postwar political struggle between small and large firms and the regional organizations subcontractors developed and utilized to obtain protection from larger firms, see Friedman (1988, chap. 4–5); Nishiguchi (1989, chaps. 3–4).
125. Kakamigahara field study, December 1991.

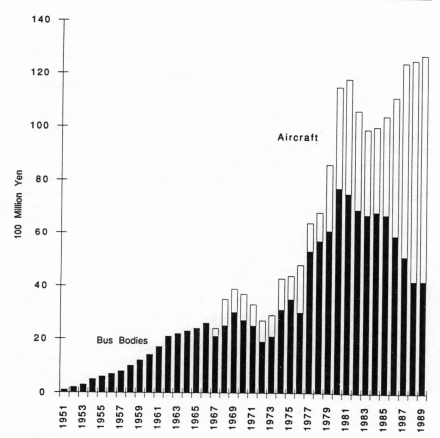

Fig. 7.1   Kakamigahara Kawasaki Kyōdō Kumiai bus bodies and aircraft business volume, 1951–89
Source: Kawasaki, Gifu Kyōdō Kumiai (1990, 128).

ies. By the mid-1980s, nineteen of the thirty-five members participated in both the bus and aircraft divisions of the *kumiai*. This enabled the subcontractors to shift their KHI production from one division to the other in response to market trends. Between 1951 and 1966, for instance, while aircraft subcontracting languished, bus-body production sustained the regional network. From 1967 onward, bus and aircraft manufacturing were largely complementary. During the oil-shock-induced 30 percent slump in KHI aircraft production of 1977–80,[126] for example, *kumiai* bus output almost doubled; as *kumiai* aircraft subcontracting grew almost 300 percent from 1983 to 1989, bus production fell by nearly 50 percent, as shown in figure 7.1.

126. Kakamigahara Shiyakusho (1987, 700).

Kumiai members also diversified their relationships with other aircraft and transportation producers and by entering other industries. In the 1950s and 1960s, the region's subcontractors relied on KHI for close to 80–90 percent of their work. By the early 1980s, however, just 35.9 percent of *kumiai* total sales were KHI-related. Over 10.5 percent of their work was with other aircraft producers, notably MHI and IHI, and 18.9 percent was with the automobile industry (table 7.5). At the same time, average *kumiai* member reliance on KHI for sales fell. Only 31 percent of the member subcontractors relied on KHI for more than 51 percent of their business (table 7.6).

Stable relations with their leading customer, KHI, therefore enabled Kakamigahara's subcontractors to diversify while maintaining their ties to the region's aircraft industry. Collectively, they were able to exploit aerospace industry technological and financial resources while pursuing other options. Some of the *kumiai* members simply used aircraft work to fill in cyclical production gaps that occurred in their primary business. For these firms, aircraft work afforded more financial than technological resources. Others actively sought to utilize aircraft technologies or process techniques in nonerospace sectors; their participation in the industry enhanced their overall manufacturing capacities. And by continually participating in and mastering military aircraft production techniques through licensed production, the region's firms developed skills that have made them increasingly competitive in commercial aerospace as well. New factories are springing up throughout Kakamigahara as the region's subcontractors, anticipating large increases in 777 subcontracting, smoothly shift from defense to civilian production. As military procurement languished in the late 1980s, large increases in international commercial project work generated for the regional aircraft industry a subcontracting growth rate of close to 300 percent for the decade.

The Kakamigahara experience contrasts squarely with American aircraft industry practices. Most U.S. primes do not form enduring regional ties or gener-

Table 7.5   **Distribution of Total Sales by *Kumiai* Members, 1981**

Kumiai Members' Customers	% of Total *Kumiai* Member Sales
KHI bus body, parts, and assembly	24.3
KHI aircraft parts and assembly	11.6
Other Japanese aircraft manufacturers	10.5
Automobile industry	18.9
Transportation-related industries	8.0
Agriculture/construction machinery	8.3
Machine tools	7.6
Electrical/construction industries	10.8

Source: Kakamigahara Shiyakusho (1985, 704).

Table 7.6   *Kumiai* **Member Reliance on KHI Bus/Aircraft Sales (percentage of total sales)**

Degree of Reliance on KHI (%)	% of Members
0–10	11.5
11–30	15.4
31–50	38.5
51–70	11.5
71–100	19.2

Source: Kakamigahara Shiyakusho (1985, 704).

ate "sticky" industrial regions; instead they actively shop for social or labor concessions from their suppliers by threatening to move, and actually moving, production to other states, regions, or countries—a process that unsettles thousands of aerospace jobs and hundreds of subcontractors. There are few, if any, arrangements in which local subcontractors collectively build regional and national political and industrial networks to bargain with U.S. primes. Interfirm information exchanges between primes and machining subcontractors are usually limited to the circulation of blueprints to several firms simultaneously for bids. Subcontracts must continually lobby teams of non–technically trained buyers at the prime even to get on a bid list, let along receive an order. Buyers move frequently from division to division and to other firms; when they do, subcontractor links with the primes can rapidly deteriorate. When asked, few American subcontractors can articulate the basis on which bids are accepted; in some cases award-winning subcontractors in one year can suddenly find, to their surprise, that their work has been cut off in the next.[127] And while Kakamigahara is flooded with investment for an expected surge in 777 orders, Puget Sound subcontractors who traditionally have close ties to Boeing have seen their work cut back so severely that many took the unprecedent step of confronting Boeing publicly with the problem.[128]

The cutbacks even prompted one of the luckier first-tier Boeing subcontractors to note that "they [Boeing] expect us to take over and maintain the links with second-tier companies. But my [subcontracting] shops are going bankrupt so fast that soon we'll have no one to subcontract to up here [in Puget Sound]."[129]

127. Puget Sound field study, January 1992.
128. There have been several accounts in the popular press about the tension between Boeing and Puget Sound subcontractors. See *Seattle News-Tribune,* December 30, and June 21, 1991; *Seattle Post Intelligencer,* June 22, 1991. According to published accounts, there are several potential explanations for the Puget Sound subcontracting work fall off, including (1) Boeing's apparent efforts to direct relationships to a smaller number of suppliers; (2) growing efforts to subcontract to non–Puget Sound regions such as Wichita, Kansas, or Tennessee; (3) moving work to foreign countries, including Japan; and (4) reducing costs by putting pressure on area subcontractors.
129. Ibid.

Kakamigahara therefore suggests how the protocol economy sustains aircraft industry producers in the game so that technology and skills accumulate and are diffused to new uses throughout Japan's production network. It is not a story of altruism or culture, but of novel organizational forms and incentives. The aircraft industry has indigenized technology, has diffused it broadly, and is organized to help assure that domestic beneficiaries are able to exploit what they learn. Even though it has not yet produced (and may not produce for several years) a competitive fly-away commercial or military aircraft, the Japanese aircraft industry is nevertheless successful because its leaders value an industry both for its ability to foster and spread knowledge and for the products it makes. They are willing to commit substantial public and private resources to maintain industries that meet these criteria, where American practice would let them die. In the process, not only does Japan build its core economic capabilities, but it also is able to embed an increasingly sophisticated defense production network in the commercial economy. In the final section, we consider some of the industrial and strategic implications of this achievement.

7.5   Conclusions

7.5.1   Ideology Matters

As we discussed above, defense and aircraft are but additional lanes on a very busy Japanese technology highway. Despite often vigorous postwar debates about how to build and maintain these lanes, it long ago became clear that commercial and dual-use technologies are racing ahead of purely military applications in Japan and in the United States. Some may argue that Japan's achievements in this regard are accidental or that Japan enjoyed a "free ride" on U.S. security guarantees during the Cold War. Still others may credit Japan's strategic vision in fostering a dual-use economy.

But none of these "explanations," we believe, sufficiently account for the institutional and strategic choices Japan made in generating its dual-use capabilities. Other nations, enjoying similar security alliances with the United States and in similar strategic circumstances, have evolved quite different dual-use capabilities. It is also difficult to credit accident with an industrial outcome that is so strikingly consistent with Japan's fundamental set of beliefs about security and the interdiffusion of technology. Finally, while Japan's particular defense industry strategies have in fact varied widely over the last century, it has nevertheless sought, if often in an ineffective and halting manner, to realize the touchstones of Japan's technology and security ideology: indigenization, diffusion, and nurturance.

The Japanese experience therefore shows that beliefs about national security and technology affect decisions about industrial structure and the way a nation evaluates its comparative global strengths and weaknesses. Japan, we believe, values industries differently than does America. Japan's security and technology ideology fosters a national consensus so basic that it is now unquestioned by virtually all industrial and political actors—that industries have importance beyond the goods they produce. Acting on this belief, the Japanese are driven to procure or develop skills and knowledge that they may lack for their domestic economy so that nonproduction benefits—especially learning and diffusion—can be realized at home. Industrial policy in Japan is guided by the effort to maintain the nation's knowledge and technology base rather than to produce a specific product to which a domestic firm might affix a nameplate.

In the United States, by contrast, companies displace one another in competition for markets or contracts, leading to wholesale capacity losses, or even complete domestic skill displacement from the American economy, which Japan would never tolerate. While many argue that the production consequences of these losses are, in fact, beneficial if overall prices fall, this position ignores the potential long-term loss that may result from the knowledge diffusion, skill development, and commercialization that will not occur. As we have seen in the aircraft industry, Japan is willing to pay (and pay dearly) for the same technical knowledge that the United States is willing to transfer abroad, because Japan values the ancillary industrial results of that knowledge as much, or more than, the ability to make specific goods.

There is, moreover, a vast gulf between U.S. and Japanese thinking about the importance of maintaining industry support mechanisms to nurture competent firms to which technology has been transferred and diffused. While Japan exerts significant efforts to assure that opportunities to form alliances, compete, and exploit learning in different ways are preserved by reducing fratricidal and exogenous market shocks, America believes that whole regions, sectors, and industries can be "given up" in the hope that new industries will emerge. But, compared to firms nurtured in systems like Japan, which consistently *build* skills and networks over time, U.S. producers may be successively weakened as they experience unshielded market shocks that are not shared by their overseas competitors.

The ideological divergence between U.S. and Japanese technology and security thinking is particularly apparent in the post–Cold War era. As the U.S. defense industrial base contracts, losing certain skills and failing to exploit commercial opportunities, the Japanese increasingly build dual-use capabilities and purchase what the Americans have incentives to discard. This is as true in defense as it is in other sectors. Japan maintains and secures across-the-board manufacturing and design technologies from abroad in a bottom-up strategy; the United States is now contemplating cutting all but top R&D functions in the defense industry on the theory that manufacturing skills are generally fungible.

Consequently, where American ideology drives firms and policymakers to seek the cheapest components regardless of the structural or domestic economic consequences, their counterparts in Japan—operating under a different set of beliefs—are motivated by a concern to obtain, diffuse, and nurture the broadest possible spectrum of skills. This striking variation in basic principles and resulting industrial choices between America and its principal economic competitor ought, we believe, to give U.S. policymakers pause. If Japan is to be our guide, the United States may be undervaluing the knowledge production and diffusion benefits domestic manufacturing networks generate. If so, a public policy concern is to ensure that indigenous production networks—in defense as in other sectors—are not sacrificed in the operation of current American industrial strategic thinking. Instead, it may be necessary to intervene to protect the nation's manufacturing networks, foster more effective collaboration among both prime contractors and their suppliers, and seek much more substantial access to foreign manufacturing networks, especially in Japan.

7.5.2   A Dual-Use Defense Industry Possible, if Not Essential

The postwar instability of domestic demand and the political impossibility of developing arms exports markets has led the Japanese defense industry to describe itself ruefully as "neither dead nor alive" (*ikasanu yō ni, kurosanu yō ni*).[130] By some measures this assessment may be correct. Although the defense industry's share of total industrial production in Japan has increased slightly since 1970, it is still less than 1 percent of total industrial production.[131] In sales, the defense industry in Japan is on the scale of the nation's sushi shops or bakeries.

But these measures greatly understate both latent Japanese defense capabilities and the country's achievements in "embedding" a military production sector within the commercial economy. By relying on the skills of its commercial producers to obtain and master dual-use technologies, as we described in the case of aircraft, Japan has generated dramatic absolute growth in its military sector. One percent of 1970 Japanese GNP is not the same as 1 percent of 1990 Japanese GNP. In any case, if Japanese defense spending is recalculated according to NATO standards (including pensions, aid, and other items that the Japanese exclude in order to stay under the nominal 1 percent ceiling), Japan actually spends 2 percent of its massive GNP on defense.[132] Despite the formal ceiling on defense expenditures that obtained until 1986, defense spending was either the first or second fastest growing item in the national budget throughout the 1980s—a decade during which the total budget more than doubled. Since the mid-1960s defense spending expanded between 5 and 8 percent each year, and actual JDA spending has risen from 300 billion yen to more than 4 trillion yen.[133] By 1984, Japan had the fourth largest naval fleet in the world, and by the late 1980s, its defense budget was third in the world. Thus, by the time Japan slowed down its defense buildup in 1993, it had built

130. Kamata (1979, 205).
131. Japan Defense Agency (1990).
132. Dekle (1989); Tomiyama (1982, 26).
133. Bōeichō . . . Kikakubu (1991, 37).

a formidable defense capability in spite of severe domestic political and international handicaps.

More importantly, unlike U.S. economic policymakers, the Japanese have never believed that silicon chips and potato chips are the same.[134] Differences between sushi and Sidewinders and between bread and ballistic missiles are profound in Japanese thinking, but not for the obvious reason that some build while others destroy. As we have described in the case of aircraft, the Japanese are convinced that advanced technology has a strategic value beyond its immediate application. Guided by this belief, the Japanese try to assess how industries contribute to the national standard of living in general. This has been true in defense as well as commercial sectors, where Japanese procurement decisions have helped to foster domestic networks and skills as well as military readiness.

The result has been the creation of a defense sector that appears particularly suited for the post–Cold War world. It might once have been arguable that Japan's defense industry choices were unsuccessful: Japan could hardly have defended itself from potential enemies such as the former USSR or even China without the equipment that the United States produced. But the view that Japan possesses a dysfunctional defense industry is losing favor as the Cold War ends, and clear, long-term military needs are being replaced by fuzzy, highly variable security options and threats. In such a world, the capability to mix and match specific design or production skills to meet military challenges, or to sustain cutting-edge technologies without bankrupting the public treasury, is becoming more valued than the ability to stamp out hundreds of guns, tanks, or fighters in publicly supported defense firms. Analysts are beginning to acknowledge that the absence of specialty aircraft makers, to cite one key element of the defense industry, is an advantage for Japan.[135]

They also have begun to acknowledge the growing confidence of the Japanese to meet national defense needs and to compete with other nations by exploiting the military capacities its commercial firms maintain. After decades of indigenizing, diffusing, and nurturing, Japanese defense production, like Japanese defense technology, is largely indistinguishable from Japanese industry as a whole. As a result, Japan is starting to appreciate that its best commercial producers could easily become the best military producers as well. The chairmen of Honda and Sony each became honorary chairmen of the Japan Defense Technology Association in 1982. As Ibuka Masaru, the chairman of Sony (and a former Naval Air Arsenal researcher) claimed when asked by the head of the Japan Defense Technology Association what targets should be set in order for Japan to achieve an autonomous defense technology base, "[It does

---

134. This analogy is usually credited to Richard Darman, the chief economic policy advisor to presidents Reagan and Bush.

135. Nihon Kikai . . . Kikin (1991, 7).

not matter what the targets are,] for as long as targets are set for us, we can build anything at all." [136]

Japanese defense capabilities show that military manufacturing can occur in networks of commercial firms, a capability that is now the goal of the United States as defense firms contract and attempt to convert to other purposes. But to have an indigenous defense production base embedded in the commercial economy like the Japanese, a full-spectrum commercial capability is essential. Without an effort to build and sustain lower-tier, sophisticated manufacturing networks in the United States, it will be difficult, if not impossible, to embed American defense capabilities in the commercial economy as the Japanese have done. Each of the pieces of upstream and downstream production must mesh into a seamless network from which defense capabilities precipitate.

Security, the Japanese experience suggests, means more than bombs or missiles. It also means knowledge, and a diverse top-to-bottom manufacturing economy is, in effect, a huge knowledge generator for the whole society. There is a direct relationship between a nation's economic capabilities and its technology and military security. America is only beginning to recognize this relationship much more explicitly in the post–Cold War environment. [137]

7.5.3 Strategic Use of Partners

Japanese firms and the Japanese government have defined their relationships with both domestic and foreign partners in strategic terms, consistent with the security and technology ideology we have described above. One Japanese scholar refers to Japan's international partnering strategy as involving a "two-track" policy: inviting foreign companies into relationships that could transfer technologies or enhance areas of Japanese weakness, while simultaneously building autonomous capabilities to supplant foreign dependencies. [138]

Domestic firms have evolved a system of protocols that ensure stability and shared risk. "Winners" do not "take all," nor do losers come away empty-handed. Relationships among prime contractors and between prime and subcontractors are exceptionally stable and—by U.S. standards—exceptionally interdependent. Prime contractors rely more than ever on the innovations of their subcontractors, and each exists in a complex network of alliances. The final assembly by prime contractors of components and equipment supplied by vendors and subcontractors masks extensive material, supply, and fabrication relationships. As we discussed above, prime defense contractors are directly responsible for only a fraction of Japan's arms and aircraft production.

The indigenization of both prime and subcontractor capabilities in Japan has been a phased process. While the defense industry was buffeted by clear policy shifts first toward and then away from domestic development, it was buttressed

---

136. Asahi Shimbunsha (1987, 150).
137. See speech by President Clinton at the Westinghouse Electric Corporation, Bethesda, MD, March 11, 1993.
138. Inoguchi (1991, 93).

and stabilized by a consistent technonational ideology. Even if Japan would not develop certain weapons systems due to political and fiscal constraints—such as the PX-L antisubmarine warfare plane that fell victim to Lockheed bribery in the 1970s—it has taken every opportunity to maximize learning from licensing.

At the same time, U.S. firms often obtained more significant revenues from licensing than from selling actual military products. The willingness to pay such premiums must be understood as part of Japanese industry's strategic use of foreign partners. Aircraft and defense technology transfers have been inbound for decades. Foreign partners are selected, not to supply cheap parts, but because they are willing to supply expensive knowledge. International cooperation, the euphemism for foreign licensing, has never been an end in itself; in the twentieth century, as in the nineteenth century, it has been a convenient means of learning the manufacturing processes that underlay the design and production of desired products. Foreign licensing has always been a second choice to domestic development, and it has served to close gaps in Japanese manufacturing technology while enhancing domestic capabilities in military as well as civilian areas. The Japanese strategic use of foreign partners is a major challenge for conventional American practices as well.

7.5.4   Reciprocity, Not Protection

Building an indigenous "full-spectrum" commercial economy that will also sustain U.S. defense capabilities is not simply a domestic problem. Rather, as the growing foreign interpenetration of American supply networks demonstrates, it is also a matter of regulating the flow and effects of overseas products and technology into the country. This may involve two seemingly opposite goals. First, to provide the kind of support and nurturing that has stimulated long-term, stable skill development in countries like Japan, U.S. firms may have to be shielded in some fashion from external shocks—including foreign competition—while domestic networks are rebuilt. At the same time, however, to obtain access and indigenize technology from abroad, the United States must avoid naked protectionism that would alienate its foreign partners. In short, the United States will have to develop its own version of the subtle blend of strategic cooperation and domestic technological nurturing the Japanese have practiced for decades.

The threat that American industrial reversals will foster crude protectionism is especially troublesome. Protectionism only ensures that, as Japan's technology highways (and those of other rapidly developing economies) become even more fully articulated, American access will be increasingly difficult and costly. Further, the day has long passed when the United States could expect to control or dominate world technology by retarding the flow of skill and know-how abroad. To do so now would be politically costly and would likely fail. Nor should America *want* to be isolated from overseas technologies, an outcome that would only ensure the nation's eventual obsolescence and generate even more profound commercial and defense consequences.

Instead, the task is to develop a rough parity with other nations in domestic full-spectrum indigenization, diffusion, and nurturing capabilities. There are several policy levers for achieving this goal. One is to spur U.S. firms to partner strategically with foreign producers to obtain technology flow-backs—that is, to obtain and then diffuse technology in the United States just as Japanese and other nations' producers have done with American know-how in the past. Another is to recognize the express connections between technology, knowledge, and national security and leverage America's substantial international contribution to international stability—especially in the Pacific Rim—for reciprocal access to manufacturing networks abroad. If global power increasingly turns on industrial capabilities, the United States will lose its capacity to bargain in the world if it fails to link itself more effectively with foreign economies in ways that assure that state-of-the-art technologies flow into its domestic economy and are exploited.

The Japanese clearly understand the subtleties involved in maintaining an open economy while seeking national advantage. They recognize that their bargaining power with other nations requires nurturing and indigenizing advanced technological capabilities. Restrictions of access to technology routinely accelerate Japanese efforts in both respects: "The United States has recently begun to increase its restrictions on technology transfer, and there has developed an increased severity of the environment hemming in the Japanese aircraft industry. We cannot expect the sorts of easy technology transfer we have experienced until now. So, it has become an indispensable premise that above all else we achieve world levels of autonomous technology by undertaking international joint development."[139] To the Japanese, building future options for accessing international networks while also localizing industrial capabilities is as essential a security task as manufacturing fighters or tanks.

Nurturing without becoming predatory and indigenizing without protectionism is a delicate and difficult task, one made more challenging by the need to insist on reciprocal treatment and access to technology networks—manufacturing associations, consortia, and regional networks—in countries like Japan that have little experience sharing.

Nevertheless, the stakes involved may require that the United States continue to press at every level for reciprocity and access—while pursuing the necessary domestic initiatives—so that at the least a stable balance of technology diffusion and indigenous capabilities with other dominant nations can be achieved. In the post–Cold War era, technology differentials will continue to affect each nation's defense capabilities. But more than in the past, a nation's defense skills will depend on the strength of its commercial economy. If differentials in commercial capabilities are allowed to widen, enriching manufactur-

---

139. Nihon Kikai . . . Kikin (1991, 2).

ing networks in one nation while they atrophy in another will result in unacceptable national security implications. The crucial task for the United States and Japan is to restructure their historical roles regarding bilateral technology diffusion while maintaining rounds for collaboration rather than conflict. Difficult though this goal might appear in an age of escalating transpacific recriminations, the likely alternatives appear much less attractive.

7.5.5   Regional Implications

Resolving current and potential conflicts attributable to divergent national technology and security ideologies is also essential for Asian stability. Bilateral United States–Japan disputes are merely one instance of more general problems centering on technology sharing and access that are likely to affect U.S.-Asian, Japanese-Asian, and regional relations in the future.

The pattern of American aerospace technology and product exchanges with Japan is strikingly similar to those involving South Korea, Taiwan, and Southeast Asian states. Both Taiwan and Korea have insisted on increased technology development roles for military projects with the United States, starting first with licensing and then codevelopment. They also actively seek to leverage their defense component and manufacturing capabilities to supply the U.S. and global defense and commercial aerospace industries.[140] In 1991, a Taiwanese company mounted a bid, backed in part by government funds, to purchase a stake in McDonnell Douglas's commercial transport (aircraft) operations. Countries as diverse as Singapore and Indonesia have discussed, or are developing, similar licensing and developmental strategies.[141]

The use of licensing and subcontracting to build domestic skills that can facilitate increasingly advanced defense and commercial capabilities exists throughout the world. But unlike Europe, where American and European mutual defense supply network interpenetration and close political collaboration promotes at least the appearance—if not the reality—of reciprocal U.S. technology access, American industrial interaction with Asian nations has generally not produced reciprocal technology flows. As in Japan, U.S. producers are technology suppliers, prime contractors, and component consumers. Should North and Southeast Asian economies substantially penetrate the U.S. defense supply base, or obtain growing shares of the global commercial aerospace business, many of the same tensions that are likely to afflict U.S. and Japanese relations may well recur throughout the region.

Consequently, even though the political and security contexts, and industrial

---

140. For an excellent review of the Korean defense industry "partnership strategy," which involves the goals of (1) supplying components to U.S. defense firms and using offsets to induce local subcontracting by American primes, (2) exporting components worldwide, and (3) collaborating in weapons technology development, see Office of Technology Assessment (1990, 133–36). A description of Taiwan's indigenization and diffusion efforts, centering on the codevelopment with General Dynamics of a two-engined fighter based on the F-16, the IDF, or Ching Kuo, and government promotion of defense-commercial industry linkages, is also found at 170–74.

141. Ibid., 164–70.

capabilities, of other Asian countries are very different form Japan, the basic issue of ensuring reciprocity and preserving a full-spectrum commercial base to support defense requirements will likely be a dominant concern for the United States in the region. Moreover, should Japanese multinationals increasingly knit the Asian region's industrial base together, purely bilateral U.S. and Japanese technology and security conflicts could well be exported throughout Asia.

Japan must also learn how to offer specific, effective reciprocal technology access to preserve its own interests in Asia. Japan's role in the region is the reverse of its historical position relative to the United States; it is a supplier, not a consumer, of technology and know-how from its Asian partners. As such it has to learn new forms of interaction with its neighbors, for as we have discussed, Japan's technology and security ideology may uneasily accommodate the transfer and sharing of industrial capabilities or opportunities. This possibility has led many Asian countries to question whether their participation in Japanese manufacturing networks could adversely affect their long-term domestic capabilities and thus their security interests. The result has been increasingly contentious efforts to force Japan to transfer technologies or to condition Japanese direct investment on reciprocity and commitments to create local business opportunities.[142]

The close and growing correlation between technology, domestic capabilities, and security may therefore drive conflict and realignment in Asia. This will likely compel America to develop strategies for obtaining reciprocity and preserving its industrial base that go beyond bilateral concerns with Japan. Japan may find that its economic efforts in Asia could be stalled if its commitment to share and develop technologies in a genuine partnership with other nations is widely questioned. Rather than observing the development of a new, Asian regional "bloc" economy, technology and security concerns could well provoke new alliances among the United States, Europe, and Asian states. The successful creation of reciprocal technology networks, or highways, could become the critical factor shaping future Asian political and economic relations. If so, technology and security issues will transcend the U.S.-Japanese bilateral relationship, and will be crucial to the stability and welfare of the Asian region as a whole.

---

142. A central point of contention between South Korea and Japan, for instance, was technology transfer, and many Korean companies are now canceling tie-ups with Japanese firms that have lasted for years. Singapore reportedly has also begun restricting Japanese investment in semiconductor facilities, absent more extensive technology sharing and transfer. Even in Malaysia, a country often cited as one of the seminal "look East" nations that actively prefer Japanese investment over U.S. or European ties, bilateral conflict over Japanese subcontracting, technology transfers, and local business development has erupted. See, for example, the account of Malaysian-Japanese struggles to develop ventures in automobiles and steel in Machado (1990).

Appendix A

Table 7A.1   **Major Japanese Foreign Airframe Subcontracting, by Firm and Project, 1991 (including helicopters)**

Firm	Aircraft	Components
	1. Mitsubishi Heavy Industries	
Boeing	737	nose landing gear steering actuator; valves
	747	inboard flaps; landing gear door actuator
	757	landing gear door actuators; fuselage longerons; valves
	767	aft fuselage; doors; landing gear actuator valves
McDonnell Douglas	MD-80	wing panels
	DC-10, MD-11	fuselage tail sections
	2. Kawasaki Heavy Industries	
Boeing	707, 727, 737, 747, 767	gearbox; machinery components
	737	inspar ribs; outside flaps
	747	outboard flaps
	767	forward, mid fuselage; cargo doors; flap actuators; wing ribs
McDonnell Douglas	MD-80	flap actuating section fairing covers
	MDX	main reduction gears
KHI/Messerschmitt-Boelkow-Blohm	BK-117	total assemblies; fuselages; main reduction gears
	3. Fuji Heavy Industries	
Boeing	747	rudder, ailerons, and fitting sheets; spoilers
	757	outside flaps
	767	fairings; main landing gear door
McDonnell Douglas	MD-11	outside ailerons
Fokker	F-50	rudders, elevators
	4. Shin Meiwa	
Boeing	757	tail unit components
	767	fuselage structural components
McDonnell Douglas	MD-80	thrust reverser components
	MD-11	engine suspenders
	5. Nihon Kokuki	
Boeing	767	structural components
	6. Teijin Seiki	
Boeing	737	landing gear actuating cylinders/ brake control valves
	747	aileron actuators; nose landing gear steering actuator
	757	aileron actuators; yaw damper

Table 7A.1   (continued)

Firm	Aircraft	Components
	767	spoiler aileron; hydraulic components; yaw damper
McDonnell Douglas	MD-11	elevator actuators
	7. Shimadzu	
Boeing	737	brake control and fuel reverse flow prevention valves
	747	aileron adjustment equipment; spoiler actuators; fuel cut-off valves
	757	aileron adjustment and cargo door actuators; gearbox
	767	gearbox; high-lift device actuators
	8. Kayaba	
Boeing	737	thrust reverser control valves
	757	valves, nose landing gear steering equipment
	767	valves; landing gear hydraulic actuators
	9. Yokohama Rubber	
Boeing	737	water tanks
	747	honeycomb structural core
	757	lavatory modules and fuel tanks
	767	composites
McDonnell Douglas	MD-11	water tanks
	10. Kobe Steel	
Boeing	737, 757, 767	titanium and steel forgings
	11. Furukawa Aluminum	
Boeing	757, 767	aluminum forgings; extrustions
	12. Japan Airline Manufacturing Company	
Boeing	757	galleys; elevators; carbon fiber pipes
	727, 737, 747, 767	galleys
McDonnell Douglas	MD-80	lavatories; cabin attendant seats
	MD-11	lavatories
Airbus	A300/310	lavatories
British Aerospace	BAe 146	galleys
	13. Minebea	
Boeing	747, 757, 767	bearings; motors
	14. Toray Industries	
Airbus	A300/310	interior component materials
	15. Mitsubishi Electric	
Boeing	747, 757	valves; actuators
	767	valves; actuators; instrument display CRTs
	16. Matsushita	
Boeing	737, 747, 757, 767	entertainment systems
McDonnell Douglas	MD-80	entertainment systems
	DC-10	entertainment systems

Table 7A.1   (continued)

Firm	Aircraft	Components
Airbus	A300/310	entertainment systems; interior component materials
British Aerospace	BAe 146	cabin entertainment
	17. Daido Steel	
Boeing	767	steel sheets
	18. Sumitomo Precision	
Boeing	757, 767	nose landing gear actuating components
Airbus	A300/340	landing gear actuating equipment
Fokker	F-50	heat exchangers and air coolers
	19. Koito Manufacturing	
Boeing	737, 757, 767	reading lights
	737, 747, 757, 767	seats
	20. Tokyo Aircraft Instruments	
Boeing	737	gyro horizons
	757, 767	spare altimeters
	21. Shinko Electric	
Boeing	747, 757, 767	cargo and general motors
	22. Tenryu Industries	
Boeing	727, 737, 747, 767	seats
	23. Japan Aviation Electronics	
Boeing	737	accelerometer
	757, 767	accelerometers; flight panel displays; air data inertial reference system
	24. Toshiba	
Boeing	767	instrument display CRTs
	25. Sony	
Boeing	767	cabin video systems
Summary: First-Tier Subcontractors		
Boeing	737 = 13	
	747 = 13	
	757 = 18	
	767 = 24	
McDonnell Douglas	MD-80 = 5	
	DC-10 = 2	
	MD-11 = 6	
Airbus	A300/A310 = 3	
	A300/A340 = 1	

Sources: Kukita (1990, 58); *Aerospace Japan Weekly,* August 26, 1991.

Appendix B

Table 7A.2   **Spinoffs from Midpostwar Japanese Military Projects, Aircraft Industry**

Technology	Spillover Effects
Production Control Technologies	
Quality control methods used for F-86 and T-33	Improved techniques of process control, inspections, vendor control, etc.
Zero defects campaign	Had impacts on a wide range of civilian industries
Reliability management techniques	Became a major turning point for improving the quality of electronics products
Comprehensive transportation production system	Improved production systems operation and design
Design Technologies	
Large-scale helicopters	Improved the designing of speed governors for ships and transmissions
F-104 hydraulic system	Improved high-pressure pipes and coupling for commecial vehicles
Ink recorder	Helped development of ink-recorder oscillographs for microquality measurement
Antivibration, antishock products	Became available for general electronics control systems
Tantalum condenser commission development	Enabled Japanese domestic test of condenser
Test/production of gyroscopes	Contributed to the development of precision equipment
Ground-air telemeter transponder	Contributed to the development of communication microwave technologies
Designing of aircraft heat exchangers	Contributed to the development/mass production of car heaters that use exhaust gas
Jet-engine bearing manufacturing technology	Contributed to the development of durable railcar bearing
Application of aircraft gas turbine to ships	Expanded the applicability to electric generators and ships
Aircraft measuring equipment technology	Enhanced the quality of general high-class measuring equipment
Ceramic brake lining for F-104	Applied the lining technology to buses and other general vehicles
Connector technology	Applied to railcars
Shield beam lamp	Applied its major characteristics—high illumination, small size, light weight, and durability—to general-purpose products
High-pressure oil filters	Contributed to the improvement of filters for automobiles and machine tools
High-pressure hose for F-104	Improved the quality of general-purpose hoses
High-temperature fuel	Contributed to the improvement of tank tester techniques for designing large-scale, high-pressure test chambers

Table 7A.2 (continued)

Technology	Spillover Effects
Manufacturing bolts for F-104 engines (J-79)	Improved the quality of bolts for automobiles
Manufacturing self-locking nuts for aircraft	Improved the quality of self-locking nuts (especially ones with nylon) for automobiles
Domestic production of navigation equipment and gyroscopes	Improved the inertial navigation technology
Domestic production of simulators	Applied to simulators for other areas (e.g., railway, automobile)
Hydraulics controller technology	Improved overall hydraulics control
Information-processing technology	Applied to other information-processing equipment to be used to process radar information
Information-display technology	Applied to other equipment to display symbolized signals

Manufacturing Technologies

Divided-sleeve technology used for F-104's valve	Improved the quality of precision servo-valves for general-purpose soil-pressure equipment
Speed limit assurance testing of T-1A	Applied to range of other transportation test and measuring equipment
Domestic production of aircraft material	Improved overall materials technology
High-pressure technology used for F-104's hydraulic	Improved the hydraulics technology for industrial products equipment such as plunger pump motors
Automatic wiring test technology	Applied computer-aided test technology to other equipment
Module technology	Applied module assembly/manufcturing technology to other equipment
Wiring identification	Applied baking method to other technologies and antiheat wirings
Electrolytic manufacturing method for turbine rotor for air gas hard processing turbine	Applied to the molding of general-hydraulic equipment material
Welding technology for rocket chambers	Achieved JIS 2-class technology and improved the overall quality of welding
Adhesive technology including honeycomb structure	Applied to general-purpose equipment such as stable panel and bus door
Aluminum welding technology	Applied to the manufacture of general-purpose heat exchangers
Prevention of bacteria corrosion of metal products	Improved the technology to prevent bacteria corrosion of metal products
Adhesive technology for aircraft copper, antiheat alloy, and ultra-heat shields	Applied adhensive technologies for antiheat alloys to automatic generation and magneto-hydro dynamics generation
Jet engine parts processing technology	Applied cutting and molding technologies in other industries
Jet engine parts forging technology	Applied to industrial gas turbine parts

Table 7A.2   (continued)

Technology	Spillover Effects
Aircraft parts electron discharge method (EDM)	Applied to industrial gas turbine parts processing technologies
Precision grinding, polishing, and processing technologies	Applied to special processing treatment of industrial products to reduce engineering tasks
Improved hydraulic technologies	Applied to the installation of industrial oil-pressure control chambers and to cylinders
Metal-plating technology	Contributed anticorrosion and high degrees of precision to the development of special metal-plating technologies for industrial products
Welding technology	Applied high-reliability spot-welding to industrial products
Heat treatment technology	Improved stability in heat treatment for industrial products
J-58 engine ignition system	Applied to antivibration, antishock treatment by reducing size and weight
Technology for plating nickel onto aluminum plate used for J-79 ignition	Applied to other industrial products in reducing size and weight of parts
Military dual-side-printed circuit board	Manufactured through-hole, circuit boards commercially
Special CRT technology	Contributed to the enhancement of high-definition CRT technology
Other Technologies	
Explosive forming technology ued for F-104 fuselage parts	Applied forming technology for metal processing, leading to the widespread use of large-scale presses
Duct hose used for F-104	Applied to the auto industry
O-rings for aircraft	Applied to the general-purpose oil-pressure equipment in other industries
Disk brakes for jet aircraft	Used in automobiles and rapid railways
Plastic tooling introduced for F-86	Used for automobiles and engine turbine blades
Anodizing process developed for F-86	Increased durability and reduced weight for other machine parts
Reinforced plastic developed for F-104	Used in YS-11 and MU-2, as well as in buses, automobiles, and general-purpose machinery
F-104 chemical milling technology	Applied to other machinery processing to cut costs
Jet engine bearing technology	Used for bullet trains
Mentor Trainer oil cooler technology	Improved heat exchangers such as general-purpose radiators, car coolers, and car heaters

Sources: Keidanren Bōei Seisan Iinkai (1965, 285); Bōei Kiki Sangyō Jittai Chōsa Iinkai (1968, 81–84).

References

Abbegglen, James C. 1991. Where Japan Does Not Succeed: The Case of the Aerospace Industry. *Newsletter of the Asia Advisory Service,* March.

Aboulafa, Richard L. 1991. World Military and Commercial Aircraft Briefing. Fairfax, VA: Teal Group Corporation.

Adachi, Tetsuo. 1981. Ririkki o Mukaeta Nihon no Kōkūki Sangyō. (The Japanese aircraft industry welcomes the take-off period). Chōsa Geppō no. 185. Tokyo: Nihon Chōki Shinyō Ginko.

Aerospace Industries Association of America. 1990. *Aerospace Facts and Figures 1990–1991.* Washington, DC.

Alexander, Arthur, 1993. Of Tanks and Toyotas: An Assessment of Japan's Defense Industry. Rand Note N-3542-AF. Santa Monica, CA: Rand Corporation.

Alexander, Arthur, C. Hill, and R. Bodilly. 1989. *Defense Department Report of Industries Independent Research and Development (IR&D).* RAND R-3649-ACQ. Santa Monica, CA: Rand Corporation.

Alic, John A. 1989. Dual-Use Manufacturing: Technology, Organization, and Management. Cambridge, MA: Dual-Use Technologies Project, John F. Kennedy School of Government, Harvard University.

Alic, John A., Lewis M. Branscomb, Harvey Brooks, Ashton B. Carter, and Gerald L. Epstein, eds. 1992. *Beyond Spin-Off.* Boston: Harvard Business School Press.

Analytic Science Corporation. 1990. *Foreign Vulnerability of Critical Industries.* Washington, DC: Analytic Science Corporation.

Anchordoguy, Marie. 1989. *Computers, Inc.: Japan's Challenge to IBM.* Harvard East Asian Monograph Series. Cambridge, MA: Council on East Asian Studies.

Asahi Shimbun Shakaibu. 1987. *Heiki Sangyō* (The weapons industry). Tokyo: Asahi Shimbunsha.

Asamuma, Banri. 1989. Manufacturer-Supplier Relationships in Japan and the Concept of Relation-Specific Skills. *Journal of the Japanese and International Economies* 3:1–30.

Bobrow, Davis B., and Steven R. Hill. 1991. Non-military Determinants of Military Budgets: The Japanese Case. *International Studies Quarterly* 35: 39–61

Bōeichō Gijutsu Kenkyū Honbu, ed. 1977. *Bōeichō Gijutsu Kenkyū Honbu Nijūgo Nenshi* (The 25-year history of the Defense Agency Technical Research and Development Institute). Tokyo: Bōeichō Gijutsu Kenkyū Honbu.

Bōeichō Gijutsu Kenkyū Honbu Kikakubu, ed. 1991. *Kenkyū Kaihatsu Katsudō* (Research and development activities). Internal data.

Bōei Kiki Sangyō Jittai Chōsa Iinkai, ed. 1968. *Bōei Kiki Sangyō Jittai Chōsa* (Research report on the actual conditions of the defense machinery industries). Tokyo: Bōei Kiki Sangyō Jittai Chōsa Iinkai, July.

Chōgin Sōgō Kenkyūjo, ed. 1991. *Kōkūki Buhin Sangyō Jittai Chōsa* (Empirical research on the aircraft and components industry). Tokyo: Chōgin Sōgō Kenkyūjo, April.

Defense Science Board. 1987. Report of the Defense Science Board Task Force on Defense Semiconductors Dependency. Office of the Undersecretary of Defense for Acquisition. Washington, DC: Defense Science Board.

Defense Technical Information Center. 1990. *Critical Technology Plan.* Washington, DC: Defense Technical Information Center.

Dekle, Robert. 1989. The Relationship between Defense Spending and Economic Performance in Japan. In J. Makin and D. Hellmann, eds., *Sharing World Leadership? A New Era for America and Japan.* Washington, DC: American Enterprise Institute.

Dore, Ronald. 1987. Goodwill and the Spirit of Market Capitalism. In Ronald Dore, *Taking Japan Seriously*. Stanford: Stanford University Press.

Frenkel, Orit. 1984. Flying High: A Case Study of Japanese Industrial Policy. *Journal of Policy Analysis and Management* (3): 406–20.

Friedman, David. 1988. *The Misunderstood Miracle: Industrial Development and Political Change in Japan*. Ithaca, NY: Cornell University Press.

———. 1993. Getting Industry to Stick: Creating High Value Added Production Regions in the United States. MIT Japan Program Working Paper 93–02. Cambridge, MA.

Fuji Sōgō Kenkyūjo, ed. 1990. Waga Kuni Kōkūki Sangyō no Genjō to Tembō (The current situation and prospects for Japan's aircraft industry). *Fuji Taimuza* (July): 2–8.

Gansler, Jacques. 1984. The Pentagon in the Sciences. In John Tirman, ed., *The Militarization of High Technology*, 163–79. Cambridge, MA: Ballinger.

———. 1989. *Affording Defense*. Cambridge: MIT Press.

Green, Michael J. 1991. *Kokusanka: FSX and Japan's Search for Autonomous Defense Production*. MIT Japan Program Working Paper 90–09.

Hall, G. R., and R. E. Johnson. 1970. Transfers of United States Aerospace Technology to Japan. In R. Vernon, ed., *The Technology Factor in International Trade*, 305–63. New York: National Bureau of Economic Research.

Hasegawa, Eichi. 1987. Draft essay for ILO.

Hirschman, Albert. 1970. *Exit Voice and Loyalty*. Cambridge, MA: Harvard University Press.

Inoguchi, Takashi. 1991. *Japan's International Relations*. London: Pinter.

Institute for Defense Analysis. 1990. Dependence of U.S. Systems on Foreign Technologies. Washington, DC.

Japan Defense Agency, ed. 1990. *Defense of Japan 1990*. Tokyo: Japan Times.

Jikibō Mondai Kentō Waakingu Gurūpu, ed. 1990. *Jiki Bōeiryoku Seibi Keikaku ni Taisuru Yōbō* (Demands for the next defense equipment program). Tokyo: Keizai Dantai Rengōkai Bōei Seisan Iinkai.

Kagaku Gijutsuchō Shigen Chōsajo, ed. 1987. Kagaku Gijutsu Shihyō no Kaihatsu ni Kansuru Kisō Chōsa: Chū Kan Hōkoku (Fundamental inquiries in science and technology indicators: midterm report). Tokyo, October.

Kakamigahara Shiyakusho. 1982. *Shishi* (City history). Kakamigahara: Kakamigahara City Government Publication.

———. 1985. *Shishi* (City history). Kakamigahara: Kakamigahara City Government Publication.

———. 1987. *Shishi* (City history). Kakamigahara: Kakamigahara City Government Publication.

———. 1990. *Shishi* (City history). Kakamigahara: Kakamigahara City Government Publication.

Kamata, Satoshi. 1979. *Nihon no Heiki Kōba* (Japan's arms factories). Tokyo: Shio.

Kamitani, Chikatoshi. 1988. *Gijutsu Taikoku Hyakunen no Kei: Nippon no Kindaika to Kokuritsu Kenkyū Kikan* (The hundred-year path of technonationalism: Japanese modernization and national research institutes). Tokyo: Heibonsha.

Kawasaki Gifu Kyōdō Kumiai. 1990. *Sōritsu Yonjūnen Kinenshi*. (A forty-year history of the producer association). Kakamigahara, Japan: Kawasaki Gifu Kyōdō Kumiai.

Keizai Dantai Rengōkai Bōei Seisan Iinkai, ed. 1965. *Kokubō Yōsan ni Kansuru Kenkyū* (Research related to the defense budget). Tokyo: Keizai Dantai Rengōkai Bōei Seisan Iinkai, March.

———, ed. 1970. *Bōei Kiki Kenkyū Jittai Chōsa* (A survey of the actual condition of the defense machinery and armament research and development). Tokyo: Keizai Dantai Rengōkai.

————, ed. 1976. *Bōeiryoku Seibi Mondai ni Kansuru Wareware no Kenkai* (Our interpretation of the defense equipment problem). Tokyo: Keizai Dantai Rengōkai.

Keizai Dōyūkai, ed. 1979. 21 Seki e no Sangyō Kōzō Bijiyon o Mitomete (Demanding a vision for a twenty-first century industrial structure). Tokyo, June.

Kelley, Maryellen R., and Todd A. Watkins. 1992. The Defense Industrial Network: A Legacy of the Cold War. Manuscript. Pittsburgh.

Kikai Shinkōkyōkai and Keizai Dantai Rengōkai Bōei Seisan Iinkai, eds. 1965. *Bōei Kiki Sangyō no Jittai* (The condition of the defense machinery and arms industries). Tokyo, July.

Kobayashi, Ushisaburō. 1992. *Military Industries of Japan.* New York: Oxford University Press.

Kōkūki Kikai Kōgyō Shingikai, Kōkūki Kōgyō Bukai. 1985. Kōkūki Kōgyō No Tōmen Suru Kihon Mondai To Seifu Jijo No Arikata ni Tsuite (Chūkan Hōkoku) (The current state of government assistance and basic problems in the aircraft industry [mid-term report]). Tokyo: MITI.

Kukita, Sanemori. 1990. *Kōkūki Buhin* (Aircraft equipment). Tokyo: Nihon Keizai Shimbun.

Kurth, James. 1990. The Follow-on Imperative in American Weapons Procurement, 1960–1990. Paper presented to the Conference on Economic Issues of Disarmament, Institute for International Peace Studies, University of Notre Dame, November 30–December 1.

Lesbriel, Haydon. 1991. Structural Adjustment in Japan: Terminating Old King Coal. *Asian Survey* (11): 1079–94.

Levy, Jonah D., and Richard J. Samuels. 1991. *Institutions and Innovation: Research Collaboration as Technology Strategy in Japan.* MIT Japan Program Working Paper 89–02.

List, Frederick. 1922. *The National System of Political Economy.* London: Longman, Green and Co.

Lockwood, William. 1955. *The Economic Development of Japan: Growth and Structural Change, 1868–1938.* London: Oxford University Press.

Long Term Credit Bank of Japan, Industrial Research Division, ed. 1986. The Japanese Aircraft Industry: Entering a Period of Progress Spurred by International Joint Development. *LTCB Research Special Issue,* May.

Machado, Kit. 1990. Japanese Transnational Corporations in Malaysia's State-Sponsored Heavy Industrialization Drive: The HICOM Automobile and Steel Projects. *Pacific Affairs* (4): 504–31.

Maema, Takanori. 1989. *Jetto Enjin ni Toritsukareta Otoko.* (Men obsessed with jet engines). Tokyo: Kodansha.

Mason, Mark. 1992. American Multinationals and Japan: The Political Economy of Japanese Capital Control, 1899–1980. Cambridge, Mass.: Council on East Asian Studies, Harvard University.

Mowrey, David C. 1987. *Alliance Politics and Economics: Multinational Joint Ventures in Commercial Aircraft.* Cambridge, MA: Ballinger.

Moxon, Richard W., Thomas W. Roehl, and J. Frederick Truitt. 1987. International Cooperative Ventures in the Commercial Aircraft Industry: Gains Sure, but What's My Share? Paper prepared for the Wharton-Rutgers Conference on Cooperative Strategies in International Business, Seattle.

Najita, Tetsuo. 1980. *Japan: The Intellectual Foundations of Modern Japanese Politics.* Chicago: University of Chicago Press.

Nakayama, Shigeru. 1991. *Science, Technology, and Society in Postwar Japan.* Melbourne: Kegan Paul International.

Nihon Kikai Kōgyō Rengōkai and Kōkū Kokusai Kyōdō Kaihatsu Sokushin Kikin, eds. 1991. *Heisei ni nen: Kōkūki Kokusai Kyōdō Kaihatsu Shinkō ni Kansuru Chōsa Kenkyū Hōkokusho* (Research report concerning the promotion of international cooperation in aircraft, 1990). Tokyo: Nihon Kikai Kōgyō Rengōkai and Kōkū Kokusai Kyōdō Kaihatsu Sokushin Kikin.

Nihon Kōkū Uchū Kōgyōkai, ed. 1979. *Waga Kuni Kōkū kiki Kōgyō no Shinkō Hōsaku: Chōsa Hōkokusho* (Programs for promoting Japan's aircraft machinery industry: a research report). Tokyo: Nihon Kōkū Uchū Kōgyōkai, March.

―――, ed. 1985. *Kōkūki Sangyō Gijutsu no Iten, Hyōka: Chōsa Hōkokusho* (Aircraft industry technology transfer and evaluation: a research report). Tokyo: Nihon Kōkū Uchū Kōgyōkai, June.

―――, ed. 1987. *Nihon no Kōkūki Uchū Kōgyō Sengoshi* (Japan's aerospace industry: a postwar history). Tokyo: Nihon Kōkū Uchū Kōgyōkai.

―――, ed. 1992. *Kōkū Uchū Kōgyō Nenkan* (The aerospace industry yearbook). Tokyo: Nihon Kōkū Uchū Kōgyō Kai.

Nihon Ritchi Sentaa, ed. 1982. *Kōkū oyobi Kōkūki Buhin Sangyō* (The aircraft and aircraft parts industry). Tokyo: Nihon Ritchi Sentaa.

Nishiguchi, Toshihiro. 1989. Strategic Dualism: An Alternative in an Industrial Society. Ph.D. thesis, Nuffield College, Oxford University.

Noble, David. 1984. *Forces of Production: A Social History of Industrial Automation.* New York: Knopf.

Noble, Gregory W. 1992. *Flying Apart? Japanese-American Negotiations over the FS-X Fighter Plane.* Policy Papers in International Affairs no. 41. Berkeley: University of California.

Office of Technology Assessment. 1989. *Holding the Edge: Maintaining the Defense Technology Base.* Washington, DC: Office of Technology Assessment.

―――. 1990. *Arming Our Allies: Cooperation and Competition in Defense Technology.* Washington, DC: Office of Technology Assessment.

―――. 1991. *Competing Economies: America, Europe, and the Pacific Rim.* Washington, DC: U.S. Government Printing office.

Ono, Eiichi, ed. 1991. *Aerospace Industry in Japan.* Tokyo: Society of Japanese Aerospace Companies.

Rubin, Paul J. 1983. Overview of Japanese Aerospace Industries. *Interavia,* October.

Samuels, Richard J. 1987. *The Business of the Japanese State: Energy Markets in Comparative and Historical Perspective.* Ithaca, NY: Cornell University Press.

―――. 1992. Reinventing Security: Japan since Meiji. In Raymond Vernon and Ethan Kapstein, ed., *Defense and Dependence in a Global Economy.* Washington, DC: Congressional Quarterly.

Samuels, Richard J., and Benjamin C. Whipple. 1989. Defense Production and Industrial Development: The Case of Japanese Aircraft. In Chalmers Johnson, Laura Tyson, and John Zysman, eds., *The Politics of Productivity.* Cambridge, MA: Ballinger.

Sanemoto, Yae. 1989. *Chūkyōken ni Okeru Kōkūki Sangyō* (The aircraft industry in the central region). Graduation thesis, Department of Geography, Ochanomizu Women's University, Tokyo.

Schumpeter, Joseph A. 1950. *Capitalism, Socialism, and Democracy.* New York: Harper and Row.

Sommers, Paul, Daniel Carlson, and Helen Birss. 1992. *Diversifying the Defense Contract Industry in Kind County.* Draft report, Northwest Policy Center, University of Washington, Seattle, January.

Takase, Shōji. 1979. Shirasezaru Nihon no Heiki Kihatsu (Japan's unknown weapons development). *Asahi Janaru,* August 3, 10–20.

Tomiyama, Kazuo. 1982. Nihon no Bōei Sangyō no Dōkō (Trends in Japan's defense industry). *Keizai Hyōron* (June): 25–36.

Ueda, Naruhiko. 1991. *Gijutsu Kokubō Ron* (A theory of technology and national defense). Tokyo: Deifensu Risaachi Sentaa.

U.S. General Accounting Office. 1982. *U.S. Military Co-production Programs Assist Japan in Developing Its Civil Aircraft Industry.* Washington, DC: U.S. Government Printing Office.

Womack, James P., Daniel T. Jones, and Daniel Roos. 1990. *The Machine That Changed the World.* New York: Rawson.

Yamazaki, Toshio. 1961. *Gijutsushi* (The history of technology). Tokyo: Tōyō Keizai.

Comment   Gregory W. Noble

This study of the Japanese aircraft industry by David Friedman and Richard Samuels, with its emphasis on the success of Japan's "bottom-up" strategy of concentrating on producing materials and composites in dual-use plants, is nothing if not provocative. It directly contradicts conventional wisdom about the weakness of the Japanese aerospace industry. Especially arresting is the description of the deepening relationship between Boeing and its Japanese suppliers. Backed by impressive technical skills and the buying power of Japanese airlines, Japanese suppliers have increased their share of value-added in each generation of Boeing aircraft and now dominate Boeing's foreign procurement, the authors say. Nor, they argue, is the Japanese role confined to standard parts: Japanese suppliers have been integrated into the design and engineering of the forthcoming 777. The material on subcontracting and small-firm networks also addresses a gaping hole in the existing literature on aerospace in both countries. If the authors are right, the American aerospace industry faces serious challenges from Japan just as Airbus is consolidating its position as chief rival to Boeing. Given the economic, technological, and symbolic importance of aerospace, intensified political struggle among the advanced industrial countries could be in the offing.

Friedman and Samuels posit three elements in Japan's aircraft industry, and in technology policy more broadly: (1) indigenization—the active acquisition of every type of technology rather than simple acceptance of some fixed position in the international division of labor; (2) diffusion—active dispersion of technology throughout assembler-supplier networks, across civilian and military products, and among prime contractors, particularly through repeated cooperative projects; and (3) nurturing—a combination of promotion and insurance against instability.

If the approach is new and provocative, and some of the data are striking, the analysis is not yet complete, and the evidence not yet sufficiently comparative. First, the paper is remarkably lacking in politics. Much could be done in this area. For example, it is possible that the balance of diffusion and nurturing,

Gregory W. Noble is assistant professor of political science at the University of California, Berkeley.

and the support for supplier networks, follows from the electoral system and patterns of political contributions in Japan: prime contractors in the aerospace industry, like large Japanese firms more generally, supply contributions on a prorated basis to the party headquarters and faction leaders of the Liberal Democratic party (LDP), while smaller producers give votes and money to individual LDP members (Curtis 1988, 176–87). Perhaps this two-tiered pattern of political intervention in Japanese technology policy has served to promote competition and innovation, and not simply rent seeking and protectionism.

Second, the discussion of ideology is sketchy. Do we actually need to look beyond specific institutions and the incentives they create? Perhaps ideology can be conceptualized as a kind of platform binding together a coalition of diverse interests. If so, closer attention to the patterns of overlap and competition among those interests is in order.

Third, the comparative evidence is not always complete and convincing. Technology spillover from military aircraft to the civilian sector in Japan may have been significant in the 1950s and early 1960s, but that was true in the United States as well. As the authors note, the picture for recent years is cloudy, because the political sensitivity of the industry has blocked more recent efforts to assess the contribution of military aircraft production to the civilian economy. On the American side, the authors stress the relative weakness of diffusion policies, but possible counterexamples exist and their effectiveness could be explored: NASA in the 1960s, the Defense Advanced Research Project Agency (DARPA), and the diffusion requirements in Department of Defense procurement regulations. A preliminary glance at the literature suggests that a possible difference is Japan's emphasis on including subcontractors and not simply primes. Similarly, the authors stress that Japanese aerospace firms are efficient and flexible partly because they mix military and civilian production—but is that a cause, or an effect of some other difference in strategy or organization? Grumman tried to move into bus production, as Kawasaki had done so successfully in Japan, but it could not compete in the civilian market. Why the difference? Finally, many first-tier subcontractors in both Japan and the United States mix civilian and military production, yet by the authors' account the Japanese subs are rapidly displacing American producers of aerospace materials and components. Why?

Even if the Japanese industry is organized differently, it is not always clear from this account exactly how it functions. If every major postwar aircraft project has been organized cooperatively, why has the result not been inefficiency and stagnation, as some foreign critics suggest (Mowery and Rosenberg 1985, 19)? If diffusion is critical, why do firms with proprietary technology not block efforts to diffuse their knowledge and skills to competitors—and to the extent that it does occur, why does diffusion not undermine the incentive to innovate? And just how do the crucial vertical regional producer associations (*kumiai*) and horizontal cooperation associations of subcontractors (*kyoryoku-kai*) actually work (Doner 1992)?

Finally, the paper takes little note of the international context. Cold War alliances made the United States willing to defend Japan and to supply it with advanced technology. The Japanese industry did not have to undertake serious defense production and was able to treat each military project as an exercise in technology acquisition and development. The American industry, in contrast, was shaped by the need to develop effective weapons and by an obsession with leading-edge technology, to offset the Soviet advantage in numbers, and with secrecy, to prevent the loss of that technological edge. The contrasting positions of the two countries in the postwar security system thus go a long way toward explaining why they adopted different industrial strategies in aerospace, particularly the greater distance between military and civilian production in the United States.

These reservations notwithstanding, the basic thrust of the article rings true: Japan's position in supplying advanced materials and parts is extremely strong, and Japan has poured tremendous effort into the acquisition and dissemination of technology; the United States has fallen behind in both areas and often fails to recognize the problem. In the FS-X case, for example, the United States was attentive to the short-term economic interests of the prime defense contractors, but paid little attention to identifying and acquiring Japanese technology, and knew little about the capabilities of American subcontractors (Noble 1992). Judging from the evidence in this paper, little progress has been made since the signing of the FS-X agreement. In the case of the space station (and the superconducting supercollider), Japan seems unwilling to support U.S. projects financially without greater opportunities to acquire technology in return.

Aerospace is, to be sure, an unusual industry: barriers to entry are almost uniquely forbidding, governmental subsidies and politicized procurement play crucial roles in the competitive struggle, and in Japan cooperative production has been the norm. Nevertheless, the broader theme of Japan's obsession with the acquisition and diffusion of technology and skills can be seen across the industrial spectrum.

References

Curtis, Gerald L. 1988. *The Japanese Way of Politics.* New York: Columbia University Press.

Doner, Richard F. 1992. Limits of State Strength: Toward an Institutionalist View of Economic Development. *World Politics* 44 (3): 398–431.

Mowery, David C., and Nathan Rosenberg. 1985. The Japanese Commercial Aircraft Industry since 1945. Occasional Paper of the Northeast Asia–United States Forum on International Policy, Stanford University, Stanford, CA.

Noble, Gregory W. 1992. Flying Apart? Japanese-American Negotiations over the FSX Fighter Plane. Institute of International Studies, University of California, Berkeley.

8   Foreign Aid and Burdensharing: Is Japan Free Riding to a Coprosperity Sphere in Pacific Asia?

Shafiqul Islam

> The Americans concentrate on a vision of Japan as a closed society, driven by totally selfish economic motives, unfairly exploiting American military protection to dump its industrial-technological products on America while driving Americans out of their jobs.
>
> ZBIGNIEW BRZEZINSKI

> The way *Japan Inc.* operates also facilitates the formation of an Asian co-prosperity zone: government and business work hand-in-glove and business moves jointly. They move together as a group, because they are so keenly aware of vulnerability on their own. The decision will be made by consensus, and the rest is routine.
>
> RUDIGER DORNBUSCH

8.1   Introduction

Americans routinely label Japan an international free rider.[1] The accusation is rooted in one simple fact: America spends 5–6 percent of its GNP on maintaining its military supremacy while Japan, committed to nonaggression formalized by its "peace constitution"—and protected by the 1960 United States–Japan mutual cooperation and security treaty—limits its military spending to about 1 percent of GNP.[2] Since neither America nor Japan's Asian neighbors wish to see Japan—already an economic superpower—engage in rearmament and emerge as a military superpower, how to prevent Japan from enjoying a security free ride to economic supremacy has become a matter of increasing

Shafiqul Islam is senior fellow for international economics and finance at the Council on Foreign Relations and a visiting fellow at the Institute for International Economics.

The author would like to gratefully acknowledge excellent research assistance and other indispensable logistical support provided by Radha Muthiah. He would also like to thank Jeffrey Frankel for encouraging him to write this paper and offering constructive criticisms on the conference draft.

1. See, among others, Johnson (1986), House Armed Services Committee (1988), Schroeder (1988), Reed (1983), and MacIntosh (1987).

2. Popular sentiment against war and the military is probably a more binding barrier against a sharp rise in Japan's defense expenditure than the war-renouncing clause (Article 9) inserted by the American victors in the 1947 "peace constitution." The 1 percent of GNP limit on defense expenditure was established by Prime Minister Miki in 1976. While this limit was broken de jure when the Diet approved a fiscal 1987 defense budget at 1.004 percent of GNP, conventional wisdom notwithstanding, the *actual* defense spending so far has not exceeded the 1 percent limit.

concern to some Americans.[3] One resolution to this conundrum is official development assistance (ODA): there is virtual consensus on both sides of the Pacific that Japan should assume greater global responsibility by substantially expanding its economic assistance to the Third World.[4]

The "foreign aid solution" to the free rider problem, however, has created a new quandary and concern: some Americans are now complaining that Japan is creating a new "coprosperity sphere" in Pacific Asia, with official aid driving private trade and investment. The accusation now is that Japan is providing aid primarily to promote its trade and investment interests in Pacific Asia, and not so much to meet the developmental needs of the recipient countries.[5]

This paper reviews the evidence and concludes that there is little basis for singling out Japan's behavior as globally irresponsible and mercantilist and regionally neocolonialist. Section 8.2 critically reviews the popular concepts of burdensharing and military free ride, and questions the notion that the U.S. national defense is an international public good. Section 8.3 presents an empirical assessment of the view that Japan engages in unfair aid practices (provides low-quality aid) and aid mercantilism (gives aid to serve its own commercial and trade interests) in Pacific Asia and elsewhere. Section 8.4 looks at additional evidence to assess the thesis that Tokyo is implementing an official aid

---

3. Johnson (1986) sums it up as a Japanese defense dilemma: "Fear of revived militarism, then, constitutes the first horn of the Japanese defense dilemma. The other horn of the dilemma is, of course, the persistent charge that Japan is taking a free ride on the backs of the Americans, Koreans, Taiwanese, and all the other peoples of the Pacific Basin who take seriously their responsibilities to try to maintain a stable and secure environment. This free ride is doubly galling since no nation profits more from international political and military security than does Japan." See also Yamamura (1989), Hellmann (1989), and Brown (1987).

4. Balassa and Noland (1988, 188) suggest this resolution: "Japan could increase its defense capabilities by building up its conventional forces, naval strength, and air defenses. Japan would still rely on the United States for nuclear protection and for the defense of distant interests and would thus remain a significant free rider in defense matters. The government could partially offset that, however, by increasing its financial assistance to developing countries." See also Kissinger and Vance (1988), McNamara (1992), Robinson (1986), Peterson (1987), Okita (1989, 1986), Murakami and Kosai (1986), Nakasone (1986), Takeshita (1991), and Kaifu (1989).

5. See, for example, Arase (1991, 1988), Harrison (1991), Maidment (1989), Brown (1991), and Garten (1989–90, 95). Two chapters in this volume also propound this thesis: Katzenstein and Rouse (chap. 6) and Doner (chap. 5). For example, Katzenstein and Rouse write: "In January 1987 MITI unveiled in Bangkok a program known as the New Aid Plan, dealing specifically with the issue of infrastructural difficulties in Asia and their relation to the developmental needs of Japanese industry and the restructuring of the Japanese economy in general. . . . The program is an attempt to relocate selected Japanese businesses to Southeast Asia through loans and technical assistance to governments. These loans will be used for the improvement of infrastructure, including industrial estates, ports, and improved telecommunication services. . . . MITI, the Overseas Economic Cooperation Fund (OECF), and the Ministry for Foreign Affairs, are attempting . . . to coordinate different aspects of this plan, the details of which are negotiated bilaterally with each government." Rich Doner says: "One of its [the New Aid Plan's] goals was to facilitate Japanese domestic restructuring. The other was to provide assistance to export-oriented industries in developing Asia, including help in targeting particular sectors for development. These may be part of MITI's efforts to extend its industrial planning and coordination activities into foreign economies in response to the expansion of Japanese FI and the lack of coherent industrial policies in host countries (Wade 1992, 290)."

plan to create a new coprosperity sphere—a regional economy in East Asia to serve Japan's economic interests. Section 8.5 examines the dynamics of United States–Japan cooperation and conflict in the Philippines and the Asian Development Bank (ADB) to further address the issue of Japan's free-riding behavior and its strategy for gaining regional hegemony with mercantilist means. Section 8.6 summarizes the key conclusions.

8.2 Burdensharing and Japan's Free Ride: Is U.S. Defense Spending an International Public Good?

Burdensharing and military (security) free ride are intimately related concepts. An ally that fails to bear its "fair share" of common defense burden, by definition, is enjoying a military free ride. (A country's burden is typically measured by its share of military spending in its GNP). When Americans first coined these terms, this burden referred to that of common defense of the members of NATO against a possible attack from the Soviet Union, and the security free riders were America's underburdened European allies.[6] By the late 1960s, Japan joined the ranks of free riders as it began to catch up with the West and posed a growing competitive challenge to American supremacy in manufacturing. During the 1980s, Japan emerged as the top "unfair burdensharer" as it transformed into an economic, financial, and technological superpower and threatened America's supremacy in high finance and high technology. Meanwhile, the United States maintained economic growth and rising living standards by borrowing huge sums from overseas—a large chunk of it from Japan—and turned almost overnight into "the world's largest debtor nation."[7] Consequently, the perception heightened that Japan had taken a free ride to economic supremacy at the expense of America, which is lying flat on its back under the burden of defending its economic adversaries.[8]

Japan, however, posed a unique conundrum to the applicability of the concept of burdensharing. Having renounced war and aggression in its 1947 "peace constitution" after massive death and destruction and a humiliating defeat in World War II, in 1976 Japan decided to limit its military (self-defense) spending to 1 percent of GNP. This nonaggressive military posture enjoys immense support within Japan and abroad. With the United States devoting 5–6 percent of its GNP to maintain its military superpower status, there is thus only one way Japan can eliminate its "defense burden deficit" and stop free riding: by increasing its defense spending by 4–5 percent of GNP. While Japan has continued to increase host nation support for U.S. military bases, has extended its defense responsibility over sea-lanes to a distance of 1,000 nautical miles,

---

6. See, for example, Bull (1964) and Pincus (1962).

7. For a detailed analysis of the causes and consequences of America's debtor status, see Islam (1988).

8. This perception appears partly to explain the popularity of "the imperial overstretch" thesis advanced by Paul Kennedy (1987).

and is now participating physically in the United Nations peacekeeping force, it has long been considered virtually impossible for Japan to increase its defense spending three- to fourfold. This is because neither the American security experts, nor the Japanese people, nor Japan's Asian neighbors think that rearming the rising sun even to a modest degree for the sake of fairer burdensharing will enhance global peace and security.

This paradox by the late 1970s led to a reformulation of the goal: how to reduce Japan's free ride without rearming it into a military-nuclear superpower. More recently, this reformulation has led to a redefinition of the global security burden: the burden now is not confined to military spending alone, but includes other "international public goods," items such as development assistance, alleviation of the Third World debt problem, international peacekeeping, preservation of the environment, the fight against international terrorism and drug trafficking, prevention of international transmission of communicable disease, and so on.[9]

Thus the reconstructed concept of burdensharing (or responsibility sharing, as more balanced and sophisticated observers correctly rephrase it[10]) envisions a division of labor in global roles. In this "new world order," the United States will continue to provide a security umbrella to Japan and other allies by carrying "the burden of being the world's only military superpower," and Japan will try to match the costs of maintaining the downsized but still massive American military machine by spending huge sums on development assistance and other international public goods. Incidentally, the Gulf War appears to have broadened the scope of burdensharing/responsibility sharing even further: now the presumption seems to be that if the United States fights a war, especially with a seal of approval from the United Nations Security Council, then Japan has a perfect one-shot opportunity to temporarily reduce its free ride by picking up a large share of America's war expenses. In other words, Japan in this post–Cold War, post–Gulf War world is to bear its fair share of the burden by paying for not only nonmilitary international public goods, but also wars that the United States decides to wage to selectively defend freedom and democracy.

Many advocates of burdensharing seem to rest their case on essentially three propositions: (1) America's relative economic decline and Japan's economic prosperity are rooted in Japan's security free ride under U.S. protection. (2) U.S. national defense spending is an international public good in the context of not only NATO, but also the 1960 United States–Japan mutual coopera-

9. See McNamara (1992) and Peterson (1987).

10. Burdensharing, by construction, is a one-sided concept: it focuses solely on a hegemonic nation's financial and human cost of assuming leadership of a collective security arrangement, and ignores the power, privilege, and prestige that comes with it. By contrast, responsibility sharing is a more balanced concept because it recognizes the positive correlation between burden and power; that is, greater burdensharing will result in greater power sharing. The adherents of the burdensharing school appear to avoid the issue of power sharing.

tion and security treaty. (3) Japanese ODA is also an international public good and is highly substitutable for Japanese and American defense spending. The rest of this section argues that these presumptions rest on faulty foundations.

The central argument supporting the first proposition runs as follows: while the United States devotes a disproportionately high share of national resources to military spending and thereby weakens its global competitive position by diverting resources away from productive investments, Japan, protected by the U.S. security umbrella, spends little on defense and devotes freed-up resources to improving economic competitiveness, and thereby beats hands down its military protector in the international marketplace (see Harrison and Prestowitz 1990).

While this is not the place to settle this debate, I would simply stress that the alleged negative security-economics linkage has little empirical grounding; it is simply another example of the fallacy *post hoc, ergo propter hoc*. The proponents of this linkage are fully satisfied with the prima facie evidence that high-defense America appears to be losing its competitive edge to low-defense Japan. One wonders whether they really believe that if Japan spent 6–7 percent of its GNP on defense in the postwar period, it would have failed to catch up with the West and to attain its legendary manufacturing prowess. One can just as easily argue the opposite: with a high proportion of resources devoted to defense, Japan would have not only become an economic superpower; it could have also achieved what it does not have today—supremacy in military technology and in other areas where this technology and the associated R&D spending have spillover effects (aviation, for example). The proponents also seem to forget that the United States reached new economic heights in the wake of two world wars while it devoted a much larger share of its GNP to military spending. During the 1950s and 1960s, the United States reached the peak of its economic supremacy; these were also the years when the nation assumed a much larger burden of defense as compared to the last two decades.[11]

Looking around the Pacific, three out of the four so-called Asian dragons—Taiwan, Singapore, and South Korea—devote a much larger proportion of GNP to defense than does Japan. (Hong Kong is a British colony where the resource allocation statistics are either unavailable or messy and difficult to interpret.) If high defense spending did not stop Taiwan—a small island with no history of past glory and power—from achieving economic prosperity, one may wonder why it should have stopped Japan—the only Asian country to have approached the level of industrial development of the Western nations before World War I—from emerging as an economic superpower. Having

---

11. One can argue that the economic ills of the 1970s and 1980s are precisely the lagged effects of excessive defense spending of the earlier decades—effects of diverting scarce resources to fight the Korean War, the Vietnam War, and above all the Cold War. The available econometric and other empirical analyses offer mixed answers. For an analysis that does not support the above thesis, see Weidenbaum (1968).

committed the sin of engaging in causal empiricism, let me absolve myself by referring to the higher authorities: the large and growing empirical literature on the subject turns up mixed evidence—there is no clear-cut linkage between a country's defense spending and its economic performance.[12] A country's saving rate and other characteristics may influence this linkage significantly. In the case of Japan, at least one study found little evidence of the free ride contributing to its economic prosperity (Okimoto 1982). Thus it does not appear that America made a mistake by providing Japan military protection—even without it, Japan would likely have emerged as an economic superpower. Indeed, those who fear Japan's militarism may wish to find comfort in that the free ride has kept Japan from becoming a military superpower, and is likely to keep it from challenging America's preeminence in the military sphere over the foreseeable future.

The second presumption that the U.S. and the Japanese defense contributions to the United States–Japan security treaty can be interpreted as *international public goods* is fraught with a series of questionable assumptions.[13] To begin with, it is difficult to statistically determine how much of the U.S. national defense expenditure (and the Japanese national defense expenditure) is a contribution to the United States–Japan security treaty (or the United States–Japan alliance, to use a term favored in the 1980s), and how much is not. Some observers implicitly assume both countries' total national defense expenditures (America's 5–6 percent of GNP defense burden and Japan's 1 percent burden) to be their contributions to the alliance, while others view the estimated costs of the U.S. military presence in Japan (or in the Pacific) as America's burden of defending Japan. Analytically the more significant issue, however, is that a hegemonic nation's international commitments cannot be neatly separated from its national interest: America's financial and human costs of assuming leadership of a collective security arrangement (NATO, the United States–Japan security treaty, and so on) are precisely what bring it various economic, political, and psychic benefits. In other words, the burden that the United States seems increasingly unwilling—and apparently unable—to bear is the burden of being the superpower: this burden forms the basis of America's global power, prestige, and privilege.

In the language of the theory of public goods, U.S. national defense at the international level is thus at best a *mixed good* with a dominant private good

12. See, for example, Benoit (1973, 1978), Deger and Sen (1990), Faini, Annez, and Taylor (1984), and Kaldor (1978).

13. Olson and Zeckhauser (1966) did the seminal work where they analyzed common defense within an alliance as a public or collective good. Murakami and Kosai (1986, 34), among others, extended the concept of international public goods beyond common defense. More recently, Balassa and Noland (1988, 173) applied the concept of international public good to U.S. and Japanese expenditures on defense and foreign aid: "The responsibilities of world leadership require Japan to take a more active role in the collective management system and in the provision of international public goods. In this chapter, we have examined two potential areas for action—military security and assistance to developing countries."

feature. Put another way, defense produces joint products—these may include anything from positive economic spillovers of military R&D spending to the ability to use the military to serve nonalliance national security objectives— that are not, or only partly, appropriable by the members of the alliance.[14] In addition to this obvious mixed good characteristic of defense in the alliance, three other shortcomings of interpreting the U.S. or Japanese defense spending as international public goods are worth stressing. First, the widely accepted notion that defense at the national level is a pure public good is only partly accurate. For example, while the deterrence resulting from national defense can be viewed as a pure public good because it meets the *nonrivalness* and *nonexclusion* criteria,[15] the same cannot be said about defense when deterrence fails. This is because the instruments of defense will not protect all communities and all regions within the country in the same way, thus failing the non-rivalness criterion.[16]

Second, the public good characteristic of defense when it is a contribution to an alliance such as NATO becomes even more diluted. Deterrence passes the nonrivalness test, but not the nonexclusion test, as one leading member (say, the United States) can lower its deterrence for a particular ally (say, France) by eroding the credibility of defense for that ally. If deterrence fails and an attack ensues, neither criterion of a pure public good is met. The defense in the wake of an attack from the common enemy fails the nonrivalness test as more attention to the security of its own citizens may prevent a member (say, the United States) from providing the same degree of protection to its NATO allies. It also fails the nonexclusion criterion. For example, the United States may give itself more protection than its European allies.

Finally, the international public good feature of common defense is further diminished when it to comes to the United States–Japan security treaty. For one, the treaty appears to have incorporated two separate objectives: to defend against the common enemy, the Soviet Union; and to ensure that Japan did not become a military and nuclear superpower. In other words, part of the agreement was actually to ensure that one ally remained the military and nuclear superpower by spending a lot on defense while the other one maintained limited national defense capability by spending much less. Put another way, Japan's "military free ride" was a mutually agreed-upon component of the treaty because both parties saw it as serving their own national interests.

While this mutually beneficial bargain is not explicitly stated in the treaty,

---

14. Olson and Zeckhauser (1966, 272) recognize this: "Another assumption in the model developed in the foregoing section was that the military forces in an alliance provide only the collective benefit of alliance security, when in fact they also provide purely national, non-collective benefits to the nations that maintain them."

15. *Nonrivalness* refers to the fact that one can consume a public good without reducing the amount consumed by others. *Nonexclusion* means one cannot prevent others from consuming a public good even if they do not pay for it. See Samuelson (1954) and Head (1962).

16. This paragraph and the next draw heavily on De Strihou (1967).

it is implicitly referred to in Article 3, with a mention of constitutional provisions: "The Parties, individually and in cooperation with each other, by
means of continuous and effective self-help and mutual aid will maintain and
develop, subject to their constitutional provisions, their capacities to resist and
attack." The significance of this seemingly innocuous reference to "constitutional provisions" becomes clear when one recalls chapter 2 of Japan's constitution.

> Aspiring sincerely to an international peace based on justice and order, the
> Japanese people forever renounce war as a sovereign right of the nation and
> the threat or use of force as a means of settling international disputes.
>   In order to accomplish the aim of the preceding paragraph, land, sea and
> air forces, as well as other war potential, will never be maintained. The right
> of belligerency of the state will not be recognized.

One interpretation of this treaty could be that the United States agreed to
provide Japan a mixed good in exchange for a limit on Japan's provision of a
mixed good. Moreover, both the United States and Japan (and many of Japan's
Asian neighbors) continue to view a substantially enlarged Japanese defense
capability as an "international public *bad*." Clearly many security experts believe that if one of the parties pulls out of this treaty—especially in the context
of deteriorating bilateral relations—Japan will sharply increase its defense expenditure, starting an arms race in the region, and perhaps inducing the United
States to respond by spending more. This brings out another interesting point:
in the absence of an alliance, national defense of individual countries can be
interpreted as partly an international public bad.[17] The central point, however,
is that Japan's low defense spending cannot be interpreted as a free ride, because both the United States and Japan appear to believe it to be in their national interest to limit Japan's military spending, as both view significantly increased Japanese defense spending as an international public bad.

The end of the Cold War does not invalidate the above arguments. With the
disappearance of the Soviet Union as the common enemy, NATO as well as
the United States–Japan alliance now face more than one "common enemy"—
they are multidimensional, diffuse, and unpredictable (for example, future ethnic wars within a nation or regional conflicts between two erstwhile friendly
countries). All of this only weakens the argument that Japan is a free rider, as
the face of the common enemy becomes fuzzier and mutual need for containing a rise of militarism in Japan becomes greater.

Finally, the GNP-share-based methodology to measure the burden and deter-

---

17. This interpretation follows directly from the theory of externalities: without cooperation or
public intervention, a public bad (pollution) will be overproduced. Olson and Zeckhauser (1966,
272) mention this result without any reference to defense as a public bad: "Allied nations may be
suspicious of one another, even as they cooperate in the achievement of common purposes, and
may enlarge their military forces because of conceivable future conflicts."

mine the bilateral burden imbalance assumes that defense and foreign aid—of the United States and of Japan—are all *highly substitutable* international public goods. This is again a dubious assumption. Applying reasons already advanced, one can see that the case for ODA as an international public good is even weaker: the political credit goes to Japan—and not to other donors— and both the nonrivalness and nonexclusion criteria fail even more clearly. For example, Tokyo's aid to Thailand does not confer on the United States the same economic benefits as it does on Japan (nonrivalness fails), and Japan can partially exclude the United States from benefits of its foreign aid to Thailand (nonexclusion fails). ODA is thus a mixed good where its private good feature seems dominant.

The practical problem arises from the way many observers treat U.S. defense spending and Japanese aid spending as perfect substitutes—a clearly invalid presumption. When it comes to measuring a country's burden, the share of GNP devoted to military spending is added to that devoted to other international public goods.

Typically, the basket of other international public goods is reduced to one good—ODA (McNamara 1992; Kosminsky and Fischer 1989; Pharr 1988; WIDER 1987). Thus the burden is often measured by adding the share of GNP spent on development aid to that spend on defense. Yamamura (1989, 229) sums up this approach succinctly: "The logical and realistic course for Japan is to increase its 'sacrifice' by sharply increasing its nonmilitary contributions to the alliance and to world peace—that is, by increasing its official development assistance (ODA)." Robinson (1986, 8) presents his burden calculations as follows: "Japan could make a commitment sufficiently large that the world would have to take notice. How large? Well, what about $60 billion a year? Where did I get this figure? The United States spends about 6.5 percent of its GNP on defense and foreign aid. Japan spends about 1.5 percent of its GNP— 5 percent less. Five percent of Japan's $1.2 trillion GNP comes to $60 billion, or roughly ¥11 trillion."

Making no distinction between one country's military spending and another's foreign aid spending, and the using combined spending on military and foreign aid as the measure of the burden, however, appears to make little economic, political, or even moral sense. For example, such an approach implies that if America decides to spend 1 percent of its GNP on "Star Wars," then Japan is being a selfish free rider if it does not follow by allocating 1 percent of its GNP to development assistance. Or that if the United States spends 5 percent of its GNP on defense and Japan spends only 1 percent, then the goal of fair burdensharing dictates that Japan spend 3–4 percent of its GNP on foreign aid or be doomed to the status of a free rider. In this view, the overriding objective is for Japan to spend some x percent of its GNP on some nonmilitary items; who gets the money and how it is used are less important. The following line of reasoning advanced by one prominent observer of United States–Japan relations, Yamamura (1989, 231), is widely shared:

Another reason to argue that even Takeshita's seemingly ambitious goal for ODA in the 1988–1992 period is inadequate is that Japan's military expenditure and ODA will remain significantly less than those of its Western allies (except Canada), which spend 4 to 6 percent of GNP for defense in addition to ODA. . . . Therefore, if Japan provides ODA of $10 billion per year as projected by the Takeshita proposal, it is still likely to be criticized by its allies for failing to do its share. Given its GNP of nearly $2.5 trillion, ODA equivalent to 1 percent of Japan's GNP (the amount needed to bring the sum of the defense expenditure and ODA to 3 percent) would be $25 billion. This suggests that, even allowing for a steady increase in Japan's military expenditure, many in the Western alliance are justified in demanding that Japan not only maintain the current pace of increase in its defense expenditures but also increase its ODA and other international contributions substantially as soon as possible from the projected level of $10 billion to about $25 billion per year.

The central point of this section is not to question the need for Japan to assume greater global responsibilities; it is to challenge the conventional premise and modalities for doing so. Japan should play a greater global role, but not because it should pick up a fair share of its burden by compensating for its military free ride. There is a much more simple and compelling reason: Japan is a global economic superpower, and despite recent progress its global commitments and obligations still fall far short of its capacity for undertaking global responsibilities. Since Japan is a nonnuclear pacifist power, and so far the international community on balance prefers it remain so, it seems sensible that Japan make contributions in nonmilitary areas by addressing the problems of poverty, economic underdevelopment, natural disasters, environmental degradation, and other transnational "common enemies."[18]

While both U.S. and Japanese political leaders are increasingly using the term "global partnership" to characterize the bilateral relationship, an adequate and satisfactory elaboration of what this term means still seems to be lacking. In my view, the concept of global partnership or "collective responsibility sharing," if properly defined and applied, can effectively deal with an increasingly unsustainable global imbalance causing much of the bilateral friction—the imbalance between monetary might and military muscle of the world's top two economic superpowers. A credible exercise of hegemonic leadership requires both monetary might and military muscle. As the Gulf War has demonstrated, if a superpower assumes the burden of flexing its military muscle but lacks the monetary means, it runs the risk of becoming the world's police-for-hire; similarly, if an economic and financial superpower unburdened with military

18. In response to the U.S. pressure—intensified during the Gulf War—for sweat and blood in addition to money, Japan has also begun to participate in the United Nations peacekeeping force. Future historians may look back at this development as a first step toward Japan's rearmament. The historical irony is that the country—the United States—that helped Japan embrace pacifism after World War II is the one that may turn out to be responsible for pushing Japan to break out of it half a century later.

prowess tries to help with money alone, it risks becoming a push-button cash dispenser.

The principle of global partnership reduces these risks arising from this monetary-military imbalance. While burdensharing assumes that America is selflessly carrying the burden of defending freedom and peace, and that it is only fair that its allies share it (through military and monetary means), global partnership rests on the premise that promoting global peace and prosperity is the collective responsibility of the leading nations, and that they should exercise joint leadership within a multilateral framework and contribute jointly according to their respective national advantages.

The underlying assumption here is that promoting global peace and prosperity is a responsibility—it is a burden as well as a source of power and influence—and that since the world is dominated by a group of major powers, this responsibility has to be shared, although not necessarily equally. Nations with greater economic, military, and leadership capacity may shoulder more of the responsibility and consequently may project more power and influence. For example, with a chronic shortage of financial resources the United States is no longer the supreme superpower it was in the 1950s, but it is still the only nation on earth that is both an economic and a military superpower. In other words, America is first among equals and thus is still the only power capable of being the leading, or senior, partner of a global partnership—or the largest "shareholder" of collective responsibility.

The principle of global partnership thus implies that mechanical formulas involving dollar figures and GNP shares may not be the way to determine Japan's monetary and other contributions to the global community; the nature and the magnitude of Japan's contributions should be assessed on a case-by-case basis depending on the needs in a particular area relative to Japan's capacity in meeting them. It also implies that America's unilateralist instinct in dominating multilateral organizations should be contained; the tendency to hold on to political power while prodding Japan to shoulder the ever-growing financial burden only erodes the credibility of American leadership and subverts the emergence of a true United States–Japan global partnership or of a new world order promoting peace and prosperity.[19]

8.3   How Unfair and Mercantilist Is Japanese Aid to Pacific Asia?

Many of America's Japan experts believe that Japan provides low-quality aid primarily to meet its own commercial needs. For example, Hellmann (1989, 262) asserts: "Roughly 70 percent of aid is tied—in fact, if not formally—to the Japanese economy." Pharr (1992, 18) says: "In all these [quality of aid, grant element, terms, and portion of grant to loan aid] areas, Japan repeatedly has been found wanting in OECD reviews"; however, she adds that

19. For more details on the concept of global partnership, see Islam (1991, 216–24).

"Japan is committed to making improvements."[20] Indeed, the view that Japan gives aid to serve its own narrow economic interests constitutes an important bridge between the theme of global free ride and that of an East Asia co-prosperity sphere. The purpose of this section is to see whether this bridge can take the weight of empirical evidence.

It is useful to classify the myriad criticisms of Japanese development aid into two broad categories: unfair aid practices and aid mercantilism. I focus on two specific criticisms under the category of *unfair aid practices* (low aid quality): the share of grants in total ODA is too low, and the loans are not concessional enough; and too little aid goes to support "basic human needs" of the poorest of the poor (too much goes to finance economic infrastructure). While overlapping indirectly with unfair aid practices, *aid mercantilism* subsumes the following specific criticisms: Japan makes extensive use of *tied aid* (limits aid money to procurement from Japan) and *mixed credits* (subsidizes sales of Japanese goods by spicing up export credits with concessional developmental loans) to boost exports; and it promotes Japanese high-technology sales with excessive focus on capital projects and physical infrastructure.

Before trying to assess the empirical validity of these criticisms for Pacific Asia, it may be useful to address the criticism that Japan gives too little aid (low aid quantity) and most of it goes to Asia (inequitable geographical distribution) (Pharr 1988; Bloch 1991, 76). Table 8.1 reports the relevant aid data for the Group of Seven (G-7) countries. On aid volume, three points are worth emphasizing. First, while in nominal dollar terms Japan replaced the United States as the top donor nation in 1989 for the first time in the "history of ODA" (ODA is a post–World War II phenomenon with a very short history) before returning to the number two position in 1990, it had to provide only 0.31 percent of GNP to accomplish this feat. That is because the United States spent only 0.15 percent of its GNP on ODA in 1989 and was able to recapture its traditional top donor position in 1990 with a 0.21 percent of aid-to-GNP ratio. While 0.31 percent of GNP looks pitifully small, Japan should not be singled out for being "stingy": in 1990, two (the United States and the United Kingdom) of the other six major countries did worse, and one (Italy) did about the same. To put it the other way, only half of the other six did modestly better. Indeed, Japan's 0.31 percent of GNP contribution was only 0.04 percent less than the Development Assistance Committee (DAC) average of 0.35 percent. The issue here is not to argue that these numbers are necessarily adequate, but to point out that Japan is not behaving particularly differently from the other G-7 countries.

The comparison with the Nordic countries that contribute a much higher percentage of GNP to ODA is misleading because it ignores the enormous difference in economic size. For example, Norway contributes more than 1

---

20. See also Pharr (1988), Pyle (1989), and Preeg (1989b). Yamamura's (1989, 230) comment is typical: "Japanese ODA has been known for both its high proportion of tied loans and the high interest rates it charges."

Table 8.1   **G-7 Countries, ODA Disbursements and Geographical Distribution**

| | Net Disbursements | | | | Bilateral ODA: % of Gross Disbursements | | | | | | | | | |
| | $ million | | % of GNP | | Sub-Saharan Africa | | South Asia | | Other Asia and Oceania | | Middle East and North Africa[a] | | Latin America and Caribbean | |
	1989	1990	1989	1990	79/80	89/90	79/80	89/90	79/80	89/90	79/80	89/90	79/80	89/90
Japan	8,965	9,069	0.31	0.31	10.4	13.5	32.6	16.9	41.3	52.5	8.6	8.8	7.1	8.2
United States[b]	7,676	11,366	0.15	0.21	12.7	14.0	11.8	10.3	10.1	7.1	54.4	48.2	11.0	20.5
Germany	4,948	6,320	0.41	0.42	32.5	36.4	20.9	12.3	7.2	13.6	29.6	26.2	9.8	11.4
France[c]	5,162	6,571	0.54	0.55	45.2	54.3	2.0	2.7	14.4	14.0	13.0	9.7	25.3	19.2
United Kingdom	2,587	2,647	0.31	0.27	36.3	50.5	40.7	26.7	9.4	10.5	6.8	4.5	6.8	7.8
Italy	3,613	3,395	0.42	0.32	54.1	55.9	3.1	4.4	10.4	6.0	21.2	13.5	11.3	19.9
Canada	2,320	2,470	0.44	0.44	41.1	53.4	35.3	14.1	4.9	12.0	7.6	6.7	11.1	13.9
Total DAC	46,712	54,077	0.34	0.35	29.2	34.3	18.4	11.8	16.7	21.2	22.9	18.4	12.9	14.5

Source: OECD (1991a).

[a]Includes small amounts of ODA to southern Europe.

[b]For 1990, includes forgiveness of non-ODA military debt of $1.2 billion.

[c]Excludes net ODA flows to the Overseas Departments and Territories (DOM/TOM).

percent in GNP, but in 1989 it came to less than $1 billion; that year Japan's GNP was more than thirty times that of Norway. If Japan's net disbursement of ODA were 1 percent of GNP in 1989, it would have provided $30 billion. That sum is equal to the two-thirds of the 1989 total net DAC disbursement. It is not clear how Japan could have effectively disbursed such a huge volume of aid.

Second, while avoiding a formal commitment to reach the United Nations target of 0.7 percent of GNP within a specified period of time, Japan pledged to "improve steadily the ratio of its ODA to GNP" in its Fourth Medium-Term Target of ODA announced in June 1988 (OECD 1991, 12; Ministry of Foreign Affairs 1990, 155). By contrast, the United States has rejected such a target and has made no commitment to increase its ODA/GNP ratio. Given the domestic political and administrative constrains as well as the limited—and slowly expansive—absorptive capacity of the recipient countries, it seemed until recently that Japan would be unable to raise its aid/GNP ratio substantially in the near future. With rising demand for official resources in some new areas—especially environmental challenge in the Third World, opening up of Indochina, and economic reform and development of nations (old and new) in central and eastern Europe and the former Soviet Union—a window of opportunity has, however, opened for Japan to increase its contribution rapidly through bilateral as well as multilateral channels.

Finally, without denying the role of additional external resources in promoting growth and development in the Third World, the important issue is not how to reach a magic quantitative target for aid: it is how to use the money effectively to promote equitable, environment-friendly, and self-sustaining development. Excessive focus on who gives what percentage of GNP can distract one from the real goal, which is how to employ foreign assistance as an effective catalyst in the development process and help the developing countries to help themselves. This point is particularly important in view of the fact that ODA so far seems to have been more successful in creating a growing ghetto of aid-addicted dependencies rather than in assisting countries to "graduate" and take off on a path of sustainable development (Lele and Nabi 1990; OECD 1985; World Bank 1990, 127–37).

Two observations are in order with regard to the criticism that Japanese aid is excessively concentrated in Asia. First, it is true that almost 70 percent of Japanese aid goes to Asia. But the intra-Asia distribution has changed dramatically during the 1980s—there has been a shift away from South Asia toward Southeast Asia and China. For example, while the share of Japanese aid going to South Asia has dropped from 33 percent in 1979/80 to 17 percent in 1989/90, the share going to "other Asia and Oceania" (largely Southeast Asia and China) has risen from 41 percent to 53 percent (table 8.1). Before one jumps to the conclusion that Japan is diverting resources from poor South Asia to richer and getting-even-richer Southeast Asia to serve its own economic and commercial interests, it should be noted that the absolute dollar volume of Japanese aid to South Asia has actually risen, although not sharply. The share shift has largely occurred due to a sharp rise in Japanese net aid disbursements to two countries: China and the Philippines (table 8.2). While Indonesia has remained the number-one recipient of Japanese aid, its share has actually declined over the 1980s. These countries are where much of the poor—not only of Asia, but of the world—live. This is one reason why despite this shift to the east from the south within Asia, Japanese share of aid to the least-developed countries has actually increased during the 1980s (table 8.6). It is also noteworthy that the increase in Japanese aid to the Philippines has been very much in response to the U.S. request for support of the military bases there and to the overall American (and Japanese) security interests in Pacific Asia. Increased aid to China reflects U.S.-Japanese interests in fostering market reforms there as well as the Japanese goal of improving relations with Beijing. And it is essentially a continuation of an old policy to expand dollar volume aid to Indonesia, the poorest and most populous country in Southeast Asia, where Japan's energy policy interests mesh well with its developmental goals.

Second, there is no economic logic why a donor should distribute its ODA more or less equally among various geographical *regions* of the world. An appeal for a better balance in distribution in terms of *sectors* (say, physical infrastructure versus basic human needs), or *income levels* (middle-income versus low-income countries), or *allocation channels* (bilateral versus multilateral) is at least more compelling, though not necessarily convincing. On geographical distribution, however, one can sensibly reason that bilateral aid is likely to be more effective if it is allocated in areas with which the donor country has close historical, political, and economic relationships, and where it is more familiar with and knowledgeable about the nature of local institutions, values, and attitudes. Indeed, this is the norm among the major donor countries: the British and the French allocate most of their bilateral aid to their former colonies. Once again Japan is no different in this respect, except that none of its major aid recipients is its former colony, although Japan had colonial ambitions toward some of them before the Second World War.

Interestingly, the United States is the outlier here whose security interests dominate its regional and country allocation of aid (table 8.1). Almost half of U.S. aid goes to the Middle East and North Africa, with 30 percent allocated to two countries out of political/security motivations: in 1989/90, 17 percent of its aid was allocated to Egypt and 12 percent to Israel (a high-income country with the 1989 per capita income of $9,790). While the share of those two countries in U.S. aid has declined, in 1989/90, they received more economic aid than all countries of Latin America and the Caribbean combined (20.5 percent).

Having questioned the economic logic of criticizing Japanese aid's Asian concentration, it is useful to point out that Japan is poised to become the world's top donor nation and remain so over the foreseeable future. That means the geographical distribution of Japan's aid can no longer be dictated by economic logic alone: political, security, and other considerations will begin to

Table 8.2 Net Disbursements of ODA to Asia, Japan and the United States (millions of U.S. dollars)

	Japan							United States						
	1980	1985	1986	1987	1988	1989	1990	1980	1985	1986	1987	1988	1989	1990
NIE	81	5	3	20	27	56	49	13	−24	−28	−26	−30	−39	34
South Korea	76	−4	−14	7	13	41	50	21	−19	−23	−22	−26	34	−31
Taiwan	0	0	0	0	0	0	0	−8	−5	−5	−5	−5	6	5
Hong Kong	1	1	2	3	3	4	9	0	0	0	0	0	0	0
Singapore	4	8	15	11	11	11	−10	0	0	0	1	1	1	2
ASEAN-Four	700	791	897	1,666	1,905	2,118	2,308	184	202	444	289	164	253	309
Indonesia	350	161	161	707	985	1,145	868	117	43	46	36	22	31	31
Malaysia	66	126	38	276	25	80	373	1	0	−1	0	−1	−1	0
Philippines	94	240	438	379	535	404	648	50	135	367	230	121	192	248
Thailand	190	264	260	302	361	489	419	16	24	32	23	22	31	30
South Asia	587	525	1,066	1,132	1,346	1,139	947	362	452	542	341	616	529	405
India	37	22	227	304	180	257	87	83	29	49	39	91	69	24
Bangladesh	215	122	249	334	342	371	374	174	165	146	146	120	138	169
Pakistan	112	93	152	127	302	178	194	42	144	194	90	339	263	167
Myanmar	153	154	244	172	260	71	61	0	8	9	11	10	2	1
Sri Lanka	45	84	127	118	200	185	176	55	85	127	35	41	43	75
Nepal	24	51	68	77	62	77	55	8	21	17	20	15	14	17
Indochina	4	8	11	14	17	23	18	0	1	1	3	5	7	7
Vietnam	4	1	6	0	5	2	1	0	1	1	1	1	2	2
Kampuchea	0	0	0	1	1	2	2	0	1	0	2	4	5	5
Laos	0	8	5	14	11	19	17	0	0	0	0	0	0	0
China	4	388	497	553	674	832	723	0	0	0	0	0	0	0
Grand total	1,375	1,717	2,440	3,385	3,968	4,168	4,045	559	631	959	607	755	750	687

Source: OECD (1992, 1991b, 1988, 1982).

shape Japan's national and regional aid allocation. This implies not only some equitable geographical distribution of Japanese aid, but also future shifts in the distribution within Asia and around the globe. For example, Indochina and central Asian republics of the former Soviet Union are likely to become increasingly important recipients of Japanese economic assistance, and some Latin American nations, say, Brazil and Mexico, may receive substantial environmental aid.

Having dealt with two global criticisms of Japanese aid, we can now turn to assessing the empirical validity—in Pacific Asia—of the criticisms summarized earlier. But before doing so, it would be useful to look at the evolution of Japanese and U.S. aid to the developing countries of Asia as a whole. Table 8.2 reports dollar figures for net disbursements of Japanese and American ODA to developing Asia. The numbers reveal several interesting facts. First, the much talked-about phenomenon of Japanese aid driving trade and investment in the four Asian NIEs—South Korea, Taiwan, Hong Kong, and Singapore—if present earlier, certainly ceased to exist by the 1980s. This is because since 1980 Japan has given little or no aid to these countries. Therefore, the oft-discussed aid-trade-investment linkages with Japan only apply to the four ASEAN countries and China. This is well known yet often forgotten in a broad discussion of these linkages in East or Pacific Asia.[21]

Second, as regards the rest of developing Asia, South Asia is the largest recipient of Japanese aid. Indochina receives very little at this moment, but given the recent Cambodian settlement and Vietnam's market reforms, this region can soon become a major absorber of Japanese development assistance.

Third, even the raw dollar figures on the destination of Japanese aid money seem to contradict the view that Japan's aid program is driven only by commercial motives. For example, until recently Japan had provided substantial sums of aid to Myanmar. This has a lot more to do with the history of Japan's relations with Myanmar than with profit motive of Japanese companies. Similarly, private business interests do not explain Japanese aid to Bangladesh; development and humanitarian considerations do.

Finally, the United States is no match for Japan when it comes to development aid in Asia. Among ASEAN countries, the Philippines is the only country to receive substantial U.S. aid, although it is still less than half of Japanese aid disbursement. South Asia is the only other region where the United States has a significant presence, but it also gets more than double the U.S. aid from Japan. A closer look reveals that Pakistan and Bangladesh account for the lion's share of U.S. aid to South Asia. In 1991, however, the United States suspended all aid to Pakistan. All this boils down to a striking observation: the United States provides nontrivial amounts of development assistance to only two

---

21. For example, Katzenstein and Rouse (chap. 6 in this volume) assert: "Japanese business and government elites view ASEAN (and the NICs) as one economy, requiring a comprehensive perspective on aid, trade, and investment. The provision of the necessary infrastructure . . . will serve the interests of Japanese companies and promote economic growth in Asia."

countries in Asia—the Philippines and Bangladesh. And both of these countries receive from Japan more than double what the United States provides.

Experts on United States–Japan relations often talk enthusiastically about the potential for United States–Japan aid cooperation in Pacific Asia (for example, CSIS 1991). One cannot help wondering, however, how Japan can cooperate with the United States in an area where the United States has little presence. With withdrawal of military bases, the Philippines may not even remain an exception for too long, as U.S. aid to that country is likely to dry up as well. With little U.S. aid going to Pacific Asia, United States–Japan aid cooperation in that region may remain alive only in conference rooms filled with United States–Japan relations experts.

The purpose of table 8.2 is partly to identify the major Asian recipients of Japanese development aid. The rest of this section will focus on those countries, namely, four ASEAN countries, five South Asian countries (India, Pakistan, Bangladesh, Sri Lanka, and Nepal), and China. Although this paper is concerned with Pacific Asia, the data on South Asia will serve as a point of reference and comparison, especially vis-à-vis the United States. Also, whenever possible, Japan's performance will be compared with that of the United States or that of the DAC donors, so that Japan's behavior is assessed not against an absolute standard but against the existing U.S. or international norm.

Table 8.3 reports Japanese and U.S. aid to ASEAN, South Asia, and China in shares of total ODA these countries receive from the DAC members. The data confirm the increasing dominance of Japan in the regions' aid arena, accompanied by a shrinking American role. As early as 1980, Japan dwarfed the United States as an aid donor to the region. For example, while Japan accounted for almost half of the DAC aid going to ASEAN countries, the U.S. share was only 15 percent. The gap widened by the end of the 1980s. The only exception is Pakistan, where the share of U.S. aid rose during the 1980s. But that reflected U.S. response to Soviet invasion of Afghanistan.

By the end of the 1980s, two-thirds of the DAC aid going to ASEAN came from Japan, while the U.S. share dropped below 10 percent. The Japanese aid share in South Asia rose one-third. The U.S. share in South Asia remained at about 15 percent, thanks to the temporary Afghanistan bonanza to Pakistan; the share of U.S. aid in every other country of South Asia fell. Finally, the Japanese share of aid to China rose from one-fifth to a peak of three-fourths in 1986, and has since declined to about a half by the end of the decade. It is worth noting that the United States does not give any aid to China.

With this preliminary review of the trend and pattern of Japanese and U.S. aid to Asia, we can now try to assess the specific criticisms of Japanese aid. Within the category of unfair aid practices, we begin with the criticism that the quality of Japanese development assistance is low because the share of grants in it is "too low" and ODA loans charge excessively high interest rates. For

Table 8.3   Net Disbursement of ODA to Asia, Japan and the United States (percentage of total net ODA from DAC countries)

	Japan							United States						
	1980	1985	1986	1987	1988	1989	1990	1980	1985	1986	1987	1988	1989	1990
ASEAN-Four	48	52	44	64	66	65	61	14	15	22	13	8	8	9
Indonesia	41	32	27	63	66	67	57	14	9	8	3	1	2	2
Malaysia	62	62	22	78	26	60	81	N.A.	N.A.	N.A.	N.A.	N.A.	N.A.	N.A.
Philippines	46	55	49	54	68	53	59	24	31	41	33	15	25	23
Thailand	62	69	67	69	70	74	57	5	6	8	5	4	5	4
South Asia														
India	6	4	22	32	19	23	12	13	6	5	4	10	6	3
Bangladesh	25	20	33	36	37	38	34	20	27	19	16	13	14	15
Pakistan	33	22	25	29	30	26	30	12	34	32	20	34	39	26
Sri Lanka	15	25	33	36	46	47	44	19	25	17	11	9	11	19
Nepal	29	41	40	41	28	31	23	10	17	10	11	7	6	7
China	19	68	75	64	56	56	51	0	0	0	0	0	0	0

Source: OECD (1992, 1991b, 1988, 1982).

N.A. = not applicable; zero or negligible.

example, according to Pyle (1989, 51), "The quality of aid has been low: Japan gave away less and lent more on tougher terms than most other donors."

Table 8.4 confirms that the share of grants in Japanese ODA is indeed low, although the country-specific shares vary a great deal from year to year. For example, the grant ratio for Indonesia was 17 percent in 1980, rose to 47 percent in 1985, declined to 13 percent in 1989, and rose to 19 percent in 1990. These variations, however, do not obscure the low grant shares: in 1990 the grant ratio was about 25 percent for ASEAN, 45 percent for South Asia and 30 percent for China. These figures contrast sharply with grant shares of 90 to 100 percent for other major donors, including the United States.

A sole focus on the *grant ratio,* however, is somewhat misleading. A better measure of the overall degree of concessionality of ODA is the average *grant element,* which takes into account the interest rate, grace period, and maturity of all loans. By definition, the grant element of a grant is 100 percent, whereas the grant element varies from loan to loan even for the same donor. Table 8.5 reports the average grant element of ODA for Japan, the United States, and the DAC countries as a group (unfortunately, similar data on the grant element for specific Asian countries are not available). Two points are worth highlighting. First, while the Japanese grant element is lower than that of the United States and the DAC countries, the difference is insignificant when it comes to the least-developed countries. In other words, Japan takes into account the income levels of the recipient countries in determining the concessionality of its aid across countries, and this is reflected in Japan's aid to the poorest countries, which is as concessional as aid provided by the United States and other donors.

Table 8.4   **Net disbursements of Japanese ODA Grants**

	Grants (millions of U.S. dollars)				Grant Ratio (% of Japan's Total ODA)			
	1980	1985	1989	1990	1980	1985	1989	1990
ASEAN-								
Four	178	287	586	552	25	36	28	24
Indonesia	59	76	147	167	17	47	13	19
Philippines	36	70	176	153	38	29	44	24
Thailand	70	117	205	172	37	44	42	41
South Asia	160	174	427	392	37	47	40	44
India	28	14	35	34	76	64	14	39
Bangladesh	53	62	152	152	25	51	41	41
Pakistan	29	43	89	68	26	46	50	35
Sri Lanka	30	14	94	91	67	17	51	52
Nepal	20	41	57	47	83	80	74	85
China	3	43	164	201	75	11	20	28
Total	341	504	1,177	1,145	30	33	29	29

Source: OECD (1992, 1991b, 1988, 1982).

Table 8.5   **Grant Element of ODA, 1989–90 (percentage)**

	Japan	United States	Total DAC
Grant element of			
total ODA	81.2	98.8	92.8
ODA loans	59.8	63.1	58.6
ODA to least-			
developed countries	96.8	98.9	97.8
Grant equivalent of			
ODA (% of GNP)	0.27	0.19	0.35

Source: OECD (1991a).

Notes: Grant element figures are based on ODA commitments data, excluding debt reorganization. Grant equivalent figures are calculated on a gross disbursement basis.

ªThe figure for total DAC excludes several member countries for which data are not available.

Second, while the grant equivalent of Japan's ODA in percentage of GNP is lower than that of the DAC countries as a group, it is higher than that of the United States. Put more simply, when all is said and done, Japan contributes a higher percentage of GNP to concessionality-adjusted aid than the United States does. The point once again is that, if the Japanese quantity of "quality-adjusted" aid is low relative to its economic capacity, that of the United States is even lower.

More important, the share of grants in total ODA or even the grant element per se says little about the quality of aid. Whether a particular project should be financed by grants or loans depends on the nature of the project. There is no reason why a commercially near-viable fertilizer factory should be financed by grants, and there is every reason to provide grants for a primary school or a health center. Also, given the differences in development requirements, a low-income country is likely to be a candidate for a higher share of grants than a middle-income country. The World Bank does not give any grants; that does not lower the quality of its aid. The quality of development assistance depends on its effectiveness in promoting self-sustaining development and not on some mechanical mix of grants and loans. If the leading bilateral donors believe grants are always better than loans, that does not make it necessarily right.

The preference for loans over grants in its development assistance program also reflects Japan's own growth experience as well as its development philosophy, that the most effective way to help countries to help themselves onto a path of sustainable development is not to get them addicted to an unending flow of foreign charity, but to pressure them to build up their productive capacity in a financially responsible way. This does not mean that the Japanese aid authorities believe that development assistance should be provided in terms of loans at market rates. They understand full well that the developing countries can boost their economic growth rates with the help of grants and concessional loans, as these foreign resources typically finance projects that private capital, foreign or domestic, will not touch (economic and social infrastructure—from roads and bridges to schools and hospitals), and yet are critical to promoting productive capacity and productivity. A case for concessional aid can also be made on the ground of low total factor productivity of developing countries, and in some situations, of raising consumption of basic necessities of the poor. As table 8.5 illustrates, Japan's aid program reflects these considerations. While one can question the appropriateness of loans for a particular project, or the mix of grants and loans for a particular country, there is little economics behind the view that the "quality" of loans is by definition lower than that of grants. Finally, Pyle's assertion notwithstanding, Japan does not lend on tough terms: in 1990, Japan's ODA loans carried an average interest rate of 2.5 percent (Ministry of Foreign Affairs 1991).

One of the more defensible global indicators of quality of aid is the proportion of aid allocated to the poorest countries. On this criterion, the quality of Japan's aid is higher than that of the United States. In 1988–89, Japan allocated 70 percent of its aid to low-income countries, whereas the United States gave them a little over 46 percent (table 8.6). Japan also gave more of its aid to the least-developed countries than the United States did (20 percent as opposed to 17 percent), but both countries fell below the DAC average of 25 percent. Given all the criticisms of Japanese *bilateral* aid, it is also noteworthy that Japan gives on average a greater share of aid to multilateral institutions than do the United States and the DAC countries.

The other major unfair aid practice Japan is accused of is that it spends too much aid money on economic infrastructure and large industrial projects, and not enough on social infrastructure and "basic human needs" (BHN). Detailed data to adequately assess this criticism in the case of Pacific Asia are not available. However, the 1989 data on sectoral distribution of aid put together by the DAC can throw some light (table 8.7). First, the proportion of its total ODA (18 percent) Japan allocated to social and administrative infrastructure (education, health, water supply, etc.) in 1989 was not much lower than what the United States (19 percent) or the World Bank (19 percent) allocated; but all three donors fell below the DAC average of 26 percent. Since there is no widely accepted definition of what constitutes aid for BHN, if we assume the

Table 8.6   **Aid to Multilateral Institutions and Poor Countries, Japan and the United States (net disbursement as percentage of total ODA)**

	Multilateral Institutions		Low-Income Countries		Least-Developed Countries	
	1983–84	1988–89	1983–84	1988–89	1983–84	1988–89
Japan	35.5	27.1	66.2	69.5	18.6	19.6
United States	28.5	23.7	53.4	46.4	16.6	16.6
All DAC countries	26.9	23.5	56.7	57.5	21.7	24.7

Source: OECD (1990, 1985).

Table 8.7   **Uses of Aid, Japan and the United States, 1989 (percentage of total ODA commitments)**

	Japan	United States[a]	World Bank[a]	All DAC Countries
Social and administrative infrastructure	17.5	19.2	18.7	25.7
Education	5.8	4.6	4.2	10.7
Health and Population	2.6	7.2	6.0	6.7
Planning and public administration	0.8	2.1	0	1.6
Other (including water supply)	8.4	5.2	8.0	6.7
Economic infrastructure	31.7	2.7	32.3	19.1
Transport and communication	19.3	1.2	13.4	11.7
Energy	6.3	1.4	18.9	5.4
Other	6.0	0	0	2.0
Production	16.9	14.3	38.1	18.6
Agriculture	10.0	9.6	24.0	11.3
Industry, mining, and construction	6.6	0.3	8.2	5.5
Trade, banking, and tourism	0.3	4.3	5.9	1.7
Multisector	1.8	0.1	0	2.6
Program assistance	20.6	22.5	10.5	12.4
Debt relief	3.6	2.1	0	2.1
Food aid	0.6	19.0	0	5.9
Emergency aid (other than food aid)	0.1	1.7	0	1.6
Administrative expenses	3.4	5.8	0	4.0
Unspecified plus support to private volunteer, agencies	3.8	13.8	0.8	8.0

Source: OECD (1990).

[a]1988 data.

social and administrative structure is a close proxy for BHN, then one has to conclude that to the extent Japan is guilty of neglecting BHN, the United States is too.[22] Second, the striking difference shows up in economic infrastructure: in 1989, Japan spent 32 percent of its aid money on transport, communication, energy, and other physical infrastructure projects, whereas the U.S. allocation was meager, less than 3 percent. The DAC average share was about 19 percent. Interestingly, Japan behaved more like the World Bank (which also allocated 32 percent of its funds to economic infrastructure) than other bilateral donors. The biggest outlier was not Japan, but the United States. It is also

22. Counting food aid or assistance for agricultural production as BHN aid is questionable. Indeed, the concept of human development is perhaps more useful than that of BHN in the context of development aid. United Nations Development Program (1991, 13) defines human development in the following way: "The real objective of development is to increase people's development choices. Income is one aspect of these choices—and an extremely important one—but it is not the sum-total of human existence. Health, education, a good physical environment and freedom—to name a few other components of well being—may be just as important. . . . A healthy, well nourished, well educated and skilled labor force is the best foundation for growth. . . . People must be at the center of human development. . . . It [development] has to be development *of* the people, *by* the people, *for* the people."

noteworthy that almost 20 percent of U.S. assistance was food aid. This aid item, however, is designed to assist U.S. farmers and not so much the developing countries; indeed numerous studies have shown that food aid—while desperately needed in situations of famine and natural disaster—if provided routinely may adversely affect food production in the developing countries.[23]

These data on sectoral distribution of aid do not, however, settle the issue of whether Japan's aid program pays too little attention to BHN and too much to economic infrastructure, because they do not tell us what the right mix is. The data show that the Japanese aid allocation to economic infrastructure significantly exceeds "the DAC norm"—although not the World Bank norm—and the divergence on social infrastructure is less pronounced. These observations raise questions that the data cannot answer: what reason is there to believe that the DAC norm represents the right mix of aid allocation, and why does each donor country have to have that same mix? It makes more sense to argue that with donors as a group coordinating their aid programs to maximize global development goals, each individual donor should design its aid program according to its own strengths and weaknesses. For example, while Japan should do its part in the area of social infrastructure, there is no reason why it cannot allocate a greater share of aid to economic infrastructure if it is relatively more effective in that sector. A much more important issue is how closely that aid is responding to the development priorities of individual recipient countries and how effectively the aid resources are being utilized.

Japan is routinely accused of aid mercantilism. Simply put, the proposition runs as follows: while the United States sacrifices its national economic interests at the altar of humanitarian considerations and global security concerns by providing untied aid to the developing countries, commercial interests motivate mercantilist Japan to provide tied aid, which primarily benefits Japan's private sector in its drive to promote exports and gain market shares in the recipient countries.[24] An adequate assessment of this proposition requires breaking it into several empirically verifiable components.

The first verifiable element is the assertion that Japan relies heavily on tied aid, whereas the United States and other leading donors do not. The data on tied aid collected by the DAC, however, suggest otherwise: Japan's aid is less tied than that of the DAC members as a group, while U.S. aid is more tied than the DAC average (table 8.8). For example, in 1989 only 17 percent of Japanese

---

23. For instance, World Bank (1986, 146–47) state: "The quantity of food aid is more closely related to the needs of donors than those of recipients. For example, U.S. legislation on food aid—Public Law 480—makes explicit mention of foreign policy considerations, surplus disposals, and the avoidance of conflict between commercial and concessional exports. Donors give food aid as a convenient way of disposing surplus stocks, particularly of milk products. . . . Food aid is also provided to supplement domestic production in normal times. As a result, domestic prices may fall, discouraging local production and reducing farm profits."

24. See, for example, Pharr (1988), Bloch (1991), Hellmann (1989), and Preeg (1989b, 179; 1989a, 9).

Table 8.8   **Tied Aid, Bilateral ODA, Japan and the United States (percentage of total ODA)**

	1982–83 (gross disbursements)			1989 (commitments)		
	Japan	United States	Total DAC	Japan	United States	Total DAC
Fully tied[a]	17.1	30.3	30.0	13.8	40.2	33.0
Partially tied[b]	15.7	10.7	7.2	3.0	17.5	5.6
Fully and partially tied	32.8	41.0	37.2	16.8	57.7	38.6

Source: OECD (1991a, 1990, 1985).

[a]Mainly aid tied to procurement in the donor country; also includes amounts available for procurement in several countries, but not widely enough to qualify as "partially untied."

[b]Contributions available for procurement from donor and substantially all developing countries.

bilateral aid was fully and partially tied, whereas the DAC group average of the proportion of tied aid was almost 40 percent. By contrast, the United States fully and partially tied 58 percent of its bilateral aid. Also note that while Japan cut back its reliance on tied aid during the 1980s, the United States seems to have headed in the opposite direction: Japan's tied aid ratio fell from 33 percent in 1982–83 to 17 percent in 1989; during the same period the U.S. ratio rose from 41 percent to 58 percent.

The adherents of "the Japanese aid mercantilism school" find these DAC data unpersuasive: they argue that though de jure Japan's aid is no longer heavily tied, de facto it is so. In this view, with the Japanese private sector playing an active role in identifying and implementing aid projects, much of the officially untied aid turns into tied aid in practice.[25] Some light can be thrown on this issue by the data collected by the Japanese Ministry of Foreign Affairs on the nationalities of procurement contractors of Japanese ODA loans (table 8.9). The evidence suggests that while the de facto tying thesis was largely valid during the early eighties, it was no longer valid by 1990. While Japanese firms obtained 63 percent of the procurement contracts generated by untied Japanese ODA loans in 1983, their share dropped to 20 percent by 1990. During the same period, the procurement share of the contractors from the developing countries rose from less than 30 percent to 55 percent, and that of the contractors from the other DAC countries increased from 10 percent to 25 percent. That only 20 percent of the untied ODA loan contracts went to Japanese firms in 1990, if true, is actually remarkable: even without any tying and subsidy in their favor, one would expect the strongly competitive Japanese firms to do much better than 20 percent in open and free competition in markets they are greatly familiar with.

25. For example, Pharr (1992, 16) states: "The real issue today is *de facto* tying that results from the informal role played by the Japanese private sector abroad in lobbying Third World governments to request Japanese aid projects that are favorable to their interests." See also Preeg (1989b).

Table 8.9   Procurement Share of Japanese ODA Loans by Nationalities of Contractors (percentage, contract basis)

	1983	1985	1987	1988	1989	1990
United ODA loans						
Japan	63	52	37	27	25	20
Other DAC countries	9	15	15	22	27	25
Developing countries	28	33	48	51	48	55
Total ODA loans						
Japan	70	68	55	43	38	27
Other DAC countries	6	8	10	16	21	21
Developing countries	24	24	35	41	41	52

Source: Ministry of Foreign Affairs.

Note: The data are for Japanese fiscal years (April 1 to March 31).

Estimates available from the U.S. General Accounting Office (GAO) support these conclusions. For example, the GAO reckons that the United States ties its aid far more tightly than Japan does: it estimates that in 1987 the share of fully and partially tied aid in total *bilateral* ODA was 48 percent for Japan and was over 90 percent for the United States. On procurement, the GAO calculations imply that, in 1987, about 60 percent of Japanese bilateral ODA was spent on Japanese goods and services, while the U.S. ratio was about 70 percent.[26] Even these statistics do not persuade the critics, who argue that many of those so-called developing country contractors are nothing but fronts for the Japanese firms. The critics, however, do not feel it is necessary to go beyond citing one or two anecdotes from Thailand or Indonesia to convince themselves and others of what the Japanese are really up to (see Preeg 1991, 115–16; Bloch 1991, 72; Orr 1990, 62).

Another way to assess the empirical validity of the proposition that the Japanese government and business work hand in glove in using ODA to promote exports is to look for such a linkage in the data on Japanese aid and exports to the region. Opting for simplicity, I propose that, if aid were indeed playing a significant role in promoting Japanese exports to Pacific Asian developing countries, we would expect the following: (1) countries that receive the largest volumes of Japanese aid tend to be the ones where Japan also exports the most; and (2) countries that are top recipients of Japanese aid, and/or have been blessed with the fastest increase in Japanese aid, are where the United States has the smallest markets, and/or has been least successful in expanding exports. Once again, none of this discussion has any relevance for the NIEs be-

26. See U.S. GAO (1990). The U.S. procurement ratio is lower than the tied aid ratio because some of the aid is only partially tied and the data modestly overstate the tying of U.S. aid. The fact remains, however, that in 1987 a higher fraction of U.S. aid was used to buy U.S. goods and services than was the case for Japan. And 1987 was not the first year when that happened; as early as 1982–83, the United States was more guilty of tied aid than Japan was.

cause they currently receive little or no aid from Japan: East Asia or Pacific Asia really boils down to five countries—four ASEAN countries and China. The data on Japanese ODA and exports to those countries and South Asia seem to contradict the above two implications of the aid-driving-trade thesis (table 8.10).

First, the top three current recipients of Japanese aid are Indonesia, China, and the Philippines, whereas the top three markets for Japanese exports are China, Thailand, and Malaysia. During 1989–90, Japan's annual average aid flow to Indonesia was $1 billion with annual exports averaging $4.2 billion; by contrast Japan exported on average $8 billion to Thailand, which received only $450 million in aid. China—the number-two recipient of Japanese aid and number-two market for Japanese exports—seems to fit the aid-driving-trade model; but with a per capita income of less than $400 and a very anti-Japan communist regime, this is not the country the critics think of when they accuse Japan of building a coprosperity sphere with interlocking wheels of aid, trade, and investment. The Philippines also poses a contradiction: it was the third largest recipient of Japanese aid in 1989–90 yet provided a strikingly small market for Japanese exports ($2.4 billion)—about the same as captured by the United States. Bangladesh adds yet another question mark to the thesis that Japan's aid is commercially motivated: Japan offered the fifth largest share of its total ODA to one of the world's poorest countries in return for about $370 million of exports.

Second, the top three largest and/or fastest growing markets for U.S. exports are China, Malaysia, and Thailand. Two of these countries—China and Thailand—are also top recipients of Japanese aid, and all three of them are top markets for Japanese exports. Note also that, though the United States gives little aid to the region, during 1977–90, U.S. exports to China and the Philippines grew faster than Japanese exports, at only a slightly lower pace for the other three ASEAN countries. By contrast, Japanese exports grew a bit faster than U.S. exports in South Asia—not a region where Japanese aid is supposed to be acting in full force to promote exports. The picture that seems to emerge from all this is that, aid or no aid, markets for foreign goods are growing rapidly in these countries, and Japan as well as the United States is benefiting from this boom.

Another simple way of examining the Japanese aid-trade linkage is to take a close look at the behavior of the ratios of Japanese exports to aid across time and countries, vis-à-vis the United States. One can propose three null hypotheses. (1) If Japan gives aid primarily to promote exports, then one would expect it to provide most aid to those countries where its exports/aid ratios are the highest, that is, where for each dollar of aid, the exports gains are the greatest. (2) If it is also true that Japanese exporters use tied aid to enter a new market and establish a foothold from which to expand market shares, then one would expect the exports aid ratio to rise over time. (3) Even assuming away possible competitive advantages of Japanese exporters over their American

Table 8.10   Trade and Aid, Japan and the United States in Asia (millions of U.S. dollars)

	Japan					United States					Change 1977–90 (%)	
	1977	1980	1985	1989	1990	1977	1980	1985	1989	1990	Japan	United States
Exports to												
ASEAN-Four	5,160	9,163	7,360	16,576	22,241	2,710	6,144	4,562	8,629	10,786	331	298
Indonesia	1,812	3,476	2,191	3,288	5,052	763	1,545	795	1,256	1,897	179	149
Malaysia	870	2,070	2,184	4,107	5,529	561	1,337	1,539	2,875	3,425	536	511
Philippines	1,108	1,692	946	2,370	2,510	876	1,999	1,379	2,206	2,472	127	182
Thailand	1,370	1,925	2,047	6,811	9,150	510	1,263	849	2,292	2,992	568	487
South Asia	1,087	2,150	3,052	3,744	3,552	1,289	2,697	2,983	4,033	3,950	227	207
India	508	920	1,610	2,007	1,711	779	1,689	1,642	2,463	2,486	237	219
Bangladesh	120	320	314	349	370	156	292	219	282	182	195	17
Pakistan	362	626	793	1,023	1,088	293	642	1,042	1,136	1,143	201	290
Sri Lanka	75	237	273	294	316	53	62	73	143	137	321	158
Napal	14	39	62	71	59	8	12	7	9	10	321	25
China	1,955	5,109	12,590	8,477	6,145	171	3,755	3,856	5,807	4,807	214	2,711

Net ODA to

ASEAN-Four	260	700	791	2,118	2,308	199	184	202	253	309	787	55
Indonesia	148	350	161	1,145	868	102	117	43	31	31	485	70
Malaysia	30	66	126	80	373	3	1	0	−1	0	1,164	N.A.
Philippines	31	94	240	404	648	86	50	135	192	248	2,018	188
Thailand	52	190	264	489	419	8	16	24	31	30	709	275
South Asia	147	433	372	1,068	886	280	362	444	527	404	504	44
India	29	37	22	257	87	64	83	29	69	−24	202	N.A.
Bangladash	66	215	122	371	374	81	174	165	138	169	468	109
Pakistan	29	112	93	178	194	88	42	144	263	167	576	90
Sri Lanka	19	45	84	185	176	37	55	85	43	75	846	103
Napal	5	24	51	77	55	10	8	21	14	17	1,070	70
China	0	4	388	832	723	0	0	0	0	0	N.A.	N.A.

Sources: OECD (1992, 1991b, 1988, 1982); IMF (1991, 1984, 1980).
N.A. = not applicable.

Table 8.11   **Exports/Aid Ratio in Asia, Japan and the United States (ratio of donor exports to net ODA disbursement)**

	Japan					United States				
	1977	1980	1985	1989	1990	1977	1980	1985	1989	1990
ASEAN-Four	20	13	9	8	10	14	33	23	34	35
Indonesia	12	10	14	3	6	7	13	18	41	61
Malaysia	29	31	17	51	15	187	N.A.	N.A.	N.A.	N.A.
Philippines	36	18	4	6	4	10	40	10	11	10
Thailand	26	10	8	14	22	64	79	35	74	100
South Asia	7	5	8	4	4	5	7	7	8	10
China	N.A.	N.A.	32	10	8	N.A.	N.A.	N.A.	N.A.	N.A.

Sources: OECD (1992, 1991b, 1988, 1982); IMF (1991, 1984, 1980).

N.A. = not applicable; net ODA disbursement was negligible, zero, or negative.

counterparts, one would also expect the U.S. exports/aid ratios on balance to be lower than those for Japan.

Exports/aid ratios reported in table 8.11 exhibit a great deal of year-to-year and cross-country variations, casting doubt on the existence of any discernible relationship between aid and exports. Indeed, they seem to contradict the three implications of the presumed aid-trade linkage mentioned above. First, Indonesia, China, and the Philippines—the top three recipients of Japanese aid— are characterized by Japanese exports/aid ratios that are lower than those for Malaysia and Thailand. Second, except for Thailand, these ratios seem to have declined since 1980. Finally, the U.S. exports/aid ratios for all these countries are much higher relative to Japan. In the framework of the aid-driving-trade thesis, this would imply that the United States is getting a much greater export bang for a buck spend on aid. The implication that the United States is generating a much larger volume of exports for a dollar of aid relative to Japan, however, casts doubt over the validity of a significant cause-and-effect linkage between aid and exports, for Japan and for the United States.[27]

The evolution of Japan's share of import markets of its major Pacific Asian aid recipients can provide further evidence on Japan's aid mercantilism (table 8.12). An increase over time of these import ratios would at least be consistent with, though by no means conclusive evidence of, the view that Japan is gaining market share with the use of tied aid. The data show otherwise: Japan's market shares since 1975 have largely remained steady, and in some cases (notably, China, Indonesia, and the Philippines) have actually declined. With no evidence of increasing market shares and no evidence of tied aid, one wonders

27. This impressionistic evidence can be supplemented by econometric analyses that test for the presumed causal effects of aid on the pattern of trade using a simple gravity model. Time constraint does not allow me to pursue this course at this time, but I hope to carry this out— perhaps for a follow-up NBER conference on the same topic!

exactly what type of research is carried out by those who continue to assert that Japan uses tied aid to gain market shares.

I conclude this section by briefly addressing the allegation that Japan's aid program promotes capital goods exports by financing capital projects with mixed credits. An April 1989 study by the U.S. Export-Import Bank showed that American companies were losing $400–800 million in potential exports each year to Japan and other foreign competitors benefiting from mixed credits from their governments. In May 1990, the U.S. Exim Bank and the U.S. Agency for International Development (U.S. AID) jointly announced a new $500 million program of mixed credits; aid money and export credits would be used together to promote export of American power plants, telecommunications gear, construction equipment, and other capital goods to four countries where Japan is the top donor—Indonesia, Pakistan, the Philippines, and Thailand. The program was to use the Exim Bank's "war chest" of $110 million in fiscal year 1990.

According to the Exim Bank report to the Congress for fiscal year 1991, the bank used virtually all of the war chest grant authority appropriated by Congress ($150 million). These transactions are expected to support $532 million in U.S. exports and include a commitment of $58 million in Economic Support Fund (ESF) money from U.S. AID. All this effort to offset an estimated loss of less than $1 billion (or even, say, $5 billion, assuming the Exim Bank severely underestimated the loss) in U.S. capital goods exports is for a country that exported $116 billion of capital goods in 1990. It is also surprising that the Exim Bank appears very proud that their program is expected to raise U.S. capital goods exports by half a billion—that is, by 0.4 percent of the U.S. 1990 exports in that category.

8.4   A Coprosperity Sphere?

Unlike burdensharing and military free ride, the "Greater East Asia Coprosperity Sphere" is a phrase that Americans did not coin; the Japanese did.

Table 8.12   **Japan's Share in Merchandise Imports of Its Major Asian Aid Recipients (imports from Japan as a percentage of total imports)**

	1975	1980	1985	1987	1989	1990	Changes 1975–90
ASEAN-Four	28	25	23	24	25	26	−2
Indonesia	31	31	26	28	23	25	−6
Malaysia	23	23	23	22	24	24	1
Philippines	25	20	14	17	19	18	−7
Thailand	32	21	26	26	30	31	−1
South Asia	15	8	10	12	11	10	−5
China	34	27	22	16	16	14	−20

Sources: OECD (1991b, 1988, 1982); IMF (1991, 1984, 1980).

Japanese militarists and imperialists came up with this concept as early as 1919 and popularized it to give a positive economic meaning to their military campaign in the 1930s to replace the European colonial domination over East Asia with their own (Storry 1979). The death and destruction the Japanese war machine imposed on Asian countries in pursuit of this colonial goal transformed the term *coprosperity sphere* into a symbol of Japanese ruthlessness and steamroller approach to establishing regional dominance. The recent return of this phrase to the discussion of Japan's emerging economic relations with its Asian neighbors reflects this history. But it also constitutes yet another example of the problem of "damned if you do and damned if you don't" that Japan often seems to face: while some are accusing Tokyo for being a selfish free rider spending too little on foreign aid, others are indicting it for using aid money to build a coprosperity sphere in Pacific Asia. Growing Japanese economic presence in East Asia is fueling the perception that since the 1980s Japan has begun to do by peaceful economic means what it could not do by violent military means during the 1930s.

Dornbusch (1989, 270) asserts, "The Asian co-prosperity scheme is the most likely option for Japan," but the concept of a coprosperity sphere harks back to subservient economic, political, and military relationships many of today's developing countries had with their European colonial masters before World War II; those relationships do not describe Japan's current economic and political interactions with the dynamic and vibrant economies of Pacific Asia. To begin with, it is useful to remind ourselves that, unlike the United States, Japan does not project military power in Asian countries with which it has economic relations. Indeed, while economic domination does lead to political influence, in an ultimate showdown, the relative leverage of the dominant country (Japan) is muted when it has no military power to back up its economic and political power.

There are at least two additional reasons why *coprosperity sphere* is the wrong phrase to describe Japan's relations with East Asia. First, Japan is not forcing its growing aid-trade-investment linkages upon its Asian neighbors; these are two-way relations reflecting comparative advantage and the stages of development from which both sides are benefiting. If that were not the case, these Asian economies would not be wooing and welcoming Japanese goods, services, capital, and technology. Clearly, the economic boom these countries are enjoying does not seem to indicate economic relations serving only Japan's economic interests. Incidentally, the only country performing poorly in this region is the Philippines, a country that ranks at the bottom within Southeast Asia in terms of its economic relations with Japan and one that has had a long colonial economic and military relationship with the United States.

Second, the view that Japan is gradually consolidating its hold on its Asian neighbors in the sense that it is increasingly influencing their economic policies and domestic politics is at best an unwarranted fear, and at worst an insult to the people of these sovereign countries. These independent nations are no longer the weak colonies of imperialist powers unable to thwart foreign domination and assert sovereignty; they are some of the most dynamic economies of the world with highly proud people and powerful nationalist governments guarding against any possible encroachment on their sovereignty. With the memory of Japanese militarism still alive, they are specially sensitive to any hint of Japanese influence in their internal affairs.

With these general remarks, let me turn to two interrelated specific theses advanced by some Japan watchers. One is that in the wake of the 1985 *endaka* (the yen appreciation) triggered by the Plaza currency accord, the Japanese government articulated a plan to use public resources (development finance, technical cooperation, and MITI planning) to help Japanese private capital and technology develop a regional East Asian economy to serve Japan's current restructuring needs and its long-term global economic interests (Arase 1988, 1991; Maidment 1989). The other related thesis is that Japan is developing neocolonial economic relationships with the East Asian economies, in particular the ASEAN countries, where trade and investment flows primarily serve Japan's economic interests and not the development requirements of the recipient/host countries (Smith and do Rosario 1990; Sinha 1982).

One clear articulation of the thesis that Japan Inc. is implementing a plan to create and manage regional economic hegemony can be found in a survey article in *The Economist*. It identifies a 1988 study by the Economic Planning Agency (EPA) and a series of MITI white papers released during the late 1980s as the official intellectual source of this new "Asian Industries Development (AID)" plan. In particular, the EPA study with a mouthful of a title, "Promoting Comprehensive Economic Cooperation in an International Economic Environment Undergoing Upheaval: Towards the Contribution of an Asian Network," is credited with formulating the goal of this plan: to integrate the East Asian economies into a greater Japan Inc. According to the *Economist* piece (Maidment 1989, 11–13),

> Industrial policy would be coordinated from Tokyo. The EPA study talks of this being done by something it dubs the "Asian Brain." This would control the disposition of industrial investment throughout Japan, the NICs and the new NICs and co-ordinate the necessary policy support by the governments of those countries. The "Asian Brain" is clearly intended to be the Japanese civil service, just as MITI was the brain behind Japan Inc. in the 1960s. . . . the Japanese government is now committed to taking the initiative in promoting greater regional economic co-operation, starting in East and South-East Asia. It would do so not on the basis of bilateral relations or even with ASEAN as a block, but by regarding Japan, the NICs and the new NICs as one economy. . . .
>
> Japan's new hidden agenda is different, because the needs of the country's economy are different. (It is also better concealed.) The New AID Plan commits government money for the relocation of Japanese industry into lower-cost Asian countries as an inducement for private industry to serve whatever policies the civil servants want to pursue.

Arase (1991, 270–71) summarizes this plan in the following way: "Since 1987, Japan has been seeking to coordinate ODA, trade and FDI to construct a regional economy managed from Tokyo. [It] points to the deliberate construction of an economic sphere in the Asian-Pacific region. . . . This is different from the old ODA policy because the new one attempts to structure production and trade within the Asian-Pacific region according to a grander conception of Japan's regional and global economic role."

Katzenstein and Rouse (chap. 6 in this volume) explain that this New Aid Plan is supposed to work in four stages: "First, Japanese loans support the development of roads, ports, and other infrastructural supports. Second, the Japanese government sends technical experts to assist in coordinating industrial plans for each country. Third, Japanese loans are extended to various industries within participating countries. Finally, Japanese bureaucrats and businessmen take steps to facilitate access to Japanese markets and to ensure the distribution of products imported from offshore factories to Japan. . . . In short, the plan suggests that Japanese business and government elites view ASEAN (and the NICs) as one economy, requiring a comprehensive perspective on aid, trade, and investment. The provision of the necessary infrastructure, as one part of this plan, will serve the interests of Japanese companies and promote economic growth in Asia."

A closer look at the available evidence leads to the following conclusion: as usual, the Japanese civil servants and the MITI bureaucrats are getting way more credit than they deserve for their ability to carry out such a complex, comprehensive, and coordinated plan, but to the extent they are succeeding it is a good thing for not only Japan but the developing economies of the region as well. If the United States had been able to do in the Latin American economies with its Alliance for Progress initiative in the 1960s what Japan is allegedly doing in East Asia in the 1990s, it would have been hailed for promoting democracy and development in its poorer neighbors with a second Marshall Plan, and not indicted for serving its political and economic interests with a mercantilist industrial policy program.

More specifically, four points are worth emphasizing. First, while the New Aid Plan reportedly targets "the NICs and the new NICs," by definition it cannot involve the NICs because they receive little or no official aid from Japan. Among the ASEANIEs, the plan evidently is not working so well for the Philippines, which is getting lots of aid from Japan but not much private money or capital. Malaysia can only be a partial participant in the New Aid Plan, where Japan is cutting back its official aid while the private trade and investment linkages are growing by leaps and bounds. That leaves Indonesia and Thailand. If there are only two (or at most three) countries for which the Japanese New Aid Plan can possibly be relevant, then one cannot help doubt the validity of the proposition that Japan Inc. is creating and managing a greater East Asian economy to serve its own economic interests.

Second, even though the East Asian regional economy boils down to Indonesia and Thailand with Japan at the center, it seems worthwhile to examine how effectively the New Aid Plan is being implemented in these two countries. The first point to note is that the complex cooperation and stage-by-stage coordination between the Japanese visible hand and the invisible hand is much harder to discern than one might expect from the blueprint presented by Arase (1991) or Katzenstein and Rouse (chap. 6 in this volume). To be sure, a lot of Japanese aid is going to both countries to build physical infrastructure—highways, bridges, railroads, ports, dams, telephone lines, power plants, and so on. But Japan has been devoting a large chunk of its foreign aid budget to build infrastructure in the recipient countries since long before the advent of the New Aid Plan, and it has been doing so from Bangladesh to Burundi. This is so because Japan correctly believes that a minimum level of physical infrastructure is critical to long-term development of a poor and backward economy. The World Bank did the same to put war-devastated Western Europe on a path of long-term recovery and growth, and has been building physical infrastructure in the member developing countries since the 1950s. It is true that the Japanese private sector is heavily investing in both Indonesia and Thailand to establish low-cost production bases for exports of manufactures; it is also continuing its investment in the oil and energy sector in Indonesia. And finally, it does not require sophisticated analysis to see that new and improved infrastructure financed by Japanese official aid is greatly facilitating the task of establishing profitable export bases by the Japanese private companies and enhancing their efficiency and productivity.

But the argument that Tokyo is using aid money to essentially serve the interests of Japanese multinationals is misleading.[28] The Japan-financed highways and telephone networks are essentially public goods: they are not closed to the local investors and consumers and non-Japanese foreign companies. Nor is it the case that the American companies are paying higher tolls and fees for their use of these transport and communication facilities. Indeed, one can reasonably argue that American multinationals are getting a free ride on Thai highways built with Japanese taxpayers' money. The central point, however, is that what is good for Japanese business in Thailand is on balance also good for Thailand's economic development.

While Japanese public aid is benefiting the Japanese private business in Thailand and Indonesia, there is little evidence that a regional economy is being created and managed by MITI with various Japanese government and private agencies working hand-in-glove with clockwork precision. On the contrary, various features of the Japanese aid machinery—severe interministry rivalry, serious shortage of aid staff, too many agencies involved in the decision-making process, too few staff people on the ground, bilateral nature

---

28. Katzenstein and Rouse (chap. 6 in this volume) state: "Evidence from Thailand suggests that the Japanese have met with some success both in creating the types of infrastructures that will benefit Japanese multinationals and their partners, and in obtaining large contracts for Japanese companies for building such infrastructure."

of the aid request and delivery process, and so on—make it virtually impossible to implement a plan for the region with any sort of consistency and precision. Interviews with the recipient aid authorities and experts also do not seem to indicate that decisions are being made under the directives and guidelines of a single and well-coordinated Japanese plan.

This conclusion is shared by two veteran observers of Japanese aid. Orr (1991, 38) refers to MITI's New Aid Plan as an example of "how Japanese aid policy is hampered by its turf-conscious aid decision making system" and points out that "the Foreign Ministry, which usually makes aid-related announcements, had no perceivable involvement in the policy nor was there much support within MOFA for this undertaking." Rix (1992) argues that "the aid implementation mechanisms for individual projects remain unchanged and in this sense, MITI is unable to exert control over the ASEAN aid process."

Third, to the extent the MITI bureaucrats are able to implement the New Aid Plan, it is a good thing not only for Japan but also for the recipient countries. ODA that encourages flows of foreign private capital and technology to take advantage of regional division of labor and creates an infrastructural and policy environment conducive to their effective operation has the greatest chance of succeeding in helping the recipient country get on a path of self-sustaining development. Such aid strategy is much more likely to promote economic development than the current American strategy of assisting countries where the United States has political, security, and military interests, and using the money to meet multiple—and often contradictory—domestic and foreign objectives ranging from helping U.S. farmers, to keeping the pro-American antidevelopment governments in power, to burning coca crops in Bolivia in its fight against the drug problem in the Bronx, to funding various and sundry development projects on an ad hoc basis. So the Japanese plan for regional development should not be greeted with anxiety and alarm; it should perhaps be welcomed as a model for development assistance with valuable lessons for the veteran donors.

Finally, the idea that Japan is pursuing a "regional industrial policy" in East Asia may be seen as yet another Japanese attempt to threaten "the liberal world economic order." But this is an emotional response to what is more a matter of semantics than of substance. Many economists and some political free market idealogues respond to the phrase "industrial policy" with allergic reaction. Industrial policy is considered a Japanese and Asian phenomenon, reflecting anti-Western values—in short, a bad thing to be avoided and resisted at all costs. The reality is that not a single major industrial nation of today developed without an industrial policy (see Hobsbawm 1969, 225–48; Mukherjee 1974, 397–406), and even today each one of them, including the United States, has a de facto industrial policy. The only issue worth debating is to what extent each of them pursues industrial policy, and to what extent the policy is helping or hurting the industrial restructuring and international competitiveness of the economy in question. This is not the place to debate this issue. Instead, the point that needs emphasis is that regional industrialization in East Asia is primarily being driven by market forces, with the Japanese private sector playing a significant role within that context; the extent to which the Japanese government is aiding this process is, if unique, not undesirable.

Now we turn to the other version of the coprosperity sphere thesis that propounds Japan's alleged neocolonial economic relationship with its Southeast Asian neighbors. One can identify three major elements that underpin this view.

First, there is concern that Japan has captured too high a market share of imports of its poorer neighbors. We can see from table 8.12 that Japan's share in imports of the four ASEAN economies has ranged from about 15 to 30 percent: in 1990, Japan's market share was the highest in Thailand (about 30 percent), and lowest in the Philippines (about 20 percent). Also, as noted earlier, these shares have not grown relative to the levels prevailing in 1975. They are, of course, quite sizeable, but that is what one would expect, given Japan's relative economic size, its relative geographical proximity to these countries, and the long history of their economic interactions. The United States supplied over 60 percent of Canada's imports in 1990. Economic nationalists may not like this degree of "economic dominance" in their country by an economic superpower, but that is exactly what results from growing regional and global economic integration.

Second, another often-heard complaint is that as elsewhere Japan pushes its exports to its Third World neighbors while keeping its doors closed to imports from them and building up huge trade surpluses. By contrast, the United States is viewed as the importer of least resistance, absorbing massive and growing volumes of goods from these trade partners of Japan.

There are at least two problems with this view. (1) Japan is a major importer of ASEAN goods. Japan's persistent surpluses with these economies are no evidence of closed markets: it makes sense for the fast-growing developing economies to run deficits with savings-rich advanced countries; indeed, that is the only way they can import much-needed foreign capital vital for their growth and development. (2) With *openness* properly defined, it does not appear that the United States is more open to imports from the ASEAN countries than Japan is. A larger economy is likely to import more from its trading partners in absolute volume than a smaller economy. To adjust for the difference in size of the importing economy, it is necessary to see how U.S. imports relative to its GDP compares with Japanese imports relative to its GDP. On this measure, Japan is more open to the countries in question than the United States is (table 8.13). For example, while U.S. imports from the ASEAN countries in 1989–90 were 0.3 percent of its GDP, the comparable ratio for Japan was about 0.8 percent. Looked at from this perspective, the real difference between Japan and the United States is not that Japan imports too little from the ASEANIEs but that the United States exports too little.[29]

Finally, we turn to the aspect of Japan's rising economic presence in Asia

29. A more satisfactory way to look at this issue would be to make use of a gravity model.

Table 8.13   Merchandise Imports from Asian Recepients, Japan and the United States
                    (percentage of importing country GDP)

	1975		1980		1985		1989		1990	
	Japan	United States	Japan	United States	Japan	United States	Japan	United States	Japan	United States
ASEAN-Four	1.2	0.3	1.7	0.4	1.2	0.3	0.8	0.3	0.8	0.3
Indonesia	0.7	0.2	1.1	0.2	0.8	0.1	0.4	0.1	0.4	0.1
Malaysia	0.1	0.1	0.3	0.1	0.3	0.1	0.2	0.1	0.2	0.1
Philippines	0.2	0.1	0.2	0.1	0.1	0.1	0.1	0.1	0.1	0.1
Thailand	0.1	0.0	0.1	0.0	0.1	0.0	0.1	0.1	0.1	0.1
South Asia	0.2	0.0	0.1	0.1	0.1	0.1	0.1	0.1	0.1	0.1
China	0.3	0.0	0.4	0.0	0.5	0.1	0.4	0.2	0.4	0.3

Sources: OECD (1991b, 1988, 1982); IMF (1991, 1984, 1980); *International Financial Statistics,* various issues.

that seems to create the most anxiety—Japanese direct investment. As noted earlier, the rapid rise in Japanese labor cost since the 1985–87 yen appreciation and increasing labor shortage have induced many Japanese companies to shift their production base to the low-labor-cost ASEAN countries. Japanese direct investment has indeed surged in these economies, and Japan appears to have already become the dominant direct investor in the region.[30]

Is Japanese direct investment in the ASEANIEs primarily benefiting Japan at the expense of the host countries? The answer is no. The ASEAN governments are welcoming these investments with open doors because Japanese capital and technology are contributing significantly to their growth and development. To be sure, profit-seeking private business, unrestrained by government regulation, often causes various negative externalities, such as environmental damage, health and safety problems for workers, sector-specific or economy-wide booms and busts, and so on. In a situation where the host country is economically and politically much weaker than the home country and thus has less leverage and an inferior bargaining position, the foreign investors will have a greater capacity to cause these negative externalities. If the history of U.S. direct investment in Asia and Latin America is any guide, it would be naïve to believe that there are no negative consequences of Japanese investment in ASEAN economies. Also, the complaints that Japanese companies are reluctant to transfer advanced technologies to the host nations and that they rarely promote local employees to top management positions are largely valid. This is exactly what the American and European multinationals did in the past and still do today. Japan is hardly different in this regard. It is also true that, with growing economic presence, Japan will wield greater political power in the region. All of this, however, does not negate the central point: Japanese direct

30. The bad quality of available data prevents one from being sanguine on this point.

investment in the ASEAN economies is not a neocolonial phenomenon bene-fiting mostly the foreign invaders—it is an economic relationship voluntarily entered into and beneficial to both parties.

The alarm over surging Japanese foreign direct investment (FDI) in the ASEANIEs appears to be much stronger in the United States than in the host countries themselves. This American anxiety seems to reflect a concern, not about the economic welfare or political sovereignty of the ASEAN countries, but over the loss of this country's long-held status as the dominant direct inves-tor in the region. This is yet one more element of the overall reaction of America—long used to being the number-one economic power with world-wide dominance and influence—to its economic hegemony challenged by an economically ascending Japan. Clearly the shifts in relative economic domi-nance will have major political and security implications for the region. And it is a subject worth analyzing. But the point here is there is little evidence that Japanese FDI is more neocolonial in nature than American FDI.

I would like to conclude this section with two broad observations. First, on the issue of an Asian coprosperity sphere, it is instructive to note that the Japa-nese New Aid Plan is not too dissimilar from the 1961 United States–initiated Alliance for Progress to utilize $10 billion of official funds and $10 billion of American private capital over a ten-year period to develop a regional Latin American economy. This plan was and is interpreted as an act of American benevolence to help its southern neighbors. Infrastructure financed by Japanese aid in Indonesia and Thailand is seen as a part of an official plan to benefit the Japanese investors, yet this was precisely a major goal of the Alliance for Prog-ress. In emphasizing this objective of the alliance, its U.S. coordinator, Teo-doro Moscoso, in a 1963 speech criticized the view that "all that Latin America needs is a friendly climate for private enterprise" and pointed out that "this view disregards the need for building roads, ports, power plants, and communi-cations systems which must be built at least in great part with public funds and which in many areas are a prerequisite for the effective and profitable invest-ment of private capital" (Horowitz 1970, 57). One key difference between the Japanese New Aid Plan and the American Alliance for Progress is, of course, that the ASEAN economies are growing rapidly with little direct implementa-tion of the Japanese plan, whereas most of Latin America remained trapped in underdevelopment despite the launching and implementation of the alliance with much fanfare.

The Enterprise of the Americas Initiative (EAI) announced by President Bush in June 1990 appears to be a reincarnation of the Alliance of Progress three decades later. According to the U.S. undersecretary for international af-fairs, David Mulford (1991), the initiative "is designed to deepen and expand for our mutual benefit the wider array of trade and investment ties which link the United States with its neighbors in Latin America and the Caribbean. . . . our long term goal is to establish a hemispheric free trade area. . . . By itself, a free trade agreement would not necessarily succeed in bringing substantial economic benefits. But free trade is a cornerstone of a broader economic system based on market principles. It is that broader system that the Enterprise for the Americas Initiative seeks to foster jointly through its trade, investment and debt pillars." No one is calling this a U.S. plan for a Greater American Co-prosperity Sphere; the only complaint is that the United States is mostly talking and not doing enough. But one can imagine the Western reaction if tomorrow Prime Minister Miyazawa announced an Enterprise for Greater East Asia Initiative with a long-term objective of creating a regional free trade area.[31]

The final broad observation is that Japan's ODA policy is not based on one-dimensional commercialism: it has numerous economic, political, security, and moral objectives, and it is becoming increasingly multidimensional and complex over time. In that sense, Japan's ODA policy is becoming more like that of the other major donors, including the United States. In the area of human rights and production of armaments, Japan, at least in principle, has now gone beyond the United States: on April 12, 1991, Prime Minister Kaifu announced that, in giving aid, Japan would take into account the recipient nation's human rights record, its promotion of democracy, and whether it is developing and manufacturing weapons of mass destruction, including nuclear weapons. To be sure, Japan will not be able to stick to these guidelines with any semblance of consistency; China alone will make a mockery of this. But this announcement should still be considered a great leap forward.

The diversity and the nonuniqueness of Japanese aid policy is summed up well by Koppel and Orr (1992):

> ODA is a post World War II invention. It was born from a marriage of anti-communism with needs for supporting economic reconstruction. . . . Japan's ODA was born from the same impulses as American and European aid, but unlike any other donor, its ODA was not born from a desire, however tacit, to maintain colonial links (as was the case e.g. with French aid), not to build, in effect, neo-colonial networks, but rather from a recognition that her own development depended on peaceful international economic relations, especially in Asia and an acknowledgement that damages she had caused during the war required reparation.

8.5   The Politics of Japanese Money and American Power: The Philippines and the Asian Development Bank

The thesis that Japan shirks global responsibility but is using aid money to achieve regional economic hegemony can be further assessed with a deeper probe into two Asian entities. One is a country, the Philippines, and the other

31. Academics and experts must face squarely this issue of double standard and asymmetric interpretation of facts; if they fail to do so, they will only supply emotional views under the guise of objective analysis, and thereby contribute significantly to the confusion and conflict that continue to characterize the United States–Japan relationship in Pacific Asia and elsewhere.

is a multilateral regional organization, the Asian Development Bank (ADB). Both have something in common—special and close involvement with Japan as well as the United States. No other country or institution appears to offer a more suitable real-life laboratory for examining the dynamics of cooperation and conflict between Japan and the United States than the Philippines and the ADB.

I take up the Philippines first. The evidence does not fit the image of a free-riding Japan gaining economic domination with aid money. On the contrary, facts seem to paint a picture of a cooperative Japan extending a generous helping hand to the United States: Japanese development aid to the Philippines has increasingly compensated for what the Filipinos see as an inadequate American aid package to pay for "rents" of the U.S. military bases.

I have already argued that the linkage between the visible hand of Japanese official aid and the invisible hand of Japanese trade and investment appears very tenuous in the Philippines. The Japanese government has been pouring massive amounts of development aid into the Philippine economy, but Japanese business is not exactly rushing in with their goods, capital, and technology. Indeed, American aid seems to be twice as effective in commercial and economic terms as the Japanese aid: the United States provides less than half of what Japan gives, yet the American economic presence in the Philippines in terms of exports and direct investment flows is comparable to that of Japan. These facts suggest that Tokyo's aid is not playing a very active role in helping expand Japanese economic presence in the Philippine economy or in shaping it to fit into a regional economy serving Japan's economic and commercial interests.

Three additional observations are worth emphasizing. First, an "aid plan" for the Philippines was drawn up in July 1989; it was initially proposed not by the MITI bureaucrats in Tokyo, but by members of Congress in Washington. With the prospect for economic crisis and communist insurgency growing as People Power overthrew former U.S. ally President Ferdinand Marcos, and with negotiations for the renewal of the 1947 military bases agreement under way, some concerned American politicians argued that only a mini–Marshall Plan could save democracy and foster development in the debt-ridden economy of the Philippines (Japan Economic Institute 1988). The only twist was that this mini–Marshall Plan, unlike the original, was to be financed multilaterally and the lion's share was to come, not from the United States, but from Japan.

In July 1989, nineteen countries and seven international organizations met in Tokyo and pledged a total of $3.5 billion ($2.8 billion, according to the Philippines authorities) for the 1989–90 period as the first installment of a $10 billion package to be disbursed over five years. With the World Bank acting as the coordinator of what became known as Multilateral Assistance Initiative (MAI) or the Philippine Assistance Program (PAP), Japan pledged the largest amount, $1.6 billion. By contrast, the United States promised $200 million, of which Congress ultimately appropriated $160 million. The MAI donors met again in February 25–26, 1992, in Hong Kong and pledged a total of $3.3 billion. Japan again topped the list with $1.57 billion, with the United States promising $160 million. These facts do not exactly paint a picture of a free-riding Japan. What they say about the United States is, however, less clear: one interpretation could be that America is turning into a Japanese aid–dependent military superpower.

Second, while Japan is likely to continue its massive development assistance program for the Philippines, the United States will sharply cut back its aid as it withdraws its military bases. The United States may appropriate less than $100 million for MAI funds, and there is pressure to cut base-related aid from $363 million in FY 1992 to zero (Awanohara 1992). These facts add up to a simple conclusion: until recently, both Japanese and American aid to the Philippines had at least one common strategic purpose—to pay for America's military bases. With the military bases gone, America seems poised to simply disengage financially from the Philippines, which is increasingly viewed as a former colony with little strategic importance, while Japan would likely continue to provide assistance to promote regional peace and stability as well as regional economic development. Paradoxically, the only argument that may persuade the United States to provide aid to the Philippines is precisely the neocolonial and mercantile one that Japan is routinely accused of: aid would promote America's economic and commercial interests; a complete disengagement will only create an economic vacuum that Japan will surely fill.

Finally, the Japanese private sector is already stepping in to fill the vacuum—one not created by U.S. cut-off of aid, but by the scheduled withdrawal of the U.S. military from Subic Bay Naval Base in late 1992.[32] The Philippine authorities have already approved a three-stage plan to transform the naval-base complex into an industrial zone with a Hong Kong–style free port. At the time of this writing, at least seventeen major Japanese private enterprises—trading companies, banks, and construction companies—have lined up to capture a part of what appears to be potentially a rich and growing pie. While the Japanese companies seem to be ahead of the line, others are not far behind. Philippine, other Asian, and American businesses have joined the competition. Some twenty-eight Philippine companies, businesses from Singapore and Hong Kong, and twenty-one U.S. firms have already showed interest. Even H. Ross Perot, the third candidate in the 1992 U.S. presidential race, plans to operate Subic Bay airfield as a regional air traffic hub and to participate in the construction of a coastal road linking Subic Bay to Manila. So far, none of this is being funded by Japanese official aid. Only the World Bank and the ADB are

---

32. There is much less interest in nearby Clark Air Base, which the United States abandoned in June 1991 in the wake of severe damage from the eruption of Mount Pinatubo. The conversion plan of this former home of the U.S. Thirteenth Air Force has been hampered by continued ash emissions from the volcano, as well by the loss of air communication due to the damaged runways. See Baguioro (1992, 23) for more details.

considering funding feasibility studies and technical assistance. This example seems to indicate that, while security-motivated official development aid to the Philippines may decline, private capital—from Japan and elsewhere—will probably more than make up for it, and in all likelihood will generate higher growth and development.

The ADB constitutes an excellent case study for examining the evolution of Japan's assumption of global (or at least regional) responsibility, the U.S. response to this evolution, and United States–Japan cooperation and confrontation on economic policy and political power in Pacific Asia. This case study offers yet another illustration of Japan's shouldering its international responsibilities; it also rejects the view that Tokyo is using foreign aid and its dominant role in the ADB to establish economic hegemony in the region. Instead, the ADB experience demonstrates forcefully that, while the U.S. government and opinion leaders continue to prod Japan to assume greater global responsibility, their attitudes and actions often keep Japan from doing so.

I would like to substantiate the above conclusion with six specific observations. First, the ADB is perhaps the earliest and most significant demonstration of Japan's willingness to assume regional, if not global, responsibility, Tokyo played a leading role in planning, designing, and founding the bank in 1966. And it guided and managed the bank actively in its formative years. Japan was intimately involved in formulating the legal structure of the bank and setting its agenda. It also took responsibility for dispatching bank presidents and a large cohort of professional staff, as well as putting up the necessary amount of money (Yasutomo 1983). Japan did not undertake this initiative under U.S. pressure or *gaiatsu*. The United States insisted on equal status in terms of voting power, and Japan apparently agreed.

Second, the criticism that Japan uses the ADB to promote its commercial interests while the United States does not, if true earlier, seems no longer valid (see Wihtol 1988, 43). To begin with, it should be noted that the United States has prevented the bank from funding palm oil, sugar, and citrus fruits in response to domestic commercial interests (Yasutomo 1992). There have been no such analogous efforts from Tokyo. In the area of procurement for ADB projects, by the end of 1989, Japan won 21 percent of all contracts funded by the Ordinary Capital Resources (OCR), 19 percent of Asian Development Fund (ADF) contracts, and 5 percent of Technical Assistance Special Fund (TASF) contracts. It is worth noting here that, by the end of 1988, Japan provided almost 40 percent of ADF money and 57 percent of TASF money. The procurement share of Japanese companies has declined in recent years. For example, Japanese share of the OCR and ADF contracts in 1988 was only 12 percent, and it fell to 7 percent in 1989. Similar data for the United States are not available, but one piece of information is relevant. These contracts include goods, relative services, civil works, and consulting services. The U.S. companies have been the leading contractors of goods for some time and have recently taken the top position in consulting services. Note that by the end of

1988, the United States contributed 18 percent to the ADF and 2 percent to the TASF (Yasutomo 1992, n. 30).

Third, Japan's role in the ADB is going through a critical transitional period, creating new grounds for conflicts as well as cooperation with the United States. While playing a leading role in establishing and organizing the bank during its infancy, Tokyo adopted a low-key approach (the so-called SSS approach of "silence, smile, and sleep") when it came to projecting its vision and participating in the policy debate. The main focus was to cooperate with the United States, adequately fund the bank, ensure its survival and prosperity, and maintain its reputation and, with it, that of Japan. This survival-cum-image-oriented vision-shy approach continued through the 1970s and the early 1980s.

During the second half of the 1980s, however, there was a dramatic change: prodded by the international community and especially the United States to assume much greater global responsibility as Japan became the world's largest creditor and capital-exporting nation boasting a superstrong yen, it became an activist development-aid power with profound implications for its role in all multilateral financial institutions, including the ADB. It dispatched a new breed of "young Turks" to the ADB, who were more articulate and assertive and who were more willing to voice their views in what should be the philosophy and policy agenda of the bank. Also, Japan wanted to end voting-right parity with the United States and be the number-one shareholder of the bank. This shift toward forward-looking activism has created two types of tensions. One is more like a Japanese schizophrenia—the clash between the traditional habits of old SSS and the move toward a new SSS—"speak, smile, and snap." The other is a U.S.-Japanese bilateral conflict—over a Japanese desire to be the bank's top shareholder and over the bank's development philosophy and its future direction.[33]

Fourth, with rising Japanese activism, Japan's relationship with the United States can still be characterized as one of overall cooperation with underlying differences and tensions, which occasionally surface as outright conflicts. Japan's efforts to maximize cooperation with the United States and minimize conflicts within the ADB reflect the imperatives of maintaining an overall friendly bilateral relationship with the United States, as well as concerns over the effectiveness and reputation of the bank. Japan's cooperative attitude and actions toward the United States—however reluctant it may be at times—shows up in various ways. One recent example is Tokyo's support for the U.S. nominee for ADB vice president in the face of opposition not only from some developing member countries (DMCs), but even from European members. Another is Japan's support for the U.S. opposition to resumption of lending to China and its conspicuous silence on concessional loans to China and India. Yet another example would be Japanese hesitation in expressing its views on the U.S. rejection of a $10 billion infusion of new funds into the ADF.

33. This paragraph and the rest of this section draw heavily from Yasutomo (1992).

Fifth, within the overall cooperative framework, conflicts between Japan and the United States have rocked the ADB repeatedly since 1985. These frictions have arisen from a variety of sources, ranging from mundane personality clashes among top personnel to lofty disagreements over development philosophy and lending policy and practices of the bank. And then, of course, there is the issue of a persistent and perhaps increasing money-power gap, with the Japanese running a deficit and the Americans a surplus—a point I elaborate in my sixth observation. In the domain of personality clashes, the United States and some other members saw Masao Fujioka, appointed president in 1981, as a major problem. He was criticized for his policies and management skills, and more for his abrasive temperament. He earned the nickname Shogun for his assertive, acerbic, and arrogant personality. On the other hand, many saw the American executive director Joe Rogers as an inexperienced ideologue with little understanding of Asia, trying to use his "textbook knowledge" to help develop Asia.

Japan has tried to mitigate the "Fuji-friction" within the top management by selecting in 1989 a low-key, conciliatory, and amiable Ministry of Finance official as flamboyant Fujioka's successor. The new president, Kimimasa Tarumizu, is noted for his typical Japanese bottom-up consensual management style and considers himself an honest broker in mediating differences between Tokyo and Washington. Japan has, however, balanced Tarumizu's kinder and gentler approach to management and decision making by appointing high-posture, assertive, and articulate executive directors. These directors are not hesitant to speak their minds at board meetings: they challenge their American counterparts on policy issues and express their disagreements even with the Japanese president himself. For example, the current executive director, Ken Yagi, is young, knowledgeable about bank operations, and not shy about expressing his opinions.

On the policy front, the U.S.-Japanese differences go deeper and are not easily reconcilable. To resolve these differences as well as to review the bank's roles and missions in the 1990s, an independent five-member advisory panel led by the Japanese wiseman Saburo Okita produced a report in 1989. Among other things, it called for a greater bank role in two areas—poverty alleviation and arresting environmental degradation, including an emphasis on designing environment-friendly projects. The report also recommended increased private sector lending. While Tokyo and Washington agree on these goals, the divergence shows up in the means and methods of achieving them. For example, Japan (and the DMCs) find the American insistence on strict conditionality for policy-based lending contentious and counterproductive. Some Japanese and Asian members feel that the United States does not really understand Asia, and its inflexible across-the-board ideological approach is inherently incapable of appreciating the diversity of Asia and thus a threat to development. Many Asian DMCs enjoying rapid economic growth consider the perceived American obsession with dubious policy conditionalities as wrong-headed conde-

scension in view of the lackluster performance of borrowing members of the
Inter-American Development Bank (IDB)—a regional development bank
where the United States plays the dominant role in enforcing policy conditionalities. They also find it annoying that the U.S. hand is unduly heavy in imposing policy conditionality, but when it comes to funding the bank, the same
hand suddenly turns empty.

Finally, the fundamental source of conflict is neither personality clash nor
policy difference, but the politics of power and purse. More specifically, Japan
wants to expand the capital base and strengthen the financial health of the ADB
and take a leading role in doing so. But the U.S. insistence on maintaining
parity in voting rights combined with its unwillingness to put up additional
money essentially prevents the ADB from playing a greater role and Japan
from assuming greater responsibility. For example, in 1988, Tokyo wanted to
achieve the top shareholder position by increasing its share in the bank's OCR
through a special capital increase. This was motivated by Japan's frustration at
not getting representation commensurate with taxation, and its desire to have
others recognize that reality. By 1988, Japan's contributions accounted
for nearly 40 percent of the ADF and 57 percent of the TASF. By contrast,
the U.S. share was 18 percent of the ADF and less than 2 percent of the
TASF. Currently, the United States is also running an arrear of $175 million
in the ADF.

Japan wanted to formalize this "U.S. free ride" by ending the parity in voting
rights, but Washington insisted on maintaining the traditional parity by matching the Japanese contributions to the OCR, thus continuing its representation
with insufficient taxation. U.S. Treasury secretary Nicholas Brady argued
(1991, 6) that the voting right parity with Japan "will enable us to maintain our
influence in the ADB. We will thus avoid ceding a measure of our influence in
Asia in general, the world's most rapidly growing region." In congressional
testimony, one Asia watcher put this rationale more forcefully: "I think the
Asian Development Fund offers an effective channel for American support for
the economic development of both India and China, two giant subcontinental
political conglomerates that cannot be easily absorbed into the Japanese-
centered economic grid now being consolidated in much of the rest of Asia.
So the main reason I present for the new emphasis that I would like to see on
the Asia Development Fund is the need for a long-term American effort to
build countervailing economic power in Asia to offset that of Japan."[34]

Another example of America's (and some European members') efforts to
undermine Tokyo's leadership at ADB is its vehement opposition to President
Fujioka's 1989 proposal to establish a private sector lending affiliate—the
Asian Finance and Investment Corporation (AFIC)—capitalized jointly by

---

34. See Harrison (1991, 23–24). Elsewhere in the same congressional testimony, Harrison
claims, "Japan has attempted to make Bank lending policies serve its effort to establish a latter-
day 'Co-prosperity Sphere' centered in nine countries of East and Southeast Asia" (89).

ADB and private banks and financial institutions. This opposition partly reflected genuine policy differences, but the politics of economic competition perhaps played a more important role: while most Asian DMCs generally supported the idea, America and other European competitors of Japan saw it as Tokyo's ploy to give business to the Japanese banks. The proposal was finally approved when an agreement was reached to reduce the maximum share of Japanese private financial institutions from 40 to 30 percent, and the ADB made special efforts to recruit American financial institutions to join AFIC. The irony in this AFIC fiasco is that Washington objected vociferously to a Japanese proposal that in fact was a response to the U.S. criticism of the ADB for its excessive focus on the public sector and to the U.S.-supported advisory panel's recommendation that the ADB establish a body to grant private sector loans.

The ADB represents a microcosm of the overall United States–Japan relationship, in Pacific Asia and elsewhere. The bilateral money-power imbalance seems to drive the dynamics of conflicts in an otherwise cooperative relationship. The United States wants to preserve the old power structure, but it is unable to put up the money to sustain it. That puts Japan in a no-win situation: on the one hand, Tokyo is chastised for practicing checkbook diplomacy and not exercising global leadership; on the other hand it is blocked from doing so by the U.S. refusal to cede its own power and status.

8.6   Conclusions

This paper reaches four key conclusions.

1. There is little analytical foundation for the view that the national defense and foreign aid of the United States (and of Japan) within the context of the 1960 United States–Japan security treaty can be considered as international public goods. The analytical and empirical basis for viewing Japan as a military free rider is also weak. Thus the notion that Japan can compensate for its military free ride with a huge expansion of its foreign aid budget is highly questionable. It is, however, perfectly reasonable to argue that as a global economic power Japan has global responsibilities and should play a greater role in various nonmilitary areas, including foreign aid and measures for addressing environmental and other transnational problems.

2. There is little evidence that relative to the United States and other donors, the quality of Japan's aid is relatively low. Also, Japan gives less tied aid than do other donors to promote exports and gain market shares. The Japanese foreign aid program, in Pacific Asia and elsewhere, seems to be becoming increasingly multidimensional in nature, embracing economic, political, security, humanitarian, and developmental objectives.

3. The interpretation of Japan's growing economic ties with Pacific Asian economies as a Japanese plan to create a coprosperity sphere to serve its own economic interests is a complete misapplication of a colonial concept of yes-

terday to the new realities of modern international economic relations. It is also factually incorrect. Japan provides little or no aid to the so-called NIEs. Out of the four ASEAN economies, its recent aid allocation to Malaysia has been modest, and its trade and investment linkages with the Philippines are quite weak, leaving only Indonesia and Thailand where the coprosperity thesis could be potentially valid. Available evidence, however, does not validate the thesis that Tokyo is using ODA incentives and instruments to essentially promote trade and investment interests of Japan's private sector in those two countries. There is also little evidence that the Japanese bureaucrats are implementing a foreign aid plan for creating and managing a regional economy to serve Japan's economic interests; market forces are largely responsible for these increased regional linkages.

4. A closer examination of the U.S.-Japanese interaction in the Philippines and in the ADB turns up additional evidence against the view that Japan is a free rider or that it is attempting to build a coprosperity sphere in Pacific Asia. Instead, Japan seems to be genuinely cooperating—financially and politically—with the United States to support security interests of both nations. Conflicts arise inevitably, especially at the ADB, when Japan attempts to assume greater responsibility and challenge the U.S. tendency of maintaining a "power free ride."

References

Arase, David. 1988. Japanese Objectives in Pacific Economic Cooperation. Honolulu: East-West Center Resource Systems Institute.

———. 1991. U.S. and ASEAN Perceptions of Japan's Role in the Asian-Pacific Region. In Harry H. Kendall and Clara Joewono, eds., *Japan, ASEAN, and the United States*. Berkeley: University of California, Institute for East Asian Studies.

Awanohara, Susumu. 1992. Out of Pocket. *Far Eastern Economic Review,* 6 February, 17.

Baguioro, Maria. 1992. Global Firms to Fill Subic Bay Vacuum. *Nikkei Weekly,* 11 April, 23.

Balassa, Bela, and Marcus Noland. 1988. *Japan in the World Economy*. Washington, DC: Institute for International Economics.

Benoit, Emile. 1973. *Defense and Economic Growth in Developing Countries*. Lexington, MA: Lexington Books.

———. 1978. Growth and Defense in Developing Countries. *Economic Development and Cultural Change* (January): 271–80.

Bloch, Julia Chang. 1991. A U.S.-Japan Aid Alliance? In *Yen for Development: Japanese Foreign Aid and the Politics of Burden-Sharing,* ed. Shafiqul Islam. New York: Council on Foreign Relations Press.

Brady, Nicholas. 1991. Statement to the Subcommittee on Foreign Operations, Committee on Appropriations, U.S. House of Representatives, Washington, DC, 5 March.

Brown, Donna. 1991. Whither Japan's MITI? *Management Review* (April): 54–55.

Brown, Harold. 1987. *U.S.-Japan Relations: Technology, Economics, and Security.* New York: Carnegie Council on Ethics and International Affairs.

Brzezinski, Zbigniew. 1990. Looking beyond Trade: Post–Cold War Politics and Portents. Speech delivered at TV Asahi Seminar, Tokyo, 29 May.

Bull, Hedley. 1964. *Strategy and the Atlantic Alliance: A Critique of the United States Doctrine.* Princeton, NJ: Princeton University, Center of International Studies.

Center for Strategic and International Studies (CSIS). U.S.-Japan Working Group. 1991. *A Policy Framework for Asia-Pacific Economic Cooperation.* Washington, DC, May.

Deger, Saadet, and Somnath Sen. 1990. Military Security and the Economy: Defense Expenditure in India and Pakistan. In *The Economics of Defense Spending: An International Survey,* eds. K. Hartley and T. Sandler. London: Croom Heim.

De Strihou, Jacques van Ypersele. 1967. Comment on Olson and Zeckhauser. In *Issues in Defense Economics,* ed. Roland N. McKean. New York: Columbia University Press.

Dornbusch, Rudiger. 1989. The Dollar in the 1990s: Competitiveness and the Challenges of New Economic Blocs. Paper presented to Monetary Policy Issues in the 1990s, a symposium sponsored by the Federal Reserve Bank of Kansas City, 30 August–1 September.

Faini, R., P. Annez, and L. Taylor. 1984. Defense Spending, Economic Structure, and Growth: Evidence among Countries and over Time. *Economic Development and Cultural Change* 32:487–98.

Garten, Jeffrey. 1989–90. Japan and Germany: American Concerns. *Foreign Affairs* (Winter): 84–101.

Harrison, Selig. 1991. Pacific Agenda: Defense or Economics? Testimony to the Subcommittee on International Development, Finance, Trade, and Monetary Policy, Committee on Banking, Finance, and Urban Affairs, U.S. House of Representatives, Washington, DC, 30 May.

Harrison, Selig, and Clyde Prestowitz, Jr. 1990. Pacific Agenda: Defense or Economics? *Foreign Policy* 79 (Summer): 56–76.

Head, John G. 1962. Public Goods and Public Policy. *Public Finance* 17 (3): 197–219.

Hellmann, Donald C. 1989. The Imperatives for Reciprocity and Symmetry in U.S.-Japanese Economic and Defense Relations. In John H. Makin and Donald C. Hellmann, eds., *Sharing World Leadership? A New Era for America and Japan.* Washington, DC: American Enterprise Institute for Public Policy Research.

Hobsbawm, Eric. 1969. *Industry and Empire.* Suffolk: Pelican Books.

Horowitz, David. 1970. The Alliance for Progress. In *Imperialism and Underdevelopment: A Reader,* ed. R. Rhodes. New York: Monthly Review Press.

House Armed Services Committee. 1988. *Report of Defense Burden-Sharing Panel.* Washington, DC: U.S. Government Printing Office.

International Monetary Fund. 1980. *Direction of Trade Statistics.* Washington, DC: IMF.

———. 1984. *Direction of Trade Statistics.* Washington, DC: IMF.

———. 1991. *Direction of Trade Statistics.* Washington, DC: IMF.

Islam, Shafiqul. 1988. America's Foreign Debt: Fear, Fantasy, Fiction, and Facts. In *The Dollar and the Trade Deficit: What's to Be Done?* CRS Report for Congress, 88–430E. Washington, DC: Congressional Research Service, 7 June.

———. 1991. Beyond Burden-Sharing: Economics and Politics of Japanese Foreign Aid. In *Yen for Development: Japanese Foreign Aid and the Politics of Burden-Sharing,* ed. Shafiqul Islam. New York: Council on Foreign Relations Press.

Japan Economic Institute. 1988. Report 16B. Washington, DC, 22 April.

Johnson, Chalmers. 1986. Reflections on the Dilemmas of Japanese Defense. Speech before the International House of Japan, Tokyo, 16 January.

Kaifu, Toshiki. 1989. U.S.-Japan Cooperation for Results: Sharing Responsibility to Solve Major World Issues. Speech before the National Press Club, Washington, DC, 1 September.

Kaldor, Mary. 1978. The Military in Third World Development. *World Development* 4:459–82.

Kennedy, Paul. 1987. *The Rise and Fall of Great Powers: Economic Change and Military Conflict from 1500 to 2000*. New York: Random House.

Kissinger, Henry, and Cyrus Vance. 1988. Bipartisan Objectives for American Foreign Policy. *Foreign Affairs* 66 (Summer): 899–921.

Koppel, Bruce, and Robert Orr, Jr., eds. 1992. *Japan's Foreign Aid Power and Policy in a New Era*. Boulder, CO: Westview Press.

Kosminsky, Jay, and R. Fischer. 1989. *A Ten-Point Program for Increasing the Allies' Share of Defense Costs*. Washington, DC: Heritage Foundation.

Lele, Uma, and Ijaz Nabi, eds. 1990. *Transitions in Development: The Role of Aid and Commercial Flows*. San Francisco: International Center for Economic Growth.

MacIntosh, Malcolm. 1987. *Japan Re-armed*. New York: St. Martin's Press.

McNamara, Robert. 1992. The Role of Japan in the Post–Cold War World. Speech at the Council on Foreign Relations, New York, 5 February.

Maidment, Paul. 1989. The Yen Block: A New Balance in Asia? *The Economist*, 15 July, Survey 5–20.

Ministry of Foreign Affairs. 1990. *Japan's Official Development Assistance*. Tokyo: Ministry of Foreign Affairs.

———. 1991. The ODA Loan Activities in FY90. Tokyo: April.

Mukherjee, Ramakrishna. 1974. *The Rise and Fall of the East India Company*. New York: Monthly Review Press.

Mulford, David. 1991. Statement before the Senate Committee on Finance, U.S. Senate. Washington, DC, 24 April.

Murakami, Yasusuke, and Yutaka Kosai, eds. 1986. *Japan in the Global Community: Its Role and Contribution on the Eve of the 21st Century*. Tokyo: University of Tokyo Press.

Nakasone, Yasuhiro. 1986. Community of Interests: Free-World Solidarity for Peace and Prosperity. Speech before the Parliament of Canada, Ottawa, 13 January.

OECD. 1982. *Geographical Distribution of Financial Flows to Developing Countries*. Paris: OECD.

———. 1985. *Development Co-operation: Efforts and Policies of the Members of the Development Assistance Committee*. Paris: OECD.

———. 1988. *Geographical Distribution of Financial Flows to Developing Countries*. Paris: OECD.

———. 1990. *Development Co-operation: Efforts and Policies of the Members of the Development Assistance Committee*. Paris: OECD.

———. 1991a. *Development Co-operation: Efforts and Policies of the Members of the Development Assistance Committee*. Paris: OECD.

———. 1991b. *Geographical Distribution of Financial Flows to Developing Countries*. Paris: OECD.

———. 1992. *Geographical Distribution of Financial Flows to Developing Countries*. Paris: OECD.

Okimoto, Daniel I. 1982. The Economics of National Defense. In *Japan's Economy: Coping with Change in the International Environment*, ed. Daniel I. Okimoto. Boulder, CO: Westview Press.

Okita, Saburo. 1986. Japan Is Advised to Diversify Investments to Aid Developing Nation's Economic Growth. *Japan Economic Journal*, 30 August, 7.

———. 1989. Japan's Quiet Strength. *Foreign Policy* 75 (Summer): 128–45.

Olson, Mancur, Jr., and Richard Zeckhauser. 1966. An Economic Theory of Alliances. *Review of Economics and Statistics* 48 (3): 266–76.

Orr, Robert, Jr. 1990. Collaboration or Conflict? Foreign Aid and U.S.–Japan Relations. *Pacific Affairs* (Winter): 476–89.

Peterson, Peter. 1987. A New Pacific Compact. Paper prepared for the joint meeting of the Keidanren and Atlantic Institute, 9 April.

Pharr, Susan. 1988. Statement before the Subcommittee on Asian and Pacific Affairs, Committee on Foreign Affairs, U.S. House of Representatives, Washington, DC, 28 September.

———. 1992. Japanese Aid in the New World Order. Paper presented at the Woodrow Wilson Center's Japan and the World conference, 27–28 January.

Pincus, John A. 1962. *Sharing the Costs of Military Alliance and International Economic Aid.* Santa Monica, CA: Rand Corporation.

Preeg, Ernest. 1989a. *The Tied Aid Credit Issue: U.S. Export Competitiveness in Developing Countries.* Washington, DC: Center for Strategic and International Studies.

———. 1989b. Trade, Aid, and Capital Projects. *Washington Quarterly* 12 (Winter): 173–85.

———. 1991. Comment. In *Yen for Development: Japanese Foreign Aid and the Politics of Burden-Sharing,* ed. Shafiqul Islam. New York: Council on Foreign Relations Press.

Pyle, Kenneth. 1989. The Burden of Japanese History and the Politics of Burden Sharing. In *Sharing World Leadership? A New Era for America and Japan,* ed. John H. Makin and Donald C. Hellmann. Washington, DC: American Enterprise Institute for Public Policy Research.

Reed, Robert. 1983. *The U.S.-Japan Alliance: Sharing the Burden of Defense.* Washington, DC: National Defense University Press.

Rix, Alan. 1992. Managing Japan's Aid: ASEAN. In *Japan's Foreign Aid Power and Policy in a New Era,* ed. Bruce Koppel and Robert Orr, Jr. Boulder, CO: Westview Press.

Robinson, James D., III. 1986. Defusing the Time Bomb: A Proposal for the Tokyo Economic Summit. Speech delivered before Keidanren, Tokyo, 18 February.

Samuelson, Paul. 1954. The Pure Theory of Public Expenditure. *Review of Economics and Statistics* 36: 387–89.

Schroeder, Pat. 1988. The Burden-Sharing Numbers Racket. *The New York Times,* 6 April.

Sinha, Radha. 1982. Japan and ASEAN: A Special Relationship? *The World Today* 38 (12): 483–92.

Smith, Charles, and Louise do Rosario. 1990. Empire of the Sun. *Far Eastern Economic Review,* 3 May, 46–48.

Storry, Richard. 1979. *Japan and the Decline of the West in Asia, 1894–1943.* New York: St. Martin's Press.

Takeshita, Noboru. 1991. Japan's International Cooperation Initiative. In Ministry of Foreign Affairs, *Outlook of Japan's Economic Cooperation.* Tokyo: Ministry of Foreign Affairs, November.

United Nations Development Program. 1991. *Human Development Report.* New York; Oxford University Press.

U.S. Export Import Bank. 1989. Report to the U.S. Congress on Tied Aid Credit Practices. Washington, DC, April.

———. 1991. Report to the U.S. Congress on Tied Aid Credit Practices. Washington, DC, October.

U.S. General Accounting Office (GAO). 1990. *Economic Assistance: Integration of Japanese Aid and Trade Policies.* Washington, DC: U.S. Government Printing Office.

Wade, Robert. 1992. East Asia's Economic Success: Conflicting Perspectives, Partial Insights, Shaky Evidence. *World Politics* 44 (2): 270–320.

Weidenbaum, Murray. 1968. Defense Expenditure and the Domestic Economy. In *Defense, Science, and Public Policy,* ed. Edwin Mansfield. New York: W. W. Norton.

Wihtol, Robert. 1988. *The Asian Development Bank and Rural Development.* New York: St. Martin's Press.

World Bank. 1986. *World Development Report.* New York: Oxford University Press.

———. 1990. *World Development Report.* New York: Oxford University Press.

World Institute for Development Economic Research (WIDER). 1987. *Mobilizing International Surpluses for World Development: A Wider Plan for a Japanese Initiative.* Study Group Series no. 2. Helsinki: WIDER Publications.

Yamamura, Kozo. 1989. Shedding History's Inertia: The U.S.-Japanese Alliance in a Changed World. In *Sharing World Leadership? A New Era for America and Japan,* ed. John H. Makin and Donald C. Hellmann. Washington, DC: American Enterprise Institute for Public Policy Research.

Yasutomo, Dennis. 1983. *Japan and the Asian Development Bank.* New York: Praeger Special Studies.

———. 1992. Japan and the Asian Development Bank: Multilateral Aid Policy in Transition. In *Japan's Foreign Aid Power and Policy in a New Era,* eds. Bruce Koppel and Robert Orr, Jr. Boulder, CO: Westview Press.

Comment   Stephen D. Krasner

Shafiqul Islam's discussion of Japanese official development assistance (ODA) takes on virtually every objection that has ever been raised about Japan's behavior and concludes that almost all of these criticisms are unwarranted. The issue that activates Islam's paper is whether Japanese ODA is different from that of other major donor countries and whether it is worse or better in terms of the benefits that it provides to recipients.

Foreign aid is a new development in the history of the international system. Before the Second World War there were no public capital transfers designed to promote the general development of poorer countries as opposed to the specific economic, political, or security interests of the lending state (Lumsdaine 1993). Much of the current transfer of development assistance cannot be explained by the narrow national interests of the donor countries. This is most obvious for small wealthy European countries such as the Netherlands or the Nordic countries, which commit relatively large proportions of their GNP to ODA yet cannot expect to reap much in the way of specific security or economic benefits.

Is Japanese ODA more closely related to identifiable economic interests than is the case for other donor countries? This volume is concerned specifically with Pacific Asia. In this area, as Islam points out, the ties between Japanese trade and investment interests and foreign aid may not always be obvious. At the global level, however, there is a closer relationship between Japanese ODA and Japanese economic interests than is the case for any other major

Stephen D. Krasner is Graham H. Stuart Professor of International Relations at Stanford University.

donor country. As table 8.1 points out, in 1989/90 69 percent of Japan's bilateral disbursements went to Asia, the developing area where Japan has, or might expect to have, the most concentrated economic interests. In contrast, about half of American assistance goes to the Middle East, specifically to Israel and Egypt. This assistance is designed to enhance the military and economic security of the region, a benefit that accrues to all oil importers, not just to the United States. The bilateral assistance of the major European countries is concentrated in Africa, an area of limited economic consequence. (In 1987 3.2 percent of Western Europe's exports went to Africa and 2.8 percent of Western Europe's imports originated in Africa. The Middle East accounted for 3 percent of North America's exports and 2 percent of its imports. In contrast, South and East Asia accounted for 23 percent of Japan's exports, and 29 percent of its imports [GATT 1988, table AA10].)

Correlation coefficients between the level of trade (exports plus imports) and the level of bilateral aid for the ten largest recipients of ODA were .68 for Japan, .41 for the United States, −.12 for France, and .54 for Germany—the four largest donors.[1]

This is a simple measure. Trade is not the only indicator of economic involvement. These figures do suggest, however, that there is a closer relationship between aid and economic interest for Japan than for any of the other three largest donor countries.

The fact that Japan's aid is concentrated in Pacific Asia, the developing area where it has the highest level of economic interest, does not imply that this aid is in any way economically harmful to the recipients. On the contrary, the more favorable the terms of aid, the greater the likelihood of generating dependent relations that would limit the options available to aid recipients. It is the creation of asymmetrical opportunity costs of change that allows one economic actor to exercise power over another. Coercive threats can only be credible if the implementation of the threat would be more costly for the target than for the threatener; that is, if the donor country can explicitly or implicitly threaten to withdraw aid at little cost to itself and the target country would suffer if the threat were implemented. This relationship between economic transactions and political power was analyzed more than fifty years ago by Albert Hirschman (1945). Japan's relations with East Asia in aid, investment, and trade are completely consistent with an effort to create a set of economic links that engender asymmetrical opportunity costs of change and thereby enhance Japanese power.

Such a policy is neither mysterious nor reprehensible. On the contrary, given the level of global uncertainty engendered by the end of the Cold War and the fear if not the reality of rising regionalism, Japanese efforts to establish a more predictable and stable environment in Asia, by making Asian countries more dependent on Japan than Japan is on them, reflects a prudent concern with

1. Derived from figures in OECD (1990, section E, table 43) and International Monetary Fund (1990, country pages).

Japanese national interests. Such a motivation is, however, different from the more diffuse and altruistic concerns that have motivated ODA from many other countries.

Islam asserts that "the view that Japan is gradually consolidating its hold on its Asian neighbors in the sense that it is increasingly influencing their economic policies and domestic politics is at best an unwarranted fear, and at worst an insult to the people of these sovereign countries. . . . they are some of the most dynamic economies of the world with highly proud people and powerful nationalist governments." This is a vacuous analytic argument. The extent to which one state can exercise influence over another as a result of economic transactions is a function of relative opportunity costs of change, not national pride. Aid, trade, and investment can all contribute to such asymmetries. So long as the United States remains actively engaged in Asia both economically and militarily, Japanese leverage will be limited. But if Asian trade and investment do become more focused on Japan, such leverage would increase.

Of the many specific points made in Islam's paper that bear closer scrutiny, the most provocative is his assertion that "Japan is more open to the countries in question [the ASEAN-Four] than the United States is." The data supporting this argument are presented in table 8.13. Islam admits that assessing openness in terms of the percentage of GNP accounted for by imports is not the best measure. Large countries generally have lower trade ratios; the normal expectation would be that the United States would import less from the ASEAN-Four than Japan does.

This point aside, many of the complaints about the closed nature of the Japanese market have emphasized manufactures rather than general merchandise imports. Table 8C.1 shows the percentage of Japanese and American imports accounted for by manufactures (SITC numbers 5–8) from the ASEAN-Four, as well as from other major Asian trading countries.

In every instance a substantially higher proportion of American imports from Asian countries is accounted for by manufactures. Japan is markedly more closed to manufacturing imports than the United States is.

The U.S.-Japanese relationship is, as Islam points out, troubled in the area

Table 8C.1   **Manufacturing Imports as a Percentage of Total Imports**

	United States	Japan
Indonesia	48	15
Malaysia	86	18
Philippines	83	33
Thailand	77	48
Singapore	96	41
South Korea	99	80
Taiwan	98	69

Source: Figures in OECD (1992, 3:11–86, 4:11–85).

of foreign aid and elsewhere. Japan is now the second largest economy in the world. Its GNP, which was about 10 percent that of the United States after the Second World War, is now 60 percent. Japan, unlike any of the European states, has continued to grow at a faster rate than the United States. The growth of Japan, coupled with the collapse of the Soviet Union, constitutes a major change in the international distribution of power. Neither the United States nor Japan has yet found an effective way to manage this power transition.

Islam points out in his discussion of U.S.-Japanese relations in the Asian Development Bank that American policymakers have not been enthusiastic about sharing decision making with other states, including Japan. The ADB is no exception. At the same time, Japan's behavior in the area of ODA, as in other arenas, has been closely oriented toward specific Japanese interests. Japan has not exercised effective leadership in any global issue area.

The bilateral relationship between the United States and Japan is the most important in the world; it is not being handled well by either country at either the regional or the global level. Asia is not inherently stable. Without the United States, Japan would be threatening to its neighbors but would not be strong enough to impose a stable order. Establishing a viable long-term relationship between the United States and Japan must involve a recognition by the United States that power configurations have changed and that policymaking must be more bilateral, if not multilateral, in Asia.

At the same time, Japan must recognize that stability can be maintained only if Japan is willing to give other countries a greater stake in the Japanese market. Such a stake can be created only if Japan becomes more open to the manufactured products of other Asian countries as well as of the United States and Europe. The most effective leadership that could be offered by Japan would be to make the Pacific more truly interdependent. Unfortunately, Japan shows fewer signs of doing this than American policymakers do of truly sharing decision making. For Japan, as opposed to any other advanced industrialized country, real leadership means changing internal behavior more than foreign policy.

Since 1945 Japan has consistently pursued a policy in ODA and elsewhere that has been closely related to specific Japanese national interests. The United States has been much more oriented toward milieu goals. Japan is now too big, and the United States too small, to continue such policies in the future. Glorifications of Japanese behavior, such as Islam's paper, do no more to contribute to viable long-term U.S.-Japanese cooperation than do similar celebrations of America's faltering leadership.

References

GATT. 1988. *International Trade, 1987–1988*. Geneva: GATT.

Hirschman, Albert. 1945. *National Power and the Structure of Foreign Trade*. Berkeley: University of California Press.

International Monetary Fund. 1990. *Direction of Trade Statistics, Yearbook 1990*. Washington, DC: IMF.

Lumsdaine, David H. 1993. *Moral Vision in International Politics: The Foreign Aid Regime, 1949–1989.* Princeton: Princeton University Press.

OECD. 1990. *Development Co-operation, 1990 Report.* Paris: OECD.

————. 1992. *Foreign Trade by Commodities, 1990.* Paris: OECD.

Comment   Robert Dekle

Some analysts have claimed that Japan after World War II has been one of the principal beneficiaries of an international political stability that came mostly at the expense of U.S. taxpayers (Prestowitz 1988, 331; Schroeder 1988). This potential "free ride" is said to have provided Japan with the resources to grow at over 9 percent per year between 1951 and 1971 and at an average annual rate of over 4.3 percent thereafter.

In this comment, I critique the above claim by reviewing recent studies that have shown that even a markedly higher level of Japanese defense spending would not have significantly lowered Japan's real economic growth rate, especially until 1970. The literature suggests that had Japan raised its defense budget–GNP level from its customary 1 percent to the U.S. level of approximately 6.5 percent, Japan's annual real output growth rate would have declined by an average of only 0.5 percent between 1970 and 1985. During Japan's rapid economic growth period that lasted until 1971, this fall is negligible, although a 0.5 percent annual fall is more significant during the subsequent slower growth period. However, I argue that, after 1970, part of the potential fall caused by the increased defense spending could have been offset by increased technological progress, a possible externality arising from defense.

This comment has three parts. In part 1, I review Japan's defense spending and provide adjustments to Japan's defense budget to make it comparable to America's. In part 2, using a result from the theory of public goods, I argue that during the Cold War era it was probably not unreasonable for Japan's allies to expect Japan to contribute between 3.4 and 6.5 percent of its GNP on security-related activities. In part 3, I review two recent studies on the relationship between defense spending and economic performance in Japan.

1. Table 8C.2 lists Japanese defense expenditures for 1991. The American and Japanese defense budgets over time are compared in table 8C.3, which shows that during the 1980s American defense spending was on average ten times higher than that in Japan. American and Japanese defense budgets are not directly comparable. The American budget includes spending on regular military forces and military pensions. The Japanese defense budget omits military pensions. In addition, the Japanese government's support for U.S. forces

Robert Dekle is assistant professor of economics and international relations at Boston University.

Table 8C.2   **Japanese Defense Expenditures, 1991**

	Billions of Yen	Billions of Dollars (135 yen = $1)
Salaries, food	1,757	12.86
Procurement of equipment	1,216	9.0
Research and development	103	0.824
Maintenance of facilities (airports, housing)	136	1.00
Maintenance of equiment, training	697	5.16
Maintenance of civilian areas surrounding military bases	425	3.15
Other	53	0.39
Total	4,387	32.49

Source: Japanese Self-Defense Agency (1991).

stationed in Japan, listed as $1.2 billion in the 1991 defense budget, is probably an underestimate of Japan's true economic cost.

Military pensions actually paid by the Japanese government in 1991 totaled 310.1 billion yen or $2.29 billion. In Japan, there are sixteen American bases, including eight in Okinawa prefecture. These bases house 50,800 people in the American military. The Japanese government is partially responsible for the physical maintenance of these bases and for the salaries and benefits of the Japanese working there. Surprisingly, the economic opportunity cost of the use of Japanese government land is omitted from the Japanese defense budget. For the six bases in the greater Tokyo area, the opportunity costs seem very high.[1] It is estimated that American bases occupy 20 percent of the total area of Okinawa island and almost 60 percent of the prefecture's navigable harbors. The U.S. Defense Department's *Allied Contributions to the Common Defense* lists an estimate of the opportunity cost of the use of Japanese land in 1991 as $0.71 billion. Assuming that this estimate is based on official land price data, the true opportunity cost could be five times as large.[2] Accordingly, we multiply $0.71 by 5 and obtain $3.55 billion. Adding to the 1991 Japanese defense budget the $2.29 billion of military pensions and the $3.55 billion of land use opportunity costs, we get $38.33 billion, or 1.09 percent of Japan's 1991 GNP.

In the spring of 1991, Japan completed its $13 billion payment to the Gulf Peace Fund to underwrite the Multinational Force's war against Iraq. As does the United States, Japan omits military aid from its defense budget. U.S. mili-

1. Yokota, Zama, Atsugi, Yokohama, Kamiseya, Yokosuka.
2. After the rapid rise in land prices in the late 1980s, the market price of land can be up to five times the official price reported by the Japanese government (Ito 1992, 417).

Table 8C.3   **Japanese and American Defense Expenditures Compared**

| | Japanese | | | | United States | |
	Defense (billions of 1988 yen) (1)	Defense (billions of 1988 dollars) (2)	Defense/GNP (3)	Defense/Government Budget (4)	Defense (billions of 1988 dollars) (5)	Defense/GNP (6)
1955	1480		1.78	13.61		
1965	1568		1.07	8.24		
1975	2008		0.84	6.23		
1976	2169		0.9	6.22		
1977	2270		0.88	5.93		
1978	2476		0.9	5.54		
1979	2617		0.9	5.43		
1980	2625		0.9	5.24		
1981	2727	21	0.91	5.13	221	5.7
1982	2863	22	0.93	5.21	241	6.3
1983	3004	23	0.98	5.47	259	6.5
1984	3127	24	0.99	5.8	271	6.4
1985	3268	25	0.997	5.98	290	6.6
1986	3439	26	0.993	6.18	305	6.7
1987	3571	27	1.004	6.5	301	6.4
1988	3700	28	1.013	6.53	296	6.1
1989	3775	29	1.006	6.49	289	5.8
1990	3968	31	0.997	6.28	268	5.7

Sources: Columns (1), (3), and (4) are from Japanese Self-Defense Agency (1991). The figures are deflated by the deflator for Japanese government expenditures. Columns (2), (5), and (6) are from SIPRI (1991).

tary aid, called "security assistance," is in the budget of the State Department, and in 1991, it totaled $8.8 billion. When Japan's $13 billion Gulf payment is added to its defense budget, Japan's defense GNP share rises to 1.47 percent. Since the Gulf contribution is unlikely to be repeated, we omit it from Japan's defense budget in the discussion below.

2. The 1.09 percent of GNP figure puts Japan's security contribution below those of Italy (2.7 percent), Canada (2.2 percent), and even the non-NATO European nations, Austria (1.3 percent) and Finland (1.4 percent). In Dekle (1989), I argued that in the immediate aftermath of the Reagan defense buildup, Japan's benefits from world security were consistent with its spending between 3.4 and 6.5 percent of its GNP on defense. The argument rests on a well-known principle in public finance: to have an optimal supply of a public good, it is sufficient to tax each person an amount equal to his marginal benefit from the public good. If the marginal benefit of defense is proportional to GNP, then Japan's defense contribution should be between 3.4 and 6.5 percent of GNP, the defense-GNP shares of Germany and the United States, respectively. Japan's GNP is between America's and Germany's in size.[3]

3. Changes in a country's defense spending affect the country's economic performance from both the aggregate demand and supply sides. The demand-side effects predominate in the short and medium runs when the economy is adjusting to a different full-employment level. Most large-scale econometric models emphasize the demand side, and these models usually predict the following effects when, say, the United States runs a fiscal or defense expansion without monetary accommodation. The dollar, the U.S. real GNP, and the real interest rates rise, and the U.S. multilateral current account deteriorates. Imports increase due to higher GNP and higher prices for domestically produced goods. Exports fall because of more expensive exportables. Depending on the model, the current account worsens more than the trade balance; the higher interest rate on foreign debt raises interest payments made abroad. For example, the Japanese Economic Planning Agency predicts that a 1 percentage point increase in the U.S. government spending–GNP ratio will worsen America's current account–GNP ratio by 0.77 percentage points (Economic Planning Agency 1988).

In the medium to long run, most economists would argue that the supply-side effects dominate in the world. Recently Dekle (1989) and Wong (1989) have separately examined the supply-side effects of increases in defense spending, the former for the period between 1961 and 1971, the latter using data between 1970 and 1985.

From the aggregate production function, making some simplifying assumptions, we know that growth in output is equal to

---

3. There is no presumption that this allocation is fair. To make an assessment of fairness, we must make an assumption of what distribution of national income among allied nations is desirable. Such an assumption will always be arbitrary.

$$\frac{\text{Output}}{\text{Growth}} = \frac{\text{Capital}}{\text{share}} * \frac{\text{Growth in}}{\text{capital stock}} + \frac{\text{Labor}}{\text{share}} * \frac{\text{Growth in}}{\text{labor stock}} + \text{Residual.}^4$$

An increase in defense spending will draw capital and labor from productive use. The degree to which output is affected depends on the size of the residual, which is said to represent technical progress. The larger the residual, the smaller is the effect on output of a change in the factor inputs, assuming that technological progress is disembodied from capital. In Japan, the residual is large, accounting for over 55 percent of the Japanese economic growth rate, which may explain why Japan's economic growth is lowered by only 0.5 percent when Japan's defense spending–GNP ratio is raised from 1 percent to 6.5 percent (Denison and Chung 1976).[5] If technological progress is embodied in capital, the results below may underestimate the negative impact of defense spending.[6]

Dekle (1989) borrows from the growth accounting framework of Denison and Chung and shows that, if Japan's defense-GNP ratio had been approximately the U.S. level of 6.5 percent, Japan's national income would have grown between 1961 and 1971 at 8.76 percent a year, instead of the actual 9.29 percent, a decline of 0.53 percent. The reason for the relatively small fall is that many other factors besides the growth of capital were responsible for the rapid growth of Japanese national income. Dekle assumes that defense spending crowds out investment in nonresidential structures and equipment one for one. Unlike Wong (1989), Dekle assumes that investment in different years is uncorrelated, and declines in the capital stock are not cumulative.

Wong's (1989) study takes into account changes in both capital and labor. He finds that an increase in defense spending seriously dampens the accumulation of the capital stock in the private sector. An increase in the Japanese defense expenditure–GNP share to the U.S. share of 6.5 percent lowers the Japanese capital stock by 37 percent between 1970 and 1985. The reason the capital stock falls so much is that, in Wong's model, investment is a function of GNP. A fall in investment this year is said to lower current GNP, which lowers investment next year. That is, the damage to the capital stock is cumulative. Private sector labor also falls as more people are enlisted in the Japanese armed forces. Since labor supply is less plausibly related to GNP, next period's labor supply is unaffected by this period's labor, so the fall in labor supply is not cumulative and is negligible, declining by only 2 percent between 1970 and 1985. The

---

4. Note that the equation is not structural; determinants of the growth in capital and labor are not specified.

5. The growth accounting literature pioneered by Denison (1967, 1974) has found that, for almost every country, output growth cannot be explained by the growth in capital and labor. There are often difficulties in accurately measuring the growth in capital and labor, and the size of the residual may partly reflect measurement error in addition to technical change.

6. The assumption of technological disembodiment from capital is probably false. It is well known that Japanese technological progress has proceeded by the rapid introduction of the latest vintage of capital equipment. The Japanese steel industry, for example, became highly efficient by incorporating oxygen-processing and large-scale, open-hearth furnaces.

combined effects of the annual declines in both capital and labor result in Japan's 1985 GNP being lower by about 7 percent than otherwise. The reason for the rather small decrease in GNP relative to the large decline in capital is that the capital share of output in Japan is only about one-fourth. A cumulative 7 percent decline occurring over fifteen years (1970–85) implies a 0.48 percent fall in the annual growth rate of output, which is very close to Dekle's estimate above. In contrast, however, to the near double-digit growth in the 1960s, Japanese GNP grew at only an average real rate of 4.38 percent between 1970 and 1985.

By assuming disembodied technical progress, both Wong and Dekle have ignored the relationship between defense and technical progress. The effect of defense spending on technical progress depends on what the spending is used for and which component of private investment is on the margin crowded out. If increased defense expenditures results in more military manpower at the expense of private R&D, technical progress may be retarded.

Zvi Griliches (1987) cites econometric results showing the differential impacts of military and private R&D. He finds that all R&D spending increases the annual growth rate of U.S. corporate output by 33 to 62 percent, depending on the year. Basic R&D has a premium over general R&D spending by several hundred percent. Griliches, however, does show that basic research undertaken by the private sector has a higher return than basic research undertaken by the government. Defense R&D is often characterized by inefficient featherbedding and cost-plus-profit procurement.

During the 1960s, most of Japan's technological progress was due to its catching-up with the best practice in the United States. The marginal value of defense R&D during this period was probably very low. In fact, it might have been negative if technological progress were embodied in capital; a crowding-out of private capital accumulation would have been detrimental to technological progress. Since the mid-1970s, however, Japan has almost caught up with the United States technologically. Higher military R&D could have helped Japan move up further along the technological frontier. While the U.S. government finances about half of the total U.S. R&D expenditures, the Japanese government supports only about 20 percent. Japan is not strong in rocketry, supercomputing, and computer software. The development of these fields entails a high degree of problem solving and unpredictability and requires an ability to integrate complicated systems. With no guarantee of government demand for new products, Japanese companies have followed a fairly conservative approach to R&D, emphasizing projects with a high degree of commercial feasibility. The absence of risk taking may have slowed Japanese technological development since the early 1970s, especially in frontier areas such as aerospace, satellites, and new materials. Increased defense R&D could have also improved Japan's basic research capacity. Relative to its strength in applied research, Japan is weak in basic research. A counting of citations in international scientific journals has revealed that Japan is fifth in the world in physics, fifth in chemistry, and third in the biological sciences.

References

Dekle, R. 1989. The Relationship between Defense Spending and Economic Performance in Japan. In J. Makin and D. Hellmann, eds., *Sharing World Leadership*. Washington, D.C.: American Enterprise Institute for Public Policy Research.

Denison, E. 1967. *Why Growth Rates Differ: Postwar Experience in the Western Countries*. Washington, D.C.: Brookings Institution.

———. 1974. *Accounting for United States Economic Growth, 1929–1969*. Washington, D.C.: Brookings Institution.

Denison, E., and William Chung. 1976. *How the Japanese Economy Grew So Fast*. Washington, D.C.: Brookings Institution.

Economic Planning Agency. 1988. External Balance Effects of Exchange Rate Changes and Macroeconomic Policies. In *Papers and Proceedings of the Fourth EPA International Symposium, March 15–17*. Tokyo: Economic Research Agency.

Griliches, Z. 1987. *Science,* July 3, 31–35. R and D Productivity: Measurement Issues and Econometric Results.

Ito, T. 1992. *The Japanese Economy.* Cambridge: MIT Press.

Japanese Self-Defense Agency. 1991. *Defense White Paper* (Boei-Hakusho). Tokyo: Ministry of Finance Printing Office.

Prestowitz, C., Jr. 1988. *Trading Places: How We Allowed Japan to Take the Lead.* New York: Basic Books.

Schroeder, P. 1988. *New York Times,* April 6, editorial page.

Stockholm International Peace Research Institute (SIPRI). 1991. *Yearbook: World Armaments and Disarmament.* Oxford: Oxford University Press.

U.S. Department of Defense. 1991. *Allied Contributions to the Common Defense.* Washington, D.C.: U.S. Government Printing Office.

Wong, K. 1989. National Defense and Foreign Trade: The Sweet and Sour Relationship between the United States and Japan. In J. Makin and D. Hellmann, eds., *Sharing World Leadership*. Washington, D.C.: American Enterprise Institute for Public Policy Research.

Comment   Takashi Inoguchi

It seems that the organizing concept of the conference was regionalism in Pacific Asia. By regionalism I mean possible or actual Pacific Asian regional arrangements that might affect positively or negatively what is seen as the United States' stake in the region. It is a good strategy to organize such a conference. In my view, it has been a successful strategy too. Yet it is somewhat narrow when one looks at the daunting set of issues confronting Pacific Asia in the beginning of the post–Cold War era.

Global Context

Let me briefly summarize what I see as the essential features of the world order after the end of the Cold War in general and those in Pacific Asia in

Takashi Inoguchi is professor of political science at the Institute of Oriental Culture, University of Tokyo.

particular (Inoguchi n.d.): (1) U.S. military dominance and the increasingly shaky foundations to sustain it in the longer term; (2) concurrent movements toward globalization and regionalization; and, (3) trends for liberalization and democratization and their destabilizing potentials.

With the end of the Cold War, the United States has emerged as the sole military superpower. Yet its longer-term economic and technological underpinnings are increasingly called into question in the United States. More vigorous efforts to counteract such deterioration in its competitive position are wanted. Political temptations to go isolationist are on the rise, especially in the year of the presidential election. Furthermore, potentials for competition and destabilization among regional powers abound in the longer term, at least when the United States' steady downsizing of its presence in the region is not yet made up for by some imaginative regional arrangements.

Technological progress has made the globe smaller and global economic transactions much easier. At the same time, intermittent structural adjustments become more or less unavoidable even to less competitive countries. The result is the increasing temptation to protectionism and regionalism of a malign kind. Pacific Asia needs global market access because the region as a whole has a much smaller market than its actual and potential productive capacity. Hence its vigorous movement to globalize its economic activities. Its need for globalization is made imperative, furthermore, first because the other two major regions of dense economic activities on the globe, Western Europe and North America, are manifesting increasing self-closure and second because the momentum for successfully concluding the Uruguay Round of GATT seems to be waning somewhat. Hence the need for the two concurrent tasks of globalizing Pacific Asian economic activities and enhancing intraregional economic transactions.

The entire globe has of late been in the process of economic liberalization and political democratization. The end of the Cold War has coincided with the trend of unraveling excessive economic regulation and control and of loosening political tyranny and authoritarianism. If Francis Fukuyama calls these processes the end of history, one might as well call these processes in Pacific Asia the midway of history. Economic liberalization in Pacific Asia has been slower than the other regions of dense economic transactions on the globe. Political democratization in Pacific Asia has been slower than in many Northern Hemisphere countries. The fact that Pacific Asia enjoys a high economic growth rate means that structural adjustments are both unavoidable and rapid. However, structural adjustments, when mishandled, tend to create social strains and political instability. Hence the need for the careful management of liberalization and democratization in Pacific Asia.

America's Anxiety

In the conference, the first and third sets of issues were not well addressed, while the second set of issues such as trade, aid, investment, technology, and bloc formation were more closely examined. While these mainly economic issues were discussed, the occasional surfacing of America's anxiety points to the importance of recognition of at least three themes that were not discussed but that underlay the whole discussion: (1) compatibility of Japan with the rest of the world (read the United States); (2) competitiveness of Japan vis-à-vis the rest of the world (read the United States); and (3) contributions of Japan to the rest of the world (read the United States).

Compatibility. America's anxiety is that Japanese may not be compatible with Americans; the Japanese look different and we may not be able to go along with them; they should be made compatible with us, as in further market openings; if not, we should close our door to them, whether it is trade, investment, or technology.

Competitiveness. America's anxiety is that Japan has unfairly acquired its advantage over the United States: the Japanese would be well advised to play the game on the level playing field. Furthermore, their unfairly acquired competitiveness should be reduced by encouraging them to divert their resources to two major tasks: more global financial contributions (e.g., the Gulf War) and more social infrastructure investment (e.g., the Structural Impediments Initiative talks).

Contributions. America's anxiety wavers between two extremes of "Japan's contributing too little, too late" and "Japan's contributing too much, too fast." The former extreme is America's reaction to Japan's reactiveness in the Gulf War, while the latter extreme is America's reaction to the Seattle-based business firms' purchase of the Seattle Mariners, in which Nintendo America contributed most by shouldering 60 percent of the whole cost of the purchase.

America's anxiety over Japan's possible or actual rise to predominance in Pacific Asia has been real. A number of questions come to mind immediately. How should the United States counteract Japan's rise to regional economic hegemony? How should the United States take advantage of its security hegemony to block Japan's rise to overall regional hegemony? How should the United States draw a strategy to keep Japan's neighbors closer to the United States than to Japan? These and related questions were raised in the conference, although they were much more textured and nuanced most of the time.

Creating Vulnerability through Technology?

It seems to me that, by allowing oneself to be guided by these questions, one is deliberately creating new sources of strain between Japan and the United States. For example, the argument advanced by David Friedman and Richard Samuels (chap. 7 in this volume), augmented by Peter Katzenstein and Martin Rouse (chap. 6 in this volume), is an impressive one, coming from those who know the subject so well. Yet their policy prescription is located in the sense of America's anxiety. They argue that, given Japan's tenacious way of borrowing, developing, and indigenizing technology from abroad without subsequently sharing much of their technological improvement with others, the United States should press Japan to open the market of technology so that technology learning would become a two-way flow. If this strategy fails—as their argument would go, I suspect—the United States should legitimately cut off technology flows to Japan. Furthermore—as their argument would go, I suspect—the United States should not allow Japan to penetrate the U.S. electronic and other markets in order to undermine the technological and manufacturing foundations of U.S. national security, since Japan's ingenious strategic use of economic and technological interdependence creates U.S. vulnerability to Japan by supplying parts of military weapons.

Japan's counterargument would be as follows: Japan is devoid of natural resources, especially energy and food, and does not enjoy strategic depth in national defense. Japan's many eggs—food, energy, technology, and security—are predominantly and thus dangerously in one basket called the United States. In other words, Japan's vulnerability to the United States is incredibly deep and manifold. Thus it is natural for Japan to enhance its autonomous ability in some of these areas to a certain extent and at the same time to divert some of its eggs from the United States to other regions, such as Pacific Asia and Western Europe, especially when the United States is increasingly critical of Japan. Even if Japan is able to create U.S. vulnerability to Japan in a few areas, that would be a much lighter kind of vulnerability than Japan's overall vulnerability to the U.S. Recognizing mutual vulnerability is one of the essential points of economic interdependence, after all. Even if mutual vulnerability is not symmetrical, it could lead to a more stable and sustainable friendship when it is managed with self-confidence and mutual trust. To resurrect the already stereotyped suspicion of Japan so tenaciously held in the United States, if inadvertently, by overemphasizing Japan's technonationalistic policy and its alleged negative effect on the United States, could spoil the overall friendship of the two countries and undermine the otherwise more productive interdependence between them. And the entire globe will suffer from more restricted flows of technology. More speculatively, the tendency to rely on patent fees for benefits might accelerate U.S. firms' tendency to make profits out of nonmanufacturing and their decline in competitiveness. It would be more productive to develop the scheme of sharing the R&D and manufacturing system and to allow a wider range of people to enjoy the benefits of technological progress while giving due credit to the innovators of science and technology.

Aid as a Trojan Horse?

Turning to Japan's aid, it seems to me that two kinds of perspective mingle nonsystematically in the minds of many Americans. One is that of burdensharing while the other is that of hegemonic cycle (Islam, chap. 8 of this volume). The former perspective says that Japan's aid is fundamentally commercially motivated. Thus Japan is seen as using aid to benefit Japanese business firms more than recipients; it is seen as being less interested in grants than loans; it is seen as being not so interested in raising the income level of ordinary people; it is seen as using aid to promote Japan's exports to recipients. The latter perspective says that Japan's aid is used to promote the state-designed scheme of economic hegemony in Pacific Asia. Thus Japan's aid is seen as an instrument of economic bloc formation; it is seen as an instrument of political-economic domination of recipient countries. What is confusing to me is that these two perspectives are arbitrarily chosen in order to advance whatever argument one wants to make about Japan's aid.

In order to make Japanese counterarguments, one needs to say a little about how Japan's foreign aid is conducted. It started as Japan's war reparations to some neighboring countries of Pacific Asia. Japan was obliged to pay them reparations because it inflicted suffering on them during the war, and defeated Japan had to pay them before the resumption of diplomatic relationships. Japan made the best use of these payments to increase commercial opportunities for Japanese business firms and to accelerate its own economic reconstruction. It does not seem that at that time there was any conception of war reparations as public goods either by Japan or by the United States, let alone any cooperation on the allocation of public goods between the two countries. Japan's official development assistance grew larger, in tandem with its steady economic growth. Japan's official development assistance has been based on its philosophy of thrift and self-help (Oshin, the heroine of a highly popular TV program in the early 1980s, and the Ministry of Finance are two good exemplars) and of "manufacturing matters" (Noboru Makino of the Mitsubishi Research Institute and the Ministry of International Trade and Industry speak for this). Related to these is an implicit Japanese developmental model (Inoguchi 1990): that developing countries must rely primarily on themselves, that too many grants spoil recipients, that recipients must be able to yield more benefits than mere interest payments by their ideas and efforts, that manufacturing is the basis of industrialization, that industrial infrastructure must be built ahead of almost anything else, and that, in doing all this, market forces take command, not politics, in the longer term. These tenets of the Japanese developmental model have surfaced recently in the publication of a World Bank study on industrialization of India, Indonesia, and South Korea. Masaki Shiratori, one of its executive directors, pushed this study against the mainstream view of the World Bank about developmental finance. The study underlined the importance of the government in economic development along with market forces.

Aside from these philosophical tenets, Japan's developmental assistance assigns a major role to two actors: recipient countries and Japanese business firms. The Japanese government has been working until recently on the strict principle that only upon request from recipients does it consider giving aid concretely. Naturally not only recipient governments but also local business firms and Japanese business firms cooperate in drawing up requests for aid, as many requests are in the areas of manufacturing and industrial infrastructure. Here is how market forces are mingled with Japanese aid, perhaps relaying Japan-led economic dynamism to recipient economies. Also important in Japan's official development assistance is that a large bulk of it comes from postal savings and government pension programs for which the government must be ready to make interest and other kinds of payments. Because of this heavy foundation, the Japanese government can make its aid sustainable for a long time, largely independent of economic vicissitudes from which normal tax revenues tend to suffer.

Since the basic picture of Japan's official development assistance should be clear by now, I should summarize the thrust of Japanese counterarguments.

First, as for the criticism of burdensharing, Japan's counterargument is simple and straightforward: one does not need to carry the Cold War ideological baggage in order to assess aid practices. Having moved into the post–Cold War era, one needs to fathom more carefully the ideas and institutions evolving within national borders and to think what kind of cooperation can be done on that basis toward the enlargement of global welfare, or more specifically in terms of economic development, technological progress, social equality, and political democracy. Here the notion of global contributions may be more helpful in assessing aid practices than burdensharing. According to this view, the wide-ranging areas of common policy agendas, like controlling carbon dioxide, arms control, telecommunications networks, codevelopment and comanufacturing of industrial technologies and commodities, and training bureaucrats and business managers, are to be taken as global contributions of one sort or another, especially when these endeavors are conceived and implemented as multilateral action, with Japan embedding itself in international institutions (Inoguchi 1992). When the post–Cold War era witnesses many competing perspectives on how the globe will evolve and how it should be managed, such a global-contributions perspective ought to be taken up more widely, even when the role of Japan and the United States is the main subject.

Second, as for the criticism of Japan's attempting to use aid as a Trojan horse for economic bloc formation or political domination, Japan's counterargument is simple and straightforward: one does not need to be awed by Japan. Japan's power tends to be exaggerated in the United States, if only to mobilize Americans for self-revitalization. Japan would not benefit in the longer term from bloc formation. Japan (and Pacific Asia) needs global market access, not access to one bloc. Bloc formation is counterproductive in Pacific Asia. Japan would not benefit from political domination, either. If Japan's official development assistance is termed a success, it is due in no small part to its largely market-conforming aid policy. No less important is the resilience of recipient countries, especially in Pacific Asia. Their nationalism is very strong. It is a force in Pacific Asia that has never been fully fathomed by Americans, even after the Vietnam War.

Pride and Prejudice

In working out the relationship between Japan and the United States in Pacific Asia, I would like to evoke the themes of Jane Austen's novel *Pride and Prejudice*. Both Japanese and Americans have pride. The United States has its hegemonic pride, while Japan has pride in its manufacturing competitiveness. That it has pride is natural and legitimate. We cannot suppress it. We should use it for good purposes. Both Japanese and Americans are prejudiced against each other, sometimes poisonously, often in racist terms. Their prejudices should not be encouraged to grow so far as to reach the level of the 1940s. Both Japanese and Americans need to moderate pride and mitigate prejudice to work out their relationship.

More specifically, the two peoples may be encouraged to think about themselves in a new fashion. I believe that Americans should be encouraged to think in terms of "America among equals" and that Japanese should be encouraged to think in terms of "Japan among responsibles." America has been the leader until now and will be for some time to come. Yet America's power will be found more in its ability to coordinate among equals as *primus inter pares*. Its attempt to hold onto its position of absolute preponderence, for a longer time to come than its own power bases suggest, would accelerate its downscaling in power and prestige. Its attempt to punish and mold others in its own fashion beyond the direction of market forces would be like spitting against Heaven, resulting in its own spit falling down back onto its face. Japan has so far been a half-hearted supporter of the United States–led global community. As Hegel says, however, Minerva flies out only in the dusk. In other words, only in the declining phase of the leadership can its leader theorize its world vision and ideology in a clear, consistent fashion. Japan is not the leader; it has been on the rise for only the last two decades; its plateau-like stagnation is speculated to come around 2010. Therefore it is not difficult to find that Japan's role in the global community has tended to be largely partial, piecemeal, pragmatic, and sometimes problematic. Yet Japan's role should be increasingly a responsible supporter. Its attempt to flirt with the notion of an autonomous, independent molder of global affairs is bound to be a farce in the era of global interdependence. Nor would its attempt to evade the exercise of coleadership in global management promise success. In the final analysis, however, I am of the view that both Japanese and Americans can adapt to the new environment and to their respective new roles, as they are two of the most dynamic nations on the globe.

References

Inoguchi, Takashi. 1990. Japan's Politics of Interdependence. *Government and Opposition* 25 (4): 412–37. Reprinted in Takashi Inoguchi, *Japan's International Relations,* 103–24. London: Pinter, 1991.

————. 1992. Japan's Role in International Affairs. *Survival* 34 (2): 71–87.

————. n.d. Dialectics of World Order: A View from Pacific Asia. In *Whose World Order? Uneven Globalization and the End of the Cold War,* eds. H.-H. Holm and G. Sorensen. Boulder, Colo.: Westview Press. Forthcoming.

9   U.S. Political Pressure and Economic Liberalization in East Asia

Takatoshi Ito

9.1   Introduction and Summary

The objective of this paper is twofold, first, to evaluate U.S. pressure for economic liberalization in Japan; second, to discuss its implications for economic and political aspects of the East Asian regional future.

I argue that there have been three types of U.S. pressure on Japan: (1) the traditional type with voluntary export restraints (VERs) and other export-limiting measures on Japan; (2) the Structural Impediments Initiative (SII) type in which market access of Japan improves the Japanese consumers' welfare; and (3) the super 301 type in which unilateral U.S. gains are sought (see table 9.1).

Although various administrations of the United States have put pressure on Japan to limit exports (starting with cotton textiles in 1956), the efforts by the Reagan-Bush administration throughout the 1980s have been marked by widened coverage of issues and heightened political tensions. Rather than more import quotas and VERs, the United States demanded market access and market shares in Japan. The logic was clear. It is better to increase U.S. exports to Japan, achieving an equilibrium with higher volume, than to limit Japan's exports to the United States, achieving an equilibrium with lower volume.

Financial deregulation in Japan was explicitly mentioned in the Yen-Dollar Agreement in May 1984. More liberalized financial markets were supposed to invite foreign investment and financial companies to Japan, thus correcting for

Takatoshi Ito is professor of economics at the Institute of Economics Research, Hitotsubashi University; visiting professor at the John F. Kennedy School of Government, Harvard University, 1992–93; and a research associate of the National Bureau of Economic Research.

The author is grateful for helpful comments by Jeffrey Frankel, Jeffry Frieden, Frances Rosenbluth, and other conference participants.

Table 9.1   **Types of Trade Conflicts between the United States and Japan**

	Winners	Losers	Examples
Export-limiting measures: VERs and OMAs	U.S. producers	U.S. consumers	Textiles, color TVs, steel, machine tools, autos
	Japanese producers (long run)	Japanese producers (short run)	
Market access measures: MOSS-SII type	Japanese consumers U.S. producers	Japanese producers	Large retail store law, rice, deposit interest deregulation, antimonopoly law enforcement, satellite procurement
Revisionist measures: results-oriented type	U.S. producers	Japanese producers Japanese consumers	Semiconductor agreement, super 301, January 1992 agreement on U.S. autos

Note: Winners and losers can be verified using a standard partial equilibrium model.

the dollar overvaluation at that time. The Market-Oriented Sector Selective (MOSS) talks targeted several products. Beef and citrus became symbolic issues of the mid-1980s. In 1987, the SII started to address many issues in the Japanese economy. Among others, the large retail store law in Japan was heavily criticized by the United States. The law, the United States contended, prevents an expansion of the number of large retail stores (such as discount stores), which carry more imports than do traditional corner stores, thus contributing to lower imports of manufactured goods. The single most important issue concerning import restrictions and market access of Japan at present is how to liberalize rice imports. At the Uruguay Round, the United States insisted that Japan move to the tariff system and gradually reduce the tariff rate, while Japan insisted on exceptional treatment of rice for Japan.

The pattern of the United States' pressuring Japan and Japan's conceding to U.S. demands is best understood as a reflection of domestic politics in the two countries. In the United States, with the split government in the 1980s, external economic issues, especially mounting trade deficits, were used, or exploited, as effective political charges and countercharges. Congress tends to blame the president for lack of a program to reduce the current account deficits, and attempts to take matters into its own hands, as in the Omnibus Trade Bill with super 301. The administration, especially the U.S. Trade Representative (USTR), trying to head off congressional meddling, pushed Japan to agree on a series of "liberalizations."

In some quarters in the Japanese government, the U.S. demands were seen as "foreign pressure," which would help dismantle vested interest with minimal political costs. The U.S. pressure was perceived as something beyond the Japanese government's control, so that no one, neither government officials nor politicians, had to assume responsibility for taking away vested interests and oligopolistic rents from producers and big corporations.

In summary, U.S. pressure of the SII type was used to liberalize and deregulate the Japanese economy, benefiting Japanese consumers and foreign producers. It recently backfired, however, because the ritual of U.S. "bullying," if not "bashing," Japan and Japan's giving "concessions" produced anti-Japan sentiment in the United States and dislike of the United States in Japan. The relationship in the 1990s will be much more strained than before.

The new type of U.S. pressure is unilateralism, pursuing U.S. unilateral gains. U.S. demands became more results oriented; that is, the United States defines a market share in Japan in an agreement and has Japan commit to it under threat of retaliatory measures.

The target of U.S. demands has not been limited to Japan but includes other Asian countries, such as Korea and Taiwan. Textile VERs were also applied for these countries in the 1960s and 1970s. In the 1980s, Korea and Taiwan were accused of artificially pegging their currencies to the U.S. dollar so that their exports to the United States did not decrease after the sharp yen appreciation triggered by the Plaza Agreement.

U.S. demands for economic liberalizations in Japan and other Asian countries have several implications. First, if the current tendency of U.S. demands cum Japanese concessions continues, Japanese resentment against the United States may turn into a desire to have stronger relations with Asian neighbors. However, this possibility is limited by lack of political leadership in Japan and by suspicious reactions to Japanese overtures by Asian neighbors. Second, fast-growing intraregional trades have been rather specialized. Typically, Japan exports parts and intermediate goods, and newly industrialized economies (NIEs) export final goods to the United States. Unless Japan imports much more from Asian neighbors, it would not replace the United States as an absorber of Asian goods. Hence, the link between Japan and the Asian countries remains weak. In other words, Japan is not ready to take a leadership role to replace the United States in the Asian region as a nexus of political and economic links.

Signs of change, however, are abundant. Japan for the first time sent mine sweepers to the Persian Gulf, though after the war. This is regarded as a sign of change in Japan's commitment to political change. Japan's trade structures are rapidly changing, partly due to U.S. demands. The share of manufactured imports now reaches almost 50 percent. Japan may increase imports from Asian neighbors in the future.

The biggest stumbling block to Japan's becoming a regional economic and political leader is lack of principles. Would Japan tolerate political suppression to achieve an economic order? Would Japan help technological transfers with direct investment? Would Japan continue saving a large portion of income even if the standard of living were sacrificed? Asian neighbors will not fully trust Japanese leadership, unless the principles of the Japanese political economy become clear. If Japan cannot project its economic-political principles, then Asian neighbors will remain suspicious of its hegemony in the region.

9.2   United States–East Asian Countries Conflicts, 1956–81

9.2.1   Conflicts of the Traditional Type

U.S.-Japan Conflicts, 1950s–1970s

Traditional conflicts between the United States and Japan (and other East Asian countries) originate from sharp increases in export of a particular product. Producers in the United States bring complaints to the U.S. government, sometimes with formal antidumping charges but most often with political pressures. Complaints might start when the market share of imports increases sharply. As long as an "injury" is felt, the level of market share might be as little as 5 percent, as in the case of cotton. The U.S. government negotiates with the exporting country. With political pressures and threats, sometimes also linking other issues, the United States always succeeds, if with a long delay, in negotiating some kind of export-limiting measures, VERs and orderly marketing agreements (OMAs).[1] This pattern was repeated in cotton, synthetics, color TVs, steel, and automobiles, for example (table 9.2).

The textiles issue was the first trade conflict between the United States and Japan in the mid-1950s, and resulted in the first VER between the two countries in 1957.[2] The textile issue, changing the focus of particular products, remained a major issue between the two countries until the 1970s.

Hence, the traditional U.S. pressure on East Asian countries was a measure to limit exports, burdening the exporting countries, such as VERs or OMAs. The political process is like that summarized above.[3]

Yoffie (1983) analyzed the dynamics of U.S. pressures and responses by

1. See Hillman and Ursprung (1988) for why VERs could be politically preferable to tariffs. In the GATT framework, tariffs were not an option. Yoffie (1983) contrasts VERs of the 1950s through the 1970s with tariffs in the 1930s.

2. In 1956, the United States tried to limit Japanese exports. "Although Japanese textile imports represented a small portion of American consumption (approximately 2 percent), in a few categories such as gingham, velveteen, and women's blouses, Japanese sales were reaching two-thirds of apparent consumption and putting some American producers out of business" (Yoffie 1983, 45). After several rounds of negotiation (described in Yoffie 1983, 44–58), "on January 16, 1957, the Departments of State, Commerce, and Agriculture released a joint statement concerning the 'details of the Japanese program for the control of exports of cotton textiles to the United States'" (58). This set the precedent for VERs.

3. This section is in broad agreement with opinions in Yoffie (1983), Destler and Sato (1982), Destler, Fukui, and Sato (1979), and Destler (1986). Yoffie (1983, 4–5) pointed out three characteristics of VERs and OMAs, as opposed to the interwar tariff war: (1) they are negotiated and bargained between two countries; (2) they use quantitative limits; (3) they are selective and so discriminate among exporters.

Table 9.2   **Historical Overview of U.S.–Japan Trade Conflicts**

1957, Jan.	Cotton textiles, VER.
1958	Japan "voluntarily" restricted woolen fabric export (Yoffie 1983, 124).
1961	Negotiations started for short-term agreement under President Kennedy's initiative.
1962–63	One-year short-term agreement on cotton textiles.
1963	Long-term agreement on cotton textiles.
1966	Steel, VER (until 1974).
1969	Negotiations for multifiber textile arrangement started. "Textile wrangle." Linkage to Okinawa and to Nixon shocks.[a]
1971, Oct. 15	The United States announced new bilateral accords with each of the four Asian exporters and the removal of the 10 percent surcharge on textiles.
1977	Color TV, OMA (until 1980). Steel, trigger pricing (until 1982).
1981, May	First automobile VER.
1983	Yen-dollar working group started.
1984	Yen-dollar working group final report. Steel, VER (renewed in 1989).
1985, Jan.	MOSS talks.
1985, March	Senate resolution.
1986	Machine tools, VER.
1986, Sept.	Semiconductor agreement.
1987, March	Findings on semiconductor agreement violation.
1988	Super 301 signed into law.
1989, May	Designation of Japan as an unfair trading partner.
1989	SII started.
1990	SII final reports.
1992, Jan.	Bush-Miyazawa agreement on United States automobiles and parts.

[a]President Nixon announced on July 15, 1971, that he would be the first American president to visit Beijing and on August 15, 1971, that he would suspend the convertibility of the dollar and introduce a 10 percent import surcharge.

Japan, Korea, Taiwan, and Hong Kong from the mid-1950s to the early 1980s. The U.S. government aimed to maximize a political effect in appeasing domestic interest groups (complaining industry) while "minimizing" the damage to the international relationship. Given U.S. pressures, exporting countries are faced with two choices: to resist pressures or to accept VERs and OMAs. By resisting VER demands initiated by the administration, exporting countries run the risk of being restricted by even more severe measures, such as unilateral quotas and high tariffs initiated by Congress. On the other hand, by accepting VERs and OMAs too quickly, exporting nations lose export revenues. Even though limited by VERs demanded by the United States, Japan, Korea, Taiwan, and Hong Kong have managed to prosper in the long run. Their success comes from (1) pursuing long-run gains by upgrading products and shifting targeted markets; (2) negotiating for delay, ambiguity, and flexibility; (3) demanding compensation for restriction (linkage); (4) cheating outright and exploiting loopholes; and (5) aiming at bureaucratic splits in the United States (Yoffie 1983, 37).

Automobiles

Let us first examine the automobile VER between the United States and Japan, which is in fact a traditional type of conflict. The automobile VER began in 1981, limiting the number of exported passenger automobiles to 1.68 million per year. This restraint was not really voluntary, but was requested by the United States and negotiated and agreed upon between the two countries. The agreement was extended for a one-year period, from April 1984 to March 1985, with a higher limit of 1.85 million. In the spring of 1985, President Reagan announced that he would not seek an extension of the VER, putting the Ministry of International Trade and Industry (MITI) in a difficult position. If the limit were lifted, MITI feared that Japanese automobile companies would increase exports sharply, almost certainly causing a backlash; maintaining the VER lends itself to managed trade. MITI chose a new, "truly voluntary" export restraint with a 2.3 million limit. The increase in the number angered Congress (Ito 1992, 370–71).

The ceiling was binding (that is, the actual number of exports was 2.3 million cars) only in 1985 and 1986. The number of cars exported from Japan to the United States declined steadily from 1987 to 1991, reflecting an increasing number of Japanese cars produced in the United States. Throughout the 1980s, the quota encouraged Japanese automakers to build factories in the United States, which became operational in the late 1980s. In fact, the market share of "Japanese brands"—a total of those exported from Japan and made in the Japanese factories in North America—steadily increased to 30 percent in the early 1990s. In 1992, MITI announced that the quota was lowered to 1.65 million.

In summary, upon the introduction of VER, prices of Japanese cars were raised, which benefited Japanese automakers as well as U.S. automakers, and direct investment by the Japanese makers in North America circumvented the restriction.[4]

Japanese automakers proved to be competitive even in making cars on U.S. turf. The fact that VER does not hinder growth of Japanese (or East Asian countries') products is very familiar. The episode shares features with events in the textile and steel industries, described by authors such as Yoffie and Destler.

9.2.2 Consequences

Yoffie (1983) emphasizes the importance of dynamic responses of the Asian countries, quickly upgrading products and moving into the area not restricted by the VER, for the success of their economic growth.[5] With few exceptions,

---

4. Throughout the 1980s, direct investment by Japanese automakers in the United States was encouraged and welcomed by the United Auto Workers and local communities as job creation.

5. When cotton textiles were restricted in the 1950s, Japan, Korea, and Taiwan moved into synthetics. At the time, the United States basically outbargained Japan in bilateral negotiations for VERs to obtain rather restrictive numbers. Japan lost cotton market share to other Asian countries, especially Hong Kong. "Ironically, the VER accelerated the movement toward synthetics, which was indeed the most dynamic market segment" (Yoffie 1983, 63). In the 1960s, a similar trend

Asian countries successfully pursued long-run gains over short-run sacrifices.[6]

He also points out the Asian countries' success was not matched by the promotion of domestic industry by the United States. The U.S. government lacked a coherent policy to protect or promote the domestic industry. Protected industries in the United States could not convert the short-run gains obtained by VERs and OMAs into long-run investment. The U.S. government tried but failed to revitalize industries already in trouble, focusing only on providing domestic makers with protection from imports, without measures to increase competitiveness.

Another interpretation, a more cynical one, of the last aspect is that the U.S. government did not seriously intend to protect the domestic industry, in favor of consumers' interests and commitment to the free trade principle. Hence, the negotiations with Japan, Korea, Taiwan, and Hong Kong were more for politically appeasing than for helping (in the industrial policy sense) the domestic industry. If this interpretation is correct, the outcome of Asian countries' economic success is not surprising. (This interpretation is more likely to be the case in Republican administrations.)

9.3   U.S.-Japan Bilateral Relations in the 1980s

9.3.1   The New Type of U.S. Pressure and Japan's "Concessions"[7]

As summarized above, U.S.-Japan trade conflicts have been commonplace since the late 1950s. Textiles, color TVs, and steel are famous cases of quotas and price controls from the late 1950s through the 1970s. The conflicts took a

---

continued. The long-term agreement (LTA) was on "*quantities* of *cotton* textiles. An exporting country could increase export *earnings* by upgrading existing product lines and diversifying into synthetics. The irony behind the LTA was that it provided Japan, as well as other exporting nations, with an additional incentive to move into synthetics, which was fast becoming the most lucrative textile market" (Yoffie 1983, 105).

Hong Kong was a different case. Its hard bargaining apparently defeated the U.S. attempt to restrict cotton exports in the late 1950s. The apparent short-run success had long-run costs. The United States had more severe restrictions under the STA and LTA in the early 1960s, and Hong Kong fell behind in the movement toward synthetics (Yoffie 1983, 64–79, 110–13). "An ironic twist in Hong Kong's success was that it did not move into synthetic textile fibers as quickly as Japan, Taiwan, or Korea" (112).

The U.S. nonrubber footwear OMAs with Korea and Taiwan in 1977 resulted in upgrading Korean and Taiwanese footwear from low-price footwear into middle-price footwear, which was the only category in which the U.S. producers had a competitive advantage (Yoffie 1983, chap. 5).

6. One of the mistakes Japan made, according to Yoffie's evaluation, was the "textile wrangle" of 1969–71. Japan should have compromised earlier for better terms for an industry that was losing overall importance for Japan and competitiveness against other Asian countries. Japan "had no long-run future in the sector, yet it promoted confrontation for the sake of short-run gains. . . . Japan jeopardized the return of Okinawa to Japanese sovereignty, and only narrowly escaped passage in the United States Congress of a highly restrictive trade bill. . . . While textiles may not have directly contributed to the Nixon 'shocks'—the overtures to China and the monetary declarations—they played a major role in disrupting the alliance" (Yoffie 1983, 155).

7. This section is partly based on Ito (1992, chap. 12).

different form in the 1980s. The Republican administration, with its philosophy of free trade, did not want to push protectionistic measures. Except for the first four years of the automobile VER, the Reagan-Bush administration avoided attempts to limit imports from Japan (see below). Instead, much more effort was given to opening up Japanese markets.[8] The 1980s were a decade of U.S. demand for market access, and sometimes a market share, in Japan. U.S. officials correctly argued that correction of trade imbalances by increasing Japan's imports is far better than by limiting Japan's exports to the United States. On the Japanese side, U.S. pressure was largely effective in persuading vested interest groups that obviously oppose less protection from imports, or in dismantling regulations that increase oligopolistic rents. This section summarizes the history of the U.S.-Japan trade conflict before the 1980s, foreign pressure (*gaiatsu*) from the United States, and Japan's response in liberalization (*jiyuka*) or deregulation (*kisei kanwa*) of various markets in the 1980s.[9]

9.3.2   The MOSS-SII Conflicts of the 1980s

1. The yen-dollar group meeting of 1983–84 and follow-up meetings illustrate essential features of the pattern of the United States' demanding liberalization and Japan's responding to it.[10] The United States demanded, among other things, deregulation in Japan's domestic financial market. As a result, foreign trust banks entered the market; a direction, if not a schedule, of deregulation of deposit interest rates was decided; and Euroyen markets were deregulated. A rationale for the U.S. demands was that to liberalize Japanese financial markets would invite foreign financial services into Japan, and foreign funds would be attracted to the Japanese stock and bond markets, thus putting pressure to appreciate the yen, the agreed objective at the time. However, as Frankel (1984) forcefully argued, negotiated measures included steps to lower barriers for Japanese capital to flow abroad (that is, purchasing Treasury bonds), putting pressure to further appreciate the dollar, contrary to the stated objectives. Perhaps a posture of being tough was more important than substance;[11] or perhaps the Republican administration was just trying to export deregulation.

---

8. This evaluation is in accordance with Destler (1991, 252): "There was, over the decade, a significant shift in policy emphasis. Both branches became much more aggressive in pressing for the opening of foreign markets."

9. There may be a subtle difference between liberalization and deregulation. Liberalization may include cases of interpreting and implementing regulations "liberally" so that market forces can work within the framework of regulation. For example, the deposit interest rate for money market certificates in Japan is set by a formula tied to the market rate. Deregulation usually refers to dismantling regulations completely. For example, the deposit interest rates on money market saving and checking accounts in the United States have been deregulated since the beginning of 1983, as have large time deposits in Japan since 1985.

10. See Frankel (1984) and Rosenbluth (1989, chap. 3) for background and detailed items of the yen-dollar working group negotiation.

11. It is well publicized that the Japanese side was not particularly happy about American theatrical toughness, such as Treasury Secretary Don Regan pounding a table to demand concessions from the Japanese.

2. Beef and orange (juice) imports into Japan were intensively negotiated from 1985 to 1987. According to the agreed-upon schedule, the import quota was raised in steps and was finally replaced by a tariff in 1991. The tariff rate for beef stood at 70 percent in April 1991 and was scheduled to decrease by 10 percent each year for the next seven years. (It became 60 percent in April 1992.) The switch from quota to tariff is significant. Under the quota system, a government agency (*Chikusan Shinko Jigyodan*) was the sole agency that could import beef, through the Japanese large trading houses. Although the quota was increased, no one could import directly from producers. The agency bought beef at the world price and "stabilized" the domestic price, that is, did not sell under a certain price. As a result, the agency accumulated beef and kept it literally frozen in the warehouse, instead of lowering the domestic price.[12] Since April 1991, wholesalers, trading houses, and large retail stores have directly imported from foreign producers, with a 70 percent tariff. Although increased consumption of beef certainly improves the utility of an average Japanese, a contribution to the trade balance is minimal. If every Japanese suddenly consumed twice as much beef and all the increase came from abroad, it would reduce Japan's trade surpluses by $2 billion.[13]

3. The construction business was targeted by the USTR. The USTR has demanded on many occasions that a government procurement procedure should be changed to allow bidding from foreign companies. The New Kansai Airport became a focus of attention. The design of a freight terminal and the construction of a passenger terminal were won by a consortium including U.S. companies.

Another aspect of the construction issue is bid rigging (*dango*) by construction companies, which has long been suspected. It came under scrutiny when

12. The Sumitomo Trading Company published a survey of various retail prices as of late July 1990 (with conversion at 150 yen/dollar). Beef (medium quality) cost 3,900 yen per kilogram in Tokyo, while comparable beef in New York cost 1,088 yen (that is, $3.25 per pound) (*Toyo Keizai Statistics Annual*, 1991, 374). The Economic Planning Agency's survey (in February 1990) put the beef (clod) price in Tokyo at 3,790 yen per kilogram, while it is 980 yen per kilogram in New York (Bank of Japan, *Comparative Economic and Financial Statistics*, 1991, 103). Yet another survey by the Ministry of Agriculture, Forestry, and Fisheries (which has a conflict of interest in conducting a survey) showed the beef (clod) price at 1,300 yen per kilogram in New York, while it was 3,830 yen per kilogram in Tokyo in November 1990 at 145.83 yen/dollar (*Toyo Keizai Statistics Annual*, 1991, 258).

The beef price seems to have come down in 1991, after retailers directly imported beef from the United States and other countries. On October 1991, a well-advertised sale at Ito-Yokado (a supermarket chain) priced a 250-gram steak from Nebraska at 1,000 yen (about $13.85 per pound at 130 yen/dollar), still about two to three times the U.S. retail price. Allowing for the 70 percent tariff, the beef price is judged to be converging to a reasonable range.

13. The following estimating method was employed in this statement. An average employee household spent 32,675 yen on beef consumption in 1989. There were 3.72 persons per employee household. Since the Japanese retail price was about four times the U.S. retail price, the imported beef price would be as little as one-fifth of the Japanese domestic price. This gives an estimate of 1,756 yen per person for beef at an import price of one-fifth of the Japanese retail price. The population in Japan was about 123 million in 1989. Hence, with 150 yen/dollar, this translates into $1.4 billion for beef imports.

the U.S. military base in Japan sued for damages and won a large settlement for construction work on the base.

4. In 1985, negotiations between Japan and the United States started on the access of specific products to Japanese markets.[14] The initial MOSS talks took up four products: electronic communication service and products, pharmaceuticals and medical equipment, electronics, and lumber products. For these products, the United States felt that U.S. firms had a competitive edge and that the Japanese markets were closed by unnecessary regulations. For example, the definition of "electronic communication products" included satellites, and of "electronics" included supercomputers. Procurement procedures of the Japanese government and its agencies for computers and satellites became a focus of discussions resulting in an agreement satisfactory to the United States.[15] Import procedures and license applications for pharmaceutical products have also been simplified, resulting in high marks from U.S. firms and trade organizations.

Imports of satellites, service of cellular phones, and a license to trans-Pacific cables were negotiated from 1985 to 1987. Motorola applied to introduce cellular phones in Japan. The Japanese government divided Japan into half and gave the less-populated western half to Motorola's joint venture and gave the eastern half, inclusive of Tokyo, to NTT. After much protest from Motorola and the USTR, the Japanese government finally gave a five-megahertz band in Tokyo to Motorola.

The Japanese government has been developing satellites domestically. Under pressure from the U.S. government, it agreed to purchase U.S.-made satellites. When two companies applied for transpacific cables, the Ministry of Posts and Communications decided to allow only one company, possibly a merged consortium. British Cable and Wire protested in vain in 1985.

5. The large retail store law in 1989 and 1990 came under attack in the SII talks.[16] The law itself, and ministry guidance in conjunction with the law, practically prohibited a large retail store from constructing a new branch without consent from the neighboring retail business.[17] Hence, the law, which essentially limits and discourages construction of department stores, discount stores, and large supermarkets, was heavily criticized by the United States during the SII. The United States contended that large stores carry more imported goods than do smaller stores; thus the law was an impediment to more imports. An application of Toys "R" Us became a symbol of the case. In 1990, MITI changed the procedure of the law, so that it became easy to open a large store.

14. The MOSS talks started as a result of the summit between Prime Minister Nakasone and President Reagan in January 1985.

15. In 1991, supercomputer procurements at Tohoku University and Kyoto University resulted in sales of Clay computers, because NEC withheld a bid.

16. For detail on the large retail store law and its impact on the Japanese distribution system, see Ito (1992, chap. 13).

17. "Large retail store" is defined as any retail store with 3,000 square meters or more in large cities, or 1,500 square meters in smaller cities. See Ito (1992, chap. 13).

The law remained intact but was revised in 1991 to speed up the license examination. The quantitative impact on trade balance is not known. What is certain is that Japanese consumers will benefit from more large retail stores with reasonably priced goods, and traditional corner-store owners are losers in the relaxation of the law. The SII talks certainly tipped the scale in the debate.

Other issues covered in the SII had implications, namely, to change the Japanese industry structures to allow more imports.[18]

6. Rice imports to Japan have been banned. The reason given by the Ministry of Agriculture, Forestry, and Fisheries is that a country has a right to "national security in food," that is, to produce basic staples (*kiso shokuryo*) 100 percent domestically. Moreover, GATT has allowed the ban on imports for a food item that is under a domestic production quota. Dependence on imported "basic food" is considered dangerous.[19] The Japanese Diet unanimously passed a resolution opposing rice imports.

The Rice Miller Association (RMA) twice brought the case to the USTR, on the basis of article 301 of the Omnibus Trade Act, and each time it was rejected. The second time it was rejected with a condition that rice imports to Japan would be discussed in the Uruguay Round. So far, the Uruguay Round has not produced a comprehensive agreement on agriculture in general. Japan is in no hurry for the talks to move toward agreement.

From late 1990 to the spring of 1991, some leaders in the Liberal Democratic party (LDP) floated the idea of an import quota, or minimum access, for rice. The idea was heavily criticized by the agricultural lobby in Japan, how-

18. See Sheard (1991) for the viewpoint of industrial organization on the SII issue in general.

19. A favorite example that illustrates the dangers of depending on imported food is the case of the U.S. soybean embargo in 1973 (and in the same line of reasoning, but less well known in Japan, the wheat embargo to the USSR after its invasion of Afghanistan). Japan heavily depended on American soybeans for tofu and soy sauce production in 1971, and the announcement shocked Japan.

There are several problems with "national security in food" arguments, however. First, processed rice, for example, rice mixed with shrimp for pilaf, can be and has been imported. This may be a logical inconsistency. Second, dependence on imports may be dangerous, but if the sources are diversified, it is much less dangerous. The wheat embargo of 1979 against the USSR was not effective because the USSR could purchase wheat in the world market, in particular from Argentina. It is much more dangerous to be isolated in the world community. How could Japan function without oil, for example, even if rice is abundant? Third, by importing the goods, Japan can have a lobby in the United States, namely, U.S. farmers will protest an export embargo, as they did the soybean embargo of 1971 and wheat embargo of 1979. The soybean embargo lasted for only three months. Fourth, suppose for the moment that it is dangerous to depend on food imports. How would the Ministry of Agriculture, Forestry, and Fisheries explain the rising trend in the import-dependency ratio for food other than rice? Japan depends on imports for most of its grain and a large part of its fish. The import-dependency ratio based on calories is more than 60 percent, among the highest in the OECD countries. Is it safe to have 100 percent self-sufficiency on rice alone? Strong national security should be based on efficient production, that is, minimizing costs, given consumption. (Rice consumption is considered to be price inelastic.) However, the production quota is decided, not by cutting off the least efficient producers, but by cutting across the board. Scale economies exist in farming but are not exploited in Japan. Driving up production costs, how could one argue the security benefits? (The cost argument is painfully familiar to the U.S. defense industry, although the situation is slightly different.)

ever, and by U.S. officials who insisted on a tariff instead of a quota.[20] The rice farmers are very cautious, for beef and orange imports were liberalized despite the earlier pledge from LDP officials not to liberalize imports. The rice farmer learned that, if a partial import quota, or minimum access, is allowed, complete liberalization (zero tariff) will arrive sooner or later.

The rice issue again is politically very sensitive in Japan, and consumers are unlikely to lobby for import liberalization. Corporations tend to favor minimum access because they fear some kind of retaliatory backlash in automobiles and semiconductors if rice ignites protectionism in the United States. Again, foreign pressure might be working, but it may take a while to settle the rice problem.

9.3.3   Analysis and Evaluation

Reviewing issues discussed between the United States and Japan (summarized in section 9.3.2), one might wonder how much of a dent these measures made in the (bilateral) trade balances. The expected small effect has always been questioned by the Japanese in negotiations. The Japanese government maintained that the major cause of the U.S.-Japan trade imbalance rested on the large U.S. fiscal deficits and consumers' impatience (spending instead of thriftiness).[21] U.S. policymakers tended to respond either that these liberalization and deregulation measures are for the benefit of Japanese consumers or that deregulation and free trade should be defended as a matter of principle. More succinctly, many members of Congress and business leaders felt Japanese firms have unfair advantages in getting government help (subsidies) and protection (nontariff barriers for foreigners). Correcting the imbalance requires prying open the Japanese markets. Moreover, the United States should push Japan, so that Japan becomes "more like us," that is, run under perfect competition and free trade.

In any case, the particular size of an expected correction for a single negotiated item was not the major concern. It may be that what was at stake was the principle of less government intervention and free trade, the Republican economic agenda, rather than maximizing deficit reduction.

A more likely explanation of the U.S.-Japan trade conflicts in the 1980s is that the White House used Japan as a scapegoat for domestic conflicts, while

20. Many politicians and bureaucrats feel that the effective tariff rate that would minimize imports would be embarrassingly high, because Japan's rice price is said to be eight times the world price. Japanese prefer short grain, however, and comparison may be difficult. The Forum for Policy Innovation (*Seisaku Kohsoh Forum*) estimated, taking into account transportation and warehouse costs, that a tariff of about 164 percent would make Kokuho Rose, a top-brand (short-grain) Californian rice, as expensive as the government sale price of domestic rice, and of 269 percent would make Kokuho Rose as expensive as the top-brand Sakanishiki (Forum for Policy Innovation 1990).

21. It can be easily shown from the GNP identity relationship that a trade deficit must result if domestic private saving is short of domestic private investment and the government runs fiscal deficits.

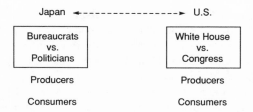

Fig. 9.1   Conceptual framework of domestic and international conflicts

the Japanese government in some quarters used foreign pressure to achieve an agenda of deregulation and to increase the slice of economic pie for consumers. In addition to the U.S.-Japan negotiations that take place officially, domestic negotiations and games are played within each country. In the United States, the White House and Congress often oppose each other, and in Japan, bureaucrats and politicians often argue over the issues. In each country, various political groups represent various producer and consumer groups, according to their political orientations and electoral needs.[22]

Figure 9.1 shows a conceptual framework for this type of two-level game: first a struggle between domestic players, bureaucrats versus politicians in Japan and White House versus Congress; then an international negotiation between Japan and the United States. Domestic players represent consumers' and special producers' interests. What follows is a detailed elaboration of this hypothesis.

The U.S. Domestic Situation and Its Reflection in Trade Issues

When a protectionist request is presented by a special interest group, the U.S. government weights several economic and political trade-offs. In those calculations, arguments against protection come from domestic users of imported products as well as from exporting countries' government and consumer groups.[23]

Another important ingredient of this scenario is that the United States was under a divided government for most of the 1980s.[24] The House, and the Senate

22. See Weingast and Marshall (1988) for an attempt to analyze legislatures (Congress) in an industrial organization framework. See McCubbins, Noll, and Weingast (1987) for how administrative procedures, such as rules of who bears the burden of proof, could be used politically. Hillman and Ursprung (1988) show that trade policy can be understood as a tool for gaining domestic political support. A VER is used to please a specific interest group, while tariffs may be divisive, so that no candidate has an interest in formulating a trade policy position using a tariff if a VER is a policy option.

23. See Destler and Odell (1987) for an analysis of domestic antiprotection activities.

24. Divided government has become more common in American political history, according to Alesina and Carliner (1991). It may be "the result of a conscious attempt by the voters to achieve moderate policy. . . . Voters in the middle of the political spectrum desire policies in between those advocated by the median members of the two parties" (2–3).

also after 1986, wanted to criticize the administration for its lack of trade policy.[25] On the other side, the executive office tried to deflect protectionist pressure and, sometimes, to steal the opportunity to initiate pressures on other countries, in order to score points domestically. The executive office may be unenthusiastic in obtaining protectionistic concessions from other countries, but is certainly not reluctant to press for opening markets for U.S. goods. In order to preempt a criticism from Congress, the White House wanted to appear tough on Japan.

One of the obvious issues in the 1980s was trade deficits. Over 30 percent of trade deficits were against Japan. Hence, Japan was chosen as an instrument for congressional criticism of the administration. This instrument is quite useful and effective, because the Japanese economy seems to behave differently than other economies.

Traditionally, Republicans advocated smaller government and fewer regulations, compared to the Democrats. The administration's stated goal was to make trade free and to let the market determine the outcome. Hence, whenever Congress threatened to pass protectionistic bills and to promote imports and put surcharges on imports, the Republican administration tried to focus on the issue of opening the Japanese market. A tough posture was maintained by the administration in order to outdo Congress. The Republican administration was interested in scoring domestically by criticizing Japan rather than by reducing the deficit, although the latter was always a pretext for negotiation. The administration was willing to take up issues that fit the Japanese agenda, so long as they also fit the Republican agenda. In that sense, Japan was a scapegoat, but a fortunate one: the scapegoat was not for sacrifice, but for window dressing.

Of course, U.S.-Japan conflicts have a long history (as shown in table 9.2) and occur even in the period without a divided government. During the last twelve years when divided government prevailed, the conflicts developed a distinctive MOSS-SII feature. MOSS-SII negotiations attempted to open Japanese markets instead of closing the American market, in order to remedy the trade imbalance. This fit the Republican White House agenda and acted to counter congressional pressure. By using MOSS-SII negotiations, the Republican administration took an initiative in domestic politics on the international trade front.

Hence, it is fair to say that the divided government in the 1980s likely explains the Republican administration's adoption of MOSS-SII demands on Japan, as opposed to the traditional VER type (which is more of a Democratic party approach).

However, it also spawned congressional counterattacks using the results-oriented pressure, because the MOSS-SII negotiations were seen as insuffi-

25. It is not important in this context whether Congress is truly interested in protectionist measures, as often charged by the conservative press and the Republicans, or is interested in appearing tough rather than passing tough legislation with teeth, as suggested by Destler (1991).

cient to remedy the imbalance in merchandize trade with Japan. The new approach also is employed to seize the initiative in domestic politics from the White House.[26]

The Japanese Domestic Situation and Its Reflection on Trade Issues

The Japanese economic and political system has produced remarkable economic development and progress. Elements that produced 10+ percent high-speed economic growth (*kodo seicho*)[27] included high saving rate, high fixed investment rate, export subsidies, and import restriction. Even after the first oil crisis, the Japanese economy overcame two oil crises and the yen-appreciation recessions (1978 and 1986) to maintain 5 percent growth rates. During all these years, what occupied the minds of Japanese business leaders, political leaders, and bureaucrats was how to cut costs, how to earn foreign currencies (dollar), how to improve quality of goods, and how to produce goods better. Economic growth, with the balance of payments constraint, was the "principle" used to evaluate funding and political priority. If cost-benefit analyses for exports and growth did not justify projects, they were not funded.

Of course, political priorities have shifted from agriculture to heavy industrial products and to high-technology products. Unfortunately, when an entire process is geared toward production as opposed to consumption, it is difficult to switch priorities.

In fact, Japan has not seriously switched its economic goal for more than forty years. The political process *added* objectives but did *not switch* objectives. Shifting weights among priorities was not a hard choice, when the entire pie, to be sliced and distributed among participants, was inflating at 10 percent per annum.[28] This is partly because severe political resistance arises when the

---

26. If this working hypothesis is correct, dissolving a divided government by electing a Democratic president would make the U.S.-Japan conflict less confrontational (less use of results-oriented pressure), hence more productive for the U.S.-Japan relationship. This contradicts a popular notion in Japan that a Democratic president would be a protectionist and a disaster for Japan.

27. The era of high-speed economic growth is defined as 1955–73, when real GNP grew on average at more than 10 percent a year, doubling income every seven years. See Kosai (1986).

28. Of course, some items are rigid even in their share, instead of the budget amount. The shares among different uses (ministry turf) of public works in the national general budget was surprisingly stable. For example, see Sakakibara (1990, 87):

Public works budget share		
	1979	1987
Agriculture infrastructure	14.11	14.13
Irrigation	13.55	13.72
Road	30.77	28.92
Housing	11.25	12.44
Sewerage	10.71	10.91
Forestry	4.53	4.56
Fishery	2.87	2.95
Seaport infrastructure	4.20	4.17

absolute value of the budget declines, and partly because the Japanese electoral system favors vested interest groups. The downward rigidity of the budget may be not a result of "rational choice," but a reality.[29]

Under slow growth, it is much more difficult to add a new agenda (say, sewerage, city parks and playgrounds, or even airports), because it means cutting a stale agenda (say, irrigation or seaports for commercial fishing). But when "better quality of life" has clearly overtaken "more exports" as the national priority, why does a new agenda not arise?

Who steers the ship in Japan? How is the social consensus on priorities determined? This may be a mystery. There is no clear leadership. Important policy items seem to be decided behind closed doors. Politicians cannot ignore business lobbyists; business leaders are subject to ministry guidance; and bureaucrats seem to be influenced by politicians' needs.[30] No one seems to be in charge, but somehow a group of powerful players form a consensus.

It was clear by the mid-1980s that the traditional value of maximum growth did not fit contemporary Japan. Foreign countries, the United States and Europe alike, criticize Japan for working too hard and exporting too much.[31] American and European economists, as well as government officials, argued that if Japan invested more on infrastructure for improved life, such as parks, sewerage, roads and sidewalks, and public transportation, then it would increase the standard of living, or quality of life. Domestic demand expansion would reduce exports to foreign countries, reducing trade conflicts. The current account surplus/GNP ration exceeded 4 percent in 1986, which was not sustainable from the international political point of view.

The difficulty in shifting political priorities in Japan has two main causes

---

However, other means of budget allocation, especially through the Fiscal Investment and Loan Program (FILP), have changed their priorities. See Ito (1992, chap. 6).

29. Myopic or uninformed voters may justify this. Suppose that farmers would not resist if the subsidies or public work budget (after inflation adjustment) did not decline, while the agricultural share in the budget did.

30. This nontransitive relationship among politicians, bureaucrats, and business is commonly nicknamed in Japan the "stone, paper, scissors" (*jankenpon*) structure. It is also known as a "truncated pyramid" (van Wolferen 1989, 5): "Today, the most powerful groups include certain ministry officials, some political cliques and clusters of bureaucrat-businessmen. . . . There is, to be sure, a hierarchy or, rather, a complex of overlapping hierarchies. But it has no peak; it is a truncated pyramid." See Sakakibara (1990, 71=88) for the way the Ministry of Finance and the ruling party have to negotiate the budget.

31. In 1985, the average number of working hours for manufacturing production workers in Japan was 43.2 hours per week, while it was 38.3 hours per week in the United States.

	Japan	U.S.	U.K.	Germany	France
1985	43.2	38.3	41.8	42.0	38.6
1990	42.3	38.2	41.6	40.7	38.8

Source: Bank of Japan, *Comparative Economic and Financial Statistics* (1991, 109, 111).
Notes: Japan in 1985 and 1990 has a discontinuity in statistical method. Germany (West) in 1990 is actually 1989.

connected to the electoral system. First, the House of Representatives electoral system, that is, the single nontransferable vote, multimember district system, makes interest groups very important. The ruling LDP candidates in the same district usually divide their support bases through trade groups. (Another way is to divide their support bases by subdistricts.) For example, votes are strongly tied to small and medium-sized shops in commercial districts, to the construction industry, and to farmers.[32]

Second, it is well known that apportionment is seriously behind reality in Japan. In an extreme case, the number of registered voters per representative in a rural district is about one-third of that in a metropolitan area. Political interests of the agricultural and fishery businesses are overrepresented in the House of Representatives.

"Quality of life giant" (*seikatsu taikoku*) became a code phrase of the Miyazawa cabinet for changing a national priority away from investment toward consumption, and away from exports toward infrastructure for a better standard of living. Indeed, a desire among the Japanese for higher satisfaction with life grew rapidly in the second half of the 1980s, because the citizens, as portrayed in the mass media, started to realize the gap between the standard of living, especially the poor quality of housing, and macroeconomic strength, such as Japan's new status as the world's largest creditor. The Maekawa report (April 1986) clearly stated that one of the national priorities is improving the quality of life.

However, concrete steps toward better life have come very slowly. There were two kinds of problems. First, it was difficult to divert resources from, say, agricultural infrastructure to that related to quality of life, especially under relatively slow growth. This pitted farmers against a silent mass of consumers. Second, increasing consumers' welfare often involves deregulation, while Japanese government officials and business leaders tend to rely on a plan and coordination between business and the government.[33]

A big push from influential foreign countries was much needed in the mid-1980s. Foreign pressure (*gaiatsu*) is most effective when it funds a big, though silent, constituency in Japan. Successful liberalization, as for beef and oranges, and deposit interest rates fit into this pattern. Japan used foreign pressure to take steps toward a new national priority, better quality of life.

There are two reasons why the MOSS-SII pressure of the 1980s has worked in Japan. First, the U.S. list of demands was in accordance with the new emphasis on better quality of life (increasing consumers' surplus, instead of pro-

32. The importance of the electoral system in making political decisions in Japan was mentioned and emphasized by my discussant, Frances Rosenbluth, at the conference. This paragraph was added to incorporate her comments.

33. The concept of "excess competition" (*kato kyoso*), which is analogous to destructive, cutthroat competition, is used as a rationale for regulation in Japan. Many government officials and business leaders think perfect competition, or laissez-faire, does not necessarily optimize social relations.

ducers' surplus); second, those who lose vested interests or oligopolistic rents in the wake of liberalization had a political and psychological bias in favor of the United States. They felt that if the U.S. government wanted liberalization, they could give in (*shoganai*).

Those who suffer from regulatory changes are traditional supporters of the LDP and friends of the United States: they feel grateful to the United States for successful help, during the occupation period and later, in various economic and political areas. With U.S. pressure, Japan could achieve liberalization that accords with a shift in priority at minimal political cost.

In summary, giving in to U.S. demands was a face-saving excuse that could be used by bureaucrats to politicians, and by politicians to voters. Leaders in big business did not bark at deregulation because they were afraid of being squeezed out of the U.S. market in retaliation.

U.S. pressure (the MOSS-SII type) and liberalization benefited Japanese consumers most. To a lesser extent, U.S. firms and Japanese new entrants received benefits. Losers were mainly those who had been protected by regulation. Politically, both the U.S. government and the Japanese government used foreign pressure for their benefit: the United States used it as a scapegoat for the inability to manage the size of fiscal and trade deficits, while the Japanese used it to minimize political damage caused by deregulation and liberalization.

9.3.4 Signs of a Dangerous Current: Unilateralism and Resentment

U.S. Unilateralism

A turning point for U.S. frustration came in 1985, after the administration lost its grip on Congress (see Destler 1986, appendix). In the spring of 1985, the Senate passed, 92–0, a resolution condemning Japan as an unfair trading partner. In September 1986, a semiconductor agreement was signed by the U.S. and the Japanese governments, only to result in a U.S. finding of Japan's violating the agreement in 1987. The Congress finally passed the Omnibus Trade and Competitiveness Act of 1988 with the super 301 clause.

Let us call this kind of approach U.S. unilateralism: (1) the issue (or the product) is singled out without being considered in a broader framework; (2) the United States unilaterally determines whether a trading partner is engaged in unfair trade (dumping, market closed to American products); and (3) the United States unilaterally imposes retaliatory fines (or tariffs) if it determines that the country violates a United States-imposed rule. The super 301 is a perfect example of U.S. unilateralism.[34]

U.S. frustration was compounded by a series of MITI mistakes and miscalculations. In the spring of 1985, President Reagan announced that he would not seek the continuation of the automobile VER. MITI, however, opted to continue the VER with a higher ceiling.[35] The ceiling was increased from 1.85

---

34. See Bhagwati and Patrick (1990) for discussions among economists in the United States.
35. See Ito (1992, 381–82, n.4) for a detailed account of this episode.

million cars to 2.3 million cars. This infuriated the president and Congress. Reagan denounced the decision because he had not asked for another VER, and the Congress was upset because of the 24 percent increase in the number of exports. Congressional frustration contributed to the passage in March of the resolution denouncing Japan. Faced with U.S. criticism, Prime Minister Nakasone admitted that MITI's decision to increase the number was a mistake. MITI also miscalculated the significance of the semiconductor agreement in July 1986. MITI thought that signing the agreement would alleviate pressures for Japanese purchase of American-made semiconductors. However, the United States found that Japan violated the agreement on two counts in March 1987, transshipping with a lower price through Hong Kong and failure to increase imports to Japan (Prestowitz 1988, 61–70). The MITI miscalculated the seriousness of the United States about the market share target (or commitment) in the agreement.

Hence, the second half of the 1980s was characterized by a mix of two types of conflicts, market access such as SII, and U.S. unilateralism such as super 301 and the semiconductor agreement.

Revisionist Influence

The so-called revisionists argue that Japan operates in a different economic system. Since the Japanese economy is different, different rules should be applied. For example, in order to open the Japanese market, normal negotiation is inadequate, because even if one barrier to imports (say, quota) is removed, another problem (say, procurement procedure and *keiretsu* trading) emerges to keep imports out. Hence, the most effective measure against Japan is to have it commit to a concrete number, such as the market share in Japan, and have it figure out how to carry out the commitment.

Revisionists think that in traditional trade negotiations, the Japanese bureaucrats outmaneuvered the American counterparts through delaying tactics and by not understanding the spirit of an agreement. The Japanese took advantage of a Republican government that promoted free trade, by exporting more to the United States while not lowering import barriers. Some go on to argue that Japanese manufacturers engage in "adversarial exports," maximizing the market share by exporting products without importing.[36]

Revisionists emphasize Japan's preference for in-group trading, such as *keiretsu* trading, as a source of low import ratio. The rules of the game are different in Japan: *keiretsu* trade, low capital costs (due to high saving rate and a capital market closed to foreign firms), long working hours, low wage, low-quality social infrastructure (such as sewerage), and low quality of housing. Essentially, the Japanese firms can take advantage of these characteristics to enhance international competitiveness.

36. See Drucker (1986). A similar line of argument, considering Japan as "Japan, Inc.," a big, social, conspiratory entity, is common from Prestowitz to Cresson. However, this kind of conspiratory argument would not stand up to a close scrutiny of the Japanese political and economic system. See Krugman (1990, 120) for a similar assessment.

There are possibly three arguments that, I think, could barely justify the revisionist policy recommendation (from the U.S. point of view), which essentially advocates an expanded import commitment (quota) for Japan. I discuss the arguments and then the Japanese reactions to them.

First, some policymakers and critics in the United States, who emphasize domestic interests (America first), finally realize that traditional types of pressure (that is, VERs and OMAs) give oligopoly rents to foreign producers as well as to domestic producers. The new market-access types (SII) mainly enhance the Japanese consumers' welfare, with little gain to the U.S. producers. Hence, the "fruits" did not come from political shows of beating Japan using the traditional or the new type of pressure. It is now time to seek U.S. interests aggressively. (Recall table 9.1.) The revisionist side, of course, would not present the argument this way. (However, implications are clear from what they advocate, that is, "import this much or retaliate.") They argue that the Japanese are restricting imports by broadly defined nontariff barriers. An extraordinary low ratio of manufactures imports proves the point, and no further pinpointing of the problem is necessary, according to revisionists.[37]

Second, a more sophisticated theory could be used to justify the market access negotiations. New trade theory states that pursuing the market share may pay off in the long run, if the market for the product expands in the future. In the same logic, export subsidies may be justified as a strategy. The new theory possibly justifies industrial policy and infant industry protection. When there are scale economies in technology, it is important to get the market share first, by securing the domestic market by protection or by expanding into foreign markets by subsidies or by thin margins (if not by dumping). Revisionists in this vein regret that the United States allowed Japan's infant industry protection for automobiles, shipbuilding, and other products that later dominated the world market. They also believe that the best chance for the United States would be to aggressively promote industries with a competitive, technological edge in the 1990s. This is managed trade, but it is better than free trade.[38] The best chance for the United States is to pry open the Japanese market, denying MITI's infant industry protection. Products in this category include satellites, aircraft, supercomputers, some types of chemicals, and pharmaceuticals.

Third, the logic of affirmative action, which is an application of Spence's signaling theory, may justify a line of revisionist argument. Suppose that, whatever the reason, American products are perceived to be of inferior quality. Consumers would not buy American commodities (say, automobiles) if their prices

37. See Dornbusch (1990) for this kind of argument: "Japan actively participated in the GATT tariff-cutting rounds but avoided opening its market through keeping in place a second layer of trade restriction" (Dornbusch 1990, 108). "Japan seems to be somewhat of an onion with multiple layers of protection of one kind or another" (Dornbusch 1990, 120). Dornbusch does on to cite a low "intra-industry" trade index for Japan as an evidence of closed Japanese market. However, Dornbusch himself points out that the number is consistent if the Japanese consumer has a "preference" for the Japanese goods (buy Japanese) without formal import barrier. You cannot blame preference.

38. I classify Tyson (1990) in this category.

are similar to those of comparable Japanese commodities. This is discrimination by the origin of manufacturing. American producers would not make efforts (investment and concentration) to make high-quality goods, because efforts would not pay off. The result would be that American products *are* of inferior quality. Hence, this is the case of self-fulfilling perceptions. The American commodities are trapped in a low-reputation equilibrium. If the perception changes, Americans would respond by changing the quality, moving to a high-quality equilibrium. This kind of multiple equilibrium justifies the use of quotas both in affirmative action of racial preferences and in international trade.

Japan's Resentment

Japanese reactions to U.S. pressure have changed gradually through the 1980s. To traditional U.S. pressure say, the automobile VER, the reaction was like making a deal with a bully. Although it was not optimal to "concede" to a U.S. demand, it was not a "resentment." For MOSS-SII pressure, the Japanese reaction was mixed. One group of Japanese thought that SII pressure was interference in internal affairs, while another group welcomed it as foreign pressure, which improves the welfare of the Japanese consumers. However, there is little sympathy in Japan for the super 301 pressure. It is clear that more people were offended by SII pressure than by VER pressure; and still more people were offended by super 301 pressure than by SII. The United States is losing its friends and constituents in Japan very quickly with super 301 pressure.

Japan's resentment at result-oriented demands is threefold. First, the Japanese, especially business leaders, tend to think that they earned their competitiveness by hard work and endless innovations. The Japanese saved a lot of household income and reinvested saving into machines, structures, and R&D. As a result, Japanese products have become better and have won a high market share in the United States and in the world. That is nothing to be ashamed of. In fact, Japanese products have overcome a reputation, or "signaling," problem, described as a possible justification of the revisionist argument.[39] Moreover, automobile and consumer electronics industries were not actively helped by government industrial policies: no export subsidy, no low–interest rate loan programs, and no depression cartels to allow oligopoly rent.[40] Meanwhile, the United States consumed a lot and failed to save. It is a U.S. management problem that U.S. manufacturers could not keep up with technological innovations by investment, the Japanese argue.[41] As for the current account imbalance in

39. It took more than ten years after its first export attempt for Toyota to make a successful entry into a U.S. market.

40. In the 1960s, the automobile industry fought off the MITI attempt to merge several automakers into two or three, and to restrict a passenger model to a particular type, "Folkscar," (*kokumin-sha*). See Yakushiji (1984) for this episode.

41. At this point, many Japanese recite a well-known Aesop fable, "The Ant and the Grasshopper."

the 1980s, many economists point out that it was mainly caused by U.S. fiscal deficits.

Second, many Japanese resent most unilateralism, that is, the United States telling Japan "import this much or we retaliate." This treats Japan not like an important ally of the Western world, but almost like an enemy. In fact, a retaliatory measure was taken after the United States found Japan guilty of violating the semiconductor agreement. An implicit agreement, believed by MITI, during the market access negotiations was that Japan should suggest topics fit to talk about, while the United States took opportunities to pretend to be tough on Japan. Hence, real bashing, or retaliation with teeth, was seen as violating the rules of the game. The super 301 was also intensely disliked by the Japanese, because it did not enhance Japanese consumers' welfare, and it appeared much more unfair to the Japanese because the United States played both prosecutor and judge.

Third, some Japanese feel that Japan is singled out as a villain (not just a scapegoat). For example, when Fujitsu had to stop its take-over of a Californian semiconductor company that is owned by a French firm because of opposition from the U.S. government on national security grounds, many Japanese felt that they were not regarded as a friendly nation. Similar resentment was registered when U.S. pressure halted a Japanese plan to develop its own design for the next generation of the Japanese fighter jet, FSX.[42]

Morita and Ishihara (1989) were the first among influential Japanese who recorded the resentment in a dramatic way. They advocated that Japan say no to U.S. pressure. Morita's and Ishihara's work got high praise from those who did not see that U.S. pressures of the MOSS-SII type worked for Japanese consumers and became increasingly irritated by U.S. "interference in internal affairs" of Japan.

The Gulf War

The Gulf War tested the relationship between the United States and Japan. Many Americans were predictably upset with countries, such as Germany and Japan, that did not help fight Iraq.

The Japanese government, on the one hand, explained that the constitution prohibits the self-defense force to go abroad to engage in fighting; on the other hand, it unsuccessfully tried to send some personnel as a support (nonfighting) team.

A new word was created in Japan to express this feeling: *Ken-bei,* or "dislike the United States."[43] This is different from the anti–United States feeling that

42. With pressure from the United States, the United States and Japan decided to develop jointly the new fighter jet in October 1987. In November 1988, the two countries signed an agreement for a joint development, with Japan paying for the entire development cost, $165 billion. In 1989, however, Congress pushed for a revision of the plan in order to minimize technological transfer to Japan.

43. *Ken* (with a particular Chinese character) means to "dislike," or "disapprove," but it could go as far as "abhor" or "hate." *Bei* (with a particular Chinese character) is an acronym for the

is typically expressed by the socialists and the communists. *Ken-bei* people may be quite knowledgeable about the United States. Yet they are either disillusioned by the United States' being unable to solve domestic problems—crimes, drugs, homelessness, education, twin deficits, S&Ls, and so forth—or frightened and alienated by a seemingly trigger-happy attitude against Iraq. Many Japanese observers took the January 15 deadline as a bluff; few predicted an immediate attack. Even after the success of the attack, many Japanese did not approve of the attack, for pacifist reasons.[44]

A fiasco over contribution to the Gulf War chest from Japan did not help sentiments in both countries.[45] The same pattern was repeated. The United States asked for action (in this case, monetary contribution), and Japan delayed a decision. When Japan decided to contribute $9 billion, in addition to $4 billion pledged earlier, it was considered to be too late. Then the Japanese side felt that Japan's contribution was not appreciated enough. Moreover, currency depreciation made actual payments short of $9 billion. Apparently, the finance minister pledged in the dollar denomination, while the budget was made in yen.[46] After a protest from the United States, Japan made up the difference, with a lot of reluctance.

9.4 U.S. Pressure and Regional Implications

This section examines what kind of implications U.S. pressure has for the relationships among nations in the Pacific region.

9.4.1 The U.S.-Japan Conflict and Japan's Attitude toward Asia

Will U.S.-Japan conflicts make Japan turn to the East Asian countries, possibly as a market or as a diverted export base? There have been strong economic relations between Japan and the East Asian nations. It has been established that Asian countries provide high-quality labor for assembly and component production. They have become an important production base for U.S. as well as Japanese companies.

Although Asia has not reached the point of replacing North America as a market for Japan, its importance as a market has grown substantially. During the first half of the 1980s, China looked like a new frontier for Japanese exports, but the export amount decreased substantially during the second half. Instead, the Asian NIES and other ASEAN countries became important mar-

---

United States. The *ken-bei* became popular in 1990–91. In 1992, another word was created, *en-bei* (avoid or despise the United States), and a most recently created word is *bu-bei* (contempt of the United States).

44. These pacifists ignored the fact that the United States carefully crafted the consensus in the United Nations, to which Japan has always pledged strong support. In fact, Japan's diplomacy is said to give most weight to the United Nations.

45. See Inoguchi (1991) for analysis of Japan's response to the Gulf crisis.

46. News of the United States' asking Japan to make up the exchange rate loss contributed to *ken-bei* feeling.

kets for Japan. In 1990, the United States and Canada combined absorbed about $100 billion (up from $70 billion in 1985) of Japanese goods, while East Asian countries absorbed about $80 billion (up from $30 billion in 1985). See table 9.3 for details.

The pattern has been that Asian countries run trade deficits against Japan while exporting final goods to the United States to keep net trade surpluses (table 9.3). Typically, Asian NIES import technology and parts from Japan and manufacture reasonably priced consumer electronics goods and automobiles for export to the United States, but not to Japan. For Asian NIES, Japan was a good source of parts, but not a good customer. In 1981, Asian NIES imported about $81 billion from Japan and exported only $9 billion to Japan, and eight to one ratio. In 1990, however, Asian NIES imported $57 billion from Japan, while they exported $26 billion to it, a close to two to one ratio. The gap is still large, and even if the trend continues, it would take another decade or more, until the Asian NIES–Japan trade balance would break even.

Table 9.3   Exports and Imports of Japan, by Region (in millions of dollars)

	1981	1985	1990
Export from Japan			
United States	38,609	65,278	90,322
Canada	3,399	4,520	6,726
NIES	20,841	22,493	56,667
Thailand	2,251	2,030	9,126
Malaysia	2,424	2,168	5,511
Philippines	1,928	937	2,504
Indonesia	4,113	2,172	5,040
Europe (west)	23,748	25,199	63,332
China	5,095	12,477	6,130
USSR	3,259	2,750	2,563
Total	152,030	175,638	286,947
Import into Japan			
United States	25,297	25,793	52,329
Canada	4,464	4,773	8,392
NIES	8,524	9,838	25,973
Thailand	1,061	1,027	4,147
Malaysia	2,927	4,330	5,401
Philippines	1,731	1,243	2,157
Indonesia	13,305	10,119	12,721
Europe (west)	11,541	12,356	42,617
China	5,292	6,483	12,054
USSR	2,020	1,429	3,351
Total	143,290	129,539	234,799

Source: Ministry of Finance, Customs Bureau, cited in *Toyo Keizai Statistics Annual* (1991, 231–32).

Note: Based on customs figures. NIES = Korea, Taiwan, Hong Kong, Singapore.

Since much of Japanese exports to Asian countries have been components and parts that are used for goods destined for the United States, one might suspect the U.S.-Japan conflict would cause Japanese companies to set up a diverted base of exports from Asian countries. It is difficult to speculate how much of Asian exports to the United States are by subsidiaries of Japanese companies. Much of the increase in Korean and Taiwanese exports to the United States comes from their own companies, though parts might come from Japan.

Worsening of the U.S.-Japan relationship at this point would not promote more intraregional trade, for two reasons. First, such a conflict would likely spill over to other Asian countries. The United States became extremely cautious toward Asian NIES, for fear of a repetition of the success of Japanese penetration into the United States. The United States has been tough on Korean trade surpluses against the United States, considering that Korea only recently paid back foreign debts. Second, the size of markets for final products such as automobiles is still small in Asia. Unless China with its large population changes its regime and continues to grow quickly, or the CIS turns to Asia for trade relations, markets are simply not present. (There is a limit how many cars and VCRs one family wants. Population is an important factor.)

However, if the political integration of the European Community results in an economic fortress and if the North American Free Trade Agreement (NAFTA) becomes a reality, the Asian nations may have no choice but to unite as a regional trading bloc.[47]

In summary, the trend shows signs of Japan's becoming mature enough to absorb Asian goods, and Asian nations' becoming mature enough to export to Japan. But it is too soon to expect intraregional trade to dominate U.S. trade with Asian countries (including Japan). The heightened tension between Japan and the United States would be counterproductive at this point for regional trade and relationship. The Pacific Asian intraregional trade is not an alternative to Asian–North American trade, unless North American and European markets become closed against Asian products.[48]

9.4.2   U.S. Pressures on Asian Countries

As explained in section 9.4.1, U.S. traditional and SII pressures on Japan have worked (or worked until recently) because of Japan's domestic political situation. That is, those who had vested interests to be lost in liberalization are those who sided with the LDP and the United States in its ideology. Moreover,

47. Such a regional trading bloc was first proposed by Prime Minister Makathir of Malaysia in 1990 by the name of East Asian economic grouping (EAEG), including Japan, Korea, China, Taiwan, Hong Kong, Vietnam, and the ASEAN-Six (Singapore, Thailand, Burnei, Indonesia, the Philippines, and Malaysia). The United States insisted that it be included in the bloc. With U.S. pressure, Japan is hesitant to commit to the EAEG plan.

48. This assessment should not give the United States a free hand to put more pressure on Japan and other Asian countries. The strain from pressure is already too much, so that resentment might become overwhelming.

internal pressure was already mounting for a better life. U.S. pressure only tipped the balance.

As explained in section 9.2, similar pressures have been applied to Korea, Taiwan, and other Asian nations.[49] However, the impacts of U.S. protectionistic measures are more serious on Korea and Taiwan than on Japan, because of their relatively lower GNP and relatively higher dependence on the U.S. market.

There is a strong tradition in economic policy and economic management, that government planning and regulation would be good for economic growth. Government intervention for infant industry protection (and more generally, for progress from import substitution to export substitution) is considered to be desirable. Until the economy becomes mature, government is unlikely to give up economic planning to maximize growth.

In summary, U.S. pressure for liberalization would not work unless the receptive environment is already there. The time is too soon.

9.4.3   Problems of Japan's Relationship with Asia

Political Aspects

A stable U.S.-Japan political relationship is no less important than export-import ties. Many Japanese and Asians feel that Japan has not apologized enough for its behavior before the Second World War. Unless Japan as a nation is accepted by its Asian neighbors, the United States is needed as a countervailing power. However, feelings toward Japan vary among the Asian nations.

Lack of Principles in Japan

It is extremely difficult to read the positions of leaders in various Japanese groups and parties. It is rare to see potential leaders compete for a top post with principles and positions. It is rare that different projects and ideas are evaluated in public, with different executives taking positions.

Is it culture? Or does it derive from an economic structure? The Japanese are known for their group orientation and consensus building. Japanese students and office workers are trained not to express opinions and not to debate with logic over different positions in public. A durable leader in a Japanese hierarchy is the one who does not reveal his position (in extremely rare cases, her position), having subordinates and colleagues debate and fight over positions, and having them turn to him for a decision that prevails as a "consensus" of the group. Minority opinions should not be revealed once the group makes the decision. Since it is a consensus, the leader does not have to take the blame even if the project fails, at least from internal pressure. Leadership may be lethal because it comes with conflicts. Is this a unique culture? Perhaps. Education contributes heavily to homogeneous thinking.

---

49. For the Korean case, see Nam (1991).

The Japanese hierarchy in big corporations, government, academics, and political parties is extremely rigid in promotion. It goes by age.[50] Unless one goes to a top post, a good retirement is not guaranteed. Hence, people become extremely cautious in taking sides and expressing opinions in public. There is no fast track, so group discipline works.[51]

Assertiveness

Taking positions and debating over ideology were much more common in the 1950s and 1960s. Labor-management conflicts and left-right political conflicts were common. However, as the fruits of high-speed growth trickled down to all participants of the society, different agents seem to have engaged in a truce. The turf is defined, and they agree to fix the border.

To take just one example, the LDP proposed in 1991, in the wake of political corruption cases, to reform the electoral system. The draft included introduction of the one representative per district (*sho senkyoku sei*) system, along with proportional representation. The former works for the LDP, while the latter works for smaller opposition parties. The pretext was to reduce the need for fund-raising. But the proposal favored the LDP as a whole. The other parties opposed it for good reason. What was unusual was the opposition within the LDP, and the proposal was abandoned. If the LDP were serious about attracting voters and dominating the majority, it would have persuaded the members to adopt the proposal.

9.4.4 Japan's Agenda for Leadership in the Region

Japan has not projected what kind of role it would play in the Pacific region or in the world. The lack of principles in the international context is not unrelated to the lack of positions in the domestic environment. This would not change even with U.S. pressure. It is deeply rooted in the Japanese society and workings of hierarchy.

Without projecting a position and an agenda, Japan will not be able to become a regional superpower.[52] Possible scenarios for Japan's taking leadership are described here.

50. In many cases, *age* means natural age. To be precise, however it is the years since an individual joined the bottom of the hierarchy. Corporations hire students fresh out of college, and promotion, through screening and attrition, goes with age. Government hierarchy (in the fast track) goes with years since joining the ministry. Academic promotions in universities depend on criteria 99 percent dominated by age, not by merit or publication. Probably 90 percent of positions for ministers are allocated by number of reelections to the House of Representatives. No one is supposed to slide into the top or the middle of Japanese hierarchy.

51. Literature in labor economics shows that shirking among workers could be avoided by an incentive structure. One solution is deferred payments, such as higher wages with longer tenure and pensions, with a threat of dismissal. This works in extreme form in a Japanese hierarchy.

52. Of course, there are costs and benefits to being politically assertive. Gilpin (1981) discusses this point. His assumption states: "A state will seek to change the international system through territorial, political, and economic expansion until the marginal costs of further change are equal to or greater than the marginal benefits" (106). In this section, my working hypothesis is that it

East Asian model of development. The World Bank and International Monetary Fund, with influence from the United States, have promoted a free market approach to developing countries. The approach emphasizes deregulating import controls, price controls, and other restrictions right from the beginning. However, the Japanese model of economic development seems different from this approach. The development strategy carefully nurtures infant industries by protecting domestic markets from imports and by giving tax breaks or preferential government loans or subsidies. The pattern has been repeated by Korea and Taiwan in developing export industries. The strategy appears to be successful in transforming low-income countries into newly developed nations. It is crucial to those countries to have markets for their exports to earn foreign currency. If Japan could stand up and defend the economic policies of up-and-coming nations, such as Thailand and Malaysia, from the U.S. assault on regulations and import restrictions as well as pressure on export restraints, this would be leadership. There is some sign of change in Japan's attitude toward a development strategy, especially in World Bank policymaking. However, it remains to be seen how strong Japan's challenge to the traditional approach would become.

Human rights. Human rights violations occur periodically in Asian countries, as in any other region in the world. Until now, the United States responded to human rights violation quickly and decisively. Japan and some European countries are reluctant to take measures against human rights violations. Japan responded very late to the Tiananmen Square incidents, compared to the United States and Europe. Japan was the first to resume aid to China after the incident. Japan did little against the Myanmar government for its house arrest of San Suu Kyi, the Nobel Peace Prize winner of 1991, or Indonesia for its killings in the East Timor incident. In either case, Japan could have used its official development assistance (ODA) muscle to press for democracy. However, this does not seem to be Japan's style so far.

Antiweaponry policy. A principle that Japan could embrace more easily than human rights is an ODA for peace enforcement. As its constitution dictates, Japan has a clean record for not exporting weaponry. In order to enforce regional stability, Japan may take up a principle of not providing ODA for countries that export or import weaponry.

Regional bloc. In a sense, Japan could respond to the call from Mahathir for forming the EAEG. It could be a regional counterproposal to the European Community (EC) and NAFTA. If this regional development takes place, Japan

---

is neither sustainable nor desirable in the long run to have a strong economic presence without political assertiveness.

will have to play a significant role, whether it likes to or not. Given that the United States firmly opposed a move such as the EAEG, this will be on Japan's agenda only when the EC and NAFTA are closed to Asian nations. I consider this to be only remotely possible.

9.5   Concluding Remarks

In this paper I have argued the following points: First, U.S. pressure in the past can be classified into three types. Second, the traditional and market access pressures on Japan and other East Asian countries were not necessarily resisted, though neither were they welcomed, by Asian countries, because of some domestic merit to the pressure. Third, the results-oriented pressure has been intensely hated by Japan and others because it unilaterally benefits U.S. producers. Fourth, resistance to pressure is not likely to turn Japan away from the United States in favor of Asian countries, because the trade relationship needs the United States as an absorber of Asian countries' products and Japan lacks leadership in the region.

References

Alesina, Alberto, and Geoffrey Carliner, eds. 1991. *Politics and Economics in the Eighties*. Chicago: University of Chicago Press.

Bhagwati, Jagdish, and Hugh T. Patrick. 1990. *Aggressive Unilateralism*. Ann Arbor: University of Michigan Press.

Destler, I. M. 1986. *American Trade Politics: System under Stress*. Washington, DC: Institute for International Economics; New York: Twentieth Century Fund.

————. 1991. U.S. Trade Policy-making in the Eighties. In Alberto Alesina and Geoffrey Carliner, eds., *Politics and Economics in the Eighties*, 251–81. Chicago: University of Chicago Press.

Destler, I. M., Haruhiro Fukui, and Hideo Sato. 1979. *The Textile Wrangle: Conflict in Japanese-American Relations, 1969–71*. Ithaca, NY: Cornell University Press.

Destler, I. M., and John S. Odell. 1987. *Anti-protection: Changing Forces in United States Trade Politics*. Policy Analyses in International Economics, vol. 21. Washington, DC: Institute for International Economics.

Destler, I. M., and Hideo Sato. 1982. *Coping with U.S.-Japanese Economic Conflicts*. Lexington, MA: Lexington Books.

Dornbusch, Rudiger W. 1990. Policy Options for Freer Trade: The Case for Bilateralism. In Robert Z. Lawrence and Charles L. Schultze, eds., *An American Trade Strategy: Options for the 1990s*, 106–33. Washington, DC: Brookings Institution.

Drucker, Peter F. 1986. *Frontiers of Management*. New York: Harper and Row.

Forum for Policy Innovation. 1990. Toward Tarrification for Opening the Rice Market in Japan. July.

Frankel, Jeffrey A. 1984. *The Yen/Dollar Agreement: Liberalizing Japanese Capital Markets*. Washington, DC: Institute for International Economics.

Gilpin, Robert. 1981. *War and Change in World Politics*. Cambridge: Cambridge University Press.

Hillman, Arye L., and Heinrich W. Ursprung. 1988. Domestic Politics, Foreign Interests, and International Trade Policy. *American Economic Review* 78 (4): 729–45.

Inoguchi, Takashi. 1991. Japan's Response to the Gulf Crisis: An Analytic Overview. *Journal of Japanese Studies* 17 (Winter): 257–73.

Ito, Takatoshi. 1992. *The Japanese Economy.* Cambridge, MA: MIT Press.

Ito, Takatoshi, and Masayoshi Maruyama. 1991. Is the Japanese Distribution System Really Inefficient? In Paul Krugman, ed., *Trade with Japan: Has the Door Opened Wider?* 149–73. Chicago: University of Chicago Press.

Kosai, Yutaka. 1986. *The Era of High-Speed Growth.* Tokyo: University of Tokyo Press.

Krugman, Paul. 1990. *The Age of Diminished Expectations.* Cambridge, MA: MIT Press.

McCubbins, Mathew D., Roger G. Noll, and Barry R. Weingast. 1987. Administrative Procedures as Instruments of Political Controls. *Journal of Law, Economics, and Organization* 3 (2): 243–77.

Morita, Akio, and Shintaro Ishihara. 1989. *Japan That Can Say No* (in Japanese). Tokyo: Kobunsha. Translated version is authored by Shintaro Ishihara (New York: Simon and Schuster, 1991). It omits Morita's chapters and adds some writings of Ishihara.

Nam, Chong-Hyun. 1991. Protectionist U.S. Trade Policy and Korean Exports. Paper presented in the second NBER East Asian Seminar in Economics, Seoul, June.

Prestowitz, Clyde V., Jr. 1988. *Trading Places: How We Allowed Japan to Take the Lead.* New York: Basic Books.

Rosenbluth, Frances McCall. 1989. *Financial Politics in Contemporary Japan.* Ithaca, NY: Cornell University Press.

Sakakibara, Eisuke. 1990. *Japan beyond Capitalism* (in Japanese). Tokyo: Toyo Keizai Shinpo-sha.

Sheard, Paul. 1991. The Economics of Japanese Corporate Organization and the "Structural Impediments" Debate: A Critical Review. *Japanese Economic Studies* 19 (4): 30–78.

Tyson, Laura D'Andrea. 1990. Managed Trade: Making the Best of the Second Best. In Robert Z. Lawrence and Charles L. Schultze, eds., *An American Trade Strategy: Options for the 1990s,* 142–84. Washington, DC: Brookings Institution.

van Wolferen, Karel. 1989. *The Enigma of Japanese Power.* New York: Alfred A. Knopf.

Weingast, Barry R., and William J. Marshall. 1988. The Industrial Organization of Congress; or, Why Legislatures, like Firms, Are Not Organized as Markets. *Journal of Political Economy* 96 (1): 132–63.

Yakushiji, Taizo. 1984. The Government in a Spiral Dilemma: Dynamic Policy Interventions vis-à-vis Auto Firms. In M. Aoki, ed., *The Economic Analysis of the Japanese Firm.* Amsterdam: North-Holland.

Yoffie, David B. 1983. *Power and Protectionism.* New York: Columbia University Press.

Comment   Frances McCall Rosenbluth

I commend Takatoshi Ito for taking seriously the charge of the conference organizers to integrate politics and economics in his analysis. He examines the

Frances McCall Rosenbluth is professor of political science at the University of California, Los Angeles.

history of United States–Japan economic relations and looks for ways macroeconomic forces and micropolitical incentives interact. I agree with much of the paper. But as the designated political scientist kibitzer, I would like to focus on Ito's characterization of Japan's political system. A more complete model of Japanese politics will allow us to understand Japan's actions better and therefore to predict Japan's responses to pressures from the United States more accurately.

Ito's characterization of Japan's political system is perhaps best illustrated by a subtheme running through his paper, decrying Japan's lack of political leadership. Ito raises the leadership issue in the introduction and returns to it again periodically, concluding that the "biggest stumbling block to Japan's becoming a regional economic and political leader is lack of principles." Ito seems to suggest that this stems from a domestic political system that deters decisive action, hence robbing Japan of important opportunities to assert itself on the international stage.

Although Japan's political system has difficulty acting speedily, as I will argue later, this depiction of an indecisive and clumsy Japan tripping over its own feet is not entirely convincing. Japan has good reason, in fact, to maintain a low international profile. Even in a post–Cold War world, Japan continues to rely on the United States for much of its defense. Second, as long as Japan's exporters rely disproportionately on U.S. markets for their viability, it is unrealistic to assume Japan could improve its welfare by asserting itself more forcefully. Japan's leadership still sees the country's interests served better by supporting than by challenging the United States.

Japan is not likely to deviate substantially from its tried-and-true course of action, short of important changes in the benefits and/or the costs of the status quo. True, the benefits of strong ties with the United States could decline, particularly if the United States begins to close its markets to Japanese products. Alternatively, the costs of challenging the United States could decline, due to a diversification of export and investment patterns away from the United States. But neither of these has yet occurred to a significant degree.

To call Japan, as does much of the popular press, a "headless monster" incapable of concerted action is misconceived. Japan has a unitary, parliamentary system of government that is more streamlined in many ways than the U.S. system, where power divides vertically between federal and state governments and horizontally between the executive and legislative branches. That Japanese bureaucrats rather than elected officials appear to handle many important decisions is precisely what one should expect in equilibrium in a parliamentary system. Politicians *prefer* to delegate routine policy decisions, and need to monitor and intervene extensively only when they face competition from an executive branch controlled by a different political party.

However streamlined, Japan's political system is incapable of moving quickly for other reasons. Japan's electoral rules amplify the importance of blocs of votes and hence delay decisions that could hurt any group of constituents. It is commonly assumed in any representative government that, because of collective action problems, organized groups are more advantaged than unorganized voters or consumers. But collective action problems operate with a vengeance in Japan. Japan's single nontransferable vote (SNTV), multimember district electoral system pits members of the ruling Liberal Democratic party (LDP) against *each other.* This forces members of that party (or any party seeking to gain a majority) to supply private goods—budgetary and regulatory favors, for example—to mutually distinct groups of voters rather than to appeal to a common party platform or label.

Given the importance to LDP members of personal support networks and of campaign financing to nurture these blocs of votes, the party leadership faces ferocious opposition from within the party's own ranks to policy measures—trade liberalization, for instance—that alienate groups of supporters.[1] Because Japan's government is a parliamentary system, the LDP leadership hypothetically could force its backbenchers to support policy decisions that are in the party's overall best interests. But the LDP leadership also has to ensure the reelection of a Diet majority. As long as the LDP faces a vote-division problem, the party cannot shift from a private goods, favor-based electoral strategy to a public goods strategy that emphasizes the interests of the unorganized populace. Until the LDP undertakes electoral reform, Japan's political leadership will liberalize Japan's markets as little as possible but as much as necessary to avoid a showdown with the United States.

In conclusion, I return to policy implications of Japan's political system for the United States. I was intrigued by Ito's open-minded attitude toward the "revisionists," which separates him from most of his economist brethren. I agree that Japan's markets are not open. But it is important that the United States pursue policies that will not backfire.

I share Ito's profound skepticism about the wisdom of a Fallowsian economic containment strategy against Japan. The LDP is slowly opening Japan's markets because of pressure from Japan's exporters, for whom the probability and expected costs of U.S. trade retaliation have risen steadily in recent decades. Demographic change, in particular the rising proportion of urban salaried workers as a proportion of voters, is also forcing the LDP to reconsider its proproducer policies.

The United States would do well to support the voices in Japan that favor market opening by pressing for greater access to foreign competitors, without alienating the Japanese public through unilateral market closure or high-profile posturing. But the United States should be prepared to be patient in the short run. Only when the LDP manages to jettison farmers and other uncompetitive sectors from its coalition—which it is attempting to do through electoral reform—can the United States expect to see dramatic changes in Japan's trade policy.

---

1. Note that the LDP would have little incentive to retain the malapportionment of districts in favor of farmers were it not for the farmers' organizations that help the LDP divide the vote in rural districts.

10   Domestic Politics and Regional Cooperation: The United States, Japan, and Pacific Money and Finance

Jeffry A. Frieden

10.1   Introduction

International monetary and financial issues are central to Pacific economic relations. Financial flows in the Pacific region are of great size and economic importance. Movements in exchange rates and related macroeconomic variables affect almost all economic activities in the region.

The future of Pacific monetary and financial policies is, however, uncertain. Japan's role in regional financial policymaking is not commensurate with its financial importance. Regional policies toward currency values and macroeconomic trends are nonexistent or embryonic. Interstate relations on these two dimensions might go in any number of directions, and the direction taken will have broad and deep implications for economic and noneconomic developments in the Pacific.

This paper examines prospects for monetary and financial relations in the Pacific by focusing on Japanese and American policy in these arenas. It looks primarily at the domestic politics of international money and finance, particularly how the distributional impact of different policies within the United States and Japan affect policy choice. Its tentative conclusion is that groups favorable to international monetary and financial cooperation are gaining ground in Japan, where they have typically been relatively unimportant. Conversely, "internationalist" groups are slipping in influence in the United States, although they remain very influential.

Section 10.2 explores the contours of regional monetary and financial issues, the variety of conceivable outcomes, and analytical tools to understand policy

Jeffry A. Frieden is professor of political science at the University of California, Los Angeles.

The author acknowledges support from the Social Science Research Council's Program in Foreign Policy Studies and from the German Marshall Fund, and comments and suggestions from conference participants, especially Jeffrey Frankel, Takeo Hoshi, Miles Kahler, and Frances Rosenbluth.

trends, especially the economic interest groups expected to affect the domestic politics of different international monetary and financial policies. In section 10.3, these tools are applied to an important previous case in which similar issues were raised, that of the United States in the interwar years. Section 10.4 looks at the economic interests at play in the formulation of Japanese policy toward international money and finance, and where they appear to be leading; section 10.5 does the same for the United States. In section 10.6, the essay's implications and conclusions are summarized.

10.2   The Problem: Cooperation or Conflict in Regional Money and Finance

The principal concern for monetary and financial relations in the Pacific is that they might become unstable, which in turn might dampen regional flows of goods and capital. Most scenarios for such a breakdown involve one of two expectations of Japanese and American international monetary and financial policies.

A first pessimistic scenario is that of "Japan as free rider" on increasingly reticent American leadership. In this picture, the United States continues to act more or less alone in attempting to manage Pacific monetary and financial relations, and incurs substantial costs to do so. Japan, however, is content to enjoy the benefits of American policies without paying for any of their costs. This would, in other words, be something of a continuation of the postwar pattern, in an era in which Japan is far better able to contribute to regional monetary and financial management than it once was—and perhaps better able than the United States now is. Japanese refusal to play a bigger part in regional monetary and financial issues would probably precipitate an American refusal to continue its leadership, and an era of hostility and conflict between the two nations.

A second pessimistic scenario is that of "Japan as bloc leader." In this picture, Japan responds to its newfound financial strength by carving out a zone of more or less exclusive monetary and financial influence in Asia. It seeks a formal or informal "yen zone," with preferential treatment of the Japanese currency and Japanese financial flows and discrimination against the dollar and American finance. Such Japanese policies would also precipitate a rupture with the United States.

In both instances, Japanese-American conflict in monetary and financial realms would almost certainly reduce the level of financial flows in the region, increase the unpredictability of exchange rates, and hamper trade. This would presumably bode ill for the economic and political stability of the region.

The two pessimistic scenarios outlined above contrast implicitly with two optimistic scenarios in which Japan and the United States cooperate. The first is not regional at all and simply looks toward global cooperation among the world's leading nations, including Japan and the United States, on whatever issues may be important at the global level. A second optimistic view involves Japanese-American cooperation within the Pacific region, to ensure a favorable environment for regional financial flows, and to provide generally predictable regional exchange rates. Both scenarios seem to require that the Japanese government play a more important role in global or regional financial policy; and that the Japanese government collaborate with other governments in the region or the world to stabilize macroeconomic conditions. In other words, the two governments would either participate in joint management of global money and finance, or would themselves jointly manage the region's monetary and financial affairs. Either way, the outcome would be cooperative: the jointness of the management would guard against conflict among governments; the management itself would provide economic and policy predictability.

Both the optimistic and pessimistic scenarios imply a general model of the politics of international money and finance, specifically of the role of conscious government supervision in these arenas and of intergovernmental cooperation in such supervision. The implicit model is one in which the smooth functioning of international or regional monetary and financial systems requires certain enabling government policies, the enactment of which is difficult without explicit interstate cooperation.

The most common assertion along these lines is that there are certain international public goods in money and finance, which improve the welfare of all but which no one government has an incentive to provide. Analogies are typically made to domestic money and finance, where price stability and a lender-of-last-resort function are the most commonly discussed public goods and a central bank often supplies them (a seminal discussion is in Kindleberger 1973, extended in Kindleberger 1985; see also Fratianni and Pattison 1982).

It is unlikely that the cooperative ventures under discussion in this realm involve true public goods. Most of them aim at stabilizing international monetary and financial flows, in the interest of increasing levels of international payments and trade. However, stability is not necessarily the best possible outcome for all concerned, especially as it typically involves maintenance of the status quo. Stabilizing exchange rates might involve setting relative prices that harm many producers or consumers, or that involve social welfare costs. Coordinating macroeconomic strategies might simply allow policymakers to reinforce each others' socially undesirable policies. Protecting cross-border financial contracts might involve soaking poor debtors for the benefit of rich creditors. It may be morally comforting for supporters of such measures to consider them public goods, but analytically they are probably club goods whose benefits accrue to some relatively limited group of actors. In this case, the concerns in question are of primary interest to those most heavily involved in international trade and payments, rather than public goods that benefit all without exception. This point will resurface in my discussion of the domestic politics of interstate cooperation on these dimensions. To avoid definitional controversy, I call the ventures in question club goods; those who believe they are truly public goods can simply regard the club in question to be society (or international society) as a whole.

Whether or not the sorts of goods in question are primarily of public or club interest, their provision still creates problems of collective action. Even if only national monetary authorities have an interest in macroeconomic coordination (against the interests of their citizens, let us assume), they still need to work out a way to cooperate among themselves. The cooperation problems raised can be divided into monetary and financial components.

The club goods associated with *international financial relations* have to do with monitoring and enforcing cross-border loan contracts, maintaining open markets for debtor exports, supervising international financial institutions, and providing international liquidity in times of crisis. International lending depends on the credibility of borrower commitments to make debt service payments; this credibility is a function both of the information available to lenders and of the ability of lenders to sanction errant borrowers. The provision of this information and the carrying out of these sanctions create significant collective action problems for real or potential lenders: once the information is available and the sanctions are in place, there is an incentive for individual lenders to free ride by not helping gather information and by evading sanctions. By the same token, international finance cannot long endure a major closure of goods markets—debtors need to earn foreign exchange to service their debts. Creditor countries have an interest in open markets for debtor exports, but they might prefer that other countries' markets be more open than theirs.

The supervision of financial institutions involved in the international arena has become especially important, as electronic funds transfers can magnify the impact of an international bank failure. All international financial actors gain from the stability cooperative supervision can provide. However, all banks have an incentive to evade supervision, and all countries have an incentive to skimp on supervisory expenses and supervisory requirements in order to give their banks an advantage in international competition. Similar conditions apply to the role of national monetary authorities in providing liquidity in times of international financial difficulty.

In a sense, these considerations reflect the disjuncture between a regionally or globally integrated financial system and the absence of regional or global financial authorities. National authorities and judicial systems safeguard contracts, supervise financial markets, and provide lender-of-last-resort facilities within nations. As no international agency does similar duty, these functions must be carried out by national governments acting together. However, there are real incentives for free riding on the part of national governments.

The club goods associated with *international monetary relations* raise similar problems. Again by a somewhat shaky analogy to the domestic order, just as national monetary authorities act to provide price stability, so does the international monetary system function best when international relative prices are most stable. This involves both policies toward predictable exchange rates, and the coordination of national macroeconomic measures. In this sense, the crux of the regional problem on the monetary front is cooperative exchange rate and macroeconomic policies among national monetary authorities.

For large countries, another major international monetary issue is the degree to which the national currency functions as a key currency for global or regional trade and payments. Just as a national money substantially lowers transactions costs and facilitates exchange domestically, so do reliable key currencies allow for higher levels of global exchange. For a national currency to function well as a key currency, however, generally requires certain commitments from the currency's home authorities. Especially important is stability in the real value of the currency—low rates of inflation and nominal exchange rate volatility—and generally deep and unencumbered national financial markets in which economic agents can trade freely in assets denominated in the currency (Krugman 1984; Tavlas 1991). These commitments, too, imply scope for national free riding (although there are direct advantages to key currency status for the issuing country).

In any case, most visions of Pacific monetary and financial futures, whether pessimistic or optimistic, involve an implicit model of the provision (or underprovision) of these club or public goods. Some pessimistic views expect that Japan, the United States, or both will try to avoid paying the costs involved in helping provide these goods. Others anticipate that the two regional leaders will attempt to provide these services within smaller, more exclusive zones of influence—the United States as monetary and financial dominator of the Western Hemisphere, Japan of East Asia. Optimistic sentiments are motivated by the expectation that the region's nations will recognize the gains associated with the cooperative provision of these collective goods and will act accordingly. They might do it as a joint U.S.-Japanese consortium, for the Pacific region; or globally, for the world as a whole.

The general analytical approach appropriate to an evaluation of the likelihood of international cooperation has two component parts: the domestic politics of national foreign policies, and strategic interaction among potentially cooperating nations (Putnam 1988). The first component part involves investigating different domestic socioeconomic and political realities. "National interests," in this context, vary widely along with the interests of those in national societies. A state dominated by foreign debtors in financial distress is more likely to downplay the importance of respecting cross-border loan contracts than a state dominated by major international creditors. This step looks at national priorities, as determined by domestic interests and institutions, to see what they might imply for the success of international or regional cooperation.

Along these lines and for heuristic purposes, we can think of national political economics as divided into two camps: cooperative and competitive (for similar domestic approaches to foreign policy, see Gourevitch 1986; Ferguson 1984; Nolt 1992). This flows from the observation that most of the regional monetary and financial collective goods discussed above involve subordinating domestic economic conditions to the demands of regional cooperation. For example, regional macroeconomic policy coordination by definition means that policymakers' goals involve more than purely domestic economic conditions. Allowing foreign debtors access to creditor markets may be good for regional financial flows, but bad for domestic producers of goods with which debtor producers compete.

Those in the cooperative or "internationalist" camp regard the costs associated with their home country's helping carry out global or regional monetary and financial leadership functions as minor compared to the benefits associated with smoothly running global or regional monetary and financial systems. Not surprisingly, those in this camp tend to be heavily committed to global or regional trade and payments; anything that hampers international money and finance impinges directly on their well-being. The camp includes international financial investors and intermediaries, global corporations, major exporters, and consumers of imports.

Competitive or "nationalist" economic groups are loathe to forgo the primacy of domestic conditions in national economic policymaking. They may not actively desire a reduction of cross-border goods and financial movements, but their priority is the state of the domestic economy—even if this means that their government eschews international cooperative agreements. Again, it is not surprising that such groups are concentrated among those who make and sell goods and services for the home market, especially producers of nontradables and of goods in direct competition with imports. Simply put and all else equal, the stronger the "internationalist" camp in any given national society, the more likely it is to desire and pursue cooperative international policies. To the extent that the internationalists are regionally oriented, their representatives will want to pursue regional cooperation; a global business orientation should lead to support for broader and more sweeping cooperative measures at the truly international level. On the other hand, the stronger the "nationalist" camp, the more likely it is to embark on unilateral ventures.

Domestic politics is only the beginning of the story, however, for by definition international politics involves strategic interaction among nations. The second step, then, is to bring the tools of the trade to bear on analyzing the problems of international cooperation (as, for example, in Oye 1986; Eichengreen 1989a; Frankel 1988b). Even where states have similar interests in outcomes, problems associated with interstate cooperation may arise due to the perils of collective action. Where these perils are reduced—where accurate information is available, where commitment mechanisms reduce the risk of cheating, where it is possible to provide selective incentives to cooperators—regional cooperation is more likely to be forthcoming.

The general method, then, involves looking both at the domestic politics of policies associated with regional cooperation and at the problems of interstate collective action. An examination of regional collaboration toward international debt, for example, could specify the interests of different governments on the basis of the domestic political realities they face. It could then go on, within this context, to discuss how, given their interests, these different governments might be able to work out cooperative agreements.

For the purposes of this essay, I essentially ignore considerations of strategic interaction in order to focus on domestic political considerations associated with the provision of regional collective goods in the monetary and financial arenas. This is not to downplay collective action problems in general. It is driven largely by the belief that, at least in the Pacific monetary and financial realm, collective action problems are relatively unimportant. There are only two major actors, the United States and Japan, and their interactions are multidimensional and iterated. In this context, free riding would be hard to ascribe to the severe constraints of such games as a single-shot prisoner's dilemma. Failures of cooperation are more liable to be the result of underlying policy differences—of domestically entrenched interests with divergent preferences. Even if strategic interaction between the United States and Japan were indeed problematic, we could not speak intelligently of it without a clear picture of the two countries' preference functions. The point, then, is to clarify the domestically derived national preference orders of the two major nations in the region. In this sense the analysis presented in this paper is simply the first step of the two-step process described above. My purpose is to understand the nature of these preferences more fully. I leave to others a more extensive exploration of strategic interaction between the two nations.

In the Pacific context, the provision of the "infrastructure" necessary to sustain regional financial and monetary flows is first and foremost a function of American and Japanese policy. While strategic interaction between these two actors may color outcomes, I think the goals of the two countries are particularly important to explaining outcomes. The remainder of the paper uses historical and contemporary evidence to clarify the issue and its potential paths.

10.3 The American Precedent

A fascinating example of the effects of domestic political conflict on a country's participation in managing the world monetary and financial system is given by the interwar United States. The parallels to today's Japan are striking. In the space of a few years, the United States leapt to a predominant international financial position. It was faced with many of the problems of international cooperation currently facing Japan, and there was much domestic conflict over how to confront these challenges. The interwar American experience with the domestic politics of national commitments to international cooperation in money and finance was grim. During the interwar years, indeed, opposition from nationalistic forces practically stymied U.S. government participation in efforts at international monetary and financial cooperation.[1] In this context, it is worth seeing what lessons the American episode may hold for Japan.

World War I catapulted the United States to international financial leadership. The Allies were deeply in debt to the U.S. government, and the financial reconstruction of European economies was largely entrusted to American private bankers. American trade and investment had come to predominate in Latin America, and even in Europe's colonies and protectorates.

The United States was at least as important an actor in the international financial system in the 1920s as Japan is today. By 1929, the United States accounted for 31 percent of the stock of all international loans and investments outstanding (calculated from Staley 1935). In capital flows, the American position was overwhelming: while reliable figures are not available, the United States accounted for well over half of all new international loans and investments in the 1920s. By comparison, Japanese investors now account for about 30 percent of all international direct investment flows; Japanese international banks account for 33 percent of the global stock of cross-border bank assets. The total international and foreign assets of Japanese banks are, in fact, larger than the combined cross-border assets of banks from the next three most important countries (the United States, Germany, and France) combined (foreign direct investment [FDI] figures from Froot 1991; bank asset figures from Bank for International Settlements 1991, 19).

International finance and investment were also important to the U.S. economy. Foreign bonds floated on Wall Street averaged over a billion dollars a year in the 1920s, equivalent to more than one-sixth of annual corporate bond flotations. Foreign direct investment averaged over a half-billion dollars a year. In 1922, the stock of overseas loans and direct investments totaled $9.1 billion, equivalent to 12 percent of American gross national product (GNP); by 1929, it was $15.2 billion, equivalent to 15 percent of GNP.[2]

The importance of U.S. loans and investment to the interwar international economy was clear to contemporaries. American private capital financed large portions of total investment in Germany and in other central and southern European nations. American bankers arranged stabilization programs for Germany, Poland, Rumania, Italy, Belgium, and other nations. In Latin America, American loans and direct investment fed an economic euphoria known as "the dance of the millions." Princeton economics professor Edwin Kemmerer— the "money doctor"—roamed the Western Hemisphere to supervise economic policies and certify their reliability to American investors (Drake 1989).

---

1. What follows draws on Frieden (1987, 25–78; 1988). Only where information is not taken from these publications will exact citations be given. A parallel story involves the evolution of American domestic economic-policy institutions in response to changes in the international position of the U.S. economy; for one treatment see Broz (1992).

2. Figures are from the *Economic Report of the President,* various issues. GNP for 1922 is actually net national product plus 10 percent, the average difference for this historical period.

Important as the United States might have been to the world economy in the 1920s, there were very divergent views among Americans about what policies were appropriate to this new reality. These different views reflected the divergent interests of major economic interest groups. "Internationalism" was rooted in those associated with the country's international economic predominance, especially money-center banks and multinational corporations; it also found support among exporting farmers and a few industries with important foreign markets. Internationally oriented bankers and industrialists belonged primarily to the internationalist wing of the Republican party or were Wilsonian Democrats; export agriculture was important to the southern Democratic party. For these groups, the world economy had come to be significant indeed, and they had a clear and present belief that the U.S. government should lead in stabilizing international monetary and financial relations.

The internationalists believed that the U.S. government should reduce or forgive European war debts: "Those debts should be canceled," J. P. Morgan, Jr., said in 1922 (Forbes 1981, 125). The Allies owed the U.S. government $10 billion, and American insistence on repayment helped destabilize European financial and monetary affairs. War debts complicated economic policymaking in Allied countries; they encouraged the French and Belgian governments to press demands for higher German reparations; and they reduced the ability of indebted nations to borrow privately.

The international monetary agenda was also full and required American involvement. The dollar was the only major currency that had not suffered serious disturbances during World War I, and it was the centerpiece of attempts to reconstruct the gold standard and stabilize European currencies. This required coordination of the policies of the United States, Great Britain, and France, especially cooperation among central banks.

Internationally oriented groups also wanted reduced American trade barriers. Those with overseas loans needed the American market open to their debtors, as investment banker Otto Kahn explained: "Having become a creditor nation we have got now to fit ourselves into the role of a creditor nation. We shall have to make up our minds to be more hospitable to imports" (Maltz 1963, 204–5). American exporters feared that protection would lead foreigners to close their markets to American products.

However, the internationalists' plans for international cooperation were thwarted by the hostility of the politically powerful isolationists. Isolationism found its principal socioeconomic base in portions of the U.S. economy unconnected to the foreign sector. Despite a rapid expansion of overseas investment and trade, indeed, this activity was narrowly concentrated. Many manufacturers and farmers faced serious import competition and had no desire to see the U.S. government engage in cooperative ventures that would increase world trade and payments or otherwise open the economy further (Eichengreen 1989b).

The isolationists adamantly opposed trade liberalization, since they were

under competitive pressure from abroad. By the same token, they saw no reason to spend taxpayers' money to stabilize the currencies or regularize the finances of their European competitors. Inasmuch as war debt forgiveness would
make European economies more competitive with the United States, it was
undesirable; inasmuch as it would reduce U.S. Treasury income and perhaps
require tax increases, it would depress domestic economic activity. Reconstructing the gold standard would only make it easier for foreigners to sell to
the American market, especially as most monetary plans called for a strong
dollar. On all counts, then, the isolationists opposed the country's internationally integrated banks and corporations.

Isolationist opposition thwarted most of the internationalists' attempts to get
an American government commitment to international monetary and financial
leadership. Despite the prominence of American banks and corporations in
the world economy of the 1920s, American officials were absent from most
discussions of international money and finance. At the Versailles Conference,
the United States under Woodrow Wilson presented elaborate designs for the
postwar political and economic order, including money and finance. After Wilson was unable to obtain congressional approval for American membership in
the League of Nations, however, the U.S. government was largely forced to
abdicate the international scene.

Most American official involvement in international monetary and financial
negotiations was foreclosed by the predominance of isolationist sentiment
within the United States. Supporters of a greater role for the U.S. government
were unable to prevail in domestic debates over foreign policy. This forced the
internationalists to cobble together private schemes for international monetary
and financial management, and these schemes typically were fragile enough
that they collapsed under strong economic and political pressure.

The isolationists were anything but a fringe group. They were economically
important, and the strength of localist interests in Congress reinforced their
influence. For all intents and purposes, the isolationists controlled Congress
and the cabinet in the 1921–33 Republican administrations. However, economic internationalists were often able to influence government agencies out
of the public eye. Foremost among these was the Federal Reserve Bank of New
York, which was supportive of the interests of money-center banks. The State
Department, too, tended to sympathize with international businessmen. In both
cases, however, participation in attempts at international cooperation had to be
carried out surreptitiously, for Congress blocked whatever it discovered.

The limitations placed on the U.S. government by domestic isolationism
made it extremely difficult for official American delegations to be openly involved in the most important monetary and financial negotiations of the period.
For example, the stabilization of the German economy, carried out under the
Dawes and Young plans, required American support, but the U.S. government
could not be involved. While other parties to the agreements were represented
by their central banks, the American delegation was composed of partners and

friends of J. P. Morgan and Company, which provided the bulk of the original German stabilization loan. When, as part of the Young Plan, the Bank for International Settlements was established in 1930, partly to oversee German finances and partly to provide a framework for international monetary and financial cooperation, again the members were the European central banks and Morgan and Company.

The Federal Reserve did participate in a series of international monetary conferences in the 1920s and did cooperate with the Bank of England and the Bank of France on a number of dimensions. However, the Fed's room to maneuver was severely hamstrung by congressional sniping at the allegedly Europhilic central bank, and less directly by the unwillingness of Congress and the administration to make concessions in domestic economic policy that might smooth the path of international monetary cooperation (Clarke 1967).

Important as trade liberalization may have been for financial reconstruction, the protectionists within the United States prevailed at almost every turn. The trend toward liberalization begun under Wilson was reversed by the Republican protectionists, and tariffs were raised in 1921 and 1922. In 1930, the Smoot-Hawley Act raised American tariffs to extremely high levels (Eichengreen 1989b).

The inability of the U.S. government to commit to international cooperation seriously undermined these ventures (Eichengreen 1992). On the one hand, American private investors were at the center of international finance. On the other hand, the U.S. government was almost nowhere to be found. American private bankers organized financial and monetary stabilization programs with the support of European governments, but without the support of the U.S. government. U.S. overseas lending grew by leaps and bounds, along with the progressive closure of the U.S. market to foreigners. The refusal of the U.S. government to involve itself in international monetary and financial negotiations, and its unwillingness to take into account the international consequences of its policies, probably contributed to the collapse of the already-fragile international monetary, financial, and trading orders during the Depression.

The American example is one in which private overseas financial interests grew far more rapidly than the government's willingness or ability to act on behalf of these interests. This meant, specifically, that the U.S. government simply did not help provide many of the club goods we have identified as potentially important to stable global monetary and financial relations. This was so much the case that American private bankers often found themselves driven to carry out these functions themselves, although the experience of private businesses acting on these dimensions without government support was rarely positive. The disparity between economic activities and government support was large and grew larger with time. If this were to happen in Japan, we might expect difficult times both for Japan's partners and for world money and finance generally.

The principal inference that can be drawn from the interwar American experience is that entrenched domestic interests can impede the evolution of government policies to help stabilize international money and finance—even in a country that dominates the international monetary and financial systems. This makes it crucially important to understand the political balance of power among various domestic economic interest groups in countries faced with important international policy choices along these lines. The next sections survey the balance of power in contemporary Japan and the United States.

10.4 Contemporary Japan

Japan has come to dominate international money and financial markets, and international conditions have become extremely important to many Japanese firms. Japan's rise to predominance has been almost as rapid as that of the United States during and after World War I. In the late 1970s, Japanese investors accounted for 6 percent of direct investment outflows from the major industrial nations, 2 percent of equities outflows, 15 percent of bond outflows, and 12 percent of short-term bank outflows. By the late 1980s, the figures were 20 percent of FDI, 25 percent of equities, 55 percent of bonds, and 50 percent of short-term bank outflows (calculated from Turner 1991, 42–75; a general survey is Thorn 1987). Temporary difficulties can slow this process, but they are unlikely to alter the overall trend: Japan's role in Pacific financial and investment flows is extremely large and likely to grow larger.

This process has made major Japanese banks and firms far more integrated into the international financial system. Japanese financial investors and intermediaries have enormous overseas positions; as of 1991, the international assets of Japanese banks were $1.9 trillion, one-third of total international bank assets (Bank for International Settlements 1991, 19). The number of Japanese bank affiliates abroad went from 253 in 1975 to 913 in 1988, while affiliates of securities firms went from 54 to 196 in the same period (Tavlas and Ozeki 1991, 15). In 1990, foreign securities were 15 percent of total bank securities holdings, up from less than 3 percent in 1980 (Turner, 1991, 77). The Japanese offshore market grew from nearly nothing in 1985 to almost half a trillion dollars in 1991.

Similar patterns characterize major Japanese multinational corporations. The explosion of Japanese FDI in the late 1980s was concentrated in some of the country's leading sectors: finance, real estate, and sophisticated manufacturing (especially electrical machinery and transportation equipment). At this point, FDI is important to many major Japanese industries, including traditional export producers that have located production facilities in lower-cost regions (Froot 1991; Naya 1990).

Many Japanese firms have come to depend on global financial markets as a source of funds. Indeed, Japanese issuers accounted for one-third of all international bonds issued in 1990–91 (Bank for International Settlements 1991, 15). Between 1984 and 1988, approximately half of all corporate bonds issued by Japanese residents were bought abroad, while the share of foreign bonds in total corporate securities issues went from 11 percent in the late 1970s to 35 percent in the late 1980s (Osugi 1990, 15, 55).

Japanese predominance in world and Pacific money and financial markets is not reflected in the corridors of international and regional policymaking. Japan's decision-making role in such multilateral financial institutions as the International Monetary Fund (IMF) is quite small, and more generally Japanese involvement in structural adjustment in the Pacific region is minimal. The United States continues to dominate at both the global and regional levels, even though Japan is a far more important provider of external finance to the world and the Pacific. The same is true of the position of the yen in international currency affairs. The dollar remains the world's vehicle currency, with the yen typically third or fourth (depending on the use in question) after the deutsche mark, the ecu, or the pound sterling.

Nonetheless, Japan's global and regional positions in international money and finance have been changing. Perhaps the most easily measurable change is in fact in the use of the yen in international trade and payments. Yen are but a small portion of total world official foreign exchange reserves, only about 8 percent in the late 1980s, but this is up from just 3 percent in the late 1970s. The proportion in selected Asian countries is much higher, about 25 percent in the late 1980s, nearly double the figure of a decade earlier (Tavlas and Ozeki 1991, 46). The use of the yen in international finance has also increased. In mid-1991, some 17 percent of all international fixed-rate bonds outstanding were denominated in yen, compared to 33 percent in dollars, but the two years up to mid-1991 saw more net new yen issues (23 percent) than dollar issues (19 percent) (Bank for International Settlements 1991,12). And the foreign debt of the major Asian borrowers (Indonesia, the Philippines, Korea, Malaysia, and Thailand) is much more heavily denominated in yen than in dollars, 38 and 27 percent respectively (Tavlas and Ozeki 1991, 45).

Qualitatively, Japan has been participating more actively in regional and international negotiations over monetary and financial issues. This has perhaps been most prominent in discussions of currency values across the Pacific, in which the yen-dollar rate has been a constant topic. Nonetheless, there is little doubt that the Japanese government is inconclusive about its commitment to systematic regional or global leadership.

Many of the reasons for Japanese official ambivalence concerning regional and international monetary and financial relations can be traced to the domestic political economy. For purposes of simplicity, we can identify two broad groups in Japanese society, those with interests in more determined Japanese leadership in international and regional money and finance, and those whose interests lie more in safeguarding domestic conditions regardless of their external consequences.

The sorts of policies in question consist of a wide range of issues. Japanese monetary and financial leadership would require the following measures, some of which are already under way:

- The liberalization of the domestic financial system, in order to provide a broader and deeper market for yen-denominated assets. This would permit the yen to develop toward full key currency status.
- Continued commercial liberalization, especially toward the products of countries with net liabilities to Japan.
- A major Japanese role in multilateral financial institutions.
- Domestic macroeconomic policies undertaken with a strong eye toward their international effects. This implies monetary and fiscal stability, and high levels of cooperation with American and European policymakers.

These policies have differential effects within Japan and thus attract both political support and opposition. Those most inclined toward international cooperation are, not surprisingly, major Japanese banks and corporations with global interests. For them, whatever domestic price may be paid for Japan to help manage regional and world financial and monetary conditions pales in comparison to the benefits associated with stability in these arenas. Leading financial institutions may have reservations about financial deregulation, but these are outweighed by the recognition that such deregulation is a prerequisite to a greater Japanese role (Rosenbluth 1989; Pauly 1988; for background see Suzuki 1987; Friedman 1986; Semkow 1985). The same may be true about the attitude of major exporters and multinationals toward trade liberalization, and toward the strong yen that macroeconomic policy coordination tends to imply (Rosenbluth 1991; Funabashi 1988, 87–107; Frankel 1984; Green 1989; Cargill and Hutchison 1988; Suzuki 1989, 91–171). Their general sense that the trade-off of domestic for foreign goals is worthwhile is heightened by the greater ability of internationally oriented firms to make up abroad for what business they lose at home.

Other groups in Japan are unenthusiastic about sacrificing domestic economic goals on the altar of regional or international cooperation. Such groups include producers of nontradable goods and services: construction, wholesale and retail trade. They also include many small and medium-sized manufacturing companies. While these companies often produce for export or subcontract for large export-oriented firms, they often concentrate in the production of standardized goods for which price competition is crucial. Such firms are thus very hard hit by a strong yen and trade liberalization, while larger firms in markets where nonprice competition is more important (automobiles, sophisticated electrical equipment) are less adversely affected. (Rosenbluth [1991,

6–12] has a good summary of the interests and organization of these business groups.)[3]

The influence of small- and medium-scale businesses has traditionally been magnified by the character of Japan's political system. Liberal Democratic party (LDP) politicians have depended on local supporters in the small business sector, and have been quite responsive to their demands. This pattern was unproblematic so long as the policy preferences of small business were not in conflict with those of big business—especially in foreign economic policy. However, as big business has become more international, strife on these issues has increased.

Although conflict between internationalist and nationalistic groups in Japan continues, there are reasons to believe that the balance of power is swinging in favor of the internationalists. The first reason is that internationalization of the Japanese economy continues apace. Unlike in interwar America, the process affects broad segments of Japanese business. Second, the increasing importance of unattached urban voters in Japan has reduced the relative influence of such localist groups as farmers and small businesses, which have tended to be nationalistic on economic policy. Third, the central LDP leadership is generally able to enforce its policy preferences on LDP backbenchers, and the party leadership's ties to big business tend to make it favorable to internationalist policies (Rosenbluth 1991). All these factors tend to push Japan toward more cooperative policies at the regional and international level, regardless of foreign pressure—albeit not without difficulties and opposition.

The possibilities for a regionalist Japanese, or even Japanese-American, sphere of monetary and financial influence in Pacific Asia are often discussed. Most of the evidence, regarded from the political economy standpoint taken here, does not seem favorable to such an outcome. Indeed, the traditional concentration of Japanese foreign loans and investments in Asia has eroded in the past ten years; Japanese FDI has grown more slowly in Asia than in any other region. The United States and the European Community (EC) combined accounted for four-fifths of all long-term capital outflows from Japan in the late 1980s: the most rapid relative growth in Japanese foreign investment was in the EC (Tavlas and Ozeki 1991, 31–33; Froot 1991, 8–9). This implies that policies that might cut Japan off from the European or North American markets in favor of an exclusive Asian zone are unlikely to be supported by major externally oriented sectors.

While the jury is most definitely still out, then, there are indications that Japan's domestic political economy has become more hospitable to the country's playing an important role in regional and international monetary and fi-

---

3. There is no doubt that this typology is far too crude for nuanced analysis. Japan exports some construction services; there are many dynamic and internationally oriented small firms; and exceptions could be found to many of the patterns discussed here. I do not claim to have devised a detailed map of Japanese economic interests, only to have summarized some of the broad patterns.

nancial policymaking. Those who stand to benefit directly from Japanese provision of collective or club goods in these arenas have become more numerous, economically important, and politically influential. There are plenty of political obstacles to thoroughgoing Japanese commitment to these policies. If current trends continue, however, Japan is likely to avoid a repetition of the interwar American experience, and to move into a position of leadership in regional—and eventually international—money and finance. Of course, regional trends depend also on the policies of the United States, to which we now turn.

10.5   Contemporary United States

Concern about Japanese policy focuses on incomplete progress toward a greater international role, but the problem in the United States is the opposite: the possibility of a retreat into traditional economic nationalism. Although internationally oriented economic groups remain politically very important, they appear to be in danger of losing ground to those less interested in American cooperation with Japan over regional and international monetary and financial, or other economic, issues.

To be sure, the United States remains heavily involved in the world economy, as do many major banks and corporations. Indeed, explicit pressure for trade protection seems to be on the wane, as the result of three factors: the increased globalism of American industry, the development of greater export interests, and the generally weak dollar (Destler and Odell 1987; Milner 1988). Nonetheless, there are residual demands for trade barriers from remaining import-competers, and these demands could rise if the domestic economy grows slowly.

Probably the major source of future nationalistic pressures on economic policy will be the accumulated liabilities of the United States, and of the U.S. government, to the rest of the world. It is indeed ironic that, while in the 1920s the principal axis of debate over the role of the United States in the international economy had to do with foreign debts to the U.S. government, in the 1990s the principal axis of debate will likely have to do with U.S. government debts to foreigners.

Foreign holdings of over a trillion dollars in U.S. government securities, and of hundreds of billions more in corporate stocks and bonds, represent claims on future government and private revenues. As these claims come due, they will be met by pressures to give them less priority than domestic economic needs. Perhaps the simplest way to reduce the external debt burden would be to inflate it away, as almost all of the liabilities are denominated in dollars. Support for such measures will come from those whose economic activity is wholly or primarily domestic—nontradables producers, import-competers— for whom external debt service is an unmitigated drain. Support for more internationally cooperative policies will be centered in those tied to such internationally oriented activities as international banks and multinational corporations, for whom the costs of debt service are outweighed by the benefits of untrammelled access to the global economy. Of course, temptations to shift some of the adjustment burden onto the shoulders of holders of government securities will face opposition both from foreigners and from wealth holders within the United States. This set of issues will be crucial to resolution of America's regional and international positions, but the contours of the debate and its outcome are still too murky to forecast—and they depend too importantly on the underlying state of the U.S. economy (Frankel 1988a).

A related issue has to do with the conflict between domestic and international macroeconomic policies. The dollar remains the centerpiece of international trade and payments, and its stability is clearly of interest to most of those involved in the Pacific and world economies. However, confidence in the dollar can often be obtained only at the expense of policies to spur domestic economic activity—and vice versa. As above, interests on the relative importance of stability in the international value of the dollar as against efforts to stimulate domestic economic activity vary according to how involved the actors in question are in external as opposed to domestic business. And while the influence of more internationally oriented businesses—those more interested in international macroeconomic policy cooperation—has grown, the portions of the U.S. economy still relatively unaffected by external conditions remain very large (Destler and Henning 1989; Gowa 1983; Odell 1982; on specific episodes see Funabashi 1988, especially 65–86; Cohen and Meltzer 1982, 15–64; Destler and Mitsuyu 1982).

A specific problem that has long been contentious in American politics is that of support for multilateral institutions, including the IMF–World Bank system. Indeed, congressional support for the 1983 general increase in IMF quotas, which amounted to an $8.4 billion increase in the U.S. quota, was extremely weak. The quota bill passed only because it was tied to a public housing bill that the administration supported in return for the vote of key congressional Democrats on the IMF. The IMF bill's problems were compounded by domestic economic weakness at the time and by a very strong dollar—all of which inflamed the opposition of import-competers, nontradables producers, and many others (Frieden 1987, 179–190). Such conflict will undoubtedly recur and will undoubtedly be exacerbated if the U.S. economy is not growing rapidly at the time.

Other difficulties arise on the financial front, where the snail's pace of financial deregulation in the United States risks impeding American contribution to more integrated global financial markets. As is well known, the slow speed of deregulation is largely due to jockeying for position among financial institutions of different size and functional specialization. Although the cost to the taxpayers of the savings and loan crisis and the potential cost of similar problems in the commercial bank sector give an impetus to reform of the financial system, the economic and political barriers to rapid regulatory change are quite high. It is unlikely that the desire of the most competitive and international of financial institutions to move the American regulatory environment into lockstep with that of Europe and Japan will prevail rapidly, costlessly, or without compromise.

The political institutions through which economic interests are mediated in the United States are not especially favorable to those who desire more internationalist policies. The interwar pattern of political institutions, with a highly decentralized government that was especially responsive to localist (and typically nationalistic) groups, is still largely intact. Unlike in Japan, central party leaderships cannot impose the preferences of big business on local politicians more concerned with local conditions and pressure groups. The closest American analogue is the executive branch, and the relative power of the president is constrained by congressional and bureaucratic institutions quite responsive to local political influences. The Treasury and the Federal Reserve System are closer to international business and somewhat autonomous from day-to-day political pressures, but even this is tightly circumscribed by legislative oversight capabilities—as has been demonstrated, most recently, by battles over financial deregulation. American political institutions thus tend to reinforce the position of those least sympathetic to the sacrifice of domestic for foreign economic goals.

Unlike in Japan, the intermediate position of a U.S. zone of economic influence does not seem quite so far-fetched as Japanese resurrection of the Greater East Asia Co-prosperity Sphere. Although the relative share of Canada and Latin America in U.S. trade, lending, and investment has declined since the 1950s, it is still quite high—on the order of one-third to one-half depending on the arena. Negotiations on free trade agreements with Canada, Mexico, Chile, and other Latin-American nations are progressing; preliminary discussions are taking place about macroeconomic (especially exchange rate) policy in the region. However, considerations similar to those mentioned in the case of Japan tend to apply for the United States as well: most internationally oriented American businesses are not specifically concentrated in the Western Hemisphere and would not welcome Pan-American initiatives if they would threaten markets or investments in Asia and Europe.

The future of American international monetary and financial policy is unusually difficult to predict because the domestic politics of American foreign economic policy are particularly sensitive to the state of the domestic economy. This is especially the case with the debt overhang and its impact on macroeconomic policy. If U.S. economic growth is weak, there is likely to be much more significant opposition to measures that might threaten macroeconomic performance in the interest of regional or international cooperation. If growth is strong, such opposition will be mitigated.

Nonetheless, there are some reasons to anticipate that nationalistic economic-policy pressures in the United States, although powerful, will not prevail. The level of overseas commitments of major American firms is now higher than ever before. The rapid growth of inward direct investment has also increased the size of another support group for international economic-policy cooperation: managerial and production employees of foreign firms. Should the U.S. economy collapse, these more internationalist groups will be hard-pressed to prevail politically, but in the absence of serious macroeconomic disturbances, they are likely to remain politically predominant, albeit not without a struggle.

10.6 Implications and Conclusions

The analysis presented here can be used to evaluate the probabilities of the various scenarios discussed at the outset of this paper. The two pessimistic scenarios—one in which Japan free rides on American Pacific leadership, the other in which Japan creates an exclusive monetary and financial zone in the Pacific—both presuppose that inward-looking or exclusivist, regionally oriented groups will prevail over internationalist interests in Japanese domestic politics. Most of the evidence weighed here runs in the opposite direction, to indicate that internationalist groups have gained in influence and are likely to prevail in policy debates. Similarly, there is little evidence for bases of support for a primarily regional, as opposed to global, approach that would involve cooperation between the United States and Japan solely within the Pacific region. However, this does not necessarily mean that optimism should prevail. Indeed, most of my analysis of the American political economy indicates how conditional policy outcomes are on unpredictable events, especially the state of the domestic economy.

Indeed, one inference that can be drawn from this analysis of the domestic politics of Pacific money and finance is that the dangers of conflict come more from the American side than from Japan. Given the reversal in the net asset position of the United States, it is not unreasonable to expect growing dissatisfaction with the tradeoffs involved in continued American commitment to regional and international cooperation. Whether this dissatisfaction will translate into an all-out assault on current American policy, and whether it will predominate against the persistent strength of internationalist interests, depends in large part on the state of the domestic economy.

In this context, an aspect omitted from this analysis can be reintroduced. Strategic interaction among national governments can affect the domestic politics of regional and international negotiations (Putnam 1988). Specifically, the Japanese response to American demands, and to American political realities, can help reinforce the domestic political position of those in the United States who would like to maintain cooperative regional ties. This would require recognition of the need to mitigate the cost of such regional cooperation to domestically oriented economic groups, and of the desirability of reinforcing the benefits of cooperation to already-supportive internationalist groups. Although there may be little justice in asking Japan to bear greater sacrifices than

America for the good of regional cooperation, realization of domestic political realities in the two countries probably leads to the conclusion that this injustice may be the price paid for the maintenance of an open and stable regional monetary and financial order.

This analysis is unquestionably tentative, partial, and schematic. However, the very contours of the issues it addresses are still not entirely clear, and the information available to assess them is very sparse. As the issues and the data become more definite, more robust analyses and predictions may be possible. For now, I am content to insist on the importance of the domestic political lineup—both the economic interests involved and the mediation of these interests by political institutions—for the future of Pacific money and finance. The specifics of this future will be resolved by both domestic politics and interstate negotiations, but we cannot understand one without understanding the other.

References

Bank for International Settlements. 1991. *International Banking and Financial Market Developments during the Second Quarter of 1991.* Basle: Bank for International Settlements.

Broz, Lawrence. 1992. Wresting the Sceptre from London: The International Political Economy of the Founding of the Federal Reserve. Ph.D. diss., University of California, Los Angeles.

Cargill, Thomas F., and Michael M. Hutchison. 1988. The Response of the Bank of Japan to Macroeconomic and Financial Change. In Hang-sheng Cheng, ed., *Monetary Policy in Pacific Basin Countries,* 227–46. Boston: Kluwer.

Clarke, Stephen V. O. 1967. *Central Bank Cooperation, 1924–1931.* New York: Federal Reserve Bank of New York.

Cohen, Stephen D., and Ronald I. Meltzer. 1982. *United States International Economic Policy in Action.* New York: Praeger.

Destler, I. M., and C. Randall Henning. 1989. *Dollar Politics: Exchange Rate Policymaking in the United States.* Washington, DC: Institute for International Economics.

Destler, I. M., and Hisao Mitsuyu. 1982. Locomotives on Different Tracks: Macroeconomic Diplomacy, 1977–1979. In I. M. Destler and Hideo Sato, eds., *Coping with U.S.-Japanese Economic Conflicts,* 243–69. Lexington, MA: Lexington Books.

Destler, I. M., and John S. Odell. 1987. *Anti-protection: Changing Forces in United States Trade Politics.* Washington, DC: Institute for International Economics.

Drake, Paul. 1989. *The Money Doctor in the Andes.* Durham, NC: Duke University Press.

Eichengreen, Barry. 1989a. Hegemonic Stability Theories of the International Monetary System. In Richard Cooper, Barry Eichengreen, Randall Henning, Gerald Holtham, and Robert Putnam, *Can Nations Agree?* 255–98. Washington, DC: Brookings Institution.

———. 1989b. The Political Economy of the Smoot-Hawley Tariff. *Research in Economic History* 12: 1–43.

———. 1992. *Golden Fetters.* New York: Oxford University Press.

Ferguson, Thomas. 1984. From Normalcy to New Deal. *International Organization* 38: 41–94.

Forbes, John Douglas. 1981. *J. P. Morgan, Jr.* Charlottesville: University Press of Virginia.

Frankel, Jeffrey A. 1984. *The Yen/Dollar Agreement: Liberalizing Japanese Capital Markets.* Washington, DC: Institute for International Economics.

———. 1988a. International Capital Flows and Domestic Economic Policies. In Martin Feldstein, ed., *The United States in the World Economy,* 559–627. Chicago: University of Chicago Press.

———. 1988b. *Obstacles to International Macroeconomic Policy Coordination.* Princeton Studies in International Finance no. 64. Princeton: International Finance Section.

Fratianni, Michele, and John Pattison. 1982. The Economics of International Organizations. *Kylos 35:* 244–62.

Frieden, Jeffry A. 1987. *Banking on the World: The Politics of American International Finance.* New York: Harper and Row.

———. 1988. Sectoral Conflict and U.S. Foreign Economic Policy, 1914–1940. *International Organization 42 (1):* 59–90.

Friedman, Robert Alan. 1986. *Japanese Financial Markets: Deficits, Dilemmas, and Deregulation.* Cambridge, MA: MIT Press.

Froot, Kenneth. 1991. Japanese Foreign Direct Investment. NBER Working Paper no. 3737. Cambridge, MA: National Bureau of Economic Research.

Funabashi, Yoichi. 1988. *Managing the Dollar: From the Plaza to the Louvre.* Washington, DC: Institute for International Economics.

Gourevitch, Peter. 1986. *Politics in Hard Times.* Ithaca: Cornell University Press.

Gowa, Joanne. 1983. *Closing the Gold Window: Domestic Politics and the End of Bretton Woods.* Ithaca: Cornell University Press.

Green, David Jay. 1989. Exchange Rate Policy and Intervention in Japan. *Keizai-Shirin* (Hosei University Economic Review) 57: 129–167.

Kindleberger, Charles. 1973. *The World in Depression.* Berkeley: University of California Press.

———. 1985. The Functioning of Financial Centers: Britain in the Nineteenth Century, the United States since 1945. In Wilfred Ethier and Richard Marston, eds., *Internationl Financial Markets and Capital Movements.* Princeton Essays in International Finance no. 157. Princeton: International Finance Section.

Krugman, Paul. 1984. The International Role of the Dollar: Theory and Prospect. In John Bilson and Richard S. Marston, eds., *Exchange Rate Theory and Practice,* 261–78. Chicago: University of Chicago Press.

Maltz, Mary Jane. 1963. *The Many Lives of Otto Kahn.* New York: Macmillan.

Milner, Helen. 1988. *Resisting Protectionism: Global Industries and the Politics of International Trade.* Princeton: Princeton University Press.

Naya, Seiji. 1990. Direct Foreign Investment and Trade in East Southeast Asia. In Ronald Jones and Anne Krueger, eds., *The Political Economy of International Trade,* 288–312. Cambridge: Basil Blackwell.

Nolt, James. 1992. *Business Power and National Strategy in the American Century.* Ph.D. dissertation, University of Chicago.

Odell, John S. 1982. *U.S. International Monetary Policy: Markets, Power, and Ideas as Sources of Change.* Princeton: Princeton University Press.

Osugi, K. 1990. Japan's Experience of Financial Deregulation since 1984 in an International Perspective. BIS Economic Paper no. 26, Basle: Bank for International Settlements.

Oye, Kenneth, ed. 1986. *Cooperation under Anarchy.* Princeton: Princeton University Press.

Pauly, Louis. 1988. *Opening Financial Markets: Banking Politics on the Pacific Rim.* Ithaca: Cornell University Press.

Putnam, Robert. 1988. Diplomacy and Domestic Politics: The Logic of Two-Level Games. *International Organization* 42, (3): 427–60.

Rosenbluth, Frances McCall. 1989. *Financial Politics in Contemporary Japan.* Ithaca: Cornell University Press.

———. 1991. Japan's Response to the Strong Yen: Party Leadership and the Market for Political Favors. San Diego. Mimeo.

Semkow, Brian. 1985. Japanese Banking Law: Current Deregulation and Liberalization of Domestic and External Financial Transactions. *Law and Policy in International Business 17 (1): 81–155.*

Staley, Eugene. 1935. *War and the Private Investor.* Garden City, N.Y.: Doubleday, Doran, and Company.

Suzuki, Yoshio, ed. 1987. *The Japanese Financial System.* Oxford: Clarendon Press.

———. 1989. *Japan's Economic Performance and International Role.* Tokyo: University of Tokyo Press.

Tavlas, George S. 1991. *On the International Use of Currencies: The Case of the Deutsche Mark.* Princeton Essays in International Finance no. 181. Princeton: International Finance Section.

Tavlas, George S., and Yuzuri Ozeki. 1991. The Japanese Yen as an International Currency. IMF Working Paper 91/2. Washington, D.C.: International Monetary Fund.

Thorn, Richard S. 1987. *The Rising Yen: The Impact of Japanese Financial Liberalization on World Capital Markets.* Singapore: Institute of Southeast Asian Studies.

Turner, Philip. 1991. Capital Flows in the 1980s: A Survey of Major Trends. BIS Economic Paper no. 30. Basle: Bank for International Settlements.

Comment   Takeo Hoshi

Jeffry Frieden's paper examines the possibility of international cooperation in money and finance between Japan and the United States. As the paper correctly points out, such an analysis must be carried out in two stages: analysis of domestic politics and analysis of the international game. This paper focuses on the domestic politics and classifies the major political actors into two camps: internationalists and nationalists. Comparing the relative power in each camp in each country, the paper concludes that Japan and the United States are likely to achieve cooperation. Internationalists are likely to be more influential than nationalists in both countries, although there is some possibility that the U.S. nationalists could gain enough power to impede the process toward cooperation.

Focusing on the domestic politics, the paper gives us a good starting point for an examination of the likelihood of international cooperation. This is just

Takeo Hoshi is assistant professor of economics at the Graduate School of International Relations and Pacific Studies, University of California, San Diego.

a starting point, however, and the analysis has to be refined and expanded to get firm conclusions. The analysis is preliminary not only because of its exclusive focus on the first stage of the two-stage game but also because of the lack of depth in its discussion of domestic politics.

The paper identifies two camps that have opposing views about internationalization, but it is too quick to conclude on the relative power of these groups. For example, the paper mentions three reasons the internationalists are likely to dominate in Japanese politics. The supporting evidence is, however, weak and not very convincing.

The first reason internationalists are likely to dominate in Japan is because the Japanese economy will continue to become more international. It may be true that internationalization will increase the number of people who will gain from international cooperation, but this does not necessarily mean that the power of internationalists will be enhanced. In fact, a larger population of internationalists may make the internationalist camp weaker relative to the nationalist camp because of a classic collective action problem. The larger number of internationalists aggravates the collective action problem within the camp and makes the group politically less effective.

The second advantage for internationalists mentioned in this paper is increasing importance of urban voters relative to localist groups such as farmers. If this means that the number of urban voters is increasing, then again the argument ignores the collective action problem, which becomes more serious as the size of a group increases. If this refers to some radical changes in the Japanese political system that make urban voters more important, the paper should show exactly what these are. As long as the current election system continues, in which most Diet members are elected in local districts, it will always be important for politicians to maintain local support in order to be reelected. Thus the influence of localist groups is not likely to decline in the near future.

It is also interesting to point out that farmers are not necessarily nationalists and urban voters are not necessarily internationalists. A good example is the recent discussion on liberalization of rice imports in Japan, in which large farmers often expressed a favorable view toward liberalization. They hoped that import liberalization would pressure the government to abandon its food control system, which is government planning of production and distribution of rice. Consumer groups generally opposed the import liberalization. They claimed that rice imports should continue to be prohibited so that they can enjoy safe Japanese rice.

The third advantage of internationalists in Japan is the significant power exercised by the central LDP leadership over its members. This statement, however, is an exaggeration. One can find several examples that show the LDP leadership often fails to force its policy preferences on individual members. One example is Prime Minister Nakasone's attempt to introduce the sales tax in 1987 (see Nakamura 1988). As soon as Nakasone suggested the introduction of sales tax in January 1987, the local chapters of LDP started to voice their opposition. They were afraid of the voters' response in the unified local elections scheduled in April. The central leadership made several attempts to convince the members that they would be able to persuade the voters. First, they advertised that the tax reform package, which includes the sales tax, actually reduces the total burden of taxpayers, and the key issue is not the introduction of sales tax but the implementation of a tax cut. Then, the LDP National Convention for Advancement of Tax Reform was held on February 10, and Nakasone made a forty-minute speech asking the members' support for the tax reform. All these efforts failed, and many individual members continued to voice opposition to the tax reform. In March, a candidate from the LDP lost in a supplementary election for the House of Councilors in Iwate prefecture, where the LDP had traditionally been very strong. And in April, the LDP lost several important seats in the unified local elections, just as the local offices had anticipated. At this point, Nakasone had no choice but to drop the sales tax bill.

In each case discussed above, the analysis would be significantly improved by paying serious attention to some important factors that are not appreciated in the paper. Here I suggest three such factors. The first one is the collective action problem among the members of each camp: internationalist and nationalist. The second suggestion is an explicit consideration of institutional constraints, such as the election system. It is important to know if the existing election system favors one camp or the other, or one group or another. The third factor is the resource constraint for each camp, or what each party can do to influence the government. For example, the paper argues that, if the U.S. economy grows slowly, there will be more opposition to international cooperation from import-competers. The slow growth, and hence lower profits for the nationalists, however, affects their capability of influencing the government at the same time. Because lobbying is costly, although the nationalists' incentive to oppose the international cooperation may increase following the slow growth, their ability to influence the government will be reduced.

Another possible improvement of the paper is a general theory of what determines the line between the internationalists and the nationalist camps. There seem to be two factors that determine to which camp a political agent belongs. The first one is industry affiliation. If a firm belongs to an industry that benefits from international cooperation, then the firm becomes internationalist; if the industry gains little or is actually hurt by internationalization, then the firm becomes nationalist. The second factor is the position of the firm within the industry; whether it is large or small. The American experience after World War I discussed in the paper is useful to clarify the first factor, but it is not very helpful in identifying the second factor, the size of the firm. Looking at the experience in the same period in Japan may help establish that the size of the firm matters. During the late 1920s, the biggest policy debate in Japan was whether Japan should go back to the gold standard. Since the government planned to restore the gold standard at the prewar parity and the yen had depreciated in the postwar period, going back to the gold standard also meant revaluation. Some of the supporters of the gold standard were large *zaibatsus* (family-owned business conglomerates), like Mitsubishi and Mitsui (Nakamura 1978). They knew that the Japanese industries would be hurt by the revaluation, but they argued for the revaluation, because the troubles at weak firms would help increase their monopoly power. This episode shows that the size of the firm often affects its preference for internationalist and nationalist camps. Another example is the Japanese farmers' attitude toward rice liberalization in contemporary Japan, mentioned above. Large farmers are for the liberalization, and small farmers are against it.

The strategic interaction at the international level, which is omitted from the analysis in this paper, can potentially be important even for the analysis of the domestic level game, as Frieden correctly argues in his conclusion. The paper argues that the favorable Japanese response to American demands may strengthen the internationalists in the United States. The argument, however, could go in the opposite direction. Seemingly opportunistic demands from the United States may strengthen the nationalists in Japan. Or if the internationalists in the United States see that cooperation is more likely because of Japan's efforts, they may reduce their lobbying effort, which gives nationalists a better chance. Again, more substantial analysis is necessary.

References

Nakamura, Akio. 1988. Jimin-to no Han'no (LDP's response). In *Zeisei Kaikaku o Meguru Seiji Rikigaku* (Politics of tax reform), ed. K. Uchida, M. Kanazashi, and M. Fukushima, chap. 7. Tokyo: Chuo Koron-sha.

Nakamura, Takafusa. 1978. *Shyowa Kyoko to Keizai Seisaku* (Shyowa depression and economic policy). Tokyo: Nihon Keizai Shimbun-sha.

11   National Security Aspects of United States–Japan Economic Relations in the Pacific Asian Region

Martin Feldstein

Several years ago the National Bureau of Economic Research began a major project on the economics of national security. We wanted to look beyond the traditional issues of defense budgeting and military procurement to focus on the broad economic forces that could affect the security of the United States in future decades. One aspect of this research has been a major study of economic transformation in Eastern Europe and the Soviet Union, since economic developments there are likely to be important for the political and military stability of that region and therefore of Europe and the Middle East.[1] The second major area of our research on national security has focused on the relationship between the United States and Japan.

The present conference was designed to explore the frequently raised question, "Are United States–Japan relations in the Pacific Asian region a potential national security risk for the United States?" In a departure from our usual approach, the research team for this project was expanded to include political scientists as well as economists, and the project was co-managed by economist Jeffrey Frankel and political scientist Miles Kahler.

Three types of questions were posed to the economic researchers in the project. Is the Pacific Asian area becoming an economic "bloc" with an unusual concentration of trade, finance, and investment? Does Japan dominate the economic relations of the region, including trade flows, finance, and investment? Are the Pacific Asian countries becoming dependent on Japan for trade, finance, investment, and foreign aid?

We asked the political scientists three much more difficult questions. If an

Martin Feldstein is professor of economics at Harvard University and president of the National Bureau of Economic Research.

1. Many of the NBER studies of this subject will be published in O. Blanchard, K. Froot, and J. Sachs, eds., *The Transition in Eastern Europe,* vols. 1 and 2 (Chicago: University of Chicago Press, forthcoming).

economic bloc centered on Japan is forming in the region or will develop in the future, what effect will that have on the political alliances of the region's countries with the United States and with Japan? Similarly, what effect will it have on potential security relations in the area? And, more generally, can these developments pose a military or more general national security risk for the United States?

Although the political scientists were not able to answer the questions as we had posed them, they did teach us a number of quite different but very important things about how to think about the relation between national security and economics. The political scientists emphasized that there is more to a "bloc" than nonsymmetric patterns of trade, finance, and investment, and that it is therefore necessary to look in a more disaggregated way at specific industries and economic relations in order to understand the changing patterns of power and influence that follow changing economic relations. They reminded the economists that observed patterns of economic activity do not reflect just natural comparative advantage and geographic distance but depend on government policies and that policies in turn reflect interests within countries. And they noted that Japanese foreign policy and foreign economic policy are evolving and this evolution can be understood only by recognizing the existence of heterogeneous forces within the Japanese bureaucracy and the Liberal Democratic party. I found these comments very useful in themselves and important as a guide to future research.

My task now is to summarize what I have learned about the original subject: the national security risk to the United States implied by the evolving United States–Japan relations in the Pacific Asian region. It will be helpful if I do this in terms of five questions.

1. Is the Pacific Asian region becoming an economic bloc centered on Japan? Jeffrey Frankel's statistical analysis has shown that there is nothing about the overall trade pattern to suggest that this area is becoming a trading bloc, any more than geography alone would suggest, or that Japan is playing a particularly central role in trade within the region. Future studies at a more disaggregated level will be necessary, however, to determine whether this is also true in key industries and products.

In contrast to trade, there is no doubt that Japan has become the dominant source of foreign direct investment in the region, far outstripping the level of investment from the United States and Europe. The political scientists have persuasively urged that the next step should be an analysis of patterns of ownership and control that determine the extent of influence and dependence. A similar predominance of Japan has also developed in the flow of development assistance in the region.

The pattern of financial flows is more unclear, but the trends suggest a growing role for Japan and the yen in the financial relations of the region. Whether the recent weakness of the Japanese banks will change this remains to be seen.

2. Is Japan acting in ways that could lead to a hegemonic position in the Pacific Asian region? There is a range of voices in Japan calling for a more inward-looking policy for Pacific Asia with a dominant role for Japan. In the extreme, this is summarized with the slogan, "Asia for the Asians." The advocates of such a policy point to similarities of East Asian culture in the broadest sense (e.g., the Asian emphasis on consensual politics), of religion (i.e., the importance of Confucianism and Buddhism and the minor role placed by Christianity), and of race.

At a more practical level, businessmen and government officials in Japan point to the development of EC92 in Europe and the North American Free Trade Agreement and argue that Japan (or Asia) needs to protect itself with a similar Asian economic bloc. Some Japanese are talking about the desirability of developing an East Asia coprosperity sphere, despite the very negative historic connotations of that term.

Some of the actions of the Japanese government and of private Japanese businesses are consistent with trying to establish a hegemonic position in the region. The most obvious of these is the dominant role of Japanese direct investment in countries like Thailand and Indonesia, where Japan's activity far outstrips that of the United States and Europe.

There is also no doubt that Japanese official development assistance is generally targeted for Asian countries, with much of it going to rapidly growing countries rather than to those countries with the greatest poverty. Although there is evidence that most of the aid is not literally tied with "buy Japan" requirements, critics complain that the aid is given in a form that is advantageous to Japanese business interests (like the financing of transportation and other infrastructure that would be useful for international trade).

Such criticism seems excessive. Even if Japanese development assistance is helpful to Japanese business, that is not inconsistent with its helping the recipients as well and even with its benefiting businesses in the United States and other trading partners as much as it helps Japanese businesses. Moreover, Japan is not unusual in restricting its aid in various ways.

A third way in which Japan may be strengthening its role in the region is by dealing more actively than the United States with China and Vietnam. But here the explanation is that U.S. domestic politics impedes American activity rather than that Japanese policies in the area have been particularly aggressive.

In short, there is some behavior that may increase Japan's relative strength in the region, but it would be difficult to interpret this as evidence that Japan is seeking to establish itself as a hegemonic power in East Asia.

3. Does Japan want to establish a hegemonic position in the future? Although current behavior cannot be interpreted as an active pursuit of hegemonic status, it is interesting to ask whether the Japanese want to establish such a position and will take steps to do so in the future.

There is not doubt that there are potential economic rewards of being the local hegemon. By excluding others from the market or restricting their access, a Japanese hegemon could enjoy the benefits of being a monopoly supplier or a monopsony purchaser. More subtle advantages could accrue to firms that use exclusive access to develop more advantageous integrated production arrangements.

Another reason Japan might want to develop a hegemonic status in the region is to promulgate its development strategy. Many Japanese officials and academics have recently contrasted the Japanese approach to economic development with the approach advocated by the United States, the World Bank, and other "Western" authorities. The Japanese emphasize a greater role for government at the early stage of development, a different approach to domestic competition, different intercorporate financial arrangements, and so forth. The desire to promote the Japanese approach to development may reflect honest differences of development philosophy. It may also (or alternatively) reflect a desire to have neighboring countries pursue development strategies that are more compatible with current Japanese industrial policy and with the mode of operation of Japanese private industry.

Finally, the Japanese may want to establish a hegemonic role in the region as a matter of national pride. At a time when the major industrial countries are calling on Japan to exercise more "leadership" in world affairs, it is easy to confuse hegemony with leadership.

But even if there are many in Japan who would like to see a Japanese hegemony in the Pacific Asian region, I believe it is unlikely to occur. The desire to play such a role and the benefits of establishing a hegemonic position are simply not great enough to outweigh the costs of doing so.

The greatest such cost would be the conflict that would result with the United States. The United States is not only the largest market for Japan's exports but also Japan's strongest ally in global affairs. A new generation of political leaders in Japan could be willing to pay this cost, but there is no indication of such an inclination at the present time.

A second cost of achieving hegemony would be the resistance from the individual countries of East Asia. The history of Japan as an aggressive power in the region, not only in World War II but ever since the opening of Japan in the mid-nineteenth century, makes these countries nervous about seeing Japan increase its power in the region. These countries will therefore seek to keep the United States and other nations involved in order to prevent the development of Japanese monopoly and monopsony power.

4. Will the collapse of the Soviet Union change United States–Japan relations in ways that affect U.S. national security? In many ways this is the most speculative of the five questions, particularly because of the recentness of developments in the former Soviet Union. Moreover, although there is much talk about the end of the Cold War and the elimination of the Soviet threat, substantial military risks to both the United States and Japan remain. Russia still has thousands of nuclear warheads on missiles that are potentially targeted at the United States and Japan. Moreover, the Japanese are acutely aware that they still have no treaty with Russia and that Russian soldiers still occupy the four northern islands that belonged to Japan before World War II and that Japan regards as Japanese territory.

But, to the extent that Russia (and the other parts of the former Soviet Union) is no longer a security threat to Japan and the United States, the United States–Japan bilateral relation is weakened in five distinct ways.

First, the elimination of the Soviet Union as a military threat to Japan means that Japan no longer needs the protection of the U.S. nuclear umbrella. The reduced dependence of Japan on the United States gives Japan greater freedom to develop its own policies, including polices that create conflicts with the United States.

Second, from the American point of view, there is no longer as great a need to use Japan as a base for American military presence in the Pacific area. Military considerations are therefore no longer as much of a check on potential trade conflict or other conflicts between the United States and Japan.

Third, the collapse of communism highlights the varieties of capitalism. As long as the world was divided into capitalist and communist camps, the United States and Japan were clearly members of the same club. Now the contrast between U.S. capitalism of independent shareholder-owned firms and Japanese *keiretsu* capitalism appears more sharply. This is a source of conflict not only in United States–Japan trade relations but also in the shaping of development assistance.

Fourth, the absence of a Soviet military threat makes it easier for Japan to normalize relations with China. Many in Japan look to China as the source of markets and indirectly of manpower for Japan in the twenty-first century. Although Japan's pursuit of close relations with China requires overcoming the memories of Japan's role there before and during World War II, the Japanese are making major efforts in this direction. These developments could reverse the relative importance of the United States and Japan in China. Given China's geographic size and its overwhelming population, any potential shift in China's link from the United States to Japan could have substantial long-term security ramifications for the United States.

Finally, the decline of Soviet power in the Middle East provides an opportunity for Japan to develop a Middle East policy that serves its own interests without worrying about the implications for the U.S.–Soviet conflict. Japan clearly has strong interests in the region because of its dependence on oil imports from the area. There is no reason to expect that Japan's interests in this complex part of the world coincide with the interests of the United Sates. A current example of this may be Japan's active cultivation of ties with Iran through official as well as business channels.

In each of these five ways, the collapse of the Soviet Union has changed the likely future relations between the United States and Japan. Each is now militarily less dependent on the other and therefore more likely to pursue policies that have adverse effects on the other country.

5. Is the United States vulnerable to a shift in United States–Japan relations? Despite the trade conflict, the United States and Japan have been strong allies that share a common philosophy. It is possible, however, that a combination of developments—shifting economics relations in East Asia, pressure inside Japan for that country to play a hegemonic role in the area, and the end of the Soviet military threat—could cause a significant change in the relations between the Untied States and Japan. Even if that is unlikely, it is worth asking whether such a shift could create a serious national security risk for the United Sates. Put succinctly, is the United States potentially vulnerable to a shift of Japanese policy toward the United States?

There is no doubt about the converse; Japan is vulnerable to a shift in U.S. policy toward Japan. Japan must import its food and energy. The large amount of foreign direct investment that Japan has in the United States is a hostage that is not matched by comparable U.S. investment in Japan. An antagonistic U.S. government could change tax rules in a way that drastically reduces the economic value of those investments to their Japanese owners. The hundreds of billions of dollars of portfolio investments that Japanese companies have in U.S. securities are a further hostage that could be effectively destroyed by a change in U.S. tax policy. Closing the U.S. market to the nearly $100 billion a year that the U.S. imports from Japan would do substantial damage to Japanese industry.

The Japanese are very much aware of this vulnerability to the United States. Their awareness of this vulnerability is likely to be a positive force that keeps our bilateral relationship from degenerating.

The United States does not share the same types of vulnerability vis-à-vis Japan. Our investments in Japan are very much less than Japanese investments in the United States. Our exports to Japan are also very much less, and agricultural products are a large part of those exports; a decision by Japan to reduce agricultural imports from the United States in favor of other producers would not change the global demand for U.S. agricultural products.

Many Americans worry about the "financial vulnerability" of the United States to Japan. They are concerned that the Japanese government might cause Japanese financial investors to stop the annual flow of funds to the United States or, in the extreme, might cause those investors to sell their bonds and other financial investments in the United States "and bring that capital back to Japan."

Neither of these should be a real source of concern. Because of the sharply reduced U.S. trade deficit, the United States no longer needs a substantial inflow of capital each year; the current account deficit for 1992 was only 1 percent of our GDP. In any case, if Japanese institutions stopped buying U.S. securities and redirected their annual capital outflow to investments in other countries, the funds that they displaced would flow to the United States. The most harm that would result from an unwillingness of the Japanese to make financial investments in the United States might be a very small increase in the interest rate on U.S. bonds.

The idea that Japan could "sell their bonds and bring the funds home" is based on a misconception. Even if Japanese investors wanted to sell all of their U.S. bonds (thereby precipitating a capital loss for themselves), they could not "bring the funds home" unless Japan shifted from having a large trade surplus to a large trade deficit; that is, a capital flow into Japan is only possible if Japan has a large trade deficit. A decision by Japanese investors to sell dollar bonds and shift the funds to other countries would put downward pressure on the U.S. dollar (relative to the yen and to the currencies in which the Japanese invested) and upward pressure on our interest rates relative to other interest rates in the world financial markets. The combination of a depressed dollar and higher U.S. interest rates would induce the funds displaced elsewhere by the shift of Japanese investments to flow to the United States. When the dust settled, there would be little change in the value of either the dollar or the level of U.S. interest rates. To the extent that the dollar remained lower than it had been before, the effect would be to stimulate U.S. exports (and to reduce our imports).

But although the United States is not financially vulnerable to Japan, technological vulnerability may be a real problem with potential consequences for U.S. military security. The United States now depends on Japan for semiconductors, machine tools, and many of the components of aircraft and military equipment. How vulnerable does this makes us? If Japan decided to ban the sale of such items to the United States, how long would it be before American firms could make these things? Is the number of such products increasing? Is the time that it would take the United States the substitute for such products becoming greater? I cannot answer these questions, but I believe that it is important to have answers and to keep those answers up to date.

Although the possibility of such a rupture of United States–Japan relations may seem remote, it may not be, particularly if there is a change of political power in Japan. Except for a very short period, the government of Japan has been controlled by the Liberal Democratic party. The opposition Socialist party has very different views from the LDP about military activities in general and about United States–Japan military relations in particular. It is certainly not inconceivable that the LDP could at some time during the next few years lose control of the Diet and have to form a coalition with the Socialist party or allow the Socialist party to form the government. Japan already has a policy that bans exports of weapons. This is currently interpreted in a way that allows Japan to sell critical components of military equipment to the United States. We should not assume that this interpretation would always be sustained, especially if the Socialist party were to come to power or even to be a part of the government coalition. A ban on military exports to the United States could even occur during a period of attempted U.S. military activity like the recent Gulf War, because of a general antiwar sentiment in Japan or because of a sense that the current specific U.S. policy is contrary to Japan's interests.

The United States needs to recognize this risk and consider what actions should be taken now to deal with this technological vulnerability. There are, I believe, four possibilities.

First, the United States could simply accept the new military vulnerability to Japan, recognizing that Japan is at least as vulnerable to the United States. While it would therefore be irrational for Japan to exercise its strength, the risk would remain. The existence of that risk would limit our ability to contemplate independent military actions of the sort that we did in Iraq and, more generally, would limit our ability to assure our own self-protection and our ability to use force to maintain global stability.

Second, the United States could seek to eliminate the technological vulnerability by producing the needed military components instead of importing them from Japan. Because we would not have the economies of scale associated with production for civilian as well as military use, this form of procurement could be much more expensive than importing. The costs look even more formidable if we consider the need to do the product design research and to develop the manufacturing equipment that would be needed to make the military equipment. For example, how much of a "nonmarket" machine tool industry would we need to support in order to have the capability to manufacture products that we now import, and how expensive would it be to maintain such an industry?

Third, the United States could use trade barriers to protect those industries that make products that are important for military purposes. This includes not only the final military components but also such industries as semiconductors, computers, numerically controlled machine tools, critical materials, and so forth. The United States already does this to a limited extent, most recently by protecting the U.S. machine tool industry on the basis of its military importance. In principle, the products that would be protected would be chosen on the basis of their military importance only and not as a matter of domestic industrial policy. In practice, however, it would be difficult to decide where lines should be drawn, especially since protecting products like machine tools would artificially raise the cost of making various consumer products. Should the producers of those nonmilitary products be penalized by the military decision to protect machine tools or should they be "compensated" by the protection of their products?

Finally, the United States could seek to achieve greater access to Japanese technology of military significance through joint production or other arrangements that eliminate U.S. vulnerability. Taken by itself, there is no reason for Japanese firms to voluntarily allow U.S. firms to share their technology and to produce many of the relevant products under license in the United States. The government of Japan might, however, have a different view about this if they perceived that the alternative response of the U.S. government to our current technological vulnerability might be broad protectionist legislation of the type described in the previous paragraph. The Japanese government would also recognize that, even if such protectionist legislation was not passed and the United States accepted a relation of mutual vulnerability, that could lead under the type of scenario described above to a very costly rupture of United States–Japan relations if some future Japanese government blocked the exports of Japanese products of military significance. In comparison to these alternatives, cooperative sharing of technology might seem attractive.

Contributors

Robert Dekle
Department of Economics
Boston University
270 Bay State Road
Boston, MA 02215

Richard F. Doner
Department of Political Science
Emory University
Atlanta, GA 30322

Martin Feldstein
President and Chief Executive Officer
NBER
1050 Massachusetts Avenue
Cambridge, MA 02138–5398

Jeffrey A. Frankel
Department of Economics
787 Evans Hall
University of California, Berkeley
Berkeley, CA 94720

Jeffry A. Frieden
Department of Political Science
University of California, Los Angeles
Los Angeles, CA 90024

David B. Friedman
Tuttle & Taylor
Fortieth Floor
355 South Grand Avenue
Los Angeles, CA 90071

Kenneth A. Froot
Graduate School of Business
Harvard University
Soldiers Field Road
Boston, MA 02163

Robert Gilpin
Center of International Studies
The Woodrow Wilson School
Princeton University
323 Bendheim Hall
Princeton, NJ 08544

Stephan Haggard
Graduate School of International
  Relations and Pacific Studies
University of California, San Diego
9500 Gilman Drive
La Jolla, CA 92093

Takeo Hoshi
Graduate School of International
  Relations and Pacific Studies
University of California, San Diego
9500 Gilman Drive
La Jolla, CA 92093

Takashi Inoguchi
Institute of Oriental Culture
University of Tokyo
27–3-1 Hongo Bunkyo-ku
Tokyo 113
Japan

Shafiqul Islam
Council on Foreign Relations
58 East 68th Street
New York, NY 10021

Takatoshi Ito
Institute of Economic Research
Hitotsubashi University
Kunitachi, Tokyo 186
Japan

Miles Kahler
Graduate School of International
Relations and Pacific Studies, 0519
University of California, San Diego
9500 Gilman Drive
La Jolla, CA 92093

Peter J. Katzenstein
Department of Government
Cornell University
Ithaca, NY 14853

Stephen D. Krasner
Department of Political Science
Stanford University
Stanford, CA 94305

Lawrence B. Krause
Graduate School of International
Relations and Pacific Studies, 0519
University of California, San Diego
9500 Gilman Drive
La Jolla, CA 92093

Robert Z. Lawrence
John F. Kennedy School of Government
Harvard University
79 John F. Kennedy Street
Cambridge, MA 02138

Robert E. Lipsey
NBER
269 Mercer Street, 8th Floor
New York, NY 10003

Gregory W. Noble
Department of Political Science
210 Barrows Hall
University of California
Berkeley, CA 94720

Marcus Noland
Institute for International Economics
Sixth Floor
11 DuPont Circle, NW
Washington, DC 20036

Peter A. Petri
Department of Economics
Brandeis University
Waltham, MA 02254

Frances McCall Rosenbluth
Department of Political Science
University of California, Los Angeles
Los Angeles, CA 90024

Martin Rouse
Department of Government
McGraw Hall
Cornell University
Ithaca, NY 14853

Richard J. Samuels
Department of Political Science
E-53–400
Massachusetts Institute of Technology
Cambridge, MA 02139

Gary R. Saxonhouse
Department of Economics
University of Michigan
Ann Arbor, MI 48109

Wing Thye Woo
Department of Economics
University of California, Davis
Davis, CA 95616

David B. Yoffie
Graduate School of Business
Harvard University
Morgan Hall, Room 247
Soldiers Field Road
Boston, MA 02163

Author Index

Subject Index